Discovering The Magic Kingdom:
An Unofficial Disneyland Vacation Guide

By
Joshua C. Shaffer

WITHDRAWN

To order autographed copies of my book,
please visit my website

DiscoveringTheMagicKingdom.com

facebook.com/DiscoveringTheMagicKingdom
Instagram @DisneyGuides
Email: DisneyGuides@yahoo.com

Front cover and back cover photos taken by Joshua C. Shaffer

Front cover and back cover designed and edited by Craig Johnson and Joshua C. Shaffer

Illustrations and inserted photos by Joshua C. Shaffer, unless otherwise stated

TESTIMONIALS

"This book has a lot of great information for your trip to Disneyland. What I especially loved about it though was the extra sections that tell you a lot of the the back story, or little known facts, about the Park, the attractions, and characters. The book was filled with lots of fun information that makes it beneficial even for the experienced Disney traveler." - Russell D. Flores (author of *Seen, Un-Seen Disneyland*), Sacramento, CA.

"Unless you live in SoCal and can frequent the park, you need to make the most of your time. This book gives you lots of options, not to mention the fascinating facts and trivia along the way. Whether you're a first timer or a season pass holder, this book is a must!!!" - Nancy L., Martinez, CA.

"I bought a copy of this book for my next trip to Disneyland. My father found it on my book shelf and decided to read it from cover to cover. He isn't a big fan of the Disney parks because they are too crowded and hasn't been since sometime in the 80's. Well, after reading all the Fun Facts, trivia, Hidden Mickeys, and the history of the park, he is excited to finally go back." - Val P., San Pablo, CA.

"This is a very thorough, well researched book on Disneyland. As Ed MacMahon would say to Johnny Carson, "Everything you ever wanted to know about Disneyland is in this book." If you love Disneyland, you will love this book. Well done!" - George M., San Diego, CA.

"I had not been to Disneyland for 20 years and this book brought me back up to speed. This book has so much information about the park, rides, and movies. I brought my family with me and we would go through the book and mark pages for different areas of the park we really wanted to see. The author has really taken time to explain the ins and outs of Disney. With so much information, it's a great book to keep out on the coffee table. It makes a great conversation piece for company." - Shelly W., Vacaville, CA.

"We got your book before we left for Disneyland/CA Adventure. It was helpful to know how to maneuver through the parks and see the most we could in two days. The 'Fun Facts' kept us distracted while standing in line. Others around us asked how we knew so much about the rides. My son just held up the book. We found a grocery store by our hotel as well as a restaurant. Thanks for all the tips." - Sandra S., Brentwood, CA.

"Before my first trip to Disneyland I was told by a lot of friends that I needed to do this, that or something else. I thought why not get some kind of guide to have to read on the ride there. My favorite thing about Josh's guide was I was able to use it to plan my run around the park. Hidden mickeys were great, fun facts made for some great conversations, and of course the best part was having it with me in the park. I'm glad I have his guide." - David A., Oakley, CA.

"These books are a must have in the parks! I love using the book to search for Hidden Mickey's and learning fun facts about each ride while waiting in line. I have had numerous people come up to me while holding the book to ask where I got it and if they can look at it to learn more for themselves! Josh's books are very informative and have everything you'd ever want to know about the parks and movies." - Andrea and Ryan M., Berkeley, CA.

"There are so many elements to Discovering the Magic Kingdom: An Unofficial Disneyland Vacation Guide. First of all, it's just super interesting reading. I read it through twice and thoroughly enjoyed it both times! So many fun things to learn about Disneyland all in one book. It's great that it's in paperback book form to easily carry in a backpack or stroller for reference throughout the park. And, while you're standing in lines waiting for rides, it's a great time to share the facts about that particular ride with all the other people around you. It helps make the time go faster for you and them. And, you get to meet lots of people and help make their day a little more fun. You'll find out how to get free coffee refills while in the park, how to make the trip more affordable, how to maneuver the park in one day (if needed), where to save money on food outside the park, where to stay, ghost stories, information that Cast Members have shared, and just so many fun facts about the rides, the people who have been instrumental in all things Disneyland, and more information about Walt Disney himself. I could go on and on about this book because there's just so much material in it. And, there's even a whole section dedicated to Disney movies and the studio. Especially fun in the Disney movie section is reading little tidbits about things to look for in the different movies (like characters from one movie in the background of another movie). Now, I have to watch all the movies and look for the items that Joshua points out in the movie section. I truly can't wait until Joshua's new book comes out because I know there will be so much more fun stuff to discover about Disneyland. And, one more thing--the price is great!!!!This is a wonderful, affordable gift idea for family and friends who also like Disneyland." - Harry & Sue F., Pittsburg, CA.

TABLE OF CONTENTS

Planning Ahead

Disneyland History

Disney The Film Industry

What's Inside

I am going to just start this book off with an awesome story, and with a photo of the guy who created all of this, Walt Disney. I met Gil and he had an awesome story to tell about the time he met the legend. Jump back to 1956, just one year after Disneyland opened and put youself near the Disneyland Hotel.

"I met Walt Disney as a kid in Disneyland. Here's the proof — I'm on the right, my twin brother is on the left and our sister is in the middle.

Our father saw him about 20 yards away in front of the Disneyland Hotel, walked up to him and said, "Mr. D? Dan Zeimer. Would you mind taking a picture with my kids? We're big fans." Walt was very gracious and even signed an autograph. The photo and signature are framed and hanging on my office wall.

Now, I can't say that the chance meeting in the late 50s made me become a writer decades later, but it did inspire my creativity. And about 10 years later, on another of my frequent visits to Disneyland, I bought a Mickey Mouse watch at Tinkerbell's Toy Shop in the Fantasyland Castle. Since then, I've worn it virtually every day for over 40 years to remind me of Walt, the Disney magic, and the power of creative thinking."

-Gil Zeimer
(*zeimer.com*)

PREFACE

I have spent years now trying to gather as much information as I possibly could for my favorite place to visit. Disneyland is full of rich and interesting history that needs to be shared with everyone. I began writing in 2006, and had the first edition of this book published in 2010. That couldn't be all there was to learn about this massive company and one of the most visited places in the world. I set out to write this second edition, now having more material about the company than ever before. I have read lots of books, articles, blogs, listened to interviews, watched documentaries, etc. about the topic of Disney and realized that the information is too paragraphical. It was all presented as large paragraphs full of information. While reading, I realized I could break up the paragraphs into individual "fun facts." It is much easier to read and remember information this way. I also read books that presented fun facts, but the facts were short and not very detailed. The much-quoted line, "Did you know?" seemed to start off these fun fact phrases, but, there was no supporting information included. Each fact was a nice piece of information, but didn't tell why was it so, when it was, and who was involved with it. By adding the extra information, it made the fun facts that much more fulfilling. I went so far as to add history that is not even about Disney, but the information ties into Disney. This book was everything I wanted it to be, and I spent hundreds of hours putting it together for everyone to enjoy.

FOREWORD

One of the things I always stress to artists and creative people that ask for advice is, "do your homework." Well, Joshua has taken that advice to the next level. Anyone interested in all there is to know about Disneyland, will find that and so much more in the pages of this informative book.

Rolly Crump
Former Disney Imagineer

FOREWORD

What could be better than reading the first edition of *Discovering the Magic Kingdom: An Unofficial Disneyland Vacation Guide* by Joshua C. Shaffer? It can only be the opportunity to read the **second edition** of *Discovering the Magic Kingdom: An Unofficial Disneyland Vacation Guide*.

As an Imagineer, I can tell you that a *Guide* like this one can be the most valuable tool in your vacation toolbox, if you want to get the most out of your trip to one of the most magical places on earth.

Joshua is not only an amazing author and cartoonist, but a true fan when it comes to the Walt Disney Company and the parks that Disney has created all over the world; most notably Disneyland.

Even though fans are in love with all the parks, there is only one park that Walt Disney actually walked. He was on-site overseeing its creation every day. Only one park that has the lingering warmth of the dreamer that started it all, and that park is Disneyland. Walt Disney's fingerprints are all over this magical place.

Disneyland isn't the largest of the parks. And, it's not the smallest. But, it is the jewel of them all. This is because it bares the mark of its creator and that's incredible. Nowhere else will you get to see, touch, and experience what Walt Disney felt as he painstakingly worked with Disney Imagineers to bring his vision to life.

This book helps you to capture that feeling, and get a taste before you go to Disneyland. It gives you the little secrets that only the fans can give you. This is because fans like Joshua and I are passionate in our love for this park. Joshua knows every little nook and cranny, every delicate detail, and he shares those with you.

Joshua gives you step-by-step assistance on how to make your trip extra magical. He also gives you specific chapters on some of the extremely special events that you can sign up for that will elevate your experience. And, for special secrets that the casual visitor might miss, he guides you where to find them.

Imagine feeling a little like Walt Disney as you walk, touching, smelling, tasting, seeing, and hearing experiences the same way he must have. This *Guide* will help you do just that.

So, what are you waiting for? Open this book and get started.

Terri Hardin
Show Designer, Sculptor
Walt Disney Imagineering

11

COPYRIGHT AND TRADEMARK INFORMATION

THE BOOK HISTORY

Throughout the years during my *Disneyland* visits, I started to learn more and more about the parks, the attractions, and the history from talking to *Disneyland* Cast Members, friends, and other park visitors. While waiting in lines and walking around the park, I would randomly strike up conversations with other people and would always land on the topic of *Disneyland* facts. Spending lots of time with these people, I transferred the information that I already knew over to them. In 2006, I wanted to make a list of all the random *Disneyland* facts that I had learned. I wanted a list that I could share with others while I was at the park. While compiling the list, I decided to look up some information online to verify statements or to learn something new. After discovering there was so much more information out there than I could have ever imagined, I started adding it to my existing list. In the beginning, I had everything divided up by lands and then by attractions. That's when I decided to make a little book. I added in some information about the FastPass and how to get cheap tickets and so on. Not putting a whole lot of effort into the book, it got pushed to the wayside for a little while. In the beginning of 2008, I started to pick it back up and completed my first draft. I printed up several copies of this book, then containing 67 pages, and sold them to friends and on Ebay. Friends began to ask me questions about items that were not in my book. That's when I made a complete overhaul. By mid-2008, I decided to accommodate the queries of everyone and added another 152 pages with more photos and information. That was the completion of the 1st edition that was published in October 2010. As time went on, prices went up and things got added or taken away, so I started working on my second edition. The second edition was in the works for nearly 7 years. With the completion of the second edition, readers can learn over 2,500 more fun facts and read the nine newly added sections.

Since publication of the first edition, it has been used as a reference on numerous Wikipedia pages, including *Disney Theatrical Group, Fathoms Below, Mulan, Ariel, Ernie Newton, Jack Lindquist, Walt Disney Animation Studios, Who Wants to Be A Millionaire* (attraction), *Who Wants To Be A Millionaire* (game show), *Belle,* and the *Golden Age of American Animation*. I have made great contacts and met lots of Disney fanatics like myself. I was asked to be the Public Relations Manager for Gina Rock, the longest flying Tinker Bell in Disneyland history, and I was invited to be in several documentary DVD's for *Theme Parkology* to talk about the park and to be on the Disney podcast *The Magic Behind The Ears*.

ACKNOWLEDGMENTS

There are so many people I would like to thank for helping me with information for this book. Some of the contributors are the frequent visitors of the parks that I have met over the years, the Cast Members, and friends that I visit with at the parks. I went to many websites and blogs to learn the information. Much of the information in this book was gathered from random websites; none of the information contained in this book is copyrighted information. All the photos contained in this book were taken by me or given to me. I would like to give credit to the websites that contributed information to this book;

➤ **wikipedia.com** and **disney.wikia.com** for supplying most of the information about:
- the attractions
- the attraction lengths
- the dates and times
- the attractions of the past
- the biography of Walt Disney
- some of the random *Disneyland* facts
- the complete list of all the Disney movies
- the history of the Walt Disney Productions Company
- the information about the Disney Princesses

➤ **disney.com** for providing:
- the attraction height requirements
- the visitor pass prices
- the restaurant information

➤ **hiddenmickeys.org** and **oitc.com** for providing:
- a list of Guest findings of the Hidden Mickeys
- some of the random base facts about *Disneyland*

➤ **imdb.com** for providing:
- some of the random movie facts
- actors' acting history

Special thanks to:

Sue Fujita for promoting and proofing this whole book in two weeks.

Sandy Shaffer for special support and proofing this book.

A special thanks to my fiancée, **Ashley Oliver,** soon to be **Ashley Shaffer**, for all the support, for proofreading the first draft, and for giving up many hours without me while I was lost in my writing.

Jerry Cornell, owner of *Theme Parkology* and *The Magic Mehind The Ears Podcast*, for putting me into contact with many new Disney Legends and people connected to the Disney company. Our friendship has been a wild and exciting journey.

Cast Member **Louise Pitt** for helping me gather information I didn't have.

Jeanie Ramos and **Marg Orlando** for also proofing the first edition.

Courtney Shaffer for designing the first edition cover and consulting for the design of the second edition.

Chris Lyndon, owner of *DisneyChris.com*, for book cover ideas and writing the history of the parades section.

Craig Johnson, owner of the travel blog *NomadicGuys.com*, for desiging my second edition cover.

Linda C. for the assistance with the book cover.

Diane H. of Clyde, CA, for the photo of the little girl with the princesses.

Caesar M. of San Jose, CA, for the English translation of the "Hawaiian War Chant" in *The Enchanted Tiki Room*.

Kaitlin M. of Antioch, CA, for having me be a guest speaker for her class at the *Antioch Learning Academy*.

Craig & Angela C. from Concord, CA. for the side-view photo of the Neuschwanstein Castle.

Rob J. and Leila M. from Pleasanton, CA. for the front-view photo of the front of the Neuschwanstein Castle.

Trish C. from Pleasant Hill, CA. for some of the photos from inside Guardians of the Galaxy- Mission: Breakout!

Darby G. from Huntington Beach, CA. and **Jillian L.** from Anaheim, CA. for the Disneybounding photo as Chip & Dale.

Mikayla F. from Brentwood Ca. provided the photos of her Disneybounding

Nicole B. from San Bruno, CA. for some of the photos from inside Guardians of the Galaxy- Mission: Breakout!

Jennifer E. and **Della E.** from Charlotte, NC. for the photo of Disneybounding as the Mayor from Nightmare Before Christmas.

Robert P. from Mission Viejo, CA. for the photo of Johnny Depp as Jack Sparrow.

Justin Brown from San Diego, CA. for the photo of the Disneyland train.

Rolly Crump for the wonderful Foreword and the sketch.

Terri Hardin for the very long and awesome Foreword.

Jessica M from Ilwaco, WA. for providing the photo of the Tour Guide.

Stephanie D. from Rohnert Park, CA. for introducing me to Gil.

14

Gil Zeimer for providing the photo of Walt Disney along with his story.

Thank you to those who helped with promotions or book signings for my first edition: **Golden Gate Disneyana Club**, **The Travis Exchange** in Faifield, CA, **John Young** and **Ron Brown** from the Hometown Morning Show on *95.3 KUIC* in Vacaville, CA, **Contra Costa Times**, **Dogs4Diabetics** in Concord, CA., **Mouse-Con**, the **Disneyana Club**, and **Barnes & Noble**.

Thank you to my local book stores who were kind enough to keep my book stocked on the shelves and allowed for book signings: **Railroad Book Depot** in Pittsburg, CA, **All Inked Up Books & Hometown Memories** in Brentwood, CA, and **Barnes & Noble** in Antioch, CA.

I read through many books, listened to podcasts, and watched documentaries to build up a culmination of information for this edition. So, a special thank you to:
- *The Haunted Mansion: Imagineering a Disney Classic* by Jason Surrell
- *Pirates of the Caribbean: From the Magic Kingdom to the Movies* by Jason Surrell
- *The Unauthorized Story of Walt Disney's Haunted Mansion* by Jeff Baham
- *Seen, Un-Seen Disneyland* by Russell D. Flores
- *More Seen, Un-Seen Disneyland* by Russell D. Flores
- *Cleaning the Kingdom* by Lynn Barron and Ken Pellman
- Many books written by Dave Smith
- *Walt Disney: The Triumph of the American Imagination* by Neal Gabler
- *The Wisdom of Walt: Leadership Lessons from the Happiest Place on Earth* by Jeff Barnes
- *The Hidden Mickeys of Disneyland* by Bill Scollon
- *The Sweep Spot Podcast* hosted by Lynn Barron and Ken Pellman
- *Disney Vault Talk Podcast* hosted by Steve Glosson and Teresa Delgado
- *The DoomBuggies Spook Show Podcast* hosted by Jeff Baham
- *Theme Parkology* documentary DVDs produced by Jerry Cornell
- *The Magic Behind the Ears Podcast* hosted by Jerry Cornell and Joshua Shaffer

INTRODUCTION

This guide is to assist you with working your way through the Wonderful World of *Disneyland* and *California Adventure*. It will also give you several tips on how to save money during your stay. Also listed are lots of interesting facts about the park and other Disney-related trivia.

I do not work for the Disney Corporation in any way. I am a huge fan of the *Disneyland* theme parks, and I go there quite frequently with my family using our season passes during several different seasons of the year.

Disneyland has attracted millions of visitors since it first opened its gates in 1955. When you enter *Disneyland*, the cares and worries of the day are left behind. You're transported to a fantasy world where elephants can fly, pirates serenade, and a ghost will follow you home.

Disneyland is most certainly a land of enchantment where children and the young at heart find that dreams really do come true. The park is a seamless blend of yesterday, today, and tomorrow. Smiling train conductors, marching bands, and the clip-clop of the horses pulling the carriages bring you back to carefree days. You can also rocket through the galaxy, meet a mermaid, or trek through the jungle. Laughter is always in the air with friendly smiles all around. The secret to *Disneyland* is its ability to change, yet remain the same.

Walt Disney had said, Disneyland will never be completed. It will continue to grow as long as there is imagination left in the world.

I hope you find this guidebook very useful for informing and showing you how to save a few bucks on your visit to the happiest place on earth. Every *Fun Fact* and the other information listed in here are true and accurate to the best of my knowledge and research.

Keep in mind that the park is continually changing, opening new attractions, and removing old ones. This book had its most recent update prior to publishing in early 2017.

WHY ADULTS LOVE DISNEYLAND

"Why do adults like to go to *Disneyland*?" I have been asked this question numerous times now. For me, the word "like" is an understatement, whereas, the word "love" seems better suited. People would not spend their time on a day off from work to travel hundreds of miles just to experience something they simply "like." You have to love something to give it that much dedication.

In the past, I have responded with, "Because they just do." But now, after having experienced *World of Color* in *California Adventure*, I have a better answer for them. The scene, in which I had my mini-epiphany, was between Mufasa and Scar from *The Lion King*. In conjunction with the video clips on the enormous screen, there is actual fire that bursts into the air while loud, exciting music plays. Then a deep gravelly voice says, "*Long live the King!*" Simba shouts "*Nooooooo...*" as Mufasa falls backward and the screen dramatically goes black. "*Daaaad? Dad?*" is played in the darkness, and then silence. The soft piece "So Close from Enchanted" begins to slowly play, while giving us clips of love scenes from other animated films.

Noticing the huge lump in my throat, it was then that I realized why I had such a huge attraction to a "place for children." I was only a child when I first saw The Lion King. It was at a time when I had no control over my emotions and simple things could work their way into my heart. That moment during *World of Color* made me access my childhood emotions.

That part of the brain, where those memories lie, is what brings me back to *Disneyland*, again and again. I walk through the gates, turn off my phone to disconnect myself from the outside world, breathe in deeply, and just explore the park. Everything connects to my childhood. Seeing Tinker Bell fly across the castle during the fireworks narrated by Mary Poppins, riding through the dark rides in *Fantasyland,* seeing Pinocchio dance or Peter Pan fly, hearing the group of Pirates sing "yo ho, yo ho, a pirate's life for me," feeling the chills as a disembodied ghost welcomes you into the *Haunted Mansion*. All this just hits home, straight to memories of a happier, less stressful time in life, when all you had to worry about was playing outside with your friends, watching cartoons, and making sure your room was clean. Who wouldn't want to have this feeling? Who wouldn't want to get rid of all the stresses of adult life, if not just for a few days?

Furthermore, I don't find it weird to see an adult running up to Mickey Mouse to give him a big hug and pose for a picture. I don't think it's odd for an adult to stand in line for 20 minutes just to get a Dole Whip to enjoy while watching the audio-animatronic birds sing, that I happen to know all the lyrics to.

It is interesting how one can go decades without seeing a Disney movie, but as soon as part of a song is played, or part of a movie is quoted, we instantly sing along, most of us knowing all the words. For example, when I hear "That's not a

17

flower," I picture a fluffy gray bunny rolling around on the ground, laughing, "No, no, no, that's not a flower." A skunk replies, "Oh that's all right. He can call me a flower, if he wants to." My brain doesn't do that with recent movies. Movies are generally a more important part of our lives as children than they are now. As adults, we watch movies while thinking of our other obligations: when we have to go to work next, if we have to stop at the bank on the way home, if we need to pick up milk, etc. Kids don't think that way; they are not distracted by adult problems. They are completely submersed in a movie and relate to it so much that they become one with the characters. Kids want to be Peter Pan and fly over Neverland or have a mermaid fin like Ariel and swim through the ocean with a yellow fish sidekick. These thoughts don't usually cross an adult's mind because we view it as impossible.

Being a parent and taking your child to *Disneyland* is a whole other ballgame. Just watching your daughter experience what it is like to visit with Princess Merida after she has been obsessing over the movie, watching it dozens of times, is just a sight to behold! Handing your son a Mickey ice cream bar just to see him get it all over his face while watching all the characters dancing down *Main Street, U.S.A.* in sync with the music. Showing them what a pirate's life used to be like, "Yeaaaar." Best of all, is seeing the glow of the multicolored bursts of light on their faces as fireworks explode in the sky. All of this is worth going time after time.

Think about when you were a kid. Like 30 years ago, there were only a total of 154 movies that had been made by Disney. Up until 1980 when Disney released *Pete's Dragon* on VHS, the only way to get a Disney "fix" was to wait for a movie to show up on TV or to rent one of the few movies that were available on VHS. Today our children have access to 374 movies. Nearly all of them are available on DVD or digital download. They can watch them on iPhones, iPads, in the car, anywhere. Just about every room nowadays has a DVD player so they can experience the magic anytime they want. I can only imagine what it will be like for them when they grow up. There is so much more magic at their fingertips.

Now think about the park crowds. In 1980, there were 11.5 million visitors to the park. In 2012, there was nearly 16.5 million. I can guarantee you that number will only multiply over the next 20 years. The draw to the park will become stronger and stronger with the more children that are introduced to it. I know numerous adults that had never even gone as a child, but have recently gone as adults and are now season pass holders; they can't get enough of it. It's the timeless magic, the freedom we feel, and the relaxing atmosphere that first draws us in. But, most important are the ties to our childhood from everything we see, hear, and taste around the park that keeps us adults coming back for more.

People don't realize how much of an impact their childhood experiences will have on them after they grow up. Children are like little sponges, soaking up everything, and those memories stay with us; we just don't access them daily. Simply thinking about *Disneyland* (or anything Disney related, for that matter) triggers that part of the brain that is about happy experiences. This is why I still LOVE going to *Disneyland*. What about you?

Planning Ahead

VISITING TIMES

The best times to visit *Disneyland* or *California Adventure* are from the second week in January through April and the first part of September because they are less crowded. The last two weeks in December are very busy due to Christmas and New Year's Day. Thanksgiving week is busy, and so is mid-September through October because of the Halloween décor and *Mickey's Halloween Party* nights. Avoid Saturdays if you can; they are the busiest. Saturdays are when most of the Meet and Greet characters are out.

Recently, they have been closing the park early starting the second week in September through the end of October for trick or treaters to attend *Mickey's Halloween Party*, which is only held on select nights.

Selecting the "best" time to visit the *Disneyland* Resort depends upon your interests. If you want to visit when the number of guests is fairly low, plan to stay mid-week (Tuesdays-Thursdays) during:

- mid-September through mid- November

- mid-January through mid-March

- mid-April through mid-May

The benefit of visiting the Resort during lower attendance is that wait times are shorter enabling you to do more. However, *California Adventure* and *Disneyland* typically reduce their operating hours making for fewer events (i.e., Fireworks, *World of Color*, *Fantasmic!*, and the parades) and entertainment. Frequently, more attractions are closed for refurbishing.

If you want to visit while the parks have extended hours, entertainment, events, and most attractions are operating, plan your stay for weekends, including extended holiday weekends during Christmas and Spring Break or June-August. During these times, the number of Guests is usually increased. *Disneyland* has a maximum capacity, though they do not release the exact number to the public. There are two stages of capacity.

Stage #1: This admits about 60,000 Guests. When this amount is reached, they stop selling tickets for the day. If you get your hand stamped, you can leave and still go back in, or go to *California Adventure,* if you wish.

Stage #2: This admits about 80,000 Guests. If you leave, you can't get back in, even if your hand is stamped. I have known someone resorting to watch the fireworks from their car. So, ask before you leave if you will be able to re-enter.

The ticket booths have been known to allow people admittance to *California Adventure,* giving them a free upgrade from a single park pass to a hopper pass so they can try to get into *Disneyland* later in the evening. The gates have been known to close at 10:00 a.m. on holidays such as Veterans Day, Fourth of July, Thanksgiving week (but not Thanksgiving Day), and the whole week of Christmas through New Year's Day. Choosing to go on these days will be rough. A wait time for *Dumbo* alone has been known to reach four hours and *Indiana Jones* can be two hours. The park hours are longer so you will have more time in the day, but fewer attractions to can get on. On New Year's Eve Day, *Disneyland* is open from 8:00 a.m. to 2:00 a.m., totaling 18 hours. Adults may be able to do it, but don't expect your kids to. Most people aren't even awake for that many hours in a day, let alone being active for all of them.

The maximum capacity of *California Adventure* is about 45,000 Guests. There are far fewer attractions in *California Adventure* for people to be waiting in lines, so they fill the walkways in the park.

The hours of operation vary from day to day, year to year and seasonally (also see *Magic Morning* on *page 65*). Use the following chart to help base your visitation time. Times are estimates and subject to change.

Disneyland
WINTER / FALL Weekdays: 10 a.m. – 8 p.m. Weekends: 9 a.m. – 9 p.m.
SUMMER Weekdays: 8 a.m. – midnight Weekends: 8 a.m. – midnight
SPRING Weekdays: 10 a.m. – 8 p.m. Weekends: 8 a.m. – midnight

California Adventure
WINTER / FALL Weekdays: 10 a.m. – 6 p.m. Weekends: 10 a.m. – 7 p.m.
SUMMER Weekdays: 10 a.m. – 9 p.m. Weekends: 8 a.m. – midnight
SPRING Weekdays: 10 a.m. – 6 p.m. Weekends: 10 a.m. – 9 p.m.

AN EXAMPLE OF A TRIP

The following is an example of what it may cost a family of four to visit the parks for 5 days. I talk about each item later on in more detail and how to save money. This is all an estimation based on prices in early 2017.

- Tickets-2 adults (from AAA): $670
- Tickets-2 children over 3 years (from AAA): $650
- Hotel for 6 nights, walking distance, about $55 a night (off season): $330
- Food-pre-purchased sandwich stuff and snacks at a grocery store, carry in food, eat breakfast at the hotel, possibly return to hotel for dinner: $100
- Travel expenses: depends on mode of travel
- No souvenirs

Your total trip, not including travel, would be about: $1,750

Now if you decide to do things the more expensive way, this is a rough total you would be looking at.

- Tickets-2 adults: $700
- Tickets-2 children over 3 years: $670
- Hotel for 6 nights, walking distance, about $119 a night (off season): $714
- Food-two meals in the park, not including snacks, prices vary for meals from $6-$28 each: $400
- Travel expenses: depends on mode of travel
- Average for souvenirs a family might spend: $200

Your total trip, not including travel, would be about: $2,684

OTHER THINGS TO DO

If you are on a long trip or just want to mix up your Disney days with other activities, there are a multitude of places nearby. The following list contains places within driving distance of the *Disneyland* Resort. Prices and info are current as of 2013.

Knott's Berry Farm	MILES FROM *DISNEYLAND*: 8	
ADDRESS: 8039 Beach Boulevard	CITY: Buena Park	PHONE: (714) 220-5200
1-Day TICKET PRICE: $26.99 - $59.99	WEBSITE: www.knotts.com	
DESCRIPTION: Themed park with roller coasters, water slides, and is adhorned with the Peanuts characters created by Charles M. Schulz (Charlie Brown, Snoopy, Woodstock, Linus, etc.)		
Legoland	MILES FROM *DISNEYLAND*: 65	
ADDRESS: 5885 The CrossingsDrive	CITY: Carlsbad	PHONE: (877) LEGOLAND
1-Day TICKET PRICE: $66.00-$76.00	WEBSITE: california.legoland.com	
DESCRIPTION: With more than 60 rides, shows and attractions it's an interactive, hands-on theme park experience for families with children 2-12. The Resort is also home to SEA LIFE Aquarium and the world's first LEGOLAND Water Park.		
Medieval Times Dinner/Tournament	MILES FROM *DISNEYLAND*: 8	
ADDRESS: 7662 Beach Blvd.	CITY: Buena Park	PHONE: 1-866-543-9637
1-Day TICKET PRICE: $35.95 - $57.95	WEBSITE: medievaltimes.com/buenapark.aspx	
DESCRIPTION: A dinner show with knights competing with jousting, sword fighting, a horse show, and some falconry while you eat with your hands and root for your knight.		
Page Museum La Brea Tar Pits	MILES FROM *DISNEYLAND*: 35	
ADDRESS: 5801 Wilshire Blvd.	CITY: Los Angeles	PHONE: (323) 934-PAGE
1-Day TICKET PRICE: $5.00 - $12.00	WEBSITE: www.tarpits.org	
DESCRIPTION: A museum that has a working tar pit excavation, exhibits, and educational videos about what happened to the mammoths and other prehistoric animals.		
Pirates Dinner Adventure	MILES FROM *DISNEYLAND*: 8	
ADDRESS: 7600 Beach Blvd.	CITY: Buena Park	PHONE: (714) 690-1497
1-Day TICKET PRICE: $41.15 - $60.15	WEBSITE: www.piratesdinneradventure.com	
DESCRIPTION: A dinner with special effects, wizardry, swashbuckling swordplay, duels, fantasies of would-be pirates of all ages become uncannily real.		
San Diego Zoo	MILES FROM *DISNEYLAND*: 94	
ADDRESS: 2920 Zoo Drive	CITY: San Diego	PHONE: (619) 231-1515
1-Day TICKET PRICE: $36.00-$46.00	WEBSITE: www.sandiegozoo.org/zoo/index.php	
DESCRIPTION: The 100-acre Zoo is home to over 3,700 rare and endangered animals representing more than 650 species and subspecies, and a botanical collection with more than 700,000 plants.		
Sea World	MILES FROM *DISNEYLAND*: 91	
ADDRESS: 500 Sea World Drive	CITY: San Diego	PHONE: (800) 25-SHAMU
1-Day TICKET PRICE: $63	WEBSITE: seaworldparks.com/en/seaworld-sandiego	
DESCRIPTION: Themed after marine life, enjoy watching killer whales, dolphins, sea lions, and other animals perform stunt shows. You can also go on roller coaster and other rides.		
Six Flags Magic Mountain	MILES FROM *DISNEYLAND*: 61	
ADDRESS: 26101 Magic Mountain Pkwy	CITY: Valencia	PHONE: (661) 255-4100
1-Day TICKET PRICE: $42.99-$67.99	WEBSITE: https://www.sixflags.com/magicmountain	
DESCRIPTION: With 18 roller coasters, Six Flags Magic Mountain holds the world record for most roller coasters in an amusement park.		

Universal Studios Hollywood	MILES FROM *DISNEYLAND*: 36	
ADDRESS: 100 Universal City Plaza	CITY: Universal City	PHONE: 1-800-864-8377
1-Day TICKET PRICE: $72.00 - $80.00	WEBSITE: www.universalstudioshollywood.com	
DESCRIPTION: A themed park run by the film company Universal Studios, with shows, rides and working movie sets.		

SAVE MONEY STEP BY STEP

The following are examples of ways to save money on your next trip to the park.

➤ First off, if you contact Disney, they will send you **a free *Disneyland* Vacation Planning DVD**. Just go to https://www.disneyvacations.com.

➤ If you get coffee in the park *on Main Street, U.S.A.*, save your receipt and your cup for a **free refill on *Main Street, U.S.A***. This only works for regular coffee, not espressos or mochas, etc.

➤ **Carry your food in with you**. It is okay to carry in food and drinks. You can't, however, take in rigid ice chests. If you need an ice chest, take a soft-sided one. There are grocery stores nearby where you can purchase food. *Target* is on S. Harbor and *Food 4 Less* is on Katella. Some foods you can take in could include trail mix, corn nuts, dried fruit, fresh fruit, mixed nuts, sandwiches (I suggest not taking in meat and cheese unless it is in an ice chest), juice bottles, beef jerky, candy, and just about anything else. If it is going to be hot out, I don't recommend anything that could melt, like chocolate. Also, place your sandwich in a small Tupperware-type container to prevent it from getting smashed.

➤ **Take in water bottles**. You will need to drink plenty of water while walking around to avoid dehydration. I suggest getting mix-in drink packets to add flavor to the water to make it more desirable. Lipton makes great flavors and there is a water enhancer called Mio (little silver teardrop-shaped bottle with over two dozen flavors to squirt any amount in your water bottle for desired flavor strength). If your bottle gets empty, there are water fountains everywhere for refills. This is where the flavor packets would work best. For ease of carrying your water bottle, they sell lanyards that strap to the water bottle for around $7.00. They also sell key chains with a rubber ring shaped like Mickey or Minnie for around $3.50 to put on the bottle and clip to your pants, backpack, or wherever. They are very convenient and work as a reminder to drink more fluids.

➤ Ice **water or just a cup of ice is free;** just ask for it. It is great if your water bottle has gotten warm in the sun.

➤ If you take in a mini ice chest to hold your lunch, **you can get a locker** on *Main Street, U.S.A.* to hold it for you while you romp around the park. Also, you can use frozen water bottles in place of ice packets to save space.

➤ **When booking a hotel:**

- Contemplate on how important it really is for you to have a higher-end hotel. If you are only down there to go in the parks, do you need a hotel with a full restaurant, room service, a gym, a full-size pool, free cable, and other amenities? Or will you just be sleeping there and spending all your time in the parks? These questions will have an impact of the hotels and the many price ranges you have to choose from.
- Book in advance for lower price rates. If you plan a few months ahead and are only needing a bed to sleep in, then you can get a room for around $34-$55 a night.
- Try to "room share" if you are traveling with others.
- Get a room with a microwave and mini fridge for eating in and storing food. You have to check this ahead of time to find out if there is a microwave in the room already or if you will need to rent it for $10 a day. One time, I got a room and found out it was going to be $10 a day to rent the hotel's microwave. So, I got one down at Target for less and then kept it.
- Find a hotel within walking distance to the park. This will save on parking or shuttle service (some hotels have it included). The main streets surrounding the park are Katella Ave., Disneyland Dr., Walnut St., Harbor Blvd., and Ball Rd.

➤ **When parking:**

- Walk-in #1: Off of Ball Road on West Place is a small parking lot for employees. You can walk across that small parking lot, proceed across the parking structure, and then take the tram into the park.
- Walk-in #2: From Katella Ave., you can walk down Disneyland Way and enter *Downtown Disney* by the *AMC Theater*, then ride the *Monorail* into *Tomorrowland*.
- Walk-in #3: The main entrance to the parks is located across the street from McDonalds and Denny's.
- If you will be visiting *Disneyland* for two hours or less, you can park in the *Downtown Disney* parking lot for free. You can get an additional two hours of free parking with validation from *AMC Theater* or select table service dining restaurants. Every hour thereafter is $12.
- If you are going to be upgrading your ticket to a season pass, then take the parking pass you are given upon entering the parking garage with you. They will subtract the amount on the ticket from your season pass parking upgrade. If you have already parked there for multiple days, take all your parking stubs for maximum savings.

➤ **When buying tickets:**

- Tickets at the gate or *Disneyland's* website can be up to $25 more than other places. Check with your local AAA office or credit union for savings. Safeway also has cheaper tickets.
- A 1-Day pass can only be purchased at the park gate or from *Disneyland's* website; there is no other place.

- You might also think about upgrading your hopper pass to a season pass if you will be visiting a second time within the next year.
- Read more details about ticket pass upgrading information on page 27.
- If there is a long line at the ticket booth, you can order tickets online with your phone. They will send a barcode to the phone to scan to get in the park, which is where they will hand you a ticket. This only works for the 1-Day and 1-Day Hopper tickets.
- Keep an eye on Disney's website. They used to offer 10-Day Park Hopper "No Expire" *Disney World* Tickets that could be used in Florida and in California if you plan on visiting both parks. They stopped the offer the summer 2013. That doesn't mean they won't start it again.

➤ **When traveling to the parks:**
  - See *Getting to The Parks & Parking* on page 34 for details on traveling to *Disneyland* by train, plane, bus, or car.

ATTENDANCE OF THE DISNEYLAND RESORT

DISNEYLAND VISITORS BY THE MILLIONS

Year	1955	1956	1957	1958	1959	1960	1961	1962	1963	1964
Guests	1	4	4.5	4.6	5.1	5	5.3	5.5	5.7	6
Year	1965	1966	1967	1968	1969	1970	1971	1972	1973	1974
Guests	6.5	6.7	7.8	9.2	9.1	10	9.3	9.4	9.8	9.5
Year	1975	1976	1977	1978	1979	1980	1981	1982	1983	1984
Guests	9.8	9.8	10.9	11	11	11.5	11.3	10.4	9.9	9.8
Year	1985	1986	1987	1988	1989	1990	1991	1992	1993	1994
Guests	12	12	13.5	13	14.4	12.9	11.6	11.6	11.4	10.3
Year	1995	1996	1997	1998	1999	2000	2001	2002	2003	2004
Guests	14.1	15	14.2	13.7	13.5	13.9	12.3	12.7	12.7	13.3
Year	2005	2006	2007	2008	2009	2010	2011	2012	2013	2014
Guests	14.26	14.73	14.87	14.72	15.9	15.98	16.14	15.96	16.2	16.77
Year	2015	2016	2017	2018	2019	2020	2021	2022	2023	2024
Guests	18.28	17.9	????	????	????	????	????	????	????	????

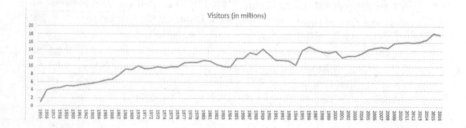

Visitors (in millions)

CALIFORNIA ADVENTURE VISITORS BY THE MILLIONS

Year	2001	2002	2003	2004	2005	2006	2007	2008	2009	2010
Guests	5	4.7	5.31	5.6	5.8	5.95	5.68	5.566	6.095	6.287
Year	2011	2012	2013	2014	2015	2016	2017	2018	2019	2020
Guests	6.341	7.775	8.514	8.769	9.383	9.3	????	????	????	????

In the 58 years since *Disneyland* first opened its gates, 689.21 million, well over half a billion, patrons have passed through those turnstiles. That means about 9.19% of the entire world population, or more than double the entire population of North America (United States, Canada, Mexico=484,250,000), has been to *Disneyland*.

Disneyland commemorates their landmarks with visitors. As I understand it, the special Guest gets a lifetime pass to the park. Here are the millions of Guest landmarks.

- 1 Millionth Guest: Elsa Marquez - September 8, 1955
- 10 Millionth Guest: Leigh Woolfenden - December 31, 1957
- 25 Millionth Guest: Dr. Glenn C. Franklin - April 19, 1961
- 50 Millionth Guest: Mary Adams - August 12, 1965
- 100 Millionth Guest: Valerie Suldo - June 17, 1971
- 200 Millionth Guest: Gert Schelvis - January 8, 1981
- 250 Millionth Guest: Brook Charles Arthur Burr - August 24, 1985
- 300 Millionth Guest: Claudine Masson - September 1, 1989
- 400 Millionth Guest: Minnie Pepito - July 5, 1997
- 450 Millionth Guest: Mark Ramirez - March 15, 2001
- 500 Millionth Guest: Australian Bill Trow - January 12, 2004
- In September 1994, Disney celebrated having its 1 billionth guest; this takes into account all of the Disney parks around the world.

TICKETS AND PASSES

The current cost for a ticket varies upon point of purchase. Buying it at the park will cost more. A "Park Hopper" is a ticket that lets you go back and forth from *Disneyland* to *California Adventure* throughout your stay and on the same day.

This section was difficult to keep current as *Disneyland* bumped up the ticket prices about seven times in the past five years. They also keep changing the block out dates for season pass holders, and changing the payment plan rules. Please bear with me as I try to keep this section as current as I can by the time it is published, and please double check actual prices online.

When *Disneyland* first opened, it only cost $1 to get in the park. Once inside, patrons had to individually pay to ride each attraction. It wasn't until October that Disney started the ticket program. Those tickets were called "A-E Tickets,"

27

and ranged in price from 10¢ to 35¢. The "A" tickets were used for the simpler and cheaper attractions like *King Arthur Carrousel* and the vehicles on *Main Street, U.S.A.* (added in 1959). The "E" tickets were for the more expensive attractions like the *Matterhorn Bobsleds*, *Monorail*, and the *Mine Train*. You can read more detail about the "E-ticket" in *Disney Things Explained* on page 278.

Ticket Prices Of The Past							
Date	1981	1982	1984	1985	1986	1987	1990
Price	$10.75	$12.00	$14.00	$17.95	$18.00	$21.50	$25.50
Date	1991	1993	1994	1999	Jun-00	Nov-00	Mar-02
Price	$27.50	$28.75	$31.00	$39.00	$41.00	$43.00	$45.00
Date	Jan-03	Mar-04	Jan-05	Jun-05	Jan-06	Sep-06	Sep-07
Price	$47.00	$49.75	$53.00	$56.00	$59.00	$63.00	$66.00
Date	Aug-08	Aug-09	Aug-10	Jun-11	May-12	Jun-13	May-14
Price	$69.00	$72.00	$76.00	$80.00	$87.00	$92.00	$96.00
Date	Feb-15	Feb-16		Feb-17		2018	2019
Price	$99.00	$95/$105/$119		$97/$110/$124		$0/$0/$0	$0/$0/$0

Current ticket prices as of *May 2017* (ticket prices may go up):

AGES 2 & UNDER		
Always free		
AGES 3-9		
Single Day Theme Park (varies based on attendance)	$91	Low
Single Day Theme Park (varies based on attendance)	$104	Medium
Single Day Theme Park (varies based on attendance)	$118	High
1-Day Park Hopper (varies based on attendance)	$151	Low
1-Day Park Hopper (varies based on attendance)	$159	Medium
1-Day Park Hopper (varies based on attendance)	$168	High
2-Day 1-Park Per Day	$187	Any 2 days
2-Day Park Hopper	$232	Any 2 days
3-Day 1-Park Per Day	$258	Any 3 days
3-Day Park Hopper	$303	Any 3 days
4-Day 1-Park Per Day	$275	Any 4 days
4-Day Park Hopper	$320	Any 4 days
5-Day 1-Park Per Day	$290	Any 5 days
5-Day Park Hopper	$335	Any 5 days
Deluxe Annual Passport	$619	314 days
Signature Passport	$849	350 days
Signature Plus Passport	$1,049	365 days
Disney Premier Passport (entrance to every Disney park in US)	$1,439	365 Days

AGES 10 & OVER		
Single Day Theme Park (varies based on attendance)	$97	Low
Single Day Theme Park (varies based on attendance)	$110	Medium
Single Day Theme Park (varies based on attendance)	$124	High
1-Day Park Hopper (varies based on attendance)	$157	Low
1-Day Park Hopper (varies based on attendance)	$165	Medium
1-Day Park Hopper (varies based on attendance)	$174	High
2-Day 1-Park Per Day	$199	Any 2 days
2-Day Park Hopper	$244	Any 2 days
3-Day 1-Park Per Day	$270	Any 3 days
3-Day Park Hopper	$315	Any 3 days
4-Day 1-Park Per Day	$290	Any 4 days
4-Day Park Hopper	$335	Any 4 days
5-Day 1-Park Per Day	$305	Any 5 days
5-Day Park Hopper	$350	Any 5 days
Deluxe Annual Passport	$619	314 days
Signature Passport	$849	350 days
Signature Plus Passport	$1,049	365 days
Disney Premier Passport (entrance to every Disney park in US)	$1,439	365 days

NOTE: You can only purchase a 1-Day ticket at the park, not online or anywhere else.

NOTE: If you are going for only one day, check ahead of time as the price varies depending on how busy the day is.

NOTE: Tickets that are 3-Day tickets or more get a free *Magic Morning*. Read more details in *Magic Morning* on page 65.

NOTE: Guests who stay in one of the three Disney hotels can have *Early Entry*, also called *Extra Magic Hour*, every day of the week. With possession of the hotel room key, Guests can enter *Disneyland* one hour early every Tuesday, Thursday, and Saturday. They can also do the same in *California Adventure* every Monday, Wednesday, Friday, and Sunday.

NOTE: If you stay at one of the three Disney hotels, you can use the *Grand Californian* entrance into *California Adventure* which places you by *Grizzly River Run;* you just need your room key.

NOTE: The difference between a *Signature Passport* and a *Signature Plus Passport* is being blocked out 15 days at the end of December. Basically, with the Plus Passport, you are paying $200 to visit the park during the busiest time of the year.

NOTE: Disney doesn't offer a block-out ticket anymore for season passholders. It was set up before that a season pass holder could pay $50 at the ticket booth to get a 1-day pass and get in on a block-out day.

In February 2015, Disney bumped the ticket price up to $99 a day for a single day theme park ticket. At the time, *Magic Kingdom* skyrocketed to $105 a day, making it the first Disney Park to pass the $100 mark.

Disney is trying to figure out a way to cut down its attendance for busy days in the park. In 2016, they inducted the three-tier pricing system. On a busy day, it costs more to get into the park than on a slower day. The three levels are $97 for a slow day, $110 for a regular day, and $124 for a peak day. A peak day being summer days, weekends, and holidays, regular days being week days during non-summer days and some weekends, and regular days being all the other days.

Deluxe Annual Passport Includes:

➤ 314 pre-selected days of admission to both *Disneyland* Resort Theme Parks and unlimited enjoyment of attractions during regular operating hours. Blocked out days are Saturdays, March through August (days may change; you can verify the blockout days on disneyland.com, and keep in mind that Saturdays are the busiest days), the last two weeks in December, and any major holidays.

➤ 10% dining discount at select *Disneyland* Resort restaurants. Special rates at the hotels of the *Disneyland* Resort.

➤ Exclusive benefits at select *Downtown Disney District* locations.

Premium Annual Passport Includes:

➤ 365 consecutive days of admission to both *Disneyland* Resort Theme Parks and unlimited enjoyment of attractions during regular operating hours.

➤ 20% merchandise discount at select locations throughout the *Disneyland* Resort.

➤ Exclusive benefits at select *Downtown Disney District* locations.

➤ Free annual parking pass for the *Mickey & Friends Parking Sructure*.

➤ 10-15% dining discount at select *Disneyland* Resort restaurants.

➤ Special rates at the hotels of the *Disneyland* Resort.

Disneyland Premier Passport Includes:

➤ This pass covers entrance to all of the Disney parks from California and Florida. Including:
   • *Disneyland* Park
   • Disney *California Adventure* Park
   • *Magic Kingdom* theme park
   • *Epcot* theme park
   • Disney's *Hollywood Studios* theme park
   • Disney's *Animal Kingdom* theme park
   • Disney's *Blizzard Beach* water park
   • Disney's *Typhoon Lagoon* water park
   • *DisneyQuest* Indoor Interactive Theme Park
   • *ESPN Wide World of Sports Complex* (valid only on event days; some events require an additional admission charge)
   • Disney's *Oak Trail Golf Course* (greens fee only; tee time reservations are required and are subject to availability)

➤ In addition to unlimited park admission with no block-out dates, a Disney Premier Passport entitles you to all the Premium Passholder benefits at both *Walt Disney World* Resort and *Disneyland* Resort, including:
   • Complimentary parking at all theme parks
   • Merchandise discounts at select locations (save up to 20%)
   • Dining discounts at select locations (save up to 15%)

30

- Discounts and special offers (from time to time) on select car rentals and *Disney* Resort hotel stays
- Exclusive special events and privileges (excluding special events requiring separate admission charge)
- Subscription to the *Mickey Monitor* newsletter and *Backstage Pass*
- Disney Photo Pass Downloads
- Special Events tickets (save up to 20%)

➤ Disney Premier Passports are available for purchase only at select Disney Parks locations:
- *Disneyland Resort* theme park ticket booths
- *Guest Relations* windows at **Walt Disney World** theme parks
- *Downtown Disney* area at *Walt Disney World* Resort

At any time during your trip, the visitor can take the purchased ticket to the ticket booth and trade it in, adding the difference to upgrade to a season pass. For example; $350 for a 5-day pass plus $269 will get you a pass for one year from the day you first used your card. Basically, it will cover a complete second trip. Technically, it really wouldn't save you money unless you went for a third time. If you cannot pay for the whole amount at once, they have a payment plan available for California residents. You just put down $97 and make 12 monthly payments of $79.34 (Signature Plus), $62.67 (Signature), and $43.50 (Deluxe).

You can purchase your tickets online at:
- http://www.disneyland.com
- http://www.mousesavers.com
- http://www.cheaptickets.com
- http://www.citypass.com

Or you can pick them up locally:
- AAA card members can get great deals on tickets at your local AAA office.
- You can also find passes at Safeway grocery stores.
- Your local credit union may have deals on tickets as well.

The good thing about getting a discount ticket from a credit union or AAA is that the ticket still has the selling price on it. Example: I just got a 3-Day pass for $225 from my credit union, but the ticket was marked $250. This comes in handy when upgrading your ticket to a season pass; you are only required to pay the difference between the cost of the season pass and the price listed on the ticket.

WARNING about getting tickets from places like:
- http://www.craigslist.com
- http://www.ebay.com
- http://www.diztix.com

People used to be able to get a cheap season pass if someone was selling their partially-used ticket online on such sites as *craigslist.com* or *ebay.com*. Sometimes people cut their visit short after purchasing a 5-Day Hopper Pass, but only used 4 days of it. You can use their ticket to take advantage of Disney's offer as long as:

- there is one day left on it
- it is still within the 13 days of its first use
- if the seller didn't take advantage and pay the difference between a season pass and the price listed on the ticket

The problem now is *Disneyland* doesn't stamp the entry date on the ticket. The start date is stored in the computer system, so there is no way to check out the validity of a ticket when you buy it "used." Sites like *diztix.com* have strict rules about returning their passes to them by the end of a certain day. If you fail to return them on time, they charge your credit card an outlandish amount of money to compensate them because the buyer kept the ticket. The *Disney* Resort now takes your photo to attach to hopper passes over three days. This makes it virtually impossible to use someone else's ticket. *Disney World* takes a thumbprint of the user, and it is unsure whether or not that technology will be used in California in the future. *Universal Studios Hollywood* is already doing it.

There are sometimes ways to get free admission into *Disneyland*. During some years, has special promotions to get people into the park for free. Check online to find out what will be happening in future years.

FUN FACTS

When the park first opened in 1955, the **cost to get in was $3.50** ($1 for the entrance ticket and $2.50 for a book of tickets). After taking inflation into account, it would be $30.90 to enter the park in 2015, but instead it is $99.

The "ticket book" system (*see photo*) was discontinued in 1982. This was when Disney established a set price to get in and go on all the attractions. The cost to get in back in 1982 was $10.75. Taking into account the cost of inflation, the **$10.75 admission ticket in 1981 would cost you $27.98 now**. But instead, a ticket is $99.

In 1957, the **average person spent $4.90 a day** in the park. This included admission, attractions, food, and souvenirs.

In 2009, anyone was **free on their birthday**. They just had to register online ahead of time. If you already had a season pass to the park, then they gave you a $72 gift card for use in the parks.

In 2010, they had **"Give a day, get a Disney day."** The first one million people to register and work a day as a volunteer got in for one day. They were all registered for the one million volunteers by January 20.

In 2012, the park opened at 6:00 a.m. on February 29, and **didn't close for 24 hours** because of Leap Year; they called it *One More Disney Day*, or *Disney Leap Day*. The first 2,000 people in the park received a collectible Mickey ears hat.

WARDROBE FOR THE TRIP

Since you will be in Southern California, you can dress according to the seasons. During the summer months, pack light clothing, shorts, bathing suit, sunscreen, and a light jacket. During the winter months, be prepared to dress in layers. Pack jeans and t-shirts or long-sleeved shirts for the daytime and a sweatshirt or jacket for early mornings and evenings. Come prepared for the unexpected. Pack an umbrella and the appropriate clothing in case the weather suddenly turns wet or unseasonably warm or cool. Check a weather site like *http://www.weather.com* and type in Anaheim, CA, for a listing of the 10-day forecast, and pack accordingly.

Wear comfortable tennis shoes. I do not recommend wearing sandals, boots or any kind of dress shoes. Pick something you don't mind standing or walking in for 10 hours.

I also recommend taking a small jacket. Try not to bring in something that will fill up your whole backpack. You will be moving around a lot and standing in lines that go inside buildings, so it is easy to get toasty.

Check with the park before going that day to see if it has been a busy week for them. During the weeks of Thanksgiving, Christmas, and New Year's, the park is known for reaching maximum capacity and closing its front gates for re-entry. That means if you leave to get your jacket from the car, you won't be getting back in.

Here is a chart of the average and record temperatures for Anaheim.

	Jan	Feb	Mar	Apr	May	Jun	Jul	Aug	Sep	Oct	Nov	Dec
Rec. High	95°	94°	97°	106°	106°	104°	107°	102°	108°	107°	99°	89°
Avg. High	69.7°	69.9°	72.2°	74.6°	77.1°	80.2°	85.2°	86.9°	85.8°	81.3°	73°	70.2°
Avg. Low	47.3°	48.4°	50.4°	52.9°	57.3°	60.6°	64°	64.4°	62.2°	57.8°	50.2°	47.4°
Rec. Low	30°	30°	37°	38°	45°	50°	54°	53°	51°	45°	33°	32°

PACKING FOR THE TRIP CHECKLIST

___ Address book and stamps to send a postcard from a *Disneyland* Mailbox
___ Autograph book and fat pen (big pens make it easier for the characters to hold)
___ Backpack (with zippers, not buttons, clips or draw strings; things fall out)
___ Camera and batteries, video camera
___ Cash and credit cards
___ Driver's license
___ Emergency numbers or contacts from home
___ Fanny packs (*giggle* do people still use these?)
___ Hat
___ Health insurance card
___ Insect repellent (in the summer)
___ Lip balm with sunscreen
___ "Mister" (sprays a mist of water during the hotter months)
___ Motion sickness pills (if you get car sick on attractions)
___ Pennies & quarters for the souvenir penny press machines
___ Purse pack sized tissue
___ Rain ponchos/umbrella (plastic ponchos are $7.50 in the park)
___ Re-sealable plastic bags (big and small)
___ Sunglasses
___ Sunscreen (Disney Sun Pals SPF 45 has been approved by dermatologists)
___ Sweatshirt or jacket
___ Veterinarian records if you are bringing your dog or cat and leaving them at the *Kennel Club*
___ Walking shoes
___ Wet wipes and hand sanitizer

GETTING TO THE PARKS & PARKING

There are many ways to get to the parks. You can fly, drive, take a train, or take a bus.

ARRIVAL BY FLIGHT

Make sure you book your flight as far in advance as you can for maximum savings. Land at Los Angeles airport, LAX. The airport is 35 miles from *Disneyland*, or just a 38-minute drive, depending on traffic, at 1 World Way, Los Angeles, CA 90045. If you get a rental car, just take highway **105 east** for 12 miles, highway **710 south** for 2 miles, highway **91 east** for 12 miles, then highway **5 south** for 5 miles and finally exit onto **Disneyland Drive**. Depending on your city of departure, flying can cost several hundred dollars per person. The best place to check for flight prices is *orbitz.com* and *expedia.com*.

ARRIVAL BY TRAIN

Make sure you book your train as far in advance as you can for maximum savings. Not all areas have trains leaving on the days you plan to leave on your trip. You might have to find a departure time and location first, before booking your hotel. The Amtrak station is only 2 ½ miles down Katella Ave from *Disneyland*, at 2150 East Katella Avenue. Depending on your city of departure, taking the train can cost several hundred dollars per person. You can visit *amtrak.com* for schedules and pricing.

ARRIVAL BY BUS

Make sure you book your bus as far in advance as you can for maximum savings. The Greyhound bus station is a little over a mile from *Disneyland*, at 100 W Winston Rd. Depending on your city of departure, taking the bus can cost under a hundred dollars per person. You can visit *greyhound.com* for schedules and pricing.

ARRIVAL BY CAR

If you decide to drive, just exit **highway 5** at **Disneyland Drive** in Anaheim, California, from north or south. Drive straight through to the entrance of the *Disneyland* parking lot on Ball Road. If you have family or friends that live within a reasonable distance from *Disneyland*, then this is the best way to travel to the parks. Even if you have to stop for the night in a hotel, it is still cheaper than flying if you have a car full of people.

You can easily budget for gas by figuring out your gas costs ahead of time. Just take the average miles per gallon that your car gets, go to *maps.google.com,* and figure out the distance you have to travel. Then, divide your mpg into the amount of miles you have to travel, and multiply it by the current cost of a gallon of gasoline. Example: mpg = 25, divided into 400 miles = 16 gallons, multiply by current gas costs of $3.98 a gallon = $63.68 for a one-way trip.

Currently, the parking price is $20.00 a day. This is continually going up, so check ahead of time.

 The *Disneyland* parking structure is the **sixth largest parking structure in the world,** but when it opened on June 27, 2000, it was the largest in North America. It can hold over 10,000 vehicles.

 There are **over 23,000 parking spaces** at *Walt Disney World*.

Because the parking lot is so huge, it is easy to lose your vehicle. When leaving your car, write down what area you are parked in. If you don't have a pen and paper with you, just text yourself the location or take a temporary photo with your cell phone camera for easy reference.

Parking for Guests with disabilities is available throughout the *Disneyland* Resort, including the *Mickey and Friends Parking Structure* and the *Toy Story Parking Area* off of **Harbor Boulevard**. A valid disability parking permit is required.

If you would like to save money on parking, just walk in.

- Off of **Ball Road** on **West Place** is a small parking lot for employees. You can walk across that small parking lot, proceed across the parking structure, and then take the tram into the park.

- From **Katella Ave.**, you can walk down **Disneyland Way** and enter *Downtown Disney* by the *AMC Theater;* then ride the *Monorail* into *Tomorrowland*.

- If you will be visiting *Disneyland* for two hours or less, you can park in the *Downtown Disney* parking lot for free. Every hour thereafter is $12 (which is cheaper than the regular parking fee).

- If you plan on eating at one of the table service restaurants in *Downtown Disney*, you can get an extra two hours validated, giving you four hours of free parking. They also validate if you are going to watch a movie at the *AMC Theater*.

- If you are going to be upgrading your ticket to a season pass, then take the parking pass you are given upon entering the parking garage with you. They will subtract the amount on the ticket from your season pass parking upgrade.

- Besides the savings on parking costs (especially if you are an annual passholder without parking on your pass), the *Downtown Disney* lot affords you the convenience of not having to deal with the parking lot trams. You can board the *Monorail* and enter *Disneyland* in *Tomorrowland*. This can be a huge time saver and lots of fun for the kids.

HOTELS

The main streets surrounding the *Disneyland* theme parks are **Katella Ave., Disneyland Dr., Walnut St., Harbor Blvd.,** and **Ball Rd.** If you can find a hotel on these streets, then you're set for a straight shot to the parks. When making reservations, you can usually find a cheap hotel room for around $35 to $55 a night, depending on the time of year, days of the week, and how far in advance you book. You can get some great deals at the following sites:

- http://www.travelocity.com
- http://www.orbitz.com
- http://www.expedia.com

About 95% of the hotels that I have researched in the area have microwaves and mini-fridges. If this is important to you, look into it before making your reservation. One time, my hotel said they had a microwave. But, I found out upon arrival that it was for rent at $10 a night. So, find out in advance if a microwave is included in the price or if it costs extra.

Some hotels offer a transit pass to get to *Disneyland*. Others offer a bus pass. If you are on the main streets, walking may be just fine.

The following list is for convenience only; not for advertisement.

- If you need some food to take into the park, take **Katella** to **Food 4 Less**.

- If the weather changes and you don't want to spend $35 on a sweater in the park, take **Harbor** to **Target**.

- If you don't want to spend $80 to eat lunch in the park, walk down **Katella** to **Del Taco**, or right outside the entrance to **McDonald's** (prices there are inflated due to its location).

- If you don't want fast food, go to **Tiffy's** on **Katella** (by the back corner of *California Adventure*).

- If you are leaving the parking structure and you need gas before entering the freeway, go to the **Arco** on **W. Ball**.

COST TO EAT IN THE PARK
A CROSS SECTION

FOOD

Small Hamburger	$6.50
Hot Dog	$5.39
Chili Dog	$6.39
French Fries	$3.00
Large Pizza (Pizza Port)	$31.99
Blue Bayou Average Plate	$27.99 - $35.00
Clam Chowder Bread Bowl	$8.95
Gumbo Bowl (in sour dough)	$8.95
Corn Dog	$5.39
Turkey Leg	$9.00

SNACKS

		DRINKS	
Soft Pretzel	$3.00	Soda 20 oz.	$2.99
Churro	$3.00	Water Bottle	$2.75
Popcorn	$2.75 - $5.50	Lemon Icee	$4.00
Cotton Candy	$3.00	Coffee (free refill w/receipt @ Market House)	$2.50
Dole Whip	$3.75	**DESSERT**	
Candy Apple	$3.47	Häagen-Dazs Ice-cream Bar	$5.00
Fresh Fruit (Apple, Banana, Orange)	$1.75	Frozen Chocolate Dipped Banana	$3.75
Pickle	$2.50	Ice-cream Sandwich	$3.00

Many *Disneyland* visitors have their favorite Disney food that they have to get every trip, or even every day. Keep your eyes open for these "favorites" provided by a fan poll on my Facebook fan page:

Pomme Frites	Chocolate-Dipped Caramel Apple	Gumbo Bread Bowl
Creme Brule	Broccoli & Cheddar Bread Bowl	Corn on the Cob
Giant Pickle	Main Street Ice Cream Sundae	Frozen Lemonade
Dole Whip	Mickey-shaped Ice Cream Bar	Pineapple Spears
Mint Julep	Mickey Rice Crispy Treats	Goofy Sour Balls
Turkey Leg	Monte Cristo Sandwich	Dole Whip Float
Crab Cakes	Honey Pot Candy Apple	Mickey Beignets
Kettle Corn	Bengal Barbeque Skewer	Mickey Waffle
Macaroons	Cream Cheese Pretzel	Fresh Cupcake
Chili Dog	Mac and Cheese Dog	Mickey Pretzel
Corn Dog	Tie Dyed Cheesecake	Frozen Banana
Popcorn	New Orleans Fritters	Fried Chicken
Churro	Clam Chowder Bowl	Cotton Candy
Fudge	Chocolate Croissant	Pork Shank

FOOD FUN FACTS

🎈 The **only restaurants that offer all-you-can-eat** are *Ariel's Grotto* in *California Adventure* and *Plaza Inn* offer a breakfast buffet.

🎈 There are **only three restaurants that offer free refills on sodas:** the *Plaza Inn, Rancho del Zocalo,* and *Pizza Port.*

If you are looking for a **table service breakfast meal**, *Carnation Café* on *Main Street, U.S.A.* is the only restaurant that offers it. There are only four table service restaurants in *Disneyland*: *Blue Bayou, Cafe Orleans, Carnation Café*, and *Plaza Inn*.

Even though the menus offer full meals when you order, **you can ask for items à la carte and get charged separately**. The same goes for not wanting an item. If you order a hot dog and don't want the bag of chips, the Cast Member can subtract it from your order, so you don't have to pay for it.

On select days during the Christmas season, **handmade candy canes are prepared** at *Candy Palace* in *Disneyland* and *Trolley Treats* in *California Adventure*. Lines form for these early (before park opening) and numbers are distributed. So, if you want one, don't expect to stroll up to these candy shops in the middle of the day and just pick one up. Despite the fanfare, there really isn't anything all that special about these candy canes. The fun is in watching Cast Members make the candy canes at the open-air bakeries (which anyone can do, regardless of whether you purchase a candy cane or not). They will only make about 160 of them a day in several batches.

If you are not very hungry, **adults can order from the Kid's Menu**.

For reservations, call (714) 781-DINE or (714) 781-3463. Disney doesn't offer what we think of as "Reserved Seating;" they offer "Priority Seating." It is recommended that you show up 15 minutes prior to your "reserved" time. They will fit you in with the next available seating. If you have any special requests, like sitting next to the water in the *Blue Bayou*, you could be waiting a little longer than anticipated. You can make reservations up to 60 days in advance.

Right now, the **most popular restaurant that you will definitely need a reservation** for is the *Carthay Circle Restaurant* in *California Adventure*. It is the newest and most formal. Because of this, the *Blue Bayou* is less busy, which used to be the most popular.

RESTAURANT FUN FACTS

Disneyland **goes through a lot of food every year**. Visitors from all over the world want to try out different foods to make their tummies enjoy the happiest place on earth. This is how much food is eaten every year.

- Hamburgers   4 million
- Hot Dogs/Corn Dogs   1.6 million
- French Fries   3.4 million orders
- Popcorn   43.7 million boxes (that's 18.4 million gallons)
- Ice Cream   3.2 million servings
- Soft Drinks   1.2 million gallons
- Churros   2.8 million

There has been **enough ice cream served up to make a life-size replica** of the *Matterhorn Bobsleds Mountain*.

If there is a particularly delicious dish that you fancy in one of the restaurants, visit *City Hall;* **they keep copies of recipes on hand** for some of the more popular dishes. Asking your waiter could result in a visit from the kitchen's chef.

The popular golden triangle chip ***Doritos* were invented in *Disneyland*.** There was a restaurant in *Frontierland* called *Casa De Frito*, which is now *Rancho del Zocalo Restaurante*, and was sponsored by Frito-Lay. It opened shortly after the park did in 1955. This was a sit-down restaurant and was well known for its Frito Pie. At the end of the day, the restaurant would throw out old corn tortillas supplied by Alex Foods. A distributor for Alex Foods noticed this happening and suggested to the chef to turn the unwanted corn tortillas into corn chips. The chef did this and added seasonings to the final product to resemble the Mexican chilaquiles. Over time, they became so popular that the restaurant began selling them in bags for 5¢ in 1964. "The Frito Kid" was the mascot and had a statue standing near the restaurant while people inserted their money into the "vending machine." "The Frito Kid" had two locations from which you could purchase the chips. One was by the entrance to *Casa De Frito* and the second was at *Aunt Jemima's Kitchen*, which was the original location for *Casa De Frito* before moving to where the building is today, near where *Pirates of the Caribbean* is now.

Frito-Lay figured out that they could mass produce these phenomenal chips and wanted to make them available outside the park. Up until then, Frito-Lay didn't have any corn-based chips in their arsenal of products available elsewhere; their main seller was potato chips. In 1966, Frito-Lay made "Doritos," which means "little golden things," available nationwide, making it the first nationally-distributed corn chip. Not sure if this part is true, but when the original logo was made, it resembled the original *Disneyland* entrance sign.

The ***River Belle Terrace* wasn't always what it is today.** The restaurant started out as *Casa de Fritos* (1955-1957) before it moved to the center of *Frontierland*, when it became the *Silver Banjo Barbeque* (1957-1961). When the *Banjo* closed, it became part of the expansion to give extra space to the restaurant on the corner of *Adventureland* and *Frontierland*, *Aunt Jemima's Pancake House* (1955-1962), which became *Aunt Jemima's Kitchen* (1962-1970), then *Magnolia Tree Terrace* (1970-1971), and then *River Belle Terrace* (1971-Present).

Here is a list of the restaurants, listed by land. All the prices do not include the drinks, which can vary depending on what you get. A soda is $2.99-$3.49. This is the key for the meals: Breakfast=**B**, Lunch=**L**, Dinner=**D**, and Snacks=**S**.

Disneyland

Main Street, U.S.A.

Carnation Café

TYPE: American, Vegetarian	
FOOD: Soup, salad, sandwich, breakfast foods	
PRICE RANGE: $6 to $13 per person	
Character Meet & Greet: No	
RESERVATIONS: Walk-In	MEALS: B, L, D

Gibson Girl Ice Cream Parlor

TYPE: American	
FOOD: A selection of flavors for a cone, a sundae, or milkshakes	
PRICE RANGE: $4 - $6 per person	
Character Meet & Greet: No	MEALS: S
RESERVATIONS: N	

Main Street Cone Shop

TYPE: American	
FOOD: Ice cream cones and very large ice cream sandwiches	
PRICE RANGE: $4 - $6 per person	
Character Meet & Greet: No	MEALS: S
RESERVATIONS: Walk-In	

Plaza Inn

TYPE: American, Vegetarian	
FOOD: Fried chicken, pasta, pot roast, salad, breakfast buffet	
PRICE RANGE: $4 - $24 per person	MEALS: B, L, D, Buffet
Character Meet & Greet: Yes	
RESERVATIONS: Recommended	

Refreshment Corner

TYPE: American	
FOOD: Sourdough bread bowls and hot dogs	
PRICE RANGE: $3 - $9 per person	MEALS: B, L, D, S
Character Meet & Greet: No	
RESERVATIONS: Walk-In	

Jolly Holiday Bakery Café

TYPE: American	
FOOD: Sandwiches, soups, salads and bakery items	
PRICE RANGE: $7 - $10 per person	MEALS: L, D
Character Meet & Greet: No	
RESERVATIONS: Walk-In	

41

Little Red Wagon	
TYPE: American	
FOOD: Hand dipped corndogs only	
PRICE RANGE: $7 each	MEALS: L, D, S
Character Meet & Greet: No	
RESERVATIONS: Cart	

Market House Coffee Counter	
TYPE: Drinks	
FOOD: Coffee and hot chocolate (keep receipt for free coffee refill)	
PRICE RANGE: $3 - $5 per person	MEALS: Drinks
Character Meet & Greet: No	
RESERVATIONS: Walk-In	

Adventureland

Bengal Barbecue	
TYPE: American, Vegetarian	
FOOD: Meats on skewers with a variety of flavors	
PRICE RANGE: $4 per person	MEALS: L, D, S
Character Meet & Greet: No	
RESERVATIONS: Walk-In	

Tiki Juice Bar	
TYPE: American	
FOOD: Dole whip, Dole whip floats, fruit bowls, pineapple spears	
PRICE RANGE: $3 - $5 per person	MEALS: S
Character Meet & Greet: No	
RESERVATIONS: Walk-In	

Tropical Imports	
TYPE: American, Healthy Selections, Vegetarian	
FOOD: Prepackaged snacks and fruits	
PRICE RANGE: $2+ per person	MEALS: S
Character Meet & Greet: No	
RESERVATIONS: Walk-In	

Critter Country

Harbour Galley	
TYPE: American	
FOOD: Soups, chili, clam chowder, salads	
PRICE RANGE: $9 - $10 per person	MEALS: B, L, D
Character Meet & Greet: No	
RESERVATIONS: Walk-In	

Hungry Bear Restaurant	
TYPE: American, Vegetarian	
FOOD: Sandwiches, burgers, salads	
PRICE RANGE: $3 - $11 per person	MEALS: L, D
Character Meet & Greet: No	
RESERVATIONS: Walk-In	

Fantasyland

Edelweiss Snacks

TYPE: American	
FOOD: Turkey legs, chimichangas, corn on the cob	
PRICE RANGE: $5 - $9 per person	MEALS: S
Character Meet & Greet: No	
RESERVATIONS: Walk-In	

Troubadour Tavern

TYPE: American, Vegetarian	
FOOD: Bratwurst, corn on the cob, baked potatoes, ice cream, fruit	
PRICE RANGE: $4 - $9 per person	MEALS: L, D, S
Character Meet & Greet: No	
RESERVATIONS: Walk-In	

Village Haus Restaurant

TYPE: American, Vegetarian	
FOOD: Burgers, pizza, salads	
PRICE RANGE: $6 - $11 per person	MEALS: L, D
Character Meet & Greet: No	
RESERVATIONS: Walk-In	

Frontierland

The Golden Horseshoe

TYPE: American	
FOOD: Chicken strips, fish & chips, ice cream	
PRICE RANGE: $5 - $10 per person	MEALS: L, D
Character Meet & Greet: No	
RESERVATIONS: Walk-In	

Rancho del Zocalo Restaurante

TYPE: American, Healthy Selections, Mexican, Vegetarian	
FOOD: Grilled chicken, enchiladas, tacos, soups, salads	
PRICE RANGE: $5 - $14 per person	MEALS: L, D
Character Meet & Greet: No	
RESERVATIONS: Walk-In	

River Belle Terrace

TYPE: American, Healthy Selections, Vegetarian	
FOOD: Breakfast foods, sandwiches, soups, salads	
PRICE RANGE: $3 - $13 per person	MEALS: B, L, D
Character Meet & Greet: No	
RESERVATIONS: Walk-In	

Stage Door Café

TYPE: American	
FOOD: Chicken strips, fish & chips, funnel cakes	
PRICE RANGE: $5 - $10 per person	MEALS: B, L, D, S
Character Meet & Greet: No	
RESERVATIONS: Walk-In	

Mickey's Toontown

Clarabelle's

TYPE: American	
FOOD: Sandwiches, salads, desserts	
PRICE RANGE: $4 - $9 per person	MEALS: L, D, S
Character Meet & Greet: No	
RESERVATIONS: Walk-In	

Daisy's Diner

TYPE: American	
FOOD: Pepperoni or cheese personal pizzas	
PRICE RANGE: $8 per person	MEALS: L, D, S
Character Meet & Greet: No	
RESERVATIONS: Walk-In	

Pluto's Dog House

TYPE: American	
FOOD: Hot dogs, cheesy macaroni	
PRICE RANGE: $6 per person	MEALS: L, D, S
Character Meet & Greet: No	
RESERVATIONS: Walk-In	

Toon Up Treats

TYPE: American	
FOOD: Fresh fruit and other snacks	
PRICE RANGE: $3 - $4 per person	MEALS: S
Character Meet & Greet: No	
RESERVATIONS: Walk-In	

New Orleans Square

Blue Bayou

TYPE: Cajun-Creole, Healthy Selections, Vegetarian	
FOOD: Seafood, ribs, chicken, filet mignon	
PRICE RANGE: $25 - $47 per person	MEALS: L, D
Character Meet & Greet: No	
RESERVATIONS: Recommended	

Café Orleans

TYPE: American, Cajun-Creole, Healthy Selections, Vegetarian	
FOOD: Soups, sandwiches, salads	
PRICE RANGE: $6 - $19 per person	MEALS: L, D
Character Meet & Greet: No	
RESERVATIONS: Recommended	

French Market Restaurant

TYPE: American, Cajun-Creole, Healthy Selections, Vegetarian	
FOOD: Roasted chicken, roast beef, seafood, pastas, salads	
PRICE RANGE: $12 - $15 per person	MEALS: L, D
Character Meet & Greet: No	
RESERVATIONS: Walk-In	

Mint Julep Bar	
TYPE: American	
FOOD: Alcohol-free mint juleps, Mickey shaped beignets	
PRICE RANGE: $3 - $7 per person	MEALS: S, Drinks
Character Meet & Greet: No	
RESERVATIONS: Walk-In	

Royal Street Veranda	
TYPE: American, Cajun-Creole, Vegetarian	
FOOD: Clam chowder, gumbo, coffee	
PRICE RANGE: $4 - $10 per person	MEALS: L, D, S
Character Meet & Greet: No	
RESERVATIONS: Walk-In	

Tomorrowland

Redd Rockett's Pizza Port	
TYPE: American, Healthy Selections, Italian, Vegetarian	
FOOD: Pasta, pizza, salads (whole pizza $32)	
PRICE RANGE: $8 - $10 per person	MEALS: L, D
Character Meet & Greet: No	
RESERVATIONS: Walk-In	

Tomorrowland Terrace	
TYPE: American, Healthy Selections, Vegetarian	
FOOD: Breakfast foods, hamburgers, sandwiches, salads	
PRICE RANGE: $9 - $11 per person	MEALS: B, L, D
Character Meet & Greet: No	
RESERVATIONS: Walk-In	

California Adventure

Golden State

Alfresco Lounge at the Golden Vine Winery	
TYPE: American	
FOOD: Bruschetta, salads, paninis, wine	
PRICE RANGE: $7 - $11 per person	MEALS: L, D
Character Meet & Greet: No	
RESERVATIONS: Walk-In	

Wine Country Trattoria	
TYPE: Healthy Selections, Italian, Vegetarian	
FOOD: Salads, pastas, fish, sandwiches	
PRICE RANGE: $12 - $23 per person	MEALS: L, D
Character Meet & Greet: No	
RESERVATIONS: Recommended	

Mendocino Terrace Wine Bar	
TYPE: American	
FOOD: Wines, cheese, fruit	
PRICE RANGE: $10 - $20 per person	MEALS: Alcohol
Character Meet & Greet: No	
RESERVATIONS: Service Counter	

Pacific Warf

Cocina Cucamonga Mexican Grill	
TYPE: Healthy Selections, Mexican, Vegetarian	
FOOD: Tacos, burritos, tamales, grilled chicken	
PRICE RANGE: $10 - $14 per person	MEALS: L, D
Character Meet & Greet: No	
RESERVATIONS: Walk-In	

The Lucky Fortune Cookery	
TYPE: Asian, Healthy Selections, Vegetarian	
FOOD: Rice bowl with vegetables and chicken, beef or tofu	
PRICE RANGE: $10 per person	MEALS: L, D
Character Meet & Greet: No	
RESERVATIONS: Walk-In	

Pacific Wharf Café	
TYPE: California, American, Healthy Selections, Vegetarian	
FOOD: Breakfast foods, soups, salads, sandwiches	
PRICE RANGE: $4 - $10 per person	MEALS: B, L, D, S
Character Meet & Greet: No	
RESERVATIONS: Service Counter	

Rita's Baja Blenders	
TYPE: American, Mexican	
FOOD: Margaritas	
PRICE RANGE: $7 - $9 per person	MEALS: Drinks
Character Meet & Greet: No	
RESERVATIONS: Service Counter	

Smokejumpers Grill	
TYPE: American, Vegetarian	
FOOD: Burgers, salads, sandwich, chili fries	
PRICE RANGE: $6 - $13 per person	MEALS: L, D, S
Character Meet & Greet: No	
RESERVATIONS: Service Counter	

Hollywood Land

Award Wieners	
TYPE: American	
FOOD: Philly cheese steak, hot dogs	
PRICE RANGE: $6 - $9 per person	MEALS: L, D, S
Character Meet & Greet: No	
RESERVATIONS: Service Counter	

Fairfax Market

TYPE: Healthy Selections, Vegetarian	
FOOD: Prepackaged snacks and fruits	
PRICE RANGE: $2+ per person	MEALS: S
Character Meet & Greet: No	
RESERVATIONS: Service Counter	

Schmoozies

TYPE: American, Healthy Selections, Vegetarian	
FOOD: Smoothies, coffees	
PRICE RANGE: $3 - $5 per person	MEALS: Drinks
Character Meet & Greet: No	
RESERVATIONS: Service Counter	

Studio Catering Co.

TYPE: American	
FOOD: Chips, coffee, sodas	
PRICE RANGE: $3 - $4 per person	MEALS: S, Drinks
Character Meet & Greet: No	
RESERVATIONS: Service Counter	

Paradise Pier

Ariel's Grotto

TYPE: American, Healthy Selections, Vegetarian	
FOOD: Pasta, tri-tip, fish, ricotta	
PRICE RANGE: $25 - $45 per person	MEALS: B, L, D, Buffet
Character Meet & Greet: Yes	
RESERVATIONS: Recommended	

Bayside Brews

TYPE: American	
FOOD: Pretzels, beer	
PRICE RANGE: $4 - $7 per person	MEALS: S, Drinks
Character Meet & Greet: No	
RESERVATIONS: Walk-In	

Boardwalk Pizza & Pasta

TYPE: Healthy Selections, Italian, Vegetarian	
FOOD: Pizzas, pastas, salads	
PRICE RANGE: $8 - $10 per person	MEALS: L, D
Character Meet & Greet: No	
RESERVATIONS: Walk-In	

Corn Dog Castle

TYPE: American	
FOOD: Corn dogs	
PRICE RANGE: $7 per person	MEALS: L, D, S, Drinks
Character Meet & Greet: No	
RESERVATIONS: Service Counter	

Cove Bar

TYPE: American	
FOOD: Buffalo wings, tacos, pizza, tri-tip sliders, nachos	
PRICE RANGE: $9 - $11 per person	MEALS: L, D, S
Character Meet & Greet: No	
RESERVATIONS: Service Counter	

Dulce Aventura

TYPE: American	
FOOD: Caramel apples, cookies, sweets	
PRICE RANGE: $3 - $9 per person	MEALS: S
Character Meet & Greet: No	
RESERVATIONS: Service Counter	

Hot Dog Hut

TYPE: American	
FOOD: Hot dogs, corn on the cob	
PRICE RANGE: $5 - $6 per person	MEALS: L, D, S
Character Meet & Greet: No	
RESERVATIONS: Service Counter	

Don Tomas

TYPE: American	
FOOD: Turkey legs, corn on the cob, chimichangas	
PRICE RANGE: $5 - $9 per person	MEALS: L, D, S
Character Meet & Greet: No	
RESERVATIONS: Service Counter	

Paradise Garden Grill

TYPE: Healthy Selections, Mediterranean, Vegetarian	
FOOD: Mediterranean skewers, Greek salad	
PRICE RANGE: $8 - $11 per person	MEALS: L, D
Character Meet & Greet: No	
RESERVATIONS: Service Counter	

Paradise Pier Ice Cream Company

TYPE: American	
FOOD: Vanilla or chocolate soft serve ice cream, beachfront floats	
PRICE RANGE: $4 - $5 per person	MEALS: S
Character Meet & Greet: No	
RESERVATIONS: Service Counter	

World of Color Picnics Dessert Party

TYPE: Dessert, beverage	
FOOD: Dessert-This is to reserve your spot for *World of Color*	
PRICE RANGE: $79 per person	MEALS: Dessert
Character Meet & Greet: No	
RESERVATIONS: Recommended	

Cars Land	
Cozy Cone Motel	
TYPE: American, Healthy Selections, Vegetarian	
FOOD: Churro bites, soft serve, bacon-scrambled egg cone, pretzel bites, chili	
PRICE RANGE: $3 - $12	MEALS: B, L, D, S
Character Meet & Greet: No	
RESERVATIONS: Service Counter	
Fillmore's Taste-In	
TYPE: American, Healthy Selections, Vegetarian	
FOOD: Fruit, chips, juice, soda, veggie cups	
PRICE RANGE: $2 - $4	MEALS: S, Drinks
Character Meet & Greet: No	
RESERVATIONS: Cart	
Flo's V8 Café	
TYPE: American, Healthy Selections, Vegetarian	
FOOD: Spit-fired rotisserie, turkey salad, veggie tater bake	
PRICE RANGE: $4 - $12	MEALS: B, L, D
Character Meet & Greet: No	

(Mint Julep, Ghirardelli Chocolate Sundae, Boysen Apple Freeze, Dole Whip)

(Monte Cristo Sandwich, Corn Dog, Matterhorn Macaroon, Mickey Beignets)

49

THE DISNEY HOTELS

DISNEYLAND HOTEL

The *Disneyland Hotel* is noted as the first hotel to officially bear the Disney name. It has been in operation since 1955, although it was not owned by The Walt Disney Company until 1988. When Walt Disney constructed *Disneyland* in 1955, the cost to build the park exceeded $17 million, and he did not have the money to build and operate a hotel. Adjusting for inflation, it would cost $150,381,492.54 to build *Disneyland* today with the materials and building techniques of 1955. Walt Disney negotiated a deal with Jack Wrather to build and operate the hotel. The contract gave Wrather the

rights to use the *Disneyland Hotel* name on any hotel in the state of California until the year 2054. The history of the hotels is mainly from Wikipedia.

The Hotels Infancy 1955-1984

Designed by the firm of Pereira & Luckman, the original *Disneyland Hotel* consisted of a two-story guest room complex (later known as the South Garden Rooms) with shopping, dining, and recreational facilities, including the Plaza Building and Restaurant Row. It was one of the first hotels in the region to offer accommodations for four persons per room. Guests traveled between the hotel and *Disneyland Park* main entrance via a tram. Over the years, the hotel has expanded to include another two-story guest room complex, North Garden, and three guest room towers: Sierra, Marina, and Bonita. The *Disneyland Monorail* was extended from its original 1959 configuration and a station was opened at the hotel in 1961. Recreational areas, attractions, and a convention center were also added over the years.

Disney Takes Over

When Michael Eisner became Chairman & CEO of Walt Disney Productions in 1984, he desperately wanted to get out of Disney's agreement with the Wrather Corporation and bring the *Disneyland Hotel* under the Walt Disney Company's umbrella. However, every time Wrather was approached by Disney, he said that he was happy with the contract. When Jack Wrather died in late 1984, The Walt Disney Company bought the entire Wrather Corporation. As a result, Disney owns the *Disneyland Hotel*, along with the RMS Queen Mary (a retired ocean liner), *The Lone Ranger*, and the TV series *Lassie*. In 1988, the hotel came under the ownership of the Walt Disney Company.

The Resort Expansion 1999-2001

In 1999, a significant portion of the hotel was demolished to make way for *Downtown Disney* and parking areas for the newly-expanded *Disneyland* Resort. Most buildings east of the Sierra Tower and north of the Marina Tower were demolished including the original hotel buildings. The only original buildings remaining in these areas are the convention center, parking garage, and the second-level monorail station which was significantly renovated but still in its original location. Recreational facilities were built in the quad between the three towers, previous site of the *Water Wonderland*, to replace those that were located east of the Sierra Tower. Streets used to access the hotel by car were re-grated and/or outright eliminated, and new streets were built to access the hotel. Tram service from the hotel was also discontinued, leaving the monorail as the only vehicular mode of transportation from park to hotel.

The loss of hotel rooms was offset with the opening of *Disney's Grand Californian Hotel* in 2001, but many of the restaurants and amenities that existed prior to 1999 were never replaced. The hotel contains 990 rooms.

The *Disneyland Hotel* Today

Today none of the original hotel buildings from 1955 remain standing. Original signs and other artifacts from several of the demolished stores and restaurants are on display in the hotel's employee cafeteria.

ESPN Zone, *Rainforest Café*, and *AMC Theater*, all *Downtown Disney* venues, now occupy much of the former hotel space east of the Sierra Tower. Mickey Mouse theming is employed in many interior furnishings and details. In 2007, the Marina, Sierra, and Bonita Towers were renamed Magic, Dreams, and Wonder. Other buildings in the sprawling hotel complex house restaurants, stores, offices, recreational facilities, and convention and banquet facilities. The complex also features gazebo and garden areas that are used for *Disney's Fairy Tale Weddings* (*see page 57*).

In keeping with the re-drawn hotel boundaries, the monorail station was re-designated the *Downtown Disney Monorail Station*, and is still used to takes guests to *Tomorrowland* inside *Disneyland* Park along the same beamway that existed prior to the 1999-2001 expansion. An exclusive entrance to *Disney's California Adventure* for guests staying at Disneyland Resort hotels is a short walk away.

There is a waiting room inside the lobby that is used for *Goofy's Kitchen* restaurant. Disney movies are shown in the air-conditioned room. Sit, relax, and cool off. There is also a mural wall in an enclosed case that contains old Disney memorabilia (*see photo*). Some walls contain lots of old Disney photos.

Today none of the original hotel buildings from 1955 remain standing. Very little of the hotel, other than parking areas and service facilities, sit outside of the perimeter created by the three remaining guest room towers. Original signs and other artifacts from several of the stores and restaurants demolished with the Plaza are on display in the hotel's employee cafeteria.

ESPN Zone, Rainforest Café, and *AMC Theatres,* all *Downtown Disney* venues, now occupy much of the former hotel space east of the *Sierra Tower*. Mickey Mouse theming is employed in many interior furnishings and details. In 2007, the *Marina, Sierra,* and *Bonita Towers* were renamed *Magic, Dreams,* and *Wonder,* respectively. Other buildings in the sprawling hotel complex house restaurants, stores, offices, recreational facilities, and convention and banquet facilities. The complex also features gazebo and garden areas that are used for *Disney's Fairy Tale Weddings & Honeymoons*.

A new *Downtown Disney Monorail Station* was built on the same site as the old *Disneyland Hotel* station, and still takes Guests to *Tomorrowland* inside *Disneyland,* along the same beamway that existed prior to the 1999–2001 expansion.

The *Disneyland Hotel* started a major renovation in 2009, beginning with the

Dreams Tower. Renovation of the hotel included new windows, wallpaper, carpeting, and decor. The *Dreams Tower*, completed in 2010, became the *Adventure Tower*. The *Wonder Tower* became the *Frontier Tower* after its completion in 2011, and the *Magic Tower* became the *Fantasy Tower* in 2012.

The *Neverland Pool* area also received a redesign which was completed in 2012. This transformation includes six new cabanas and two new water slides featuring the iconic original park signage at the top, along with replicas of Mark I Monorails encasing both slides. A new four-foot pool was built between the former *Neverland Pool* and water play area. (*see photo*)

52

On May 25, 2011, the two new dining locations at the *Disneyland Hotel* opened, replacing the former *Hook's Pointe, Croc's Bites* and *Birs, The Wine Cellar*, and *The Lost Bar* locations. *Tangaroa Terrace* is the new location that serves casual dining in a new innovative way. There are touch screens to place an order and select your side. *Tangaroa Terrace* is a casual dining experience with Tahitian architecture based on *Adventureland*, most specifically the *Jungle Cruise* and *The Enchanted Tiki Room*. The new bar, *Trader Sam's Enchanted Tiki Bar*, is based on the *Jungle Cruise's* head salesman, Trader Sam. These two new locations are rather small inside, but there is plenty of outdoor seating, including seating by a giant fireplace by the pool entrance. Also, a new pool area opened when the *Neverland Pool* closed for renovations. There is a new pool, located between the monorail-inspired slides and the closed *Neverland Pool*, which is called the *'D'-Ticket Pool* inspired by the D-ticket admission.

Hotel Facilities

➤ **Restaurants:**
- *Goofy's Kitchen*
- *Steakhouse 55* (formerly Granville's Steak House)
- *The Coffee House*
- *Tangaroa Terrace* – Casual Island Dining

➤ **Bars:**
- *Trader Sam's Enchanted Tiki Bar*
- *The Lounge at Steakhouse 55*

➤ **Shops:**
- *Disney's Fantasia Shop*
- *Small World Gifts & Sundries* (formerly *Donald's Gifts & Sundries*)

GRAND CALIFORNIAN HOTEL AND SPA

Disney's Grand Californian Hotel & Spa was added as part of a major expansion of the *Disneyland* Resort in 2001. It is the Resort's flagship hotel and is the first and only hotel there to have been originally built and operated

53

since inception by The Walt Disney Company. This luxury hotel is designed to celebrate the early 20th Century Arts and Crafts era, showcasing the architectural style of Northern California. It also features a Disney Vacation Club wing that opened in September 2009. The hotel contains 1,019 rooms for Guest accommodations.

The theme was based on the "arts and crafts" design of the western culture. The interior is designed after the *Ahwahnee Hotel* in *Yosemite National Park* and the Old Faithful Inn in Yellowstone National Park.

The reception hall is loosely based on the interior design of the Swedenborgian Church in San Francisco.

The central lobby has a living room feel to it, but on a much larger scale. There is a massive fireplace and vast arching beams overhead, and furnished with chairs and sofas arranged around small coffee tables.

Some of the hotel's rooms and features are tributes to various Craftsman-era architects and designers.

- Two of the guest suites, and the *California Boardroom*, pay homage to Frank Lloyd Wright.
- The *Napa Rose* restaurant features a rose motif in the glass design which was inspired by Charles Rennie MacKintosh.
- The *Storytellers Cafe* features a large tile mural that is a reproduction of an original design by the Gladding, McBean Company for a Robin Hood Room in the Wilmington, California, public library.

Its name is based on *Disney's Grand Floridian Resort & Spa*, its sister resort and *Walt Disney World's* flagship resort hotel. The two hotels do not share themes, though, as the *Grand Californian* is a Craftsman theme, and while the *Grand Floridian* is of a Victorian theme, but both are Disney's two finest resort properties in the world. It does, however, share many thematic elements with *Disney's Wilderness Lodge* with its national park lodge theming at *Walt Disney World*.

The hotel has its own entrance to *California Adventure*, located at the *Grizzly Peak* area. You have to show your room key to use that entrance, as they have their own security check point. They do not check for exiting the park. So you can cut through there after *World of Color* at night while everyone squishes to the front of the park.

The hotel opened on January 2, 2001.

➤ **Restaurants:**
- *Napa Rose*
- *Napa Rose Lounge*
- *Storytellers Café*
- *White Water*

➤ **Shops:**
- *Acorn's Gifts and Goods*

PARADISE PIER HOTEL

Disney's Paradise Pier Hotel is a resort hotel located at the end of *Downtown Disney* across the parking lot from *The Disneyland Hotel*. The hotel was originally built and owned by Japan-based Tokyu Group, and opened in 1984 as the *Emerald of Anaheim*. It was renamed *Pan Pacific Hotel Anaheim* in 1989. Disney purchased the hotel from Tokyu Group in 1995 and renamed it *Disneyland Pacific Hotel*. The hotel was rebranded as *Disney's Paradise Pier Hotel* on December 15, 2000, named after the waterfront land in *California Adventure* that the hotel tower overlooks.

The hotel complex consists of a high-rise guest room tower with 489 rooms, which includes 29 suites. An odd thing about the hotel is the presence of a 13th floor. Generally, in the United States, due to the superstition associated with the number 13, the floor numbering omits that number. At the base of the tower is the lobby, restaurants, a gift shop, recreational facilities including a video arcade, over 30,000 square feet for meeting space, and a 7,250-square-foot ballroom. There is also an outdoor swimming pool and *California Screamin'* themed waterslide located on the third floor.

➤ **Restaurants:**
- *Disney's PCH Grill*
- *Surfside Lounge*

➤ **Shops:**
- *Mickey in Paradise*

55

DOWNTOWN DISNEY

The *Downtown Disney District* is an outdoor shopping, dining, and entertainment area themed after a garden walk. It was constructed during the *Disneyland* Resort expansion which also included the construction of Disney's *California Adventure* opening in 2001. The *Downtown Disney District* occupies a space between Disney's *California Adventure* Park and *Disneyland* Park on the western side of the resort, east of the *Disneyland Hotel*. Part of Anaheim's *Downtown Disney* is built on a bridge over Disneyland Drive (formerly West Street). Currently, no admission ticket is required for *Downtown Disney District* and parking is free for the first two hours. The location of the *Disneyland Hotel Monorail Station* was incorporated into the *Downtown Disney District* area while never physically moving the station's location.

➤ **Stores**
- *Alamo Rent-A-Car*
- *Apricot Lane Boutique*
- *Blink, by Wet Seal*
- *Build-A-Bear Workshop*
- *Disney's Pin Traders*
- *Disney Vault 28*
- *D Street*
- *Fossil*
- *House of Blues Store*
- *Lego Imagination Center*
- *Little MissMatched*
- *Marceline's Confectionery*
- *Pearl Factory*
- *Rainforest Cafe' Retail Shopping Village*
- *Roxy @ Quiksilver Boardriders Club*
- *Ridemakerz*
- *Sanuk*
- *Sephora*
- *Something Silver*
- *Studio Disney 365*
- *Sunglass Icon*
- *Travelex*
- *WonderGround Gallery*
- *World of Disney*

➤ **Restaurants**
- *Catal*
- *Earl of Sandwich*
- *ESPN Zone*
- *Häagen-Dazs*
- *House of Blues*
- *Jamba Juice*
- *La Brea Bakery Cafe*
- *Naples Ristorante e Pizzeria*
- *Napolini*
- *Rainforest Cafe*
- *Ralph Brennan's Jazz Kitchen*
- *Tortilla Jo's*
- *Tortilla Jo's Taqueria*
- *Uva Bar*
- *Wetzel's Pretzels*

➤ **Other**
- *AMC Theatres Downtown Disney 12*
- *A Walt Disney Travel Company Info Center*
- Live musicians (CD's available for purchase)
- *House of Blues Anaheim*
- *Swing Dancing*

DISNEY'S FAIRY TALE WEDDING

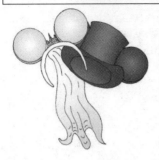

Walk down the aisle of your very own fairy tale come true. Enjoy the enchantment of ceremonies and receptions set against magical backdrops, unparalleled entertainment, and savory meals as your personal "fairy godplanner" grants your every wish and ensures your wedding day, vow renewal, or commitment ceremony is everything you have always dreamt it would be. This is the magic of Disney's Fairy Tale Weddings.

Elegant Wedding Options

Your Disney Wedding Planner will help customize your Elegant Wedding to meet your wishes and your budget with the following elements:

➤ Ceremony in one of the magical and unique locations of the Hotels of the *Disneyland* Resort with accompaniment of a classical harpist

➤ Classic floral to include bridal bouquet, three bridesmaids' bouquets, groom's boutonniere, and three groomsmen's boutonnieres

➤ A unity candle arrangement

➤ Hosted self parking for your guests

➤ Cocktail reception in one of our resort hotel garden locations to include menu items such as cheese and vegetable displays

➤ Open Bar throughout event (based on a five-hour event)

➤ Sit down dinner with menu items such as:

   • Roasted Butternut Squash Soup or Romaine Salad

   • Roasted Meyer Lemon Chicken Breast

   • Whipped Yukon Gold Potatoes mixed with Garlic Asparagus & Red Pepper Strips

   • Tahitian Vanilla Bean Crème Brûlée with Seasonal Berries

   • Freshly Baked Rolls and Butter

   • Coffee, Decaffeinated Coffee, and Specialty Teas

➤ Champagne Toast

➤ Classic design Wedding Cake

➤ Table centerpieces (based on 10)

➤ Chair covers and bows

➤ Disc Jockey

➤ Landscaping Package

Total pricing, including all applicable taxes and gratuities, for above-described event could range from $15,000 — $25,000.

57

For more information, call (321) 939-4610, or visit their website *www.disneyweddings.go.com. (see photo of the gazebo at The Disneyland Hotel)*

DISNEYLAND BIRTHDAY PARTY

Celebrate your birthday with a meal at a full-service restaurant in *Disneyland*, Disney's *California Adventure*, or the *Disneyland* Resort Hotels, and add to the fun with a Sorcerer Mickey or Disney Princess birthday bucket! Both buckets are topped with an individual-sized birthday cake and contain terrific birthday treats, including a collectible toy, a cloisonné pin, and a few special surprises. Birthday buckets are also available from room service at *Disneyland* Resort Hotels. Price: $20

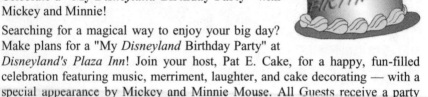

Celebrate a **"My *Disneyland* Birthday Party"** with Mickey and Minnie!

Searching for a magical way to enjoy your big day? Make plans for a "My *Disneyland* Birthday Party" at *Disneyland's Plaza Inn*! Join your host, Pat E. Cake, for a happy, fun-filled celebration featuring music, merriment, laughter, and cake decorating — with a special appearance by Mickey and Minnie Mouse. All Guests receive a party hat, souvenir sipper cup, mini birthday cake, icing, and cake toppings.

➤ Inform Cast Members/travel agents when you book your reservation that it is a birthday celebration and provide them with the name and age of the birthday child and the child's favorite character.

➤ Let your Resort/Hotel know when you check-in. Sometimes they will do something special for your child ranging from autographed character pictures and birthday buttons to balloons in your room. This does not always happen, but there have been many instances where it has.

➤ Visit City Hall on *Main Street, U.S.A.* in *Disneyland* or *Guest Services* in *California Adventure* for a complimentary Birthday Button.

➤ Make sure your child has an autograph book when they wear the button. They will receive special birthday greetings from the characters.

➤ Tell the server about the birthday at all meals in the parks and *Disneyland* Resort Hotels on this day.

➤ Let the band at *New Orleans Square* know about the birthday for a special birthday serenade.

Lilo & Stitch Birthday Set up

Guests dining at the PCH Grill can add this birthday celebration to their meal. It includes a birthday hat, plate, cup, blowout, and goodie bag with stickers and candy treats for $5.00 each plus tax. This is only available during Character meals.

Goofy's Kitchen Birthday Set up

Guests dining at *Goofy's Kitchen* can add this birthday celebration to their meal. It includes a birthday hat, balloon, and goody bag with Goofy-themed maraca, pen, and puzzle cube for $5.00 each plus tax. For $1.50 per item you can also add a birthday balloon and/or cupcake.

"Happiest Birthdays on Earth"

You can enjoy a 45-minute to 1-hour birthday party at the *Plaza Inn*, which is located at the end of *Main Street, U.S.A.* Priority seating can be made at the *Plaza Inn*, *City Hall*, and any *Guest Relations* Information kiosk. Or, call (714) 781-DINE up to 30 days in advance. Prices are $15.99 per guest. Children under the age of 2 are free (prices are subject to change). Price includes cake, punch, party hat, a special happy birthday cup, and a Mickey Mouse Plate. Park admission is required. Premium Annual Passholders get 10% discount.

During the party, there will be a cake-decorating contest and each participant will receive a special sticker. Your party host will be Mr. Patrick Edward Cake (AKA Pat E. Cake). Joining the party will be two Disney characters. While Mickey Mouse and Minnie Mouse usually attend, other characters may appear in their place.

Birthday Buckets

These are available for $20 in two themes. It is recommended that you check with the restaurant to confirm availability.

1. **Disney Princess-** a 4" round birthday cake with candle, Sleeping Beauty magnetic dress up doll, kid-sized purse with a brush and comb, and a happy birthday cloisonné pin in a souvenir birthday bucket.

2. **Sorcerer Mickey-** a 4" round birthday cake with candle, Mickey plush key ring, happy birthday cloisonné pin, and a sticker sheet in a souvenir birthday bucket.

Available at the following locations while dining:

- *Blue Bayou*
- *Carnation Cafe*
- *Ariel's Disney Princess Celebration*
- *Wine Country Trattoria*
- *Vineyard Room*
- *Storytellers Cafe*
- *PCH Grill*
- *Yamabuki*
- *Goofy's Kitchen*
- *Hook's Pointe*
- *Granville's*

If you are not dining, they are available at the *Plaza Inn* or any of the three Disney-owned hotels with room service.

Fantasy Celebrations Events

If you want a celebration customized to commemorate a special occasion, Disney's Fantasy Celebration Event staff can roll out the red carpet for you and help make dreams come true complete with entertainment, characters, special prizes, food, beverages and more, in a variety of magical locations and themes. Just let them know your plans at least 30 days in advance (restrictions and fee minimums apply).

For reservations, information, and current pricing, call (714) 781-DINE.

KENNEL CLUB & SERVICE DOGS

Kennel Club

An indoor kennel facility for your dogs and cats at the *Disneyland* Resort are located to the right of the Main Entrance of the *Disneyland* Park. The *Disneyland*  *Kennel Club* is available for day-use only. The cost is **$20.00** per pet per day and reservations are not necessary. No overnight accommodations are available. Please note; the Hotels of the *Disneyland* Resort do not permit pets.

The *Disneyland Kennel Club* and County of Orange require dogs to have the rabies, distemper, and hepatitis vaccination certificates from your vet in order to board dogs over four months of age. Cats over four months old need proof of vaccination for rabies, distemper, hepatitis, panleukopenia, rhinotracheitis, and calicivirus. Dogs and cats are allowed to ride on the *Mickey & Friends Parking Structure* trams, but are not allowed on the *Toy Story Parking Lot* buses. They open 30 minutes before the earliest park opening time and close 30 minutes after the latest park closing time. If you have any *Kennel Club* questions, you can call (714) 781-4565.

When the *Kennel Club* first opened, it was called "Ken L Land," and it was only 50¢ a day for them to house your pet.

Cast Members have stated that other pets have been left in their care including a tortoise, iguana, and even a pig.

Service Dogs & Guide Dogs

Service dogs and guide dogs are welcome throughout most of the *Disneyland* Resort. The dogs must remain on a leash or harness at all times. Cast Members are not allowed to handle the dogs for any reason. Attractions are accessible to all Guests with service dogs and guide dogs via the standard queue. Guide/assistants dogs are as described by the ADA (Americans with Disabilities Act): *"Service animals are defined as dogs that are individually trained to do work or perform tasks for people with disabilities. Examples of such work or tasks include guiding people who are blind, alerting people who are deaf, pulling a wheelchair, alerting and protecting a person who is having a seizure, reminding a person with mental illness to take prescribed medications, calming a person with Post Traumatic Stress Disorder (PTSD) during an anxiety attack, or performing other duties. Service animals are working animals, not pets. The work or task a dog has been trained to provide must be directly related to the person's disability. Dogs*  *whose sole function is to provide comfort or emotional support do not qualify as service animals under the ADA."* Beginning on March 15, 2011, only dogs are recognized as service animals. This information can be viewed on *ada.gov.*

Due to the nature of the following attractions, service dogs and guide dogs are not allowed on them:

➤ *Disneyland*

- *Big Thunder Mountain Railroad*
- *Gadget's Go Coaster*

- *Indiana Jones Adventure*
- *Matterhorn Bobsleds*
- *Space Mountain*

- *Splash Mountain*
- *Star Tours: The Adventures Continue*

➤ *Disney California Adventure*

- *California Screamin'*
- *Goofy's Sky School*

- *Grizzly River Run*
- *Jumpin' Jellyfish*
- *Mater's Junkyard Jamboree*

- *Radiator Springs Racers*
- *Silly Symphony Swings*
- *Soarin' Around the World*

- *Guardians of The Galaxy*
- *Tuck and Roll's Drive 'Em Buggies*

If there is an attraction that you want to go on but can't because of the dog, you can utilize the **Switch Pass** (see page 339) with a friend/family member so you can go on it. There are also dog crates available at some attractions to temporaily kennel the dog. I have seen them on *Space Mountain* and *Splash Mountain. (see photo)*

 There are designated potty areas for the dog, but Guests are welcome to use any open grass area for service dog relief. You can check with *City Hall* for the locations of the doggy bathrooms. Please notify a Cast Member to make arrangements for proper disposal. Service dogs and guide dogs are also allowed anywhere in the hotels. They must remain on leash or harness at all times except in

61

the hotel room. (*see photo*)

Emotional Support Dogs

Disneyland does not allow emotional support animals or therapy dogs in the park as they do not fall under the ADA laws as a service animal. Service dogs must be with the human they are serving at the time they enter the park. Disney recently had to become more strict with their policy and leniency of letting visitor's "service dogs" into the park due to incidents. Service dogs are trained to handle all situations like large crowds, fireworks, going on low-key attractions, and other issues that a dog would have to deal with in a theme park. Emotional Support Animals are not.

PACKAGE CHECK SERVICE

The *Disneyland* Resort offers a Package Check Service. If you are staying at one of the hotels of the *Disneyland* Resort, you may have your purchases sent directly to the hotel. If you are just there for the day or are staying at a non-Disney hotel, you may check your purchases until you leave at:

➤ Disneyland Resort Stroller Shop

➤ *Elias & Company* in Disney's *California Adventure*

➤ *Pioneer Mercantile* in *Disneyland* Park

➤ *The Star Trader* in *Disneyland* Park

➤ *Port Royal* in *Disneyland* Park

TAKE A TOUR

There are many tours that you can take, if you are interested in learning about the park from behind the scenes. If you have an annual pass, you could get 20% off the tour price. Call (714) 781-TOUR (8687) to book your tour up to one month in advance. Always check the weather to wear appropriate clothing, and comfortable shoes for walking as most of the tours will keep you on your feet for hours. Check with *City Hall* for any special or temporary tours. I went on a tour that was just for the *Dream Suite*. Here is the list of tours and prices (prices may change);

Art of the Craft Tour at *Disney's Grand Californian Hotel & Spa* - FREE - Length aproximately 1 ½ hour – As a Disney Resort Guest, you can get an insider's look at Disney's integration of the Arts & Crafts Movement in the hotel décor.

The tour usually runs on Sundays, Mondays, Thursdays, and Fridays at 1:00 p.m.

- Learn some of the history behind the architecture and designs of the hotel
- If it is vacant, peek inside the *Presidential Suite*

Rove the *Carthay Circle Restaurant* Tour – FREE - Length aproximately <u>15 minutes</u> – this is a free tour of the stately *Buena Vista Street* icon, the *Carthay Circle Restaurant*. A look around the elaborate theater building and dining interior, the tour is led by a restaurant host or hostess who will help Guests "...explore the history of the theater and its connections to the Walt Disney Company." If you're interested, meet in front of the building at 10:30 a.m. to join in.

Welcome to *Disneyland* Tour - $25 - Length approximately <u>2 ½ hours</u> - Make the most of your stay with this overview of both *Disneyland* and *California Adventure*. This tour only runs on Fridays, Saturdays, and Sundays at 10:30 a.m. The tour includes;
- Going on multiple attractions.
- A collectible souvenir pin (changes yearly) and lanyard
- Priority seating for a show like *Aladdin: A Musical Spectacular*
- FastPasses for attractions later in the day
- Learn some neat trivia and fun facts about the parks, but probably nothing new if you have read this book.

Cultivating the Magic Tour - $49 – Length approximately <u>2 hours</u> - Discover the power of plants and how beautiful botanicals help tell the story in each of the *Disneyland* Park lands. The tour includes;
- Select attraction experiences
- Collectible souvenir pin that changes annually.
- Seed packet

Discover the Magic Tour - $59 - Length aproximately <u>2 ½ hours</u> - Search popular attractions for hints, solve puzzles, receive a sweet treat, and delight in a special surprise! The tour includes;
- Embark on a scavenger hunt around *Disneyland* to find hidden pirate treasure and meet characters along the way.
- Select attraction experiences
- Collectible lanyard and medallion

Disney's Happiest Haunts Tour - $75-$145 - Length approximately <u>3 hours</u> - Starting at sunset, journey through both theme parks led by your own "ghost host" and enjoy an eerie evening of merry pranks, lively adventures, and tracking down villains. This tour is only available every night for the Halloween season 9/14-10/31. The tour includes;
- An awesome adventure that can combine, on certain nights, with the trick-or-treating of *Mickey's Halloween Party*.
- Riding some attractions and enjoying some entertainment (some of the attractions have a 42-inch height requirement and some physical considerations).
- Each tour Guest will receive a collectible souvenir pin (changes yearly), personalized button, and a tasty treat.

"Walk in Walt's *Disneyland* Footsteps" Tour - $109 - Length approximately <u>3 hours</u> - Discover what inspired Walt Disney to create *Disneyland* Park, his first theme park, and original *Magic Kingdom*.

- Walk around the whole park and learn some trivia and historical stories
- A visit into Walt's apartment above the *Firehouse*
- A view inside the lobby of *Club 33*
- Ride on two attractions
- A collectible souvenir pin (changes yearly)
- You will be fed lunch

"Holiday Time at Disneyland" Tour - $75 - Length aproximately 3 hours - Celebrate the Holidays in *Disneyland* and see how the magic shines brightest during this spectacular season! It is available for booking at the end of November through the first week in January.

- Walk around the whole park and learn some trivia and holiday stories from the past
- Ride on two attractions
- A collectible souvenir pin (changes yearly)
- A snack and hot beverage
- Reserved seating for the Christmas Parade

VIP Tour Services - $175/hour with a minimum of 6 hours (good for 10 Guests at a time) - Design a perfect day around your schedule and revel in an exceptional personalized adventure at the *Disneyland* Resort.

- Personalized service, professional insight, and insider stories throughout your tour from your highly knowledgeable VIP Tour Guide.
- A flexible start time during normal park operating hours. VIP Tour Services have no established time; you chose when you start.
- Visits to one theme park or to both *Disneyland* and Disney *California Adventure* in one day. Separate theme park admission is required and not included in the tour price.
- VIP viewing or seating for parades, select stage shows, and nighttime spectaculars.
- Special seating at exceptional restaurants.

Private Tours

Prices to be negotiated. If you search around online, you can find someone to give a private tour. Like an Imagineer. Terri Hardin gives private tours of the park. **You can contact her at TerriHardinSpeaks@gmail.com** to set something up. You can also Google her name, look her up on FaceBook, or visit her website terrihardin.com.

FUN FACTS

🔴 Julie Reihm was the **first tour guide chosen as a Disneyland Ambassador** in 1965 and was given the title of Miss Tencennial. You can see her in the ten year anniversary special from *Walt Disney's Wonderful World of Color* (1961-1969).

🔴 **Walt Disney wanted female tour guides** for guests when they entered the park. Possibly because men used to be the main controller of the household income and, therefore, would make the decision to hire a guide. It is rumored that Walt would only hire women who were naturally beautiful like fairy tale princesses because they weren't allowed to wear makeup.

🏰 **The tour guides had to weigh in** to make sure they were under the maximum weight requirement specified by Walt. Since then, times have changed and so has the Disney standard. This was told to me by an actual tour guide.

🏰 **Their most popular tour** is "Walk in Walt's Footsteps Tour."

🏰 The tour guides costume is similar to a jockey's outfit giving them **the nickname "Guest Jockeys."** (*see photo*)

🏰 **Disney employees have a special bond with their job,** fellow co-workers, and the visitors. They put their whole heart into the job that they do every day. Tour Guide Jessica Murfin (2007-2012) recalls her last days as a Tour Guide....*"I had the hardest time leaving that place. I even remember my second to last shift, it was Holiday Tour Support, and I went home and sat in the middle of my living room floor, in that tour guide costume, and just sobbed knowing I had to turn it in the next day and may never wear it again!!"* (*see photo*)

MAGIC MORNING

Magic Morning (formerly "Early Entry") at *Disneyland* is quite a bit different than the "Extra Magic Hours" feature at *Walt Disney World* that many people are familiar with. It is offered only at *Disneyland* **Park** and not at **Disney's** *California Adventure* for the time being.

Rather than being limited to Disney resort Guests only, **Magic Morning** is available to those who have an admission ticket which includes the "Magic Morning" feature. Magic Morning is included with **3-, 4-, and 5-day park hoppers** that are purchased from the *Disneyland* web site and also with certain travel packages. Guests do not necessarily have to stay at the Disney resorts; a number of local "Good Neighbor" hotels are also included. The feature can only be used on one day.

Presently, Guests at any of the Disney resorts, *Disneyland Hotel, Disney's Grand Californian*, or *Paradise Pier*, may take advantage of **Magic Morning** any day that it is offered during their stay. They must show their resort ID at the gate. This is subject to change without notice.

Magic Morning is generally offered every **Tuesday, Thursday, and Saturday**. It allows Guests to enter *Fantasyland* and *Tomorrowland* one hour before park opening. The following attractions are usually available (subject to change without notice):

- *Alice in Wonderland*
- *Astro Orbitor*
- *Buzz Lightyear Astro Blasters*
- *Disneyland Monorail*
- *Dumbo the Flying Elephant*
- *Finding Nemo Submarine Voyage*
- *King Arthur Carrousel*
- *Mad Tea Party*
- *Matterhorn Bobsleds*
- *Mr. Toad's Wild Ride*
- *Peter Pan's Flight*
- *Pinocchio's Daring Journey*
- *Sleeping Beauty Castle Walkthrough*
- *Snow White's Scary Adventures*
- *Space Mountain*
- *Star Tours: The Adventures Continue*

During the **Magic Morning** hour, some shops and restaurants on *Main Street, U.S.A.* are also open. **"Mickey's Toontown Morning Madness - Interactive Guest & Character Experience"** is another "extra" type of feature that is offered. Unlike **Magic Morning**, this feature is only available to Guests with certain **WDTC** (Walt Disney Travel Company) travel packages. Guests can use this feature on one day of their visit to enter *Toontown* an hour early. (*Toontown* typically opens at least one hour after the rest of *Disneyland* opens.) During this hour, there's a **Toontown Citizenship** ceremony led by Mayor Mickey Mouse. An abundance of characters are there to greet guests, sign autographs, or show off their respective homes. This feature is available **Mondays, Wednesdays, Fridays,** and **Saturdays**.

It *IS* possible to attend "**Magic Morning**" and "**Mickey's Toontown Morning Madness**" on the same day since **Magic Morning** begins an hour BEFORE the park opens and **Mickey's Toontown Morning Madness** begins WHEN the park opens.

Extra Magic Hour Is a special benefit offered to guests who are staying in one of the three Disney hotels; *The Disneyland Hotel, Grand Californian Hotel*, and *Paradise Pier*. Seven days a week the guests staying in the Disney hotels can enter the parks an hour earlier than regular guests. *Disneyland* early entry is on Tuesdays, Thursdays, and Saturdays. *California Adventure* early entry is Mondays, Wednesdays, Fridays, and Sundays. Disney hotel guests have to share the early entry with regular guests who are utilizing their Magic Morning option.

NOTE: During an early entry, the FastPass machines are not in service, with the exception of the one for *World of Color* which is located over by *Grizzly River Run*. Generally guests use part of this time to line up for *Radiator Springs Racers* FastPass machines for when the park does open.

NOTE: *Disneyland* has its limited attractions open in the list on the previous page. *California Adventure* offers *Cars Land*, select other attractions, food venues, and shops during that hour. At this time, *Hollywood Land* is not open for that hour. People line up at the land's entrance for the "rope drop" and briskly walk to *Guardians of the Galaxy – Mission: Breakout!* to be the first to get a FastPass and also hop on the attraction.

LOST AND FOUND

Whatever gets lost, can be found. It can be something pretty unusual. Up to 40,000 hats and 20,000 glasses are recovered annually. Passports, a glass eye, and a toilet seat are among the other things found. Two hundred thousand items are turned in each year to the *Lost and Found*. Most of the goods are returned to their rightful owners. About 70 percent of lost items are returned to their owners within a day. One worker retrieved a diamond ring in the restroom. A woman who, 25 years ago, lost her glass eyeball on *Main Street, U.S.A.,* ended up getting it back. There was a wallet found with $18,000 inside it. Unclaimed cell phones are donated to firefighters for reprogramming for battered women. Boxes of articles unclaimed for more than 60 days are hauled to the Santa Ana Goodwill Store for a periodic "Disneyland Lost & Found Sale." It is recommended that you write your name and phone number on all cameras and input your home phone number in your cell phone.

If a tourist has left the theme parks without an item that was lost and found in the park, *Disneyland* mails the item free of charge.

The best way to find an item lost at the Disneyland Resort is to visit the *Lost & Found*, which is located next to *Guest Relations* to the left of the *Main Entrance* of Disney's *California Adventure* Park. If you are not able to visit *Lost & Found* in person, you can call (714) 817-2166. This building covers lost and found for *Disneyland, California Adventure,* and the *Downtown Disney District.*

FOREIGN CURRENCY EXCHANGE & DISNEY DOLLARS

The Disneyland Resort offers currency exchange through Travelex Exchange Services. Foreign currency may be exchanged for U.S. dollars at:

- *City Hall* in *Disneyland*
- *Guest Relations* Lobby just inside *California Adventure Main Entrance*
- *Guest Relations* Window located to the left of the *California Adventure* Entrance
- The front desks at the Hotels of the *Disneyland* Resort.

Disney Dollars

Disney dollars are a form of corporate scrip or tokens sold by Disney and accepted at the company's theme parks, the Disney cruise ships, The Disney Store, and at certain parts of Castaway Cay, the Disney cruise-line's private island. Disney dollars are somewhat similar in size, shape, and design to the currency of the United States. Most of them bear the image of *Mickey Mouse, Minnie Mouse, Donald Duck, Goofy, Pluto,* or a drawing of one of the landmarks of *Disneyland* or *Walt Disney World* Resort. Two small monochrome reproductions of Tinker Bell float to the sides. There is sometimes the signature of the Treasurer, Scrooge McDuck.

Series

Disney dollars come in A dollars and D dollars. The former were created for *Disneyland* in Anaheim, California, hence the A. The latter, D, were created for *Walt Disney World* in Florida. Since 2005, they also have T dollars (for The Disney stores).

History of the Currency

On May 5, 1987, Disney dollars were released to the public. The idea for the specialized bills came from the Disneyland President Jack Lindquist. The bills came in one- and five- dollar denominations from 1987 to 1989 and in 1990 they added the ten-dollar bill to the list. The bills are redeemable for goods or services at the Disney theme parks, the Disney cruise ships, Disney's Castaway Cay port of call, and the Disney stores, unless indications to the contrary are printed on the individual bills. Also, they can simply be exchanged back to U.S. currency. They were first issued in 1987 and are collected by Disney memorabilia fans. Special editions are sometimes sold to Disney Cast Members as a form of incentive.

In 2005 only, *Disneyland* (A) and *Walt Disney World* (D) released a $50 bill that were designed by Disney artist Charles Boyer (Mr. Boyer personally signed a select amount of these bills) for *Disneyland's* 50th Anniversary Celebration.

Parity with the US Dollar

Disney dollars are exchanged on a one-for-one basis with U.S. currency - one Disney dollar for each U.S. dollar tendered. Disney dollars can be 'purchased' using non-currency methods, such as credit and debit cards. The Disney dollar program is a source of revenue for the Walt Disney Company. The company assumes that a certain number of Disney dollars will never be redeemed. The assumption is that a substantial percentage of the Disney dollars will be thrown away, kept as souvenirs, or forgotten.

Printing History

New Disney dollars have been produced every year since 1987, except 1992, 2004, and 2006.

Recent News

Because of the recent negative performance of the U.S. dollar, to which the Disney dollar is pegged, reports have surfaced that the Walt Disney Company will soon be printing currency that would be pegged to the Euro and called Disney Euros, to be used at the *Disneyland Paris* Resort and Disney Stores that are within the European Economic Community. The same reports do not disclose if the company will print Disney Yens and *Disney Hong Kong* dollars, to be used at parks and stores in Japan and Hong Kong, respectively.

Security Features

Disney dollars are created with anti-counterfeiting features such as micro printing, and hard-to-scan/copy reflective ink and imprinting on the front and back of the bill. In addition, the bills are printed with serial numbers and letters which are unique to each bill.

NOTE: Disney discontinued the Disney Dollars. They sold what was in stock until they sold out in May 2016.

HEIGHT REQUIREMENTS FOR SMALL VISITORS

Disneyland Park
Mickey's Toontown
- *Gadget's Go Coaster* = Minimum Height – 35"

Adventureland
- *Indiana Jones Adventure* = Minimum Height – 46"

Critter Country
- *Splash Mountain* = Minimum Height – 40" - (Under 8 years must be accompanied by someone 16 or older)

Frontierland
- *Big Thunder Mountain Railroad* = Minimum Height – 40"

Tomorrowland
- *Autotopia* = Minimum Height – 52" to Drive (No Children under 12 months)
- *Space Mountain* = 40" (Under 8 years must be accompanied by someone 16 or older)
- *Star Tours: The Adventures Continue* = Minimum Height – 40"

Fantasyland
- *Matterhorn Bobsleds* = Minimum Height – 35"

California Adventure Park
'a bug's land'
- *Tuck & Roll's Drive 'Em Buggies* = Minimum Height – 36" to Drive

Paradise Pier
- *California Screamin'* = Minimum Height – 48"
- *Jumpin' Jellyfish* = Minimum Height – 40"
- *Goofy's Sky School* = Minimum Height – 42"
- *Silly Symphony Swings* = Minimum Height – 48"

Hollywood Land
- *Guardians of the Galaxy- Mission Breakout!* = Minimum Height – 40"

Grizzly Peak
- *Soarin' Around The World* = Minimum Height – 40"
- *Grizzly River Run* = Minimum Height – 42"
- *Redwood Creek Challenge Trail Log* = Minimum Height - 32"
- *Redwood Creek Challenge Trail Traverse Climbing Wall* = Minimum Height - 42"
- *Redwood Creek Challenge Trail Cable Slide Zip Line* = Minimum Height - 42" - No taller than 63" and 12 years old or younger.

69

Disneyland History

CREATION OF THE PARK

The concept for *Disneyland* began one Sunday when Walt Disney was visiting Griffith Park with his daughters, Diane and Sharon. His idea was simple: a place that both adults and children could enjoy. His dream would lie dormant for many years. Walt Disney's father helped build the grounds of the 1893 World's Fair in Chicago. This perhaps gave Disney the creative spark from whence *Disneyland* originated. The fairgrounds for the World's Fair were a cheaply constructed set of individual "Country" areas from around the world and areas representing various time periods of man. It also included many "attractions" including the first Ferris wheel, sky ride, a passenger train that circled the perimeter, Wild West Show, etc. The 1893 World's Fair was meant only to last a summer in Chicago. In Southern California, the weather was accommodating to a "Fair Grounds" of stucco buildings that would otherwise disintegrate in the rain, snow, and ice of other climates. One can see the resemblance of a "Land" filled with "attractions" and fair grounds with differently-themed areas to the *Disneyland* created 60 years later in the 1950's as the population of America for the first time shifted west into desert climates.

While many people had written letters to Walt Disney about visiting the Disney Studio, Walt realized that a functional movie studio had little to offer to the visiting fans. He then began to foster ideas of building a site near his Burbank studios for tourists to visit. His ideas then evolved to a small play park with a boat ride and other themed areas. Walt's initial concept, his "Mickey Mouse Park," started with an eight-acre plot across Riverside Drive.

Walt visited other parks for inspiration and ideas, documenting what he liked and did not like. Some of these included Tivoli Gardens, Greenfield Village, Playland, Children's Fairyland, and Republica de los Niños. He started his designers working on concepts, but these would grow into a project much larger than could be contained in eight acres.

Walt hired a consultant, Harrison Price from Stanford Research Institute, to gauge the area's potential growth. With the report from Price, Disney acquired 160 acres of orange groves and walnut trees in Anaheim, south of Los Angeles, in neighboring Orange County.

Difficulties in obtaining funding prompted Disney to investigate new methods of fundraising. He decided to use television to get the ideas into people's homes, and so he created a show named *Disneyland,* which was broadcast on the then fledgling ABC television network. In return, the network agreed to help finance the new park. For the first five years of its operation, *Disneyland* was owned by Disneyland, Inc., which was jointly owned by Walt Disney Productions and ABC. In 1960, Walt Disney Productions purchased ABC's share. In addition, many of the shops on *Main Street, U.S.A.,* were owned and operated by other companies who rented space from Disney.

Construction began on July 18, 1954, and would cost $17 million to complete and was opened exactly one year later. U.S. Route 101 (later Interstate 5) was under construction at the same time just to the north of the site. In preparation for the traffic that *Disneyland* was expected to bring, two more lanes were added to the freeway even before the park was finished.

The city of Anaheim was originally founded in 1857. The first half of the name, Ana, was derived from the name of the Santa Ana River. The "heim" comes from a German word that means home.

One of the main roads through the area is Katella Ave. In 1896, walnut farmers John and Margaret Rea moved to Anaheim with their two daughters, Kate Rea (1876-1972) and Ella Rea Wallop (1881-1966). John wanted to come up with a different name for their ranch other than Rea Ranch. One night he called, "Kate-Ella, supper," and thought of the name Katella. That is how Katella Ranch was born. The ranch existed from about where the *Jungle Cruise* is all the way down to where *World of Color* is performed. Later on a schoolhouse was built and was named Katella School. The dirt road that went alongside the family property was named Katella Road. It wasn't until 1934 did the name change to Katella Ave.

OPENING DAY 1955

Disneyland Park was opened to the public on **Monday, July 18, 1955**. However, a special "International Press Preview" event was held on **Sunday, July 17, 1955,** which was only open to invited Guests and the media. The Special Sunday events, including the dedication, were televised nationwide and anchored by three of Walt Disney's friends from Hollywood: Art Linkletter, Bob Cummings, and Ronald Reagan.

Walt Disney's opening day speech: *"To all who come to this happy place; welcome. Disneyland is your land. Here age relives fond memories of the past...and here youth may savor the challenge and promise of the future. Disneyland is dedicated to the ideals, the dreams, and the hard facts that have created America...with the hope that it will be a source of joy and inspiration to all the world."*

The event did not go smoothly. The park was overcrowded as the by-invitation-only affair was plagued with counterfeit tickets. All major roads nearby were empty. The temperature was an unusually high 101°F (38°C), and a plumbers' strike left many of the park's drinking fountains dry. The asphalt that had been poured just the night before was so soft that ladies' high-heeled shoes sank in. Vendors ran out of food. A gas leak in *Fantasyland* caused *Adventureland*, *Frontierland*, and *Fantasyland* to close for the afternoon. Parents were throwing their children over the shoulders of crowds to get them onto attractions such as the *King Arthur Carrousel*. There were even patrons outside the park charging people $10 to climb over the wall on their ladder.

The park got such bad press for the event day that Walt Disney invited members of the press back for a private "second day" to experience the true *Disneyland*, after which Walt held a party in the *Disneyland Hotel* for them. Walt and his 1955 executives forever referred to the first day as ***"Black Sunday,"*** although July 17 is currently acknowledged by Disney as the official opening day. On July 17 every year, Cast Members wear pin badges stating how many years it has been since July 17, 1955. For example, in 2004 they wore the slogan "The magic began 49 years ago today." But for the first ten years or so, Disney did officially state that opening day was on July 18, including in the parks own publications.

On Monday, July 18, crowds started to gather in line as early as 2 a.m. The first person to buy a ticket and enter the park was David MacPherson with admission ticket number 2, as Roy O. Disney arranged to pre-purchase ticket number 1. Walt Disney had an official photo taken with two children instead, Christine Vess and Michael Schwartner, and the photo of the two carries a caption along the lines of "Walt Disney with the first two Guests of *Disneyland*." Vess and Schwartner both received lifetime passes to *Disneyland* that day, and MacPherson was awarded one shortly thereafter, which was later expanded to every single Disney-owned park in the world.

DISNEYLAND RESORT

In the late-1990's, work began to expand on the one park property. *Disneyland* Park and its Hotel, the site of the original parking lot, as well as acquired surrounding properties, were earmarked to become part of a greater vacation resort development. The new components of this resort were another theme park, Disney's *California Adventure* Park, a shopping and entertainment precinct, *Downtown Disney*, and a remodeled *Disneyland Hotel*, *Paradise Pier Hotel*, and *Grand Californian Hotel*. Because the old parking lot (south of *Disneyland*) was built upon by these projects, the six-level, 10,250 space *"Mickey and Friends" Parking Structure* was constructed, making it the largest parking structure in the U.S. and the second largest in the whole world. It is now the sixth largest.

The park's management team of the mid-1990's was a source of controversy among *Disneyland* fans and employees. In an effort to boost park profits, various changes began by then park executives Cynthia Harriss and Paul Pressler. While their actions provided a short-term boost in shareholder returns, it drew widespread criticism from employees and Guests alike. With the retail background of Harriss & Pressler, *Disneyland's* focus gradually shifted from attractions to merchandising. Outside consultants McKinsey & Co. were also brought in to help streamline operations which resulted in many changes and cutbacks. After nearly a decade of deferred maintenance, Walt Disney's original theme park was showing visible signs of neglect. Fans of the park decried the perceived decline in customer value and park quality and rallied for the dismissal of the management team.

Disney The Film Industry

A FULL LIST OF EVERY DISNEY FILM

Here is a listing of every Disney film ever made including the animated films, computer animated, stopmotion, live action, documentary, and nature films. This list is current at the time it was created in early 2017.

Type	Description	Type	Description
DOC	True Life Adventures	LIVE ANI	
			Animation / Live Action
ANI	Animated features	DOC	Documentary
COMP ANI	Computer Animated	LIVE	Live Action Movie

1937	Snow White and the Seven Dwarfs	ANIM
1940	Pinocchio	ANIM
1940	Fantasia	LIVE ANIM
1941	The Reluctant Dragon	LIVE ANIM
1941	Dumbo	ANIM
1942	Bambi	ANIM
1943	Victory Through Air Power	LIVE ANIM
1943	Saludos Amigos	ANIM
1945	The Three Caballeros	ANIM
1946	Make Mine Music	ANIM
1946	Song of the South	LIVE ANIM
1947	Fun and Fancy Free	ANIM
1948	Melody Time	ANIM
1949	So Dear to My Heart	LIVE ANIM
1949	The Adventures of Ichabod and Mr. Toad	ANIM
1950	Cinderella	ANIM
1950	Treasure Island	LIVE
1951	Alice in Wonderland	ANIM
1952	The Story of Robin Hood and His Merrie Men	LIVE
1953	Peter Pan	ANIM
1953	The Sword and the Rose	LIVE
1953	The Living Desert	DOC
1954	Rob Roy, the Highland Rogue	LIVE
1954	The Vanishing Prairie	DOC
1954	20,000 Leagues under the Sea	LIVE
1955	Lady and the Tramp	ANIM
1955	The African Lion	DOC
1955	The Littlest Outlaw	LIVE
1955	Davy Crockett, King of the Wild Frontier	LIVE
1956	The Great Locomotive Chase	LIVE
1956	Davy Crockett and the River Pirates	LIVE
1956	Westward Ho, The Wagons!	LIVE
1957	Johnny Tremain	LIVE
1957	Perri	DOC
1957	Old Yeller	LIVE
1958	The Light in the Forest	LIVE
1958	White Wilderness	DOC

1958	*Tonka*	LIVE
1959	*Sleeping Beauty*	ANIM
1959	*Darby O'Gill and the Little People*	LIVE
1959	*The Shaggy Dog*	LIVE
1959	*Jungle Cat*	DOC
1959	*Third Man on the Mountain*	LIVE
1960	*Pollyanna*	LIVE
1960	*Toby Tyler*	LIVE
1960	*Kidnapped*	LIVE
1960	*The Sign of Zorro*	LIVE
1960	*Ten Who Dared*	LIVE
1960	*Swiss Family Robinson*	LIVE
1961	*One Hundred and One Dalmatians*	ANIM
1961	*The Parent Trap*	LIVE
1961	*Nikki, Wild Dog of the North*	LIVE
1961	*Babes in Toyland*	LIVE
1961	*The Absent-Minded Professor*	LIVE
1961	*Greyfriars Bobby*	LIVE
1962	*Bon Voyage!*	LIVE
1962	*Big Red*	LIVE
1962	*Almost Angels*	LIVE
1962	*Moon Pilot*	LIVE
1962	*The Legend of Lobo*	LIVE
1962	*In Search of the Castaways*	LIVE
1963	*Son of Flubber*	LIVE
1963	*Summer Magic*	LIVE
1963	*Miracle of the White Stallions*	LIVE
1963	*Savage Sam*	LIVE
1963	*The Sword in the Stone*	ANIM
1963	*The Incredible Journey*	LIVE
1964	*Mary Poppins*	LIVE ANIM
1964	*The Misadventures of Merlin Jones*	LIVE
1964	*A Tiger Walks*	LIVE
1964	*The Three Lives of Thomasina*	LIVE
1964	*The Moon-Spinners*	LIVE
1964	*Emil and the Detectives*	LIVE
1965	*That Darn Cat!*	LIVE
1965	*Those Calloways*	LIVE
1965	*The Monkey's Uncle*	LIVE
1966	*Follow Me, Boys!*	LIVE
1966	*The Ugly Dachshund*	LIVE
1966	*Lt. Robin Crusoe, U.S.N.*	LIVE
1967	*The Jungle Book*	ANIM
1967	*The Adventures of Bullwhip Griffin*	LIVE
1967	*The Gnome-Mobile*	LIVE
1967	*The Happiest Millionaire*	LIVE
1967	*Monkeys, Go Home!*	LIVE
1968	*Blackbeard's Ghost*	LIVE
1968	*The Horse in the Gray Flannel Suit*	LIVE
1968	*Never A Dull Moment*	LIVE
1968	*The One and Only, Genuine, Original Family Band*	LIVE
1968	*The Love Bug*	LIVE
1969	*Rascal*	LIVE
1969	*My Dog The Thief*	LIVE
1969	*The Computer Wore Tennis Shoes*	LIVE

1969	Doctor Syn, Alias the Scarecrow TV	LIVE
1970	The Boatniks	LIVE
1970	The Aristocats	ANIM
1971	Bedknobs and Broomsticks	LIVE ANIM
1971	The Barefoot Executive	LIVE
1971	The Million Dollar Duck	LIVE
1972	The Biscuit Eater	LIVE
1972	Napoleon and Samantha	LIVE
1972	Now You See Him, Now You Don't	LIVE
1973	Robin Hood	ANIM
1973	Snowball Express	LIVE
1973	Superdad	LIVE
1973	The World's Greatest Athlete	LIVE
1974	Herbie Rides Again	LIVE
1974	Castaway Cowboy	LIVE
1974	The Island at the Top of the World	LIVE
1975	The Strongest Man in the World	LIVE
1975	Escape to Witch Mountain	LIVE
1975	The Apple Dumpling Gang	LIVE
1975	One of Our Dinosaurs Is Missing	LIVE
1976	Freaky Friday	LIVE
1976	Gus	LIVE
1976	No Deposit, No Return	LIVE
1976	The Shaggy D.A.	LIVE
1977	The Rescuers	ANIM
1977	The Many Adventures of Winnie the Pooh	ANIM
1977	Pete's Dragon	LIVE ANIM
1977	Herbie Goes to Monte Carlo	LIVE
1977	Candleshoe	LIVE
1978	Hot Lead and Cold Feet	LIVE
1978	Return from Witch Mountain	LIVE
1978	The Cat From Outer Space	LIVE
1979	Unidentified Flying Oddball	LIVE
1979	The Apple Dumpling Gang Rides Again	LIVE
1979	The Black Hole	LIVE
1979	The North Avenue Irregulars	LIVE
1980	Herbie Goes Bananas	LIVE
1980	The Last Flight of Noah's Ark	LIVE
1980	Midnight Madness	LIVE
1980	Popeye	LIVE
1981	Condorman	LIVE
1981	Dragonslayer	LIVE
1981	The Devil and Max Devlin	LIVE
1981	The Fox and the Hound	ANIM
1981	Night Crossing	LIVE
1981	The Watcher in the Woods	LIVE
1982	Tron	LIVE ANIM
1982	Tex	LIVE
1983	Never Cry Wolf	LIVE
1983	Trenchcoat	LIVE
1983	Something Wicked This Way Comes	LIVE
1985	One Magic Christmas	LIVE
1985	The Black Cauldron	ANIM
1985	Return to Oz	LIVE
1985	The Journey Of Natty Gann	LIVE
1986	Flight of the Navigator	LIVE

1986	The Great Mouse Detective	ANIM
1987	The Brave Little Toaster	ANIM
1987	Benji the Hunted	LIVE
1988	Oliver & Company	ANIM
1988	Return to Snowy River	LIVE
1989	Honey, I Shrunk the Kids	LIVE
1989	Cheetah	LIVE
1989	The Little Mermaid	ANIM
1990	DuckTales the Movie: Treasure of the Lost Lamp	ANIM
1990	The Rescuers Down Under	ANIM
1991	White Fang	LIVE
1991	Wild Hearts Can't Be Broken	LIVE
1991	Beauty and the Beast	ANIM
1991	The Rocketeer (Film)	LIVE
1992	Newsies	LIVE
1992	Honey, I Blew Up the Kid	LIVE
1992	Aladdin	ANIM
1992	The Mighty Ducks	LIVE
1992	The Muppet Christmas Carol	LIVE
1993	Homeward Bound: The Incredible Journey	LIVE
1993	The Three Musketeers	LIVE
1993	Cool Runnings	LIVE
1993	A Far Off Place	LIVE
1993	The Adventures of Huck Finn	LIVE
1993	Hocus Pocus	LIVE
1994	Iron Will	LIVE
1994	Blank Check	LIVE
1994	D2: The Mighty Ducks	LIVE
1994	White Fang 2: Myth of the White Wolf	LIVE
1994	The Lion King	ANIM
1994	Angels in the Outfield	LIVE
1994	Squanto: A Warrior's Tale	LIVE
1994	The Santa Clause	LIVE
1994	Rudyard Kipling's The Jungle Book	LIVE
1995	Heavyweights	LIVE
1995	Man of the House	LIVE
1995	Tall Tale	LIVE
1995	A Goofy Movie	ANIM
1995	Pocahontas	ANIM
1995	Operation Dumbo Drop	LIVE
1995	A Kid in King Arthur's Court	LIVE
1995	The Big Green	LIVE
1995	Toy Story	COMP ANIM
1995	Tom and Huck	LIVE
1996	Muppet Treasure Island	LIVE
1996	First Kid	LIVE
1996	Homeward Bound II: Lost in San Francisco	LIVE
1996	D3: The Mighty Ducks	LIVE
1996	James and the Giant Peach	LIVE ANIM
1996	The Hunchback of Notre Dame	ANIM
1996	101 Dalmatians	LIVE
1997	Jungle 2 Jungle	LIVE
1997	Hercules	ANIM
1997	George of the Jungle	LIVE
1997	Air Bud	LIVE

1997	Flubber	LIVE
1997	Mr. Magoo	LIVE
1997	That Darn Cat	LIVE
1997	RocketMan	LIVE
1998	Mulan	ANIM
1998	A Bug's Life	COMP ANIM
1998	Meet the Deedles	LIVE
1998	Mighty Joe Young	LIVE
1998	The Parent Trap	LIVE
1998	I'll Be Home for Christmas	LIVE
1999	My Favorite Martian	LIVE
1999	The Straight Story	LIVE
1999	Doug's 1st Movie	ANIM
1999	Tarzan	ANIM
1999	Inspector Gadget	LIVE
1999	Toy Story 2	COMP ANIM
2000	Fantasia 2000	LIVE ANIM
2000	The Tigger Movie	ANIM
2000	Dinosaur	COMP ANIM
2000	Disney's The Kid	LIVE
2000	Remember the Titans	LIVE
2000	102 Dalmatians	LIVE
2000	The Emperor's New Groove	ANIM
2001	Recess: School's Out	ANIM
2001	Atlantis: The Lost Empire	ANIM
2001	The Princess Diaries	LIVE
2001	Max Keeble's Big Move	LIVE
2001	Monsters, Inc.	COMP ANIM
2002	Snow Dogs	LIVE
2002	Return to Never Land	ANIM
2002	The Rookie	LIVE
2002	Lilo & Stitch	ANIM
2002	The Country Bears	LIVE
2002	Tuck Everlasting	LIVE
2002	The Santa Clause 2	LIVE
2002	Treasure Planet	ANIM
2003	The Jungle Book 2	ANIM
2003	Piglet's Big Movie	ANIM
2003	Ghosts of the Abyss	DOC
2003	Holes	LIVE
2003	Finding Nemo	COMP ANIM
2003	Pirates of the Caribbean: The Curse of the Black Pearl	LIVE
2003	Freaky Friday	LIVE
2003	The Lizzie McGuire Movie	LIVE
2003	Brother Bear	ANIM
2003	The Haunted Mansion	LIVE
2004	Teacher's Pet	ANIM
2004	Miracle	LIVE
2004	Confessions of a Teenage Drama Queen	LIVE
2004	Home on the Range	ANIM
2004	Sacred Planet	DOC
2004	America's Heart and Soul	DOC
2004	Around the World in 80 Days	LIVE
2004	The Princess Diaries 2: Royal Engagement	LIVE
2004	The Incredibles	COMP ANIM

2004	*National Treasure*	LIVE
2005	*Aliens of the Deep*	DOC
2005	*Pooh's Heffalump Movie*	ANIM
2005	*The Pacifier*	LIVE
2005	*Ice Princess*	LIVE
2005	*Herbie: Fully Loaded*	LIVE
2005	*Sky High*	LIVE
2005	*The Greatest Game Ever Played*	LIVE
2005	*Chicken Little*	COMP ANIM
2005	*The Chronicles of Narnia: The Lion, the Witch and the Wardrobe*	LIVE
2006	*Glory Road*	LIVE
2006	*Roving Mars*	DOC
2006	*Eight Below*	LIVE
2006	*Bambi II*	ANIM
2006	*The Shaggy Dog*	LIVE
2006	*Cars*	COMP ANIM
2006	*Pirates of the Caribbean: Dead Man's Chest*	LIVE
2006	*Invincible*	LIVE
2006	*The Santa Clause 3: The Escape Clause*	LIVE
2007	*Bridge to Terabithia*	LIVE
2007	*Meet The Robinsons*	COMP ANIM
2007	*Pirates of the Caribbean: At World's End*	LIVE
2007	*Ratatouille*	COMP ANIM
2007	*Underdog*	LIVE
2007	*The Game Plan*	LIVE
2007	*Enchanted*	LIVE ANIM
2007	*National Treasure: Book of Secrets*	LIVE
2008	*Hannah Montana & Miley Cyrus: Best of Both Worlds Concert 3D*	LIVE
2008	*College Road Trip*	LIVE
2008	*The Chronicles of Narnia: Prince Caspian*	LIVE
2008	*WALL-E*	COMP ANIM
2008	*Tinker Bell*	COMP ANIM
2008	*Beverly Hills Chihuahua*	LIVE
2008	*Morning Light*	DOC
2008	*High School Musical 3: Senior Year*	LIVE
2008	*Roadside Romeo*	COMP ANIM
2008	*Bolt*	COMP ANIM
2008	*Bedtime Stories*	LIVE
2009	*Jonas Brothers: The 3D Concert Experience*	LIVE
2009	*Race to Witch Mountain*	LIVE
2009	*Hannah Montana: The Movie*	LIVE
2009	*The Boys: The Sherman Brothers' Story*	LIVE
2009	*Up*	COMP ANIM
2009	*G-Force*	LIVE ANIM
2009	*A Christmas Carol*	LIVE
2009	*Old Dogs*	LIVE
2009	*The Princess and the Frog*	ANIM
2010	*Alice in Wonderland*	LIVE
2010	*Waking Sleeping Beauty*	DOC
2010	*Oceans*	DOC
2010	*Prince of Persia: The Sands of Time*	LIVE
2010	*Toy Story 3*	COMP ANIM
2010	*The Sorcerer's Apprentice*	LIVE
2010	*The Crimson Wing: Mystery of the Flamingos*	DOC

2010	Secretariat	LIVE
2010	Tangled	COMP ANIM
2010	The Boys: The Sherman Brothers' Story	DOC
2010	Tron: Legacy	LIVE
2011	Mars Needs Moms	COMP ANIM
2011	African Cats	DOC
2011	Prom	LIVE
2011	Pirates of the Caribbean: On Stranger Tides	LIVE
2011	Cars 2	COMP ANIM
2011	Winnie the Pooh	ANIM
2011	High School Musical: China	LIVE
2011	The Muppets	LIVE
2012	John Carter	LIVE
2012	Chimpanzee	DOC
2012	Brave	COMP ANIM
2012	The Odd Life of Timothy Green	LIVE
2012	Frankenweenie	STOPMOTION
2012	Wreck-It Ralph	COMP ANIM
2013	Oz the Great and Powerful	LIVE
2013	Wings of Life	DOC
2013	Monsters University	COMP ANIM
2013	The Lone Ranger	LIVE
2013	Planes	COMP ANIM
2013	Frozen	COMP ANIM
2013	Saving Mr. Banks	LIVE
2014	Muppets Most Wanted	LIVE
2014	Bears	DOC
2014	Million Dollar Arm	LIVE
2014	Maleficent	LIVE
2014	Planes: Fire & Rescue	COMP ANIM
2014	Alexander and the Terrible, Horrible, No Good, Very Bad Day	LIVE
2014	Big Hero 6	COMP ANIM
2014	Into the Woods	LIVE
2015	McFarland, USA	LIVE
2015	Cinderella	LIVE
2015	Monkey Kingdom	DOC
2015	Tomorrowland	LIVE
2015	Inside Out	COMP ANIM
2015	ABCD 2	LIVE
2015	The Good Dinosaur	COMP ANIM
2016	The Finest Hours	LIVE
2016	Zootopia	COMP ANIM
2016	The Jungle Book	LIVE
2016	Alice Through the Looking Glass	LIVE
2016	Finding Dory	COMP ANIM
2016	The BFG	LIVE
2016	Pete's Dragon	LIVE
2016	Queen of Katwe	LIVE
2016	Moana	COMP ANIM
2017	Beauty and the Beast	LIVE
2017	Born in China	DOC
2017	Pirates of the Caribbean: Dead Men Tell No Tales	LIVE
2017	Cars 3	COMP ANIM
2017	Untitled Disney live-action film	LIVE

2017	Coco	COMP ANIM
2017	Magic Camp	LIVE
2018	Wreck-It Ralph 2	COMP ANIM
2018	A Wrinkle in Time	LIVE
2018	The Incredibles 2	COMP ANIM
2018	Untitled Disney live-action film	LIVE
2018	Mulan	LIVE
2018	Gigantic	COMP ANIM
2018	Mary Poppins Returns	LIVE ANIM
2019	Untitled Disney live-action fairy tale film	LIVE
2019	Untitled DisneyToon Studios film	COMP ANIM
2019	Toy Story 4	COMP ANIM
2019	Untitled Disney live-action fairy tale film	LIVE
2019	Untitled Disney Animation film	COMP ANIM
2019	Untitled Disney live-action fairy tale film	LIVE
2020	Untitled Pixar film	COMP ANIM
2020	Untitled Pixar film	COMP ANIM
2020	Untitled Disney Animation film	COMP ANIM
TBA	Aladdin	LIVE
TBA	Alien Legion	LIVE
TBA	Artemis Fowl	LIVE
TBA	Bob the Musical	LIVE
TBA	Captain Nemo	LIVE
TBA	Untitled Chip 'n Dale Rescue Rangers film	LIVE
TBA	Christopher Robin	LIVE
TBA	Untitled Chronicles of Prydain film	LIVE
2018	Cruella	LIVE
TBA	Dashing Through the Snow	LIVE
TBA	Untitled Delilah Dirk film	LIVE
TBA	Disenchanted	LIVE ANIM
TBA	Don Quixote	LIVE
TBA	Dr. Q	LIVE
TBA	Dumbo	LIVE
TBA	Frozen 2	COMP ANIM
TBA	Genies	LIVE
TBA	Happily Ever After	LIVE
TBA	Hotfuss	LIVE
TBA	Inspector Gadget	LIVE
TBA	It's a Small World	LIVE
TBA	James and the Giant Peach	LIVE
TBA	The Second Jungle Book	LIVE
TBA	Jungle Cruise	LIVE
TBA	Kiki's Delivery Service	LIVE
TBA	Untitled Maleficent sequel	LIVE
TBA	National Treasure 3	LIVE
TBA	Nicole	LIVE
TBA	Night on Bald Mountain	LIVE
TBA	Nottingham & Hood	LIVE
TBA	Oliver Twist	LIVE
TBA	Overnight at 42nd Street	LIVE
TBA	Untitled Oz the Great and Powerful sequel	LIVE
TBA	Peter Pan	LIVE
TBA	Untitled Phineas and Ferb movie	LIVE ANIM
TBA	Pinocchio	LIVE
TBA	Untitled Prince Charming live-action film	LIVE
TBA	Rose Red	LIVE

TBA	*Ruse*	LIVE
TBA	*Sky High 2*	LIVE
TBA	*Snow White and the Seven Dwarfs*	LIVE
TBA	*Something Wicked This Way Comes*	LIVE
TBA	*Untitled Splash remake*	LIVE
TBA	*The Haunted Mansion*	LIVE
TBA	*The Lion King*	LIVE
TBA	*The Little Mermaid*	LIVE
TBA	*The Nutcracker and the Four Realms*	LIVE
TBA	*The Rocketeers*	LIVE
TBA	*The Sword in the Stone*	LIVE
TBA	*The Water Man*	LIVE
TBA	*Tink*	LIVE
TBA	*Tower of Terror*	LIVE
TBA	*Tribyville*	LIVE
TBA	*Wild City*	LIVE
TBA	*Untitled Disney Animation film*	COMP ANIM

A FILM COMPANY IN THE MAKING

Disney owns more film companies than just Walt Disney Pictures. I tried to find as many mergers and buyouts as I could find for this list.

- 1923 – **The Walt Disney Animation Studio** was started by Walt Disney and is the oldest existing animation studio in the world.

- 1943 – The **American Broadcasting Company (ABC)** was started up by the **Blue Network**, a radio production and distribution service.

- 1953 – **Buena Vista** was originally created by Walt Disney to distribute his film and television productions.

- 1958 – **The Jim Henson Company** was created by Jim Henson, but was called **Muppets, Inc.**

- 1960's – **ABC News** was a division of **ABC** created to air the news.

- 1960's – Disney bought the rights to use **Winnie the Pooh** from Alan Alexander Milne's widow, and renews its rights to use it every year since.

- 1971 – **Lucasfilm Ltd., LLC** was founded by George Lucas in San Rafael, CA.

- 1977 – **CBN Cable** television network was started by Pat Pobertson's **Christian Broadcasting Network**.

- 1979 – **Miramax Films** is the art-house/independent film division of **Walt Disney Studios Motion Pictures** and acts as both producer and distributor for its own films or foreign films. It was founded in 1979 by Bob and Harvey Weinstein, named after their parents Miriam and Max. They later created **The Weinstein Company**.

- 1979 – **ESPN** was launched by Scott Rasmussen and his father Bill Rasmussen.

- 1979 – **Pixar** was founded as the "Graphics Group," which was one third of the Computer Division of **Lucasfilm**.

- 1980 - **Walt Disney Home Entertainment** was created to released its first videotapes.

- 1981 – **Amblin Entertainment** was founded in 1981 by Steven Spielberg.

- 1981 – **Touchstone Pictures** releases typically feature more mature themes than those that are released under the **Walt Disney Pictures** banner. **Touchstone Pictures** is merely a brand and does not exist as a separate company. The two companies behind it are the **Walt Disney Motion Pictures Group** and **Walt Disney Pictures and Television**.

- 1983 – **The Disney Channel** was created and has made numerous "made for TV" movies.

- 1985 – **Studio Ghibli** is a Japanese animation film studio created in June.

- 1986 - Steve Jobs buys a portion of George Lucas' animation department for $5 million, and names it **Pixar**.

- 1986 - The name changes from **Walt Disney Productions** to **The Walt Disney Company**.

- 1986 - **Brizzi Studios** was created in France by Paul and Gaëtan Brizzi to work on animated short films and commercials.

- 1988 - **Walt Disney Pictures Television Animation Group** was started to release films that went straight to home video and was in charge of the production of the animated series. In the mid-1980's the name was shortened to **Walt Disney Television Animation**. Then re-named again in 2009 to **Disney Television Animation**.

- 1988 - **Walt Disney Animation Australia** was founded by Disney as a foreign branch of their animation department to work on animated series and home video releases. It was primarily used for comedic scenes and facial expressions on characters.

- 1988 - **Walt Disney Animation Japan** was an animation studio located in Japan that worked on both feature length Disney films and television series. It was primarily used for action sequences in the films.

- 1989 – **Brizzi Studios** was bought out by **Walt Disney Animation France**.

- 1990 – **Fox Kids** was started by **Fox Family Worldwide**.

- 1990 – **Hollywood Pictures** was started by **The Walt Disney Company** for the same purpose as **Touchstone Pictures** was - to release films for adults.

- 1992 – **Dimension Films** was formerly used as Bob Weinstein's label within **Miramax Films**.

- 1994 – **Walt Disney Theatrical** was created and has produced *Beauty and the Beast, Lion King, Hunchback of Notre Dame, Aida, Mary Poppins, Tarzan, High School Musical,* and *Little Mermaid*.

- 1994 – **Dream Works** was co-founded by Steven Spielberg, Jeffrey Katzenberg, and David Geffen and has distributed many **Amblin Entertainment** films since then.

- 1994 – The name **Walt Disney Animation France** was re-named to become one with **Disney Television Animation**. The France animation department was closed in 2004.

- 1995 – **The Walt Disney Company** bought out **ABC** for $19 billion and renamed it **ABC, Inc**. They also own the other divisions, **ABC News** and **ABC Family**.

- 1995 – When the **Walt Disney Company** bought **ABC,** they inherited 80% ownership of **ESPN** and its family networks: **ESPN2, ESPNEWS, ESPN Classic, ESPNU, ESPN Deportes, ESPN PPV, ESPN Plus, ESPN on ABC, ESPN 360, ESPN Mobile**, and **ESPN Radio**.

- 1996 – **The Walt Disney Company** entered a deal with **Studio Ghibli** to have full rights to distribute their movies to theaters and home release VHS, but not to DVD at first due to the unknown future of DVDs. Since then, Disney acquired the rights to the DVDs as well.

- 1997 –The **Disney Channel** started airing **Playhouse Disney** as competition for **Nick Toons**.

- 1998 – **Toon Disney** was created by **The Walt Disney Company**.

- 2001 – **CBN Cable** had its name changed numerous times ending on **Fox Family Worldwide**. It sold to **The Walt Disney Company** for $3 billion. **Fox Family Worldwide** was already $2.3 billion in debt, so **The Walt Disney Company** had to pay that off totaling the buyout at $5.3 Billion.

- 2001 – **ABC, Inc.** bought **Fox Kids** in the deal as well.

- 2001 – Disney buys the full copyrights to **Winnie the Pooh** for $350 million. Copyright expires in 2026.

- 2002 – **Fox Kids** was renamed **Jetix**. It was a block of time used for airing action cartoons.

- 2003 – **The Jim Henson Company** was bought by the Henson family for $78 million.

- 2003 – The **Walt Disney Animation Australia's** name was changed to **DisneyToon Studios** after that name was created. Its purpose was to create sequels to other Disney films.

- 2004 – **The Jim Henson Company** sold the rights to *The Muppets* and *Bear in the Big Blue House* to **Disney**, but retained the rights to *Fraggle Rock*, *Sesame Street*, *The Labyrinth*, and *The Dark Crystal*.

- 2004 – **Walt Disney Animation Japan** was shut down.

- 2005 – The Weinstein Brothers took **Dimension Films** with them when they left **Miramax Films**.

- 2005 – **The Weinstein Company** was created by Harvey and Bob Weinstein after leaving **Miramax Films**.

- 2006 - **Walt Disney Animation Australia** or **DisneyToon Studios** building was shut down.

- 2006 – **The Walt Disney Company** bought **Pixar** for $7.4 billion.

- 2006 – **The Walt Disney Company** bought out 14.85% stake in the Indian media and entertainment company **UTV Software Communications Ltd.** or UTV.

- 2007 – In April, Disney decided to retire the **Buena Vista** brand and rename it **Walt Disney Studios Motion Pictures**.

- 2007 – **DisneyToon Studios** is now only responsible for creating spin-offs of other Disney animated films.

- 2008 – On April 21, **Disneynature** was created and made is debut on Earth Day April 22, 2009, with the release of the film *Earth*.

- 2008 – **The Walt Disney Company** stake in **UTV** jumped to 32.1%.

- 2009 - **Dream Works** entered a 5-year/30-film contract with the **Walt Disney Motion Pictures Group** that will begin in 2010. The films will be co-released under the **Touchstone Pictures** banner, but only the live-action films and not the animated films.

- 2009 - **The Walt Disney Company** renamed **Toon Disney** and **Jetix,** now calling them **Disney XD.**

- 2009 - On August 31, Disney announced that they were buying out **Marvel Entertainment, Inc.** The deal was finalzed December 31 for $4 billion.

- 2009 – The **Maker Studio, Inc.** company was created to produce videos for multiple channels on YouTube.

- 2010 - On July 27, **The Walt Disney Company** bought **Playdom**, the largest online social game developer of its time.

- 2010 - On August 2, **The Walt Disney Company** sold **Miramax** to **Filmyard Holdings** for $663 million; the deal was completed in December 2010.

- 2012 - As of February 2, **The Walt Disney Company** owns 100% of **UTV**.

- 2012 – On December 4, **The Walt Disney Company** purchases 100% of **Lucasfilm Ltd., LLC** for $4.05 billion.

- 2014 – On March 24, Disney bought **Maker Studio, Inc.** for over $500 million.

- 2017 – On May 2, Disney absorbed the **Maker Studio, Inc.** into their newly formed company **Disney Digital Network**.

IT ALL STARTED BY A MOUSE

Always remember that all of *Disneyland* was made possible because of a little cartoon mouse. Here are some pieces of trivia about the world-famous rodent called Mickey Mouse.

FUN FACTS

- After getting fired from Universal as the director of the shorts *Oswald The Lucky Rabbit,* Walt Disney first drew Mickey during a train ride back to Los Angeles

- Walt started calling him Mortimer Mouse, but Lillian didn't like it so she suggested using a friendlier name. Walt suggested Mickey Mouse, and she agreed.

- Contrary to the popular belief, *Steamboat Willie* was not Mickey's first film; it was actually *Plane Crazy.* Walt, Lillian, and Ub Iwerks worked in secret on the film in a garage behind the Disney's home.

- *Plane Crazy* had a sneak preview at a Hollywood movie house in May 1928. The film was received and liked very well, but the idea of Mickey Mouse on the big screen was shot down by the theater due to lack of interest. This film had no audio yet, which is why most don't count it as Mickey's first film.

- Mickey's second film was *Gallopin' Gaucho,* August 7, 1928; also with no sound.

- The first two films, *Plane Crazy* and *Gallopin' Gaucho,* cost Walt $2,500 each to create.

- Mickey's third and most famous film, *Steamboat Willie,* played in the Colony Theater in New York on November 18, 1928.

- Now, Mickey's official birthday is November 18, 1928.

- Walt was the first one to provide the voice for Mickey Mouse from 1929-1947. Walt was a smoker, which made his voice become raspy. Because of this, he couldn't do the high pitch of Mickey's voice. Mickey was then voiced by:
  - Jimmy MacDonald (1947-1977)
  - Wayne Allwine (1977-2009)
  - Bret Iwan (2009-present)
  - Chris Diamantopoulos (2013-present)

- Walt Disney provided the voice of Mickey Mouse until 1947. James MacDonald took over and was Mickey's voice for three decades until he retired. In 1987, Wayne Allwine started providing Mickey's voice until his death in 2009. Bret Iwan took over after Wayne passed, but only for the video games and other Mickey Mouse voice work. The current Mickey Mouse series that started in 2013 uses the voice of comedian Chris Diamantopoulos because Disney wanted a more retro sound to Mickey's voice.

- Mickey's first words ever spoken were "Hot Dogs" in the 1929 film *Karnival Kid*.

- The first merchandise to feature Mickey was a school tablet in 1929.

- Mickey Mouse is ranked third most recognizable character in the world, right after Santa Claus and Ronald McDonald.

- Mickey Mouse is his name in America, in Sweden he is Musse Pigg, in Iran he is known as Mickey Moosh, in Iceland they call him Mikki Mus, and in Italy he is referred to as Topolino.

- In the 1930's, **Betty Boop** became more popular than Mickey Mouse.

- At one point, Max Fleischer's (animator for *Betty Boop* and *Superman* in the 30's and 40's) ***Popeye the Sailor*** also surpassed Mickey in popularity.

- Mickey received his own star on the Hollywood Boulevard Walk of Fame on November 13, 1978.

- At the Fox Dome Theater located in Ocean Park CA, the first Mickey Mouse Club was formed in 1929. Following this startup, other Mickey Mouse Clubs started up in movie houses around the country.

- The first Mickey Mouse comic strip was published on January 13, 1930. They were drawn by Ub Iwerks back then. After that, Win Smith, Ub Iwerks' assistant, drew them for 3 months. He was succeeded by Floyd Gottfredson, who drew the comic strip for 45 years.

- The first Mickey Mouse book was *The Mickey Mouse Book*, published in 1930 by Bibo-Lang.

- In 1932, a special Academy Award was given to Walt Disney for the creation of Mickey Mouse.

- The *Encyclopedia Britannica* gave Mickey Mouse his own entry in 1934.

- The first Mickey Mouse cartoon in color was *The Band Concert*, which premièred on February 23, 1935. *The Silly Symphony Swings* in *California Adventure* are themed after it.

- The last black and white cartoon was *Mickey's Kangaroo*, which premièred April 13, 1935, only 1 ½ months after *The Band Concert*.

- In 1935, The League of Nations awarded Walt Disney a medal for the creation of Mickey Mouse.

- Mickey was originally drawn with circles for his head, body and ears. In 1939, that design was changed to the more pear-shaped appearance we see now. Also, pupils were added to his eyes. The first film Mickey appeared in with his new features was *The Pointer* on July 21, 1939, and the first full-length feature, as Sorcerer Mickey, was *Fantasia* (1940).

- Fred Moore was the animator who redesigned Mickey with the new look. It is said that he was sweating bullets in a group meeting when the new look of Mickey was revealed to Walt. Then Walt said, "That's the way I want Mickey to be drawn from now on."

- The 1935 Macy's Thanksgiving Day Parade in New York City was led by a 55-foot high Mickey Mouse.

- Mickey's first appearance in a feature film was in *Fantasia (1940)*, where he appeared in his most famous role as the Sorcerer's Apprentice. His image was modified for this feature film debut to include eye pupils and a more three-dimensional appearance.

- One of Mickey's greatest honors came in 1944 when the Allied Forces, under General Dwight D. Eisenhower, prepared to invade the continent of Europe. Eisenhower's password for the mission was "Mickey Mouse."

- Between 1928, *Steamboat Willie*, and 1995, *Runaway Brain*, Mickey Mouse starred in 120 films. However, there was a 30-year gap between *The Simple Things* in 1953 and *Mickey's Christmas Carol* in 1983.

- According to Walt Disney, Mickey and Minnie Mouse have never been married on screen. But, in 1933, during an interview with Film Pictorial, Walt said, "In private life, Mickey is married to Minnie... What it really amounts to is that Minnie is, for screen purposes, his leading lady." Two years later in 1935, he told Louise Morgan in the News Chronicle "There's no marriage in the land of make-believe. Mickey and Minnie must live happily ever after." The discussion of Mickey and Minnie's wedding has been fueled by the 1932 film *Mickey's Nightmare* in which Mickey falls asleep in the armchair instead of meeting Minnie at the local dance. Mickey dreams of being married to Minnie and is surrounded by numerous little Mickey mice. Then in 1935, a cover for the sheet music "The Wedding of Mister Mickey Mouse" shows a picture of a beaming Mickey, dressed in a tux, leading Minnie, dressed in a veil, from the church to the happy cheering of Horace Horsecollar and Clarabelle Cow. This music was a Novelty Fox-trot with music by Franz Vienna and words by Edward Pola with special permission by Walt Disney.

- In 1950, Walt Disney started the *The Mickey Mouse Club* television show.

- A 90-minute television show aired on November 19, 1978, to celebrate Mickey Mouse's 50th birthday. Guest appearance on the show were made by Gerald Ford, Billy Graham, Lawrence Welk, Willie Nelson, Gene Kelly, Roy Rogers and Dale Evans, Edgar Bergen, Jodie Foster, Goldie Hawn, Eva Gabor, Anne Bancroft, Jo Anne Worley, and Burt Reynolds.

- *The Runaway Brain* was made in 1995. Dr. Frankenollie transplants Mickey's brain. The name of Dr. Frankenollie was inspired by the famed animators Frank Thomas and Ollie Johnston.

- Mickey Mouse's favorite sayings are: "Gosh!" "Oh boy!" "That sure is swell!" "Aw, gee..." "See ya soon!"

- Mickey Mouse is the official greeter of *Disneyland* and *Walt Disney World*.

1928	*Plane Crazy*	1937	*Moose Hunters*
1928	*Steamboat Willie*	1937	*Mickey's Amateurs*
1928	*The Gallopin' Gaucho*	1937	*Hawaiian Holiday*
1929	*The Barn Dance*	1937	*Clock Cleaners*
1929	*The Karnival Kid*	1937	*Lonesome Ghosts*

1929	Mickey's Choo-Choo	1938	Boat Builders
1929	Mickey's Follies	1938	Mickey's Trailer
1929	The Plowboy	1938	The Fox Hunt
1929	The Jazz Fool	1938	The Whalers
1929	Wild Waves	1938	Mickey's Parrot
1929	Jungle Rhythm	1938	Brave Little Tailor
1929	Haunted House	1939	Society Dog Show
1930	Minnie's Yoo Hoo	1939	Mickey's Surprise Party
1930	The Barnyard Concert	1939	The Pointer
1930	Fiddling Around	1940	Tugboat Mickey
1930	The Cactus Kid	1940	Pluto's Dream House
1930	The Fire Fighters	1940	Mr. Mouse Takes a Trip
1930	The Shindig	1940	Fantasia
1930	The Chain Gang	1941	The Little Whirlwind
1930	The Gorilla Mystery	1941	A Gentleman's Gentleman
1930	The Picnic	1941	Canine Caddy
1930	Pioneer Days	1941	The Nifty Nineties
1931	The Birthday Party	1941	Orphans' Benefit
1931	Traffic Troubles	1941	Lend a Paw
1931	The Castaway	1942	All Together
1931	The Moose Hunt	1942	Mickey's Birthday Party
1931	The Delivery Boy	1942	Symphony Hour
1931	Mickey Steps Out	1943	Pluto and the Armadillo
1931	Blue Rhythm	1946	Squatter's Rights
1931	Fishin' Around	1947	Fun & Fancy Free
1931	The Barnyard Broadcast	1947	Mickey and the Beanstalk
1931	The Beach Party	1947	Mickey's Delayed Date
1931	Mickey Cuts Up	1948	Mickey Down Under
1931	Mickey's Orphans	1948	Pluto's Purchase
1932	The Duck Hunt	1948	Mickey and the Seal
1932	The Grocery Boy	1949	Pueblo Pluto
1932	The Mad Dog	1951	Plutopia
1932	Barnyard Olympics	1951	R'coon Dawg
1932	Mickey's Revue	1952	Pluto's Party
1932	Musical Farmer	1952	Pluto's Christmas Tree
1932	Mickey in Arabia	1953	The Simple Things
1932	Mickey's Nightmare	1954	Walt Disney's Wonderful World of Color
1932	Trader Mickey	1973	The Walt Disney Story
1932	The Whoopee Party	1983	Mickey's Christmas Carol
1932	Touchdown Mickey	1986	DTV Valentine
1932	The Wayward Canary	1987	DTV 'Doggone' Valentine
1932	The Klondike Kid	1987	Down and Out with Donald Duck
1932	Mickey's Good Deed	1987	Funny, You Don't Look 200: A Constitutional Vaudeville
1933	Building a Building	1987	DTV Monster Hits
1933	The Mad Doctor	1988	Totally Minnie
1933	Mickey's Pal Pluto	1988	Who Framed Roger Rabbit
1933	Mickey's Mellerdrammer	1988	Mickey's 60th Birthday
1933	Ye Olden Days	1988	Disney Sing-Along-Songs: Very Merry Christmas Songs
1933	The Mail Pilot	1990	The Muppets at Walt Disney World
1933	Mickey's Mechanical Man	1990	Disney Sing-Along-Songs: Disneyland Fun
1933	Mickey's Gala Premier	1990	The Prince and the Pauper
1933	Puppy Love	1991	Muppet*vision 3-D
1933	The Steeplechase	1991	The Best of Disney: 50 Years of Magic

1933	The Pet Store	1993	Disney Sing-Along-Songs: Friend Like Me
1933	Giantland	1993	Bonkers"
1934	Shanghaied	1993	Disney Sing-Along-Songs: The Twelve Days of Christmas
1934	Camping Out	1994	A Day at Disneyland
1934	Playful Pluto	1994	Mickey's Fun Songs: Let's Go to the Circus
1934	Gulliver Mickey	1994	Mickey's Fun Songs: Campout at Walt Disney World
1934	Hollywood Party	1995	Disney Sing-Along-Songs: Beach Party at Walt Disney World
1934	The Hot Choc-late Soldiers	1995	A Goofy Movie
1934	Mickey's Steam Roller	1995	Runaway Brain
1934	Orphan's Benefit	1998	The Spirit of Mickey
1934	Mickey Plays Papa	1999	Disney's Mouseworks Spaceship
1934	The Dognapper	1999	Mickey's New Car
1934	Two-Gun Mickey	1999	How to Haunt a House
1935	Mickey's Man Friday	1999	Mickey's Once Upon a Christmas
1935	Mickey's Service Station	1999	Fantasia 2000
1935	Mickey's Kangaroo	1999	Mickey Mouse Works
1935	Mickey's Garden	2001	Mickey's Magical Christmas: Snowed in at the House of Mouse
1935	Mickey's Fire Brigade	2001	Mickey's House of Villains
1935	Pluto's Judgement Day	2001	House of Mouse
1935	On Ice	2003	The 75th Annual Academy Awards
1936	Mickey's Polo Team	2003	Mickey's PhilharMagic
1936	Orphans' Picnic	2004	Mouse Heaven
1936	Mickey's Grand Opera	2004	The Lion King 1½
1936	Thru the Mirror	2004	Mickey, Donald, Goofy: The Three Musketeers
1936	Mickey's Rival	2004	Mickey's Twice Upon a Christmas
1936	Moving Day	2005	Mickey's Around the World in 80 Days
1936	Alpine Climbers	2006	Mickey Saves Santa and Other Mouseketales
1936	Mickey's Circus	2007	Mickey's Great Clubhouse Hunt
1936	Mickey's Elephant	2007	Mickey's Treat
1937	The Worm Turns	2009	Mickey's Adventures in Wonderland
1937	Magician Mickey	2006	Mickey Mouse Clubhouse
2013	Get A Horse		

Walt Disne had once said, I hope that we never lose sight of one thing, that it was all started by a Mouse. We shall never forget the history of the park.

DISNEY PRINCESS COLLECTION

Disney Princess is a Walt Disney Company franchise, based on fictional characters that have been featured as part of the Disney character line-up. When Disney started the Princess Collection, these were the already-existing eight princesses: Snow White, Cinderella, Aurora, Ariel, Belle, Jasmine, Pocahontas, and Mulan. Later they added Tiana, Rapunzel, Merida, and soon-to-be, Anna and Elsa. On March 14, 2010, Princess Tiana from *The Princess and The Frog* (2009) was added, then they added Rapunzel from the computer-animated film *Tangled* (2010) on October 3, 2011, and Merida from *Brave* (2012), in May 2013. It was announced that Princess Anna and Elsa, from the top grossing *Walt Disney Animation Studio's* film *Frozen* (2013), will be added sometime in the future as well. Merida is the first Pixar princess added to the Collection, and also the first princess that came from an original story and not a film adaptation of a previously-designed character or based off of real life. The franchise has released dolls, sing-along videos, and a variety of other children's products, apparel, and even adhesive bandages featuring the Disney Princesses.

Andy Mooney was hired by Disney's Consumer Products Division to help stop the drop in sales. Andy attended a show of *Disney on Ice* and noticed little girls dressed up in princess attire. It wasn't character specific; it was just princess garb. He realized the huge demand for princess products and soon the Disney Princess line was born.

After the release of the Disney Princess items, they became a huge success. Disney's sales went from $300 million in 2001 to $3 billion by 2006. There are over 30,000 princess products donning the princess characters.

Princesses were chosen from the classic Disney films, not necessarily based on the fact that they were royalty, but that they fit the Disney ideology of a good role model and strong character. Mulan was chosen because of her strong character. Tinker Bell was in the Collection in the beginning, but was then dropped in 2005 to add her to the Disney Fairies collection.

It is said that Roy Disney, Walt's nephew, was against the idea of putting the different girls together, stating that they would never see each other because they are from different worlds. They were instructed to keep the different characters from acknowledging each other. This is why they aren't making eye contact with each other and are always in a posed manner.

Four years after the film's release, Disney has yet to add Anna and Elsa to the official Collection. It is believed that because of the success of the *Frozen* film, Disney could keep the sisters in their own separate collection to make more money. Hence, the reason for whole stores dedicated to just *Frozen* merchandise. Or, it could be that Queen Elsa is a queen and not a princess; it would look odd to have Anna in the Collection, but not Elsa.

The Princess Collection

This information is the most accurate I could come up with during my research. Actress ages are approximate because different movies take different amounts of time to create; some can take years.

PRINCESS	MOVIE	YEAR	VOICE ACTRESS	DOB	AGE WHILE FILMING
Anna	*Frozen*	2013	Kristen Bell	07/18/80	31
Ariel	*The Little Mermaid*	1989	Jodi Benson	10/10/61	27
Aurora	*Sleeping Beauty*	1959	Mary Costa	04/05/30	28
Belle	*Beauty and the Beast*	1991	Paige O'Hara	05/10/56	34
Cinderella	*Cinderella*	1950	Ilene Woods	05/05/29	20
Elsa	*Frozen*	2013	Idina Menzel	05/30/71	40
Jasmine	*Aladdin*	1992	Linda Larkin	03/20/70	21
Merida	*Brave*	2012	Kelly Macdonald	02/23/76	34
Moana	*Moana*	2016	Auli'i Cravalho	11/22/00	14
Mulan	*Mulan*	1998	Ming-Na Wen	11/20/63	34
Pocahontas	*Pocahontas*	1995	Irene Bedard	07/22/67	27
Rapunzel	*Tangled*	2010	Mandy Moore	04/10/84	26
Snow White	*Snow White and the Seven Dwarfs*	1937	Adriana Caselotti	05/16/16	18
Tiana	*The Princess and the Frog*	2009	Anika Noni Rose	09/06/72	36

Extra Princess Info

This information is the most accurate I could come up with during my research.

PRINCESS	AGE	HEIGHT	HER PRINCE
Snow White	14	5' 2"	The Prince
Cinderella	19	5' 4"	Prince Charming
Aurora	16	5' 6"	Prince Phillip
Ariel	16	5' 4"	Prince Eric
Belle	17	5' 5"	Prince Adam (The Beast)
Jasmine	15	5' 1"	Prince Alí Ababwa (Aladdin)
Pocahontas	18	5' 2"	John Smith
Mulan	18	?	Captain Li Shang
Tiana	19	?	Prince Naveen
Rapunzel	18	?	Eugene Fitzherbert (Flynn Rider)
Merida	16	?	None
Anna	18	5'	Kristoff
Elsa	21	5' 4"	None
Moana	16	?	None

The Era and Location

This information is the most accurate I could come up with during my research.

Snow White and the Seven Dwarfs	1300s	Germany
Cinderella	1600s	France
Sleeping Beauty	1600s	England
The Little Mermaid	1700s	Atlantis/Denmark
Beauty and The Beast	1600s	France
Aladdin	1100s	Middle East
Pocahontas	1607	America
Mulan	386–533	China
The Princess and the Frog	1926	America
Tangled	1780s	Germany
Brave	900-1600	Scotland
Frozen	1840s-50s	Norway
Moana	1017 AD	Polynesia

The Movie's Origin Story

MOVIE	ORIGINAL TITLE	DATE	AUTHOR
Snow White and the Seven Dwarfs	Sneewittchen	1812	Brothers Grimm
Cinderella	Cendrillon, ou La petite Pantoufle de Verre	1697 republished in 1812	Charles Perrault first, then Grimm
Sleeping Beauty	La Belle au bois dormant	1697 republished in 1812	Charles Perrault first, then Grimm
The Little Mermaid	Den lille havfrue	1836	Hans Christian Andersen
Beauty and the Beast	La Belle et la Bête	1740	Gabrielle-Suzanne Barbot de Villeneuve
Aladdin	Les Mille et Une Nuits	1709	Antoine Galland
Pocahontas	N/A	1607	American History
Mulan	Ballad of Mulan	420-589 AD	Chinese Folklore
Princess and the Frog	Der Froschkönig	1812	Brothers Grimm
Tangled	Rapunzel	1812	Brothers Grimm
Brave	N/A	2012	Brenda Chapman
Frozen	Snedronningen	1844	Hans Christian Andersen
Moana	N/A	2016	7 Disney Writers

Disney Princess Movie Trivia

Snow White and the Seven Dwarfs

The first Disney Princess, Snow White, **was voiced by 18-year-old Adriana Caselotti**, for which she was paid $970. Walt Disney owned the rights to her voice, so she was not allowed to do any radio interviews or be in any other movie with a voice character. Walt had her blacklisted so no one would hire her. He didn't want to ruin the illusion of Snow White. She did, however, have one exception with a small, uncredited part in *The Wizard of Oz*. She was the voice of Juliette the cat during the Tin Man's song. She was paid $100 for this part. She attempted to sue Disney for part of the profit from the *Snow White* film, but lost. Later, she became a professional opera singer. In 1983 when the *Snow White Grotto* at *Disneyland* was refurbished, Caselotti re-recorded "I'm Wishing" for the *Snow White Wishing Well,* at the age of 75.

Some believe that **the prince's name is Ferdinand**, but it isn't. The only Ferdinand from back then was Ferdinand the Bull from 1938. Fans thought this was his name due to a reference by Shirley Temple while giving the academy award to Walt Disney. She had said "Snow White, and the Seven Dwarfs, Mickey Mouse, Ferdinand...," but she was referring to the bull, since it was nominated for Best Short Subject. Children already knew about Ferdinand the Bull because of the book, *The Story of Ferdinand*, published in 1936.

The average animated film needs 24 frames of animation to make up one second of screen time. **Snow White needed about 100,000 hand painted frames** to complete it.

Snow White had a sister named Rose Red. This is a misconception that people have about the original story by The Brothers Grimm. Their published fairytale book from 1812 contained a short story called *Snow White and Rose Red,* a story about two sisters. This story has nothing to do with *Snow White and the Seven Dwarfs*. The original title of *Snow White and Rose Red* was *The Ungrateful Dwarf*, and was originally written in the late 1700's. The only thing the two stories have in common is a girl named Snow White, and the fact that there was a dwarf in the story.

In the original story, the dwarfs didn't have any names. They received their first names in 1912 when the *Snow White* play debuted on

93

Broadway. The dwarfs' names were Blick, Flick, Glick, Plick, Quee, Snick, and Whick.

🔱 Before receiving the names of Doc, Grumpy, Happy, Sleepy, Bashful, Sneezy, and Dopey, **Disney went through a myriad of other possible names**. There was even concept art drawn up with the other dwarfs, like a scene with Grumpy and Deafy, in which Grumpy gets mad at Deafy because he is always off topic for improperly hearing everyone. The names from the cutting room floor: Awful, Baldy, Biggo-Ego, Biggy-Wiggy, Blabby, Burpy, Busy, Chesty, Crabby, Cranky, Daffy, Deafy, Deafy, Dippy, Dirty, Dizzy, Doleful, Dumpy, Flabby, Gabby, Gaspy, Gatsby, Gloomy, Goopy, Graceful, Helpful, Hickey, Hoppy, Hotsy, Hungry, Jaunty, Jazzy, Jumpy, Lazy, Neurtsy, Nifty, Puffy, Sappy, Scrappy, Shifty, Shorty, Silly, Slutty, Snappy, Sneezy-Wheezy, Sniffy, Snoopy, Snurfles, Soulful, Strutty, Stuffy, Tearful, Thrifty, Tubby, Weepy, Wheezy, Wistful, and Woeful.

🔱 The first **live version of the film was released in 1916**, starring Marguerite Clark (1883-1940), and was a silent film. It is said that this was an inspiration for Walt when he was making his animated version. Walt would have been 15 years old when he saw it.

🔱 The film was re-released 7 years after its first showing to make Disney some extra money during hard times. This set the **standard for the 7-year wait** for Disney cartoons to be re-released to VHS or DVD.

🔱 Dopey was **originally supposed to speak**, but since no one suitable was found to do the voice, they made him mute.

🔱 Convinced that the film would fail, the Hollywood film industry **labeled the film "Disney's Folly."**

🔱 "The Prince" from *Snow White* was originally a **much more major character**, but the difficulty found in animating him convincingly forced the animators to reduce his part significantly.

🔱 People believe that this movie was the first full-length animated film ever released; however, it's **not the first full-length animated movie**. *Die Abenteuer des Prinzen Achmed (The Adventures of Prince Achmed)* released in 1926 is the first, but since the whole movie was just silhouettes, they didn't count it. *Snow White* is in full color.

🔱 It was the **first film to ever have a soundtrack** recording album released for it.

🔱 **Scenes that were planned** for *Snow White*, but never fully animated:
- The queen holds the prince in the dungeon and uses her magic to make skeletons dance for his amusement.
- Fantasy sequence accompanying "Some Day My Prince Will Come" in which Snow White imagines herself dancing with her prince in the clouds beneath a sea of stars.
- Dwarfs building Snow White a coffin with help from woodland creatures.

94

- The song "Music in Your Soup" where the dwarfs sing about the soup that Snow White had just made them.
- The musical number "You're Never Too Old to Be Young" featuring the dwarfs. It was pre-recorded, but never animated.

Scene records indicate that **this production employed 32 animators**, 102 assistants, 167 "in-betweeners," 20 layout artists, 25 artists doing water color backgrounds, 65 effects animators, and 158 female inkers and painters. Two million illustrations were made using 1500 shades of paint.

It was one of the first films to have **related merchandise available** at the time of its premiere.

The Evil Queen's actual **name is Grimhilde**.

At a recording session, Lucille La Verne, **the voice of the Wicked Queen**, was told by the Disney animators that they needed an older, raspier version of the Queen's voice for the Old Witch. Ms. Laverne stepped out of the recording booth, returned a few minutes later, and gave a perfect "Old Hag's voice" that stunned the animators. When asked how she did it, she replied, "Oh, I just took my teeth out." Snow White was her last film.

It held the title of **highest grossing film ever for exactly one year**, after which it was knocked out of the top spot by *Gone with the Wind* (1939).

Marge Champion, who is one of the greatest dancers and choreographers in both movies and stage, served as a **movement model for Snow White**. Some of this animation was later reworked for Maid Marion in *Robin Hood*.

In the original fairy tale, the Queen dies when she is forced to **dance in burning metal shoes**. Disney dropped the idea.

Disney Studios in Burbank was **built with the profits**.

Cinderella

There have been many tellings of the *Cinderella* story over the past almost 2,000 years. **It originated in the T'ang Dynasty 618-907 AD.** Cinderella's name then was Yeh-Shen. In 1697, the author, Charles Perrault, rewrote the story and included the pumpkin, fairy godmother, and the glass slipper. The Grimms Brothers then rewrote the story in 1812.

There have been **350-1,500 different versions of Cinderella recorded**, circulating around the world throughout time.

- Not only is the **name of the prince never revealed**, he is nowhere in the film mentioned as "Prince Charming."

- Ilene Woods **was chosen over 309 other girls for the part** of Cinderella, after some demo recordings of her singing a few of the film's songs were presented to Walt Disney. However, she **had no idea she was auditioning** for the part until Disney contacted her; she initially made the recordings for a few friends who sent them to Disney without telling her.

- **Lucifer was modeled after** animator Ward Kimball's (the designer of Jiminy Cricket and the one who redesigned Mickey Mouse) cat. Animators were having trouble coming up with a good design for that cat, but once Walt Disney saw Kimball's furry calico, he declared, "There's your Lucifer."

- When Cinderella is singing "Sing, Sweet Nightingale," **three bubbles float around** and form the head and ears of Mickey Mouse.

- According to Marc Davis, one of the directing animators of Cinderella, at least **90% of the movie was done in live action** model before animation. Dancer Ward Ellis was the live action model for Prince Charming.

- You can hear a **"Goofy holler"** when both the King and the Grand Duke fall from the chandelier.

- The transformation of Cinderella's torn dress to that of the white ball gown was considered to be **Walt Disney's favorite piece of animation**.

- Walt Disney had not had a huge hit since *Snow White and the Seven Dwarfs*. The production **of this film was regarded as a major gamble** on his part. At a cost of nearly $3,000,000, Disney insiders claimed that if this movie had failed at the box office, it would have been the end of the Disney studio. The film was a big hit. The profits from its release, with the additional profits from record sales, music publishing, publications, and other merchandise, gave Disney the cash flow to finance a slate of productions (animated and live action), establish his own distribution company, enter television production, and begin building *Disneyland* during the decade.

- Disney restored and re-mastered the movie for its October, 2005, DVD release as the sixth installment of Disney's Platinum Edition series. According to the Studio Briefing, Disney **sold 3.2 million copies** in its first week and earned over $64 million in sales.

- The story takes place roughly in June. In the movie, the sun rises slightly before 6:00 a.m. (in France), as it would within a few weeks of the summer solstice. Also by this time, a **pumpkin would have grown to 20-40 pounds**.

- **Gus' full name is Octavius**, presumably after the Roman Emperor.

- Cinderella's **carriage is actually a live-action model** painted white with black lines. This was the first time this technique had actually been used.

- Ranked #9 on the **American Film Institute's list** of the 10 greatest films in the genre "Animation" (as of 2008).

- The carriage that Cinderella and the prince take after the wedding has an emblem of a sword and **two Hidden Mickey Mouse heads** around it.

- **Elaenor Audley, who was used to do the voice** of Lady Tremaine (and also voiced Maleficent in *Sleeping Beauty* (1959) and Madame Leota in the *Haunted Mansion*), was also the live action reference model for the animators.

- At the end of the film, Cinderella and Prince Charming hop in the carriage and ride away. Prior to entering the carriage, Cinderella is wearing a long sleeve wedding dress, but **after she is in the carriage, it is sleeveless.**

Sleeping Beauty

- The **original story first appeared between 1330 and 1344,** but was first put into print in 1528. In 1634, Giambattista Basile published the story and named it *Sun, Moon, and Talia*. Charles Perrault published it as *Little Briar Rose* in 1697.

- The **cookies that the fairies eat with their tea** are shaped like Mickey Mouse's head and ears.

- **Helene Stanley was used as the live action model for Aurora.** She was also used as the reference model for Cinderella and Anastasia in *Cinderella* (1950) and Anita in *One Hundred and One Dalmatians* (1961). Helene retired from acting in 1961, after *One Hundred and One Dalmatians*, at the age of 32.

- Sewing the dress Helene Stanley wore as Briar Rose was the **first wardrobe design Alice Davis did for Disney,** after receiving a call from her husband, Marc Davis, who was animating Aurora.

- Now, imagine that you are a 15 almost 16-year-old girl wandering around a forest all alone. Some strange man in his early 20's comes up to you and starts dancing and singing to you. When you try to leave, he grabs your arm and demands that you don't leave. **That is what happened to Aurora when she first met Prince Phillip**.

- In both this film and *Cinderella*, **Aurora's and Cinderella's friends** surprise them with new dresses, calling out, "Surprise! Surprise! Surprise! Happy birthday!"

- There is no record as to **who provided the voice for the queen**, Briar Rose's mother.

- They used a **flame thrower to create the dragon breath** sound effect for the climax of the movie. Castanets were used for the sound of its snapping jaws.

- In active production from 1951 until the end of 1958, setting a record (for which it is tied with another 70mm film, *The Black Cauldron*) for being the Disney animated film with **the longest production schedule**.

- Aurora's long, thin, willowy body shape was **inspired by that of Audrey Hepburn**.

- There were **originally going to be seven fairies** instead of just the three.

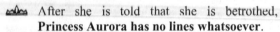

- **Briar Rose is Sleeping Beauty's name from the German version** of the original fairy tale. Princess Aurora is Sleeping Beauty's name in the Italian version of the original fairy tale.

- The ominous piece of music to which Maleficent hypnotizes Aurora into pricking her finger is called **"Puss-in-Boots and the White Cat."** In Pyotr Ilyich Tchaikovsky's ballet, it is used for a comic number in which two cats snarl at and try to scratch each other.

- After she is told that she is betrothed, **Princess Aurora has no lines whatsoever**.

- In the original fable, **the princess sleeps for 100 years**, and the Prince finds her and wakes her up after the aforementioned century has passed. This idea was dropped for the Disney film so that the Prince could be introduced much earlier in the story.

- In the original fable, Princess Aurora is the result of a **spell cast on the Queen by a magical fish** that she had thrown back into a pond after it wound up lying on the bank.

- **Elaenor Audley, who was used to do the voice** of Maleficent (and also voiced Lady Tremaine in *Cinderella* (1950) and Madame Leota in the *Haunted Mansion*), was also the live-action reference model for the animators.

- The evil character of Maleficent is favored as **the top Disney villain of all time**.

- Mattel Entertainment was in the **process of making the film *Barbie as the Sleeping Beauty***, but had to cancel it because Disney had been granted licensing rights for their movie *Maleficent* (2014).

The Little Mermaid

- Jodie Benson did the voice of Ariel in all three *Little Mermaid* movies and the TV series. At the time she recorded the first *Little Mermaid*, she was about 26 years old. Jodie has done voices for other characters such as Tour Guide Barbie in *Toy Story 2*, Aquagirl in *Batman Beyond*, Jenna from *Balto 2*, Lady from *Lady and the Tramp 2: Scamps Adventure*, Princess Atta from *A Bug's Life*, the video game, and Weebo from the movie *Flubber*. You can see her as Sam (the secretary) in the movie *Enchanted*.

- This was the **last Disney animated feature to use hand-painted cells** and analog camera and film work. One thousand different colors were used on 1,100 backgrounds. Over one million drawings were done in total.

- Originally, our favorite red-headed princess, the other being Cinderella who is strawberry blonde, **was supposed to be blonde**. After the 1984 release of their popular film *Splash*, Disney felt it would be too similar to Daryl Hannah's mermaid form.

- This was considered to be the **first Disney animated feature using all digital processes,** but, at the time, CAPS (Computer Animation Production System) wasn't ready. Disney's next animated feature, *The Rescuers Down Under* (1990), was going to be the first 100% digitally processed film.

- Disney artists had considered an **animated film of "The Little Mermaid" in the late 1930's**, and illustrator, Kay Nielsen, prepared a number of striking story sketches in pastels and watercolors. For this film, the artists received inspiration from the Nielsen story sketches that were brought out of the Archives for them to study, and they gave Kay Nielsen a "visual development" credit on the film.

- Another first for recent years, live actors and actresses were filmed for reference material for the animators. **Sherri Stoner acted out Ariel's key scenes**. Not all of Disney's animators approved the use of live-action reference. Glen Keane, the co-supervising animator of Ariel, said in an interview with the Orange County Register that one artist quit the project rather than work with live-action reference.

- This film was the **most effects-animation-heavy Disney animated feature since** *Fantasia* in 1940. The two-minute storm sequence alone took 10 special effects animators over a year to finish. Effects animation supervisor, Mark Dindal, estimated that over a million bubbles were drawn for this film, in addition to the use of other processes such as airbrushing, backlighting, superimposition, and some flat-shaded computer animation.
- The **directors insisted that every one of the millions of bubbles should be hand-drawn**, not Xeroxed. The sheer manpower for such an effort required Disney to farm out most of the bubble-drawing to Pacific Rim Productions, a China-based firm with production facilities in Beijing.
- Ariel's **lip lines were created with hand-inking**.
- Ariel's treasure cave **includes the painting "Magdalene With the Smoking Flame"** by 17th-century artist Georges de La Tour.
- In the opening scene when King Triton arrives at the arena, you can briefly see **Mickey Mouse, Goofy, and Donald Duck in the crowd of sea-people as mermen** when he passes over them.

- The story **"The Little Sea-Maid,"** by **Hans Christian Andersen**, was slated by Walt Disney to be a *"Silly Symphonies"* short. However, another Andersen classic, *The Ugly Duckling* (1939), replaced it.
- **Sebastian the Crab's full name,** according to the movie script, is Horatio Thelonius Ignatius Crustatious Sebastian.
- When **Ben Wright got the part of Grimsby,** Prince Eric's butler, the current Disney folks had no idea that he had been the voice of Roger in *One Hundred and One Dalmatians* (1961). He had to tell them.
- In Greek mythology, the **"God of the Sea" is Poseidon**. Triton, however, is one of his sons.
- This was the **first Disney film to receive an Academy Award** since *Bedknobs and Broomsticks* (1971), though other films had been nominated.
- The **name of the human woman** that Ursula transforms herself into is Vanessa.
- A few of the backgrounds used during the "Kiss the Girl" **scene are taken from** *The Rescuers* (1977).
- There are several shots of Ariel, forlornly sitting on a rock, in a pose reminiscent of the **"Little Mermaid" statue that sits in Copenhagen harbor**.

100

- Originally, **Sebastian was to have an English accent**. It was lyricist/producer Howard Ashman who suggested he be Jamaican. This opened the door to calypso style numbers like "Under the Sea," which won the Academy Award.

- **Songwriting team Alan Menken and Howard Ashman** were brought to the attention of Disney Animation Chair Jeffrey Katzenberg by longtime colleague (and future Dreamworks co-founder), David Geffen, who was producing the team's off-Broadway musical "*Little Shop of Horrors.*"

- While writing "Part of Your World," Alan Menken and Howard Ashman discovered that **the song shared contextual and rhythmic similarities** with "Somewhere That's Green," a song from their earlier musical, *Little Shop of Horrors* (1986). Hence, leading the duo to humorously nickname "Part of Your World" as "Somewhere That's Dry."

- When Scuttle (voiced by Buddy Hackett) is providing "vocal romantic stimulation" to Eric and Ariel while they are rowing in the lagoon, **he is actually squawking his own version** of Tchaikovsky's "Romeo and Juliet."

- Jodi Benson **sang "Part of Your World" in the dark** to get that "under the sea" feeling.

- Ariel was quite **deliberately made a redhead** in order to distinguish her from Daryl Hannah's character in *Splash* (which was produced by Touchstone Pictures; it is subsequently owned by Disney).

- **"Part of Your World" was nearly cut**; Jeffery Katzenberg felt that it was "boring," as well as being too far over the heads of the children for whom it was intended. At a test screening, children were restless during the song which did not have finished animation - in particular, one child that sat in front of Jeffery Katzenberg spilled his popcorn and was more interested in picking it up than watching the sequence.

- **Deleted scenes:**
  - An extended "Fathoms Below" sequence in which it is revealed that Ursula is Triton's sister, thereby making her Ariel's aunt
  - Alternate version of "Poor Unfortunate Souls" explaining why Ursula was banished by Triton
  - A scene just before the concert in which Sebastian finds out Ariel is missing
  - Extended scene of Sebastian lost in Eric's castle
  - Sebastian giving additional advice to Ariel at bedtime
  - The fight with Ursula to the ending with no dialog

- There is a **Hidden Mickey on the scroll** that Ursula gets Ariel to sign. It is in the middle of the words when it pans over the scroll from top to bottom.

- The shot of Ariel reaching out through **the skylight of her grotto was the last shot to be completed**. It took four tries to get the optical effects just right.

101

- Before recording "Poor Unfortunate Souls," **Pat Carroll asked Howard Ashman to sing the song** one more time to get it right. He obliged, and as he sang he added little spoken ad-libs that Carroll then incorporated into her performance. These included Ursula saying "Pathetic" at the mer couple she conjures up as an example, and the line "Life's full of tough choices, innit?"

- At the beginning of "Kiss the Girl," the **reeds blowing in the wind are taken from *The Old Mill*** (1937).

- The animators created the character of **Ursula with the intention of having Bea Arthur** provide the voice. By the time Arthur was approached, she was already well into the sitcom *The Golden Girls* (1987) and declined the Disney offer.

- The idea to give Ursula a pair of sneaky, identical pets as henchmen was **inspired by Madame Medusa's two alligators** (also identical and with similar personality traits), Brutus and Nero, from *The Rescuers* (1977).

- Scheduling conflicts with "*Star Trek: The Next Generation*" (1987) **forced Patrick Stewart to turn down the role** of King Triton.

- Carlotta, Eric's maid at the castle who bathes Ariel and serves dinner, is **wearing the same outfit from *Cinderella*** (1950), except for the scarf on her head.

- **Jennifer Saunders auditioned for the role of Ursula** but was turned down. In 2002, Steven Spielberg got hold of her audition recording and, after hearing it, insisted to the three directors of *Shrek 2* (2004) that she be cast as the scheming Fairy Godmother.

- When Eric is waiting for Ariel to arrive, **one of the portraits is that of Princess Aurora** and Prince Phillip from *Sleeping Beauty* (1959).

- During Eric's alleged wedding to Vanessa, **the King and Grand Duke from *Cinderella*** (1950) both make appearances.

- When Ariel is singing "Part of Your World," there is **a bust of Abraham Lincoln**. It was placed there to pay homage to one of Walt's favorite American icons. This is why Walt had the *Great Moments with Mr. Lincoln* attraction created for the World's Fair, then later moved it to *Main Street, U.S.A.*

- There is **a Hidden Mickey in the scene where the animals are trying to break up the wedding**, right as the seals are jumping onto the deck of the boat from the ocean. There is a woman with black hair in a red gown with her back to the camera. The shape of her hair clearly outlines a Mickey head until she turns sideways.

- The movie was **adapted as a Broadway musical** in 2007.

- The names of **Flotsam and Jetsam** have a meaning. Traditionally, flotsam and jetsam are words that describe goods of potential value that have been thrown into the ocean. There is a technical difference between the two: jetsam has been voluntarily cast into the sea (jettisoned) by the crew of a ship, usually in order to lighten it in an emergency; while flotsam describes goods that are floating on the water without having been thrown in deliberately, often after a shipwreck. In modern usage, flotsam also includes driftwood, logs, and other natural debris in oceans and waterways.

- To **tell the difference between Flotsam and Jetsam** isn't an easy feat since they are both almost identical, aside from the opposite glowing eye in each. Flotsam has a glowing left eye and Jetsam has a glowing right eye.

- **Ursula was only animated with six tentacles**, instead of eight tentacles like a real octopus. However, she technically has eight limbs if you count her two human arms.

- Several **elements from the original Hans Christian Andersen** story were kept in the movie:
  - Ariel being the youngest of many sisters
  - The secret white marble statue
  - Sea anemones along the entrance to Ursula's cavern
  - Ariel asking what she'll have left without her voice and the sea-witch's response

- During planning for the film, **Ursula was not originally designed as a cecaelia** (a composite mythical being, combining the head, arms and torso of a woman, and from the lower torso down, the tentacles of an octopus or squid as a form of mermaid or sea demon). It was thought that she would be another sea creature, such as a rockfish-like mermaid. The film's director, Mike Peraza, saw a documentary about octopuses, and decided that their multiple arms and overall imposing appearance would be perfect for the character they were creating. Pat Carroll, who was cast to voice Ursula, envisioned the character as "part Shakespearean actress, with all the flair, flamboyance, and theatricality, and part used-car salesman with a touch of con artist." Carroll, who is a contralto, deliberately deepened her voice for the role.

- The release of *The Little Mermaid* (1989) holds the record for **the longest period of time between** Disney "princess" movies. Its predecessor "princess" film 30 years before was *Sleeping Beauty* (1959).

- Ariel is the **only princess in the official Disney Princess line-up** to have had a baby.

- Ariel is the **only princess that isn't human.** She isn't an animal, either; she is a mythological entity.

- The only princess from Walt Disney Animation Studio **to have biological siblings**, until the release of *Frozen* (2013). Merida had three brothers, but *Brave* (2012) was made by Pixar.

- **Ariel's sisters' names** are Aquatta, Andrina, Arista, Adella, Alana, and Attina.

- The **movie was re-released November 14, 1997**, the week prior to the release of the Don Bluth film *Anastasia* (1997), which was released on the

21st and is sometimes mistaken for a Disney film. It was also planned to be re-released as a 3D film September 13, 2013. But, in January it was announced that wasn't going to happen due to the lack of popularity with the other films that were re-released in 3D prior to that: *Beauty and the Beast* (1991) on January 31, 2012, *Finding Nemo* (2003) on September 14, 2012, and *Monsters, Inc.* (2001) on January 18, 2013. The first re-released 3D film was *The Lion King* (1994) on Aug. 27, 2011, which grossed almost $178 million worldwide, but the 3D Disney movie popularity dropped off after that.

Beauty and the Beast

- It was the **first full-length animated feature to be nominated** for an Oscar for Best Picture losing to *The Silence of the Lambs*. It was also the first full-length animated feature to win the Golden Globe for Best Picture (Musical or Comedy).

- **Sherri Stoner was used as the model** for Belle.

- "Be Our Guest" **was originally animated with Maurice** (not Belle) as the guest, but they decided not to waste such a wonderful song on a secondary character.

- **Chip originally had only one line**, but the producers liked Bradley Pierce's voice so much that extra dialogue and business was written and storyboarded for the character.

- The **original "cute" character of the movie was a music box** which was supposed to be a musical version of Dopey. When Chip's role was expanded, the music box idea was scrapped. However, the music box can be seen for a brief moment on a table next to Lumière just before the fight between the enchanted objects and the villagers in the Beast's castle.

- The last phrase of Cogsworth's line "Flowers, chocolates, promises you don't intend to keep..." **was ad-libbed by David Ogden Stiers**.

- The **first animated movie to win the Annie Award** for Best Animated Film.

- A **song sung by the enchanted objects entitled "Human Again" was cut** before production started. The song was later added to the *Disney on Ice* and theatrical productions and was recorded and animated for the 2001 IMAX re-release. It was also added to the special edition released on October 8, 2002, making the movie a bit longer.

- Art director Brian McEntee color keyed Belle so that **she is the only person in her town who wears blue**. This is symbolic of how different she is from everyone else around. Later, she encounters the Beast, another misfit, who also ends up wearing blue.

- Belle was also wearing blue to show that she was a good person and **Gaston was wearing red to show that he was evil**. When Maurice and Belle first meet Beast, he, too, is wearing red as we are to believe that he is evil at this point in the movie. Later he gets to know Belle and he is seen wearing purple, meaning he is in transition to being good. Blue and red makes purple. At the end, in the ballroom scene, he is wearing blue to indicate that he is now one of the good guys.

- While songwriters are writing the melody to a song, they **often use dummy lyrics** to help with writing the melody. In the song "Gaston," the writers liked the dummy lyrics so much that they used those in the final production.

- Computer technology was considered for the rooftop fight and the forest chase, but the primitive state of the technology only allowed time to use it for the ballroom scene. Even for that scene, **they had a fallback strategy**: what they called the "Ice Capades" version with just a spotlight on the two characters against a black background.

- In the French release, **Cogsworth's name is Big Ben**, after the famous clock in London.

- When Beast and Gaston are having their life-or-death struggle on the castle, Gaston yells, "Belle is mine!" **Originally, he was supposed to say, "Time to die!"** but the writer changed it to fit Belle back in the scene.

- Chip **is the only object in the movie to mention Belle by her name**. All of the other objects refer to her as "mademoiselle," "she," "her," "the girl," etc.

- This was the **first Disney-animated movie to use a fully-developed script** prior to animation. In previous films, the story was developed through the use of storyboards only, and was further developed during animation. Several previous films had gone way over budget when the animators spent time and effort animating scenes that, it was eventually decided, did not fit the movie, and producers realized that they could save money by having a script written first.

- The dance between Belle and her Prince in the finale is **actually reused animation of the dance** between Princess Aurora and Prince Phillip in *Sleeping Beauty* (1959). The original *Sleeping Beauty* (1959) pair had been drawn over to become the new *Beauty and the Beast* (1991) pair, and this was done because they were running out of time during the production of the movie.

- In the 1930's and again in the 1950's, **Walt Disney attempted to adapt *Beauty and the Beast*** (1991) into a feature but could not come up with a suitable treatment, so the project was shelved. It wasn't until *The Little*

Mermaid (1989) became hugely successful that they decided to try it for a third time.

- The **second Disney-animated feature to use their proprietary CAPS** (Computer Animation Production System) system entirely, a digital ink, paint, animation, and camera process used to put the film together. *The Rescuers Down Under* (1990) was the first film to use the system.

- Angela Lansbury, the voice of Mrs. Potts, thought that **another character would be better suited to sing the ballad** "Beauty and the Beast." The director asked her to make at least one recording to have for a back up if nothing else worked, and that one recording ended up in the film.

- The film was previewed at the New York Film Festival in September 1991 in a "Work-In-Progress" format. Approximately 70% of the footage was the final color animation. The other 30% consisted of storyboard reels, rough animation pencil tests, clean-up (final line) animation pencil tests, and computer animation tests of the ballroom sequence. This marked the **first time that Disney had done a large-scale preview of an unfinished film**.

- Julie Andrews was **considered for the role of Mrs. Potts**.

- Among the trophy heads on Gaston's tavern is what **appears to be a frog's head**, visible in the scene where Gaston spits.

- When the Beast is getting his hair cut for Belle, the **hair style he is given is the same as Lion's** in The *Wizard of Oz* (1939).

- The smoke seen during the transformation of the Beast to the Prince is **actually real smoke**, not animated. It was originally used in *The Black Cauldron* (1985) and was re-used for *Beauty and the Beast* (1991).

- Linda Woolverton, an animator, drew her inspiration for the screenplay, not from Jean Cocteau's *La belle et la bête* (1946), but from *Little Women* (1933), admitting that **there's a lot of Katharine Hepburn in the characterization of Belle**.

- Many of the **paintings on the walls of the castle are undetailed** versions of famous paintings by such artists as Vermeer, Rembrandt, and Goya.

- Art **directors working on the film traveled to the Loire valley in France** for inspiration, and studied the great French romantic painters like Fragonard and Boucher to give their settings a European look.

- It was lyricist Howard Ashman who **came up with the idea of turning the enchanted objects into living creatures** with unique personalities.

- Glen Keane, the supervising animator on the Beast, **created his own hybrid beast** by combining the mane of a lion, the beard and head structure of a buffalo, the tusks and nose bridge of a wild boar, the heavily muscled brow of a gorilla, the legs and tail of a wolf, and the big and bulky body of a bear.

- Songs take up 25 minutes of the film and **only five minutes were without any musical score** at all.

- Three hundred and seventy men and women were involved in the film's production, of whom 43 were animators.

- The movie uses **1,295 painted backgrounds** and 120,000 drawings.

- **Caricatures of the directors, Kirk Wise and Gary Trousdale, can be seen** in the scene where Belle is given the book as a gift. As she is leaving the store, three men are seen pretending to not look through the window and then they sing, "Look there she goes. The girl who's so peculiar. I wonder if she's feeling well." They are the two men on the outside of the large blonde man.

- Robby Benson's **voice was altered by the growls of real panthers** and lions so that it is virtually unrecognizable. This is why near the end, when the Beast transforms into the prince, his voice changes. His voice is also not changed on the original motion picture soundtrack.

- This was the first Disney-animated feature to **have a pop version of the film's main song play over the end credits**.

- The **film is dedicated to Howard Ashman**, the lyricist, who died before the movie's completion. At the end of the final credits, you can read the dedication: "To our friend Howard, who gave a mermaid her voice and a beast his soul, we will be forever grateful."

- **Many scenes were storyboarded but never animated**. Those include a scene where Gaston visits the asylum and a scene where the Beast is seen dragging a carcass of an animal he killed. Both where considered too gruesome for the film and the ideas were dropped.

- The majority of the **sculptures seen in the castle are different earlier versions** of the Beast.

- In the beginning, the **Beast is more monster than man**. He walks on all fours, leaps across whole balconies, and his wardrobe is not complete. At the same time, Gaston starts off as a man and slowly becomes more of a monster.

- **Alan Menken composed two different musical scores** for the Beast's death scene. The original (which is part of the Transformation piece on the original motion picture soundtrack) was considered too happy for the feeling needed, so Alan Menken changed it to the version now heard in the film.

- Disney was **originally going to have Jodi Benson**, the voice of Ariel in *The Little Mermaid* (1989), also provide the voice for Belle. However, it was decided that Belle needed a more "European" sounding voice. Howard Ashman remembered working with Paige O'Hara and suggested she try out for the part.

- **All of the dialog spoken by Tony Jay** (Monsieur D'Arque, the head of the local insane asylum) heard in the film was recorded during his audition.

- Tony Jay's brief role as the asylum owner **led to him being cast as Judge Claude Frollo** in *The Hunchback of Notre Dame* (1996).

107

- Scheduling conflicts with *Star Trek: The Next Generation* (1987) forced **Patrick Stewart to turn down the role** of Cogsworth.

- The **first Disney animation movie to have Spanish dubbing**. Until that, all Disney animation movies were sent to Spain with Puerto Rican accented dubbing.

- When Paige O'Hara was auditioning, a **bit of her hair flew in her face and she tucked it back**. The animators liked this so they put it in the movie.

- The **stained-glass window that is seen** at the very end of the movie was built in *Disneyland* after the film's release.

- The name of **Gaston's sidekick, Lefou,** pronounced just like the French words meaning "the idiot," "the fool," or "the insane."

- **Ranked #7** on the American Film Institute's list of the 10 greatest films in the genre "Animation" as of 2008.

- Jerry Orbach intended **Lumiere's voice to be similar to Maurice Chevalier's**, and even pays tribute to him in the middle of the "Be Our Guest" number (right as he says "course by course, one by one...").

- **Almost the entire cast are stars of Broadway musicals** (most notably Angela Lansbury and Jerry Orbach), and Disney intended it that way, hoping that a theatrical backer could finance a future stage version of the film.

- This was the **only animated film to be nominated for the Academy Award** for Best Picture until the release of *Up* (2009) and then *Toy Story 3* (2010). It isn't that they weren't allowed to be nominated, it is just that the Academy Awards created the Best Animation category in 2001 so that they wouldn't compete with live-action films. This point was argued in 2008 when Wall-E was released and was regarded as the best film of the year and it should have been allowed to be nominated for that award.

- Disney's **30th animated feature**.

- The **stage version of *Beauty and the Beast* opened at the Palace Theater** on April 18, 1994, and ran for 5,461 performances (closing on July 29, 2007), making it the sixth longest running play on Broadway. The Broadway production is based on this film and was nominated for the 1994 Tony Award (New York City) for the Best Musical.

- **Rupert Everett auditioned for the role of Gaston**, but was told by the directors he didn't sound arrogant enough. He remembered this when he voiced Prince Charming in *Shrek 2* (2004).

- During the song "Belle," when Belle goes to the bookshop and picks out another book, she describes this book as her favorite "with far off places, daring sword fights, magic spells, and a prince in disguise." **The story she describes is *Beauty and the Beast*.**

- The sugar bowl in Mrs. Potts' tea set is the **same sugar bowl from *The Sword in the Stone*** (1963), but with a slight color change

108

- The character of **Gaston was not in the original fairy tale of *Beauty and the Beast*.** Rather, he was inspired by the antagonist of the French film *La Belle et la Bête* (1946), *Avenant*, who also was in love with Belle and tried to kill the Beast upon learning that she loved him, losing his life in the process. Reportedly, a direct-to-video sequel to the Disney movie was to feature a character named Avenant as the villain, this time as Gaston's revenge-seeking younger brother, but the project was scrapped in favor of *Beauty and the Beast: The Enchanted Christmas*.

- Though the **Beast/Prince is never mentioned by name in the film**, it is revealed by the CD-ROM game The D Show that his name is Adam.

- In the first song where Belle sings in the town, she sits by a fountain. As she reads the book (described earlier, as an adventure with a prince in disguise sounding just like Beauty and the Beast), she flips to a page with a picture. Look closely, and **you will see that she is in the bottom right**, the beast in the middle left, and the prince's castle in the middle.

- In *Hunchback of Notre Dame* (1996), **Belle appears during the film's second musical number**, the sequence in which Quasimodo sings "Out There" from atop the roof of the Notre Dame cathedral. As the camera slowly pans down and along a street reminiscent of Belle's home town in *Beauty and the Beast* towards a small group of people, Belle appears in the bottom right-hand corner of the screen, walking, and reading a book (and wearing her blue dress, of course). In the same scene, a sharp-eyed viewer can catch glimpses of a rooftop satellite dish, The Lion King's Pumbaa being carried by two men with a pole, and a street merchant shaking out the flying carpet from *Aladdin*.

- Considering Gaston had no culture and didn't read, it is odd that he would sing "Screw your courage to the sticking place," during "The Mob Song." **This was a line penned by William Shakespeare** 140 years prior to the setting of *Beauty and the Beast*. He cited it in the play *Hamlet* (1599-1602). Nobody has discovered its meaning. It may not have one, as Shakespeare sometimes made up his own words or phrases. Some theorize that the "sticking place" is the catch that holds the string on a crossbow.

- While Gaston is singing his song, he swallows three eggs. The "gulp, gulp, gulp" **sound you hear was provided by voice actor Bill Farmer**, the voice of Goofy.

Aladdin

- Animator Eric Goldberg **based the Genie on the drawings done by caricaturist Al Hirschfeld**.

- This was a **turning point for Disney in voice acting**. They realized they could bring in a larger fan base if they used big name actors to do the voices, even if they aren't professional voice actors. In this case, it was Robin Williams.

- The opening **scene with the street merchant was completely unscripted**. Robin Williams was brought into the sound stage and was asked to stand behind a table that had several objects on it and a bed sheet covering them all. The animators asked him to lift the sheet and, without looking, take an object from the table and describe it in character. Much of the material in that recording session was not appropriate for a Disney film.

- Some of the **Genie's imitations were cut from the film**, including John Wayne, George Bush, and Dr. Ruth Westheimer.

- Robin Williams provided the voice for the Genie at union scale rate (the lowest legal pay rate a studio can give an actor) on the provisos that his voice was not used for merchandising (i.e. toys and such) and that the Genie character not take up more than 25% of the space of a poster, ad, billboard, or trailer. When these wishes were not granted, **he withdrew his support for Disney and the film**. As a result, his name was not included in "The Art of Aladdin" book (it makes constant references to "the voice of the Genie"), and he was not available for the direct-to-video sequel, *The Return of Jafar* (1994), or the "*Aladdin*" (1994) TV show (Dan Castellaneta filled in as the voice of the Genie for these productions). In an attempt to get back on good terms with Williams, Walt Disney Co. CEO Michael Eisner apologized to him with a peace offering of an original Pablo Picasso painting. Still angered and feeling betrayed by Disney, Williams would not accept the gift. It was not until Jeffrey Katzenberg was fired and a new producer hired did Williams return to Disney. Through this new producer, a public apology was given (by the producer). Promises were made to right wrongs, and Williams was so touched that he came back as the Genie for the second direct-to-video sequel, *Aladdin and the King of Thieves* (1995). Disney was so thrilled that they threw out the previously completed recording sessions with Castellaneta.

110

- This film became the 14th (and the first animated movie for Disney) to **gross more than $200,000,000**.

- The **most successful film of 1992**, earning over $217 million at the US box office and over $504 million worldwide.

- This was the first major animated film which was advertised on **the strength of having a major movie star** providing one of its voices (Robin Williams in this case). This has since become the norm with animated features.

- John Candy, Steve Martin, and Eddie Murphy **were all considered at one point** to provide the voice of the Genie.

- Robin Williams **recorded most of his scenes in between filming breaks** on *Hook* (1991) and *Toys* (1992).

- During the course of recording the voices, Robin Williams improvised so much **they had almost 16 hours** of material.

- **Eight other songs were written for the film** but were later removed.

- When the film was first released on VHS in October 1993, it **sold over 10.8 million copies in its first week** and went on to sell over 25 million in total. This record stood for only two years when it was beaten by the release of *The Lion King* (1994).

- An **IMAX version was planned** but never released.

- **Linda Woolverton, who had written the screenplay** to *Beauty and the Beast* (1991), did a first draft screenplay for *Aladdin*.

- Howard Ashman and Alan Menken originally **conceived the opening song "Arabian Nights" to be recurrent** throughout the film, acting as narration. This idea was dropped when the visuals and storytelling proved strong enough in their own right.

- The color design of the film was **inspired by old Persian miniatures** and Victorian paintings of the Middle East.

- Layout supervisor, **Rasoul Azadani, traveled to his hometown of Ispahan** in Iran in 1991 to get a feel for the look of the film. He took nearly 2000 pictures there.

- The artists **videotaped capuchin monkeys at the Los Angeles Zoo** to give them an understanding of the physical characteristics of Abu.

- To capture the movement of Aladdin's low-cut baggy pants, animator **Glen Keane looked at videos of rap star M.C. Hammer.**

- **Alan Menken had tentatively written a love song for Aladdin and Jasmine's** magic carpet ride called "The World at Your Feet." When lyricist Tim Rice came on board, he changed it to "A Whole New World."

- In early visual development, **Aladdin resembled Michael J. Fox**. As the film developed, Jeffrey Katzenberg didn't think Aladdin had enough appeal to women, so he asked that Aladdin be beefed up a bit to resemble Tom Cruise.

111

👑 The **genie appears in the following guises**:

Arsenio Hall	game show host	Robert De Niro
baseball pitcher	goat	Rodney Dangerfield
bee	Groucho Marx	script prompter
boxing trainer	hammock	sheep
Carol Channing	harem	submarine
certificate	harem girl	tailor
cheerleaders	Jack Nicholson	talking lampshade
chef	Jafar	teacher
dragon	Julius Caesar	the moon
drum major	little boy	tiger
Ethel Merman	magician	tourist with a Goofy hat
Fantasia-like devil	muscle man	TV parade hosts
fat man	one-man band	ventriloquist
fireworks rocket	pair of lips	Walter Brennan
flight attendant	pink rabbit	William F. Buckley
French maître d'	Pinocchio	zombie of Peter Lorre
Frenchman in a beret	roast turkey	

👑 **Jasmine's appearance was influenced by Jennifer Connelly**, as well as the sister of her animator, Mark Henn.

👑 The stack of wooden toy animals that Jasmine's **father plays with has a toy of the Beast** from *Beauty and the Beast* (1991).

👑 When the **Genie changes Abu into a car**, the license plate reads "ABU 1."

👑 The two men in the crowd that Aladdin pushes through are caricatures of a couple of the directors, John Musker and Ron Clements. The original plan **was to use film critics Gene Siskel and Roger Ebert**, but they wouldn't grant permission.

👑 A rumor circulated in late 2001 that, during Aladdin's balcony scene, **he says, "Take off your clothes."** He is talking to Raja at the time, and his exact words are, "Nice kitty, take off and go, go on." This has been cut in the DVD version.

👑 The idea of adapting the Aladdin story as a **Disney-animated musical was first proposed by Howard Ashman in 1988** at the time that he and Alan Menken were still working on *The Little Mermaid* (1989) and before work had begun on *Beauty and the Beast* (1991). Ashman wrote an initial treatment for the project and collaborated on six songs with Menken. When John Musker and Ron Clements finished directing duties on *The Little Mermaid*, they turned their attention to writing a first draft of this film's script, and eventually became its directors.

112

In the first draft, **Aladdin had three friends** (Babkak, Omar, and Kassim), a magic ring, and two genies.

Some of the original **songs before the story was rewritten and half of the characters were cut**: "Proud of Your Boy" (supposed to be sung by Aladdin to his mother while she was sleeping, but was later removed); "Call Me A Princess;" "Omar, Babkak, Aladdin, Kassim;" "Humiliate The Boy" (sung by Jafar, cut as it was considered too cruel for the film); "High Adventure;" "Count on Me" (which was something Aladdin sang to his friends and family, then it was changed to "A Whole New World").

Not only is **the plot similar to *The Thief of Bagdad*** (1940), but character names Jafar and Abu were apparently borrowed from the 1939 script by Lajos Biró. The characters in the silent original, *The Thief of Bagdad* (1924), were not given names.

In the original folktale, **Aladdin is actually Chinese**.

Andreas Deja **based Jafar on Marc Davis' design for Maleficent** in *Sleeping Beauty* (1959). The two villains share more than just looks: both carry a staff which they use to execute evil magic; both have bird henchman (Maleficent's is a raven, Jafar's a parrot); and both turn themselves into gigantic animals in their respective films -- Maleficent as a dragon, Jafar as a snake. UltimateDisney.com featured Maleficent and Jafar in their Top Villain Countdown at #1 and #2.

Bill Plympton turned down a seven-figure offer to work on this film because any ideas and concepts he developed for his other projects while under contract with Disney would become their intellectual property.

While filming this movie, **Robin Williams frequently received calls from Steven Spielberg** who, at the time, was working on *Schindler's List* (1993). He would put him on speaker phone so he could tell jokes to the cast and crew to cheer them up. Some of the material he was using was from this film.

Originally, the peddler who introduces the movie **would be revealed to be the Genie at the end**, hence the reasoning behind having Robin Williams voice him, too. Notice the similarities in the design of the two, especially the eyebrows, the beard, and the four-fingered hands. (All the other human characters have five fingers.)

Jafar at first was more hot-tempered, while Iago was a cool, haughty British type. The filmakers felt that having Jafar losing his temper too much made him less menacing, so the personalities of the two characters were switched around.

Production designer **Richard Vander Wende devised a simple color scheme for the film**, inspired by its desert setting. Blue (water) stands for good, red (heat) for evil, and yellow (sand) is neutral. For example, the villainous Jafar is clad in blacks and reds, while the virtuous Jasmine wears blue. Another example is in the Cave of Wonders, where the lamp's chamber is blue and the ruby that tempts Abu is bright red.

- The **fire walker in the "One Jump Ahead" number is a caricature of T. Hee**, a former Disney story man who later taught caricature at CalArts, where many of the film's artists studied.

- Crazy Hakim, the "discount fertilizer" salesman in the opening chase, is a **caricature of animator Tom Sito**.

- Whenever **Aladdin tells a lie**, the plume on his hat falls and covers his face.

- The **fireworks seen at the end of the film are reused** special effects from *The Rescuers* (1977).

- When Howard Ashman began work on the movie, **he developed the story as a fast-paced comic adventure** about a young boy trying to prove his worth to his parents. But, in 1991, Ashman died, and the story problems stalled the movie. The plot was reworked to be about a teenager, Aladdin, seeking self-respect instead of the approval of others.

- In the original recording for the opening song "Arabian Nights," **part of the song originally went "where they cut off your ear, if they don't like your face."** After the movie's release, Arabic Americans took offense, so the line was changed to "where it's flat and immense, and the heat is intense." If you listen closely, you can hear a distinct vocal change when he sings.

- There are **513 people listed** in the credits.

- In the throne scenes, the **decorations at the top of the columns are the same designs** used for Mrs. Potts and her teacups in *Beauty and the Beast* (1991).

- During script and storyboard development, the writers were already considering Robin Williams for the role of the Genie but had not approached him for the project. In order to convince Williams to do the role, Eric Goldberg **animated the Genie doing several minutes of Williams' stand-up routines** and screened it for him. Williams was so impressed that he signed almost immediately.

- This is (as of 2006) the **only traditionally animated film to be nominated** for the MTV Movie Award for best picture.

- When Aladdin asks Genie if he can make him into a prince, Genie consults his "cookbook." One of the things he **pulls out of the book is Sebastian** from *The Little Mermaid* (1989).

- Scheduling conflicts with *Star Trek: The Next Generation* (1987) **forced Patrick Stewart to turn down the role** of Jafar. He has said in interviews that this is his biggest regret.

- In the preview screenings for the movie, nobody applauded after the big song numbers. The animators wanted applause and so **somebody stuck the Genie with an "Applause" sign** at the end of "Friend Like Me." The joke worked and the sign was kept for the movie.

114

- Because Robin Williams ad-libbed so many of his lines, the **script was turned down for a Best Adapted Screenplay** Academy Award nomination.

- On what came to be **known among the Aladdin animators as Black Friday**, then Disney head Jeffrey Katzenberg told the team to scrap virtually everything they'd been working on for months and start all over again. He also refused to move the film's release date. Directors John Musker and Ron Clements were able to completely turn around the film's new plot and screenplay in just eight days.

- Aladdin's personality and, initially, his look **were initially based on that of Michael J. Fox**. In the film, Aladdin is chased by burly, unintelligent brutes, who end up falling into a large pile of manure, which was much the situation of Fox's Marty McFly in *Back to the Future* (1985).

- Princess Jasmine is the **only princess to kiss the villain** of her movie.

Pocahontas

- A song titled **"If I Never Knew You" was cut** after children in test audiences found it boring. At the time, it was almost fully animated with the exception of color. For the film's 10th anniversary DVD release, the animation was completed and the song inserted back into the film as well as a short reprise in the final scene.

- Actress Irene Bedard, who provided the **voice of Pocahontas, was also the physical model** for the animated character.

- When ABC aired *Pocahontas* (1995) in 1997, **they showed the cut music scene** for "If I Never Knew You" sung by Mel Gibson and Judy Kuhn. The animation was just the black-and-white pencil sketches (no color).

- The Disney executives had all the secondary animal characters, such as **Meeko and Flit, lose their entire dialog** in order to make the film a bit more serious.

- Animators working on the film regarded *Pocahontas* as being **one of the hardest films ever produced** by the studio. The complex color schemes, angular shapes, and facial expressions meant that the film was in production for 5 years. The hard work paid off, however. Pocahontas herself is now frequently cited as being one of the most beautifully and realistically animated characters in the Disney canon; her fluid movements mainly being attributed to rotoscoping.

- This is **one of the Disney animated movies inspired by a true story**; the other being *Mulan* (1998).

- In their quest for authenticity, the **Disney studios hired mostly Native American actors** to do the voices. They also employed Native American consultants and had a session with a real shaman. Despite these efforts, prominent Native American activists issued an open letter condemning the film for its historical inaccuracies and stereotyping of the Indian people.

- The **first film to feature Mel Gibson singing**.

- *Pocahontas* was put into production at the same time as *The Lion King* (1994). Much of the animating **talent at the studio opted to work on** *Pocahontas* as they saw it as more of a prestigious production than the latter film.

- The **animation style is of a more flat and geometric appearance**, first employed by the studio back in 1959 on *Sleeping Beauty* (1959) and on *One Hundred and One Dalmatians* (1961). It would be a style that was re-used on *Hercules* (1997) and, to a lesser extent, on *Mulan* (1998).

- **"Colors of the Wind" was the first song written for the production**; it helped define the tone and direction of the film.

- John Pomeroy, the supervising animator for John Smith, **watched a number of Erroll Flynn movies** to get the movements of the character down pat. Once the look of Smith was finalized, 14 other animators were drafted in to make him come to life.

- At the time, Disney cartoons **traditionally featured a show-stopping musical number**. Previous examples would include the "Kiss the Girl" segment from *The Little Mermaid* (1989), "Be Our Guest" from *Beauty and the Beast* (1991), and "Friend Like Me" from *Aladdin* (1992). However, this proved to be problematic with *Pocahontas* as the story didn't really lend itself to such an ornate production number. Stephen Schwartz and Alan Menken penned several songs, of which the leading contender was a song called "In the Middle of the River," but it was eventually dropped when it was decided that the song simply didn't fit within the dramatic context of the story.

- **John Candy had provided a large amount of voice work** into a character named "Redfeather," a turkey, and Pocahontas's sidekick. However, after Candy's death in 1994, the concept was scrapped.

- The film's premiere was a huge event in Central Park, NYC on June 10, 1995. With **over 100,000 people attending**, it holds the record for the largest movie premiere. The 70 mm prints were projected on three enormous screens, and the sound was offset by twelve frames to accommodate the vast seating area.

- Many at **Disney had high hopes for the movie** upon initial release. Then studio head Jeffrey Katzenberg regarded it as a more prestigious project than *The Lion King* (1994), and even believed that it had a chance of earning an Academy Award nomination for Best Picture following in the steps of *Beauty and the Beast* (1991). However, the movie was less successful commercially than was hoped. Because the film dealt with more adult themes and tones, it did not appeal to younger children as much as earlier hits had.

- In the very first draft of the script, the character of **"Grandmother Willow" was written as a male character** who was the spirit of the river; the character was named "Old Man River." The song "Just Around the Riverbend" was written for this character to be sung. Gregory Peck was offered the role and, as much as it pained him to do it, he turned down the role because he felt the title character needed a motherly figure to turn to for advice. Soon the filmmakers agreed with him and the character was changed.

- **Howard Ashman was going to write lyrics for the songs** of this film as soon as he finished writing lyrics for the songs in *Aladdin* (1992). He died before he could finish the lyrics for the songs in *Aladdin*.

- Pocahontas is the **only princess to have a visible tattoo;** the other would be Kida from *Atlantis: The Lost Empire* (2001), but she isn't an official Disney princess.

- In true American history, Pocahontas was born around 1595 and met 28-year-old John Smith in early 1608. That would make **Pocahontas around 13-years-old at the time** she met him.

- **Pocahontas' real name was Matoaka.** "Pocahontas" was only a nickname, and it means "the naughty one," spoiled child," or "playful."

- When Pocahontas and Nakoma are walking to see John Smith tied up, they are holding hands, but **the shadow that preceeds them is not holding hands.**

- **Nakoma is the first of two human sidekicks for princesses.** The second is Charlotte for Tiana in *The Princess and the Frog* (2009).

Mulan

- When Mulan sings "Reflection" in her father's shrine, her reflection appears in the polished surface of the temple stones. The names of the Disney animators who worked on the film **are written in ancient Chinese on the temple stones**.

- The scene where Mulan disarms Shan-Yu with a fan **shows an actual martial art technique**.

- This was the **first full-length movie animated only at the Florida** animation studio.

- **Likenesses of the directors, Tony Bancroft and Barry Cook, appear** as the fireworks attendants frightened by Mushu in the climax.

- In the scene where Mushu awakens the ancestors, one set of grandparents worry that Mulan's quest will ensure her family loses their farm. This couple appears to be the **couple on the farm in Grant Wood's famous painting, "American Gothic."**

- **Bruce Willis (Shang's martial arts model) was originally** cast as Li Shang.

- One of the beauty parlor ladies preparing Mulan for the matchmaker **was drawn in the likeness of Rita Hsiao**, the screenplay writer for *Mulan* and *Toy Story 2*.

- **Jackie Chan voices Shang** in the Chinese release of this film.

- The **only Disney score from Jerry Goldsmith**. It was also his last Academy Award nomination.

꧁ The scene where Mulan finds a **child's doll in the burnt-out Chinese village is a tribute to Hayao Miyazaki's** *Kaze no tani no Naushika* (Nausicaä) (1984), where an explorer/warrior finds the same doll in an abandoned village.

꧁ The family names called out when the conscription notices are being handed out (with the exception of the Fa family) are **actually family names of Rita Hsiao's childhood friends**.

꧁ "Fa" is the Cantonese pronunciation of Mulan's family name. "Hua" is the correct Mandarin pronunciation, and means "flower." "Hua Pin," **Mulan's fake name, means "flower vase"** or just "vase."

꧁ In one of the original versions of the film, Mulan was engaged to Li Shang and **matching Yin-Yang necklaces were bestowed upon them**. Although that part was removed, the Yin-Yang necklaces survive in the sequel, *Mulan II* (2004), as wedding gifts to them after Shang's proposition.

꧁ According to Robert D. San Souci, who retold and researched the original story, **Disney didn't like the idea of putting in a dragon as a companion for Mulan;** they feared it would be too big and menacing. San Souci explained to them that in Chinese lore, dragons can be any size, so a small dragon was approved. Thus, Mushu was born. This change is acknowledged when Mulan calls him "tiny" and Mushu replies, "Of course! I'm travel size for your convenience! If I was my REAL size, your cow (Khan) here would die of fright!"

꧁ The English translation of the Chinese characters on the rocket Mushu has strapped to his back is "The Big Bamboo," a place in Kissimee, **Florida, where the Mulan crew liked to hang out**.

꧁ The voice for the old "American Gothic" ancestor, (his only line: "Not to mention, they'll lose the farm!") was **provided by an uncredited Barry Cook**, one of the film's directors.

꧁ Chi Fu's name **literally means, in Chinese, "to bully."**

꧁ The movie's artistic supervisors spent three weeks in China sketching, photographing, and soaking up the culture. Computer animators used the latest technology to add detail and mimic camera techniques that were previously unavailable in animation, like crowd scenes of up to 30,000 people. **They used a computer program called "Atilla"** to make the sequence featuring 2,000 Huns on horseback.

꧁ In the original Chinese legend, upon which this film was based, **Mulan succeeds in her deception and leaves the battlefield with great honors**. Months later, Mulan's fellow soldiers come in search of their "brother"-in-arms, and are shocked to discover that she's a woman.

꧁ Eddie Murphy **recorded his dialog during the breaks** of *Holy Man* (1998).

꧁ Tony/Olivier Award Winning actress **Lea Salonga originally auditioned for Mulan's voice,** but was deemed 'not deep enough' for when Mulan is

118

impersonating a male soldier. Instead, Lea provided Mulan's vocals in this film and for Princess Jasmine in *Aladdin* (1992).

- When Shang asks Mulan for her name, her response was "Ah Chew." This was a possible **reference to the voice of the Emperor,** Pat Morita, who portrayed Mr. Miyagi in *The Karate Kid* (1984) because "Ah Chew" was Morita's character on *Sanford and Son* (1972).

- The **36th Disney animated feature**.

- This was originally planned as an animated short entitled "China Doll" about an oppressed and miserable Chinese girl who is whisked away by a British Prince Charming to happiness in the West. Then Disney consultant Robert San Souci, suggested making a movie of the Chinese poem, "The Song of Fa Mu Lan," so **the 2 projects were combined**.

- **Development first began in 1994,** with Disney sending a select group of artistic supervisors to China for a 3-week acclimatization and inspiration course.

- Disney was very **keen to gain the support of the Chinese government,** hoping that it might help smooth over relations following the upset that had been caused by the Disney-funded release of *Kundun* (1997).

- Credited with **launching the career of Christina Aguilera,** whose first song to be released in the US was the film's song "Reflection." The song went down so well that it landed her a recording contract with RCA Records.

- **Donny Osmond, who sings several songs on the soundtrack**, noted that his children only ever really thought that he had made it in show business when he worked on a Disney film.

- The **first Disney animated film to openly deal with warfare**.

- The **first Disney cartoon to feature an Asian heroine**.

- After the departure of Jeffrey Katzenberg in 1994, the story was infused with a lighter touch and **handed over to the fairly new Florida feature unit**. Up until that point, they had been mainly responsible for the Roger Rabbit shorts.

- This marks **Eddie Murphy's first comic relief role in an animated film**. He would, of course, go on to greater success with the *Shrek* films.

- At one point **Stephen Schwartz was lined up to be the lyricist for the film**. When he couldn't do it, the job went to David Zippel, who had been working on *Hercules* (1997).

- Both **Mulan and her father were animated by the same team**, which was supervised by Mark Henn, as this helped make them seem related to each other.

- In total, **nearly 700 artists, animators, and technicians** worked on the film.

- Co-director **Barry Cook cites David Lean, producer/director of *Lawrence of Arabia* (1962), as one of his influences**. This is particularly

119

evident given the epic sweep of the Hun mountainside advance of 2000 soldiers on the Imperial troops and the later crowd sequence of 30,000 in the Imperial City.

- *Mulan* was **Disney's first ever DVD**, released in November 1999.

- The **opening titles were put together by simply putting water color** on rice paper.

- **Crickets are considered good luck in China**, hence the inclusion of one as a character.

- Mushu was **animated by director Tony Bancroft's twin brother,** Tom.

- Mushu says at one point that he wanted to have an "entourage." A **persistent joke during Eddie Murphy's career** was that he had a large entourage.

The Princess and the Frog

- Princess Tiana was **added to the official Disney Princess Collection** on March 14, 2010.

- *The Princess and the Frog* is **the first Disney movie to feature an African American princess**, Tiana. *Atlantis: The Lost Empire* (2001) was the first to feature a black princess, Kida.

- The **first hand-drawn Disney animated film** since *Home on the Range* (2004).

- This is the **first 2-D animated Disney film for composer Randy Newman**, who previously scored the Disney/Pixar films *Toy Story* (1995), *A Bug's Life* (1998), *Toy Story 2* (1999), *Monsters, Inc.* (2001), and *Cars* (2006). Alan Menken and his new lyricist, Glenn Slater, were originally going to do the music for the film, but John Lasseter didn't want the public to feel that Disney was becoming repetitive because Menken had been scoring another fairy tale film, *Enchanted* (2007). Newman had also previously done a jazz-inspired score for Turner's 2D animated film, *Cats Don't Dance* (1997).

- Anika Noni Rose (Tiana) **requested that Tiana be a left-handed** princess, because she herself is left-handed.

- The alligator character in the film is named Louis **in honor of jazz great Louis Armstrong**.

- During the *Walt Disney Company's* annual shareholder meeting in March 2007, **Randy Newman performed a new song written for the movie**. He was accompanied by the Dirty Dozen Brass Band.

- **Musical alligators, like Louis the Jazz trumpeter**, had been a part of a previous Disney animated classic, *The Rescuers* (1977), in which Madame Medusa's two pet reptiles, Brutus and Nero, play a tune on an organ in order to blast the two mice heroes from their hiding place. The character, Louis, in this film also has a strong connection to the "Orangutan King" character in *The Jungle Book* (1967), who is also named Louis ("King Louie") and who is also a talking animal that sings a song about wanting to be human ("*I Want to Be Like You*"). Although the ape is not a trumpeter, he was voiced by New Orleans Jazz trumpeter **Louis Prima**. Incidentally, the music supervisors used some musical elements of the latter film as the basis to create Louis' song for this film.

- The band that **Louis plays for is named the *Firefly Five Plus Lou*,** a reference to the Dixieland jazz band *Firehouse Five Plus Two,* which consisted of Disney animators.

- *The Princess and the Frog* (2009) **contains several references to the plays of Tennessee Williams**, who despite having been born in Mississippi, growing up in Missouri, being nicknamed "Tennessee," and eventually dying in New York, was strongly associated with New Orleans, the setting for this movie (Williams lived for many years in New Orleans, wrote and set several of his plays there, and met his longtime boyfriend, Frank Merlo, there, and New Orleans hosts an annual literary festival named for Williams). References include: Charlotte calls her father "Big Daddy" (the name of the wealthy patriarch character in "*Cat on a Hot Tin Roof*"), and during the party, La Bouff calls for his dog, Stella, using the distinctive cry from "*A Streetcar Named Desire.*" John Goodman, the voice of La Bouff, lives in New Orleans and has starred in several productions of William's plays, including A *Streetcar Named Desire* (1995) and a 2005 Geffen Playhouse production of "*Cat on a Hot Tin Roof*" (as the original "Big Daddy").

- During the prologue, **the princess characters from other Disney films** can be seen as toy dolls on young Charlotte's bookshelf.

- **Charlotte is the second of two human sidekicks for princesses**. The first is Nakoma for Pocahontas in *Pocahontas* (1995).

- While the **film takes place in the mid-1920's**, the time when Prohibition was still enforced until 1933, alcohol is seen being served in Tiana's restaurant, on the riverboat, and at the La Bouffs' masquerade ball.

- The firefly, Ray, is in love with the **Evening Star he named "Evangeline"** and thinks it's another firefly. Evangeline, *A Tale of Acadie,* is a poem published in 1847 by the American poet Henry Wadsworth Longfellow. The poem follows an Acadian girl named Evangeline and her search for her lost love, Gabriel. Ray is a Cajun, an ethnic group consisting of the descendants of Acadian exiles.

- The star Ray calls "Evangeline" is, **in fact, the planet Venus**. Venus is known as the Roman goddess of love.

- Early in the musical number "*Down in New Orleans,*" there is an establishing shot of the city streets. On the right side of the frame, a woman can be seen beating the **Magic Carpet from *Aladdin*** (1992) over the side of the balcony.

121

- When Louis the alligator begins playing the trumpet, he **plays a few bars of *Dippermouth Blues***, which was recorded originally by King Joe Oliver and Louis Armstrong in the 1920's. Louis Armstrong was nicknamed 'Dippermouth' and 'Satchelmouth'.

- **Animator Bruce W. Smith described Dr. Facilier** as "the love child of *Peter Pan's* (1953) Captain Hook and *One Hundred and One Dalmatians'* (1961) Cruella DeVil." Both are Disney villains and literary characters.

- **The Prince of Maldonia is called Naveen**. Naveen is an Indian name, meaning "new," which suggests that Maldonia is a Eurasian country (the name of Maldonia is a mix between Malta and Macedonia).

- The **animation style was influenced primarily by *Lady and the Tramp*** (1955) for the city scenes and *Bambi* (1942) for the bayou scenes. Those films were, in the director's opinion, "the peak of animation in the classic Disney animation style."

- This is the first 2-D film in which **all of the voice actors do both the speaking and singing parts** since *Beauty and the Beast* (1991).

- **New Orleans celebrity chef Emeril Lagasse,** who is famous for his Cajun and Creole cuisine, plays the voice of Marlon, one of the alligators who tries to eat Naveen and Tiana in the swamp. He uses his signature "Bam!" line in some of his character's sentences. Marlon is, of course, named after Marlon Brando, star of the New Orleans drama *A Streetcar Named Desire* (1951).

- Tiana's dad, **James, received a US Army Distinguished Service Cross**. It is assumed he was bestowed this honor posthumously. The Distinguished Service Cross is awarded to soldiers for acts of extraordinary heroism.

- The **Mama Odie character was inspired and patterned after the late, famed New Orleans storyteller, Coleen Salley**, even down to the character's voice. Coleen consulted with the director several times, but never lived to see the completed movie. Her name is mentioned in the film's credits. Coleen was known especially for the telling of the old Southern children's story "*Epaminondas and His Auntie*" and her own updated version entitled "*Epossumondas.*" Mama Odie can even be heard saying a famous line from those stories: "You ain't got the sense you was born with!" Coleen passed away September 16, 2008, at the age of 79.

- Animator Eric Goldberg based the animation style of Tiana's "Almost There" fantasy sequence on the art of **African-American painter Aaron Douglas**, one of the major figures of the Harlem Renaissance. Goldberg had previously directed the stylized "Rhapsody In Blue" segment in *Fantasia/2000* (1999), which was based upon the work of Al Hirschfeld.

- Dr. Facilier, Keith David, mentions transformations during his song, "Friends on the Other Side." Is it a coincidence that **David voiced the Decepticon Barricade** in *Transformers: The Game* (2007)?

122

- Jim Cummings had **earlier voiced Fuzzy Lumpkins**, a similar American Southern character with prominent antennae, on *The Powerpuff Girls* (1998).

- **Elton John was considered for the voice of Louis**, and would have performed a version of his classic song "Crocodile Rock." He had earlier composed for *The Lion King* (1994).

- The **prologue takes place in November of 1912**, as indicated by the newspaper with the headline "Wilson Elected" being read by a streetcar passenger.

- When the Shadow Man is reading Prince Naveen's tarot cards, **the last card he pulls is of the prince's future**. It features the prince sitting on a lily-pad in a pond with the money in hand, foreshadowing his later transformation.

- During the "Down in New Orleans" montage, the newspaper featuring the image of Naveen **mentions in print that Maldonia cannot be found on the map**. This is a reference to it being a fictional country made entirely for the premise of the movie.

- At one point, **you can see the "A113" on the streetcar** that Tiana is trying to board. A113 was the classroom number used by character animation students at the California Institute of the Arts. Many of its alumni, including Brad Bird, have used the number in their professional works. It appears in some way, shape, or form in every Pixar film.

- Originally titled "*The Frog Princess*," **Disney changed several key elements of the film** after receiving numerous complaints of racial insensitivity. Besides retitling the picture to avoid the implication that the first Afro-American Disney princess was somehow ugly or an animal, the lead character's name changed from Madeline to Tiana since her nickname, "Maddie," sounded too much like "Mammy." A subplot about her working as a maid was also dropped to avoid negative stereotypes.

- **Jennifer Hudson, Alicia Keys, and Tyra Banks were all considered** for the lead role. Keyes and Banks personally lobbied the studio for the part.

- In the graveyard scene at the end, there is a face on one of the tombstones. It is the face of Madam Leota from the **Madam Leota tombstone in the graveyard** along the queue for the *Haunted Mansion* in *Magic Kingdom*. (*see photo*)

Tangled

- Rapunzel was **added to the official Disney Princess Collection** on October 3, 2011.

- **Kristin Chenoweth and Dan Fogler** were the original choices to voice Rapunzel and Flynn.

- **David Schwimmer and Burt Reynolds** were cast in roles that were eventually deleted in the pre-production stage.

- According to production manager Doeri Welch Greiner, the **original script was a quasi-sequel to Enchanted**, and had Rapunzel turned into a squirrel and her place taken by a girl in the real world.

- According to Glen Keane, the movie's visual style (a three-dimensional painting) was greatly **inspired by the romantic painting "The Swing,"** by the French rococo artist Jean-Honoré Fragonard: "A fairy tale world has to feel romantic and lush, very painterly." For a clear idea of what was intended, the animators duplicated the picture in 3D to achieve a shot containing depth and dimensions.

- Composer Alan Menken reported that **he based the film's musical score on 1960's rock.**

- The hero's **name was originally going to be Bastian** instead of Flynn.

- This was Disney's **first computer animated fairytale** film.

- Many of the techniques and tools that were required to give the film the quality Keane demanded **didn't exist when the project was started;** Walt Disney Feature Animation had to make them on their own.

- Zachary Levi auditioned **with a British accent** for the part of Flynn Rider, and got it. Later this was dropped, and Levi read the role in his own American accent instead.

- Disney's previous animated feature *The Princess and the Frog*, despite being popular with critics and audiences alike, was a box office disappointment. Disney felt that the film's princess theme discouraged young boys from seeing it. In an attempt to market *Tangled* to a broader audience, **Disney changed the title of the film from *Rapunzel* to *Tangled*,** and promoted it as a comedic adventure. An early trailer for the film focused less on Princess Rapunzel and more on Flynn Rider, the male lead character. It was originally believed that Disney's marketing campaign was a desperate attempt to search for a particular audience. However, directors Byron Howard and Nathan Greno claimed that the title change was to emphasize that Flynn has as much of a role in the film as Rapunzel.

- This is the **first animated Disney "princess" film to get a PG rating** by the MPAA. All other Disney "princess" films have a G rating.

- **Clay Aiken was, at one point, confirmed for the role of Flynn Ryder** during the film's pre-production in 2005.

- The song "When Will My Life Begin (Reprise 1)" and part of the song "Mother Knows Best" are omitted from the movie. However, the complete **renditions can be found in the soundtrack** album.

- The **sword that Maximus uses to fight Flynn at the dam is a Roman gladius**. This would normally be out of place to the time-set of the movie. However, in this case it is very fitting because the name Maximus is also a Roman name.

- It is the **most expensive Disney film** in their animated collection at $260 million.

- The character of **Rapunzel is constantly barefoot**, something she shares in common with her voice actress, Mandy Moore, who loves to perform barefoot.

- Animators have said that **Rapunzel's hair is approximately 70 feet long** and consists of about 100,000 strands. With the average weight of hair, her long flowing locks would weigh about 10.4 pounds.

- **Neither Rapunzel's parents nor the eye-patched Stabbington brother** say a word for the entire movie.

- In the Snuggly Duckling tavern, the ruffian 'Greno,' who leaves to get the guards, is named for and **modeled after the film's co-director, Nathan Greno**, only much bigger but with the same van Dyke-style goatee and the same arm tattoos.

- The teaser trailer for the movie **showed the first meeting between Rapunzel and Flynn quite differently**. After getting hit with the pan, Flynn recovers. But, Rapunzel stays out of sight while her hair punches and grabs him, and drags him around the room in slapstick fashion. When Flynn is tied to the chair and tries his smoldering look on her, she throws him out of the tower while still tied to her hair. There is also an unused scene where Flynn waits at the foot of the tower and gets the full weight of Rapunzel's hair thrown on him, which greatly amuses Maximus the horse.

- The algorithm that manages how Rapunzel's hair moves appears to be **based on a similar algorithm for cloth.** This is noticeable, for example, at the end of the "When Will My Life Begin" montage as she tosses her hair around her in a spiral.

- **"Pascal" was also the name of a character** in the 1980's drama *Beauty and the Beast*, which starred Ron Perlman, voice of the Stabbington Brothers.

- In the "When will my life begin" sequence, Rapunzel says she'll "take a climb" and climbs up her hair. The way she climbs is an **actual aerial silk climbing technique**.

- You will **find Pinocchio in the Snugly Duckling**, right after cupid is swung to the right of the screen. You will find him in the top right corner in the rafters.

- The descending lantern that Rapunzel lifted back to the sky **was the one her parents, the king and queen, launched** from the palace veranda. It was the only one with the royal symbol of the sun on it.

- Over **45,000 lanterns are used** during the 'I See the Light' sequence.

- The character design of **Flynn came from the process which was called the "hot man meeting"** by Nathan Greno and Byron Howard. They set up a meeting with all the female employees of the studio in one room and asked them for their opinions of what made a man good looking in order to create Flynn's character design with features such as eye color, hair color and style and body type. Video footage showed concept art and photos of various male celebrities, including Johnny Depp, Hugh Jackman, Brad Pitt, David Beckham and Gene Kelly on the walls of the room.

- This was **Disney's 50th animated feature**.

- **Natalie Portman was considered for Rapunzel** and her audition recording was used for a pencil animation test.

- Other actresses, among the hundreds, that auditioned for Rapunzel were **Reese Witherspoon and Idina Menzel** (who later voiced Elsa in *Frozen*).

- **Gothel's dress is from the Renaissance**, which is 400 years before the time period of the film, which takes place in the 1780's. This is an effort to emphasize how Gothel and Rapunzel don't match up and how long Gothel had been living.

- When Flynn enters the tower to save Rapunzel from Mother Gothel, she stabs him and shackles his right wrist. When Rapunzel is saying goodbye to Flynn, he touches her face with his right wrist and **the shackle is gone**, only to return a moment later from another angle.

Brave

- Princess Merida was **added to the official Disney Princess Collection** on May 11, 2013.

- Princess Merida is the **first Pixar character to be included** in the Disney Princess Collection.

- **Reese Witherspoon was originally announced** as the voice of Princess Merida, but scheduling conflicts prevented her from taking the role. Kelly Macdonald ended up replacing her.

- This is the first Pixar-produced film to have a **female main character**.

- The original working title of the film **was *The Bear and the Bow*.**

- It **took six years to make this film.** Mark Andrews was initially the consultant, providing the Scottish

themes for Brenda Chapman. However, by October 2010, Chapman left after four years of work with Andrews subsequently taking over, but still keeping the intended story that Chapman wrote. Originally 80% of the film took place in snow, but when Chapman left the project, so did much of the white stuff.

- **The Pizza Planet truck**, an "Easter Egg" in nearly every full-length Pixar film, can be spotted in the Witch's Hut.

- The Pixar team **spent three years studying curly hair** to perfect the look and movement of Merida's red curling locks.

- **None of the footage shown** in the first trailer released is in the finished film.

- The misunderstood dialect that **Young MacGuffin speaks is called Doric**. It is spoken in northeastern Scotland, including the town of Elgin. Kevin McKidd chose to speak in this manner because that is his hometown.

- The name Lord **MacIntosh is a common Scottish surname;** also, the name of a well-known variety of apple. It is a reference to the Apple computer. Steve Jobs was a co-founder of Apple and played a big role in Pixar. The movie is dedicated to Jobs with this quote at the end credits: "Dedicated to the memory of Steve Jobs, our partner, mentor, and friend." It is also a reference to the visual image of Merida being interrupted while trying to bite into an apple, which her mother considers unladylike; it is repeated several times throughout the film.

- The chess set in Merida's room is the famous **Lewis Chessmen from the 12th century**, unearthed in Scotland in 1831.

- Brenda Chapman, the film's director, **based Merida on her own daughter** while Elinor was loosely based on herself.

- Two additional **software programs were specially developed for this film** by Pixar in the period of three years. One of them allows simulation of Merida's 1500 strands of hair curls to move together with her movements.

- The first film to use the new Dolby Atmos sound system. The new system expands from the 5/7.1 channel sound **mixes to 64 discrete speaker feeds** and 128 simultaneous and lossless audio channels.

- The belt that Queen Elinor wears in the first half of the movie **forms a Hidden Mickey** when viewed from the front.

- Dingwall is a town in Scotland which once **contained the largest castle** north of Stirling and was believed to be the site of a legendary battle between the Clan Mackay and the Clan Donald in 1411. The English name Dingwall means "meeting place of the local assembly." The town's Gaelic name Inbhir Pheofharain means "the mouth of the Peffery," but it is also known as Baile Chail ("cabbage town"), appropriate for Lord Dingwall's son.

- Pixar movie-makers created the family tapestry using a **technology that allowed them to create billions** of individual threads.

- Kevin McKidd was said to have been particularly happy to work on this project because it was the first time in years that he'd been **able to use his natural Scottish accent** in a film.

- Sean Connery was **considered for the roll of King Fergus**, and Annette Crosbie as The Witch.

- **Kelly Macdonald was in her thirties** when she voiced the teenage Merida.

- The name of the evil bear, from the legend told by the Queen, is Mordu. In Gaelic, it would be spelled Mor Dubh, and **means "the large black one."**

Frozen

- It was announced that Anna and Elsa will be added to **the official Disney Princess Collection**, but a date hasn't been set yet.

- Four years after the film's release **they have yet to be added to the official Collection.** It is believed that because of the success of the *Frozen* film, Disney could keep the sisters in their own separate collection to make more money. Hence the reason for whole stores dedicated to just *Frozen* merchandise.

- This movie is **based on the story** *The Snow Queen* published in 1845 by Hans Christian Andersen.

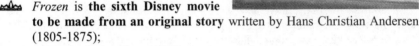

- *Frozen* is **the sixth Disney movie to be made from an original story** written by Hans Christian Andersen (1805-1875);
  - *The Ugly Duckling* (1939) – animated short
  - *The Little Mermaid* (1989) – full-length animated feature
  - *The Emperor's New Grove* (2000) – full-length animated feature based on *The Emperor's New Clothes*
  - "The Steadfast Tin Soldier" as a segment of *Fantasia 2000* (1999) – animated short
  - *The Little Match Girl* (2006) – animated short

- The names **Hans, Kristoff, Anna, and Sven were all made up** specifically for the film to pay homage to Hans Christian Anderson, the author of the original story. Just say their names in that order without pausing.

- Idina Menzel (Elsa) and Kristen Bell (Anna) **both auditioned for the roll of Rapunzel** for the animated film *Tangled* (2010). Idina was cast as Elsa based on her recordings for Rapunzel, and Kristen was cast based on a recording she had done singing "Part of Your World" from *The Little Mermaid* (1989).

- Kristen Bell stated that **she has always wanted to do voice** work for Disney ever since she saw the movies *The Little Mermaid* (1989) and *Aladdin* (1992).

- At the Wandering Oaken's Trading Post and Sauna, you can spot a plush looking **Mickey Mouse sitting on a shelf** when Anna walks toward the "winter stock."

- When Anna is singing the song "For the First Time In Forever," she exits the castle gates and **you can spot Rapunzel and Flynn from *Tangled*** (2010) entering the scene from the left. This is referred to as an "Easter Egg."

- Originally, **Elsa was going to be the villain,** like in the original story. But after the producers heard the song "Let It Go," they decided the song's theme about personal empowerment and self-acceptance was too much of a positive aspect for a villain to put across. So, they rewrote the storyline into the movie as we know it.

- While doing his recording for Olaf, Josh Gad **improvised some of his lines** to make the directors laugh; some ended up in the final film.

- The scene when Olaf is **dancing with the four seagulls** during his musical number "In Summer," was to pay tribute to Dick Van Dyke's portrayal of Bert dancing with four penguins in the film *Mary Poppins* (1964).

- A **live reindeer was brought into the studio** for the animators to study and get the body movements down for the animation of Sven. This isn't uncommon for Disney to do; they brought in live deer when animating *Bambi* (1942) and lions when they were producing *The Lion King* (1994), to name a few.

- The movie **contained 24 minutes' worth of musical numbers**. That would be almost 25% of the movie's runtime.

- Until *Frozen* (2013) was released, *The Lion King* **(1994) held the record for top grossing film of all time** during initial release almost two decades ago, which was just over $1 billion.

- *Frozen* (2013) was still playing steadily in theaters for three months, continually bringing in millions of dollars for Disney, all the way up to its digital copy release date. In fact, the **movie was re-released at the two-month mark** as a sing-a-long movie, with a "following the bouncing ball" concept, all while still playing regular showings.

- **Walt had always wanted to make *The Snow Queen*.** Back in the 1940's he was set to do a collaboration with *Samuel Goldwyn Productions* to make a live action/animated crossover movie about Hans Christian Anderson, with Disney creating the animated portions. The plan fell through and the idea was scrapped, along with *The Little Mermaid, The*

130

Emperor's New Clothes, The Ugly Duckling, The Little Match Girl, The Steadfast Tin Soldier, Thumbelina, and *The Red Shoes*.

- The song "Let It Go," which was performed by Idina Menzel, **topped out at #1 on the Billboard 200**, and remained there for five non-consecutive weeks. This is the first time a soundtrack reached #1 and stayed there for so long in 15 years. The last one to do it was the soundtrack from *Titanic* (1998) with "My Heart Will Go On" by Celine Dion.

- *Frozen* is the only Disney princess film that **doesn't reveal the main antagonist** until the end of the film.

- In the design stage for Elsa's giant snow monster, Marshmallow, animators toyed with the idea of **making him a giant looking Olaf**, and Olaf was going to refer to him as "little brother." But that idea was scrapped because it just didn't look right.

- Idina Menzel **has done three voice characters for Disney**. The first was the sorceress Circe Disney in the television series of *Hercules* (1998). The second was of Nancy Tremaine when she went to the animated realm of Andalasia in *Enchanted* (2007). And the third, most recent, and most popular roll, is as Elsa in *Frozen* (2013).

- The **animation team visited Norway** to get a feel for what they were to be creating. A lot of the architecture of the buildings and the designs for things made its way into the film. They also visited an Ice Hotel in Quebec, Canada, to get a feel for how light refracts around when everything is made of ice. A visit to Wyoming was used to experience what their winters are like to incorporate it into the film.

- The painting Anna jumps in front of is a **rendition of the famous oil painting "The Swing"** by French painter Jean-Honoré Fragonard in 1767. The Disney animators used it for inspiration when designing concept art for the film *Rapunzel*, which was later renamed *Tangled* (2010).

- Supposedly the mountain of chocolate on the plate next to Anna that she stuffs her face with is a **nod to the mountain in the game "Sugar Rush"** from the last animated film by Walt Disney Animation Studio, *Wreck-It Ralph* (2012).

- There is a **Hidden Mickey that appears briefly in the block of ice** that Elsa uses to push the guard off the balcony.

- Anna **picks up some baby ducklings** while singing her musical number "For the First Time In Forever." This was a nod to *Rapunzel* when she said, "Well, I do like ducklings," in reference to entering the Snuggly Duckling.

- When Olaf is on the beach singing "In Summer," he passes a sandwoman that is a **nod to the infamous Coppertone ad**. This ad was also placed on a billboard in *California Adventure* on *Paradise Pier*, but has since been removed.

- *Walt Disney Animation Studios* **made several attempts at making this film**. They made an attempt in 2002, but the project got scrapped when Glen Keane quit the project. Another attempt was made in 2009 when John Lasseter found directors, producers, writers, and a composer for the project before it was put on hold again, so that a proper script could be written.

- *Frozen* is the **first Disney animated feature film to win a Golden Globe** since *Tarzan* (1999), which was also directed by Chris Buck.

- Santino Fontana had **originally auditioned for the role of Flynn Rider** in *Tangled* (2010), but lost the part to Zachary Levi. After that, Santino got a call back from Disney to play the part of Kristoff. After the story was rewritten again, he auditioned for the part of Hans.

- When Kristoff and Sven are in the barn and Kristoff is serenading Sven, he is playing a four-stringed guitar. The animators added **only three tuning keys on the guitar head** instead of four, one for each string.

- Jennifer Lee was initially assigned to be a screenwriter for the film, like she was for *Wreck-It Ralph* (2012). Later Disney announced that Jennifer would be a co-director with Chris Buck, making her **the first woman to direct an animated film** for *Walt Disney Animation Studios*.

- The characters Kai and Gerda are both servants in the castle. They were both **named after the two child main characters** from the original *Snow Queen* story. Kai is the one who missprounces "Weselton."

- The Duke of Weselton is the second consecutive Disney **character antagonist to be voiced by Alan Tudyk**. The first was King Candy in *Wreck-It Ralph* (2012).

- In Wandering Oaken's Trading Post and Sauna, Oaken offers Anna a jar of "Lutefisk." **Lutefisk is a traditional dish of Nordic countries**. It is whitefish soaked in lye, or dehydrated for preservation, and is reconstituted or prepared at a later time.

- On December 22, 2011, Disney announced that "*The Snow Queen*" had been put back into development, but was called *Frozen* (2013). At that time, Disney was uncertain whether or not the **movie was going to be hand drawn or computer animated**. It wasn't until 20 days later, on January 11, 2012, it was announced that the film was going to be computer animated.

- Much of the cinematography done for the mountainous settings of the **Norwegian fjords was inspired by the look in** *Black Narcissus* (1947) and *The Sound of Music* (1965).

- When Hans is with Elsa on the ice and he tells her that her magic killed Ana, he has no visible weapons of any kind. They cut to Ana as the flurry clears and you hear a sword pulling from a sheath only to see **Hans with a sword that appeared from nowhere,** and he still doesn't have a sheath that would make the sound.

132

Moana

- Moana is the **first Polynesian Disney princess**.

- Her **full name is Moana Waialiki** and she is from the island of Motunui.

- **Auli'i Cravalho is the youngest actress to voice one of the Disney princesses.** She was only 14 years old when she was cast and was 16 years old when the movie was released, making her the same age as Moana.

- Auli'I's birthday is November 22, and the movie was released on November 23. But for diehard Disney fans, they got to see the film on premier night, **her birthday on the 22nd.**

- **This is Auli'i's first acting role.** She wasn't planning on auditioning for the part because she didn't think she would have a chance against the hundreds of other females auditioning. Oddly enough, she was the last audition on the last day of auditions.

- The **name "Moana" means "ocean"** in many Polynesian languages, including Hawaiian and Maori.

- The animators developed new software to **give Moana's hair a realistic look**. They had it vary in different styles, like when she puts it in a bun while sailing.

- Moana's **body type was designed to be the most realistic** out of all of the princesses; she doesn't have the super thin waistline.

- Moana, Chief Tui, and Sina **are the only ones to wear red**. It signifies their royalty. The other villagers wear oranges, yellows, tans, and browns.

- Heihei the rooster was **voiced by Alan Tudyk**. He was also the voice of Duke Weaselton in *Zootopia* (2016), Duke of Weselton in *Frozen* (2013), King Candy in *Wreck-It Ralph* (2012), Ludo & Butterfly King in *Star Vs. The Forces of Evil* (2015-2016), Alistair Krei in *Big Hero 6* (2014), and K-2SO in *Rogue One: A Star Wars Story* (2016).

- The vocal work for Pua the pig was **done by actual pigs**.

- In the original story, Moana was **supposed to go on a quest to save her true love**. She was to be a secondary character to Maui.

- In another variation, **Moana had nine older brothers** that she set out to rescue.

- Tamatoa is actually designed off of a real species of crab. It is known as **the Coconut Crab, or sometimes called the "robber crab"** or "leaf thief." These crabs can grow to be 3' 3" long and is the largest land living arthropod (crab). They are known for being attracted to shiny objects and are cannibalistic with their own kind. Both of these attributes were sung about in Tamatoa's song "Shiny."

- In Maori, the name *Tamatoa* means "*trophies*," which is what Tamatoa collects.

- Sven from *Frozen* (2013) can be seen when Maui gets his hook back and tries to shape-shift it into an eagle.

- In the beginning in the hut where Gramma Tala is storytelling, you can see **a tapestry with a tribal painting of Marshmello** from *Frozen* (2013).

- **Flounder from *The Little Mermaid*** (1989) can be spotted swimming with other fish during Maui's song "You're Welcome," when he takes her into the 2D world view.

- **Wreck-It Ralph can be seen right before the end of the end credits**. He is on the right side of the screen.

- After Moana boards the coconut pirates' ship, **one of the pirates can be seen with the facepaint of Baymax** from *Big Hero 6* (2014). He is toward the right side in a cluster of other coconut pirates.

- *Moana* is the **only film to not have a main protagonist**. She has to beat coconut pirates, Tamatoa the crab, and the lava demon. These are just obsticles she has to overcome on her journey.

- **Nowhere in the film does Moana have a love interest**, or someone interested in her. She is the first Disney princess to not have this. Some might argue that Merida didn't have a love interest, but the fact that there were three "princes" competing to win her hand excludes it. None of them did by the end, but they were still there. Moana had nothing.

- This was the first time in 14 years that **Disney released two animated features in the same year**. Nine months preceding the release of this film, Disney released *Zootopia*. The last time they did that was in 2002, when they released *Treasure Planet* and *Lilo & Stitch*. *Lilo & Stitch* was also the last and only other Pacific Island-themed movie that they released.

- *Inner Workings* was the short that was released before the film in the theaters. There was a scene in it when the main character had a full bladder but relieved itself while it was in the ocean. Later in Moana a similar sequence would poke fun at it when **Maui does the same thing while Moana is testing out the temperature** of the water.

- This was the **seventh film to be directed by John Musker and Ron Clements**. The first six were *The Great Mouse Detective* (1986), *The Little Mermaid* (1989), *Aladdin* (1992), *Hercules* (1997), *Treasure Planet* (2002), and *The Princess and the Frog* (2009). With *Moana* being the seventh, it was also the first to be fully computer animated. Their first film, *The Great Mouse Detective*, was the first to actually use a computer to animate specific aspects of the film, in this case the Big Ben clock tower scene showing the inner workings with the cogs.

- When *Moana* was released in Italy, it had to undergo a name change. **The film's title was changed to *Oceania* and Moana's name was changed to Vaiana**. This was because a tv miniseries was released in Italy called

Moana in 2009 and was a biographical film about the adult film star Moana Pozzi. They didn't want any confusion between the two.

- 👑 In Spain, the movie **title was changed to *Vaiana: La Légende du Bout du Monde***, which translates to *Vaiana: The Legend from the End of the Earth*. Another alternate title was *La Princesse du Bout du Monde*, which means *The Princess from the End of the Earth*. It is said this was done because of trademark issues.

- 👑 With Vaiana being her name, the 'Via' means "water" and the 'ana' means "cave," together **meaning "water cave" in Maori**. 'Wai' from her last name of Waialiki means "water" as well.

- 👑 **Moana is a wayfinder**. That is someone who searches out new places without using any form of navigational tool, like a compass, map, or satellite. She uses the sun, stars, the ocean current, and her instincts to find her way.

- 👑 Moana's story **takes place 1,000 years ago**.

- 👑 In real Polynesian history, the wayfinders stopped traveling about 2,000 years ago and stayed in one place for 1,000 years Then, all of a sudden they started traveling again around 1000 AD. The story of *Moana* **tells the story as to why they started traveling again**. Maybe they stopped because Maui stole Te Fiti's heart 1,000 years ago, and he was banished, so the humans didn't have his help anymore.

- 👑 This timeline puts **Moana's story as being the second oldest** in the princess collection. Although, Merida's could possibly be older as hers took place between 900-1600 AD. Mulan's story takes place between 386–533 AD.

- 👑 Originally, **Heihei was going to be an intelligent character** and was intended to be a protector/babysitter of Moana, much like Sebastian for Ariel. Because they were having issues writing the story with his character like that, and due to audiences not liking him much, he ended up getting cut from the film. John Lasseter gave them 48 hours to solve the Heihei problem or he would stay cut. It was then suggested that Heihei be a dumb character to add comedic bits to the film. They ended up going with this, and to celebrate the reinstating of Heihei, the directors went out for a chicken dinner.

- 👑 **Heihei is reguarded as the least intelligent Disney character**. That's pitting him against Becky and Gerald in *Finding Dory* (2016), too.

- 👑 The **story was written by seven Disney writers**; Ron Clements, John Musker, Chris Williams, Don Hall, Pamela Ribon, Aaron Kandell, and Jordan Kandell. The story was then given to Jared Bush to adapt into a screenplay.

- 👑 John Musker's **inspiration of a Polynesian theme for a film** came from the author Herman Melville, who wrote *Moby-Dick* and *Billy Budd*, and author Joseph Conrad who wrote *Heart of Darkness*, *Lord Jim*, and *Rescue*.

135

The movie wasn't fully computer animated. The **tattoos on Maui were hand drawn** and added into the animation.

Maui's tattoos were drawn by animator Eric Goldberg. He was the one who animated Genie in *Aladdin*, Phil in *Hercules*, Louis in *The Princess and the Frog*, and Rabbit in *Winnie the Pooh*.

The **tattoos act much like a conscience,** like Jiminy Cricket did for Pinocchio.

When Maui transforms into a bird, **you can see his giant fishhook in the feather pattern** under his wing.

The writers used **the storyline of *True Grit*** (1969) starring John Wayne as an inspiration for the film. It was about a washed-up US Marshal who helped a stubborn teenage girl track down her father's killer.

Writer **Taika Waititi wrote an early script for this film**. He also wrote scripts for episodes of the show *Flight of the Conchords* (2007-2009) which coincidently starred Jemaine Clement, the voice of Tamatoa. Taika is also the director for the Marvel movie *Thor: Ragnarok* (2017).

Mark Mancia worked on creating the music for *Moana*. He also worked on the music for *The Lion King*, *Tarzan*, *Brother Bear*, *Tarzan 2*, *Brother Bear 2*, *The Haunted Mansion*, *Planes*, and *Planes 2: Fire & Rescue*. As for non-Disney films, he did the music on *Speed*, *Bad Boys*, *Assassins*, *Money Train*, *Twister*, *Con Air*, *Speed 2: Cruise Control*, *Training Day*, *Shooter*, and *August Rush*.

One of the villagers was voiced by Phillipa Soo. She was nominated for Best Actress in a Broadway Musical for her role in *Hamilton*.

The scene when the coconut pirates are chasing Maui and Moana was **inspired by *Mad Max: Fury Road***.

The coconut pirates are actually called kakamora. From mythology, the kakamora are cave/tree dwelling goblins or spirits. These creatures are thought to be human-like with long nails and vary in size from a few inches to about five feet in height. They sometimes kill humans and eat their flesh. In mythology that is, not in the movie.

Moana is the **most technically-advanced animated film** with having 80% of the animation being visual effects. Compare that to *Big Hero 6* which had less than 50% visual effects. Of that 80% visual effects, 60% were water effects.

Because Disney needed such realistic water effects, they had to create a new computer program to animate the water. **The program was called SPLASH**.

Dwayne Johnson was also the singing voice of Maui. Previously, Dwayne had sung the song *"What a Wonderful World"* in *Journey 2: The Mysterious Island* (2012). On a few occasions, he sung in the ring when he was still a wrestler and went by the name "The Rock."

136

- There was an "Easter Egg" for *Moana* in the movie *Zootopia* (2016). Duke Weaselton is selling bootleg DVDs on a street corner. One of the titles is **"Meowana: Adventure in The South Purrcific."** The voice of Duke Weaselton was provided by Alan Tudyk, who is also the voice of Heihei.

- **Maui's hook can be seen in *Zootopia*** (2016) on the back, left side of Finnick's van when Judy goes looking for Nick.

- The **animators added in some of Auli'i's gestures** and movements into the animations of Moana. Like how Auli'i kept touching her hair.

- **The El Capitan Theater in Hollywood hosted movie nights** in October 2016 for Ron Clements and John Musker. They previewed all of their past films and then held a panel at the end for a Q&A with Ron and John.

- People have been associating England with fairy tales. John and Ron want to expand on what we think of fairy tales by **telling stories from other places in the world**, like the Polynesian islands.

- The animators created a program for *Frozen* (2013) to **animate the snow and called it Matterhorn**. In *Moana*, they used this program to animate the foam on the beach and the lava in Te Ka.

- *Moana* was beating *Frozen* by $4 million in the box office in its first five days of theatrical release. *Moana* ended up taking in about $643 million while *Frozen* raked in almost $1.3 billion at the end of their runs.

General Princess Trivia

Here are some trivia that pertains to all of the princesses. After I wrote this section, the movie *Frozen* (2013) and *Moana* (2016) was released and changed some of the relativity of the information. Elsa and Anna are included in this although they are not part of the princess collection at the moment. Maybe after the hype of *Frozen* melts away Disney will induct them.

- Only **nine out of the fourteen princesses are royal by birth**: Moana, Jasmine, Aurora, Snow White, Ariel, Rapunzel, Merida, Elsa, and Anna. Belle, Tiana, and Cinderella married a prince. Pocahontas is the daughter of a Native-Indian chief, who, with those standards, could be considered royalty by the English. Indian Chiefs were actually chosen for their positions, so Pocahontas was more like the "mayor's daughter." Mulan is the daughter of a war hero, and she was the only woman to receive special honor for saving the Emperor of China. Both Mulan and Pocahontas were added to the lineup for their status and acts of heroism in their films, making them good role models for young girls.

- The only princesses born into royalty that are **not included in the Collection are Princess Kida**, later a queen, born the daughter of King Kashekim Nedakh in *Atlantis: The Lost Empire* (2001), and Princess Eilonwy from The Black Cauldron (1985). Both films did poorly in theaters and so the princesses' statuses are not acknowledged.

- Even though all of the princesses come from different countries, **they all still speak English**.

- If the princesses existed in real life, the **only three that would speak English** would be Tiana, because she is from New Orleans, Pocahontas, because she learned from the English settlers, and Aurora, because she is from England.

- All of the princesses are **humans, with the exception of the mythical mermaid,** Ariel, who was human for part of her film.

- The **only princess to be an animal** is Tiana, she was a frog, at least for part of the movie.

- All of the **princesses were shown at a younger age** in their films, with the exception of Snow White, Ariel, and Pocahontas. Although, Ariel was shown as a little girl in her third film, *The Little Mermaid: Ariel's Beginning* (2008).

- There are sequels or shorts for most of the princesses. The **only ones that do not have a sequel or a short** are Merida, Tiana, Snow White, and Moana.

- Having a **birthday on film isn't a common occurrence**. In fact, Aurora, Rapunzel, and Jasmine are the only ones to have done so. Anna has her birthday in the short *Frozen Fever* (2015).

- **All of the villains are killed off at one point** in the films except in Cinderella, Moana, Pocahontas, Aladdin, and Frozen. Although Jafar does die in *The Return of Jafar* (1994).

- The princesses are either royal by blood or marriage, except for Mulan or Pocahontas. But Snow White, Aurora, and Ariel are **royal by both blood and marriage**.

- Each princess **can be seen wearing a tiara or crown** in their promotional photos. But in their films, Aurora, Cinderella, Rapunzel, Tiana, Ariel, Moana, Elsa, and Merida are the only ones to actually wear them.

- In the beginning, **Tinker Bell was a part of the Collection.** She was dropped in 2005 when she got her own franchise, *Disney Fairies*.

- Snow White and Cinderella are the **only two princesses who were orphaned** at the beginning of the film.

- Generally, the villains are killed by accident, by allies of the princess, or were not killed. The **only two that killed their own protagonist** are Mulan and Tiana.

- Disney likes to make up names for their new characters, like Merida, Moana, and Ariel. But Snow White, Cinderella, Belle, Pocahontas, Mulan, and Rapunzel **took their names from their source story**.

- Of the Disney Renaissance, Jane Porter, from *Tarzan* (1999), was the **last female heroine** to be seen on film.

- **The Disney Renaissance lasted from 1989-1999,** and the last princess to arise from that era was Mulan.

138

👑 Cinderella, Ariel, Aurora, Tiana, and Belle are the **only five princesses to have ever danced with their love interest**. Anna sort of did, but then again Hans wasn't really her love. Rapunzel had the kingdom dance, but when she connected with Flynn, the dance was done.

👑 All of the **princesses have experienced some form of magic** in their lifetimes:

- Snow White was poisoned by the Queen's dark magic.
- The Fairy Godmother used magic to create Cinderella's gown, glass slippers, and the horse-drawn pumpkin carriage.
- Aurora was put into a magical sleep by Maleficent's spinning wheel.
- Ariel was transformed into a human, both by her father, and by Ursula.
- Beast had a curse placed upon him and his kingdom by a beautiful enchantress. All of the magical, enchanted people in his castle were around Belle, and Belle broke the curse by saying she loved the Beast.
- Jasmine is friends with a magical Genie. The main villain, Jafar, has also cast spells on her.
- Grandmother Willow is a tree that holds a spirit that gives guidance to Pocahontas.
- Mushu was a dragon that was tasked with assisting Mulan by her ancestors.
- Tiana was transformed into a frog.
- The glowing hair of Rapunzel had the ability to heal the sick and bring back youth.
- Merida made a deal with a *scaffy witch* that gave her a gammy spell that turned her mother into a bear. It also turned her three bothers into bears.
- Anna's sister, Elsa, can create snow and ice with her magical powers. Anna was almost killed on two separate occasions by her sister because of that magic, both instances were accidental. Anna also has a magical talking snowman, Olaf.
- Moana teamed up with the shape-shifting demi-god Maui, met the goddess Te Fiti, and was assisted on her quest by the ocean, that had a personality of its own.

👑 There are six princesses that have brown eyes: Snow White, Jasmine, Pocahontas, Mulan, Moana, and Tiana. Of the six, **Snow White is the only Caucasian princess that has brown eyes**. Cinderella, Ariel, Merida, Anna, and Elsa are the five princesses with blue eyes; the only one with violet eyes is Aurora, Belle has hazel, and Rapunzel has green eyes.

👑 The six princesses with brown eyes are also **the only ones to have black hair**, although Moana's could be considered a very dark brown, depending on the light.

👑 **Aurora is the only naturally-blonde princess**. Rapunzel has blonde hair because of its magical powers but is genetically brunette, Cinderella has strawberry-blonde hair, and Elsa's hair is platinum blonde.

Belle was the **first heroine to teach her love interest how to read**. In 1999, Jane taught the King of the Jungle, Tarzan, how to read, making her the second.

Ariel, Merida, Cinderella, and Anna **all have red hair and blue eyes.**

Pocahontas, Mulan, Moana, Merida are the only princesses to originate or take their story from a fairy tale. They were either **made up by Disney, or were from real history**.

It is said that Pocahontas and Mulan are **the least popular of the princess collection**. They are difficult to find on merchandise for this reason.

Not counting Merida, because it wasn't a musical, **all the princesses sing their own songs** or sing their song with someone else. The exception to this is Belle as Mrs. Potts sings her song.

One of the rules Disney came up with was to not have the princesses interacting with each other or acknowledge each other's existence. This is why they all look posed and **aren't making eye contact with each other**. They all originate from different worlds and timelines.

Some of the princess characters have appeared in the series *Once Upon a Time* (2011-present). You can see Snow White, Cinderella, Belle, Aurora, Mulan, Ariel, Elsa, Anna, Merida, and Jasmine. Rumors are buzzing that Pocahontas and Moana might show up as well.

Jasmine is one of two princesses who are **not the main protagonists** of their films. Her movie is actually Aladdin's story. The other is Sleeping Beauty, because the story is told from the point of view of the fairies, and she only has 18 minutes of screen time.

Belle is the only brunette princess, although Rapunzel becomes a brunette at the end of her film.

In the official artwork of the princess collection, **Pocahontas is the only one to go unchanged**. Although, at one point she is shown wearing the dress she wore in London from *Pocahontas II: Journey to a New World* (1998).

Classical 2D animation is a thing of the past. *Princess and the Frog* (2009) was the last film to be released in this format. Although, there are certain segments of *Moana* (2016) that were hand drawn, like Maui's tattoos.

None of the princesses after Mulan were shown in *House of Mouse* (2001-2002).

If a princess becomes a queen, then **she can no longer be considered a Disney princess**.

Merida was **the first princess to break the mold**:
- She was the first to have her movie made by Pixar.
- She was the first to not have a love interest.
- Was the first to not star in a musical.

- She is also the first to not be inspired by another movie, a book, or real life.

- All of the **princesses have long to shoulder-length hair**, except for Snow White. Both Rapunzel and Mulan had short hair, either part way through or by the end of their films.

- The main focus of the franchise has been to **add more princesses** since the addition of Tiana in 2009.

- **Each princess is seen doing servant work or chores** with the exception of Ariel, Anna, Elsa, Moana, and Pocahontas.

- Four Disney Princesses **starred in live-action films** that are more of terror or action than fairy tale. Elsa, Anna, and Ariel were made up for their Disney versions, so they don't have a live verson. Merida's and Moana's stories were completely made-up, and they only exist in those films. There are lots of *Aladdin* movies going back to 1906, but Disney created the name Jasmine. These are just a few examples;
  - Snow White - *Snow White & the Huntsman* (2012)
  - Snow White - *Snow White: A Tale of Terror* (1997)
  - Mulan - *Mulan: Rise of A Warrior* (2009)
  - Pocahontas - *The New World* (2005)
  - Aurora - *Maleficent* (2014)
  - Briar Rose - *The Curse of Sleeping Beauty* (2016)

- In 2013, **the princesses were redesigned** and were franchised with their new designs.

- **Marc Davis animated Snow White**, Cinderella, and Aurora; Glen Keane animated Ariel, Pocahontas, and Rapunzel; and Mark Henn animated Belle, Jasmine, Mulan, and Tiana. The rest of the princesses were animated by different people.

- The only princess **to not have their father shown** is Snow White.

- The **only princesses to have both parents through the whole movie** are Aurora, Moana, Mulan, Rapunzel, and Merida.

- *Frozen* is the **only film to have another princess crossover** into it when Rapunzel showed up for Elsa's coronation day.

- Rapunzel, Tiana, Elsa, and Anna are the **only princesses to have the title of their movies have a different name** than the original story. *Rapunzel* was changed to *Tangled*, *The Frog Princess* was change to *The Princess and the Frog*, and *The Snow Queen* was changed to *Frozen*. Disney wanted to modernize the titles and get both boys and girls into the theater to see the movies.

- Each princess has an object, or **objects, that represent them**:
  - Snow White – red apple
  - Cinderella – glass slipper, pumpkin
  - Aurora – spindle, spinning wheel
  - Ariel – dinglehopper, seashell, trident

- Belle – red rose, book
- Jasmine – Genie's lamp
- Pocahontas – her necklace, a feather
- Mulan – peach blossom, a fan
- Tiana – lily pad flower, frog
- Rapunzel – sun, lantern, paintbrush
- Merida – bow/arrow, bear
- Anna – tulip of the royal family of Arendelle
- Elsa – snowflake
- Moana - Tiare flower

⚜ Snow White, Aurora, and Anna **"died" in their films and were revived**. Megara and Giselle also had that same fate, but they aren't in the Collection.

⚜ People like to argue about who and why other princesses or characters weren't included in the official line-up. **There is a reason as to why none of the 26 females on the following list weren't added** and I list the reasons.

- **Vanellope von Schweetz** from *Wreck-It Ralph* (2012) - she stepped down from being a princess when she became the president of her candy-covered video game world of *Sugar Rush*.

- **Sofia** from *Sofia the First* (2012) - she is considered too young to be in the Collection and she is from a television series and not from a movie.

- **Tinker Bell** from *Peter Pan* (1953) - Tink was originally in the Collection for a few years until she got her own spin-off collection, *Disney Fairies*, for which she is the main character.

- **Kida** from *Atlantis: The Lost Empire* (2001) - she becomes the queen in the sequel *Atlantis: Milo's Return* (2003). This may not be a good argument since Elsa was added to the Collection and she, too, is a queen. But, Kida came from a film before the Princess Collection started, and it was a flop film.

- **Megara** from *Hercules* (1997) - she was in a few items when the Princess Collection started out but was removed due to lack of popularity, per Disney. The same goes for **Alice** from *Alice In Wonderland* (1950), **Esmeralda** from *Hunchback of Notre Dame* (1996), and **Jane Porter** from *Tarzan* (1999), although technically Jane did end up with the "King of the Jungle," which would make her a queen, if anything. Alice did appear as one of "The Princesses of Heart" in the video game *Kingdom Hearts*.

- **Princess Eilonwy** from *The Black Cauldron* (1985) is not included in the official line-up because of the poor reception of the film. She is sometimes referred to as the "Forgotten Disney Princess." If she was to be added to the line-up, she would be the youngest one at the age of 12 years, closely followed by Snow White who is 14 years old.

- **Minnie Mouse**, **Daisy Duck**, **Faline** (*Bambi*), **Nala** (*The Lion King*), **Kiara** (*The Lion King 2: Simba's Pride*), **Princess Atta** & **Princess Dot** (*A Bug's Life*), **Jessie** (*Toy Story 2*), **Sally** (*Nightmare Before Christmas*), and **Maid Marian** (*Robin Hood*) - are all anthropomorphic. That means they are animals or something non-human that were given human characteristics, like walking, talking or human emotions. Because of this, none of them are considered. However, Nala was on a few princess items in the beginning. Daisy and Minnie are both queens in the *Kingdom Hearts* video games. Minnie is also a princess in *Mickey, Donald and Goofy: The Three Musketeers* (2004). Technically, if Sally married "The Pumpkin King" (Jack Skellington), then she would be a queen.

- **Melody** from *Little Mermaid 2: Return to the Sea* (2000) - one of the few princesses who was actually born to a queen and king, both by blood, to not be included. At the age of 12 she is said to be too young for the line-up, this only putting her two years behind Snow White. And, she was in a straight-to-DVD movie and not a theatrically-released one, so her popularity is low.

- **Wendy Darling** from *Peter Pan* (1953) is in no way royalty or with someone of royalty. In the sequel, *Return to Neverland* (2002), Wendy is married to a regular man.

- **Giselle** from *Enchanted* (2007) - due to Giselle being in human form for the majority of the movie, she isn't considered for the line-up. Rumor has it that Disney would have to pay Amy Adams royalties because of her likeness with the animated Giselle.

- **Ting-Ting**, **Su**, and **Mei** from *Mulan 2* (2004) - they had too small of a part from a straight-to-DVD movie to be considered.

- **Princess Calla** from *Adventures of the Gummi Bears* (1985–1991) isn't considered because she was a supporting character in a television series, and not in a movie.

- **Princess Tiger Lilly** from *Peter Pan* (1953) had too small of a part as a supporting character to be considered.

- **Kilala Reno** is from the manga book series *Kilala Princess*. This book series isn't made by Disney, but the producers had permission to use the characters of Snow White, Jasmine, Cinderella, Belle, Ariel, and Aurora in the animations.

- **Kairi** from the *Kingdom Hearts* (2002) video game is a "Princess of Heart," but because she is only in a video game, she isn't considered.

- **Princess Leia** from the *Star Wars Franchise* (1977-2017) - although people petitioned to have Disney add Leia to the Collection after Carrie Fisher's death, they won't because Leia is from live action and not animation. They would also have to pay out royalties for using Carrie Fisher's likeness.

DISNEY FAIRIES

Disney Fairies is a Disney franchise built around the character of Tinker Bell, whom Disney adapted in their 1953 animated film *Peter Pan* and subsequently adopted as a mascot for the company. Walt made Tinker Bell the official mascot of Disneyland in place of Mickey Mouse for fear of negative reactions to the park. He didn't want his prized mouse firstly associated with the downfall of his park, so he decided to use Tink as the promoting character.

In addition to the fictional fairy character created by J. M. Barrie, the franchise introduces many new characters, and expands substantially upon the limited information the author gave about the fairies and their home of Neverland. The characters are referred to within stories as "Never Fairies." The franchise includes children's books and other merchandise, a web site, a computer-animated Tinker Bell film series, featuring the character and several of the Disney fairies as supporting and recurring characters. The series of computer animated films featuring Tinker Bell has been releasing since 2008. Produced by *DisneyToon Studios*, and distributed by *Walt Disney Studios Home Entertainment*, the series consists of six direct-to-video films and one TV special.

1. *Tinker Bell* (September 18, 2008)
2. *Tinker Bell and the Lost Treasure* (October 27, 2009)
3. *Tinker Bell and the Great Fairy Rescue* (September 21, 2010)
4. *Pixie Hollow Games* (November 19, 2011)*
5. *Secret of the Wings* (October 23, 2012)
6. *The Pirate Fairy* (April 1, 2014)
7. *Legend of The Neverbeast* (March 3, 2015)

*It was originally intended as the last of five feature-length films in the Tinker Bell series of direct-to-DVD 3D animated films, with the title *Tinker Bell: Race through the Seasons*, and a release date in 2012. However, the movie was rescheduled and retooled as a TV special instead of a film-length movie. Unlike the previous feature films in this series, Tinker Bell is not a centrally-featured character in this special release; Rosetta is.

FUN FACTS

* In *The Pirate Fairy*, **the six main fairies have about equal screen time**. The film is about Zarina becoming a pirate and the six having to save her.

* In *Legend of the Neverbeast*, **Fawn is the main character** since she is an animal fairy and the Neverbeast is an animal.

144

✳In *The Pirate Fairy*, **Captain Hook is introduced into the series** and is voiced by Tom Hiddleston. Tick-Tock was also introduced when he hatched from an egg and imprinted on Rosetta.

✳There have been **over 45 books published** in the Disney Faries Collection.

✳Tinker Bell and her friends even **have their own meet-and-greet section** in Disneyland called *Pixie Hollow*. It is located at the back side of *The Matterhorn Bobsleds* where *Ariel's Grotto* was located. This is all on the spot where the *Monsanto House of the Future* sat from 1957-1967.

✳The movies' **worldwide gross is $493 million** for Disney just from DVD sales.

✳The **combined budgets for all the films** was about $140 million.

✳In Barrie's 1902 novel *The Little White Bird*, in which **he introduced the myth of Peter Pan and the fairies**, he wrote, "*When the first baby laughed for the first time, his laugh broke into a million pieces, and they all went skipping about. That was the beginning of fairies.*" The *Disney Fairies* are based on a similar idea: every time a newborn baby laughs for the first time, that laugh travels out into the world, and those that make their way to Neverland turn into a Never Fairy.

✳The fairies generally reside in the Home Tree, a towering, massive tree located in the very heart of Pixie Hollow in Neverland. Various groups of fairies work and live nearby as well. Most of the fairy characters are young and female, but older, taller, and male fairy characters are also included. The males are sometimes referred to as "sparrow men," though the term **"fairies" is used to refer to both female and male fairy characters**.

✳On September 21, 2010, Tinker Bell was **presented with the 2,418ᵗʰ star on the Hollywood Walk of Fame**, becoming the thirteenth fictional character and the sixth Disney character to receive this honor. Tinker Bell's star celebrated Hollywood Walk of Fame's 50th anniversary.

✳In November 2009, Tinker Bell **became the smallest waxwork** ever to be made at Madame Tussauds (a wax museum in London), measuring only five and a half inches.

✳Many have been **confused as how to write our favorite pixies name**. According to Disneyland's website it is "Tinker Bell" not "Tinkerbell" or "TinkerBell."

✳A longtime myth is that **Marilyn Monroe was the live action model for Tinker Bell** from *Peter Pan* (1953). The truth is the **live action model and pantomime was Margaret Kerry** as confirmed by Marc Davis the animator. Marilyn Monroe was just rising to popularity when Disney released *Peter Pan,* which led people to believe otherwise. Margaret Kerry was on set in the studio with large props to act out scenes as Tinker Bell for six months. Tink's well known personality was based off of what Kerry was portraying. A most memorable pose that most people have seen is the one with Margaret peeking through a large key hole. Margaret was also the model for the red-haired mermaid on the rock in the Neverland lagoon and provided the voice for her and said "We were only trying to drown her." Margaret went on to act and do voice roles mastering 21 different dialects and 53 character voices all the way up until present time.

FAIRY	TYPE	PURPOSE
Tinker Bell	Tinker fairy	Advanced knowledge to create and build
Rosetta	Plant fairy	Controls all flowers and plants
Iridessa	Light fairy	Creates light and rainbows
Silvermist	Water fairy	Controls all forms of water
Fawn	Animal fairy	Can talk to and control all animals and insects
Vidia	Wind fairy	Creates wind and tornados, fastest at flying

There is a full cast of characters in the Tinker Bell movie collection consiting of over 115 characters. Here are the main popular ones from the films.

FAIRY	VOICE ACTOR	FAIRY	VOICE ACTOR
Tinker Bell	Mae Whitman	Vidia	Pamela Adlon
Rosetta	Kristin Chenoweth	Fairy Mary	Jane Horrocks
Rosetta	Megan Hilty	Terence	Jesse McCartney
Iridessa	Raven-Symoné	Clank	Jeff Bennett
Fawn	America Ferrera	Bobble	Rob Paulsen
Fawn	Angela Bartys	Queen Clarion	Anjelica Huston
Fawn	Ginnifer Goodwin	Nyx	Rosario Dawson
Silvermist	Lucy Liu	Zarina	Christina Hendricks

NOTE: Kristin Chenoweth voiced Rosetta in the first three films; she was then replaced by Megan Hilty for the ones following. America Ferrera voiced Fawn in the first film only, and was then replaced by Angela Bartys who voiced her in all the following films up until Legend of the Neverbeast, when Ginnifer Goodwin took over.

WHO DOES THAT VOICE?

Voice actors intrigue me. Something about someone being able to play multiple characters and you don't even notice. Some of the older voice actors used the same voice for all of their characters. Like Sterling Holloway as Kaa, Pooh, Mr. Stork, and Cheshire Cat, they all sound the same. Here are a few other voice actors that you might not have noticed.

1. **Pinto Colvig** was famous for voicing Sleepy and Grumpy in *Snow White* (1937), Goofy (in 77 animated shorts), Pluto (in 83 animated shorts), Bluto from *Popeye* (1939-1940) (in 9 animated shorts), one of Maleficent's Goons in *Sleeping Beauty* (1959), the Aracuan Bird in *The Three Caballeros* (1944), *Clown of the Jungle* (1947), and *Melody Time* (1948), Gabby from *Gulliver's Travels* (1939), and other Gabby cartoons following that. Pinto was also the first Bozo the Clown for the television series *Bozo's Circus* (1949). Another little-known role he played was his portrayal of some of the Munchkins in *The Wizard of OZ* (1939).

2. **Sterling Holloway** was best known for voicing Winnie The Pooh in all his movies up until 1977. He was also the voice of the Cheshire Cat from *Alice In Wonderland* (1951), Kaa from the *Jungle Book* (1967), Roquefort the Mouse in *The Aristocats* (1970), Amos Mouse in *Ben and Me* (1953), his first Disney role of The Stork in *Dumbo* (1941), adult Flower in *Bambi* (1942), and many more. He was considered for the role of Sleepy in *Snow White and the Seven Dwarfs* (1937), but lost it to Pinto Colvig. He also was asked to reprise his role of Baloo in the 1990 TV series *TaleSpin,* and even did some reordings before getting replaced by Ed Gilbert.

3. **Peter Cullen**, better known as Optimus Prime from *Transformers* the movie and the TV series, was the voice of Eeyore in all the Winnie The Pooh movies and TV series since 1989 (except in 1995 when it was Jim Cummings and 2011 when it was Bud Luckey). You can hear him as Eeyore on the attraction *The Many Adventures Of Winnie The Pooh* in *Critter Country*.

4. In *The Aristocats* (1970), **Thomas O'Malley's full name is** Abraham De Lacey Giuseppe Casey Thomas O'Malley. He was voiced by **Phil Harris**, who also voiced the characters Little John in *Robin Hood*, Baloo in *The Jungle Book*, and for his final film, the narrator and Patou the dog in *Rock-A-Doodle* (1991).

5. The **"Pink Elephants on Parade" song in *Dumbo*** (1941) was sung by Thurl Ravenscroft, Mel Blanc (voice of Bugs Bunny, Daffy Duck, Porky Pig, Tweety, Sylvester in the Looney Toons cartoons), and The Sportsmen Quartet.

6. Comedian **Billy Gilbert** found out that one of the dwarfs in *Snow White* (1937) was going to be named Sneezy, so he called Walt and gave him his famous sneezing gag and got the part. He was also the voice of Willie the Giant from *Mickey and the Beanstalk* (1947).

7. The voice actor **Paul Winchell is best known for voicing Tigger** in 29 of the *Winnie-the-Pooh* movies (1968-1999), Gargamel in *The Smurfs* (1981), the Siamese cat named Shun Gon in *The Aristocats* (1970), Boomer the woodpecker in *The Fox and the Hound* (1981), and as Zummi Gummi in *Adventures of the Gummi Bears* (1985). In the Dr. Seuss short, *Green Eggs and Ham* (1973), he voiced Sam-I-Am. His first voice-over role was "Pig-Pen" in *It's the Great Pumpkin, Charlie Brown* (1966). In commercials, he voiced the character of Burger Chef for the fast food chain Burger Chef, opened in 1954 and closed in 1996, the leader of the Scrubbing Bubbles for Dow Chemicals, and Mr. Owl for Tootsie Roll Pops. You can hear him as Tigger in *The Many Adventures of Winnie the Pooh* attraction in *Magic Kingdom* and *Hong Kong Disneyland* versions. His final voice role for Disney was in *Winnie the Pooh: A Valentine for You* (1999). These are just a few of his voice roles in his acting career. His voice talents were just part of his life; he was also interested in medicine. He became an acupuncturist after graduating from The Acupuncture Research College in 1974. He was also an inventor. He became one of the first people to build and patent an artificial heart (US Patent #3097366), with the help of Dr. Henry Heimlich, the inventor of the Heimlich maneuver. Some of his other patents include a disposable razor, a blood plasma defroster, a flameless cigarette lighter, an "invisible" garter belt, a fountain pen with a retractable tip, and battery-heated gloves.

8. You may not know the name **Verna Felton, but you do know what characters she has voiced** from your favorite childhood movies. She started her career off with Disney by voicing the pachyderm Mrs. Jumbo in *Dumbo* (1941). Then, the Fairy Godmother in *Cinderella* (1950), the Queen of Hearts in *Alice in Wonderland* (1951), Aunt Sarah in *Lady and the Tramp* (1955), and flower fairy Flora in *Sleeping Beauty* (1959). She then voiced a second elephant, Eloise, in *Goliath II* (1960), and finished her voice acting carrier with her final film, and third elephant role, Winifred, in *The Jungle Book* (1967). She was born in 1890, and passed away the day before Walt Disney did on December 14, 1966.

8. **Wally Boag** – (Born September 13, 1920 in Oregon – Died June 3, 2011). Wally, also known as "The Clown Prince of Disneyland," was best known for his character Pecos Bill and the traveling salesman in the *Golden Horseshoe Review*. You might have seen footage of him with his onstage gag where he got hit in the face and he kept spitting out teeth. One of his famous lines is, "When they operated on father, they opened mother's male." The tenor from the *Golden Horseshoe Review* introduced Wally to Walt for an audition in 1955. Wally continued his role in the show for 27 years and completed almost 40,000 performances, holding the record in the *Guinness Book of World Records* for having the greatest number of performances of any theatrical presentation. The show ran from July 16, 1955, until October 12, 1986. Wally also appeared on television shows like the original *Mickey Mouse Club* (1955), *Disneyland* (1959), and *Walt Disney's Wonderful World of Color* (1962), as well as motion pictures,

including *The Absent-Minded Professor* (1961), *Son of Flubber* (1963), and *The Love Bug* (1968).

You can now hear Wally as Jose the Tiki bird in *The Enchanted Tiki Room*. When Walt was first making the *Tiki Room*, he made a barker bird for Wally to voice named Juan, to go to the World's Fair in 1964. When *Magic Kingdom's Tiki Room: Under New Management* opened in 1998, Wally, along with Thurl Ravenscroft and Fulton Burley (who was also in the *Golden Horseshoe Review*), were able to reprise their roles of the Tiki birds. In 2011, Disney produced a film called *Gnomeo & Juliet*, in which there was a scene when the Tiki Room birds show up and an old audio recording of Wally voicing Jose was used.

Wally was inducted into the Disney Legends Program in 1995 and had a window dedicated to him on Main Street. He passed away June 3, 2011 at the age of 90. The day after his passing, his good friend and costar of the 40,000 *Golden Horseshoe Review* shows, Betty Taylor, who portrayed Slue Foot Sue, also passed away; she was 91.

9. **Corey Burton** – (Born August 3, 1955 in Los Angeles, California). Corey is known well for his voice work. He got hired on at Disney after doing an impersonation of Hans Conried, the original voice of Captain Hook from *Peter Pan* (1953). He is recognized as the voice of many animated characters including Ludwig Von Drake (1987-present), Ziro the Hutt and Count Dooku in *Star Wars: The Clone Wars*, Dale and Zipper in *Chip 'n Dale Rescue Rangers*, Captain Hook in *Return to Never Land*, Braniac in *Superman The Animated Series*, and so many other voices for cartoons and theme park attractions. He has also done voiceover work for commercials and movies, including the narrator for films like *Planet Terror* (2007) and *The A-Team* (2010). You can go just about anywhere in Disneyland and hear him:

- The "Ghost Host" for *Haunted Mansion Holiday*
- The opening narration for *Great Moments with Mr. Lincoln*
- Chernabog, Captain Hook, and the pirates in the nighttime show *Fantasmic!*
- The loading and unloading announcement for *Pirates of The Caribbean*
- The animatronic "Pooped Pirate" looking for Jack Sparrow on *Pirates of The Caribbean*
- Captain Hook and Smee on *Peter Pan's Flight*
- Flotsam and Jetsam on *The Little Mermaid: Ariel's Undersea Adventure*
- Doc Hudson on *Radiator Springs Racers*
- The announcer and additional bug sounds for *It's Tough to Be A Bug*

10. **Candy Candido** – (Born December 25, 1913 in New Orleans, Louisiana – Died May 19, 1999). Candy is most recognizable in the movie *Peter Pan* (1953) when he voiced the Indian Chief. He was also Fidget in *The Great Mouse Detective* (1986), the angry apple tree in *The Wizard of Oz* (1939), the Captain of the Guards, the crocodile, in *Robin Hood* (1973), Maleficent's goon in *Sleeping Beauty* (1959), Ben in *Gentle Ben* (1967),

Brutus and Nero in *The Rescuers* (1967), Lumpjaw the Black Bear (growls) in *Fun and Fancy Free* (1947), and Shere Khan's roars in *The Jungle Book* (1967). You can hear Candy's menacing laugh in *The Haunted Mansion* in the graveyard scene across from the singing busts and as you exit the building. He also reprised the roll of the Indian Chief for *Peter Pan's Flight*. He was married to Anita Gordon, the voice of the Singing Harp in *Mickey and the Beanstalk* (1947).

11. **June Foray** – (Born September 18, 1917 in Springfield, Massachusetts). There have been times when Mel Blanc was referred to as the male version of June Foray. June's most notable voice role was that of Granny in the *Looney Toons Sylvester and Tweety* cartoons and *Tiny Toons*. Her career with Disney started with her role as Lucifer in *Cinderella* (1950). She then went on to voice the brunette mermaid (and modeled for it) and squaw in *Peter Pan* (1953), Mrs. Sheep in *Lambert the Sheepish Lion* (1952), Witch Hazel in *Trick or Treat* (1952), Knothead and Splinter in the *Woody Woodpecker* cartoons, Witch Hazel in the *Looney Toons* cartoons, Rocky Squirrel and Natasha in the *Rocky and Bullwinkle* cartoons, Cindy Lou Who in *How the Grinch Stole Christmas* (1966), Dorothy Gale in *Off to See the Wizard* (1967), Raggedy Ann in 1978 & 1979, Aunt May Parker in *Spider-Man and His Amazing Friends* (1981), Jokey Smurf in *Smurfs* (1981-1986), Wheezy and Lena Hyena in *Who Framed Roger Rabbit* (1988), Ma Beagle & Magica De Spell in *DuckTales* (1987-1990), Grammi Gimmi in *Adventures of the Gummi Bears* (1985-1991), Norman's Aunt in *Marsupilami* (1992), Grandmother Fa in *Mulan I* (1998) & *Mulan II* (2004), and so many others. In Disneyland, you can hear her on *Pirates of the Caribbean* as Carlos' wife shouting out the window "Don't tell him, Carlos." She also reprised her roll as Wheezy the weasel for *Roger Rabbit's Car Toon Spin*.

12. **Paul Frees** – (Born June 22, 1920 in Chicago, Illinois – Died November 2, 1986). Paul is best known for his line, "I am your host, your ghost host." He is the disembodied ghost host of the *Haunted Mansion*. He virtually voiced every character in *Great Moments with Mr. Lincoln* (except Lincoln), numerous characters in *The Pirates of The Caribbean* attraction including the auctioneer and the "pooped pirate," and was the narrator in the old *Adventure Thru Inner Space* attraction. In addition, Frees narrated many Disney TV shows and record albums. He has also provided the voice for Santa Claus in *Frosty the Snowman* (1969), Thing in *Fantastic Four* (1967), Ludwig Von Drake, the crazy haired duck scientist, and Boris in *The Bullwinkle Show* (1961). He was also in *The Little Drummer Boy* (1968), *Santa Claus is Comin' to Town* (1970), *Here Comes Peter Cottontail* (1971), *Frosty's Winter Wonderland* (1976), *Rudolph's Shiny New Year* (1976), *The Hobbit* (1977), *Rudolph and Frosty's Christmas in July* (1979), *Jack Frost* (1979), *The Return of the King* (1980), *The Last Unicorn* (1982), and many others. Frees was to Disney as Mel Blanc was to Warner Bros. He became a Disney Legend in 2006.

13. **Alan Tudyk was the voice of Duke Weaselton** in *Zootopia* (2016), he was also the Duke of Weselton in *Frozen* (2013), King Candy in *Wreck-It Ralph*

150

(2012), Heihei the rooster in *Moana* (2016), King Candy in *Wreck-It Ralph* (2012), Ludo & Butterfly King in *Star Vs. The Forces of Evil* (2015-2016), Alistair Krei in *Big Hero 6* (2014), and K-2SO in *Rogue One: A Star Wars Story* (2016).

14. The actor who is credited as doing **the most voices for animated characters of all time is Frank Welker**. He has done a multitude of Disney characters, mostly non-humans, like Abu, RC Car, Bullseye, Flit, Pegasus, Raja, Bubba the Cave Duck, Cave of Wonders, Cri-Kee, Totoro, and loads more. Frank started acting in 1967 at the age of 21. His first role for Disney was as Henry in the Kurt Russell film *The Computer Wore Tennis Shoes* (1969). His first voice role was as Fred in *Scooby-Doo, Where Are You!* (1969-1970). It just snowballed from there. Including live action films, television shows, animated movies, and video games, he has over 800 credits to his name.

15. The director of *Brave* (2012), Steve Purcell, was also **the voice of The Crow**, The Witch's sidekick.

16. **Thurl Ravenscroft** – (Born February 6, 1914, in Norfolk, Nebraska – Died May 22, 2005) – The six-foot-four-inch tall Thurl is known for his deep voice and was part of a singing quartet called *The Mellowmen*, among others. Most people will recognize  Thurl with his deep voice saying *"They're grrrrreat!"* as Tony the Tiger from the Kellogg's Frosted Flakes commercials. At Christmas time, you can hear him on the radio belting out *"...you're a mean one Mr. Grinch..."* in the animated Christmas classic *How The Grinch Stole Christmas* (1966). He only sang that song in the movie. Many people believe he was the voice of The Grinch, but that honor belongs to Boris Karloff (Frankenstein's monster in the 1930's); Thurl was also the narrator. Thurl has done many voice and singing parts for *Disneyland* and *Disney World* attractions.

Adventure Through Inner Space - Singing chorus	*The Mark Twain Riverboat* - The First Mate
Alice In Wonderland - Dandelions	*Peter Pan's Flight* - Singing chorus
Alice In Wonderland - Painting card	*Pinocchio's Daring Journey* - Monstro
Country Bear Jamboree - Buff	*Pirates of the Caribbean*- Dog jailer
Disneyland Railroad - Narrator	*Pirates of the Caribbean* - Drunk singing pirate
Enchanted Tiki Room - Fritz	*Pirates of the Caribbean* - "Yo Ho" Chorus
Enchanted Tiki Room Pre-Show - Tangaroa	*Pirates of the Caribbean* - Accordion player
Haunted Mansion - Uncle Theodore	*Pirates of the Caribbean* - "Singing" dog
it's a small world - Singing	*Splash Mountain* - Singing bullfrogs

Thurl has also been in many Disney films and television shows.

101 Dalmatians - The Captain
20,000 Leagues Under the Sea - Singing "Whale of a Tale"
Alice In Wonderland - Painting card/Dandelion
The Aristocats - Russian Cat/Billy Boss
Bedknobs and Broomsticks - Singer/animal voices
Boys of the Western Sea - Singer
The Brave Little Toaster - Kirby
The Brave Little Toaster Goes to Mars - Kirby
The Brave Little Toaster to the Rescue - Kirby
Davy Crockett - Singer
Dumbo – Singer "Pink Elephants on Parade"
Dumbo – Announcer/Lion Roaring
Dumbo – Singer "Look Out for Mr. Stork"
The Hardy Boys: Mystery of the Applegate Treasure - Singer
The Hobbit - the goblins
The Jungle Book - Shere Khan (singing)
The Jungle Book - Singing elephants/Bagheera roar
Lady and the Tramp - Singing dogs

Lady and the Tramp - the Alligator
Lambert the Sheepish Lion - Adult Lambert/Wolf
Lilo & Stitch: The Series - Singer
Lion Around - Louie the Mountain Lion
Mary Poppins - Andrew/the hog/bankers
Melody Time - Singer, Big Toot
The Mickey Mouse Club - Singer
One Hundred and One Dalmatians - Captain
Paul Bunyan - Paul Bunyan
Peter Pan - Singer/Pirates
Pinocchio - Monstro
Saludos Amigos - Singer of "Saludos Amigos Theme Song"
Sleeping Beauty - Singer
The Sword in the Stone - Black Bart/Mim as Tiger
Walt Disney's Wonderful World of Color - Jungle Cruise Skipper
Winnie the Pooh - Singer, Black Honeypot
Zorro - Singer

When *Disneyland* first opened back in 1955, Thurl was the one who said, *"Open the Fantasyland Castle in the name of the children of the world,"* before the drawbridge went down when it was recorded for ABC television.

The most recognizable thing that you can hear of Thurl in the parks is the "Grim Grinning Ghosts" song in the *Haunted Mansion*. It is sung by a barbershop-type quartet consisting of Thurl Ravenscroft, Jay Meyer, Chuck Schroeder, Verne Rowe, and Bob Ebright who were called The Phantom Five, a mixture of five excellent singers. It was composed by Buddy Baker, with the lyrics written by X Atencio, and was recorded February 14, 1969. Thurl became a Disney Legend in 1995.

17. Bill Thompson was best known for voicing the lovable Droopy Dog character, but he did quite a few voices for Disney as well. White Rabbit & Dodo in *Alice in Wonderland* (1951), Mr. Smee in *Peter Pan* (1953), Jock in *Lady and the Tramp* (1955), King Hubert in *Sleeping Beauty* (1959), and Uncle Waldo in *The AristoCats* (1970).

18. Michael Keaton, such a versatile actor. He **portrayed one of the most iconic superheroes of all time, Batman** in *Batman* (1989) and *Batman Returns* (1992). Then he was Chick Hicks in Cars (2006) and Ken in Toy Story 3 (2010). His next big role for Disney is as The Vulture in *Spider-Man: Homecoming* (2017). This role puts him in both the DC and Marvel universes.

19. Hans Conreid was the perfect model and voice for *Peter Pan's* (1953) **evil Captain Hook**, and was also the voice for Mr. Darling.

20. Actress Eleanor Audley used her commanding voice and presence to shape the wicked step-mom, Lady Tremane in *Cinderella* (1950), and Maleficent in *Sleeping Beauty* (1959). You can hear her in almost every Disney Park as the voice of Madame Leota in the *Haunted Mansion*.

21. **Ed Wynn was the live action reference model** and voice actor for The Mad Hatter from *Alice In Wonderland* (1951). He was also Toymaker in Babes in Toyland (!961), the Fire Chief in *The Absent Minded Professor* (1961), A.J. Allan in Son of Flubber (1963), Uncle Albert in *Mary Poppins* (1964), Mr. Hofstedder in *That Darn Cat* (1965), and for his final film he was Rufus in *The Gnome-Mobile* (1967).

22. Julie Walters and Robbie Coltrane, who voiced the Witch and Lord Dingwall in *Brave* (2012), **both appeared in the entire *Harry Potter* film series** as Molly Weasley (Ron's mother) and Rubeus Hagrid, respectively. Also, Kelly Macdonald had appeared as the Grey Lady in *Harry Potter and the Deathly Hallows - Part 2* (2011). And Emma Thompson appeared as Professor Sybill Trelawney in three of the *Harry Potter* films. Also Patrick Doyle, who did the voice of Martin the guard in Brave (2012), the one that had his moustache half chopped off, was one of the composers for the music in *Harry Potter and the Goblet of Fire* (2005) and for the film *Brave* (2012).

23. **Billy Connolly was the voice of King Fergus** in the movie *Brave* (2012). He was also the voice of Ben in *Pocahontas* (1995). You might have also heard him as McSquizzy in *Open Season* (2006). He also appeared in *Lemony Snicket's A Series of Unfortunate Events* (2004) and *Boondock Saints* (1999).

24. **Pat Buttram was the voice behind many Disney animated characters** including Chief in The Fox and the Hound (1981), Luke in The Rescuers (1977), Napoleon in The Aristocats (1970), Sherriff of Nottingham in Robin Hood (1973), a toon bullet in Who Framed Roger Rabbit (1988), and Possum Park Emcee in A Goofy Movie (1995). He had a cameo appearance in *Back To The Future 3* (1990).

25. **David Tomlinson is most known for his role as Mr. Banks** in the very popular film *Mary Poppins* (1964). Not only was he Mr. Banks, he was also the voice of Mary Poppins' parrot umbrella, one of the voices of the waiter penguins, and the voice of the polite jockey that allowed Mary Poppins to pass during the horse race. When David sang the song "The Life I Lead" it was the first time for him to sing professionally or on camera. He appeared in many other films during his acting career but most notably was his portrayal of Emelius in *Bedknobs and Broomsticks* (1971), and Peter Thorndyke in *The Love Bug* (1968).

DISNEY MOVIE TRIVIA

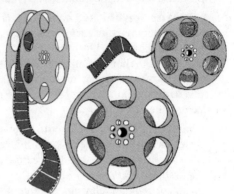

1. There was **a film that took 58 years to complete** and release. It is titled *Destino*, and was released in 2003. One day Walt approached Marc Davis while he was on his lunch break and inquired about the book he was reading. Marc showed him it was a book about the artist Salvador Dali. Walt was intrigued by his artistic style and had his secretary contact Marc to borrow the book. A short time later, Salvador was working on a project at the studio with animator John Hench. They began the project in 1945 and only worked on it for eight months before the project was put on hold. At the time, Disney was having financial problems due to World War II. Hench put together a 17-second clip of the film hoping Disney would continue with the project, but it was shot down and put on permanent hold. It wasn't until Walt's nephew, Roy E. Disney, was working on the *Fantasia 2000* project that the plans for *Destino* get uncovered. The project was put back in motion in Disney Studios France. They produced *Treasure of the Lost Lamp* (1990), 20% of the *Hunchback of Notre Dame* (1996), episodes of *TaleSpin*, *Marsupilami*, *Bonkers*, and others. The studio had to decipher Hench's and Dali's storyboards with the help of Dali's notebooks acquired from Dali's wife, and John Hench himself. With an animation staff of 25 people, they had the film completed by 2003. They succeeded in using Hench's original animations and the rest hand-drawn animation, with a few segments done on computer. After the final film of his career, John Hench passed away eight months after its release.

2. **John Williams** (born February 8, 1932) is an American composer, conductor, and pianist. John's most notable compositions include the main scores for *Fiddler on the Roof* (1971), *Jaws* (1975), *Star Wars* (1977), *Close Encounters of the Third Kind* (1977), *Superman* (1978), the *Indiana Jones* series (1981), *E.T.* (1982), *Home Alone* (1990), *Hook* (1991), *Jurassic Park* (1993), *Saving Private Ryan* (1998) and the *Harry Potter* series (2001).

3. Johnny Depp's character, Jack Sparrow, from *Pirates of the Caribbean*, has a **swallow tattoo on his right forearm** that says Jack under it. In the movie it was a fake tattoo. After the filming was completed, Johnny had the tattoo made permanent after changing the design a little. He now has the sparrow flying toward his body, rather than away like in the movie. Jack represents his son's name.

154

4. **Jim Henson** died of walking pneumonia on May 16, 1990, the weekend he was going to sell his company to Disney for $150 million. After his death, the negotiations fell through and Disney wouldn't get the opportunity to purchase the company until 2004.

5. *Song of the South* (1946) was Walt Disney's **first live-action film**, though it also contains major segments of animation. The film has never been released on home video in the USA because of content which Disney executives believe would be construed by some as racially insensitive towards African Americans and is thus subject to much rumor, although it does exist on home video in the UK. *Song of the South* was the inspiration behind the attraction *Splash Mountain*.

9. The movie *Treasure Island* was the **first full-length movie** with live actors in it. The movie was released in 1950 and consisted of a cast comprised only of males.

10. The movie *Who Framed Roger Rabbit* (1988) **marked the first-time** cartoon characters from both Walt Disney and Warner Brothers appeared together on screen. The movie was produced by *Amblin Entertainment* (founded in 1981 by Steven Spielberg). Since the movie was being co-made by Disney, *Warner Brothers* would only allow the use of their biggest toon stars, Bugs Bunny and Daffy Duck, if they got an equal amount of screen time as Disney's biggest stars, Mickey Mouse and Donald Duck. Because of this, both sets of characters are always together in frame when on the screen.

11. Remember **Saturday morning cartoons**? Remember getting home from school and turning on the television to watch shows like *DuckTales* in the afternoons? Disney tested the daily animated television slots back in 1985 with *The Wuzzles*. Disney's afternoon popularity didn't take off until they released *DuckTales*. Since the beginning, Disney has released 80 different television shows on a variety of television networks. It became so popular that they added *Disney Afternoon Avenue* into *Disneyland*. It was a temporary land set up between the *Storybook Land Canal Boats* and the entrance to *Toontown*. It was only there in 1991; *Toontown* opened in 1993. Here are all the shows that we remember so well:

The Disney Afternoon

NO.	SHOW	OnAir	OffAir
1	*Adventures of the Gummi Bears*	1985	1991
2	*DuckTales*	1987	1990
3	*Chip 'n Dale Rescue Rangers*	1989	1992
4	*Tale Spin*	1990	1994
5	*Darkwing Duck*	1991	1993
6	*Goof Troop*	1992	1993
7	*Bonkers*	1993	1994
8	*Aladdin*	1994	1996
9	*Gargoyles*	1994	1996
10	*Timon and Pumbaa*	1995	1997
11	*Shnookums & Meat Funny Cartoon Show*	1995	1995
12	*Quack Pack*	1996	1997
13	*The Mighty Ducks*	1996	1997

Disney's One Saturday Morning

NO.	SHOW	OnAir	OffAir
1	*101 Dalmatians: The Series*	1997	1999
2	*Recess*	1997	2001
3	*Pepper Ann*	1997	2000
4	*Hercules: The Animated Series*	1998	1999
5	*Mickey Mouse Works*	1999	2000
6	*The Weekenders*	2000	2004
7	*Teacher's Pet*	2000	2002
8	*Buzz Lightyear of Star Command*	2000	2001
9	*House of Mouse*	2001	2002
10	*Lloyd in Space*	2001	2001
11	*The Legend Of Tarzan*	2001	2003
12	*Teamo Supremo*	2002	2004

Other Disney Series

NO.	SHOW	OnAir	OffAir
1	*The Wuzzles*	1985	1985
2	*The New Adventures of Winnie the Pooh*	1988	1991
3	*The Little Mermaid*	1992	1994
4	*Raw Toonage*	1992	1992
5	*Marsupilami*	1993	1993
6	*Disney's Doug*	1991	1994
7	*Jungle Cubs*	1996	1998
8	*Nightmare Ned*	1997	1997
9	*Fillmore!*	2002	2004

Disney Channel Original Series

NO.	SHOW	OnAir	OffAir
1	*Kim Possible*	2002	2007
2	*Lilo & Stitch: The Series*	2003	2006
3	*Dave the Barbarian*	2004	2005
4	*Brandy & Mr. Whiskers*	2004	2006
5	*American Dragon: Jake Long*	2005	2007
6	*The Buzz on Maggie*	2005	2006
7	*The Emperor's New School*	2006	2008
8	*The Replacements*	2006	2009
9	*Shorty McShorts' Shorts*	2006	2007
10	*Phineas and Ferb*	2007	2015
11	*Fish Hooks*	2010	2014
12	*Take Two with Phineas and Ferb*	2010	2011
13	*Gravity Falls*	2012	2016
14	*Mickey Mouse*	2013	NOW
15	*Wander Over Yonder*	2013	2016
16	*Gravity Falls Shorts*	2013	2014

17	*Descendants: Wicked World*	2015	NOW
18	*The Lion Guard*	2015	NOW
19	*Elena of Avalor*	2016	NOW
20	*Tangled: The Series*	2017	NOW

Disney XD Original Series			
1	*Phineas and Ferb*	2009	2015
2	*Kick Buttowski: Suburban Daredevil*	2010	2012
3	*Motorcity*	2012	2013
4	*Tron: Uprising*	2012	2013
5	*Randy Cunningham: 9th Grade Ninja*	2012	2015
6	*Wander Over Yonder*	2014	2016
7	*The 7D*	2014	2016
8	*Gravity Falls*	2014	2016
9	*Penn Zero: Part-Time Hero*	2014	NOW
10	*Star vs. the Forces of Evil*	2015	NOW
11	*Two More Eggs*	2015	NOW
12	*Wander Over Yonder Shorts*	2015	2015
13	*Pickle and Peanut*	2015	NOW
14	*Future-Worm!*	2016	NOW
15	*Milo Murphy's Law*	2016	NOW
16	*DuckTales*	2017	NOW
17	*Big Hero 6: The Series*	2017	NOW
18	*Billy Dilley's Super-Duper Subterranean Summer*	2017	NOW
19	*Country Club*	2018	-

Playhouse Disney/Disney Junior Original Series			
1	*PB&J Otter*	1998	2000
2	*Mickey Mouse Clubhouse*	2006	2016
3	*My Friends Tigger & Pooh*	2007	2010
4	*Special Agent Oso*	2009	2012
5	*Jake and the Never Land Pirates*	2011	NOW
6	*Sofia the First*	2012	NOW
7	*The Lion Guard*	2016	NOW
8	*Mickey and the Roadster Racers*	2017	NOW

12. Remember **Flotsam and Jetsam** from *The Little Mermaid* (1989)? Their names have a meaning. Traditionally, flotsam and jetsam are words that describe goods of potential value that have been thrown into the ocean. There is a technical difference between the two: jetsam has been voluntarily cast into the sea (jettisoned) by the crew of a ship, usually in order to lighten it in an emergency; while flotsam describes goods that are floating on the water without having been thrown in deliberately, often after a shipwreck. In modern usage, flotsam also includes driftwood, logs, and other natural debris in oceans and waterways.

13. It has been believed by many that the **Walt Disney Company made the movie *The Wizard of Oz* (1939)**. This is not true. Walt Disney did want to make it, though, but MGM owned the rights to *The Wizard Of Oz* books. Walt Disney's top grossing film of all time, *Snow White and the Seven Dwarfs* (1937), was the reason behind Louis B. Mayer's determination to equal its success. In 1954, Disney aquired the rights to the Oz books so they could make the movie *Rainbow Road to Oz* for the *Disneyland* TV series, but it was scrapped. Disney did make the sequel *Return to Oz* (1985) and owns the rights to the spoof movie *The Muppets Wizard of Oz* (2005).

In 2013, Disney made a prequel *Oz the Great and Powerful*. On the attraction *Storyland Canal Boats* in *Disneyland Paris,* there is a small model of the Emerald City from the *Return To Oz* film.

14. In the film *Pirates of the Caribbean: At Worlds End* (2007), actress Takayo Fischer portrays the character Mistress Ching. **That character is a person from real life**. Ching Shih lived from 1775-1844. She was originally a prostitute who was captured by pirates and ended up marrying the pirate captain Zheng Yi. Six years after they were married, he died and she took over his command of over 300+ ships, employing 20,000-40,000 sailors. She is well known for being extremely strict and followed through with her punishments of whipping, flogging, and beheading. She defeated the Chinese government's attempts to stop her by beheading every prisoner who didn't join her. She terrorized the Chinese seas from 1807 until she received amnesty in 1810. After she retired, she kept all of her loot and opened up a gambling house. In 1844, she died at the age of 69.

15. The **actor who portrayed Dr. Terminus in *Pete's Dragon*** (1977), the one trying to capture Elliot, is Jim Dale (born 08/15/1935). He has been nominated for, and won, many awards. He holds two *Guinness World Records* spots for the most characters in a story containing 146 different voices, and holding the top six spots on the top ten chart of most popular audio books. He is well known for recording the audio books of *Harry Potter* by J.K. Rowling. His first record held in *Guinness* is for *Harry Potter and the Deathly Hallows* (2007). His most recent role is the narrator on the television show *Pushing Daisies* (2007).

16. Tick-Tock, the crocodile from *Peter Pan* (1953), has **made more cameo appearances** than any other Disney film character, ranging from films to theme parks. He appeared in films and shows such as *Goliath II, Two Happy Amigos, Chip 'n Dale Rescue Rangers, Marsupilami, TaleSpin, Darkwing Duck, Goof Troop, Aladdin: The Series, Jungle Cubs, House of Mouse, Return to Never Land, Jake and the Never Land Pirates,* and, more recently, as a recently-hatched reptile in *The Pirate Fairy*. Asside from his theatrical appearances, he has been in video games as well - *Mickey Mousecapade, Peter Pan: The Legend of Never Land, Kingdom Hearts* series, *Return to Never Land, Peter Pan: Adventures in Never Land, Epic Mickey, Kinect Disneyland Adventures,* and *Disney Universe*.  If you have been to the parks in the past or presently, you can or could have seen him in *Fantasmic!, Peter Pan's Flight, Dream Along with Mickey, One Man's Dream II: The Magic Lives On, Back to Never Land, Disney Dreams!,* and *Festival of Fantasy Parade*.

17. The **only time Tick-Tock ever spoke** was in the Donald Duck short *Two Happy Amigos* (1960), where he played an alligator and said, *"I'm a gator. Welcome Joe, do drop in."* The voice was provided by Billy Blecher, best

158

known for voicing Pete in the animated shorts. Dee Bradley Baker provides the animalistic sounds for the big ticking lizard in *Jake and the Never Land Pirates*.

18. There is a **singing quartet called The Mellomen** with lead bass singer, Thurl Ravenscroft. They have done many singing numbers for Disney films including *Alice in Wonderland* (1951), *Peter Pan* (1953), *Lady and the Tramp* (1955), and *The Jungle Book* (1967), as well as numerous animated shorts, including *Trick or Treat* (1952), *Pigs is Pigs* (1954), *Paul Bunyan* (1958), and *Noah's Ark* (1959). Remember the intro song for *Zorro* (1957)? They did that, too, along with *The Scarecrow of Romney Marsh* (1963) theme song. If you have any albums from Disneyland, they sung *Meet Me Down on Main Street*, along with some others.

19. **Fred MacMurray was the first Disney Legend** ever honored. Fred starred in films like *The Shaggy Dog* (1959), the first Disney film Kurt Russell ever starred in, *Follow Me Boys!* (1966), and again with Kurt in *Charley and the Angel* (1973). He was also in *Bon Voyage!* (1962), and he played "Steve Douglas" in 380 episodes of *My Three Sons* (1960-1972). Fred is also well known for his crazy professor persona in *The Absent-Minded Professor* (1961) and *Son of Flubber* (1963). He had the honor of working with Walt Disney in the last film he produced before passing away, *The Happiest Millionaire* (1967).

20. **Walt first discovered Julie Andrews at her play *Chamelot*** in 1962. Walt went back stage and told her he wanted to cast her as Mary Poppins. She said she would like to, but she was pregnant. Walt then told her, "That's okay. We'll wait." That is when Julie gave birth to her first daughter, Emma Walton, on November 27, 1962. Emma grew up to be an actress and a children's author with a line of books called *Dumpy the Dumptruck*, *The Very Fairy Princess*, and others.

21. In 1939, comic book artist **C. C. Beck used Fred MacMurray as his model** for the famouse superhero Captain Marvel, who was later renamed Shazam! by DC Comics. Shazam outsold Superman in comic books in the 1940's.

22. The Brazilian-based production company ***Video Brinquedo* has been in several lawsuits with Disney, Pixar, and DreamWorks.** They are accused of plagiarizing several of their films with character design and storyline. Each movie they have released was based off of a more famous title, like *The Little Cars* (*Cars*), *Ratatoing* (*Ratatouille*), *Little Bee* (*Bee Movie*), *The Little Panda Fighter* (*Kung Fu Panda*), *Tiny Robots* (*Wall-E and Robots*), *Little Princess School* (uses the Disney princesses), *Gladiformers* (*Transformers*), *Little & Big Monsters* (*Monsters vs. Aliens*), *What's Up?: Balloon to the Rescue* (*Up*), *Gladiformers 2* (*Transformers*), *The Frog Prince* (*The Princess and the Frog*), and *Little Princess School 2* (uses the Disney princesses). They are all extremely low budget films and are referred to as "Z Movies," a grade much lower than a "B Movie."

23. "The Beautiful Briny Sea" was **written by the Sherman brothers for the film** *Mary Poppins* (1964), but it was dropped from that film and later used in *Bedknobs and Broomsticks* (1971).

24. Before Disney started their own company, *Buena Vista Home Entertainment*, **they used MCA Discovision to distribute movies formatted on Laserdisc.** The first and only Disney movies to be released by them were *Kidnapped* (1960), *On Vacation with Mickey Mouse and Friends* (1956), *Kids is Kids* (1961), *At Home with Donald Duck* (1956), *Adventures of Chip 'n' Dale* (1959), and *The Coyote's Lament* (1961), which were all released May 1979 and discontinued December 1981.

25. *Pete's Dragon* (1977) was **Disney's first ever VHS/Betamax**, released on March 4, 1980.

26. Disney's **first releases on VHS tape were 13 titles** that were licensed for rental to Fotomat on March 4, 1980, initially in a four-city test (Chicago, Houston, Philadelphia, and San Francisco/Oakland/San Jose). Fotomat was a drive-up photo development kiosk that was generally located in shopping centers and mall parking lots. They were the first to offer VHS. People would order a movie from a catalogue, pick it up the next day for a $12 rental fee, and keep it for five days. In 2016, that would calculate to $34.50, FOR A RENTAL. It was later expanded to nationwide by the end of 1980. The agreement specified rental fees ranging from $7.95 to $13.95. The first batch of titles on VHS and Beta included 10 live-action movies:
    * *Pete's Dragon* (1977)
    * *The Black Hole* (1979)
    * *The Love Bug* (1968)
    * *Escape to Witch Mountain* (1975)
    * *Davy Crockett, King of the Wild Frontier* (1955)
    * *20,000 Leagues Under the Sea* (1954)
    * *Bedknobs and Broomsticks* (1971)
    * *The North Avenue Irregulars* (1979)
    * *The Apple Dumpling Gang* (1975)
    * *Hot Lead and Cold Feet* (1978)
    * *On Vacation with Mickey Mouse and Friends.* This collection includes the episodes *Canine Caddy* (1941), *Bubble Bee* (1949), *Goofy and Wilbur* (1939), *Dude Duck* (1951), *Mickey's Trailer* (1938), and *Hawaiian Holiday* (1937).
    * *Kids is Kids starring Donald Duck.* This collection includes the episodes *Donald's Happy Birthday* (1949), *Good Scouts* (1938), *Don's Fountain of Youth* (1953), *Soup's On* (1948), and *Lucky Number* (1951).
    * *Adventures of Chip 'n' Dale.* This collection includes the episodes *Two Chips and a Miss* (1952), *Chicken in the Rough* (1951), *Chips Ahoy* (1956), and *The Lone Chipmunks* (1954).
    * *Mary Poppins* (1964), being **the fourteenth**, was added on December 30, 1980.

27. *A Christmas Carol* (2009) was **Disney's first-ever 3D Blu-ray**, and was released on November 30, 2010.

28. Here you can see the **timeline release of the Disney** films in their respective formats:

The First In It's Media		
Laserdisc Rental	Kidnapped (1960)	May 1979
Laserdisc Rental	On Vacation with Mickey Mouse and Friends (1956)	May 1979
Laserdisc Rental	Kids is Kids (1961)	May 1979
Laserdisc Rental	At Home with Donald Duck (1956)	May 1979
Laserdisc Rental	Adventures of Chip 'n' Dale (1959)	May 1979
Laserdisc Rental	The Coyote's Lament (1961)	May 1979
VHS Rental	Pete's Dragon	3/4/1980
Betamax Rental	Pete's Dragon	3/4/1980
VHS Purchase	Robin Hood (1973)	12/4/1984
Blu-Ray	Dinosaur (2000)	9/19/2006
3D Blu-Ray	A Christmas Carol (2009)	11/30/2010

29. When **Dick Van Dyke starred as Bert in *Mary Poppins*** (1964), he was 38 years old, and Julie Andrews was 28 years old.

30. **There have been nine movies that begin with the opening of a bejeweled or fancy fairy tale book**. These movies are *Snow White and The Seven Dwarfs* (1937), *The Adventures Of Ichabod and Mr. Toad* (1949), *Cinderella* (1950), *Sleeping Beauty* (1959), *The Sword In The Stone* (1963), *Robin Hood* (1973), *The Jungle Book* (1967), *The Many Adventures of Winnie The Pooh* (1977), and *Enchanted* (2007). Only the books from *Sleeping Beauty*, *Snow White*, and *Cinderella* can be found in the Disney Archives.

31. **Disney had shown interest in the film rights to J.R.R. Tolkien's novels *The Lord of The Rings***, which were published in 1954. They ended up not getting the rights, but The Saul Zaentz Company did acquire the rights and made the animated film *The Hobbit* (1977), and *The Lord of the Rings* (1978). The production company that made *The Hobbit* (1977) and *The Return of the King* (1980) was Topcraft, a Japanese animation-based studio which also produced *Nausicaa* (1984). It went bankrupt in June 1986 and was purchased by three of its animators, one of them being Hayao Miyazaki, who renamed it Studio Ghibli.

32. There have been **seven films directed by John Musker and Ron Clements**. They are *The Great Mouse Detective* (1986), *The Little Mermaid* (1989), *Aladdin* (1992), *Hercules* (1997), *Treasure Planet* (2002), *The Princess and the Frog* (2009), and Moana (2016). In total, their films have grossed a little under $2 billion. Moana has been in theaters two months now and has grossed $530 million, so there is potential for it to make more.

33. The **Academy Awards created the Best Animated Feature award** for the 2002 awards show. Disney has won almost every year since the awards inception with the exception of *Monsters, Inc.* losing to *Shrek* in 2001, and *Lilo & Stitch* and *Treasure Planet* losing to *Spirited Away* in 2002. Although Disney released *Spirited Away* in English and distributed it,

nothing lost to *Wallace & Gromit: Curse of the Were-Rabbit* in 2005, because Disney didn't release an animated film that year, *Cars* lost to *Happy Feet* in 2006, and nothing lost to *Rango* in 2011 because *Cars 2*, *Winnie The Pooh*, and *Mars Needs Moms* weren't even nominated.

34. **John Musker and Ron Clements have made cameo appearances** in their films as animated characters. In *The Little Mermaid,* they appeared as two wedding guests. In *Aladdin,* they made appearances as two men on the sidelines; Aladdin stands behind them. In *Hercules,* they are two men carrying a stone block. In *Treasure Planet*, they were an android and alien that give Jim directions. In *The Princess and the Frog*, they were in fish costumes on the float in the parade.

35. You can hear **the "Jaws Chomp" stock sound** when Captain Hook is hanging from the rock overhang in Skull Rock and Tick-Tock jumps out of the water and snaps at him. That snapping sound was created by Jimmy MacDonald, who was a sound effects man for the Disney Company. He provided the voice for Mickey Mouse after Walt gave up that position in 1947. He was able to create the sound effect of jaws chomping by using castanets in an echo chamber. That same sound was also used for Maleficent's Dragon in *Sleeping Beauty*, Al the Gator in *Lady and the Tramp*, and for Madam Mim as a crocodile in *The Sword in the Stone*.

36. Other **stock sounds used in multiple movies** would be the Angry Dog Barking, Baby Elephant Trumpeting 1-2, Bear Growl, Bear Roar, Boing, Boink 1-2, Bonk, Car Screech (was used in 52 movies, shorts, or television episodes), Carnival Talking, Castle Thunder 1 (was used in 21 movies, shorts, or television episodes), Castle Thunder 2-3, Cat Growl, Cat Screeching, Cat Screeching 2 (was used in 47 movies, shorts, or television episodes), Cat Yowl, Children Laughing, Clang 1-2, Clearing Throat, Coughing 1-3, Cracking, Cranky Bird, Crash, Creaking, Crowd Cheering 1-3, Crumbling, Crying Baby 1-4, Crying Bird, Cymbal Crash, Dizzy Sound, Dog Bark 1-8, Dog Growl 1-2, Dog Howl, Dog Pack Barking, Dog Snarl, Dog Whimper 1-4, Dog Yelp, Donkey Bray 1-2, Dopey Cry, Doppler Truck Horn, Electricity, Elephant Trumpeting 1-3, Exhausted Breathing, Falling In A Distance, Ferocious Roar, Fireworks, Gasp 1-3, Goblins' Gibberish, Goofy Holler (was used in 34 movies, shorts, or television episodes that don't involve Goofy), Growl, Gulp 1-3, Gunshot 1-5, Hiccup 1-2, Horse Whinny 1-4, Hound Barking, Howie Scream, Hypnotic Gaze, Jaws Chomp, Jet Vroom, Kissing Sound 1-2, Kling, Knocking Pins Sounds, Loud Crash, Low Trumpeting, Machine Gun Getting Out Of Control, Multiple Kisses, Oof, Panting, Pete Laugh, Plugged Trumpet, Pluto Growl 1-3, Pluto Scream, Poof, Pop!, Pottery Break, Puppy Barking, Puppy Growl, Puppy Whimper, Quick Nibbling, Quickly Toys, Raccoon Growl, Rocking Chair Sound, Rooster Crow 1-6, Rumbling, Sigh, Slingshot, Smacking and Shouting, Snarling 1-2, Snoring, Splash, Splat, Tarzan Yell, Thunder Crackle, Tiny Bugle Charge, Toy-Making Machine, Transformation, Trumpet Call, Umbrella Opening Up and Poof, Wiggling Sound, Wilhelm Scream (was used in 38 movies, shorts, video games, or television

episodes), Wind Howl 1-2, Window Shatter, Witch Shriek, Wobble, Wolf Howl, Wood Crack, and Wood Crash.

37. The **Wilhelm Scream has an interesting history**. Actor Sheb Wooley let out this famously used scream when he was attacked by an alligator in the film *Distant Drums* (1951). It was later used in the film *The Charge at Feather River* (1953) when Private Wilhelm took an arrow in the thigh. It was used a few times after that, but when *Star Wars Episode 4: A New Hope* (1977) was released, it brought the stock sound to light. You can hear it when Luke and Leia are trapped on the landing. They are shooting up at the Storm Troopers when Luke manages to hit one, knocking him into the depths; the trooper is heard screaming. The sound department for Lucas dubbed it "The Wilhelm Scream." After that it was used in other *Star Wars* and *Indiana Jones* films. In total, the sound has been used in over 360 films, television episodes, and video games. Not only is Sheb Wooley known for his scream, he is also known for being the artist who wrote and performed the classic oldie *"Purple People Eater"* song in 1958.

38. Some of the **notable Disney uses of the Wilhelm Scream** would be in *Toy Story* (1995) when Buzz gets knocked out of the window by the lamp, in *Beauty and the Beast* (1991) you can hear a villager scream during the castle raid, just after Chip busts in the cellar to rescue Belle, in *Hercules* (1997) when the cyclops arrives in Thebes, in *Pirates of the Caribbean* (2003-present) it can be heard multiple times throughout all the films, in *Enchanted* (2007) right when the queen turns into a dragon, in *Up* (2009) when dogs fall off the cliff, and in *Star Wars Episode 7: The Force Awakens* (2015) when Finn and Poe are escaping the First Order and are blasting the Storm Troopers. There are many other times when it is used throughout multiple films and episodes.

39. **Goofy has his own set of 16 stock sounds** that he uses including Gawrsh, Goofy Holler, Ow, and Whaaaaugh.

40. Generally, Disney only releases one film per year in the cannon of films. This doesn't include Pixar or the straight-to-video animated films. It is common now for Disney to have one film per year in the year they are released. **There were four instances in which two movies were released to theaters in the same year**;
    - *Pinocchio* (1940) and *Fantasia* (1940)
    - *The Rescuers* (1977) and *The Many Adventures of Winnie the Pooh* (1977)
    - *Lilo & Stitch* (2002) and *Treasure Planet* (2002)
    - *Zootopia* (2016) and *Moana* (2016)

41. Back in the beginning, it wasn't as frequent of a release as one movie per year. In fact, **there were four instances of a four-year gap**, which is the longest, between the films;
    - *Lady and the Tramp* (1955) and *Sleeping Beauty* (1959)
    - *The Sword in the Stone* (1963) and *The Jungle Book* (1967)
    - *Robin Hood* (1973) and *The Rescuers* (1977)

- *The Many Adventures of Winnie the Pooh* (1977) and *The Fox and the Hound* (1981).

42. **"A113" is a Pixar and Disney inside joke or "Easter Egg."** "A113" was the room number at California Institutes of the Arts (CalArts) that many of the Disney animators attended. CalArts was established in 1961 by Walt Disney to train new animators. It was a mashing up of two previously-existing institutes; *Chouinard Art Institute* (founded 1921) and the *Los Angeles Conservatory of Music* (established 1883). The school is located in Valencia, California, just one hour north of Disneyland. It isn't just Disney and Pixar that use "A113," other films have, too. Including *Mission: Impossible – Ghost Protocol* (2011), which was directed by Brad Bird. In it there is a class ring with a needle in it, the side of the ring says "A113." Other films to include it would be T*he Hunger Games: Catching Fire* (2013), *The Iron Giant* (1999), *Terminator Salvation* (2009), *Dawn of the Planet of the Apes* (2014), and many others.

43. **The first use of "A113" was in the pilot episode** for the short-lived television series *Family Dog* (1993). The pilot episode was a part of the series *Amazing Stories* (1989-1987), which aired February 16, 1987, and was titled *The Family Dog*. It was the only animated episode of the series. The episode was written and directed by Brad Bird; later on, it became a series in 1993. The series credited Brad Bird as the creator. It was produced by Steven Spielberg and Tim Burton, music was scored by Danny Elfman, and it was written by Dennis Klein, Paul Dini, and Sherri Stoner, the model for Ariel from *The Little Mermaid* (1989) and Belle from *Beauty and the Beast* (1991). Brad Bird was the first one to use the "A113" as a license plate on the back of the robber's van in that pilot episode. Other films Brad worked on were *The Fox and the Hound* (1983), *The Iron Giant* (1999), *The Incredibles* (2004), *Ratatouille* (2007), *Up* (2009), *Toy Story 3* (2010), *Brave* (2012), *Monsters University* (2013), *Inside Out* (2015), and *Tomorrowland* (2015).

44. **The Pizza Planet Truck is an "Easter Egg"** that can be found in every Pixar film to date, with the exception of *The Incredibles* (2004). It made its first appearance in *Toy Story* (1996), and has shown up in one form or another in every Pixar film. It can't be found in *The Incredibles* (2004), but it can be found in *The Incredibles* (2004) video game. In the *Toy Story* films, the truck's license plate says "RES1536," because *Toy Story's* RESolution was 1536 x 922 pixels. The truck is said to be a 1978 Gyoza Mark VII Lite Hauler pickup truck, not a Toyota.

45. **The Pixar Ball is a common "Easter Egg" to find in the Pixar films**. It is a yellow ball with a blue stripe and a red star on it. Sometimes it is called the Luxo Ball because its first appearance was in the Pixar short *Luxo Jr.* (1986). In that short, the Luxo Jr. lamp squashes the ball flat. The Pixar Ball is not in *A Bug's Life* (1998), *Cars* (2006), or *Ratatouille* (2007). In 2014, *Luxo Jr.*

was the second Pixar short to be added to The National Film Registry. The first was *Tin Toy* (1988); it was added in 2003. (*see photo*)

46. It is important to note **the different Disney film eras**. Sometimes people refer to them, like "The Golden Age." Meaning the period of time when Walt first started making animated films. The following is a breakdown of the eras. They only include the Disney cannon films and not the straight to home video or Pixar films. These are fan made era classifications and are not predetermined by Disney.

The Golden Age (1937-1942)
- *Snow White and the Seven Dwarfs, Pinocchio, Fantasia, Dumbo, Bambi*

The Wartime Era (1943-1949)
- *Saludos Amigos, The Three Caballeros, Make Mine Music, Fun and Fancy Free, Melody Time, The Adventures of Ichabod and Mr. Toad*

The Silver Age (1950-1959)
- *Cinderella, Alice in Wonderland, Peter Pan, Lady and the Tramp, Sleeping Beauty, One Hundred and One Dalmatians, The Sword in the Stone, The Jungle Book*

The Bronze Age aka The Dark Age (1960-1988)
- *The AristoCats, Robin Hood, The Many Adventures of Winnie the Pooh, The Rescuers, The Fox and the Hound, The Black Cauldron, The Great Mouse Detective, Oliver and Company*

The Disney Renaissance (1989-1999)
- *The Little Mermaid, The Rescuers Down Under, Beauty and the Beast, Aladdin, The Lion King, Pocahontas, The Hunchback of Notre Dame, Hercules, Mulan, Tarzan*

Post-Renaissance Era aka Second Dark Age (2000-2009)
- *Fantasia 2000, Dinosaur, The Emperor's New Groove, Atlantis: The Lost Empire, Lilo and Stitch, Treasure Planet, Brother Bear, Home on the Range, Chicken Little, Meet the Robinsons, Bolt*

The Revival Era (2010-now)
- *Princess and the Frog, Tangled, Winnie the Pooh, Wreck it Ralph, Frozen, Big Hero 6*

MOVIE FUN FACTS BY INDIVIDUAL FILM

A Bug's Life (1998)

1. The character types were **based on the Aesop's Fable "The Ant and the Grasshopper,"** also known as "The Cicada and the Ant." There are over 600 fables told by the slave Aesop, who lived in 600 BC.

2. The **storyline was based on the Japanese film *Seven Samurai*** (1954). It's about a village of farmers who hire seven Ronin to protect their village from bandits who will return after the harvest to steal their crops.

3. Disney **had produced a film based on the same fable prior to this** in 1934 titled *The Grasshopper and the Ants*. It had a very different ending, and the grasshopper was voiced by Pinto Colvig, the voice of Goofy.

4. **This film was conceived in a single lunch meeting** between John Lasseter, Andrew Stanton, Peter Docter, and Joe Ranft in the summer of 1994, along with *Toy Story 2* (1999), *Monsters, Inc.* (2001), *Finding Nemo* (2003), and *WALL•E* (2008).

5. **Princess Atta was named after the genus Atta**, which is a species group of leafcutter ants.

6. A **month before its release, the *DreamWorks* film *Antz* (1998) was released** to theaters. The CEO of *DreamWorks* at the time was Jeffrey Katzenberg. Jeffrey was the CEO of *Walt Disney Studios* up until 1994 when he was let go. He then created *DreamWorks* with Steven Spielberg and with his knowledge of the storyline he created a similar film to go head to head with Disney in the box office. Jeffrey was also one of the reasons why Robin Williams didn't want to come back to the studio, but did so after Jeff left.

7. The short *Geri's Game* that preceded the film was the **first short to precede a Pixar film** in the theaters.

8. *Geri's Game* was **finished one year before the feature film**.

9. When Flik arrives at the Bug City located under the mobile home, **the Pizza Planet truck** can be seen parked outside, just like the one in *Toy Story* (1995).

10. In the bug bar a mosquito orders a Bloody Mary O+. This was **the first time blood was shown in a Pixar film**. The second time was when Dory got a bloody nose in *Finding Nemo* (2003).

11. When Flik walks up to the bug bar, there is **a cup on top of it from the Pizza Planet restaurant** in *Toy Story* (1995).

12. The animal cookie box that the circus bugs are in has the brand Casey Jr. Cookies, which is a nod to **Casey Jr., the train in the movie *Dumbo*** (1941).

13. **P.T. Flea was named after P.T. Barnum**, the financial backer for *Barnum and Bailey Circus* in 1875.

14. The two mosquitoes that get trapped in the light of the **bug zapper are voiced by John Lasseter and Andrew Stanton**, the film's directors.

15. In the scene when Flik is walking through Bug City, **you can see *The Lion King: On Broadway* poster** on the side of one of the boxes.

16. On the side of a cereal box **you can find "A113-1195."** This is a Pixar inside joke. "A113" was the room number where a lot of the Disney animators went to school. The "1195" represents the date the film was released, November 1995.

17. When the bug scouts are painting Francis, **you can spot a Hidden Mickey**.

18. The **original title of the film was going to be *Bug Story***, but Pixar thought that people would then expect them to use "Story" in the title of all their films.

166

19. This is the **first of three Pixar films to not feature any humans**, the second is *Cars* (2006), and the third is *Cars 2* (2011).

20. Hopper is the **first Pixar villain to die**.

21. In the scene when Hopper is flying away with Flik, Tuck and Roll are tossed at him. They fail by getting stuck in a branch and **Hopper flies off with both antennae attached** to his head, but then it is revealed that Tuck and Roll had just pulled one out. In the next up-close shot, he has one missing.

22. John Lassetter **originally wanted to have Robert DeNiro do the voice of Hopper**, but he kept declining. It wasn't until after John met Kevin Spacey at the 1995 Academy Awards did he fill the roll with someone who was excited to do it. Robert made his first voiceover appearance in *Shark's Tale* (2004).

23. The attraction *It's Tough to Be a Bug* **opened seven months before the film was released**. It was in the *Tree Of Life* in *Disney World's Animal Kingdom*, and in *California Adventure* in 2001. This was the second time an attraction opened before the film's release. The first was *Sleeping Beauty Castle* which opened in 1955, but the film was not released until 1959. The third was *Pirates of the Caribbean* which opened in 1967, but the film was not released until 2003. The third was *The Haunted Mansion* which opened in 1969, but the film was not released until 2003.

24. **Woody from *Toy Story* (1995) makes an appearance** in the gag reel at the end of the movie.

25. In another blooper **Flik yells out "To infinity and beyond,"** which is Buzz Lightyear's catch phrase in *Toy Story* (1995).

26. **The ant's tree is also used in the film *Toy Story 2* (1999)** when Jesse has her flashback, and again ten years later in *Up* (2009), when Elle and Carl go to have a picnic.

27. This film marks the **first time that a DVD and VHS version** of a Disney film were released at the same time, April 20, 1999.

28. This was also the **first Pixar film to be released to DVD**.

29. When it was released to home video, **there were five different character covers to pick from:** Hopper, Flick, Dot, Francis, and Heimlich.

The Adventures of Ichabod and Mr. Toad (1949)

30. This **movie is actually a collection of two films**, *The Legend of Sleepy Hollow* and *The Wind in the Willows*.

31. **This was the last of the "packaged films."** During World War II, Walt didn't have a lot of man power or resources to get full-length projects done. They had many ideas for films that were too short to be feature films and too long to be shorts. Disney came up with the idea of "packaged films." The first three are *Make Mine Music* (1946), *Melody Time* (1948), and *Fun & Fancy Free* (1947).

32. In the opening sequence when Basil Rathbone is talking about picking out the most fabulous character in English literature, he mentions Robin Hood, King Arthur, Becky Sharp, Sherlock Holmes, or Oliver Twist. **Disney ended up making all of those characters movies**, with the exception of Becky Sharp. They can be found in *Robin Hood* (1973), *The Sword in the Stone* (1963), *The Great Mouse Detective* (1986), and *Oliver & Company* (1988). Again, it is funny that the narrator is Basil Rathbone, the actor who portrayed Sherlock Holmes from 1939-1953. You also get to hear his voice in *The Great Mouse Detective* (1986) when they used archive recording from an old episode.

33. The **original title was "*Two Fabulous Characters.*"** In the early planning stages, Disney wanted to place *The Wind in the Willows* with *Mickey and the Beanstalk* and *The Gremlins* as a package film. They ended up canceling The Gremlins and were going to have the package about Mickey and Mr. Toad, but Mickey's film was done two years before Toad's film was completed. That is when they paired up Ichabod and Mr. Toad.

34. They had **originally planned for Jiminy Cricket to do the intro for the films** like he did in the previous film, *Fun & Fancy Free* (1947), but that idea was dropped.

35. **Basil Rathbone and Bing Crosby were both picked because of their popularity**. It was believed they would draw in crowds. Up until this point Disney hadn't used big name celebrities in their productions. They had a tendency to bring back characters from past films, like Jiminy Cricket to be the narrator for *Fun & Fancy Free* (1947). People knew and loved Jiminy and saw him as a celebrity and Disney could draw on that.

The Legend of Sleepy Hollow

36. *The Legend of Sleepy Hollow* was written by Washington Irving and was published in 1820. **This story has been told over 23 times in various movies**, television shows, television episodes, animated films, and shorts for over a 95-year span. It has also had dozens of audio recordings, one of which was done by Boris Karloff. There have been 17 musicals and stage productions of the story as well. In 1974, the US Post Office honored the story with a postage stamp adorned with Ichabod being chased by the Headless Horseman.

37. The **setting of the story was about thirty years before its publication,** placing it in the 1790's.

38. Washington Irving was also known for his writing of *Rip Van Winkle* (1819). **The city of Irvington, New York, was named after him**.

39. During the Ichabod tale, Ichabod Crane is frightened by some **reeds whistling** in the wind. The same drawings were first used in *The Old Mill* (1937).

40. Animating on this film **began in December 1946.**

41. The **opening narrator is Basil Rathbone**, best known as Sherlock Holmes. He was also the inspiration for naming Basil of Baker Street in *The Great Mouse Detective*.

42. The character of **Brom Bones would later become the inspiration for Gaston** in *Beauty and the Beast* (1991).

43. **Brom Bones was voiced by the late, great Bing Crosby**.

44. This film predates *Cinderella* (1950) by one year. The same animators and animation supervisors worked on the films around the same time, like Production Manager Ben Sharpsteen. Animation designs and style were all uniform between characters, which is why **Katrina looks so much like Cinderella**. Those two also share similarities with Grace from *Make Mine Music* (1946), The Golden Harp from the "Mickey and the Beanstalk" segment of *Fun & Fancy Free* (1947), and Slue Foot Sue from the "Pecos Bill" segment of *Melody Time* (1948).

45. The song "Headless Horseman," sung by Bing Crosby, **was considered dark and was almost cut from the film**. Much like the songs "Worthless" from *The Brave Little Toaster* (1987) and "Hellfire" from *The Hunchback of Notre Dame* (1996).

46. The **Headless Horseman is still notated as one of the scariest characters** created by Disney along with The Horned King from *The Black Cauldron* (1985) and Chernabog from *Fantasia* (1940).

47. Thurl Ravenscroft (see *Who Does That Voice on page 147*) **sang a version of "The Headless Horseman" song**. Thurl's version, recorded in 1963, was released on CD and is titled *Walt Disney Records: Archive Collection Volume 1*.

48. The name of **Ichabod's horse is Gunpowder**.

49. **Ichabod Crane is a gold digger**. Was Ichabod technically the villain for only wanting Katrina for her money? Was Brom actually the hero for wanting Katrina for who she was and using his storytelling ability to scare the villain out of town? That's up to you to decide.

50. In the story, **Ichabod got his surname of Crane from his appearance**. He was tall and slender, with a long nose much like a crane.

51. It is believed that **the Scarecrow villain in DC's Batman comics** was based off of Ichabod in body type and was also given the same last name, Jonathan Crane.

52. The **Headless Horseman mythology has roots in English**, German, Scandinavian, and Irish folklore. They all have their own tales of a headless rider on a horse.

53. There is a themed **restaurant in *Magic Kingdom* called *Sleepy Hollow*** that serves waffle sandwiches or funnel cakes topped with strawberries and whipped cream.

54. **The Disney version was the third telling of the story** in the film medium. The first was *The Legend of Sleepy Hollow* (1912) which was a comedic short, the second was *The Headless Horseman* (1922) which was a comedic horror film in which Ichabod Crane was played by the famed actor Will Rogers. Since then there have been 16 films, shorts, or television episodes created around the story, and more recently a four-season-long television series. Ichabod Crane has been played by Jeff Goldblum and Johnny Depp.

55. Although Ichabod doesn't speak in the film, he does sing, which Bing Crosby provides the vocals for. The instance in which Ichabod screams near the end, **his scream is produced by Pinto Colvig**, the voice of Goofy.

56. This is the **second time in a Disney animated feature when the villain wins** in the end. Although the ending of the film could be up for debate. The first instance of the villain winning was Foxy Loxy in *Chicken Little* (1943), when he ate all the fowl.

57. Some have **deduced that the Headless Horseman is just Brom** in costume, although the instance when Ichabod peeked inside his cloak would beg to differ.

Wind in the Willows

58. The **voice of the Persecutor is provided by John McLeish**. He is the narrator for the Goofy shorts including *Goofy's Glider* (1940), *"How to Ride A Horse"* segment of *The Reluctant Dragon* (1941), *The Art Of Skiing* (1941), *The Art Of Self Defense* (1941), *The Olympic Champ* (1942), *How To Swim* (1942), *How To Fish* (1942), *How To Be A Sailor* (1944), *Goofy Gymnastics* (1949), *How To Ride A Horse* (1950), *Motor Mania* (1950), and his last film, *Home Made Home* (1951). He also wrote the story segment of *"Rite of Spring"* in *Fantasia* (1940) and was the narrator for the opening of *Dumbo* (1941).

59. **Ratty had called Mr. Toad's latest obsession "Motor Mania."** Then the following year, the Goofy short was released called *Motor Mania* (1950).

60. **Ratty and Mole appear to resemble Sherlock Holmes and Doctor Watson**. Ratty is even wearing a deerstalker and smoking a pipe. This is interesting because Basil Rathbone is the narrator and he is known for his portrayal of Sherlock Holmes from 1939-1953.

61. **The weasels made appearances** in the films *Mickey's Christmas Carol* (1983), *The Prince and the Pauper* (1990), and one of them made a guest appearance in the Goofy short *How to Be a Detective* (1952). The Toon Patrol Weasels in *Who Framed Roger Rabbit* (1988) were modeled after the weasels in the film.

62. **J. Thaddeus Toad made guest appearances** in the films *Mickey's Christmas Carol* (1983) and *Who Framed Roger Rabbit* (1988).

63. **Ratty and Mole also make guest appearances** in *Mickey's Christmas Carol* (1983).

64. **In the book, Ratty is described as a European water vole.** They are sometimes called water rats, which is why he is named Ratty.

65. **The author of *The Wind in the Willows* is Kenneth Grahame.** He is also the author of *The Reluctant Dragon* (1898) which was also made into a Disney short in 1941.

66. *The Wind in Willows* was **the last publication Kenneth wrote.** He never did write a sequel to the book.

67. The original printing of the story of *The Wind in the Willows* (1908) didn't have any illustrations. They weren't added until later. One of the illustrators was Ernest Howard Shepard, **the same artist who illustrated the *Winnie the Pooh*** (1926) novelization.

68. Before a film adaptation of the book, there was a **theatrical play in 1929 that was produced by A. A. Milne**, the author of the *Winnie the Pooh* books. The play was titled *Toad of Toad Hall* and was focused on Mr. Toad as most of the rest of the story was removed.

69. Claud Allister provided the **voice of Ratty in *The Wind in the Willows* and also the voice of Sir Giles,** the Dragon Killer in *The Reluctant Dragon* (1941).

70. The **production for this segment of *The Wind in the Willows* began in 1941**, but was put on hold because of World War II and wasn't resumed until 1945.

71. Mr. Toad's **full name in the Disney film is J. Thaddeus Toad, Esquire**. In the original story he is just known as Mr. Toad.

72. The attraction *Mr. Toad's Wild Ride* in *Disneyland* was an **opening day attraction** and is still there today, over 60 years later. There was also a version that opened in *Disney World's Magic Kingdom* on their opening day in 1971. That attraction was removed in 1998 to be replaced by *The Many Adventures of Winnie the Pooh*. Parts of the attraction went up for auction. Actor John Stamos, a huge Disney fan, purchased one of the devils from the hell scene for inside his recording studio. The hell scene was added to the attraction, but it does not exist in the film.

73. A non-Disney **film that is to be released in 2017 called *Banking on Mr. Toad*** is about the writer Kenneth Grahame and the struggles he went through to get his book, *The Wind in the Willows,* published in 1908. It is going to star Brian Blessed, the voice of Boss Nass in *Star Wars Episode I: The Phantom Menace* (1999) and Clayton in *Tarzan* (1999).

Aladdin (1992) - See *Disney Princess Collection* on page 90 for Fun Facts

Alice in Wonderland (1951)

74. This movie is **based off of two books written by Lewis Carroll**, *Alice's Adventures in Wonderland (*1865) and the sequel, *Through the Looking Glass* (1871).

75. The **Doorknob was the only character in the movie** that did not appear in Lewis Carroll's books.

76. **If you want to see the Doorknob in Disneyland**, just go to the door on the left of the Roger Rabbit's Cartoon Spin queue.

77. In the *"**Walrus and the Carpenter**"* sequence, the 'R' in the word "March" on the mother oyster's calendar flashes. This alludes to the old adage about only eating oysters in a month with an 'R' in its name. Reason being that those months without an 'R' are the summer months when oysters would not keep due to the heat in the days before refrigeration.

78. Though it was a box-office flop when first released, several years later it became the Disney studio's **most requested 16mm film** rental title for colleges and private individuals. In 1974, the studio took note of this fact, withdrew the rental prints, and reissued the film nationally themselves.

79. When Ed Wynn was providing the live action reference for the **Mad Hatter, he ad-libbed the dialogue** for the scene when he was fixing the White Rabbit's watch, *"Muthtard? Don't leth be silly."* Walt wanted it in the film because it was so funny to him. The sound technicians had to work on the audio because of the background sound. Even though they were filming, it was never intended to be used in the movie. That's what recording studios were for. His ad-lib recording ended up in the final cut of the film.

80. In an earlier plot point, **Dinah was going to get lost down the rabbit hole** and was to be turned into the Cheshire Cat. Alice was to try and find Dinah with the help of the Cheshire Cat, the Mad Hatter, and the March Hare. Alice would get captured by the Queen of Hearts and the Cheshire Cat was to turn back into Dinah and escape with Alice.

81. This film is actually a **culmination of the two Lewis Carroll books,** *Adventures in Wonderland* and *Through the Looking Glass.*

82. After the cards sing the song "Painting the Roses Red" and get through the line *"not pink, not green, not aquamarine..."* the army of cards come marching into the scene with psychedelic lighting and the first set of colored cards that comes into view are **pink, followed closely by green, and then finally aquamarine**.

83. In the scene with the Walrus and the Carpenter, the mother oyster looks at her calendar. March 5th falls on the first Friday of the month. The Tim Burton-directed film *Alice in Wonderland* (2010) was released on March 5, 2010, **which also landed on the first Friday of the month**.

84. In the scene when the Dodo is lighting his pipe, you can see a **Hidden Mickey in the flames of his match**.

85. This movie has 15 songs; **more songs than any other animated Disney film**

86. There are also **more characters** than any other Disney animated film.

87. This was the **first Disney animated film that credited each actor with their character** in the credits after the film. It wouldn't be done again this way until the credits of *The Jungle Book* (1967).

88. There were plans to have **the Jabberwocky scene** occur, but either due to the pacing of the film or the scare factor, it was cut. He was going to be voiced by Stan Freberg, the voice of Beaver in *Lady and the Tramp* (1955). What did remain was the Cheshire Cat singing part of the poem; *"'Twas brillig, and the slithy toves. Did gyre and gimble in the wabe. All mimsy were the borogoves, and the mome raths outgrabe."*

89. There were also plans to have **the Bandersnatch and the Jub Jub Bird**. These two were cut, but part of the design of the Jub Jub Bird carried over to the umbrella vultures.

90. This was the **first film to be released on television**, after it had a theatrical release, on *Walt Disney's Wonderful World of Color* in 1954. It had to be edited down to fit in the one-hour time slot.

91. It was also the **first film to be re-released in the theaters** after it was released on television.

92. During the trial, **you can see Jose Carioca** from *The Three Caballeros* (1944) and *Saludos Amigos* (1942) as one of the jurors.

93. **The term "Mad as a Hatter" came about** because hat makers' long-term exposure to mercury would cause mercury poisoning, which had side effects like slurred speech, tremors, stumbling, and sometimes hallucinations.

94. This was the **first film Disney was able to promote on television**.

95. **The King was voiced by Dink Trout**. It was his final film. He died in 1950, one year before its release.

96. There were **lots of songs cut from the film**, one of which was "I'm Odd" which was to have been sung by the Cheshire Cat. When Disney released the masterpiece edition on DVD, they included the song sung by Jim Cummings as the Cheshire Cat.

97. The character of **"Puppy" was cut from the film**, but later added into *Alice in Wonderland* (2010) and given the name of Bayard.

98. In the books, The Mad Hatter is **just called The Hatter**.

99. The Mad Hatter and The March Hare both **make appearances in the television series *Bonkers*** (1993).

100. Although Tweedledum and Tweedledee are depicted as being a chubby set of twins by artist John Tenniel, **the author doesn't describe them that way**. Then, the practice of them being twins carried forward through their many reincarnations.

101. The character of the **Executioner was removed from the film**, but there were several spade cards left in the place of that character.

102. The **March Hare was given his name from the term "Mad as a March Hare."** This was a term used to describe the European hare during mating season. They would exhibit odd behavior like boxing other rabbits and jumping straight in the air for no apparent reason.

103. The artist's inspiration for the depiction of the Queen of Hearts came from the stained glass windows that were adorned with the face of **Elizabeth de Mowbray, the Duchess of Norfolk** (1443-1507).

104. It is historically said that **Alice Pleasance Liddell was the inspiration for Lewis Carroll's story.** Lewis spent time with the three daughters of Henry Liddell by photographing them and telling them stories. He made up a fanciful story about a girl named Alice who got bored and went on an adventure. Alice asked him to write down the story for her. So he did and it eventually turned into the story that we know today.

The AristoCats (1970)

105. The inspiration for this story was based on the **true events of a family of Persian cats** that inherited a large fortune around 1910.

106. The kittens were given their names based on famous aristocrats of the past.

107. **Toulouse was named after the famous French painter Henri de Toulouse-Lautrec** (1864-1901). He was known for his stylized cabaret posters, most notably the ones for the Moulin Rouge.

108. **Marie was named after Marie Antoinette** (1755-1793), a Queen of France. She is most notable for the Affair of the Diamond Necklace. She was later nicknamed Madame Déficit because of her lavish spending during famine times. Multiple movies have been made about her; the most famous one was released in 2006 and starred Kirsten Dunst.

109. **Berlioz was named after Hector Berlioz** (1803-1869), the famous French composer best known for his compositions *Symphonie fantastique* (1830), *Grande messe des morts* (1837), and *Romeo et Juliette* (1839).

110. The roly-poly trumpet playing Scat Cat was designed to look like Louis Armstrong, the musician who would be voicing the character. Due to him being sick, he was unable to do it. **Disney had trumpet musician Scatman Crothers do the voice**. He also did the voice of Jazz in all the Transformers cartoons in the 1980's.

111. This was the **last animated film approved by Walt Disney before his death.** The entirety of the film was completed after his passing.

Atlantis: The Lost Empire (2001)

112. **Marc Okrand was the language consultant on the film** who came up with the Atlantean language. He is also known for creating the Vulcan and Klingon languages for the *Star Trek* films and television shows.

113. The most popular *Star Trek* Vulcan is **Leonard Nimoy, who coincidently voices King Kashekim Nedakh**, the king of Atlantis.

114. Princess Kida is the **second princess in a Disney film to sport a tattoo**. The first was Pocahontas. Although, Kida is not in the princess collection due to this film not doing very well in the box office. She was also made a queen in her direct-to-video sequel, *Atlantis: Milo's Return* (2003).

115. The voice of Jebidiah Allardyce 'Cookie' Farnsworth was provided by Jim Varney, better known as Slinky Dog in the *Toy Story* films. He **passed away before the completion of the film**. In fact, the line "*I ain't so good at speechifying*" had to be spoken by voice actor Steve Barr.

116. The video game *Atlantis: The Lost Empire* (2001) for PlayStation was the **last acting Jim Varney did before he passed away**.

117. After Milo gets seasick on the ship, he says, "*Carrots? Why are there always carrots? I didn't even eat carrots,*" which was **ad-libbed by Michael J. Fox.**

118. Disneyland was going to **theme the *Tomorrowland Submarine Voyage* after this film**, but because it didn't do as well as they wanted, they went in the direction of making it the *Finding Nemo Submarine Voyage*.

119. The sequel, *Atlantis: Milo's Return* (2003), wasn't actually a full-length film. It was essentially **a compilation of the three episodes** that were animated for the canceled *Atlantis* television series.

Bambi (1942)

120. The name **"Bambi" comes from the Italian word "bambino."** In Italian it means "little boy."

121. Bambi's **species was actually a European roe deer**. As a male he would be referred to as a Roebuck. Walt changed his species to a white-tailed deer since they are more prevalent in North America.

122. In *Who Framed Roger Rabbit* (1988), it was going to be revealed that **Judge Doom was "Man" and was the one that killed Bambi's mother**, but that part of the film was changed.

123. "Man" killing Bambi's mother is noted as **the most horrific and infamous scene in Disney animated history**, surpassed only by Scar killing Mufasa.

124. **"Man" was ranked number 20** of American Film Institute's top *100 Heroes & Villains* (2003) of all time. On that list he was the second animated villain, The Queen was #10, and he was the only one that wasn't actually ever seen in the film.

125. Voice actress **Paula Winslowe was the voice of Bambi's mother and of the pheasant.** Both were characters killed by "Man."

126. A deleted scene was to have Bambi and his father discovering "Man" burned because he was caught in the forest fire. It was deemed too dark for the test audiences and was cut.

127. Pre-production began in 1936 and was intended to be **Walt Disney's second full-length animated film** after *Snow White and the Seven Dwarfs* (1937). Disney's perfection and quest for realism delayed the project significantly, so that *Pinocchio* (1940), *Fantasia* (1940), *The Reluctant Dragon* (1941) and *Dumbo* (1941) were released earlier than *Bambi*.

128. There are **approximately only 1,000 words** of dialogue throughout the entire film.

129. There are some scenes of woodland creatures and the forest fire that are **unused footage from *Pinocchio*** (1940).

130. This was the **first Disney film to premier outside of the US**. It premiered in London, England, on August 8, 1942. It then opened in New York on August 13.

131. The budget for the film was upward of $1.7 million, and its gross intake during the 1942 release was about $1.64 million. **This film was a huge flop for Disney**. Part of it had to do with being released during World War II. Some patrons weren't fond of the film because it lacked the fantasy that Disney was known for. American hunters protested the film, saying it didn't put them in a good light. Because of this income loss, it prompted Disney to re-release Snow White into theaters in 1944 to recuperate the money. Bambi was later re-released in 1947, 1957, 1966, 1975, 1982, and 1988. With all of the combined releases, Disney has taken in over $267 million from Box Office sales. Disney later cashed in on the VHS sales when the movie premiered in 1989.

132. Director Sidney Franklin **originally pitched *Bambi* to Disney as a live-action film project** in 1933. He had even acquired recording for the narration from actress Margaret Sullavan and Victor Jory. There were issues with the recording of the live animals, but after seeing *Snow White and the Seven Dwarfs* (1937), he decided to speak with Walt Disney about making it an animated film. "To Sidney A. Franklin - our sincere appreciation for the inspiring collaboration."

Beauty and the Beast (1991) - See *Disney Princess Collection* on page 90 for Fun Facts

Big Hero 6 (2014)

133. Marvel Comics published the **first Big Hero 6 comic in September 1998**.

134. Even though it was based off of the comics, the animators **took many liberties with redesigning the characters**, settings, and the story timeline.

135. Remember Ester the Animal Control Officer from the Disney film *Bolt* (2008)? **Her photo can be seen on the police officer's desk** right when Hiro and Baymax leave the station.

136. When Baymax is showing off his rocket fist, it shoots across the yard and smashed a statue. Look closely because **that is a statue of Hans** from *Frozen* (2013).

137. When the film was in production, the animators **watched footage of fire ants** to understand their movement for the movement of the Microbots.

138. When everyone is at Fred's mansion and Hiro is looking at the action figures on the shelf, you can see an armored **Cy-Bug from the Hero's Duty game** scene in *Wreck-It Ralph* (2012).

139. After activating Baymax, Hiro falls between his bed and the nightstand. When he looks up at Baymax, **you can see a sticker of Oswald the Lucky Rabbit** on the ceiling.

140. The **face of Baymax was modeled after the Japanese Suzu bell**. The director Don Hall had said he was inspired when he visited a temple in Japan.

141. When Hiro is on his aunt's stairs, you can see a photo on the wall of **the cat dressed as Stitch** from *Lilo & Stitch* (2002).

The Black Cauldron (1985)

142. *The Black Caldron* (1985) was Disney's first theatrical feature to receive a **PG rating**. The full film had to be edited twice to avoid being rated PG-13 by early 1980's standards.

143. This film is **based on a book series called *The Chronicles of Prydain*** that contains five novels; *The Book of Three* (1964), *The Black Cauldron* (1965), *The Castle of Llyr* (1966), *Taran Wanderer* (1967), and *The High King* (1967).

144. The movie was specifically **based on a combination of two of the books,** *The Book of Three* and *The Black Cauldron*.

145. It was also **the last film to be shot in the Super Technirama 70mm widescreen** system.

146. The film **took over twelve years to make**, five years of actual production.

147. Over **1,165 different hues and colors were used**, and 34 miles of film stock was utilized.

148. The **film was suspended from video release** for years due to its dark content.

149. **Tim Burton, who worked as a conceptual artist on this film**, wanted to incorporate minions of the Horned King that resembled the "facehuggers" from the *Alien* movie series. Some samples of his work can be seen on Disney's 2000 DVD release of this film. Tim Burton was also the animator who drew Vixey for *The Fox and the Hound* (1981) and was an animator for the movie *TRON* (1982). For his final act with Disney, he wrote and directed the short *Frankenweenie* (1984), which would later inspire the stop-motion film directed by him as well, *Frankenweenie* (2012). After he

left Disney, he directed *Pee-wee's Big Adventure* (1985), *Beetlejuice* (1988), *Batman* (1989), and *Edward Scissorhands* (1990). This was the last film he worked on for Disney until he was brought back to direct *Alice in Wonderland* (2010). He was the producer of *The Nightmare Before Christmas* (1993), but that was for Touchstone Pictures, a branch of the Disney Company. In 2006, Walt Disney Pictures did convert the film for 3D release.

150. This was also the **last film John Lasseter worked on for Disney** before they fired him. He was one of the character animators. He went on to work at Pixar, was brought back to Disney in 2006, and put in charge of all the animated Disney films.

151. Technically, this was **the first movie to be <u>released</u> using computer animation**. While working on the film, the animators were having a difficult time animating the cauldron scene when all the evil is released. They knew the animation crew working on *The Great Mouse Detective* (1986) had successfully used a computer to animate some scenes, so they visited that department and borrowed the technology to complete the difficult scene. Although it was released to theaters first, it wasn't the first to actually use a computer.

152. Some of the music sounds similar to the music in the film *Ghostbusters* (1984). That is because the **music composer Elmer Berstein composed the scores for both films.**

153. This was the **first film to not feature any musical numbers**, or any other music being sung within the film.

154. Due to its horrible box office revenue, **princess Eilonwy was not considered to be in the Disney Princess Collection** when it was created in 2001.

155. The production cost was estimated to be around $44 million. Its **box office intake was only a little over $21 million**. When the *Care Bear Movie* was released that same year, it took in $23 million, beating out the Disney movie.

156. **This was the last film produced by Ron Miller**. He previously produced 72 movies and television shows, the majority being for Disney, including *TRON* (1982), *The Fox and the Hound* (1981), *Herbie Goes Bananas* (1980), *The Watcher in the Woods* (1980), *Unidentified Flying Oddball* (1979), *The Rescuers* (1977), *Escape to Witch Mountain* (1975), and *Son of Flubber* (1963), to name a fraction. Ron was also the son-in-law of Walt Disney, as he was married to Diane Disney-Miller in 1954.

Bolt (2008)

157. When Disney needed audio recording of dogs barking for the dog pound scene, they sent an audio team from Pixar 20 minutes up highway 80 to the **Contra Costa County Animal Shelter in Pinole to record the dogs barking**. At the time, it was the newest animal shelter in California.

158. A ten-year-old Chloë Grace Moretz provided the young voice for Penny in the beginning of the film. Apparently, she was **the first one cast to play Penny** and even recorded all of her lines, but was later replaced by Miley Cyrus.

159. **The animation crew adopted a hamster named Doink** and filmed him walking around on plexiglass to see how Rhino needed to be properly animated while walking around in his hamster ball.

160. When Mittens was originally designed, **her name was going to be Mister Mittens**. It was to show that her careless owner never took the time to find out if she was a girl or a boy.

161. When Rhino is flipping through the channels in his trailer, he gets to **a clip of Mr. T talking and you can hear the Wilhelm Scream**.

162. Generally, Disney tries to create individual names for characters in their movies so there aren't multiple characters from multiple movies who have the same name. **In the case of Penny, there are others with her name.** The lead female human in *The Rescuers* (1977), the lead female in the live action version of *Inspector Gadget* (1999), Penny was one of the puppies in *One Hundred and One Dalmatians* (1961), Penny Proud is in the television series *The Proud Family* (2001-2005), the girl with the power to multiply herself in *Sky High* (2005) was named Penny Lent, and the new Japanese series called *Stitch!* (2008-2011) has a supporting character named Penny; she plays the same character as Mertle from *Lilo & Stitch* (2001). Penny Proud also had a guest appearance on the series *Lilo & Stitch: The Series* (2003-2006).

Brave (2012) - See *Disney Princess Collection* on page 90 for Fun Facts

Brother Bear (2003)

163. In the German version of the film, **Rutt and Tuke were renamed Benny and Björn** after the performers in the pop group ABBA.

164. **Michael Clarke Duncan voices Tug the bear**. He was also in *Armageddon* (1998) and played the character of Bear.

165. During the end credits, Kenai and Koda are painting on the rock walls. Kenai paints a stick figure and Koda paints a **recreation of the painting "A Sunday Afternoon on the Island of La Grande Jatte"** (1884) by Georges Seurat.

166. Rick Moranis came out of retirement to voice Rutt. In Fact, ***Brother Bear* was the last theatrically-released film that he has worked on**. He was also Rutt in *Brother Bear 2* (2006), but that was released straight to DVD.

167. Dave Thomas voices Tuke. There was a television series called *SCTV* (Second City Television) (1976-1984) which was a Canadian sketch comedy show. In 1980, there was a segment added called "Great White North" with the recurring brother characters of Bob & Doug McKenzie. Both brothers were very Canadian to the point of making fun of

179

themselves. **They were played by Rick Moranis and Dave Thomas**. They were both in a comedy movie called *Strange Brew* (1983), which was based off of these two characters.

168. When the Eskimos are catching salmon with their nets, **you can see Nemo** from *Finding Nemo* (2003) for only one frame at the point when the mammoth knocks into the net.

Cars (2006)

169. When Fillmore said, "*I'm telling you, man. Every third blink is slower*," he is actually correct. **The animators had the third blink a half second slower**. The Imagineers did the same thing in *Cars Land* in *California Adventure*.

170. One of the race cars is white with an Apple logo on the hood. The number on the roof is 84. **It is to represent 1984, the year the Macintosh computer was released by Apple**. Steve Jobs, the CEO of Apple, would purchase Graphics Group, which was part of the LucasFilm computer division, and rename it Pixar in 1986.

171. This was the **last Pixar film to be made before its purchase by Disney**.

172. Luigi's back license plate says "44.5-10.8." This is the **longitude and latitude location for the Ferrari plant** located in Maranello, Italy.

173. This was the **final Pixar film to be released on VHS**, and the first to be released on Blu-ray.

174. At 1 hour 57 minutes, this is **the longest Pixar movie made to date**.

175. **You can see the Pizza Planet truck** in the scene when the cameras are recording the crowd before the race at the end of the film.

Cars 2 (2011)

176. During the chase scene through London, you can see a tapestry in a pub that is the **car version of Merida and her family's tapestry** from *Brave* (2012). Brave would open one year later.

177. This was the **first Pixar film not to be nominated for Best Animated Picture** since the category was added to the Academy Awards in 2001.

178. The **Pizza Planet Truck, named Todd in the Cars films, can be seen twice**. His first appearance is on the television screen in the bar right before the Mel Dorado Show. His second appearance is at the end of the movie when all the cars are racing through Radiator Springs. Mater uses his rockets to speed through town, and you can see Todd as the baggage from the car next to him flies onto him.

179. After Mater and McQueen are done cow tipping the Colossus XXL dump truck, they drive past a drive-in movie theater. **The kiosk out front says "The Incredimobiles,"** which is a play on the name for the film *The Incredibles* (2004).

180

180. When Holley Shiftwell and Finn McMissile are in Paris, you can see a **poster on the left side of the street that says "Les Indestructibles,"** which is a French conversion for "The Incredimobiles."

181. Gusteau's restaurant from *Ratatouille* (2007) can be seen as **"Gastows" in Paris**.

Cars 3 (2017)

182. The **door on Sterling's office has A113** on it.

183. In *Cars* (2006), **Chick Hicks was voiced by Michael Keaton**. In this film he was voiced by Bob Peterson, the voice of Roz, Mr. Ray, Geri, and Dug.

184. The **Pizza Planet Truck** can be seen on the track in the destruction derby scene. It is most noticeable when another car crashes into him and knocks him into the crowd, dislodging his rocket.

185. **The Pixar Ball can be seen** on the hood of a red and blue car during the destruction derby.

186. This is the first of the three *Cars* films that was not directed by John Lasseter. It was the **directorial debut of animator Brian Fee.**

187. This is the **second film series to have a trilogy from Pixar**. The first is the *Toy Story* trilogy.

188. Race car driver legend **Jeff Gordon reprised his role** as the voice of Jeff Gorvette.

189. **The BNL logo can be seen** on the inner perimeter of the racetrack when Lightning McQueen loses to Jackson Storm. BNL stands for Buy N Large, a reference to the company in *WALL·E* (2008). It was also the sponsor of one of the race cars.

190. **When Lightning McQueen is watching Cruz train the three cars on the tread mills, and helping them overcome their fears, the one on the end is sad because he missis his hom. Cruz shows him video of his village to make him hapopy. This is the village that is seen in the next Pixar film, Coco (2017).**

191. When Lightning McQueen is in Sterling's office, **you can spot Cinderella's pumpkin carriage** as a trophy on the shelf behind his desk.

192. When **Mack Truck dresses up like "Jocko Flocko's Party Supplies,"** it was to pay homage to Jocko Flocko, a monkey from the 1950's that was the only known co-driver in NASCAR history. He was with Tim Flocko win the Grand National race at Hickory, NC. on May 16, 1953.

193. **Paul Newman's voice was used for Doc Hudson**. Paul died in 2008, but Pixar had hours recorded of him talking when he was in studio for *Cars* (2006), most of it was about racing. They spliced together the dialogue they needed to resurrect the character.

194. Brad Paisley performed some of the music in the film, including the destruction derby scene. When he played in Mountain View, CA. on his 2017 World Tour, **his guitarist was the film's director Brian Fee**.

195. After Lightning McQueen crashes the scene cuts to Radiator Springs. You can see Radiator Springs Curios. On the left post of the porch there is a yellow sign that says "service" and to the left and right of the sign there are **Route 66 signs that form a Hidden Mickey**.

196. The **three *Cars* films were all released in the same years as the *Pirates of the Caribbean* films**.
   - *Cars* (2006) and *Pirates of the Caribbean: Dead Man's Chest* (2006)
   - *Cars 2* (2011) and *Pirates of the Caribbean: On Stranger Tides* (2011)
   - *Cars 3* (2017) and *Pirates of the Caribbean: Dead Men Tell No Tales* (2017)

Chicken Little (2005)

197. The story model of *Chicken Little* has been around for thousands of years, but the **first time it was in print was in 1812** by the Brothers Grimm.

198. In the story, Chicken Little has also been called Henny Penny, and Chicken Licken.

199. **Disney first animated this story in 1943** as an animated short propaganda film for WWII. The storyline was different from this film in that there was a fox, Foxy Loxy, invading the chicken coop. It marks the only time a villain won at the end of the film. In this case, Foxy Loxy ate all the chickens and Chicken Little.

200. There are **250,000 feathers on Chicken Little**.

201. This is the **second computer-animated film Disney made**. The first was *Dinosaur* (2000). Every film after this was computer animated with the exception of *The Princess and the Frog* (2009), and *Winnie the Pooh* (2011).

202. **This was Don Knotts' last theatrically-released film**. He passed away three months after it was released in theaters. He returned to Disney films after a 26-year break. Previously, he was in *The Apple Dumpling Gang* (1975), *No Deposit, No Return* (1976), *Gus* (1976), *Herbie Goes to Monte Carlo* (1977), *Hot Lead and Cold Feet* (1978), and *The Apple Dumpling Gang Rides Again* (1979). He was also in two episodes of *101 Dalmatians: The Series* (1997-1998).

203. **Michael J. Fox, Matthew Broderick, and David Spade were considered for the role of Chicken Little**. All of them had have previously voiced the main character in a Disney movie; Michael J. Fox was Milo in *Atlantis: The Lost Empire* (2001), and Chance in *Homeward Bound* (1993) and its sequel, Matthew Broderick was Simba in *The Lion King* (1994), and David Spade was Kuzko in *The Emperor's New Groove* (2000).

Cinderella (1950) - See *Disney Princess Collection* on page 90 for Fun Facts

Coco (2017)

204. **Miguel's dog is a Xoloitzcuintli**, also called a Mexican Hairless, or Xolo (pronounced "sholo") for short. It is one of the older dog breeds first surfacing around 1500 BC. The legend of this breed says that they were sacrificed and buried with their owners to act as a guide for their souls on the journey to the underworld.

205. The **original working title of the film** was "Dia de los Muertos," meaning "Day of the Dead," which is a tradisional Mexican holiday that lasts from October 1, through November 2.

206. In 2013, **Disney filed a U.S. patent and trademark** request for the phrase "Dia de los Muertos," and was denied.

207. The **title of the film was changed to** *Viva* in Brazil because coco in Portuguese means "poo."

208. The movie was **accompanied by the short** *Olaf's Frozen Adventure* (2017). The short is 23-minutes long and is Pixar's longest short. The last preceding short that was released by Disney was the Mickey Mouse short *The Prince and the Pauper* (1990).

Dinosaur (2000)

209. This was Disney's **first non-Pixar computer-animated feature film**.

210. This movie was **Disney's first-ever Blu-ray**, released on September 19, 2006.

211. This was the **second film to be rated PG**. *The Black Cauldron* (1985) was also rated PG and was released 15 years prior.

212. **The film was originally not going to contain dialogue** because it would make the storyline too similar to the Don Bluth film *The Land Before Time* (1988). Michael Eisner insisted that there be dialogue in the film. They then planned to have an inner monologue style of voice-over, much like *Homeward Bound* (1993), but then ended up having mouth movement.

213. The **backgrounds in the movie are actually superimposed footage of exotic tropical locations** such as Hawaii, Australia, Asia, Venezuela, Tahiti, and The Disney Ranch.

214. In the scene with the "monster cloud," you see explosions around Aladar. **The animation team referred to this scene as the "pinball alley scene."** The debris exploding on the ground was actually filmed at the Disney Ranch in Newhall, California.

215. **One prehistoric creature that was designed but cut from the final film was a Mosasaurus**. It is a large sea-dwelling reptile that would have been used in a scene where the herd goes to a river to drink. This is the same

species that can be seen in *Jurassic World* (2015), jumping out of the water to chomp on a Great White shark.

Dumbo (1941)

216. This movie is **based on the book *Dumbo, The Flying Elephant*,** published in 1939 and written by Helen Mayer.

217. This is the only Disney animated feature that has a **title character who doesn't speak**.

218. There are only **five elephants that speak in this film**. Matriarch (pink headdress) was voiced by Verna Felton, Catty also called Fidgity (yellow/green headdress) is voice by Noreen Gammill, Giddy also called Giggles (blue headdress) was voiced by Dorothy Scott, and Prissy (red headdress) was voiced by Sarah Selby. Sarah also played Aunt Gertrude in the Disney series *The Hardy Boys* (1956).

219. The **voice of Mr. Stork was Sterling Holloway's** intro to Disney films. He went on to voice Winnie the Pooh in all his movies up to 1977. He also voiced the Cheshire Cat from *Alice in Wonderland* (1951), Kaa from *The Jungle Book* (1967), Roquefort the Mouse in The *AristoCats* (1970), Amos Mouse in *Ben and Me* (1953), adult Flower in *Bambi* (1942), and many more. He was considered for the role of Sleepy in *Snow White and the Seven Dwarfs* (1937), but lost it to Pinto Colvig.

220. This was also **the first Disney film for voice actress Verna Felton**. She voiced Mrs. Jumbo along with The Elephant Matriarch. She would end up voicing a total of four elephants for Disney. The other two were Eloise in *Goliath II* (1960), and Winifred in *The Jungle Book* (1967). Other famous characters she provided the vocals for were the Fairy Godmother in *Cinderella* (1950), the Queen of Hearts in *Alice in Wonderland* (1951), Flora in *Sleeping Beauty* (1959), and Aunt Sarah in *Lady and the Tramp* (1955). It is said that she also voiced Queen Leah in *Sleeping Beauty*, but there are no records of that. Verna passed away one day before Walt Disney, on December 14, 1966.

221. Mrs. Jumbo's **only line is "Jumbo... Junior,"** in which she states Dumbo's real name.

222. With a runtime of 64 minutes, this is **the shortest animated Disney film**, aside from *Saludos Amigos* (1942), which is a package film of shorts.

223. When **Mr. Stork has Mrs. Jumbo sign on the dotted line,** she marks it with an "X." This was how the illiterate would sign their names on legal documents. It is the reasoning behind the use of an X to indicate where someone is to sign on the line.

224. This was the first Disney-animated feature, and one of the select few **to be set in America**.

225. Timothy Mouse was created for the movie. **In the book, his character was portrayed by a red robin**. Disney used a mouse because of the myth that elephants are afraid of mice.

226. **During production, there was an animators' strike.** About half of the animators left the studio. The scene with the drunken clowns heading to ask the big boss for a raise was added in to poke fun at the incident.

227. This is said to be **Walt Disney's favorite film** made by his studio.

228. **The narrator of the film is John McLeish.** He was the narrator for all of the "How To" Goofy shorts, and also *The Reluctant Dragon* (1941).

229. This was the **first Disney film to be set in the present**.

230. **The voice actor for Timothy Mouse was Edward Brophy.** He racked up 146 acting credits to his name in his 40 years on screen, but this is the only voice work he did.

231. Although World War II began in September 1939, the United States didn't engage in the war until after the Pearl Harbor bombing on December 7, 1941. Releasing on October 31, 1941, this film would be **the last to release before the war**.

The Emperor's New Groove (2000)

232. When Yzma dumps her poisoned drink in with the potted cactus, it **turned into the shape of a llama**.

233. Patrick Warburton **improvised his mission theme song** while sneaking out to dump Kuzco. Apparently Disney had to buy the rights to the song from Patrick Warburton since he made it up.

234. John Fiedler was the voice of the old man who threw off the Emperor's groove. He is best known as **the voice of Piglet in all the Winnie the Pooh movies** (1968-2005).

235. Chicha, Pancha's wife, is **the first representation of a pregnant woman** in a Disney-animated film.

236. The ancient capital of the Incas, Cuzco, **was the inspiration for the name Kuzco**.

237. Patrick Warburton (Kronk) and David Spade (Kuzco) would later **star together in the television series *Rules Of Engagement*** (2007-2013).

238. The scene in which the fly lands on the web and says, "*Help meeee,*" **is a nod to the classic horror film *The Fly* (1958)**, in which the human fly gets caught in a web and gets eaten by a spider while screaming, "*Help meeee.*"

Fantasia (1940)

239. **Chernabog got his name from the Slavonic mythology,** which means "Black God" or "God of Evil."

240. **The sequence with Chernabog is called "Night on Bald Mountain."** Disney announced that they are making a live-action movie with the title and theme in the near future.

241. **The sorcerer's name is Yen Sid.** That is Disney spelled backward.

242. The **look of Yen Sid was inspired by the look of Walt** himself.

243. This is the only movie made by Walt Disney Animation Studios that **surpasses the two-hour runtime mark.** In fact, it is two hours and five minutes long.

244. The "Pastoral Symphony" scene with the African-American centaurette appearing to be forlorn with hoop earrings, ponytails, and gapped teeth, and serving the other centaurettes was very controversial. Sunflower was also depicted as a half human, half donkey, unlike the others who were half human and half horse. In 1940, when the film was released, this was common to see in animated films. There was a huge debate in the 1960's about the scene being very racist. In response, **Disney cut the scene from the film for the 1969 theatrical re-release**. The scene was added back in for the 1990 VHS release, but the parts with Sunflower were cropped out.

245. This is the **longest of the cannon animated films,** reaching the runtime of 2 hrs. 5 min.

246. **Animator Fred Moore redesigned Mickey Mouse for this film**. He upgraded his look and gave him pupils and whites of his eyes. By the time this movie was released in 1940, Mickey's new design had already been used in the shorts *The Pointer* (1939), *Mickey's Surprise Party* (1939), *Pluto's Dream* (1940), *Mr. Mouse Takes a Trip* (1940), and *Tugboat Mickey* (1940).

247. Mickey was originally drawn with circles for his head, body and ears. In 1939, that design was changed to the more pear-shaped appearance we see now. Also, pupils were added to his eyes. **The first film Mickey appeared in with his new features** was *The Pointer* on July 21, 1939, and the first full-length feature, as Sorcerer Mickey, was *Fantasia* (1940).

248. In the "Rite of Spring" scene, **the T-Rex has three clawed fingers**. A real tyrannosaurus rex has only two fingers. Walt told the animators he thought the dinosaur looked better with three fingers. This fact and scene were later copied for the *Disneyland Primeval Diorama* on the *Disneyland Railroad*.

Fantasia 2000 (1999)

249. **Disney intended on having a sequel to this**, *Fantasia III* (2006), aka *Fantasia 2006*, but it was scrapped. It would have been the only movie to have a part three released in the theaters. In fact, there was a short titled *Little Match Girl* (2006) that was animated for this film, but ended up being released on the DVD re-release of *The Little Mermaid* (1989) in October 2006 because, like *The Little Mermaid*, it was a Hans Christian Andersen story.

250. The "Firebird" sequence was **designed to look like the eruption of Mount St. Helens** in Washington on May 18, 1980.

251. Animator and story writer Joe Grant wrote the segment of the yo-yo-playing flamingos, "The Carnival of the Animals." He originally wanted them to be ostriches. Joe was in charge of the story direction for *Fantasia* (1940), and was the **only staff member on this project who worked on part one** 60 years before.

252. The segment "The Steadfast Tin Soldier" was the **first time a main character was done fully with a computer** outside of Pixar.

253. The whales in the "Pines of Rome" segment were computer animated. However, **their eyes were hand drawn,** as the computer program to animate eyes wasn't up to the standard the animators were looking for.

Finding Dory (2016)

254. **Riley from *Inside Out* (2014) can be seen with her class** peering into Destiny's tank after Dory is dumped into it.

255. Alexander Gould was replaced as the voice of Nemo by Hayden Rolence, because Alexander's voice changed due to puberty. **Alexander can still be heard in the film as the voice of Carl,** the truck driver of the vehicle Dory and Hank steal. When he was younger, Alexander voiced Bambi in *Bambi 2* (2006).

256. **Hayden Rolence voiced Nemo in the video game** *Disney Infinity 3.0* (2015), which came out ten months before *Finding Dory* (2016).

257. **The license plate on the truck is "CALA113,"** which is a reference to the CalArts room A113 in which many of the Disney/Pixar animators studied.

258. This is the **second Pixar film that stars a disembodied Sigourney Weaver**. In this film she is the announcement voice at the Marine Institute. In her first film for Pixar, she voiced the computer of the Axiom in *WALL•E* (2008).

259. **The photo of Darla from the dentist's office** in *Finding Nemo* (2003) can be seen on the wall in the quarantine room when Dory meets Hank.

260. In one year, **Idris Elba did three voice characters for Disney:** Chief Bogo in *Zootopia* (2016), Shere Khan in *The Jungle Book* (2016), and Fluke in *Finding Dory* (2016).

261. The setting of **the film is supposed to be one year after** the events in *Finding Nemo* (2003), even though there is a thirteen-year gap between the two films.

262. The **Pixar Ball can be seen on the steering wheel** of the truck near the end of the film. It is in the center. It looks more like a Captain America shield.

263. In the quarantine room by the shipping dock **there is an overhead pipe labeled with "TL59."** This is a reference to the overhead pipe in the queue for the *Finding Nemo Submarine Voyage* attraction in *Disneyland* that says "Seawater Supply TL59." This stands for *Tomorrowland* 1959, the year the *Submarine Voyage* first opened.

Finding Nemo (2003)

264. Since the DVD release on November 4, 2003, it has sold more copies than any other film.

265. The great white shark, **Bruce, got his name from the movie *Jaws*** (1975). The mechanical shark they used on set while filming *Jaws* was nicknamed Bruce. It was because Steven Spielberg's divorce lawyer's name was Bruce Raiman. It is also speculated that he was named Bruce after the name for the typical Australian male derived from the skit *The Bruces* from *Monty Python's Flying Circus* (1969-1974).

266. When Dory suffered a nosebleed, it was the **first time blood was ever depicted on-screen in a Pixar film**. Unless you count the droplet in *A Bug's Life* when the mosquito in the bug bar orders a "Bloody Mary O+." Most of the younger viewers, and some older ones, won't even know what that is. A bloody nose is clearly blood.

267. The dentist's **diploma on the wall was awarded by Pixar University School of Dentistry** and has a three-eyed monster on it.

268. In the waiting room of the dentist's office, **you can spot Buzz Lightyear on the floor** near the toy box.

269. The child in the dentist's waiting room is reading a **comic with Mr. Incredible on the back**.

270. While the bagged fish are rolling across the road, the **Pizza Planet truck drives by**.

271. After the bagged up fish roll out the window and into the sea, a yellow car drives by on the street. **It is actually Luigi** from the movie *Cars* (2006).

272. When the dentist is photographing Nemo, **the A113 can be seen on the front of his camera**.

273. The **computer program that was used to animate the anemones** in the sea, was also used to animate the hair on Sully in *Monsters, Inc.* (2001), the film before this one.

274. Deb and her alter ego, Flow, **was a play on the term "Ebb and Flow,"** which means a recurrent or rhythmical pattern of coming and going, like the ocean's tide.

275. The seagulls were given the blank, empty, **emotionless look after the penguin in the Wallace & Gromit** stop-motion cartoon *The Wrong Trousers* (1993).

276. Selling over 41 million copies, *Finding Nemo* is the **top-selling DVD of all time**, as of September 2015.

The Fox and the Hound (1981)

277. During the storm sequence, **old animation from *Bambi* is re-used**. This includes clips of a bird flying into her nest, ducks waddling into a pond, quails running to seek shelter, etc. Footage of young Wart as a squirrel in *The Sword in the Stone* running up a tree can be seen, too.

278. Although **this film is based on the novel *The Fox and the Hound*** (1967) by Daniel P. Mannix, it was altered so much that it barely resembles the original novel, with the exception of the title and most of the character names.

279. **The novel was dramatically darker than the film ended up being.** In the novel, Tod and Copper were never friends. Tod would tease the other dogs in the story, getting them riled up. The ages of Chief and Copper were reversed, and their character roles of who was jealous of whom were reversed. Tod intentionally leads Chief to his death by jumping out of the way of an oncoming train, tricking Chief into getting hit. Tod had two vixens that he has litters of kits with. Subsequently they were all shot by the Master, who is named Amos Slade in the movie. Master and Copper go on a hunt for Tod, and Copper chases him all night until the morning when Tod drops dead of exhaustion. Copper collapses on Tod, near-death himself. Master nurses Copper back to health before he himself was sent to a retirement home. Since no dogs were allowed there, he took Copper outside and covered his eyes while Copper licked his hand and shot him.

280. **The bear's growls were provided by voice actor Candy Candido.** He was also the snarling of Shere Khan in *The Jungle Book* (1967), Brutus and Nero in *The Rescuers* (1977), was the voice of the Indian Chief in *Peter Pan* (1953), Fidget in *The Great Mouse Detective* (1986), the angry apple tree in *The Wizard of Oz* (1939), the Captain of the Guards crocodile in *Robin Hood* (1973), Maleficent's goon in *Sleeping Beauty* (1959), Ben in *Gentle Ben* (1967), and Lumpjaw the Black Bear (growls) in *Fun and Fancy Free* (1947). You can hear Candy's menacing laugh in Disneyland's *The Haunted Mansion* in the graveyard scene and as you exit the building. He also reprised the roll of the Indian Chief for *Peter Pan's Flight*. He was married to Anita Gordon, the voice of the Singing Harp in *Mickey and the Beanstalk* (1947).

281. The **snarling sounds of the bear was provided by seasoned voice actor Clarence Nash**, the voice of Donald Duck.

282. Tod got his name from the **Middle English word "todde," which means fox.**

283. This was the **last Disney-animated feature to conclude with "The End - Walt Disney Productions."** The next animated feature to be released, The Black Cauldron (1985), was the first one with closing credits.

284. **Sandy Duncan was the voice of Vixey.** She had just come off of a three-year run on Broadway where she portrayed Peter Pan on stage.

285. **This film marks the "changing of the guard,"** if you will, between the old-school animators, Wolfgang Reitherman, Ollie Johnston, and Frank Thomas, with the new-school animators that began working on full-length animated Disney films with this one, John Musker, Michael Peraza Jr., Patricia Peraza, Brad Bird, Tim Burton, and John Lasseter. There were also, fairly new to the company, animators who had already worked on a film or two like Gary Goldman, Randy Cartwright, Glen Keane, and Ron Clements.

286. **This was the tipping point for the animation department** when they slipped into the "dark ages." Don Bluth lost interest with the Disney Animation Department and wasn't happy with how things were going, so he left and took 11 other animators, about 17% of the animation team, with him to start up his own animation company. Don Bluth and his team put out films like *All Dogs Go to Heaven*, *The Secret of NIMH*, *The Land Before Time*, and *An American Tail*, which gave Disney a run for their money. This caused a slump or dethroning of Disney in the 1980's, causing them to step up their game, subsequently producing *The Little Mermaid* (1989).

287. **This film doesn't have a main villain.** Amos Slade is just a hunter out to catch a fox, who later spares Tod's life when he saw how important he was to Copper. The bear is acting purely out of instinct, much like the rat in *Lady and The Tramp* (1955).

288. **When Chief got hit by the train, he was supposed to die.** The animation team had worries about eliminating one of the main characters and making the scene too intense for children, just as they did with Trusty in *Lady and the Tramp* (1955). They altered the storyboard and had him set up to just be injured by the train, thereby giving Copper a motive to go after Tod.

289. There is an "Easter Egg" of **Wart as a squirrel from *The Sword in the Stone* (1963).** He can be seen jumping from the tree just as it starts to storm after Tod was abandoned.

Frozen (2013) - See *Disney Princess Collection* on page 90 for Fun Facts

Fun and Fancy Free (1947)

290. This film was **the fourth of the six-package films released**. This one consisted of two shorts, *Bongo* and *Mickey and the Beanstalk.*

291. The segment, *Bongo*, was **based off of the story *Little Bear Bongo*** by Sinclair Lewis and published in Cosmopolitan in 1930.

292. *Mickey and the Beanstalk* was **based on *The Story of Jack Spriggins and the Enchanted Bean* from 1734,** which was a Cornish fairy tale. It is said that the story is much older than that and is actually about 4,000 years old.

293. This **isn't the first time Walt told the story of Jack**. His first telling was in the black and white Laugh-O-Gram studio-produced short *Jack and the Beanstalk* (1922).

294. Comedian Billy Gilbert found out that one of the dwarfs' in *Snow White* was going to be named Sneezy, so he called Walt and gave him his famous sneezing gag and got the part. **He was also the voice of Willie the Giant** from the *Mickey and the Beanstalk* segment.

295. The singing harp was voiced by **Anita Gordon. She was married to voice actor Candy Candido**, the voice of Lumpjaw in the *Bongo* segment.

296. This was the **last film in which Walt Disney provides the voice for Mickey Mouse**, although he did the short *Mickey's Delayed Date,* which was released on October 3, 1947, two weeks after *Mickey and the Beanstalk.*

The Good Dinosaur (2015)

297. The release of this film marked the **first time Pixar ever released two movies in the same year**. The first film they released in 2015 was *Inside Out* and it was in June.

298. When you see the asteroid field in the beginning of the film, **you can spot the Pizza Planet truck** over toward the left.

299. **You can spot the A113** made out of sticks in the fence around the chicken pen.

300. This is the **lowest-grossing Pixar film** ever, only taking in $332 million. *A Bug's Life* (1998) took in $363 million, which is $539 million after inflation.

301. This is the **first Pixar film to not be nominated for Best Animated Feature** that isn't a "part one." *Cars 2* (2011) and *Monsters University* (2013) were also not nominated, but they were sequels.

302. When Arlo jumps in the water to wash off after his encounter with the gopher-like creatures, **you can spot Hank from *Finding Dory*** (2016) hidden among the rocks in bottom of the water.

303. After Arlo and Spot eat the fermented fruit, they begin to hallucinate. This is the **first time Disney has had a scene like this** since the Pink Elephants on Parade scene in *Dumbo* (1941).

304. While they are hallucinating, **you can see the Pixar ball float by**.

305. One of the few times a **T-Rex is shown to be a good guy**. Another example would be Tiny from *Meet the Robinsons* (2007).

The Great Mouse Detective (1986)

306. This **movie was based on a book series titled *Basil of Baker Street*** by Eve Titus. There were five titles in the series: *Basil of Baker Street* (1958), *Basil and the Lost Colony* (1964), *Basil and the Pygmy Cats* (1971), *Basil in Mexico* (1976), and *Basil in the Wild West* (1982).

307. Basil of Baker Street **is the name of the mouse who portrays the animated mouse character** of Sherlock Holmes. The name of the actor who plays the character of Sherlock Holmes in 16 movies from 1939 to 1953 is **Basil Rathbone** (13 June 1892 – 21 July 1967). Archive recordings of Basil Rathbone as Sherlock Holmes were used for the voice of Sherlock in the beginning of the film.

308. The clock tower scene is the **first major use of computer animation** (the clock's gears) in a feature-length animated film. The same scene was also the first time traditionally-animated characters were put inside a computer-generated background by animator Phil Nibbelink.

309. **Bill, the lizard from *Alice in Wonderland*** (1951), can be seen as part of Rattigan's gang in the bar scene.

310. The **voice of Professor Ratigan was provided by actor Vincent Price**. The animators copied some of his exaggerated Shakespearean movements and incorporated them into the character.

311. The **name Basil was taken from the Sherlock Holmes book** *The Adventure of Black Peter* (1904) by Arthur Conan Doyle. In it, Sherlock goes undercover as Basil, a sea captain, and likewise, Disney's Basil also goes undercover as a sea captain.

312. When Professor Ratigan is complaining about Basil during his song "Oh Ratigan," the scene pans over to a shelf showing a voodoo doll of Basil. **The doll is a replica of the Basil from the book series;** it is even wearing his famous deerstalker hat.

313. **Candy Candido is the voice of Fidget the bat**. He was also the voice of the little mouse in the pub that shouts at the octopus "*Get off, you eight-legged bum.*" Candy's deep, gravelly voice can be heard as the Indian Chief in *Peter Pan* (1953), the Captain of The Guards rhino in *Robin Hood* (1973), the voice of Maleficent's goon in *Sleeping Beauty* (1959), the laughing voice you can hear in *Disneyland's Haunted Mansion* graveyard, and other roles.

Hercules (1997)

314. When Hercules enters Phil's hut, he bangs his head on a low-hanging mast. Phil tells him it is the mast of the Argo. In Greek mythology, Jason, the captain of the Argo, was killed when the mast hit him in the head. In the myth, **Hercules was one of the heroes on the Argo**.

315. When Meg sings her song "I Won't Say I'm In Love," **the muses become busts taking on the form of the five fallen busts** from inside *The Haunted Mansion*.

316. **Megara was voiced by Susan Egan**. She was the first actress to play Belle in the Broadway musical *Beauty and the Beast* for two and a half years. Susan is most notable for her singing voice as she was cast as the singing voice of Angel in *Lady and the Tramp 2: Scamp's Adventure* (2001), Lin in the Studio Ghibli film *Spirited Away* (2001), and Gina in the Ghibli film *Porco Rosso* (1992) (English dub in 2003).

317. Even though this is of Greek mythology, **Hercules is from Roman mythology**. In Greek he would be Heracles. If it was Roman, his father would be Jupiter and not Zeus.

318. While Hercules is posing for a painting, he is wearing a skin of a lion. After he tosses it to the ground, you can see that **the skin is that of Scar from *The Lion King*** (1994). In The Lion King, Mufasa queries, *"What am I going to do with him?"* To which Zazu replies, *"He'd make a very handsome throw rug."*

319. When Pain and Panic were pretending to be children trapped under the rocks, **they suggest to call IX-I-I,** which translated from Roman numerals is 9-1-1.

320. When Phil says to Hercules, *"Two words. I-am-retired,"* it is actually three words, which is why Hercules is counting on his fingers. **In Greek, "I-am-retired" translates to "Είμαι συνταξιούχος,"** which is two words. In English, it would be spelled Eimai syntaxiouchos.

321. Originally, Disney wanted Jack Nicholson to be the voice of Hades, but his high-salary request caused Disney to look elsewhere. **They ended up casting John Lithgow to be the voice**. He recorded the dialogue for Hades for nine months. It is said he was cut from the film due to lacking in the comedy department, at least for what Disney was looking for. He went on to star in the six-season run of *3rd Rock from the Sun* (1996-2001), one of the best sitcoms of the 90's, and Disney cast James Woods.

322. **James Woods ended up ad-libbing** quite a few lines in the film.

323. **James Woods has said that this role was one of his favorites** and offered to do the voice of Hades whenever Disney wants him to. He reprised the role for *Hercules: Zero to Hero* (1999), *Hercules* (1998-1999), *Mickey's House of Villains* (2001), *House of Mouse* (2001-2002), and six versions of the *Kingdom of Hearts* video games.

324. In the film, Hercules meets Megara at the river on his way to Themes. He saves her by beating Nessus the centaur. **In Greek mythology, this is how Herc meets his second wife, Deianira**. The river centaur would ferry people across the river on his back. He attempted to kidnap Deianira when Herc swooped in and shot him with an arrow. As he lays dying, he whispers to Deianira to save his blood and mix it with olive oil and smear it on Herc's shirt to make him remain faithful. Later on she fears that Herc will leave her so she smears the mixture on his lion-skin shirt. Instead of it making him faithful, its ends up burning his skin. It hurt him so bad, he threw himself on a funeral pyre and died.

325. **Hercules is the cousin of Ariel and Melody** from *The Little Mermaid* (1989) and *The Little Mermaid 2: Return to the Sea* (2000). Zeus is the father of Hercules. Triton is the father of Ariel. Poseidon is the father of Triton. Poseidon is the bother of Zeus. If you look at the family tree, the grey indicates the non-Greek mythology. It only exists in the Disney universe. Technically, Triton is the foster father of Athena, who is the mother of Ariel, but then that would also make her Ariel's foster sister, and Triton would be the father and foster-grandfather of Ariel. Zeus' son is Perseus, who fathered Alcmene, who had Hercules with Zeus, her grandfather. So technically, Zeus is the father and great-grandfather of Hercules. This is all so messed up. But that's Greek mythology for you. There are more people in the family tree; I just don't have room for them all.

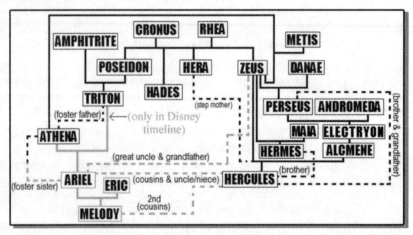

326. **Disney changed the story of Hercules' birth**. Hera isn't his birth mother; she is his step-mother. Zeus fathered Hercules with the human Alcmene. In the movie, Pain and Panic poison Hercules to take away his powers, but in actuality he was the way he was because he was half god by birth. Alcmene had two other sons, which were half-brothers to Hercules, Iphicles and Laonme. Iphicles had a son named Iolaus, the one who married Megara after she left Hercules.

194

327. Hercules actually met Megara after he saved Thebes from the Minyans at Orchomenus. **Megara was the eldest daughter of Creon, the King of Thebes**. Would that make her a princess? Creon gave her to Hercules for defending them. She and Hercules had one son and one daughter together. Hera struck Hercules with madness which caused him to lose his mind and slaughter them. Megara left Hercules and married Iolaus, the nephew of Hercules, who fought alongside him as one of the Argonauts.

328. Hermes delivering a floral arrangement to Zeus and Hera was **a parody of the FTD Florist logo Mercury**. In Roman mythology, Hermes is Mercury. He even has his winged sandals.

329. The look and easy laid back nature of **Hermes was designed after Paul Shaffer** (no relation to me), his voice actor. Paul reprised his voice role for Hermes in the television series *Hercules* (1998-1999).

330. After this film came out, **there was a television series that followed Hercules though his training** with Phil titled *Hercules* (1998-1999), and a TV movie titled *Hercules: Zero to Hero* (1999) that was about Hercules in the academy for the gods.

Home on the Range (2004)

331. The **film earned a PG rating** because of Maggie's line, "Yeah, they're real. Quit Staring," in reference to her udders.

332. This was to be Disney's **last hand-drawn animated feature**. Five years later they attempted to make the animation style popular again with the release of *The Princess and the Frog* (2009) and *Winnie the Pooh* (2011). Since Pooh, no hand-drawn films have been released.

333. With a production budget of $110 million, and only taking in $104 million, **this film is unofficially blamed for the ending of hand-drawn animation**.

334. The name **Alameda Slim was inspired by Wilf "Montana Slim" Carter**, a yodeling country singer. Montana was changed to Alameda possibly after Alameda County, the county in which Pixar is located.

335. This film's trailer was the **last Disney trailer narrated by Mark Elliot**. He started being the Disney voice trailer guy in 1983 and had his catch phrase "And now, our feature presentation," during the home video previews.

The Hunchback of Notre Dame (1996)

336. This **movie is based on the book** *The Hunchback of Notre-Dame* by Victor Hugo and was published in 1831.

337. The author of the original story, Victor Hugo, inspired the names of **two of the gargoyles**, Victor and Hugo.

338. The song "Hellfire" was almost completely cut from the movie and is **considered to be one of the darkest Disney songs** ever created.

339. Due to its dark and sexual themes, **the film almost received a PG rating**. It would have been the first to receive such a rating since *The Black Cauldron* (1985).

340. When Quasimodo and Esmeralda are in his room and she looks at the unfinished dolls, **one of the dolls resembles the baker from the opening scene of *Beauty and the Beast*** (1991), when Belle is singing "Belle."

341. While Quasimodo is singing "Out There," **you can spot Belle from *Beauty and the Beast*** (1991), Pumba from *The Lion King* (1994), and Carpet from *Aladdin* (1992) when the camera pans down through the town.

342. **You can hear the Goofy Holler** as the soldiers fall after Quasimodo pulls the rope they were climbing.

The Incredibles (2004)

343. Instead of the current title, the original **working title of the film was "The Invincibles."**

344. In the entire film you can hear about **640 gunshots, 35 explosions, and you see 189 buttons** being pressed.

345. The voice of Syndrome, Jason Lee, recorded all of his lines over a four-day span. It took Craig T. Nelson, Mr. Incredible, two years to record his.

346. **Edith Head (1897-1981), the costume designer** in Hollywood for 57 years and who has 444 movie and television episode credits to her name, was the inspiration for Edna Mode.

347. **DC Comics has a character named Elasti-Girl**, who has the power of enlarging or shrinking herself, or just one limb at a time. She first surfaced in the DC world in 1963. Pixar compromised with DC and only calls her Elastigirl in the movie and Mrs. Incredible for promotional purposes. Elasti-Girl's real name is Rita Farr, and Mrs. Incredible's name is Helen Parr.

348. **Nicholas Bird is the son of the film's director, Brad Bird.** He provided the voice of Rusty McAllister, the boy on the tricycle. He was also the voice of Squirt in *Finding Nemo* (2003).

349. The director, Brad Bird, **came up with the concept for this film in the early 1990's** when he was trying to juggle work and family life. He originally envisioned it being a cell-animation film.

350. **Sarah Vowell was 33 years old when she voiced Violet**. It is said that Brad Bird heard her on a Public Radio International program and wanted her for the role. At this point, Sarah had never done voice work before. Brad had the animators animate a segment from a show she was on, titled *This American Life*, and send it to her.

351. On the island, Elastigirl is trying to locate Mr. Incredible. On the computer terminal, she sees that he is on "Level A1" and in "Cell Block 13." **Put them together and you get A113.**

352. In the bonus footage there is an alternate opening. Amongst baby **Violet's toys, which are strewn about, is the Pixar ball**. In the attached short, *Jack-Jack Attack*, he has the Pixar ball in with his toys.

Inside Out (2015)

353. The **screams of little Riley were archived recordings of Mary Gibbs** screaming for her character of Boo from *Monsters, Inc.* (2001).

354. If you remove all of the scenes that were "inside" Riley's head, the movie would **only be 15 minutes long**.

355. When Riley and her parents are eating Chinese takeout, they are asking her about her first day of school. The take-out boxes they are eating out of are **the same take-out box that Gypsy Moth flew out of** in *A Bug's Life* (1998).

356. The scene when Riley is a toddler and her dad is trying to feed her broccoli was **changed to green bell peppers in Japan,** as the children there dislike them.

357. When Riley is recalling their trip out to San Francisco, she remembers the roadside stop where they took a photo with a triceratops. **That triceratops is the Pet Collector from *The Good Dinosaur*** (2015).

358. At that same stop, **you can see the back end and tail of Arlo** from *The Good Dinosaur* (2015).

359. When Riley is playing "The Floor Is Lava" game, you can spot **a magazine on the coffee table with Colette** from *Ratatouille* (2007) on the cover.

360. **The birds from the *For the Birds* (2000) short** can be seen sitting on a telephone line during the road trip to San Francisco.

361. **This film is set in San Francisco.** The film *Big Hero 6* (2014) was set in San Fransokyo, a hybrid city of San Francisco and Tokyo.

362. When Joy is running through long-term memory, she passes **a memory ball on the ground that has the Pizza Planet truck** in it.

363. When Riley is chasing Bing Bong through the house, they **pass the Pixar ball on the floor** next to the bookshelf.

364. When the house of cards is destroyed in Riley's mind, there is a game box in the background titled "Find Me" and **it has a picture of Nemo on it**.

365. When the train pulls up to the stop and Bing Bong is running to it, **you can spot a picture in a frame of Figment** from the *Disney World* attraction *Journey Into Imagination*.

The Jungle Book (1967)

366. This was the **last animated feature film** personally overseen by Walt Disney.

367. The **narrator of the film was Sebastian Cabot**, who also provided the voice of Bagheera. He also narrated the films *The Sword In The Stone* (1963), in which he voiced Sir Ector, and four Pooh films with *The Many Adventures Of Winnie The Pooh* (1977) being the last film of his career.

368. **The first African-American animator hired by the Disney Company**, Floyd Norman, worked on this film. He started out with Disney as a clean-up artist on *Sleeping Beauty* (1959), then moved up to assistant animator on *101 Dalmatians* (1961) and *The Sword in the Stone* (1963).

369. **There was a nearsighted character named Rocky the Rhino** that ended up getting cut from the film because Walt didn't find his comedic scenes very funny. Milt Kahl was set to be the animator of this character. Rocky ended up making an appearance in the film *Bedknobs and Broomsticks* (1971), and again in the series *Jungle Cubs* (1996-1998). He wouldn't join a Jungle Book film until the 2016 live-action release.

370. With a budget of $4 million, the film needed to succeed for the animation company to keep going without Walt. Nobody knew how things would move forward without his guidance. **The film ended up making over $205 million**, securing the jobs of the animators in the Animation Department. An almost collapse of the animation company wouldn't happen again until the mid-1980's.

371. Rudyard Kipling was the author of the original *Jungle Book* novel. According to his daughter Elsie Kipling Bambridge, **"Mowgli" is pronounced "MAU-glee,"** not "MOH-glee." It is said that she never forgave Disney for the mistake.

372. Baloo the bear (bhaaloo), Bagheera the panther (baagh), and Hathi the elephant (haathee) are **named after the words in Hindi for their species**. "Baagh" means tiger, and another name for a certain species of Black Panther is black tiger. Shere Khan (shir Khan) means Tiger King or Tiger Leader.

373. *There are **six actors in this film who also lent their voices to the Winnie the Pooh films**;*
   - *Clint Howard*, brother of Ron Howard and uncle to Bryce Dallas Howard, started out his acting career on the *Andy Griffith Show*. One of Howard's other roles as a child actor was the voice of the elephant Hathi's son, Hathi Jr. He was also the voice of Roo in *Winnie the Pooh and the Honey Tree* (1966) and *Winnie the Pooh and the Blustery Day* (1968), which were later

incorporated into *The Many Adventures of Winnie the Pooh* (1977).

- *Bruce Reitherman* did the voice for Mowgli in this film, as well as the voice of Christopher Robin in *The Many Adventures of Winnie the Pooh* (1977) and *Winnie the Pooh and the Honey Tree* (1966). His father is Wolfgang Reitherman, the movie's director.
- Sterling *Holloway* voices Kaa, as well as Winnie the Pooh in four of the *Winnie the Pooh* movies.
- Sebastian Cabot, who voices Bagheera, was the narrator for *Winnie the Pooh and the Honey Tree* (1966), *Winnie the Pooh and the Blustery Day* (1968), *Winnie the Pooh and Tigger Too* (1974), and *The Many Adventures of Winnie the Pooh* (1977).
- Hal Smith, the voice of the Slob Elephant and a monkey, was also Owl in *Winnie the Pooh and the Honey Tree* (1966), *Winnie the Pooh and the Blustery Day* (1968), and *The Many Adventures of Winnie the Pooh* (1977). He was in a total of eight movies and two television series.
- Ralph Wright, who voices Gloomy Elephant, was also the voice of Eeyore in *Winnie the Pooh and the Honey Tree* (1966), *Winnie the Pooh and the Blustery Day* (1968), *The Many Adventures of Winnie the Pooh* (1977), and *Winnie the Pooh and a Day for Eeyore* (1983). Not only did he do the voice work, he was also the one who wrote the stories for three of the Pooh films and *The Jungle Book*, along with nine other Disney films and a handful of shorts.

Lady and the Tramp (1955)

374. **The story first started development in 1937,** when animator/writer Joe Grant approached Walt with an idea for a story about dogs. He had sketched his springer spaniel, Lady, to create a storyboard. His dog, Lady, was having to deal with a new baby entering the family, so he thought it would be a great premise for a story. Walt didn't think it was that strong of a story so he negated it. In 1943, Walt read a short story in Cosmopolitan called "Happy Dan, the Whistling Dog" by Ward Greene. Walt noticed the similarities between this story and the one pitched to him in 1937. He decided to hire Ward to write the story. Production on *Lady and the Tramp* began shortly after, but came to a halt when Disney began producing propaganda films for the military in 1943 for WWII. Ward wrote the novel "*Lady and the Tramp; the Story of Two Dogs*" in 1953. Walt wanted it published before the movie was completed so the audience could familiarize themselves with the characters. The book ended up being much of the source material for the film in the end. Eighteen years after Joe Grant approached Walt with his idea, it came to fruition.

375. Peg, the dog in the dog pound, was **named after the actress who is voicing her**, Peggy Lee. She also voiced Darling, Si, and Am in the same film.

376. In 1987, Disney released *Lady and the Tramp* on VHS and earned $98 million from sales. **Peggy Lee took Disney to court** because, in her contract, she owned the rights to the songs that she wrote, "He's A Tramp" and "The Siamese Cat Song." The court settled in 1991 awarding her $2.3 million.

377. The movie was re-released in theater in 1962 as part of **a double feature with the Disney film** *Almost Angels* (1962).

378. The inspiration for having **Jim Dear give Darling a puppy in a hatbox came from Walt Disney himself**. He had given Lillian a Chow Chow puppy for Christmas in that manner. They named their puppy Sunee.

379. It is said that **Wolfgang Reitherman kept rats in his office** to study for the animation sequence he did between Tramp and the rat.

380. The film's setting was partly inspired by Walt Disney's boyhood hometown of **Marceline, Missouri**.

381. The dog that was used as the model for Tramp was adopted from the city dog pound and lived on the studio lot, and **was also a female**.

382. **Dallas "Dal" McKennon was the laughing voice of the hyenas in the zoo**. You can hear this same laughing track by the hyenas on the *it's a small world* attraction in *Disneyland*. In this same film he voiced Pedro, the Chihuahua in the pound, Toughy, the dog that banged his tail on the pail, and the human with the bowler passing the zoo that Tramp tried to pass off as his owner. He also voiced the Angel in the "Johnny Appleseed" segment of *Melody Time* (1948), Cal McNab, Paul's father, in *Paul Bunyan* (1958), the owl that dances with Aurora and also Diablo in *Sleeping Beauty* (1959), random barking dogs in *One Hundred and One Dalmatians* (1961), the fox and a hunting horse in *Mary Poppins* (1964), bees as a collective in *Winnie the Pooh and the Honey Tree* (1966), Max the dog in *How the Grinch Stole Christmas* (1966), the Bear in *Bedknobs and Broomsticks* (1971), and the voice of Gumby in that series from 1988. While you are in *Disneyland*, you can hear him doing the safety announcement for *Big Thunder Mountain Railroad*.

383. The alligator that says, "Glad to oblige" and snaps his jaws shut was **voiced by Thurl Ravenscroft**, who also does the singing fallen bust in the graveyard of the *Haunted Mansion* singing Grimm Grinning Ghosts.

384. Thurl voicing the snapping alligator being followed by Dal voicing the hyenas **isn't the first time those two actors have done vocals in a movie together**. Thurl was also a singing voice in the *it's a small world* attraction, *One Hundred and One Dalmatians* (1961), *Bedknobs and Broomsticks* (1971), *Johnny Appleseed* (1948), *Sleeping Beauty* (1959), and the hog in *Mary Poppins* (1964). Meanwhile, Dal was the fox, and Dal was Cal McNab while Thurl was Paul in *Paul Bunyan* (1958), and Dal was

200

Max in *How The Grinch Stole Christmas* (1966) while Thurl sang the popular song "You're A Mean One Mr. Grinch."

385. The young **puppy at the end of the film that resembles Tramp is Scamp**. He eventually got his own movie *Lady and the Tramp II: Scamp's Adventure* (2001).

386. At the time of its release, it was the **highest grossing Disney animated film since *Snow White and the Seven Dwarfs*** (1937).

387. **Barbara Luddy was almost 50 years old when she voiced Lady**. But she had many other rolls she played for Disney such as Merryweather from *Sleeping Beauty* (1959), Mother Church Mouse and Mother Rabbit from *Robin Hood* (1973), Rover from *One Hundred and One Dalmatians* (1961), and Kanga from all the *Winnie the Pooh* movies (1966-1977).

388. The voice of Aunt Sarah was provided by Verna Felton (Queen of Hearts, Fairy Godmother, and Flora). **She is the mother of Lee Millar**, the voice of Jim Dear and the dog catcher.

Lilo & Stitch (2002)

389. The soundtrack for *Lilo & Stitch* features seven **Elvis Presley songs** (five sung by Presley). This is more than any other movie, including ones that Elvis Presley was in.

390. Lilo's pet fish in the movie *Lilo and Stitch* is named Pudge. **He is a Humuhumunukunukuāpuaʻa (hoo-moo hoo-moo new-koo new-koo ah-poo-ah ah)**, the Hawaiian state fish, aka Reef Triggerfish. It was revealed in the film that Lilo's parents died in a car accident due to bad weather. Lilo gives Pudge the fish a sandwich every Thursday because she says, *"Pudge controls the weather."* We are to assume it is an offering or appeasement to the one who controls the weather to prevent future storms, as that is how Lilo lost her parents.

391. The film utilized **watercolors for the background art**. This is the first Disney-animated feature to do so since *Dumbo* (1941).

392. Most of the **background artwork are actual views that can be found in Hawaii**. This is most noticeable when Lilo and Stitch go on the big wheel ride around the island.

393. On November 18, 2004, *Magic Kingdom* opened the attraction *Stitch's Great Escape*. On opening day, **Disney covered *Cinderella's Castle* with toilet paper** and spray painted on the front "Stitch is king" to imply that Stitch vandalized the palace. There was even furniture strewn about near the castle's entrance.

394. Stitch was the **original character to break the barriers of another film**. Before the film's release, Disney released several teaser trailers with him crossing over into scenes of other Disney films.
   • He interrupted Aladdin and Jasmine singing "A Whole New World" and took Jasmine away in his space ship.

- He splashed Ariel with a wave while surfing to interrupt her singing "Part of Your World."
- When Mrs. Potts can be heard singing "Beauty and The Beast," Stitch sneaks into the ball room and climbs the ceiling to accidently drop the chandelier to the floor causing Beast and Belle rolling to the floor and sending Belle off to her room.
- Stitch is presented to the animals at the base of Pride Rock in place of Simba. Rafiki drops him and all the animals run off. Stitch steps up to the edge of the rock, clears his throat, and attempts to roar like Simba.

395. Due to the popularity of this film, **Disney released three subsequent films**; *Stitch! The Movie* (2003), *Lilo & Stitch 2: Stitch Has a Glitch* (2005), and *Leroy & Stitch* (2006). Stitch has also appeared in two separate television series; *Lilo & Stitch: The Series* (2003-2006) and *Stitch!* (2008-2012), which was basically a Japanese-animated series which showed what would have happened if Stitch landed on an island in Japan rather than Hawaii.

396. It always surprises people when they find out that Daveigh Chase, **the voice of Lilo, was also the creepy little girl in the horror film** *The Ring* (2002). When Disney worked on the English dub of the high-grossing Japanese animated film, *Spirited Away* (2002), but released in English in 2003, they used Daveigh to provide the voice of the main character, Chihiro. After that, Daveigh reprised her roll of Lilo in all the films, and the American series, with the exception of *Lilo & Stitch 2*, when Lilo was voiced by Dakota Fanning.

397. The name **Lilo in Hawaiian translates to "Generous One"** in English.

398. Take notice that when Lilo throws her doll to the ground, walks away, and runs back to pick her up, **the doll smiles**.

399. **Jason Scott Lee (David) and Tia Carrera (Nani) both helped the writers with the dialogue** and accents since both of them are from Hawaii. Jason was born in Los Angeles but was raised in Hawaii.

400. **Jason Scott Lee was in a Disney film prior to this film**. He was Mowgli in *The Jungle Book* (1994).

401. The photo of Elvis and the live-action monster **movie footage used was real** and was inserted into the films as it was.

402. Some of the **alien designs were inspired by other Disney characters**, like Tigger and Piglet. They can be seen on the mother ship.

403. This movie, along with *The Princess and the Frog* (2009), were **the only two films to actually do well in the theaters** from 2000-2010.

404. The character of **Cobra Bubbles was designed after the character of Marsellus Wallace** from *Pulp Fiction* (1994), which was played by Ving Rhames, who is also the voice of Cobra.

405. When Pleakley and the Grand Councilwoman visit Jamba in prison, **Dr. Jacques Von Hamsterviel can be seen in the cell to the right**. He will later be the main villain in the Lilo & Stitch series.

406. This is **one of the few Disney-animated films that actually takes place in the present**, at least at the time of the film release. The other films would be *Dumbo* (1941), *Bambi* (1942), *101 Dalmatians* (1961), *The Rescuers* (1977), *The Fox and the Hound* (1981), *The Rescuers Down Under* (1990), *Oliver & Company* (1988), *Bolt* (2008), and *Zootopia* (2016).

407. This was the **first animated Disney film to be set in the state of Hawaii**.

408. While tracking Stitch, the Galactic ship traces his whereabouts to "*Quadrant 17, Section 005, Area 51. A planet called Eee-arth.*" This is one of **several reference to the Area 51 located in Nevada**, a place where our government keeps aliens.

409. Lilo wakes Noni up in the middle of the night to show her that Stitch can play a record with his fingernail and mouth. On the wall in the background is **a poster for the movie *Mulan*** (1998).

410. When Stitch rolls into a ball and is rolling around the kitchen, **you can see the Pixar Ball on a stool** in the background.

411. When Lilo and Stitch are walking through town, **they pass a restaurant called "Mulan Wok."**

412. If you take a close look at David's hook necklace, you will see **that it resembles the magical hook of Maui**, the demi-god from *Moana* (2016).

The Lion King (1994)

413. The film **was titled *King of the Jungle*** throughout most of the animation.

414. If you adjust for inflation, the $968,483,777 the film made in the box office ranks it as the **top- grossing animated film of all time,** raking in $1,314,737,068. Without inflation, the film ranks in 6th place. It does currently stand in 1st place among the traditional hand-drawn animated films. The film in second place is *The Simpsons Movie* (2007), which took in just over $527 million, or a little over half of what *The Lion King* took in 13 years prior. Compared to all the movies ever made, live action and animated, it ranks in 29th place.

415. **For rankings in terms of attendance, it takes 1st place**. This is primarily due to the fact that an average theater ticket in 1994 was about $4.18 versus the $8.58 it cost in 2016, up to $16.09 for IMAX 3D, for a film like *Zootopia* (2016).

416. The film was **re-released on December 25, 2002, for viewing in IMAX**, and took in another $15.6 million.

417. Again, the film was **re-released for a two-week period on September 16, 2011, for IMAX 3D** viewing. It took in another $30.2 million, ranking it in 1st place for the weekend. This is the second film to ever make it to first

place again with a re-release. The first film to do so was *Star Wars: Episode VI -Return of the Jedi* (1983) in 1997.

418. **The film has spawned other films and TV shows in its wake:** T*he Lion King II: Simba's Pride* (1998), *The Lion King 1 ½* (2004), the TV series *The Lion King's Timon and Pumbaa* (1995-1999), which ran for 85 episodes, and *The Lion Guard: Return of the Roar* (2015), which was the pilot movie for the series *The Lion Guard* (2016-present).

419. **The Broadway musical *The Lion King* first debuted July 8, 1997**, at the Orpheum Theatre in Minneapolis, Minnesota, before heading to Broadway October 15, 1997. The musical went on tour and is still touring the world in 2016. It is Broadway's third longest-running performance in history and is the highest grossing Broadway production of all time, taking in over $1 billion.

420. The moment Pumbaa let one rip, was the **first time a Disney character had ever farted on-screen**. It was a bold step in the direction of bathroom humor for a brand adamant about maintaining a perfectly wholesome image.

421. It is said that **most of the senior animators that were working on the film opted to leave** the production to work on the *Pocahontas* (1996) film, due to little faith in the film's future success. This left mostly newer and first-time animators to work on the film.

422. **Mufasa was voiced by James Earl Jones and Sarabi was voiced by Madge Sinclair**. This isn't the first time they portrayed a king and queen. They both starred side-by-side in Eddie Murphy's film *Coming To America* (1988), in which they played King Jaffe Joffer and Queen Aoleon.

423. Zazu suggests to Mufasa **"He'd make a very handsome throw rug,"** referring to Scar. There is a scene in *Hercules* (1997) where Scar's likeness can be seen being worn by Hercules before tossing him to the floor like a throw rug.

The Little Mermaid (1989) - See *Disney Princess Collection* on page 90 for Fun Facts

Make Mine Music (1946)

424. This was the third of the six-package films, all of which were released in the 1940's. **This film contains the ten shorts:** *The Martins and the Coys, Blue Bayou, All the Cats Join In, Without You, Casey at the Bat, Two Silhouettes, Peter and the Wolf, After You've Gone, Johnnie Fedora and Alice Bluebonnet, and The Whale Who Wanted to Sing at the Met.*

425. Make Mine Music was the **first Disney film released after World War II**.

426. In June 2000, the film was released on VHS and DVD, but **the segment of "The Martins and the Coys" was cut from the film**. Disney felt the gun

play was too violent for children. When the film was released on DVD again in 2013, the scene was added back in.

427. The segment **"Casey At Bat" is based on a baseball poem** titled "Casey at the Bat: A Ballad of the Republic Sung in the Year 1888," which was published in The Daily Examiner (later re-named The San Francisco Examiner) in 1988. The poem was written by Ernest Thayer.

428. **Jerry Colonna is the narrator for the "Casey at Bat" segment** and recites the poem. He was also the narrator in *The Brave Engineer* short (1950), and is best known as the voice of the March Hare in *Alice in Wonderland* (1951). If you have ever looked up "vintage Mickey Mouse" costumes, he is in the photo with his kids meeting the creepy Mickey Mouse.

429. In "The Whale Who Wanted to Sing at the Met*"* segment, **the hero dies at the end.** This is unusual for a Disney film. Willie ends up singing in heaven.

430. The segment "Peter and the Wolf" was based off of the symphonic fairy tale *Peter and the Wolf,* written in 1936 by Sergei Prokofiev. One of the differences between the fairy tale and the Disney version is that **in the movie, the duck named Sonia gets eaten by the wolf**.

431. The wolf in the *Peter and the Wolf* is almost **identical to the wolf in Lambert the Sheepish Lion** (1952). Sterling Holloway is also the narrator in both films, and Candy Candido makes the wolf sounds in both films.

The Many Adventures of Winnie the Pooh (1977)

432. In 1926, English-born writer Alan Alexander Milne (A. A. Milne) had a children's book published called *Winnie-the-Pooh*. In 1928, he had the book *The House at Pooh Corner* published. The characters in the books were inspired by his son, Christopher Robin, and his stuffed animals. Christopher had a stuffed bear named "Edward." Christopher **renamed "Edward" to "Winnie" after the real Canadian black bear "Winnie,"** short for "Winnipeg." "Winnie" was a World War I mascot that was transported to the London Zoo where she lived out her 20-year life, which is where Christopher met her. "The Pooh" was apparently the name of a swan that Christopher incorporated into the full name of "Winnie-the-Pooh." Alan also included his son's other stuffed animals: Piglet, Eeyore, Kanga, Roo, and Tigger. The characters Rabbit and Owl were completely made up by Alan. The character Pooh was modeled after Christopher Robin's stuffed teddy, but the look of Pooh was actually mimicking a teddy named "Growler," the teddy bear belonging to the son of the book's illustrator Ernest Howard Shepard (E.H. Shepherd), who also illustrated the second Pooh book.

433. **The first short-lived six-episode series** *Winnie-the-Pooh* (1952) was produced and aired by the BBC (British Broadcasting Corporation). It

wasn't until Walt Disney Productions picked it up and produced *Winnie-the-Pooh and the Honey Tree* (1966) that it started to become popular.

434. Ernest Howard Shepard also did the illustrations for the book *The Wind in the Willows* (1933), which was originally published in 1908. **It was also turned into a stage play by Alan Alexander Milne in 1929.** In 1949, Disney animated it in *The Adventures of Ichabod and Mr. Toad*.

435. **This movie is actually a collection of three different shorts** that are connected together with extra animation material. The three films are *Winnie the Pooh and the Honey Tree* (1966), *Winnie the Pooh and the Blustery Day* (1968), and *Winnie the Pooh and Tigger Too* (1974).

436. **Winnie-the-Pooh** merchandise outsold Mickey Mouse merchandise for the first time in 1993.

437. **Paul Winchell, the voice of Tigger, ad-libbed the "TTFN, ta-ta for now"** line and came up with the Tigger laugh.

438. Although, **best known for the voice of Tigger in 29 of the Winnie-the-Pooh movies** (1968-1999), Paul Winchell, is also known for voicing Gargamel in *The Smurfs* (1981), the Siamese cat named Shun Gon in *The AristoCats* (1970), Boomer the woodpecker in *The Fox and the Hound* (1981), and as Zummi Gummi in *Adventures of the GummiBears* (1985). In the Dr. Seuss short *Green Eggs and Ham* (1973), he voiced Sam-I-Am. His first voice-over role was Pig-Pen in *It's the Great Pumpkin, Charlie Brown* (1966). In commercials, he voiced the character of Burger Chef for the fast food chain Burger Chef, opened in 1954 and closed in 1996, the leader of the Scrubbing Bubbles for Dow Chemicals, and Mr. Owl for Tootsie Roll Pops. You can hear him as Tigger in *The Many Adventures of Winnie the Pooh* attraction in *Magic Kingdom* and *Hong Kong Disneyland* versions. His final voice role for Disney was in *Winnie the Pooh: A Valentine for You* (1999). These are just a few of the voice roles in his acting career. His voice talents were just part of his life; he was also interested in medicine. He became an acupuncturist after graduating The Acupuncture Research College in 1974. He was also an inventor. He became one of the first people to build and patent an artificial heart (US Patent #3097366), with the help of Dr. Henry Heimlich, the inventor of the Heimlich maneuver. Some of his other patents include a disposable razor, a blood plasma defroster, a flameless cigarette lighter, an "invisible" garter belt, a fountain pen with a retractable tip, and battery-heated gloves.

439. **Paul Winchell was a ventriloquist** before he started on the Pooh movies. One of his characters was KnuckleHead Smith, who was the inspiration for the sound of Tigger's voice.

440. This was the **last film Sterling Holloway**, the voice of Pooh, ever did for Disney.

441. The character of **Gopher was not in the original book** and was created to take the place of Piglet. It was later decided to add Piglet into future Pooh films, but he was missing from the first movie.

Meet the Robinsons (2007)

442. **This film is based on the book** *A Day with Wilbur Robinson,* written and illustrated by William Joyce and published in 1990.

443. You can see a **picture in the outfield of Baloo and Mowgli** from *The Jungle Book* (1967), and Jessie, Woody, and Bullseye from *Toy Story 2* (1999).

444. On Lewis' wall in the orphanage, **you can see a picture of Nikola Tesla**, the inventor, physicist, and engineer.

445. This was the **first movie released from Disney after they changed their name** from Walt Disney Feature Animation to Walt Disney Animation Studios. Their new intro would include the clip of Mickey whistling from *Steamboat Willie* (1928), the first animated short synchronized with sound.

446. When Wilbur's dad is talking to Lewis, **he uses the Disney Point to point at Lewis.** It is the two-fingered point started by Walt Disney.

Melody Time (1948)

447. The segment "Bumble Boogie," which was utilizing the instrumentals of *Flight of the Bumblebee* by Nikolai Rimsky-Korsakov, was **originally planned to be in** *Fantasia* (1940).

448. The segment **"Pecos Bill" was edited for DVD release to remove the cigarette** from all the animation frames. They went as far as removing part of the tornado segment because he actually rolls a cigarette in his mouth and lights it with a lightning bolt. Some of the other scenes just look odd with him doing the motions of handling a cigarette, but there isn't one in animation. This is the only time Disney has edited out smoking from their films.

449. **One of the rare times Disney uses historical figures** is with the segment "The Legend of Johnny Appleseed." It is based on real-life pioneer, missionary, and nurseryman John Chapman (1774-1845), who spread apple trees throughout Pennsylvania, Ohio, Ontario, Indiana, West Virginia, and Illinois.

450. Hardie Gramatky was an animator for Disney and worked on such shorts as *Thru the Mirror* (1936), *Pluto's Judgment Day* (1935), and *Mickey's Good Deed* (1932). He started with Disney in 1931 animating the Silly Symphony short *The China Plate* and left animation in 1936 after working on *Three Blind Mouseketeers*. He has one writing credit to his name for Disney, and that was writing the script for the "Little Toot" segment for *Melody Time* (1948). The thing that is so special about this is that **he was the author and illustrator of the** *Little Toot* **books** that were first published in 1939.

451. The "Pecos Bill" segment was **introduced by Luana Patten and Bobby Driscoll**. They also starred together in *Song of the South* (1946) and *So Dear to My Heart* (1948). They were the first boy and girl to be given a signed contract to work for Disney.

Monsters University (2013)

452. John Goodman turned 61 years old on June 20, 2013, **the same day as the film's release as a premier night**.

453. When Sully enters his first classroom, the **room number on the door is A113**.

454. There is a **dinosaur on the floor of the Scare Simulator** during the first round in the final match of the scare games. This dinosaur is there as an "Easter Egg" for the next Pixar film, *The Good Dinosaur* (2015). *The Good Dinosaur* was supposed to have a May 2014 release, but was pushed back, making the next release *Inside Out* (June 2015).

455. When the students enter the Scare Building, they rub the protruding monster paw of the statue out front for good luck. This was copied from **the students from Harvard University, who do the same** to the John Harvard statue. His foot remains polished because of the constant touching; the same as the monsters.

456. **You can see the Pizza Planet truck** sitting in the driveway of the first party house that Mike busts through while riding the pig.

457. **Little Mikey, the plush, belongs to Mike** in *Monsters, Inc.*(2001), but Boo essentially takes over ownership. It would make sense for Mike's childhood plush to be seen in this prequel. It can be seen several times in Mike's living quarters. At one point, it is on the shelf in Mike and Sulley's room at the Oozma Kappa (OK) fraternity house.

458. In a scene in Monsters, Inc. (2001), Randall states to Mike and Sulley, *"Shh. Do you hear that? It's the winds of change."* In *Monsters University*, above Randall's bed, you can see a hanging poster of a tree's leaves being blown away, accompanied by the text, ***"Winds of Change. Shhh. Do you hear them?"***

459. **Roz from *Monster's, Inc.*** (2001) makes an appearance as agent 00001 near the end of the movie.

460. During the initiation ceremony at the Oozma Kappa (OK) fraternity house, you can see a car poster on the wall that **resembles the car that Mike got into in the short *Mike's New Car*** (2002). It is very similar, possibly an earlier model to the one Mike bought.

461. **The Pixar ball can be seen painted on the wall,** just before the first competition for the Scare Games.

462. Don's business card has an address on it that says 1200 Dark Ave. **The address for the Pixar studio is 1200 Park Ave.**

463. **This is the first Pixar prequel**. It is set 10 years before Monsters, Inc. (2001).

Monsters, Inc. (2001)

464. **Sully has 2,320,413 hairs** on his entire body.

465. During the chase scene when Mike and Sully are running and climbing through doors with Boo trying to escape Randal, **they not only travel to other places, but through time**. They can be in one place and it is night time, then travel to another place in a different place on the planet and it is still night time. The same thing goes for the daytime places. They are in Paris in the daytime, then a minute later they are 12 hours behind while in the South Pacific with the same daylight, and then again in Japan which is 3 hours ahead.

466. When sully takes Boo back to her room, she brings him all her toys to show them off. **One of her play things is Nemo** from *Finding Nemo* (2003).

467. In Boo's room, **you can see Jessie from *Toy Story 2*** (1999) laying on her bedroom table. She tries handing it to Sully.

468. **You can find the Pixar ball** on the floor in Boo's room.

469. If you think Randall's assistant **Fungus sounds like Yoda**, you would be spot on. Frank Oz, who voices Yoda in almost everything Star Wars, voices Fungus. He was also in the Pixar film *Inside Out* (2015) as the voice of the Subconscious Guard, Dave.

470. A special trailer for this movie was first **released as a trailer preceding the film *Harry Potter and the Sorcerer's Stone*** (2001), which opened a week after this. In it, Mike and Sully are playing charades and Mike is trying to guess what Sully is acting out. The answer is Harry Potter, but his other guesses are *Dirty Harry* (1971), *Harry Flowerpot*, and *When Harry Met Sully*, which is a reference to the Billy Crystal film *When Harry Met Sally* (1989). Sully finally put on glasses, straddled a broom, stuck a paper lightning bolt to his head, and held an owl before Mike guessed *The Sound of Music* (1965). Sully walks out of the room and Mike shouts out, "Wait. I got it. Harry Pot…" then he gets cut off by the end title card. At the very end, it is Mike's turn and he barely moves his arms before Sully guesses *Star Wars*, and is correct. It is a perfect movie to pick since, 11 years later, Disney would buy the *Star Wars* franchise for $4.5 billion.

471. While in theaters, the movie took in more than $577 million, making it **the highest-grossing animated film at the time of its release**.

472. It was difficult to record Mary Gibbs speaking as she wouldn't sit still. So, **the audio team followed her around with the microphones** and pieced together her dialogue.

473. **Mary Gibbs is the daughter of storyboard artist Rob Gibbs**. She was two years old when they were doing the principle animation and audio

recordings. She was also the voice of Sha-Ron in *Mulan II* (2004) and Baby Kiara in *The Lion King 2: Simba's Pride* (1998).

474. You can see that Boo's real name is Mary because it is written on the top of her drawings that she shows Sully. **Boo is named after her voice actor, Mary Gibbs**.

475. The story supervisor, **Bob Peterson, recorded temporary voice-over work for Roz**. They ended up liking the voice so much that they left it in the final film. He also voiced Dug and Alpha in *Up* (2009), and Mr. Ray in *Finding Nemo* (2003) and *Finding Dory* (2016), and Geri in the Pixar short *Geri's Game* (1997).

476. When Mike and Sully are warming up in the cave with Yeti, **he mentions the kids in the village** as being, *"tough kids, sissy kids, kids who climb on rocks."* This is a reference to the 1967 commercial for Armour Hot Dogs when they sing part of the jingle, *"Fat kids, skinny kids, kids who climb on rocks. Tough kids, sissy kids, even kids with chicken pox."*

Mulan (1998) - See *Disney Princess Collection* on page 90 for Fun Facts

Oliver & Company (1988)

477. This **film was based on the *Oliver Twist* stories by Charles Dickens** there were 24 serials published 1837-1839.

478. **Oliver is a homeless orphan who meets Artful Dodger**, the alpha of a gang of juvenile pickpockets that were working for the criminal Fagin. Bill Sikes is a career criminal and murderer who is also a part of the gang. The names should sound familiar as they were all characters in this movie.

479. The look of **Dodger was inspired by the look of Billy Joel**, the singer/songwriter who voices him.

480. During the song "Why Should I Worry," **you can see Jock, Peg, and Trusty** from *Lady and the Tramp* (1955) in the same shot.

481. This is **Jock's second appearance outside of *Lady and the Tramp*** (1955). His first appearance was in *One Hundred and One Dalmatians* (1961) during the Twilight Bark scene when he barked up the drain pipe.

482. Near the end of the song "Why Should I Worry," **you can see Pongo** from *One Hundred and One Dalmatians* (1961) pulling away from his owner.

483. When Oliver looks out from under the New York Yankee hat, you can see **a human walking by that resembles Roger** from *One Hundred and One Dalmatians* (1961). He is the one wearing a blue shirt and purple sweater vest.

484. To assist with animating, **photos were taken of New York City from 18 inches off the ground** to give the perspective of a dog.

485. The film **released to theaters on November 18, 1988, the exact same day as *The Land Before Time*** (1988), which was a Don Bluth film. At this point in time he was a strong competitor for Disney-animated films.

486. **Dom DeLuise voiced Fagin in this film**. He passed up the opportunity to voice a character in *The Land Before Time* (1988) so that he could voice a Disney character. This is the only movie that he voiced an animated character for Disney. He voiced characters for Bluth in six films, two television series based on Bluth films, and four sequel movies for Bluth films that weren't produced by Bluth. However, Dom did voice the character of Bacchus in the television series *Hercules* (1998-1999) later on.

487. **Sir Patrick Stewart was considered for the voice of Francis**, but his acting schedule as Captain Jean-Luc Picard on *Star Trek: The Next Generation* (1987) kept him busy. Patrick wouldn't have a chance to voice a character for Disney until his role of Mr. Woolenworth in *Chicken Little* (2005).

488. The role of **Francis ended up going to Roscoe Lee Browne**. Roscoe also voiced Mr. Arrow in *Treasure Planet* (2002). Kids from the 1990's would recognize his voice from the series *Spider-Man* (1995-1998) as Kingpin.

489. When Fagin checks his watch for the time, he has multiple watches on his wrist. **One of them is a Mickey Mouse time piece**.

490. The child actress Natalie Gregory voices Jenny. She is also credited as being **the youngest actress to portray the character of Alice** in any of the adaptations of the Alice in Wonderland story. Her *Alice in Wonderland* (1985) was produced by Columbia Pictures.

One Hundred and One Dalmatians (1961)

491. The full title of the film, *One Hundred and One Dalmatians,* is **sometimes shortened to *101 Dalmatians*.**

492. This was the **first technologically-contemporary film that Disney had released** to this point. Basically, it was set in present time. A possibility of another would be *Bambi* (1942), but since there is no visible technology to identify the timeline, we can't be sure. It could be set in the late-1800's or early-1900's. Although, the book *Bambi, A Life in the Woods* was written in 1922 and published in 1923.

493. There were **6,469,952 spots on all the Dalmatians throughout the entire movie on all the cells**. This, of course, is an estimated guess as it would be nearly impossible to count all the spots on all the original cells. It was a number that Disney threw out there for publicity materials, but was then later confirmed on the bonus footage on the Blu-ray release.

494. **Pongo has 72 spots**, Perdita has 68 spots, and each puppy has 32 spots.

495. Animators **animated clusters of puppies at a time** and would reuse the same animations and movements for the background in multiple scenes in order to cut back on animation time.

496. Due to a continuity error, there are roughly 150 Dalmatians shown in the end scene when they counted 101.

497. When *Sleeping Beauty* was released in 1959, Disney initially didn't bring in much revenue from the film. With a budget of $6 million and only bringing in $10 million, it just broke even. Disney needed a way to cut costs on their next project, *101 Dalmatians*. Ub Iwerks, who was in charge of special processes at the studio at the time, was **experimenting with Xerography photography to help in animation**. By 1959, he had altered a Xerography camera to transfer drawings by animators directly to the animation cells, eliminating the inking process and preserving the spontaneity of the penciled elements. In the past, inkers would place a cell overtop of the artist's drawing and have to trace all the lines. Then they would get sent to the paint department, where the individual cells were filled in. The Xerography process eliminated the inking step, so they could just photocopy the artist's original drawing straight onto a cell and then send it out to get painted. This is why you can see faint lines around and sometimes through the characters while watching the film. They are the artist's pencil marks that remained during the Xerography process. It is rumored that Walt disliked the look of the animation which was a result of this animation process.

498. This process **became the standard for Disney's filmmaking** covering the films *The Sword in the Stone* (1963), *The Jungle Book* (1967), *The AristoCats* (1970), *RobinHood* (1973), and *The Many Adventures of Winnie the Pooh* (1977) before it changed for *The Rescuers* (1977).

499. Due to the failure of *Sleeping Beauty*, Disney **went from a staff of 500 artists down to a staff of 100 artists**.

500. **Cruella de Vil was ranked number 39** of the American Film Institute's top *100 Heroes & Villains* (2003) of all time. It is the third animated villain on the list; the first was The Queen which was #10, and "Man" from *Bambi* which ranked #20.

501. **Eight of Walt's Nine Old Men worked on this film** with Ward Kimball absent from the collective.

502. Live-action **reference model Helene Stanley was used while animating Anita**. She was also the live-action reference for Cinderella, Anastasia (Cinderella's step-sister), and Aurora.

503. **Cruella de Vil was voiced by actress Betty Lou Gerson.** Betty also provided the voice for Miss Birdwell in the television show that Horace and Jasper are watching. She was also the opening narrator for *Cinderella* (1950). To see what the actress actually looks like, you will have to watch

Mary Poppins (1964) and keep an eye out for the old hag who scares Jane and Michael Banks after they run from the bank.

504. Actor **Rickie Sorensen provided the voice for Wart** in *Sword in the Stone* (1963) and for Spotty in *101 Dalmatians* (1961). Prior to those roles, he was known for playing "Boy," Tarzan's son, in the Tarzan films.

505. The Baduns are holding a newspaper while talking on the phone to Cruella. Along with the dognapping article, there is headline that reads "Carlsen Speaks" with a photo of a capsized ship. **This headline helps to identify the timeline of the film**. In January 1952, Captain Kurt Carlsen of the ship *Flying Enterprise*, stayed on his sinking ship for 13 days before getting forced to abandon it. They tried for those 13 days to pull the ship to shore with a tug boat, but it ended up sinking with its cargo of pig iron, coffee, peat moss, rags, 12 Volkswagen cars, antique musical instruments, typewriters, and naphthalene (main ingredient in mothballs). Nine of the ten passengers survived. Captain Kurt Carlsen was given a parade in New York for his bravery and everyone around the world learned of what happened.

506. The vocal quirks and visual appearance for Cruella were modeled after television, film, and **radio actress Tallulah Bankhead**. Her last appearance on screen was while acting the part of the villainous Black Widow in the *Batman* (1966-1968) series opposite Adam West.

507. To create the car scenes, **Disney built model cars out of cardboard** on which they drew dark black lines for angle reference. They then filmed the scenes with the movement showing the cars from all angles. They later traced each frame of the film to get the movement and the angles of the cars perfect and lifelike. The model of Cruella's car was about 18" long.

508. Cruella's car was **modeled after the Rolls-Royce Phantom**.

509. Ben Wright provided the voice of Roger with this being his first Disney film. He later voiced Rama in *The Jungle Book* (1967). If you have seen *The Sound of Music* (1965), he was Herr Zeller. His final film for Disney, and the final film of his career, was *The Little Mermaid* (1989), in which he voiced Grimsby. When he showed up to the sound studio to do his recordings, **no one there knew who he was until he said he was Roger** from *101 Dalmatians*. He never got to see the finished product of his final film before he died.

510. In the early 1990's, **Disney had released merchandise that had to be recalled** because they spelled Dalmatians as "Dalmations" and an "O" instead of an "A." Most of the merchandise was released in the parks or in the Disney stores. The film was re-released to theaters July 12, 1991, and then had its first release to VHS in April 1992.

511. There is a **stock sound called "Castle Thunder"** that was originally recorded for *Frankenstein* (1931). In this film you can hear it when Cruella enters the kitchen to purchase the puppies from Anita, and then again when she is leaving. The sound can also be heard in the *Haunted Mansion* in

Disneyland right after the Ghost Host says, *"There's always my way."* It can also be heard in other films such as *Bambi* (1942), *The Little Mermaid* (1989), *The Brave Little Toaster* (1987), *The Great Mouse Detective* (1986), *The Fox and the Hound* (1981), *Pete's Dragon* (1977), and *The Jungle Book* (1967), to name a few.

512. This was the **last feature that animator Marc Davis worked on**. He animated Cruella de Vil and then left the Animation Department and went to WED Imagineering, to develop attractions for *Disneyland*. His first was the elephant pool on *The Jungle Cruise*.

513. This was the **9th highest-grossing film in the US in 1961,** taking in $6.4 million.

514. It was the **most popular film of the year in France** after its release, earning $14.7 million. More than double what it made in the US.

515. It was re-released in theaters in 1969, 1979, 1985, and finally in 1991. **It was the 20th top grossing film of 1991**, which wasn't bad for a movie that was 30 years old. Some of the films that beat it were *Beauty and the Beast, Silence of the Lambs, Terminator 2: Judgement Day, Robin Hood: Prince of Thieves, Hook, The Addams Family,* and *City Slickers.*

516. After **all of its releases, it had grossed $216 million worldwide**, which is a higher gross than some movies of our present time.

517. This is the 17th animated Disney film. It is also the third **film made that isn't fantasy based** and is sans anthropomorphic animals. The first two are *Bambi* (1942), film #5, and *Lady and the Tramp* (1955), film #15.

518. **Bill Peet wrote the whole story by himself**. This is unusual because most films from the Disney Company to this point had multiple writers. The film *Pinocchio* (1940) had seven writers, *Cinderella* (1950), *Dumbo* (1941), *Peter Pan* (1953), and *Sleeping Beauty* (1959) all had eight writers, *The Three Caballeros* (1944) and *Alice In Wonderland* (1951) both had thirteen writers, and *Fantasia* (1940) had an outstanding twenty-five writers. Bill was also the stand-alone writer for *The Sword in the Stone* (1963). He did the complete storyboard and wrote out the dialogue for every scene himself. Almost all of it ended up in the film exactly how it was.

519. The **original story this film was based off of was titled** *The Hundred and One Dalmatians*, aka *The Great Dog Robbery*, and was published in 1956 by author Dodie Smith.

520. **Walt read the story in 1957** and had to have the rights to it to produce a film. It is said that Dodie had wanted Walt Disney to consider her book for a movie.

521. **Dodie Smith wrote a sequel book** to *The Hundred and One Dalmatians* in 1967 and titled it *The Starlight Barking*. The storyline centered on the main dogs who come to find out that all the humans won't wake up. They travel to Westminster where they find Sirius, the Lord of the Dog Star,

who invites the dogs to his house to evade nuclear war here on earth. In Astronomy, Sirius is the brightest star in our visible sky and is called the Dog Star because it is located in the constellation Canis Major, also known as the Greater Dog.

522. **There was a live adaptation of this film called** *101 Dalmatians* (1996), and a live sequel titled *102 Dalmatians* (2000). They also produced a direct-to-video animated sequel, *101Dalmatians 2: Patch's London Adventure* (2003), and an animated television series titled *101 Dalmatians: The Series* (1997-1998). None of these films had anything to do with the sequel book.

523. When the Blu-ray of the film was released in 2015, **Disney included an animated short titled** *The Further Adventures of Thunderbolt* (2015), which was the episode of the television show the puppies were watching in the film. The narrator in the short was the voice of Corey Burton, the *Haunted Mansion Holiday* overlay Ghost Host.

524. Disney is **producing an original story film for the manic puppy napper titled** *Cruella;* it is to be released in 2018. Academy Award winner Emma Stone is to play Cruella de Vil.

525. The dog character on the television show that the puppies are watching is Thunderbolt. He **was inspired by the television canine Rin-Tin-Tin**, a series that ran from 1954-1959.

526. Author Dodie Smith owned nine Dalmatians; one of them was named Pongo.

527. Dodie was inspired to write the book when one of her friends was visiting and commented *"Those dogs would make a lovely fur coat,"* referencing her pack of Dalmatians.

528. The incident when the **15 puppies are born was based on true events.** Dodie's dog birthed a litter of puppies, and her husband had to revive the last one because it was lifeless.

529. It is said that **Dodie's favorite animation in the movie** was in the opening scene, when Pongo was stretching on the window.

530. J. Pat O'Malley provided the voice of Jasper and Colonel. These two characters end up meeting each other in the barn, and **they are both voiced by the same actor**.

531. The **voice of Donald Duck, Clarence Nash**, did the vocals for the dogs barking.

532. **Lucille Bliss was the vocal artist who sang the Kanine Krunchies** commercial. She was also the voice of Anastasia in *Cinderella* (1950), the Sunflower and Tulip in *Alice in Wonderland* (1951), a mermaid in *Peter Pan* (1953), but would be most recognizable as Smurfette in *The Smurfs* series and television specials from 1982-1989.

533. **Lucky has a horseshoe shape on his back** patterned by the spots. It is easy to spot when he is standing up to watch the TV.

534. When the puppies are watching TV in Hell Hall, they are **watching the Disney short** *Springtime* **(1929).**

535. When casting the voices for the dogs, **they were cast with more dominant voices than the human owners,** so they would seem more dominant.

536. Out of the fifteen puppies Perdita gives birth to, **only six are named in this film,** Lucky, Rolly, Patch, Penny, Pepper, and Freckles. The others are named later in children's books.

537. In the film there are **several cameos of canines from** *Lady and the Tramp* (1955) during the Twilight Bark sequence. You can see Jock show up first. He is the one barking up the drain pipe. Then there is Peg and Bull in the pet shop window followed by Lady in the street and Tramp on top of the vehicle.

538. The animation used for the "Jock look-alike" when he was gasping were the **actual cells used in** *Lady and the Tramp* (1955). They were just re-photographed for this film. When he turns to bark in the drain pipe, it is new animation done with the Xerography process.

539. Opposing the patterns of previous films that contained multiple songs, **there are only three songs featured in this film.** They are "Cruella de Vil," "Kanine Krunchies" (if you count that as a song), and "Dalmatian Plantation."

540. George Bruns and Mel Leven **wrote several other songs for the film that were cut,** including "March of the One Hundred and One" and "Don't Buy a Parrot from a Sailor."

541. **There are several differences to note between the book and the film adaptation.**
   - The two dogs that had to rescue their puppies were Pongo and *Missis* Pongo.
   - Perdita was just a stray liver-and-white Dalmatian whose puppies had already been sold to Cruella by her owners and so Perdita ran away to go find them
   - Perdita's husband, Prince, was also lost.
   - Pongo's "pets" were named Mr. and Mrs. Dearly, not Roger and Anita.
   - Mr. Dearly was a financial banker of sorts and had lots of money, whereas Roger was a musician and was just getting by until his hit song "Cruella de Vil."
   - Mrs. Dearly found Perdita in the rain and took her in and utilized her as a "wet nurse" for Missis to help nurse her own fifteen puppies.
   - They had two nannies, Nanny Cook and Nanny Butler.
   - Mr. and Mrs. Dearly attend a dinner party at Cruella's place where she talks about her hatred for animals. Later they discover that their 15 puppies had been stolen.

- Perdita stays behind with Mr. and Mrs. Dearly while Pongo and Missis go after the puppies.
- Jasper stays the same, but Saul is changed to Horace.
- Tib is a grey, tabby female instead of an orange male.
- When Tib, aka Lieutenant Willow and later changed to Sargent Tibbs, finds the puppies in Hell Hall, there are 97 of them. Pongo, Missis, Perdita, and Prince make up the other four.
- The dogs make it to Cruella's house and destroy all her fur coats with the help of her cat, who is angry with Cruella for drowning all her litters of kittens.
- Cruella is a mysterious, dark, and quiet character; a complete opposite character type than what was presented to us by Marc Davis.
- Mr. Dearly buys Hell Hall and turns it into a "Dynasty of Dalmatians," a variation of the "Dalmatian Plantation."
- Prince returned home and his owners gave him to the Dearly family to make it One Hundred and One Dalmatians.

Peter Pan (1953)

542. The story of *Peter Pan*, or *The Boy Who Wouldn't Grow Up*, was **originally written as a play by J.M. Barrie** in 1904. He later published the book *Peter and Wendy* in 1911.

543. The **first mention of the Peter Pan character was in the 1902** J.M. Barrie published book *The Little White Bird*. This book was just a collection of stories with different themes and levels of appropriateness for children, as the book was intended for adults. The chapters 13-18 were children-appropriate and were about Peter Pan. They were published separately as a children's book in 1906 as *Peter Pan in Kensington Gardens*. Before that publication, in 1904, is when he wrote the play. While his play and short book were selling, he wrote *Peter and Wendy*, which came out in 1911.

544. Wendy made her first appearance in the 1911 book. This is noted as **the first time the name Wendy had ever been used as a first name**. In the recent past, it had been used as a shortened version of "Gwendolyn" or a variant of "Wanda." The author's friend, William Ernest Henley, had a 4-year-old daughter named Margaret Henley who would pronounce the word "friend" as "Fwiendy." The author used that as the inspiration for the name Wendy.

545. **Walt had intended on this film to be his second film**. He even had a team together working on the concept art and storyboarding. Peter Pan wouldn't see the big screen for another 15 years.

546. Jimmy MacDonald, who was the voice of Mickey Mouse from 1947-1977, was also the sound director for many films. He and his team would create sound effects that would be overlaid in the audio track of films. One such sound effect was the snapping jaws of Tick-Tock. That **jaw- snapping sound was achieved by using castanets**. That same sound was then used again in *Lady and the Tramp* (1955) for the snapping of the alligator's jaws trying to cut off Lady's muzzle, and then again for the snapping jaws of Maleficent's dragon in *Sleeping Beauty* (1959).

547. Marc Davis was the artist who designed and refined the temperamental pixie Tinker Bell in 1951, based off of the concept art done by John "Jack" P. Miller in 1939. **Bianca Majolie was the first known artist who worked on concept art** for her in the early 1940's. The earliest known concept art for Tink goes back to mid-1937.

548. Henry Calvin was in several Disney movies and the popular television series *Zorro* (1957-59), in which he portrayed Sergeant Garcia. In *Toby Tyler* (1960), he was Ben Cotter, and in *Babes in Toyland* (1961) he was the henchman Gonzorgo. He had a very short-lived acting career, but **he was able to record the song "Never Smile at a Crocodile" for Peter Pan**. The song was cut from the final movie and is said to be the most popular song Disney has ever cut from a film. You can hear the instrumental version whenever Tick-Tock the Croc shows up and in the final credits, but not with the lyrics. It wasn't until the movie's CD soundtrack was released in 1997, 22 years after Henry's death, can the full song be heard. The song was written by Jack Lawrence, who was also the writer for the song "Once Upon a Dream" for *Sleeping Beauty* (1959).

549. The melody for the song "Never Smile at a Crocodile" **was originally composed for a song called "Lobster Quadrille"** which was cut from *Alice in Wonderland* (1951).

550. Another song number that was repurposed from *Alice in Wonderland* (1951) was **the song "Beyond the Laughing Sky"** which was re-lyricized and renamed "The Second Star to the Right."

551. In the original book, **Captain Hook is missing his right hand**, like on the *Peter Pan's Flight* attraction in *Disneyland*. For the film, however, the animators decided to make his left hand the hook.

552. An early **approach to Peter Pan gave him wings**.

553. In the pre-production stage, **Nana was originally going to travel with the children** to Neverland, and the film was going to be from her point of view.

554. In the original story, *Peter and Wendy*, published in 1911, **Nana is described as being a Newfoundland**, or Newfie. J.M. Barrie used to have two dogs. At the time he was writing the story, he had Luath, a Newfie.

When he first came up with the concept of Peter Pan, he had Porthos, a Saint Bernard. Subsequently, Nana has been portrayed as a Saint Bernard in all of the stage plays and movies.

555. **Bobby Driscoll was the model and voice of Peter Pan**. He started his career with Disney at the age of nine, when he played Johnny in *Song of the South* (1946). He was the first male actor Disney put under contract before he went on to star in five Disney films and voiced Goofy Jr. in the Goofy shorts *Fathers Are People* (1951) and *Father's Lion* (1952). He was in Disney's *Treasure Island* (1950), which was the first all-live action film Disney ever made. His other films were *Melody Time* (1948), *So Dear to My Heart* (1948), and *The Walt Disney Christmas Show* (1951). He was sixteen when Peter Pan came out, and it was the last film he ever did for Disney. Disney didn't renew his contract because he hit puberty and developed acne.

556. On December 21, 1953, Lux Radio Theater **broadcast a 60-minute radio adaptation of** *Peter Pan* and they brought in Bobby Driscoll to reprise his role.

557. This film **produced one of the most recognizable and favorable characters** of all time, Tinker Bell. Walt used her to promote *Disneyland* on his television show, *Wonderful World of Disney*.

558. People have believed that Marilyn Monroe was the model for Tinker Bell. **The model for Tink was actually 22-year-old Margaret Kerry**. Although Marilyn Monroe would have been a good pick for the role, Marilyn wasn't trained on how to dance yet. She had been friends with Margaret in the past, after they met at a bathing suit photo shoot. It turned out that Margaret was perfect for the part. Marc Davis animated Tink while Margaret danced around and mimed with giant props. She was also the animation model for the red-haired mermaid on the rock and provided her voice by saying "We were only trying to drown her."

559. The **other two models for the mermaids were Connie Hilton and June Foray**, the voice of Grandmother Fa, Lucifer, Mrs. Goofy, Wheezy, Magica De Spell, Grammi Gummi, and many more characters for Disney and other animation studios.

560. Margaret Kerry wasn't the first model Disney went to for the test subject for Tink. Marc Davis found an **attractive 19-year-old ink and paint girl named Ginni Mack**. Previously, Ginni had been used as the face of the Ink and Paint Department for promotional material. Marc had her make facial expressions for him to sketch. He used her for that one session and then, again, a week later.

561. Now that **Marc had the face for Tink down, he needed to animate her body**. He went to Kathryn Beaumont for this part. She was already used to Marc as she was the model for him as Alice just a few years prior. Animators had her model in different poses in her bathing suit, but it wasn't what they were looking for. They needed someone more adult and

was "sexy" and shapely. This is where Margaret Kerry came in with her title of "World's Best Legs" in Hollywood in 1949. Margaret was a dancer and was able to convey the emotions of the mute pixie with her graceful movement.

562. This **isn't the first time Margaret Kerry has worked with Bobby Driscoll**. In 1948, they were both in the Warner Brother's film *If You Knew Susie* in which Bobby played Margaret's younger brother.

563. The instrumental music from "Second Star to the Right" was **originally written for *Alice in Wonderland***(1951), but was cut from that film and given new lyrics for *Peter Pan*.

564. Smee hits Hook on the heard with the oar when Tick-Tock is trying to swallow the fearful captain. When he does this, **you can hear the Goofy holler**, even though it is partially muffled by the gurgling of the water.

565. It is traditional for the actor who is portraying **Captain Hook to also portray Mr. Darling**, it was done in this film by Hans Conried.

566. This film marks the **last time all of Walt's Nine Old Men worked on a film** together.

567. This was **Ward Kimball's last theatrically-released animated film** to work on. After that, he worked on animated shorts and the animation sequences in *Mary Poppins* (1964) and *Bedknobs and Broomsticks* (1971).

568. Some people believe in the theory that the **character of Peter Pan is that of an angel** who is charged with ferrying the spirits of children to the afterlife. Also called a Psychopomp, one who escorts the souls to the afterlife. This theory is actually supported by J.M Barrie himself. In chapter one of *Peter and Wendy*, Mrs. Darling is talking to Wendy *"...after thinking back into her childhood she just remembered a Peter Pan who was said to live with the fairies. There were odd stories about him, as that when children died he went part of the way with them, so that they should not be frightened. She had believed in him at the time, but now that she was married and full of sense she quite doubted whether there was any such person."*

569. People have been under the opinion that **Hermes, the Greek god of transition, was the inspiration for Peter as a character**. Hermes could fly between the realms of the mortal and the dead. He also had a son named Peter for which it is believed was the inspiration for J. M. Barrie in his writing. In Greek mythology, Pan was a god of nature. He was half satyr and would frolic in the forests of Arcadia with nymphs and play his flute.

570. In the book, **Captain Hook spikes Peter's nightly medicine with poison**. Walt felt this would be too difficult to convey through animation, so they decided to make it a bomb instead.

571. Actor Paul Collins, the voice of John Darling, **was actually 11 months older** than Kathryn Beaumont, the voice of Wendy.

572. **Walt Disney liked Kathryn Beaumont's voice acting** so much that he had her perform two characters back to back, Alice in *Alice in Wonderland* (1951) and then Wendy.

573. The **same for Bill Thompson** as he was Smee in *Peter Pan* (1953) and also The White Rabbit and Dodo in *Alice in Wonderland* (1951).

574. Supervising animator Milt Kahl had said that the most difficult part of animating Peter and the Darling children was **animating weightlessness for the flying** and floating sequences.

575. The **term "Peter Pan Syndrome" was derived from this** film's lead character because of Peter never wanting to grow up. It is used to describe adults who still do things and act like they are still kids and are socially immature. It was first coined in the book "The Peter Pan Syndrome: Men Who Have Never Grown Up" by Psychologist Dan Kiley.

576. J.M. Barrie was the adoptive father of five boys. The parents of the Llewelyn Davies boys died, so they went to live with J.M. Barrie and became the inspiration for some of his stories. He even named characters after them. One of the boys was named Peter. Peter Llewelyn Davies went on to serve in the British Army during World War I and then later became a book publisher. **He published a little book called *Mary Poppins* by P.L. Travers** in 1934. Mary Poppins went on to become the most popular nanny of our time and inspired a movie in 1964, a musical that ran from 2004-2014, and the sequel film *Mary Poppins Returns* (2018).

577. The inspiration for J.M. Barrie to write about a boy who never grew old was **his older brother, David, who drowned in an ice-skating accident** before his 14th birthday. To him and his mother, David would never grow old.

578. It says in the book that **Peter Pan began his adventures at the age of seven days old**.

579. Although Peter Pan appears to be about 13 years old, the story says that **Peter Pan still has all of his "baby" teeth**, which would put him at the age of six or seven.

580. Two *Disneyland's Meet and Greet* character actors, Andrew and Hali, **met when they were Peter Pan and Wendy in the park**. They later married in 2012.

581. When Walt was a child, he portrayed Peter Pan in a school play.

582. When J.M. Barrie died, he **left the copyrights of Peter Pan to the Great Ormond Street Children's Hospital** in London. That way, they could continue to get funding off of the royalties.

583. Besides Roger and Anita in *One Hundred and One Dalmatians* (1961), this is the only Disney cannon film to **show both of the parents and have them live throughout the whole movie**.

Pinocchio (1940)

584. The movie is **based off of the children's book** *The Adventures of Pinocchio,* published in 1883 by author Carlo Collodi. The book is actually a collection of short stories he wrote between 1881 and 1882.

585. The book has been translated into over 260 different languages worldwide, making it the **most widely-read book in the world, second only to the Bible**.

586. The film gave the century-old talking cricket the name Jiminy. In the book he was known as "the Cricket." When Pinocchio first met the Cricket, he warned Pinocchio of the dangers of disobedience. Pinocchio didn't like hearing that so **he threw a hammer at the cricket and killed him**.

587. *Pinocchio* (1940) was **Disney's first-ever DVD**, released on October 26, 1999.

588. **The first "Easter Eggs"** can be found in this film, the second full-length Disney animated film. In the opening of the movie, you can see the title of two books over to the left when Jiminy Cricket is singing. They are *Alice in Wonderland* and *Peter Pan*. Both films were in the pre-planning stages with Disney. Whether or not this was done intentionally, I don't know.

589. Veteran animator **Ward Kimball was the artist who brought Jiminy Cricket to life**. Ward had animated the whole "Soup Song" scene for *Snow White and the Seven Dwarfs* (1937), which ended up getting cut from the film. Ward was upset that all of his work was getting stripped from the film. He marched up to Walt's office to quit. He later exited Walt's office with a grin on his face as Walt had just offered him the task of animating Jiminy for the next film. Ward stayed.

590. **Lampwick was designed to look like Fred Moore**, the one who animated him, in human form. Eric Larson animated him in his donkey form.

591. The shape of the eight ball and cue for the pool hall was **modeled after the Trylon and Perisphere** from the 1939-40 World's Fair, which was a sphere and tall, thin pyramid-shaped pair of buildings.

592. Figaro was a popular character from the film. Disney used him in half a dozen shorts as the **part of Minnie Mouse's cat**.

593. **Figaro makes an appearance in** *Alice in Wonderland* (1951) as a caterpillar that was being bothered by a copper centipede.

594. There was **a planned direct-to-video sequel** to this film titled *Pinocchio II* (2007), but it was scrapped.

Pocahontas (1995) - See *Disney Princess Collection* on page 90 for Fun Facts

The Princess and the Frog (2009) - See *Disney Princess Collection* on page 90 for Fun Facts

Ratatouille (2007)

595. In pre-production, **Remy had a mother named Desiree**, but after the story focused on the relationship between Remy and his father, her part was cut.

596. Anton Ego makes an attempt to insult the restaurant by using the name Monsieur Chef Boyardee. This really isn't an insult as **the real Chef Hector Boyardee was an award winning chef** at New York's Plaza Hotel before he started selling his food to the public. He even received special honors from Russia and the U.S.A. for feeding the troops during World War I. President Woodrow Wilson's wedding was catered by Chef Boyardee in 1915.

597. **Rats were kept in the hallway at the studio** for over a year so that the animators could study the movement of their noses, ears, fur, tails, and paws.

598. When Remy enters a house after leaving the sewer, a dog barks at him and you can see the dog's shadow on the wall. **It is the shadow of Doug from the movie** *Up* (2009), which was one of the movies following the release of *Ratatouille* (2007).

599. The debut of this film **in France set a record for their biggest opening weekend** for an animated film, taking in almost $66 million.

600. The movie was a huge success, as the first film to be released after Disney bought out Pixar, **taking in $621 million worldwide**. This makes it the third highest-grossing Pixar film (at its release) following *Finding Nemo* (2003) with $940 million and *The Incredibles* (2004) with $633 million.

601. When Skinner is chasing Remy near the river, you can **spot the Pizza Planet truck**.

602. Disney was worried that the general public wouldn't know how to pronounce "ratatouille," so **they had the promotional posters spell it phonetically** as "rat•a•too•ee."

603. The name **"Auguste Gusteau" is an anagram of itself**. If you take the "au" of the first name and put it at the end, you get the last name. And, if you take the "au" off of the end of second name and move it to the beginning, you get the first name.

604. Remy finds a bottle of Saffron in the old lady's cupboard in the beginning of the movie. **Saffron is the most expensive spice on the market**, costing close to $60 for 1 oz. Back in 1974, it was $1,000 for 1 pound of it.

605. **Disney wanted to produce a Ratatouille brand of wine** to sell in Costco. However, the California Wine Institute suggested that it would encourage underage drinking, so the idea was scrapped.

The Rescuers (1977)

606. **The Rescuers was originally a book series** published between 1959 and 1978, in which it consisted of nine books. In the second book, titled *Miss Bianca*, there were two bloodhounds named Tyrant and Torment. They were the inspiration behind the creation of Brutus and Nero, Madame Medusa's alligator minions. In turn, Brutus and Nero were the inspiration for Flotsam and Jetsam, the moray eel minions of Ursula, in the film *The Little Mermaid* (1989).

607. Disney was planning on making a sequel to this film titled *The Rescuers Down Under* (1990), which did happen. But the television series, that was going to star the two rodents prior to the film's release, didn't happen. It was to be a lead into the new movie's storyline. The series was going to star Miss Bianca and Bernard with the Rescue Aid Society and follow them on their adventures. **They ended up getting replaced with Chip and Dale** and the show's name was changed to *Chip 'n' Dale Rescue Rangers* (1989-1990) and ran for 65 episodes.

608. Eva Gabor, the younger sister of Zsa Zsa Gabor, was the voice of Miss Bianca. If she sounds familiar, it is because seven years before this she was the voice of Duchess in *The AristoCats* (1970). The **last film of her career was her voicing Miss Bianca** in *The Rescuers Down Under* (1990).

609. Like Eva Gabor, **Robie Lester was the singing voice of Duchess and Miss Bianca** and *The Rescuers* was the last film of her career. Robie recorded all the Disneyland Story Reader read- along records, and said the memorable line, "...when Tinker Bell rings her little bells like this (chimes sound)...turn the page." You can also hear her on The Story and Song of the *Haunted Mansion* record, where she played opposite Ron Howard in a duo of teens that explore the *Haunted Mansion*.

610. This was the **last Disney-animated classic film to receive an Oscar nomination** for the song "Someone's Waiting For You," until the release of *The Little Mermaid* (1989), 12 years later.

611. Rufus the cat is a caricature of animator, and **one of "Walt's Nine Old Men," Ollie Johnston**.

612. During the song "Someone's Waiting for You," **Bambi and his mother can be spotted** near the water's edge. They were traced from the exact same cells from *Bambi* (1942).

613. **The voice of Evinrude was provided by James MacDonald**. This was his last film before his death. He was the voice of Mickey Mouse from 1947, after Walt Disney retired himself from it, to 1977 when he passed away. Some other voices he vocalized would be Jaq and Gus in *Cinderella* (1950), Doormouse in *Alice in Wonderland* (1951), Chip in the Chip 'n' Dale shorts, and the Wolf in *Sword in the Stone* (1963).

614. In the Rescue Aid Society building, **there is a Hidden Mickey in the form of a Mickey Mouse watch** hanging on the wall.

615. From what animator Milt Kahl had said, **Geraldine Page got every line for Medusa correct** on her first take.

The Rescuers Down Under (1990)

616. **This film was to be a tie-in to a television series** that never happened. Well, it did happen, just not how it was supposed to. The name of the series was *Chip 'n' Dale Rescue Rangers* (1989-1990). Before animation on the series even started, Disney changed it from mice to chipmunks.

617. This was **the first sequel released into the theaters** following the release of *The Rescuers* (1977). The next one would be *Fantasia 2000* (1999) for *Fantasia* (1940).

618. **There was a third Rescuers film planned** for the late 1990's, but it was scrapped after the death of Eva Gabor, the voice of Miss Bianca.

619. This was the **first feature film to be done solely digitally**. All the animations were hand drawn, but were then scanned into a computer to combine with the scenery and have the animation colored in. They used an entire computer system called CAPS (Computer Animation Production System) that was developed with Pixar for Disney. They used it for testing with the ending sequence in *The Little Mermaid* (1989) the prior year.

620. The producers wanted the original cast to reprise their roles in this film, as they did in *The Rescuers* (1977). The voice of Orville, John Jordan, had passed away two years before this film was released. Voicing Orville in *The Rescuers* (1977) was his last film. **Instead of replacing the voice actor, they replaced the character**. That is why Wilbur stepped in to replace Orville. John Candy provided the new voice.

621. This movie was **released on the same day as another John Candy movie**, *Home Alone* (1990). *The Rescuers Down Under* had a budget of

$30 million and took home around $48 million. Home Alone's budget was $18 million and took home $476 million.

622. This is the first film since *Bambi* (1942) to have **an animal rights/environmental message**.

623. Frank Welker did the animal sounds of Marahute and Joanna. He was also **the singing voice for McLeach** when he sings his twisted version of *Home on the Range*.

624. This is the **second film in the cannon to be released that wasn't a musical**. The first non-musical release was *The Black Cauldron* (1985).

625. The **Nurse Mouse was voiced by Russi Taylor**, the voice of Minnie Mouse.

626. *The Prince and the Pauper* (1990), starring Mickey Mouse, was released with this film in the theaters. It was **Mickey's first appearance in a short since *The Simple Things*** (1953).

627. Miss Bianca and Bernard don't even make their **first appearance in the film until about 18 minutes in**. They don't even interact with Cody, the boy they are supposed to rescue, until about 56 minutes in.

Robin Hood (1973)

628. This was the **first animated Disney film to be released in VHS for home sale** on December 4, 1984. The reason why Disney chose a second-rate animated feature instead of a hugely popular one like *Cinderella* (1950), was because Disney was in the pattern of re-releasing their films to the theaters every seven years. They were afraid that releasing it to VHS would hinder the crowds from visiting the theater, so they opted for *Robin Hood* as they didn't plan on re-releasing it to the theater due to lack of popularity.

629. It is said that a few months before the film's release, the **Disney animators needed Peter Ustinov to go back to the studio** to record more dialogue for Prince John. Disney had to call London, Paris, New York, Vienna, and Tokyo to try and locate Peter. They ended up finding out that he was filming at the NBC Studios in Burbank, just a half mile down the road.

630. The **design of having a gap between Sir Hiss's front teeth** was modeled after his voice actor, Terry-Thomas, who also had a gap in his teeth.

631. The scene with Maid Marian dancing with the other animals **was traced from the cells of Snow White dancing with the Dwarfs** in *Snow White and the Seven Dwarfs* (1937). This practice is called "cell sharing" and it

was used to cut costs. Marge Champion was the dance reference model for Snow White, thereby making her the reference model for Maid Marian. The same dancing was cell shared for the dancing number for "I Wanna be Like You" in *The Jungle Book* (1967) and "Everybody Wants to be a Cat" in *The AristoCats* (1970). Marge was also the reference model for the Blue Fairy in *Pinocchio* (1040), the Hyacinth Hippo in *Fantasia* (1940), and the movement model for Mr. Stork in *Dumbo* (1941).

632. This is the **first fully-anthropomorphic film made by Disney**, meaning all the animals are humanoid, living in an "animal-run world." Not like Timothy Mouse who is also anthropomorphic, but exists in a human world. The second film to achieve this feat was *Chicken Little* (2005), followed by *Zootopia* (2016).

633. This is **only the second Disney film to not contain any humans**. The first was *Bambi* (1942).

634. **Disney brought back voice actor Phil Harris**, who voiced Thomas O'Malley in *The AristoCats* (1970), and Baloo in *The Jungle Book* (1967), to voice the role of Little John. It was a little ironic because there was cell sharing for Little John from Baloo the bear only a few years earlier.

635. In 2000, **there was a song released called the "Hamster Dance"** by Hampton the Hamster. It is the song "Oo-De-Lally" by Roger Miller that was sung in the opening scene, but was sped up to two times faster than the normal play speed. Roger Miller was the voice of the rooster, Allan-a-Dale, in the film.

636. This is the **last film that all of Disney's Nine Old Men would live to see completed**. John Lounsbery would pass away February 13, 1976, and would miss the release of *The Many Adventures Of Winnie The Pooh* (March 11, 1977) and *The Rescuers* (June 22, 1977), both of which he co-directed, and both were his only full-length films to direct.

Sleeping Beauty (1959) - See *Disney Princess Collection* on page 90 for Fun Facts

Snow White and the Seven Dwarfs (1937) - See *Disney Princess Collection* on page 90 for Fun Facts

The Sword in the Stone (1963)

637. **This movie is based on the book *The Sword in the Stone***, published in 1938 by T. H. White. It was the first part of a tetralogy (four) of novels focused on the life of King Arthur.

638. **Concept art for this film began in 1949.** The film wouldn't see completion for 14 more years.

639. **This film almost didn't get made.** Ken Anderson, Marc Davis, Milt Kahl, and director Wolfgang Reitherman spent months working on a storyboard for the film *Chanticleer*. It was the story of a cocky rooster set in a

barnyard in the early-1800's which was based on the pre-WWI French play *Chantecler* by Edmund Rostand. The entire storyboard for *The Sword in The Stone* was done solely by Bill Peet. The projects were pitched to Walt. The Board was trying to get Walt to quit animated films so they could focus their money on *Disneyland*, and the very early stages of *Disney World*. Walt ended up picking the fantasy-based story on the Arthurian legend based on the fact that humans are easier and cheaper to animate than animals.

640. A **Chantecler is a breed of chicken that was listed as extinct** in 1979, but was later listed as "critical" when small groups of them surfaced on private farms. In 1991, *Rock-A-Doodle* was made by Don Bluth based on this *Chantecler* play. It would be the last movie Phil Harris (Baloo, Little John, Thomas O'Malley) provided a voice for.

641. Due to the fact that young male voice actors age and go through vocal changes, Director Wolfgang Reitherman (animator and one of Walt's Nine Old Men) has the vocal spots filled in by his two sons, Richard and Robert Reitherman. The original **vocal talent was Rickie Sorensen, also known for voicing Spotty** in *One Hundred and One Dalmatians* (1961).

642. From the theatrically-released films, **this is the first one to be directed by one single director**, Wolfgang Reitherman. Prior to this, all the films had three or more directors. After this, he would go on to single-handedly direct *The Jungle Book* (1967), The *AristoCats* (1970), and *Robin Hood* (1973). His final films to direct were *The Many Adventures of Winnie the Pooh* (1977) and *The Rescuers* (1977), which he co-directed.

643. The Sherman Brothers had been writing music for Disney for a few years by now, but **this was their first animated movie**. They wrote the songs "The Legend of the Sword in the Stone," "Higitus Figitus," "That's What Makes the World Go Round," "A Most Befuddling Thing," and "The Marvelous Mad Madame Mim."

644. There were two songs written for the film that were later scrapped; "The Blue Oak Tree" and "The Magic Key," which was replaced with "Higitus Figitus."

645. It is said that to this point in animation, the duel between Madam Mim and Merlin is **one of the best pieces of character animation**. The characters go through multiple changes from animal to animal but still retain their distinct likenesses. Merlin always had his moustache and glasses and Madam Mim was always pink with a purple tuft of hair.

646. Wolfgang said he had auditions from 70 actors for the part of Merlin. None of them could sound the way they wanted Merlin to sound. **Actor Karl Swenson was already cast as the voice of Archimedes**, but he had what they were looking for, so he was recast as Merlin.

647. They ended up recasting the voice of **the knowledgeable owl with Junius Matthews**. He went on to voice Rabbit in the *Winnie the Pooh* films.

Tangled (2010) - See *Disney Princess Collection* on page 90 for Fun Facts

Tarzan (1999)

648. This **movie was based on the book series** *Tarzan* **by Edgar Rice Burroughs**. There were a total of over two dozen books published about Tarzan between 1912 and 1965. Books continued to get published with Edgar's works, even after his death in 1950. He was buried in Tarzana, California, a neighborhood in Southern California named after his character Tarzan.

649. At the same time Edgar Rice Burroughs published *Tarzan*, he published the *Barsoom* series. The first book in the series was *A Princess of Mars* (1912), and told the adventures of John Carter. Disney made the film *John Carter* (2012), starring Taylor Kitsch and Lynn Collins, based on this first book, making it **Disney's second film adaptation of a Burroughs novel**.

650. In the books, **Tarzan's human English name was John Clayton**.

651. To animate Tarzan sliding around on the trees in movements that mimicked skaters, the **animators watched films of Tony Hawk skateboarding**.

652. The voice of Clayton was provided by Brian Blessed. Brian also performed the "Tarzan yell" for the movie, making it **the first time an actor voiced the hero and villain** in the same movie.

653. When the gorillas hold Professor Porter upside down, items fall out of his pockets, including **a tiny stuffed dog that was Little Brother from** *Mulan* (1998), the Disney film that preceded this film.

654. **Minnie Driver improvised the dialogue for her story** to her father and Clayton of how she met Tarzan. It was so hilarious that they animated the whole sequence around it.

655. During the "Trashing the Camp" song, **you can see Mrs. Potts and Chip** from *Beauty and the Beast* (1991).

656. **The timeline of this movie is set in 1911** as deduced by the revealing of Halley's Comet. The shipwreck originally happened in 1888.

The Three Caballeros (1944)

657. In the film, the song "Mexico" by Charles Wolcott and Ray Gilbert, **was the only original song in the film**. The other songs came from Brazilian and Mexican composers but had English lyrics written by Ray Gilbert.

658. This was one of two movies, the other being *Saludos Amigos* (1942),

that **were created to improve the U.S. relations with South America** during World War II.

659. With the exception of Mickey Mouse as the conductor in *Fantasia* (1940), this is the **first time Disney has had animation with live action** since the *Alice Comedies* in the 1920's.

660. Clarence Nash, who does the voice of Donald Duck, **also does his Spanish speaking lines**.

661. The film was released February 5, 1945, in the U.S., **but was released in Mexico first** on December 21, 1944.

662. In the "Pablo the Penguin" segment, there is a penguin diving into the water. **This is the same penguin diving in Silly Symphony's** *Peculiar Penguin* (1934).

Toy Story (1995)

663. It is said that, in 1993, the **Toy Story project was almost shut down** because Woody was said to be too much of a "sarcastic jerk."

664. When Rex is playing video games, you can see a calendar on the back wall. The picture on it **shows the bugs from** *A Bug's Life* (1998), the film that would be releasing after this one.

665. It is said that **Billy Crystal was approached with the request to voice Buzz Lightyear** before Tim Allen. Billy turned it down, but after watching the final product he regretted it. John Lasseter heard about this and called him up to offer him the role of Mike Wazowski in *Monsters, Inc.* (2001). Billy's wife, Janice, answered the phone and called to Billy and said "John Lasseter is on the phone for you." Billy took the phone and replied, "Yes."

666. **Chevy Chase was also offered the role** of Buzz Lightyear.

667. Buzz Lightyear was **named after the U.S. astronaut Buzz Aldrin**, the second person to walk on the moon.

668. The carpet in Sid's house is the **same carpet from the Stanley Kubrick horror movie** *The Shinning* (1980).

669. When Woody and Buzz are on Andy's bed, you can see a sketch of Woody on the wall. It is **designed after an early concept of Woody**.

670. The animators perfected the army soldiers walk by **attaching their shoes to a skateboard** without wheels and then trying to walk around with it.

671. **Tom Hanks only provides the voice for Woody in the** *Toy Story* **movies**, and in the related shorts. He said, "After doing a line 18 different

ways, your diaphragm is busted, your throat is raw, you've spit all over your copy, and this is your fourth hour doing this." He had Disney just contact his brother, who does voice work, to do all the other recordings for Woody. Jim Hanks has done the voice of Woody for all the video games; *Toy Story Activity Center* (1996), *Toy Story* (1996), *Toy Story 2* (1999), *Toy Story Racer* (2001), *Extreme Skate Adventure* (2003), *Toy Story 3: The Video Game* (2010), *Toy Story 3* (2010), *Kinect Disneyland Adventures* (2011), *Kinect Fun Labs: Kinect Rush - A Disney Pixar Adventures: Snapshot* (2012), *Disney Infinity* (2013), *Disney Infinity: Marvel Super Heroes* (2014), and *Disney Infinity 3.0* (2015). He even provided the voice of "Sheriff Woody" in episodes of *Robot Chicken* (2012-2016), and in the talking Woody toys.

672. This movie was followed by the 37-episode television series *Toy Story Treats* (1996). **Tim Allen didn't do the voice of Woody;** his brother, Jim Hanks did.

673. There was also the spin-off television show *Buzz Lightyear of Star Command* (2000-2001) and the pilot movie *Buzz Lightyear of Star Command: The Adventure Begins* (2000) in which **Jim Hanks does the voice of Woody, when needed**.

674. When Woody is trapped under the crate, the tool box weighing down the top is a Binford brand tool box, which Buzz tries to push off. **Binford is a fictional tool company** created by Disney's television channel ABC for Tim Allen's show *Home Improvement* (1991-1999).

675. In the early stages of planning this movie, Tinny, the tin man from the Pixar short *Tin Toy* (1988), was to be the main character who went on an adventure to return home after getting lost, while being accompanied by a ventriloquist dummy. **Tinny eventually turned into Lunar Larry**, which became Buzz Lightyear. The dummy was given the identity of a cowboy and then became Woody.

676. When Woody is speaking to all the toys, you can see **all the books on Andy's shelf**. They are titled after the early Pixar shorts: *André and Wally B.* (1984), *Knick Knack* (1989), *Tin Toy* (1988), *Red's Dream* (1987). The authors on the spine are named after Pixar employees, like Lasseter on *Tin Toy*, which he wrote and directed; and Reeves, for Bill Reeves, is on *Red's Dream* because he was the Technical Director.

677. Bo Peep is based on the **character of a China shepherdess from the Hans Christian Andersen story** *The Shepherdess and The Chimney Sweep* published in 1845. The story was about toys coming to life.

678. When Andy and his mom are going to Pizza Planet, they stop to get gas at Dinoco. A **gas company later referenced** in *Cars* (2006).

679. When Buzz closes his eyes and jumps off the bed to prove he can fly, **he bounces off the Luxo Ball**. It first appeared in the short *Luxo, Jr.* (1986).

680. You can hear **the Wilhelm Scream stock sound** when Buzz Lightyear is knocked out of the window by the lamp.

681. This was the **top-grossing film of 1995**, taking in $373 million.

682. When Toy Shark sports Woody's hat and says, *"Look, I'm Woody! Howdy! Howdy! Howdy!,"* he is **referencing the Gary Larson "The Far Side" comic strip**, from the 1980's when a vulture eating a cowboy says *"Hey everyone, look at me, I'm a cowboy! Howdy! Howdy! Howdy!"*

683. In Sid's room, you can see a poster for a heavy metal band called "Megadork." **On the musician's arm is a Mickey tattoo.**

684. Penn Jillette from *Penn & Teller: Bulls**t!* (2003-2010) was the **voice of the commercial announcer** for the new Buzz Lightyear toy that the toys are watching.

685. The Buzz Lightyear **commercial makes mention of Al's Toy Barn**, which will be seen in *Toy Story 2* (1999).

Toy Story 2 (1999)

686. When Ham and Rex are looking at the TV and Ham turns it off, **the animators forgot to animate in their reflections;** it is just an empty room.

687. The tire swing in the tree from Jessie's past is **the tree from *A Bug's Life*** (1998).

688. When the newly-opened Buzz places the original Buzz under arrest, he sites Code 6404.5 as the violation ordinance. It means that all space rangers are to be in hyper-sleep. In actuality, the California **Code 6404.5 is the code that bans smoking in public places**.

689. When Jessie first meets Woody, she exclaims *"Sweet mother of Abraham Lincoln!"* This is sort of an inside joke as **the mother of Abraham Lincoln is Nancy Hanks.** Tom Hanks, the voice of Woody, is a descendant of one of her uncles. She is his third cousin, four times removed. Tom is also a distant cousin of Camille Olivia Hanks; she became Camille Cosby after she married Bill Cosby.

690. When Woody has his nightmare, Andy drops him through a pile of cards that are all the Ace of Spades. In popular history, **the Ace of Spades is the "death card."** It was made popular as such during the Vietnam War.

691. The cleaner who is called in to fix up Woody is **Geri from the Pixar short *Geri's Game*** (1997). Geri was modeled after Stuart Freeborn, a special effect makeup artist. He is referred to as the "Grandfather of modern makeup design." He fabricated the Yoda puppet for *Star Wars: The Empire Strikes Back* (1980). He worked in the film industry from 1936 until his retirement in 1990. Some of his more popular films were the original *Star Wars Trilogy* (1977, 1980, and 1983) and the *Superman* films (1978, 1980, 1983, and 1987).

692. While Hamm is flipping through channels at high speeds, **you can catch a glimpse of past Pixar shorts**, like *Luxo Jr.* (1986), *Red's Dream* (1987), *Tin Toy* (1988), and *Knick Knack* (1989). Mixed in among the shorts are

commercials Pixar created way before the release of *Toy Story* (1996); two commercials for Levis' Jeans for women, a juice box recycling commercial, three Listerine commercials, and also the original Pixar logo.

693. **There are four different Pixar balls to be seen in this film**. The first is in a blue basket on Andy's shelf, the second is in the Al's Toy Barn store, the third is outside the box in the Levi's Jeans commercial that Hamm passes when he is flipping through the channels, and the fourth is also while Hamm is channel surfing and he passes the clip from *Luxo Jr.*

Toy Story 3 (2010)

694. On the shelf in the preschool, **you can spot Mr. Ray from** *Finding Nemo* (2003).

695. When Jessie is chasing down the train, **you can spot the number 95 on the front of it**. That is the year *Toy Story* (1995) was released, and it is also the number of Lightning McQueen in the *Cars* films.

696. There is a poster on the wall in Andy's room of a blue car. It is **Finn McMissile from** *Cars 2* (2011).

697. One of Bonnie's toys is **a stuffed Totoro from the Studio Ghibli film** *My Neighbor Totoro* (1988), which Disney did the English dub for in 2005.

698. On Andy's wall you can spot a yellow diamond sign that says "Newt Crossing" with a newt silhouette on it. It is to **pay homage to the canceled Pixar film** *Newt* that was supposed to release in 2012.

699. The **bumblebee patch on Bonnie's backpack is Wally B.** from the very first Pixar short *The Adventures of André and Wally B.* (1984).

700. This film was the **first animated film to make over $1 billion** at the worldwide box office. It was then followed by *Frozen* (2013), *Minions* (2015), *Zootopia* (2016), and *Finding Dory* (2016).

701. **Ken wears 21 different outfits** throughout the film.

702. As Andy's mom is driving away, you can see **her license plate that says A113.**

Treasure Planet (2002)

703. **This film is based on the book** *Treasure Island* by Robert Louis Stevenson and was published in 1883. He was also the author of the *Strange Case of Dr. Jekyll and Mr. Hyde* (1886).

704. **You can see Stitch sitting on Jim's shelf in his bedroom**. It was there to pay homage to the previous film *Lilo & Stitch* (2002), which was released only five months before.

705. **Captain Amelia was voiced by Emma Thompson**. She would later voice Elinor in *Brave* (2012), Mrs. Potts in *Beauty and the Beast* (2017), and played P.L. Travers in *Saving Mr. Banks* (2013). Harry Potter fans will recognize her from the film series as Professor Sybil Trelawney.

706. **Jim Hawkins was voiced by Joseph Gordon-Levitt.** This film followed the release of *Angels in the Outfield* (1994) in which he played Roger only eight years before.

707. **This was the third time Disney has made an adaptation of the book.** The first incarnation was the first live-action film by Disney titled *Treasure Island* (1950), and also starred a completely male cast. The second film was *Muppet Treasure Island* (1996).

708. When Jim tells Doctor Doppler to save Captain Amelia, he responds with *"Dang it Jim. I'm an astronomer not a doctor."* **This was to make fun of a similar line quoted by Doctor McCoy** in *Star Trek* (1966-1969). Oddly enough, David Hyde Pierce was the voice of Doctor Doppler, and he played Dr. Niles Crane for 11 years on the television show *Frasier* (1993-2004).

Up (2009)

709. There are **10,286 helium balloons holding up the house**.

710. The villain, **Charles Muntz, is said to have been designed after Errol Flynn**, Clark Gable, Howard Hughes, and Walt Disney all mixed into one heroic, 1930's character.

711. Bob Peterson is the co-director of this film. In this film, **Bob voiced the ADHD dog, Dug**, and has also voiced some other memorable Pixar characters like Roz from *Monsters, Inc.* (2001) and *Monsters University* (2013), and Mr. Ray from *Finding Nemo* (2003) and *Finding Dory* (2016). He was also one of the writers for some Pixar films like *Finding Nemo* (2003), *Ratatouille* (2007), *Up* (2009), *The Good Dinosaur* (2014), and *Finding Dory* (2016).

712. When Carl's house floats by the apartment and the little girl goes running to the window, you can see **Lotso from *Toy Story 3*** (2010) in the bottom right of her room.

713. In that same room, you can see **the Pixar ball on the bottom right**.

714. In that little girl's room, you can see a poster on the wall with **Winston from the Walt Disney Animation Studio's short *Feast*** (2014). It was the short release with *Big Hero 6* (2014).

715. There is a **drawing on her wall of a "snipe,"** the same species as Kevin.

716. The grape soda bottle cap "Ellie Badge" is the **same grape soda that was in can form** in the Buzz Lightyear commercial in *Toy Story* (1995).

WALL·E

717. **Sir. Jonathan Ive, who designed the iPod, was called in for a day to the Pixar studio** at the request of Steve Jobs to help design the look of Eve for the film. He also designed the iMac and iPhone as well. Don't forget that Steve Jobs, who was the owner of Apple, started the Pixar studio.

718. **WALL·E stands for: Waste Allocation Load Lifter Earth-class**. EVE stands for: Extra-terrestrial Vegetation Evaluator.

719. When WALL·E is leaving Earth's atmosphere, there is space debris piled on him. **The last piece of debris to fall off of him is Sputnik I**. It was the first satellite sent into space by the Soviet Union on October 4, 1957.

720. Actor Fred Willard portrays Shelby Forthright, the CEO of the Buy n Large Corporation. His live-action recordings mark **the second time that Pixar has used live footage** in their full-length films. The first time it was used was earlier in this movie when WALL·E is watching the musical numbers "Put on Your Sunday Clothes" and "It Only Takes a Moment" from the movie *Hello, Dolly!* (1969).

721. The "Easter Egg" A113 can be seen as **AUTO's secret directive**.

722. **This film doesn't really have a villain**. As a computer, AUTO is only following its programming to prevent the humans from returning to earth.

723. The movie is set in the year 2805, only **700 years in the future**.

724. The musical score was composed by Thomas Newman. He also composed the music for films like *Finding Nemo* (2003), *Saving Mr. Banks* (2013), *Finding Dory* (2016), *Skyfall* (2012), *A Series of Unfortunate Events* (2004), and another 101 composing credits to his name. **Thomas' uncle, Lionel Newman, was also a composer**. He was the composer for *Hello, Dolly!* (1969), which is what was shown in this film. Lionel won Best Musical Score at the 42nd Academy Awards for that film. He actually beat out John Williams, who was nominated for his scoring of *Goodbye, Mr. Chips* (1969). Later on, Lionel would work as a music supervisor under John Williams while composing the music for *Star Wars: Episode IV - A New Hope* (1977).

Winnie the Pooh (2011)

725. This was the **last fully hand-drawn movie completed by Disney**. All the movies since have been computer animated. Although, there is the "You're Welcome" song in *Moana* (2016) which has the hand-drawn scene, along with Maui's tattoos.

726. Following *The Many Adventures of Winnie the Pooh* (1977), this is **the third time a sequel, or follow up film, was released to the theaters**. The other film partners were *The Rescuers* (1977) and *The Rescuers Down Under* (1990), and *Fantasia* (1940) and *Fantasia 2000* (1999).

727. The story supervisor for this film was Burny Mattinson. He isn't a stranger to the bear. **In the past, he was an animator** on the short *Winnie the Pooh and Tigger Too* (1974) and the film *The Many Adventures of Winnie the Pooh* (1977). He also wrote the stories for *The Rescuers* (1977), *The Fox and the Hound* (1981), *Mickey's Christmas Carol* (1983), *The Black Cauldron* (1985), *The Great Mouse Detective* (1986), *Beauty and the Beast* (1991), *Aladdin* (1992), *The Lion King* (1994), *Pocahontas* (1995), *The Hunchback of Notre Dame* (1996), *Mulan* (1998), and *Tarzan* (1999).

728. Burney Mattison's wife, **Sylvia, created the stuffed Winnie the Pooh** in the beginning of the film. The other characters were from the Disney Store.

729. This is the **only G-rated Animated Cannon Disney film** to be released in the 2010's.

730. In the opening sequence with the map, you can read "*Drawn by me*" and "*Mr. Shepard helpd.*" **This is to pay homage to the original book's illustrator** from 1926, E. H. Shepard.

731. When Tigger jumps from the mud to go find Eeyore, **you can see a Hidden Mickey** on the land.

Wreck-It Ralph (2012)

732. An early working **title for the film was *Reboot Ralph***.

733. At the end of the film, Wreck-It Ralph says that he likes it when everyone lifts him up because then he can see the Sugar Rush game. This isn't true as, **earlier in the movie, Ralph could see the whole Sugar Rush game** from further down the apartment building.

734. When the Sugar Rush game resets after Vanellope crosses the finish line and erases all existence of King Candy, **some of his décor and logos can still be seen in the background**.

735. The scene where Ralph tiptoes around the eggs containing the Cy-Bugs, and one opens and latches onto his face, was **to pay homage to the same scene from *Alien*** (1979) with the facehuggers.

736. The **film was released in the year of the 75ᵗʰ anniversary** of Walt Disney's full-length animated features, namely *Snow White and the Seven Dwarfs* (1937).

737. The **high score on Wreck-It Ralph's game is 120501**, which is Walt Disney's birthday 12/5/01.

738. **There is graffiti in Game Central Station** that says, "All your base are belong to us," which was meant to make fun of the English translation of a line in the game *Zero Wing* (1989).

739. **Another piece of graffiti says "Aerith Lives,"** which is a nod to the video game *Final Fantasy VII* (1997).

740. In Grand Central Station **you can see Vladimir from *Tangled*** (2010); he collects ceramic unicorns.

741. **Maximus from *Tangled*** (2010) can also be spotted in the same scene as Vladimir.

742. **Tiny the dinosaur from *Meet the Robinsons*** (2007) can also be seen in Grand Central Station.

743. Part of the title, "Fix-It," **was inspired by the LucasArts video game** *Night Shift* (1990) which had the two characters Fred & Fiona Fixit. Some of the style of the game was similar to the *Fix-It Felix Jr.* game.

744. Disney made a **free, downloadable version of the *Fix-It Felix Jr.* game** as an app for smartphones. It was also an arcade game that was free to play in the *Starcade Video Arcade* in *Disneyland's Tomorrowland*, but has since been removed.

745. During the 30th anniversary party in the beginning, **you can see two of the "Teddy Graham"** type characters from the Sugar Rush game from the spectator stands. They are the fans supporting the racer Crumbelina Di Caramello.

746. The jumping sound of Fix-It Felix is the **same jumping sound as Mario** from the game *Super Mario RBG: Legend of the Seven Stars* (1996).

747. In the beginning of the film there is a **Mickey Mouse on the billboard** behind the arcade.

748. The area around the Sugar Rush racetrack is decorated with lots of candy. Some of the candy are green peppermints, some of which **make Hidden Mickeys**.

749. During Ralph's Bad Guy support group meeting there is a **paper on the bulletin board with lip prints**. This is the paper from the short *Paperman* (2012), which was the short released to accompany this film in theaters.

750. The **Oreo cookies marching outside King Candy's castle are chanting** "Or-eee-oh, O-reeee-oh," and so on. It is a parody of the guards marching around the Wicked Witch of the West's castle in *The Wizard of Oz* (1939), in which they chanted "O-Ee-Yah! Eoh-Ah!" Throughout the years many have squabbled about the actual words the guards chant. Theses listed are from the script of the film. Some have chanted it as "Or-ee-oh" like the cookie, hence, the pun in the film.

Zootopia (2016)

751. **Won Best Animated Feature of 2016** at the Academy Awards.

752. Director Byron Howard **came up with the concept of *Zootopia* around the release time of *Tangled*** (2010). He drew inspiration from *The Lion King* (1994), *The Jungle Book* (1967), and *Robin Hood* (1973), the latter being Byron's favorite film growing up.

753. It took two years of research for the film to **make sure it was different than any other talking animal film** ever made.

754. In the scene with **Doug the ram**, he is dressed up in a yellow hazmat suit with a respirator. There is a knock on his door and it is two other sheep named Woolter and Jesse, who brought him a latte. This was to pay homage to the late show *Breaking Bad* (2008-2013), for which the scene of a drug lab resembled and has the main characters names of Walter and Jesse.

755. **Duke Weaselton** is the name of the weasel, which was a play on the character the Duke of Weselton in *Frozen* (2013), who was referred to as

the Duke of Weaselton. Both characters were voiced by Alan Tudyk. Judy even mispronounces Duke's last name as Weselton.

756. There are **64 different species of animals** seen in the film.

757. Assistant Mayor **Bellwether was modeled after previous Disney sheep** in the films *Fun & Fancy Free* (1947), *Melody Time* (1948), *Lambert the Sheepish Lion* (1952), *Pluto the Sheep Dog* (1949), and *Make Mine Music* (1946).

758. In every scene Bellwether is present, her outfit and glasses change. **All six of her outfits were made out of wool**, and one skirt even has a scissor pattern, to represent shears.

759. Bellwether is the **first time Disney had a female surprise villain**.

760. Bellwether is a Middle English **term used to indicate the lead sheep in a flock**. They would have a bell around their neck, and were generally a castrated male ram, which is called a "wether."

761. It is **foreshadowed that Bellwether knows Doug**, the sharpshooter with night howler pellets, because she has a post-it note on her phone with his name and number on it. You can see this when Bellwether answers her phone while she is helping Judy and Nick.

762. The whole scenario of Bellwether being the unseen villain is a reference to **the idiom "wolf in sheep's clothing."**

763. Mayor **Lionheart was inspired by the character of Mufasa** from *The Lion King* (1994).

764. **Judy Hopp's upper lip is connected**, even though real rabbits have a split upper lip.

765. Judy's uniform and **gear were inspired by U.S. Navy Seals** and horse's leg protection.

766. Judy was **given purple eyes** after the animators decided that her grey fur was too dull.

767. This is **Ginnifer Goodwin's third voice role for Disney**. Her first was in *Tinker Bell and the Legend of the Neverbeast* (2014), second was the character Gwen in *Sofia the First* (2014), and now Judy Hopps. Her character in Tinker Bell was Fawn, an animal fairy, and in *Zootopia* she is an animal. Ginnifer is most known for her character of Snow White in ABC's hit series *Once Upon A Time* (2011-present).

768. **Frantic pig was voiced by Josh Dallas**, who portrays Prince Charming on *Once Upon A Time* alongside Ginnifer Goodwin, with whom he is married to in real life.

769. Character **inspiration for Judy came from Superman** and the character Leslie Knope from *Parks and Recreation* (2009-2015), played by Amy Poehler, who is also the voice of Joy in *Inside Out* (2015).

770. **Cary Grant was an inspiration for Nick** Wilde's sly character traits.

771. Nick was **given visual similarities to Robin** from the film *Robin Hood* (1973).

772. King Richard the Lionheart from *Robin Hood* (1973) was the **inspiration for the name of Mayor Lionheart**.

773. Nick **calls Judy by her first name only one time in the film;** the rest of the time he calls her Rabbit or Carrots.

774. Nick Wilde's full name is Nicholas Piberius Wilde, a **play on the name James Tiberius Kirk** from *Star Trek*, according to co-director Byron Howard.

775. This is the Walt Disney Animation Studio's **third film starring only anthropomorphic characters**, non-humans. The first was *Robin Hood* (1973) and the second was *Chicken Little* (2005).

776. It is also the studio's **sixth film to star only animals**. The others were *Bambi* (1942), *Robin Hood* (1973), *The Lion King* (1994), *Dinosaur* (2000), and *Chicken Little* (2005).

777. About **80% of the designs made** for the film never ended up in the film.

778. There **was a computer effects program called "Keep Alive,"** which acted like a blowing machine and would continually look like leaves in trees and bushes were being blown to add a more realistic effect.

779. **Each tree has about 30,000 leaves on it**, which is continually moving, thanks to "Keep Alive." There are also 500,000 trees in the Rainforest District.

780. Generally, voice actors record their voices for a film separately because it is so hard to get everyone together for all the recording sessions. One of the rare exceptions is in this film with Ginnifer Goodwin and Jason Bateman, the voices of Judy and Nick. Ginnifer was filming *Once Upon A Time* in Canada, and Jason was filming movies here in the sates, but **they both made it in to do their recording together** to portray that onscreen chemistry. They were with the project for nearly two years from start to finish.

781. Byron Howard and Rich Moore both directed the film and **both provided the voices of Judy's nosey antelope neighbors**.

782. In the early stages of planning, **the animals of Zootopia wore collars** that prevented them from following their natural behavior of predator/prey.

783. Animated films use storyboards to help with the production process to show how the story is supposed to progress. **Zootopia's storyboard consisted of 197,136 story panels**.

784. **Animators studied muscular police officers** and noticed they couldn't button their top button, so they also did the same with Chief Bogo.

785. **Bogo got his name from "mbogo,"** which is the Swahili word for "African buffalo" or "Cape buffalo."

786. The individual strands of fur on each animal were created one strand at a time. After following the creation of *Frozen*, animators were able to master the effect of realistic looking hair. With the animals, **they were able to create different textures, colors, and lengths of fur**, which varied on each animal species.

787. **Animators studied real animal fur to get all the details and realism right**. Like the polar bears fur being clear to reflect light instead of just making it white, and the fox fur which starts out brown at the base and changes into a red as it goes out.

788. While in production, **the animators went to Kenya for two weeks to observe animals** in their natural habitat and watch how their society functioned. They also visited the San Diego Zoo's Safari Park, Walt Disney's Animal Kingdom, and the Natural History Museum.

789. While in Kenya, the film's director of cinematography, Nathan "Nate" Warner, was pecked by and ostrich, bitten by a zebra, and scratched by a cheetah. **This earned him the nickname "Nate the Bait."**

790. Part of the idea to have so many species of animals co-existing in the film came from **the film crew observing predators and prey mingling near each other** at the same watering hole and not bothering each other. This is why the city is centered around a body of water and expands outward.

791. **During production they interviewed many experts on the subject matter**, including zookeepers, anthropologists, behaviorists, and psychologists.

792. The animators had realistic amounts of hair on the different animals. **A mouse had about 400,000 strands of hair**, and a giraffe had 9.2 million strands. For comparison, Elsa from *Frozen* (2013) had 400,000 strands of hair, and Officer Hopps has 2.5 million.

793. John Lasseter, the films Executive Producer, was used as the reference model for Nick's scene of trying to eat a tiny piece of cake. **John had to struggle to eat a tiny piece of cake off of a nickel**.

794. **The story was written by Jennifer Lee** who also wrote the story and screenplay for *Frozen* (2013), *Frozen Fever* (2015), and the screenplay for *Wreck-It Ralph* (2012).

795. Officer Benjamin Clawhauser was originally going to be called Hugo, and **in concept art he wore a Hawaiian shirt like John Lasseter wears**.

796. An example of some of the animator's details can be seen in the sweater worn by Mrs. Otterton in the **fisherman knit style and with the fish patterns**.

797. The name Emmet Otterton was a nod to the **Jim Henson film *Emmet Otter's Jug-Band Christmas***(1977).

798. The elephant **owner of Jumbeaux's Café is Jerry Jumbeaux Jr.** Which is a nod to Disney's first main elephant, Dumbo, whose real name is Jumbo Junior.

799. Animator **Raymond Persi recorded some test voice recordings for Flash** in the DMV. John Lasseter and the rest of the crew liked it so much that they ended up using it in the film.

800. There are **five sections of the city of Zootopia:** Tundratown, Sahara Square, Rainforest District, The Burrows, and Rodentia.

801. **Animators looked at real cities besides New York and London** to inspire the architecture in Zootopia. Like Russia inspired *Tundratown*, Madrid's Atocha Railway Station inspired the interior of Zootopia's train station, Monte Carlo in Dubai inspired *Sahara Square* as many of the animals in the desert are nocturnal showing the need for a nightlife, and *Savanah Central* was based on the Disney Park's hub and spoke design.

802. The **animators used a size chart** when designing all of the animals so they would appear similar in size as they do in real life.

803. Tajunga and Vine were the crossroads in the Rainforest District that Judy and Nick come across when they are looking for the panther limo driver. These were **named after the streets of where the animators were located** while working on the film.

804. The **currency used in Zootopia is called Bucks**, with male deer printed on the front. This is because we refer to a dollar bill as a "buck," which goes back to the mid-1700's when a buck skin was used as a form of payment for bartering before the induction of U.S. currency in 1778.

805. Depending on **what country you live in will determine which newscaster you see** on the ZNN News. This was a detail added in, depending on which animal is more known in those regions. The U.S.A., Canada, and France have a moose, Japan has a tanuki (also called a raccoon dog, and is featured in the *Studio Ghibli* film *Pom Poko*), Australia and New Zealand have a koala, China has a panda bear, Brazil has a jaguar, and the United Kingdom has a Welsh corgi.

806. The voice of the newscaster, Peter Moosebridge, is the **Canadian news anchor Peter Mansbridge**.

807. The slow-paced voice of Priscilla the sloth in the DMV, Department of Mammal Vehicles, **was provided by Kristen Bell**, who provides the fast-paced voice of Princess Anna in *Frozen* (2013). Also, the sloth is one of Kristen's favorite animals.

808. Originally, **the storyline had Nick as the main character**, but test audiences connected better with Judy, so the storyline was changed.

809. The **scene with Mr. Big is a big nod to the film** *The Godfather* (1972), with the character of Mr. Big sounding like Marlon Brando's character, and the fact that the scene is taking place at the time of his daughter's wedding.

810. When the train arrives in Bunny Burrow to pick up Judy, it blows its horn, and again when it arrives in Zootopia. **This is the sound of the Monorail from the Disney parks.**

811. There are numerous puns consisting of **animal versions of common human brand names**, including, Lucky Chomps (Lucky Charms cereal), Urban Snoutfitters (Urban Outfitters clothes shops), Zuber (ride-hailing service Uber), Pawpsicle (Popsicle frozen pops), Lemming Bros. Bank (erstwhile Lehman Bros.), Trader Doe's (Trader Joe's food stores), Mousy's (Macy's department store), Moustercharge (MasterCharge credit cards), Furs National Bank (instead of First), Targoat (Target), among others.

812. In Europe, *Zootopia* **is called** *Zootropolis*.

813. This is the **first film from Walt Disney Animation Studio to have a non-November release** since *Winnie the Pooh* (2011).

814. The name of the nudist elephant yoga instructor is Nangi, **which means "nude" in India**.

815. **Originally, the film's setting was going to be a dystopian setting**. Basically a futuristic setting with the world in disarray and decay. Much like the film *Mad Max* (1979).

816. The **storyline portrays the evolution of animals** if humans never existed.

817. Of all the animals shown in the film, **apes can't be found**. They were left out intentionally because Rich Moore said they are too similar to humans.

818. When Judy first arrives in Zootopia, **you can see a Buy n Large building**, referencing *WALL•E* (2008).

819. The **flower shop where Emmet works is called** *Flora and Fauna*, named after two of the fairies in *Sleeping Beauty* (1959).

820. After Judy returns to the city to solve the case, she is wearing a pink shirt and blue jeans. Nick is wearing a green shirt and pants. They are both wearing the same **clothing color combination as Br'er Fox and Br'er Rabbit** in *Song of the South* (1946).

821. **The head of Baymax**, from *Big Hero 6* (2014), can be seen as an antennae topper on Finnick's van.

822. **On the back, left side of Finnick's van you can see Maui's hook**, an "Easter Egg" for the next movie to be released, *Moana* (2016). You can see it really well when Judy goes to the van to look for Nick at the end of the movie.

EASTER EGGS

What is an "Easter Egg?" An "Easter Egg" is an item or character that is placed in a movie other than the one it originated in. For example: in *Aladdin* (1992), there is a scene in which you can see Sebastian the crab from *The Little Mermaid* (1989) when Genie pulls him out of the cook book. Sebastian is not from *Aladdin* and is out of place being seen in that film, so he is considered an "Easter Egg." There can also be Hidden Mickeys or even something to pay homage to something else. Here is a listing of some other "Easter Eggs."

1. In *Lilo and Stitch* (2002) there is a scene when Lilo is in Nani's room talking next her bed; you can **see a poster for the animated film** *Mulan* (1998) on the wall.

2. In *Hunchback of Notre Dame* (1996), **Belle appears** during the film's second musical number, during the sequence in which Quasimodo sings "Out There" from atop the roof of the Notre Dame cathedral. As the camera slowly pans down and along a street reminiscent of Belle's home town in *Beauty and the Beast* towards a small group of people, Belle appears in the bottom right-hand corner of the screen, walking and reading a book (and wearing her blue dress, of course).

3. In that same scene from *Hunchback of Notre Dame* (1996), you can catch glimpses of a rooftop satellite dish. Down in the square **you can see Pumba,** from *The Lion King* (1994), being carried by two men with a pole. You can also see a street merchant shaking out **the flying carpet** from *Aladdin* (1992).

4. In *The Great Mouse Detective* (1986), there is a **lizard in Rattigan's gang**. He made an earlier appearance as Bill, the lizard with a ladder, in *Alice in Wonderland* (1951).

5. In *Cinderella* (1950), when Cinderella is singing "Sing, Sweet Nightingale," **three bubbles float around to form a Hidden Mickey**.

6. In *Cinderella* (1950), the carriage that Cinderella and the prince take after the wedding has **an emblem of a sword and two Hidden Mickeys** around it.

7. **The cookies that the three good fairies eat** with their tea are shaped like Hidden Mickeys in *Sleeping Beauty* (1959).

8. There is a **Hidden Mickey on the scroll** that Ursula gets Ariel to sign in *The Little Mermaid* (1989). It is in the middle of the words when it pans over the scroll from top to bottom.

9. In *The Little Mermaid* (1989), when Eric's maid, Carlotta, bathes Ariel and serves dinner, you can see **she is wearing the same outfit Cinderella wears,** except for the scarf on her head.

10. In *The Little Mermaid* (1989), when Eric is waiting for Ariel to arrive, **one of the portraits is that of Princess Aurora** and Prince Phillip from *Sleeping Beauty* (1959).

243

11. In *The Little Mermaid* (1989), when Ariel is singing "Part of Your World," **you can spot a bust of Abraham Lincoln**. It was placed there to pay homage to one of Walt's favorite American icons. This is why Walt had the *Great Moments with Mr. Lincoln* attraction created for the World's Fair, and then later moved it to *Main Street, USA*.

12. In *The Little Mermaid* (1989), there is a **Hidden Mickey in the scene where the animals are trying to break up the wedding**, right as the seals are jumping onto the deck of the boat from the ocean. There is a woman with black hair in a red gown with her back to the camera. The shape of her hair clearly forms a hidden Mickey, until she turns sideways.

13. During the opening scene when King Triton arrives at the arena in *The Little Mermaid* (1989), **you can briefly see Mickey Mouse, Goofy, and Donald Duck** in the crowd of sea-people as merfolk when he passes over them. In the same scene, there is a mermaid wearing a Mickey ear hat.

14. When the Beast is getting his hair cut for Belle, the hair **style he is given is the same as Lion's** in *The Wizard of Oz* (1939).

15. The sugar bowl in Mrs. Potts' tea set, from *Beauty and the Beast* (1991), is **the same sugar bowl** from *The Sword in the Stone* (1963), but with a slight color change.

16. When the sultan is being carried down the aisle in *Aladdin and the King of Theives* (1996), you can see one of the patrons on the right side near the aisle **wearing a Mickey ear hat**.

17. The stack of wooden toy animals that Jasmine's **father plays with, has a toy of the Beast** from *Beauty and the Beast* (1991).

18. There is a scene in *Aladdin* (1992) when Rajah is turning from a tiger cub into an adult tiger again; you can see one frame where they animated **Mickey's face in the place of Rajah's**.

19. In the throne room scenes from *Aladdin* (1992), the **decorations at the top of the columns are the same designs** used for Mrs. Potts and her teacups in *Beauty and the Beast* (1991).

20. In *Mulan* (1998), the spots on Shang's **horse's neck and rump are shaped like a Hidden Mickey**.

21. In *Princess and The Frog* (2009), **you can see the "A113" on the streetcar** that Tiana is trying to board. "A113" was the classroom number where character animation students at the California Institute of the Arts had classes. Many of its alumni, including Brad Bird, have used the number in their professional works. It appears in some way, shape, or form in every Pixar film.

22. When Stitch is fighting Jumba in Nani's room in *Lilo And Stitch* (2002), you can see a photo on the **night stand of people wearing Mickey ear hats**.

23. At the start of *The Great Mouse Detective* (1986), as the camera pans down to the front door of Basil of Baker Street, you can see **the silhouette of the great Sherlock Holmes**, after whom Basil was modeled.

24. In *Aladdin* (1992), during the "Whole New World" song, Jasmine and Aladdin fly past **the temple and statue from *Hercules*** (1997). Aladdin even hands Jasmine an apple from a tree just like Pagasus from *Hercules* (1997).

25. In *Hercules* (1997), during the "I Won't Say I'm In Love" singing number with Meg, the muses are posed as busts in the garden the **same way the busts are in the *Haunted Mansion*** in *Disneyland*.

26. At the end of *Aladdin* (1992), when the Genie is hugging everyone goodbye, he is **wearing a Goofy hat**.

27. After Hercules gives away his strength, listen after the titans go to Mt. Olympus. Right after the huge cyclops goes into the city, when the people are running, **you can hear the "wilhelm scream."** The "wilhelm scream" is a sound effect scream that was created for the movie *Distant Drums* (1951). Sound editors have been using it as a joke in over 130 films, including all the *Star Wars* and *Indiana Jones* films.

28. When Hercules is posing for his portrait for the vase, he is wearing a lion skin on his back. **It is Scar from *The Lion King*** (1994).

29. In *Hercules* (1997), during the singing number by the muses, one of them hangs upside down and **her hair forms a Hidden Mickey**.

30. There is a scene in *The Hunchback of Notre Dame* (1996) when Quasimodo and Esmerelda are in his room and she looks at the unfinished dolls. One of the dolls resembles **the baker from the opening scene of *Beauty and the Beast*** (1991) when Belle is singing *Belle*.

31. You can spot **Buzz Lightyear as a toy on the ground** in the waiting room of the dentist in *Finding Nemo* (2003).

32. During the opening credits to *Princess and the Frog* (2009), you can spot a woman shaking out a rug on the balcony that **looks a lot like Carpet from *Aladdin*** (1992).

33. At the end of *Finding Nemo* (2003), when the fish escape the dentist's office and are bobbing on the water in the bags, **you can see Luigi from *Cars*** (2006) drive by.

34. In *One Hundred and One Dalmatians* (1961), **you can spot Lady and Tramp** from *Lady and the Tramp* (1955) in the scene when all the dogs are barking across town.

35. When Rapunzel is running up the stairs in the opening song of *Tangled* (2010), you can spot items panted on the railing posts. One is an apple, a high heel shoe, a rose, and a cockle sea shell. All are a throwback to the **past princesses, Snow White, Cinderella, Belle, and Ariel**.

36. After Rapunzel and Flynn Ryder enter the Snuggly Duckling in *Tangled* (2010), you can **spot Pinocchio sitting in the rafters**.

37. A child sitting in the dental office waiting room in *Finding Nemo* (2003) is reading a magazine with **Mr. Incredible from *The Incredibles*** (2004) on the front cover.

38. In *Tarzan* (1999), during the "Trashin the Camp" singing routine, you can see Terk playing the drums on **Mrs. Potts and Chip from *Beauty and the Beast*** (1991).

39. Lilo wakes Noni up in the middle of the night to show her that Stitch can play a record with his fingernail and mouth in *Lilo and Stitch* (2002). On the wall in the background is **a poster for the movie *Mulan*** (1998).

40. In *Monsters, Inc.* (2001), when Sulley takes Mary (Boo) back to her bedroom at the completion of the film, she tries to hand him **a stuffed Nemo from *Finding Nemo*** (2003), a film that wouldn't be released for 2 years after *Monsters, Inc.*

41. When Merida visits the Witch in her cottage in *Brave* (2012), you can see **a carving of Sulley** from *Monsters University* (2013) on a piece of wood resting on the floor.

42. In that same scene in *Brave* (2012) when the Witch is talking by her carving table, you can spot **a wooden Pizza Planet truck** from *Toy Story* (1995).

43. In *One Hundred and One Dalmatians* (1961), when you can see in the pet shop window, **you can spot Peg from *Lady and the Tramp*** (1955) sitting against the pen wall near all the barking puppies.

44. When Genie is explaining to Aladdin about how wishes work, he **changes his head very briefly into Pinocchio**.

45. In Jim Hawkins' room in *Treasure Planet* (2002), there is **a Stitch figure sitting on his shelf** from *Lilo and Stitch* (2002).

46. In *Big Hero 6* (2014), there was a Nick Wilde poster and phone case, both referencing the future film *Zootopia* (2016).

47. In *Zootopia* (2016), in Tundra Town, there are two little girl elephants walking with their mother and **wearing an Elsa and Anna dress** from the movie *Frozen* (2013).

48. In *Zootopia*, when Judy is chasing Weaselton in Rodentia, **you can see a Hans's Pastry Shop** near the giant doughnut. This is a nod to Hans from *Frozen*.

49. In *Zootopia*, when Judy first meets Nick in Jumbeaux's Café, there are serving plates on a shelf behind the register that have the same flower pattern as the wallpaper in Ana's room from *Frozen* (2013).

50. In *Zootopia*, **Duke Weaselton is selling bootleg movies** with titles like Pig Hero 6 (Big Hero 6), Wrangled (Tangled), and Wreck-It Rhino (Wreck-It Ralph). All are nods to past Disney films. There are also nods at future films like Meowana (Moana), Giraffic (Gigantic), and Floatzen 2 (Frozen 2).

51. In Zootopia, **Genie's lamp can be seen on the shelf** in the Naturalist Club right before they walk through the doors to the outside.

52. *Zootopia* references *Frozen* when Chief Bogo tells Judy "Life isn't a cartoon musical where your dreams come true, so *let it go!*"

53. **Lucky Cat Café is seen in** *Zootopia's* **Rodentia** and in the city in *Big Hero 6*.

54. In the *Zootopia* poster, you can actually see a **young zebra holding a Mickey Mouse doll.**

55. While Nick is pushing Finnick in the stroller down the sidewalk in *Zootopia*, they pass another **stroller that is yellow; there is a plush Mickey Mouse** in it.

56. On Officer **Clawhauser's right cheek, you can see three spots making a Mickey Mouse** head in the film *Zootopia* (2016).

57. In Chief Bogo's office in *Zootopia*, you can see a **calendar on his wall with San Fransokyo** on it from *Big Hero 6* (2014).

DISNEY THINGS EXPLAINED

DUFFY THE DISNEY BEAR

Who is Duffy the Disney Bear?

Duffy the Disney Bear is a Disney character that can be found at *Tokyo Disney Resort*, *Disneyland* and *Disney's California Adventure*, *Walt Disney World*, *Hong Kong Disneyland* and *Disneyland Paris*.

The story behind how Duffy came to be is actually a very simple story. One day Mickey was preparing to set sail for a long voyage around the world. Minnie thought he should have something special to remind him of how much he was loved at home. She stayed up all night to hand make a plush teddy bear with all of her heart. Mickey adored him and named him Duffy the Disney Bear.

With Duffy in tow, Mickey toured the globe and went to ports in Hawaii, Japan, the Mediterranean, and Castaway Cay. There were plenty of stops along the way to meet old friends and make new ones. Mickey and Duffy took pictures together, always saying "Cheese!" in front of landmarks and with their pals. This is why you can see Duffy in photo opportunities at the Meet and Greet section in *California Adventure* by the bridge from *Pacific Wharf*.

Still want to know more about how this teddy bear came to the Disney parks? Although he was originally created for and briefly sold at the *Disney World Once Upon a Toy* shop in Orlando in 2002, Duffy only became popular after Oriental Land executives adopted the character, gave it a name and a backstory, and aggressively marketed it in the *Tokyo DisneySea* park. Japanese fans took to it and some of them started to carry around multiple Duffy plush bears during their visits to the park. The *My Friend Duffy* show replaced a Donald Duck-themed show at the *American Waterfront Cape Cod Cook-Off* hamburger restaurant in 2010.

Duffy was previously known as "The Disney Bear" with an entirely different backstory. The original story found on the tag of the first released bear's ear said that Mickey brought his favorite bear to the *Magic Kingdom*. Mickey sat in front of the castle wishing that he had a friend with him to share the excitement and magic of the park. Tinker Bell appears and sprinkles pixie dust on Mickey's bear, bringing it to life. Mickey then hugs the bear and a Mickey-shape appears on the bear's face, forever bonding Mickey and his new friend.

Duffy the Disney Bear joined American Disney parks on October 14, 2010. He was welcomed at *Epcot* and *Disney's California Adventure*. He then joined *Hong Kong Disneyland Resort* on November 19, 2010. He was welcomed at *Main Street, U.S.A.* in *Hong Kong Disneyland*. He joined *Disneyland Paris* on June 2011.

Duffy is also featured in the video game *Kinect Disneyland Adventures,* where the players can interact with him even though he doesn't speak.

Duffy is unique among Disney characters in that he was not first featured in a Disney movie or television show until he made his television debut in the 2010

Disney Parks Christmas Day Parade. He also is on his own Bedtime Story Channel in *Walt Disney World*.

Not only does Duffy the Disney Bear exist, but Disney has made a companion for him, Shellie May Bear. She first showed up in January 2010 at *DisneySea Tokyo*. Shellie May hasn't woked her way to California to join Duffy in the parks, but I'm sure it will happen soon.

Minnie Mouse found out that Duffy was lonely, so she created Shellie May the Disney Bear as a companion for him. Shellie May has blue eyes compared to Duffy's brown ones. Her paws are a rose pink whereas Duffy's are brown. Both Shellie May and Duffy have birth marks in the shape of a Mickey head on their backsides, but opposite of each other.

OSWALD THE LUCKY RABBIT

Have you been walking around *Disneyland* or *California Adventure* and seen articles of clothing or souvenirs with a black and white rabbit as the theme and wondered who he was? He is Oswald The Lucky Rabbit and was recently reacquired by The Walt Disney Company in 2006. In order to reaquire Oswald, Disney traded Al Michaels from Disney's ABC and ESPN to NBC Sports, which was owned by Universal at the time. They released Al from his contract so he could sign with NBC and be broadcasting with his friend John Madden again. NBC was bought by Comcast in February 2013 for $16.7 billion.

Where did Oswald come from? From 1923 to 1927, Walt and his fellow animator Ub Iwerks (see *Imagineer Mini Biographies* page 287) were animating a series called *Alice Comedies* for *Winkler Pictures*, which was run by Margaret Winkler (the first woman to produce animated films, and was the producer for the animated series of *Felix The Cat*) and her fiancée Charles Mintz, who was later Walt's producer. Due to the higher costs of producing the *Alice Comedies*, Walt and Ub Iwerks were asked to design a new cartoon character to sell to *Universal Studios,* who wanted to delve into the world of animated series production. Because of this, Walt and Ub came up with Oswald The Lucky Rabbit. Oswald was the first cartoon series produced by Universal Studios.

Oswald's first appearance was supposed to be in the short *Poor Papa* in 1927. Universal didn't like how the film turned out and said it was poorly animated and Oswald looked too old, so they turned it down. Ub touched up Oswald and made him look younger and, along with Walt, made a second film which was released September 5, 1927, and was called *Trolly Troubles*. *Poor Papa* was released August 13, 1932, but was renamed *Mickey's Nightmare* and ended up starring Mickey Mouse instead of "old Oswald." Oswald went on to star in 194 animated shorts between 1927 and 1943. He was voiced by many voice actors including Bill Nolan (1929), Pinto Colvig (voice of Pluto and Goofy) (1930–1931), Mickey Rooney (1931–1932), Bernice Hansen (1932-1938), Walter Lantz (1935), June Foray (see *Who Does That Voice* page 149) (1943), and in the video games, Frank Welker (2010–present). Until October 14, 1929, with the release of *Cold Turkey*, Oswald was a silent film character.

After creating 26 animated films with Ub, in spring of 1928, Walt traveled to New York to see his producer, Charles Mintz, to renegotiate his contract with *Winkler Pictures*. The times were hard then and the economy was in decline. Walt wanted a raise and Charles wanted to cut him 20%, along with the other animating staff. Animators, including Harman, Ising, Maxwell, and Freleng were under contract and had to stay on with Universal to continue creating the shorts. Mintz said he would start his own animation studio to produce the shorts for Universal. That is when Walt decided to quit while the rest of his staff opted to stay, or were under contract to do so. On the train ride home from New York, Walt came up with the idea for a little cartoon mouse called Mortimer. Walt shared this idea with his wife Lillian, who didn't like the name Mortimer and suggested calling him Mickey. Walt and Ub worked in secret to create the first Mickey Mouse cartoon with Walt as the director and Ub as the animator who molded the character of Mickey Mouse to star in his first film, *Plane Crazy*, but it was a silent film. They then released *Steamboat Willie* on November 18, 1928. At this point, Mickey Mouse skyrocketed past Oswald The Lucky Rabbit in popularity to become the most iconic animated character of all time.

After the cancelation of his animated shorts, Oswald began starring in comic books published by DC Comics (Superman, Batman, Wonder Woman, Green Lantern, the Justice League) from 1935 until the early 1960's. He even starred with Woody Woodpecker. Oswald was published in 201 comic books before his discontinuation with DC Comics. Through the end of the 20th century, other comic book companies from Italy and Mexico were responsible for his comics.

In 2006, Disney was able to call Oswald back home to his Disney family and in January 2007, he introduced him to everyone with a T-shirt line from *Comme des Garçons* (a Japan-based clothing design company), which would be the first Oswald merchandise. The following December, Disney released a two-disc DVD set titled *The Adventures of Oswald the Lucky Rabbit*, in the Walt Disney Treasures collection that contained 13 episodes from 1927-1928. In 2010, Oswald showed up in the popular video game *Epic Mickey*. *Disneyland* didn't see Oswald until the entrance to *California Adventure* was closed down in 2011 to turn it into *Buena Vista Street*. He was on the "under construction" walls. When *Buena Vista Street* opened in July 2012, Oswald had his own gas station themed shop called *Oswald's Service Station*. Oswald is kept primarily in *California Adventure* as Mickey Mouse is in *Disneyland*. On September 14, 2014 (nine days after his birthday), Oswald showed up as a meet-and-greet character on *Buena Vista Street* in *California Adventure*.

THE FAB FIVE
Who are the Fab Five?

"The Fab Five" is the nick-name for the grouping of Mickey Mouse, Donald Duck, Goofy, Pluto, and Minnie Mouse. Later, Daisy Duck was added in 1940 and the group was unofficially called the "Sensational Six."

MICKEY MOUSE FUN FACTS

 For Mickey Mouse fun facts, see the section *It All Started By A Mouse* on page 85.

DONALD DUCK FUN FACTS

 Donald's birthday is June 9, 1934.

 Donald's first film was *The Wise Little Hen* (1934).

 Donald was the first of the "Sensational Six" to **debut in a color film.**

 Technically, **Donald Duck has two birthdays**. A character's birthday is set depending on the air date of their first film; Donald has two. One is June 9, 1934, when the film *The Wise Little Hen* was released. His other birthday is March 13, because of the film *Donald's Happy Birthday* (1949), in which Huey, Dewey, and Louie planned to get Uncle Donald an awesome present of cigars, but Donald finds out and isn't too happy thinking his nephews are taking up cigar smoking.

 In 1949, **Donald Duck surpassed Mickey Mouse** as being the most popular Disney character.

 The quackiness of his voice is one of the **most identifiable voices** of all animated characters.

 Donald is **the mascot of the University of Oregon**. Walt had a handshake agreement with Leo Harris, the Athletic Director of the University of Oregon, in 1947 to allow them to use Donald as the mascot. After Walt's death in 1966, the Disney Company tried to get the use rights back from the university. Due to photographic proof of Walt with Leo sporting the University of Oregon attire, Disney granted them the use of Donald in 1973, but retained the right to say when and where Donald could be used. In 1984, Donald Duck was named an honorary alumnus of the University of Oregon during his 50th birthday celebration.

 He received **his own star** on the Hollywood Boulevard Walk of Fame on August 9, 2004.

 Donald has **appeared in 14 full-length animated features**, more than any of the other Sensational Six - *The Reluctant Dragon* (1941), *Saludos Amigos* (1942), *The Three Caballeros* (1944), *Fun and Fancy Free* (1947), *Melody Time* (1948), *Who Framed Roger Rabbit* (1988), *Mickey's 60th*

251

Birthday (1988), *A Goofy Movie* (1995), *Mickey's Once Upon a Christmas* (1999), *Fantasia 2000* (1999), *Mickey's Magical Christmas: Snowed in at the House of Mouse* (2001), *Mickey's House of Villains* (2002), *Mickey's Twice Upon a Christmas* (2004), *Mickey, Donald, Goofy: The Three Musketeers* (2004).

- Out of collection of the "Sensational Six," **Donald has appeared in more shorts** than any of them.

- Donald's voice **was performed by Clarence "Ducky" Nash** from 1934-1983. Nash trained Tony Anselmo, who has been the voice of Donald from 1985 to present.

- Donal's **full name is Donald Fauntleroy Duck**. This is first said in the animated short *Donald Gets Drafted* (1942).

- One of Donald's films titled ***Der Feuhrer's Face* won an academy award** in 1943, which has been the center of controversy over the decades. It depicted Donald as a Nazi who worked in the military for Hitler before finding out at the end that he was just dreaming.

- Donald **has three nephews**; Huey, Dewey, and Louie.

- Scrooge McDuck and Ludwig Von Drake are **Donald's uncles**.

- Donald's **cousin is Gladstone Gander**.

- From 1942 to 1944, Walt Disney released six short **films depicting Donald Duck's life in the U.S. Army**. This series of films came to be known as the Army shorts. Cartoons in the series include *Donald Gets Drafted* (1942), *The Vanishing Private* (1942), *Sky Trooper* (1942), *Fall Out Fall In* (1943), *The Old Army Game* (1943), and *Commando Duck* (1944).

- A rumor started in 1977 that Donald comics and books were **banned from Finland libraries and youth clubs because he wasn't wearing any pants**. The truth is that Finland felt that the money could be used elsewhere for bettering their youth programs.

- Donald Duck's **superhero alter ego is "Super Duck,"** also called "The Masked Mallard."

GOOFY FUN FACTS

- **Goofy's birthday** is May 25, 1932.

- Goofy first appeared in *Mickey's Review* in 1932. **Goofy's original name was Dippy Dawg**. Goofy is actually his nickname. The other names he has gone by are George Geef, G. G. Geef, Goofy Goof, G. G. Goof, and Goofus D. Dawg.

- The **Goofy holler is a stock sound effect** that is used frequently in Walt Disney cartoons and films. It is the cry Goofy makes when falling or being launched into the air, which could be transcribed as "yaaaaaaa-hoo-hoo-hooey!!" The holler was originally recorded by yodeller and professional ski racer, Hannès Schroll, for the 1941 short *The Art of Skiing*. The holler is also used in films and cartoons in which Goofy doesn't appear, generally in situations which are particularly "goofy" like *Cinderella, Bedknobs and*

Broomsticks, Pete's Dragon, The Hunchback of Notre Dame, Home on the Range, Enchanted, and many more.

- Goofy was **originally voiced by Pinto Colvig** in 77 animated shorts. Pinto was also famous for voicing Sleepy and Grumpy in *Snow White* (1937) and Pluto in 83 animated shorts. He was also the first Bozo the Clown for the television series *Bozo's Circus* (1949).

- Other voice actors to play Goofy are;
  - George Johnson (1939–1943)
  - Hal Smith - *Mickey's Christmas Carol* (1983)
  - Will Ryan - *DTV Valentine* (1986) and *Down and Out with Donald Duck* (1987)
  - Tony Pope - *Soccermania* (1987) and *Who Framed Roger Rabbit* (1988)
  - Bill Farmer (1986–present)

- Pinto had a falling out with Disney in 1939 and left the company. Disney still wanted to make Goofy cartoons but lost their voice actor. This started the **era of the *"How To…"* shorts** in the 1940's with John McLeish or Fred Shields as the narrator. Goofy had very few lines, and when he did, they would reuse old recordings of Pinto or hire another voice actor to impersonate him. There were a total of 10 *"How To…"* shorts made: *How to Play Baseball* (1942), *How to Swim* (1942), *How to Fish* (1942), *How to Be a Sailor* (1944), *How to Play Golf* (1944), *How to Play Football* (1944), *How to Ride a Horse* (1950), *How to Be a Detective* (1952), *How to Dance* (1953), *How to Sleep* (1953), and *How to Hook Up Your Home Theater* (2007). The last was narrated by Corey Burton.

- In the 1950's, Disney started a bunch of shorts starring Goofy as "George Geef," a regular person. **This period of shorts was called *The Everyman Years*.** They were intended to make Goofy relatable to everyday people by putting Goofy in situations that regular people faced, like quitting smoking, getting sick, raising a family, and dieting.

- Goofy's son's name is Max, and he is seen in the 90's series *Goof Troop*. Goofy had a son in the animated shorts of the 50's, but his name was Goofy Junior; Goofy (George Geef) would call him Junior or George. People believe that his first son may have been Max or at least the precursor to him. Junior appeared in four shorts including *Fathers Are People* (1951), *Father's Lion* (1952), *Father's Day Off* (1953), and *Aquamania* (1961). In Junior's first two shorts, he was voiced by Bobby Driscoll, who is also know for voicing Peter Pan in 1953, and starring in *Treasure Island* (1950), *Melody Time* (1948), *So Dear To My Heart* (1948) and *Song Of The South* (1946), to name a few.

PLUTO FUN FACTS

- **Pluto's birthday** is September 5, 1930.

- **Pluto wasn't always named Pluto**. In fact, he didn't even have a name in his first cartoon. He was one of two unnamed hounds to chase down an escaped Mickey Mouse in the short *The Chain Gang*, released September 5,

1930. In his second short he was referred to as "Rover" by Minnie Mouse, because Pluto was her dog and didn't even belong to Mickey Mouse yet. That short was released on October 23, 1930 and was called *The Picnic*. It wasn't until May 8, 1931, in the short *The Moose Hunt* that he is referred to as Pluto the Pup by his new and permanent owner, Mickey Mouse.

- Pluto has **starred in 44 short cartoons** of his own between 1937 and 1951.

- It is a little known fact that Pluto is actually **modeled after a dog breed called an English Pointer**. The design artist, Norm Ferguson, owned an English Pointer and so designed Pluto after him. Pluto is shown at his best at pointing in the animated short *The Pointer* (1939).

- Pluto was **originally voiced by Pinto Colvig** in 83 animated shorts, just like Goofy.

- **Pluto has spoken once in his career**. He whispered "Kiss Me" in *The Moose Hunt* (1931), and also had one somewhat-spoken line in *Mickey and the Seal* (1948), when he mumbled the word "Huh?" after Mickey said he was going to keep the seal.

- Besides Goofy, Pluto is the only other one in the "Sensational Six" to have offspring. **He fathered a litter of puppies** in *Pluto's Quin-puplets* in November 26, 1937. He was in an episode with one of his pups named Pluto Junior in *Pluto, Junior* on February 28, 1942.

- Pluto's wife is a **Pekingese named Fifi**, short for Flapper, a dog belonging to Minnie Mouse.

- In *Plutos Kid Brother*, April 12, 1946, we were introduced to **Pluto's brother, K.B**.

- Pluto, along with Mickey, **was in the last black & white animated short** before they started making them in color. It was titled *Mickey's Kangaroo* on April 13, 1935.

- Pluto is the only character from the "Sensational Six" **that doesn't appear in the Disney video game** *Disney Universe* (2011).

- Pluto was **named after the recently-discovered planet of Pluto** from the year before, which was later downsized to a dwarf star in 2006.

MINNIE MOUSE FUN FACTS

- **Minnie's birthday** is technically the same as Mickey's, since they both debuted together, November 18, 1928.

- Minnie Mouse is **short for Minerva Mouse.**

- **Minnie has four pets** - a cat named Figaro, who first appeared in *Pinocchio* (1940), Fifi the Pekingese, who is the mate of Pluto, Cleo the goldfish, also from *Pinocchio* (1940), and Frankie the canary from *Figaro and Frankie* (1947).

- Minnie **used to date Mortimer Mouse** before she got with Mickey.

- **Walt Disney provides the voice for Minnie in the three movies** released in 1928. The Minnie voice was then passed on to Marcellite Garner.

Marcellite was an ink and paint girl for the Disney Company. She auditioned for the role of Minnie Mouse and was partially chosen for the role because she was only one of two women there who could speak Spanish for the film *The Cactus Kid* (1930). The other woman didn't want to sing, so Marcellite acquired the role. She voiced Minnie Mouse in 50 films over an 11-year span, and that was the extent of her acting career. She is attributed for giving the personality that Minnie has today.

- For the single short *Mild Waves* (1929), **Marjorie Ralston would be the first female to privide the voice of Minnie.** Her first spoken line is, "Help!" Marjorie was an inker with Walt Disney Productions and was actually the thirteenth employee hired by them.

- Most recently, the **archive recordings of Marcellite Garner were used** to voice Minnie in the new animated short *Get a Horse!* (2013). It was released with *Frozen* (2013) in theaters.

- **Voice actress Thelma Boardman took over the voice** of Minnie from 1941-1942. She ended her voice acting career after she provided the voices of a girl bunny, the quail mother, and a female pheasant in *Bambi* (1942).

- From 1944-1952 the **role was taken over by Ruth Clifford** for a total of seven shorts.

- The current **voice of Minnie is performed by Russi Taylor** from 1986-present. Russie had been married to the late Wayne Allwine, the voice of Mickey from 1977-2009 (due to his death).

DAISY DUCK FUN FACTS

- **Daisy Duck's birthday** is May 16.

- In Daisy's first movie, *Don Donald* (1937), she **went by the name Donna Duck**. It wasn't until her second appearance in *Mr. Duck Steps Out* (1940) that she was given the name of Daisy Duck. Some don't even consider Donna to be the same character as Daisy, but a precursor female counterpart for Donald. IMDB lists Donna as being the same character as Daisy, but later in a 1951 comic, Donna was brought back to be Daisy's rival.

- What is considered **Daisy's first actual appearance** was *Mr. Duck Steps Out* (1940), but she still retained the same voice as Donna Duck.

- In her first two films, **she was voiced by Clarence Nash**, the voice of Donald. She spoke like Donald with a quack in her voice. When she made her third appearance in the movie *Donald's Crime* (1943), she was voiced by Gloria Blondell.

- **Daisy is the Countess of Disney Castle** in the *Kingdom Hearts* video games in 2002, 2005, and 2010.

CLUB 33

What is this super secret Club 33?

Club 33 is a private club located in the heart of the *New Orleans Square* section of Disneyland. Officially maintained as a "secret" feature of the theme park, the entrance to the club is located next to the *Blue Bayou Restaurant* at "33 Royal Street," and is recognizable by an ornate address plate with the number 33 engraved on it. When riding *Pirates of the Caribbean*, just as the boat departs, the *Blue Bayou Restaurant* is visible, but the balconies above it are actually a part of *Club 33*.

Membership

Club 33 members enjoy access to the club's exclusive restaurant and full bar. It is the only location within Disneyland to offer alcoholic beverages, though Disneyland has a park wide liquor license and has set up bars throughout the park for private events. *Club 33's* wine list includes vintages priced at $200. They serve Fess Parker wines up there.

Club 33 members are privileged with access to the park 365 days a year. *Club 33* offers individual and corporate memberships. As of February 2008, the current membership levels are Corporate Membership, Limited Corporate Membership, and Gold Membership. The Silver Membership is not currently being offered. As of 2011, the membership waiting list was 14 years long, and membership closed as of April/May 2007 to give the waiting list time to go down.

Those interested in membership must send a written letter of inquiry to Disney. They will then receive a confirmation letter and information packet. As memberships open, potential members are informed via a letter of intent from Disney.

Initial fees and annual dues vary by membership. The Corporate and Limited Corporate Memberships allow for transfer of members. Fees last time I checked a few years ago. I heard they made some changes to their member's policies and benefits since then.

➤ **The Corporate Membership** fee is **$27,500** plus **$6,100** in annual fees. Up to nine associate members can be designated at an annual fee of **$4,650** each. Members no longer in the employment of the corporate member's company must surrender the membership cards to Club 33. The corporate member may then designate another member of the company.

256

➤ **The Limited Corporate Membership** fee is **$13,750** with only one member at an annual fee of **$4,650**. This entitles the corporation to transfer the membership to another employee whenever necessary.

➤ **The Gold Membership** is for an individual with a member fee of **$10,450** and an annual fee of **$3,275**. Additional use of a membership card is by spouse only, with reservations accepted only from the cardholder, the spouse, or the cardholder's assistant. The Gold Membership is not transferable.

Members at any level are allowed to make personal reservations 90 days in advance and guest reservations 60 days in advance. Private parties utilizing the entire Club facilities for special occasions such as birthdays, holiday parties, business functions, and such are available upon member's request with a required minimum number of guests. Members may request any of Disney's costumed characters to appear at the Club, as Disney believes "special events are always more fun with Mickey or Donald."

Club members and up to nine guests are allowed complimentary admission to Disneyland. The member and one guest (or spouse) receives complimentary admission at anytime whether or not they eat at the Club. If the member is unable to accompany the guests to *Club 33*, the Club will arrange admission for them at no charge. The price of lunch at the Club hovers around the cost of admission. Club members receive complimentary parking.

History

There are various origins that have been claimed for the name "Club 33." One says that *Club 33* was named for Disneyland's 33 sponsors at the time, one of which was Chevron.

Atchison, Topeka and Santa Fe	Global Van Lines	Sunkist
Atlantic-Richfield	Goodyear Tire and Rubber Co.	Sunsweet Growers INC
Aunt Jemimas	Hallmark	Swift & CO
Bank of America	Hills Bros. Coffee INC.	The Upjohn CO
Bell Telephone	INA	Welch's Grape Juice Company
C & H Sugar	Ken-L Ration	Timex
Carnation	Kodak	United Air Lines
Chicken of the Sea	Lincoln Savings and Loan	Western Printing and Litho CO
Coca-Cola	Monsanto CO	Wurlitzer
Douglas Aircraft	Pendleton	-
Frito Lay	Pepsi-Cola	-
General Electric	Spice Islands	-

Another explanation is that Walt Disney chose the name simply because he liked the way "33" looked. Another, given by a *Club 33* employee, says that since Walt wanted to serve liquor in the Club, he had to obtain a liquor license - which requires a full street address. Walt, wanting to protect Disneyland's alcohol-free status, didn't want to use the park's Harbor Boulevard address, so he ordered that all the buildings in *New Orleans Square* (then under construction) be given addresses. According to the employee, "33" was chosen because Walt's lucky number was 3. One explanation, arguably the most common, is that "33" when turned on its side bears similarity to two letter "M"s, as would stand for "Mickey Mouse." In actuality, it was the address assigned to the door by chance. All of the buildings in the square have addresses, but they are internally-designated numbers. According to *Snopes.com*, the address listed on Disney's liquor license is their general-delivery location.

When Walt Disney was working with various corporate promoters for his attractions at the 1964-1965 New York World's Fair, he noted to himself the various "VIP Lounges" provided as an accommodation for the corporate elite. This gave him the idea that culminated in *Club 33*. When *New Orleans Square* was planned, this special area for corporate sponsors and VIPs was included. Disney hired Hollywood set director Emil Kuri to design the facility. *Club 33* opened in May 1967, five months after Disney's death.

Club 33 was originally intended for use by Disneyland's corporate sponsors and other industry VIPs. After Disney's death, *Club 33* was opened to individual members also.

Interior

To enter *Club 33*, a guest must press a buzzer on an intercom concealed by a hidden panel in the doorway. The member needs to insert their membership card in the slot near the buzzer and the door will open. A receptionist will ask for their name over the intercom and, if access is granted, open the door to a small decorated lobby. Guests will have the option of going to the dining area on the second floor by walking up the stairs, or going up the antique lift (photo #3). The lift is an exact replica of one Disney saw and fell in love with during a vacation in Paris, but the owner of the original refused to sell. Disney sent a team of engineers to the Parisian Hotel to take exact measurements for use in the creation of a replica; even a sample of the original finish was taken so that it could be duplicated. A staircase to the second level wraps around the lift.

The second level has two dining rooms. One room has dark wood paneling; the other room is more formal, but has a lighter environment.

Once at the dining level, guests can view antique furniture pieces collected by Lillian Disney. Walt Disney also handpicked much of the Victorian bric-a-brac in New Orleans antique stores, according to club manager Michael Bracco.

The Club is also furnished with props from Disney films. There is a fully functional glass telephone booth just off the lift that was used in *The Happiest Millionaire* (1967) and an ornate walnut table with white marble top that was used in *Mary Poppins* (1964) (photo #7). A video capture from the film on display atop the table shows actors Karen Dotrice, Matthew Garber, and David Tomlinson standing immediately to its left. A newly-installed bar prepares drinks for members and their guests.

258

A harpsichord (photo #2) which was rumored to have been an antique was, in fact, custom-built for Lillian Disney specifically for use in *Club 33*. The

underside of the lid features a Renaissance-style painting that was actually done by Disney artists. Elton John has played this harpsichord, Bracco told Bloomberg News, and it can be played by anyone who sits at it.

Walt Disney also wanted to make use of audio-animatronic technology within *Club 33*. Microphones (Photo #4) in overhead lighting fixtures would pick up the sounds of normal conversation while an

operator would respond via the characters. Though the system was never fully implemented, it was partially installed and remains so to this day. An audio-animatronic vulture (see photo) is perched in one corner of the Club's Trophy Room. The microphones are clearly visible at the bottom of each of the room's lighting fixtures. The animal trophies (Walt inherited them from a friend), for which the room was named, have been removed by Disney family members. Photos of the room with the trophies still installed can be seen on the walls now. Currently, this room is known as the Trophy Room.

Disneyland guests participating in the "Walk In Walt's Footsteps" tour are provided entrance to the lobby of *Club 33*. The tour guide will provide a brief history of the Club and explain some of the artifacts in the lobby. The tour members may be photographed in the lift, but are not allowed upstairs.

They also have their own "gift shop." The term is used loosely because the gift shop is actually a glass cabinet in the hallway (photo #1).

The food is set up buffet style for the lunch time (photo #5).

You can stand out on the balcony and catch a glimpse of the *Pirates of the Caribbean* exit and watch all the people below (photo #6).

THE DISNEYLAND DREAM SUITE

What is The *Disneyland Dream Suite*?

The *Disneyland Dream Suite* is located above the entrance to *Pirates of the Caribbean* in *New Orleans Square*. On January 31, 2008, guests were randomly selected to stay the night there as a part of the *Year of a Million Dreams* giveaway.

Measuring in at 2,200 square feet, the *Dream Suite* contains two bedrooms, a sitting room, two bathrooms, and a balcony. Walt originally planned to have this built as a larger area to entertain his guests because his apartment above the *Fire Station* was too small to do such things. He started the building of his new apartment in 1961 with the building of *New Orleans Square*. Walt attached set designer Dorothea Redmond to the project in 1966. She was the set designer for *Gone With the Wind* (1939) and was the Imagineer who designed the *Cinderella Castle* archway murals in *Magic Kingdom*. He also had Lillian and Disney set decorator Emile Kuri in charge of the interior décor design and furnishing. Emile was also in charge of the interior of *Club 33*. The project was dubbed *The Royal Suite* because of Royal Street just outside.

Walt ended up passing away in December 1966 and all construction inside the apartment halted. The continuing construction of the street was discontinued at the request of his brother, Roy Disney. He felt that the family couldn't really enjoy the suite with Walt gone.

Disney decided to continue the project in the mid-1980's. It was described as being an odd thing to see by the crew that continued the work. When they went into the suite, everything was where it was left at Walt's passing, untouched like a time capsule. *The Disney Gallery* opened July 11, 1987, in time for the park's 32nd anniversary. It housed Disney paintings, other forms or pictures, sculptures, or displays of movie props. It closed its doors on August 7, 2007. *The Disney Gallery* moved to *Main Street, U.S.A.* near *Great Moments with Mr. Lincoln*.

Disney announced that they were going to continue the work Walt wanted and complete the *Dream Suite* and use the ideas and concepts from its planning stages. Imagineers Kim Irvine (Art Director), Leslee Turnbull (Senior Show Artisan), John Gritz (Principle Concept Designer), Tino Flores (Lead, Upolstery Team), and Jim Crouch (Character Theme Paint Specialist) were responsible for making that happen.

One of the bedrooms was modeled after the *Adventureland* jungle (photo #4) and plays music that is reminiscent of *The Jungle Book*. The bedroom containing the two beds (photo #2) is *Frontierland* themed. There is a slow-moving train on a track that circles the bedroom up near the ceiling. The two arm chairs in the middle of the room were prop chairs from the Fred MacMurray movie *The Happiest Millionaire* (1960). The rooms have a special "Goodnight Kiss" button on the wall. It was named as such because Walt referred to the fireworks show as everyone's "Goodnight Kiss." After the fireworks, everyone would go home. In the room, music begins to play, a projection of a pirate ship appears on the wall, and mermaids appear in the picture of the waterfalls above the bed (painted by Jim Crouch). The button in the second bedroom starts the train on its trek around the room. As it passes through scenes, there are sound effects and some of the objects move.

The large bathrooms (photo #1) have a beautiful bathtub, and a magical show as well. There are fiber optic twinkling lights that appear overhead. If you watch closely, a Hidden Mickey will appear (photo #3)

The patio area is themed after the bayou. It is very reminiscent of the *Blue Bayou Restaurant* just downstairs. It even has bouncing fireflies, just like the bayou on *Pirates of the Caribbean*.

There are several magical things that happen in the suite throughout the night. The main clock in the sitting room has a little show for Guests to experience with music, lights, and projections on the face. There are murals of the Neuschwanstein Castle in Germany and the Chateau Chenonceau from France on the wall. They were actually ordered by Walt and were to be displayed inside the *Dream Suite* as they appeared in the conceptual designs.

A Cast Member had said it is $5,000 a night to stay there, but they don't rent out the room. It is generally given away to winners of contests or winning bidders at auctions. At a charity event, one person bid $15,000 for one night.

The balcony overlooks the *Rivers of America*. It is a prime location for viewing *Fantasmic!*. The iron filigree has two gold letters in it. WD and RD, the initials for Walt and Roy Disney.

It is rumored that they will close the suite after it has housed 266 guests.

As of 2014, it appears that the *Dream Suite* has been closed. But will we ever know for sure?

DISNEYBOUNDING

The term "Disneybounding" or "Disneybound" first showed up a few years ago, around 2012. As stated previously, you are not allowed to enter Disneyland dressed as a character if you are over the age of 14. Some adults, young adults, and teens like to dress up just as much as children do. People started showing their love for characters by dressing up like them, but not as them. They would design a color pallet and pick out clothing and accessories surrounding that pallet so it can be surmised that they are that specific character. Example: a yellow skirt/shorts, a dark blue top, a red hair bow, a little clutch shaped like an apple, and viola, you are Snow White. There are hundreds of people that go every day now as Disneybounders. It is very popular with people who are into cosplaying or just like to dress up without violating *Disneyland's* policy. This is not cosplaying, which are outfits that are more detailed. Some people will "genderbend," which means a female might Disneybound as Stitch or Wreck-It Ralph, and a male might dress up as Elsa. There is the term "steampunk" meaning the character is dressed like they are from the late 1800's in the era of steam trains and machinery, similar to *Treasure Planet* (2002) and *Atlantis: The Lost Empire* (2001), but not in the future (see photos). Then there are those who

dress "dapper." Meaning they are dressed like a dandy or a darling all neat and trim and vintage looking. Men wear bowties and fedoras and girls wear pearls, fancy hair, and high heel shoes. All this is done while color blocking and styled to look like a character. (*see photos*)

RED/YELLOW   EARS   BROWN

KHAKI SHORTS

LIGHT BLUE BLACK PEACH

DRESS IS REVERSIBLE TO SHOW THE MAYOR'S OTHER FACE

YELLOW   BLACK   RED

RED BLUE YELLOW

DISNEY MYTHS

1. _The Haunted Mansion_ - Although it is widely rumored that Disneyland acquired the coach that carried **Mormon Pioneer Brigham Young's body** to its grave in 1877, it happens that this is just another one of the many myths that surround _The Haunted Mansion._ According to Glen M. Leonard, director of The Church of Jesus Christ of Latter-day Saints' Museum of Church History and Art, said historical records are conclusive that the hearse couldn't possibly have been used for Young. "Historical evidence shows no hearse was used," he said, although he allowed for the  possibility that the vehicle may be an authentic carriage from Young's era that originated in Utah. The truth of the hearse's origins may never be known, but it can be said with reasonable certainty that neither Brigham Young (nor Joseph Smith, the Latter Day Saints church founder, for that matter) were ever transported in this particular coach. It is also reasonably certain that no carriages throughout history have ever been pulled by invisible horses, though we give Disneyland extra credit for including the horseshoes in this clever display. (_see photo_)

2. _Splash Mountain_ – The cauldron in the fireplace as you are waiting in line has been believed to be the cauldron **used in the film** _Hocus Pocus_ (1993). The one in the film is much larger than the one in the fireplace.

3. _Many Adventures Of Winnie The Pooh_ – As you are leaving the Heffalump and Woozles room, the head of **Melvin the Moose** from the long gone _Country Bear Jamboree._ It is believed that Melvin's head was the head used on the couch in the film _Return to Oz_ (1985). If the two heads are side by side, you can tell the difference between them.

4. _Pirates Of The Caribbean_ – A long-standing urban legend maintains that **Walt Disney was cryogenically frozen**, and his frozen corpse was stored underneath _Pirates of the Caribbean._ Some also believe it is under the _Sleeping Beauty Castle._ However, this was discredited due to the fact that Walt Disney was cremated, and the first known instance of cryogenic freezing of a corpse (of Dr. James Bedford) occurred a month after Walt's death in January 1967. Walt was cremated on December 17, 1966, and his ashes reside at the Forest Lawn Memorial Park in Glendale, California. That little myth probably got started in 1972, when Bob Nelson, then the president of the Cryonics Society of California, gave an interview to the Los Angeles Times. It partialy had to do with the fact that the Disney company called them and inquired about the process before Walt's death, but no paperwork was actually signed. The rumor spread was assisted by Disney animator Ward Kimball. This was verified in the book _Walt Disney: The_

Triumph of the American Imagination written by author Neal Gabler in 2006.

5. *Disneyland* – Many people believe **there are hidden tunnels underground** throughout the park. This isn't true. It is for *Disney World*, but not here. There are, however, basements below the restaurants and shops in *New Orleans Square*. These basements are connected by doorways and little hallways to get from one room to the next. *The Blue Bayou* kitchen is down there as well as an employee cafeteria. If you think about it, the basements aren't really below ground level. When you enter *New Orleans Square* you have to walk uphill to get to it. There is also a tunnel used by employees to take garbage from *Tomorrowland Terrace* out to the dumpsters. Building an underground tunnel system wasn't thought of back in 1954 while *Disneyland* was still in the planning stages. Since *Disneyland* was built in a year, they wouldn't have had the time to construct such a thing in the short amount of time.

6. *New Orleans Square* – It is rumored that the owner (back story owner) of the *Haunted Mansion* was none other than Jean Lafitte, the pirate who was a big influence in the creation of *Pirates of the Caribbean*. There were some ideas floating around to tie together *Pirates, Haunted Mansion* and *Pirates Lair on Tom Sawyer Island*. *Pirates of the Caribbean* was supposed to document the life of Jean, the *Mansion* would represent him settling down and getting married, and the *Island* would be the area where Jean kept his treasure and what he used as a base for his hideout. *Fort Wilderness* used to be on the *Island*. There was a figure of Andrew Jackson sitting in his chair with some other men. Since it was shut down, his uniform and several other articles were sent to the *Mansion* attic, thereby tying the *Island* to the *Mansion* through the friendship of Jean and Andrew. There is a crypt located by the *Rivers of America* that is bricked up. If the date is changed from 1764 to 1823 it could be the crypt of Jean. The idea to **tie together the entire land of *New Orleans Square* under one giant theme** was squashed by Chairman of Walt Disney Parks and Resorts, Paul Pressler (who was in charge of opening *The Grand California Hotel*, *California Adventure,* and *Downtown Disney*).

7. It has been believed by many that the **Walt Disney Company made the movie *The Wizard of Oz*** (1939). This is not true. Walt Disney did want to make it, but MGM owned the rights to *The Wizard of Oz* books. Walt Disney's top grossing film of all time, *Snow White and the Seven Dwarfs* (1937), was the reason behind Louis B. Mayer's determination to equal its success. After the rights to *The Wonderful Wizard of Oz* (published in 1899) book fell into public domain, Disney was then able to make the sequel *Return to Oz* (1985), the prequel *Oz: The Great and Powerful* (2013), and owns the rights to the spoof movie *The Muppets Wizard of Oz* (2005). On the attraction *Storyland Canal Boats* in Disneyland Paris, there is a small model of the Emerald City from the *Return to Oz* film. Warner Brothers and Disney are now battling it out over who will get the rights to *The Wizard of Oz* film characters.

8. I have been asked a few times, **"Why aren't there any rides for Harry Potter** in Disneyland?" To which I reply, "Because Harry Potter belongs to Warner Brothers as it states with the big WB at the beginning of each movie." If you want to go on a Harry Potter ride, you will have to travel to *Universal's Islands of Adventure* (next to *Universal Studios*) in Orlando, Florida, or just an hour north of *Disneyland* to *Universal Studios Hollywood*.

9. *Tom Sawyer Island* – It is said that when *Disneyland* opened, *Tom Sawyer Island* (now *Pirates Lair On Tom Sawyer Island*) **was given it's own Missouri zip code**. It was to pay homage to the late Mark Twain (Samuel Langhorne Clemens) because he was from that state. This is impossible because the *Island* opened on June 16, 1956, and zip codes weren't even used until the 1960's for large cities (full 5 digit zip codes on July 1, 1963).

10. A longtime myth is that Marilyn Monroe was the live action model for Tinker Bell from *Peter Pan* (1953). The truth is the **live action model and pantomime for Tinker Bell was Margaret Kerry** (born May 11, 1929 - Los Angeles, CA) as confirmed by the animator, Marc Davis. Marilyn Monroe was just rising to popularity when Disney began animations for *Peter Pan* which led people to believe otherwise. Because of this myth floating around, it prompted Margaret's children to contact Disney archivist Dave Smith and set the record straight and confirm it with Marc Davis in the late 80's. He confirmed that Margaret Kerry was on set in the studio with large props to act out scenes as Tinker Bell for six months. Tink's well known personality was based off of what Kerry was portraying. A most memorable pose that most people have seen is the one with Margaret peeking through a large key hole. Margaret was also the model for the red-haired mermaid in the Neverland lagoon and provided the voice for her as well. She began acting at the age of four in *Our Gang: The Little Rascal's* (1922-1934) television series. She later appeared in other television episodes for *The Lone Ranger*, *The Ruggles*, *Clutch Cargo*, *The Andy Griffith Show*, *Space Angel*, *The Three Stooges,* and the drama *Public Access* (1993). Margaret ended up getting into voice acting because she liked the fact that she didn't have to start work until the afternoon, and wasn't required to get dressed up or wear makeup. She ended up mastering 21 different dialects and 48 character voices in over 600 animated television episodes all the way up until present time. Nowdays, Margaret is a volunteer at Walt's Barn in Griffith Park, Los Angeles. The museum is open the third Sunday of every month. She also frequents Disney conventions and has a booth set up to meet her fans and sign autographs.

NOTE: The photobomber in the background is Jerry Cornell from ThemeParkology.com.

11. *Haunted Mansion* – **The fallen bust in the graveyard scene is of Walt Disney or Leslie Nielsen**. No, it isn't. It is actually Thurl Ravenscroft, the bass singer for the group singing the "Grim Grinning Ghosts" song. People confuse the two of them because of the moustache. To read more on Thurl, see *Who Does That Voice on page 147.*

12. *Haunted Mansion* – **The group singing the "Grim Grinning Ghosts" song is *The Mellowmen***. It is not them. In fact, Thurl Ravenscroft is the only member of *The Mellowmen* who is singing here. The other four men are actually Verne Rowe, Chuck Schroeder, Jay Meyer, and Bob Ebright. It was recorded February 14, 1969.

13. *Sailing Ship Columbia* - It is a little known Disney myth that on its maiden voyage around *Tom Sawyer's Island,* **the Mousketeers acted as the crew** with Admiral Joe Fowler there to christen and captain it. Supposedly, a young 16-year-old Annette Funicello was there with them. In actuality, Gretchen Richmond, wife of Alfred Carroll Richmond, then Vice Admiral of the U.S. Coast Guard, did the actual christening. The ships crew consisted of the Sea Scouts from Redondo Beach, CA. Sea Scouts is a group kind of like the Boy Scouts, but for water activities, and it consisted of boys and girls between the ages of 13-21. Walt Disney and Art Linkletter were also on the ship.

14. *Fantasyland* - A Disney myth is that Walt Disney was given **marble statues of Snow White and the seven dwarfs** by an anonymous Italian sculptor in 1961. What really happened is they were commissioned by Imagineer and Disney Legend John Hench (animator on *Fantasia, Dumbo, Peter Pan, Cinderella, and Alice In Wonderland*) to be made by sculptor Leonida Parbla. Unfortunately,  the sculptor made the dwarfs the same height as Snow White. They were copied from a set of soaps that were licensed to be released at the time, which is why Snow White is the same size. John contacted the sculptor to remedy the size problem, but Leonida wanted $2,000 to redo Snow White, so John worked with what he had and the technique of forced perspective was used. The dwarfs were set up along a waterfall. By setting Snow White at the top of the waterfall, and slightly back, they were able to give the illusion that she was taller than the dwarfs. In order to preserve the original marble pieces, the statues were replaced with fiberglass copies and the marble ones were stored in the Imagineer Studio. (*see photo*)

15. *Disneyland* – Walt **wanted to keep some of the original trees** from the orange grove in the park, so he had Bill Evans mark them with different colored ribbon, green meant the tree would stay, red meant the tree would be removed and planted elsewhere. Unfortunately, most of those trees got bulldozed because the operator was colorblind. This is false. Bill said he

heard this a few years after the park opened and didn't remember it happening. At the time the park was being created, Marty Sklar was a copy writer for Disney and was hurting for stories that were interesting. And that's how the myth began.

16. _Sleeping Beauty Castle_ - There is a **gold marker on the ground** that marks the geological center of _Disneyland_ (prior to _Toontown_). At least that is what most people believe. Actually, the marker was there as a surveyor's marker and was used to line up the castle with _Main Street_. There are actually several gold markers throughout the park. The center of the park is actually closer to the _"Partners"_ statue.

17. _Star Tours_ - **Jenifer Lewis, the voice of Flo in _Cars_** (2006) and Mama Odi in _Princess and the Frog_ (2009), was the African American woman in the preboarding video for the _Star Tours_ attraction up until the new attraction was opened. This isn't true. There was another woman who did the video that, too, shared the name Jenifer Lewis. Jenifer confirmed this in interviews. The rumors spread around and it stuck.

18. The Petrified Tree – It is believed that **the petrified tree was a gift from Walt to Lillian Disney** as an anniversary present. This isn't true. It was a joke started by Walt himself. On July 19, 1956, Walt sent a correspondence to purchase the petrified tree from John Baker in Colorado Springs. Mr. Baker bought and sold fossilized trees through his company, _Pike Petrified Forest Fossil_. The order was to have it delivered straight to Disneyland. Diane Disney-Miller debunked the myth in 2010 from an email correspondence with disneyhistoryinstitute.com.

19. The Last Thing Walt Wrote – It is said that on Walt's deathbed he wrote down Kurt Russell's name. Kurt was a recently-acquired commodity of the studio as they had just signed him on with a 10-year contract. He would eventually be one of the greatest actors of the past 50 years, and more to come. He would eventually star in 21 films, or serials, for the Disney Company from 1966 to today. Kurt's Disney film credits:
- _Follow Me, Boys!_ (1966) - Whitey
- _Walt Disney's Wonderful World of Color_ (1967-1976)
  - _Willie and the Yank: The Deserter_ (1967) - Pvt. Willie Prentiss
  - _Willie and the Yank: The Mosby Raiders_ (1967) – Pvt. Willie Prentiss
  - _The Secret of Boyne Castle: Part 1, 2, & 3_ (1969) – Rich Evans
  - _The Survival of Sam the Pelican_ (1976)
  - _Dad, Can I Borrow the Car_ (1972) - Narrator
- _The One and Only, Genuine, Original Family Band_ (1968) – Sidney Bower
- _The Horse in the Gray Flannel Suit_ (1968) – Ronnie Gardner
- _The Computer Wore Tennis Shoes_ (1969) – Dexter Riley
- _The Barefoot Executive_ (1971) – Steven Post
- _Now You See Him, Now You Don't_ (1972) - Dexter Riley
- _Charley and the Angel_ (1973) – Ray Ferris
- _Superdad_ (1973) - Bart
- _The Strongest Man in the World_ (1975) - Dexter Riley
- _The Fox and the Hound_ (1981) – Adult Copper
- _Captain Ron_ (1992) – Captain Ron
- _Miracle_ (2004) – Herb Brooks
- _Sky High_ (2005) - Steve Stronghold / The Commander

268

Walt did indeed write down "Kirt (sic) Russell" before he passed. The issue is that the paper he wrote on was at his desk at the studio. He hadn't been to the studio in weeks because of his failing health. The paper with Kurt's name was among other papers on the desk. There was something written below Kurt's name, "CIA-Mobley." It was for another young actor, Roger Mobley, who also starred in several Disney films. He had also written "2 Way Down Cellar," referring to a two-part serial that he possibly wanted one of the boys to be a part of. We will never know the reasoning behind Walt's note. Kurt himself confirmed that Walt did write his name down before he passed away, but didn't know why. Ron Miller had taken him up to Walt's office while he was on set filming *Now You See Him, Now You Don't* (1972) to show it to him. The conclusion is that Walt more than likely wrote other things down since his last visit to his office, not to mention that Roger's name was written after Kurt's.

DISNEY LEGENDS PROGRAM

The **Disney Legends Program** was established in 1987. It was created to recognize men and women who have made an extraordinary and integral contribution to The Walt Disney Company. The honor is awarded annually during a special ceremony. Recipients are chosen by a selection committee appointed and chaired by Disney Legend, Roy E. Disney, Walt Disney's nephew and Director Emeritus of The Walt Disney Company. The committee consists of long-time Disney executives, historians, and other authorities. It is located at Disney's corporate headquarters in Burbank, California. When Disney opened up their hall of fame, all the then major Hollywood studios considered opening up their own halls of fame, but as of 2008 Disney remains the only major Hollywood studio to have one.

In honor of the opening of the Walt Disney Studios Park at the Disneyland Resort Paris, all 2002 inductees are of European origin. The ceremony was held in the Animation building at the new park on opening day.

In honor of Disneyland's 50th anniversary in 2005, all recipients are related to Walt Disney Parks and Resorts and/or Walt Disney Imagineering, and nearly all have had some connection with Disneyland. Roy E. Disney again co-presented the awards after a two-year hiatus and a return to the company.

Class of 1987	
1	Fred MacMurray	Film
Class of 1989	
2	Les Clark	Animation
3	Marc Davis	Animation & Imagineering
4	Ub Iwerks	Animation & Imagineering
5	Ollie Johnston	Animation
6	Milt Kahl	Animation
7	Ward Kimball	Animation & Imagineering
8	Eric Larson	Animation
9	John Lounsbery	Animation
10	Wolfgang Reitherman	Animation

11	Frank Thomas	Animation

Class of 1990

12	Roger Broggie	Imagineering
13	Joe Fowler	Attractions
14	John Hench	Animation & Imagineering
15	Richard Irvine	Imagineering
16	Herb Ryman	Imagineering
17	Richard Sherman	Music
18	Robert Sherman	Music

Class of 1991

19	Ken Anderson	Animation & Imagineering
20	Julie Andrews	Film
21	Carl Barks	Animation & Publishing
22	Mary Blair	Animation & Imagineering
23	Claude Coats	Animation & Imagineering
24	Don DaGradi	Animation & Film
25	Sterling Holloway	Animation-Voice
26	Fess Parker	Film & Television
27	Bill Walsh	Film & Television

Class of 1992

28	Jimmie Dodd	Television
29	Bill Evans	Imagineering
30	Annette Funicello	Film & Television
31	Joe Grant	Animation
32	Jack Hannah	Animation
33	Winston Hibler	Film
34	Ken O'Connor	Animation & Imagineering
35	Roy Williams	Animation & Television

Class of 1993

36	Pinto Colvig	Voice
37	Buddy Ebsen	Film & Television
38	Peter Ellenshaw	Film
39	Blaine Gibson	Animation & Imagineering
40	Harper Goff	Film & Imagineering
41	Irving Ludwig	Film
42	Jimmy MacDonald	Animation-Voice
43	Clarence Nash	Animation-Voice
44	Donn Tatum	Administration
45	Card Walker	Administration

Class of 1994

46	Adriana Caselotti	Animation-Voice
47	Bill Cottrell	Animation & Imagineering
48	Marvin Davis	Film & Imagineering
49	Van France	Attractions
50	David Hand	Animation
51	Jack Lindquist	Attractions
52	Bill Martin	Imagineering
53	Paul J. Smith	Music
54	Frank Wells	Administration

Class of 1995

55	Wally Boag	Attractions
56	Fulton Burley	Attractions
57	Dean Jones	Film
58	Angela Lansbury	Film

270

59	Edward Meck	Attractions
60	Fred Moore	Animation
61	Thurl Ravenscroft	Animation-Voice
62	Wathel Rogers	Imagineering
63	Betty Taylor	Attractions

Class of 1996

64	Bob Allen	Attractions
65	Rex Allen	Film & Television
66	X Atencio	Animation & Imagineering
67	Betty Lou Gerson	Animation-Voice
68	Bill Justice	Animation & Imagineering
69	Bob Matheison	Attractions
70	Sam McKim	Imagineering
71	Bob Moore	Animation & Film
72	Bill Peet	Animation-Story
73	Joe Potter	Attractions

Class of 1997

74	Lucien Adés	Music
75	Angel Angelopoulos	Publishing
76	Antonio Bertini	Character Merchandise
77	Armand Bigle	Character Merchandise
78	Gaudenzio Capelli	Publishing
79	Roberto de Leonardis	Film
80	Cyril Edgar	Film
81	Wally Feignoux	Film
82	Didier Fouret	Publishing
83	Mario Gentilini	Publishing
84	Cyril James	Film & Merchandise
85	Horst Koblischek	Character Merchandise
86	Gunnar Mansson	Character Merchandise
87	Arnoldo Mondadori	Publishing
88	Armand Palivoda	Film
89	Poul Brahe Pederson	Publishing
90	André Vanneste	Character Merchandise
91	Paul Winkler	Character Merchandise

Class of 1998

92	James Algar	Animation & Film
93	Buddy Baker	Music
94	Kathryn Beaumont	Animation-Voice
95	Virginia Davis	Animation
96	Roy E. Disney	Animation & Administration
97	Don Escen	Administration
98	Wilfred Jackson	Animation
99	Glynis Johns	Film
100	Kay Kamen	Character Merchandise
101	Paul Kenworthy	Film
102	Larry Lansburgh	Film & Television
103	Hayley Mills	Film
104	Al Milotte	Film
105	Elma Milotte	Film
106	Norman "Stormy" Palmer	Film
107	Lloyd Richardson	Film
108	Kurt Russell	Film
109	Ben Sharpsteen	Animation & Film
110	Masatomo Takahashi	Administration

111	Vladimir (Bill) Tytla	Animation
112	Dick Van Dyke	Film
113	Matsuo Yokoyama	Character Merchandise

Class of 1999

114	Tim Allen	Film & Animation-Voice
115	Mary Costa	Animation-Voice
116	Norm Ferguson	Animation
117	Bill Garity	Film
118	Yale Gracey	Animation & Imagineering
119	Al Konetzni	Character Merchandise
120	Hamilton Luske	Animation
121	Dick Nunis	Attractions
122	Charlie Ridgway	Attractions

Class of 2000

123	Grace Bailey	Attractions
124	Harriet Burns	Imagineering
125	Joyce Carlson	Animation & Imagineering
126	Ron Dominguez	Parks & Resorts
127	Cliff Edwards	Animation-Voice
128	Becky Fallberg	Animation
129	Dick Jones	Animation-Voice
130	Dodie Roberts	Animation
131	Retta Scott	Animation
132	Ruthie Tompson	Animation

Class of 2001

133	Howard Ashman	Music
134	Bob Broughton	Film
135	George Bruns	Music
136	Frank Churchill	Music
137	Leigh Harline	Music
138	Fred Joerger	Imagineering
139	Alan Menken	Music
140	Martin Sklar	Imagineering
141	Ned Washington	Music
142	Tyrus Wong	Animation

Class of 2002

143	Ken Annakin	Film
144	Hugh Attwooll	Film
145	Maurice Chevalier	Film
146	Phil Collins	Music
147	Sir John Mills	Film
148	Robert Newton	Film & Television
149	Sir Tim Rice	Music
150	Robert Stevenson	Film
151	Richard Todd	Film & Television
152	David Tomlinson	Film

Class of 2003

153	Neil Beckett	Merchandise
154	Tutti Camarata	Music
155	Edna Francis Disney	Special Support
156	Lillian Disney	Special Support
157	Orlando Ferrante	Imagineering
158	Richard Fleischer	Film
159	Floyd Gottfredson	Animation

160	Buddy Hackett	Film & Television
161	Harrison Price	Research Economist
162	Alfred Taliaferro	Cartoonist
163	Ilene Woods	Music-Voice

Class of 2004

164	Bill Anderson	Television & Administration
165	Tim Conway	Film
166	Rolly Crump	Imagineering
167	Alice Davis	Imagineering
168	Karen Dotrice	Film & Television
169	Matthew Garber	Film
170	Leonard H. Goldenson	Television
171	Bob Gurr	Imagineering
172	Ralph Kent	Imagineering & Attractions
173	Irwin Kostal	Music
174	Mel Shaw	Animation

Class of 2005

175	Chuck Abbott	Parks & Resorts
176	Milt Albright	Parks & Resorts
177	Hideo Amemiya	Parks & Resorts
178	Hideo Aramaki	Parks & Resorts
179	Charles Boyer	Parks & Resorts
180	Randy Bright	Imagineer
181	James Cora	Parks & Resorts
182	Robert Jani	Parks & Resorts
183	Mary Jones	Parks & Resorts
184	Art Linkletter	Parks & Resorts
185	Mary Anne Mang	Parks & Resorts
186	Steve Martin	Parks & Resorts
187	Tom Nabbe	Parks & Resorts
188	Jack Olsen	Parks & Resorts
189	Cicely Rigdon	Parks & Resorts
190	William Sullivan	Parks & Resorts
191	Jack Wagner	Parks & Resorts
192	Vesey Walker	Parks & Resorts

Class of 2006

193	Tim Considine	Television & Film
194	Kevin Corcoran	Television & Film
195	Al Dempster	
196	Don Edgren	Imagineering
197	Paul Frees	Television, Film & Parks
198	Peter Jennings	Television
199	Sir Elton John	Music
200	Jimmy Johnson	Music
201	Tommy Kirk	Television & Film
202	Joe Ranft	Animation
203	David Stollery	Television & Film
204	Ginny Tyler	Television & Film

Class of 2007

205	Roone Arledge	Television
206	Art Babbitt	Animation
207	Carl Bongirno	Imagineering
208	Marge Champion	Animation
209	Dick Huemer	Animation
210	Ron Logan	Parks and Resorts

273

211	Lucille Martin	Animation
212	Tom Murphy	Animation
213	Randy Newman	Music
214	Floyd Norman	Animation
215	Bob Schiffer	Film Production
216	Dave Smith	Archives

Class of 2008

217	Wayne Allwine	Animation-Voice
218	Bob Booth	Attractions
219	Neal Gallagher	Attractions
220	Frank Gifford	Television
221	Burny Mattinson	Animation
222	Walter Peregoy	Animation
223	Dorothea Redmond	Designer
224	Russi Taylor	Animation-Voice
225	Barbara Walters	Television
226	Oliver Wallace	Music

Class of 2009

227	Tony Anselmo	Animation-Voice
228	Harry Archinal	Film
229	Beatrice Arthur	Film & Television
230	Bill Farmer	Animation-Voice
231	Estelle Getty	Film & Television
232	Don Iwerks	Film
233	Rue McClanahan	Film & Television
234	Leota Toombs Thomas	Attractions
235	Betty White	Film & Television
236	Robin Williams	Animation-Voice

Class of 2011

237	Regis Philbin	Television
238	Jim Henson	Film & Television
239	Jodi Benson	Animation-Voice
240	Paige O'Hara	Animation-Voice
241	Lea Salonga	Animation-Voice
242	Linda Larkin	Animation-Voice
243	Anika Noni Rose	Animation-Voice
244	Jack Wrather	Parks & Resorts
245	Bonita Wrather	Film
246	Guy Williams	Television
247	Bo Boyd	Consu
248	Raymond Watson	Administration

Class of 2013

249	Tony Baxter	Imagineering
250	Collin Campbell	Imagineering
251	Dick Clark	Television
252	Billy Crystal	Film & Animation-Voice
253	John Goodman	Film & Animation-Voice
254	Steve Jobs	Animation
255	Glen Keane	Animation
256	Ed Wynn	Film & Animation-Voice

Class of 2015

257	George Bodenheimer	Administration & Television
258	Andreas Deja	Animation
259	Johnny Depp	Film

274

260	Eyvind Earle	Animation
261	Danny Elfman	Music
262	George Lucas	Film & Parks and Resorts
263	Susan Lucci	Television
264	Julie Reihm Casaletto (Miss Tencennial)	Parks and Resorts
265	Carson Van Osten	Consumer Products
Class of 2017		
266	Carrie Fisher	Film
267	Clyde Geronimi	Animation
268	Manuel Gonzales	Animation
269	Mark Hamill	Film
270	Wayne Jackson	Imagineering
271	Stan Lee	Marvel
272	Garry Marshall	Film
273	Julie Taymor	Theatrical
274	Oprah Winfrey	Television

NINE OLD MEN

I believe these men should get their own section just for the sheer magnitude of things they brought to the table for the Disney Company. The term "Nine Old Men" referred to Walt's core nine animators. He gave the group that title in a joking way. The term comes from the book "Nine Old Men" by Robert S. Allen and Drew Pearson, published in 1937. It was a political book about the nine justices of the U.S. Supreme Court. None of Walt's animators were actually old men; most of them were in their 30's and 40's.

By the time *Robin Hood* (1973) was released, only four of the "Nine Old Men" (Kahl, Lounsbery, Thomas, and Johnston) were still animating for Disney. Larson was still working for Disney, but as a talent scout and trainer, Wolfgang Reitherman was only directing and producing films, and Marc Davis was helping to create the park's attractions. Lounsbery died in 1976, Kahl retired the same year and died in 1987. Thomas, Johnston and Davis retired in 1978, and Thomas and Johnston later enjoyed cameos in the Brad Bird-directed films *The Iron Giant* (1999) and *The Incredibles* (2004). Thomas died shortly afterwards in 2004, and Johnston (who was by that point the last surviving "Old Man") died in 2008.

All of the members have been acknowledged as Disney Legends.

1. **Les Clark** (November 17, 1907 – September 12, 1979) joined Disney in 1927. He was the main animator for Mickey Mouse. He was the only animator of the nine of them who had actually worked on Mickey Mouse from the beginning with Ub Iwerks. He animated all the way up until *Lady and the Tramp* (1955), when he became a director himself.

2. **Marc Davis** (March 30, 1913 – January 12, 2000) joined Disney in 1935 with animating *Snow White and the Seven Dwarfs* (1937). He later developed and animated the characters of Bambi and Thumper in *Bambi* (1942), Maleficent, Aurora, and the raven in *Sleeping Beauty* (1959), and Cruella de Vil in *One Hundred and One Dalmatians* (1961). Davis was also responsible for character design for both the *Pirates of the Caribbean* and the *Haunted Mansion* attractions in the park. The reason why part of the *Haunted Mansion*

has the funny scene of the graveyard was because of him. He was married to Imagineer Alice Davis. He became the third Disney Legend to be inducted into the program in 1989.

3. **Ollie Johnston** (October 31, 1912 – April 14, 2008) joined Disney in 1935 with animating *Snow White and the Seven Dwarfs* (1937). Some of his works include Pinocchio, Bambi, Thumper, Alice, King of Hearts, the Evil Stepsisters, Brer Rabbit, Brer Fox, Brer Bear, Mr. Smee, Lady, Jock, Trusty, Flora, Fauna, Merryweather, Pongo, Perdita, Puppies, Nanny Cook, Mowgli, Baloo, Bagheera, Duchess, Thomas O'Malley, Kittens, Prince John, Sir Hiss, Robin Hood, Little John, Maid Marian, Winnie the Pooh, Piglet, Rabbit, Kanga, Roo, Bernard, Bianca, the District Attorney, Ichabod Crane, Chairman, Rufus the Cat, Penny, Orville the Albatross, Young Tod, and Young Copper, to name a few. He also co-authored two books with his best friend and fellow animator, Frank Thomas - *The Illusion of Life* (published 1995) and *The Disney Villain* (published 1993). Rufus the cat in *The Rescuers* (1977) was modeled after Ollie. Ollie and Frank Thomas were represented by computer-animated characters with their likeness in *The Incredibles* (2004), for which they provided the voices. Frank said "Ya see that? That's the way to do it. That's old school." To which Ollie replied "Yeah. No school like the old school." These comments were to reflect on their own pasts when they used to hand draw cartoons the "old school" way, before computer animation existed. Ollie and Frank were also represented in *The Iron Giant* (1999) with their likenesses and voices as the train engineers. Both *The Incredibles* and *The Iron Giant* were directed by Brad Bird who they were an inspiration to. Brad did the voice of Edna 'E' Mode in *The Incredibles*.

4. **Milt Kahl** (March 22, 1909 – April 19, 1987) started in 1934 working on *Snow White*. His work included villains such as Shere Khan in *The Jungle Book* (1967), Edgar the butler in *The Aristocats* (1970), the Sheriff of Nottingham in *Robin Hood* (1973), and Madame Medusa in *The Rescuers* (1977).

5. **Ward Kimball** (March 4, 1914 – July 8, 2002) joined Disney in 1934 in the animation department. His works include Lucifer, Jaq, Gus and the other mice in *Cinderella* (1950), the Crows, Dumbo, and Timothy Mouse in *Dumbo* (1941), Jiminy Cricket in *Pinocchio* (1940), the Mad Hatter, Cheshire Cat, White Rabbit, March Hare, Walrus and the Carpenter, the oysters, Dormouse, and Tweedledum and Tweedledee in *Alice in Wonderland* (1951), the Dwarfs (deleted scenes) and the Vultures in *Snow White and the Seven Dwarfs* (1937), Bacchus and his pet unicorn donkey in *Fantasia* (1940), the Dragon and the Birds in *The Reluctant Dragon* (1941), Pedro in *Saludos Amigos* (1942), Donald Duck, José Carioca, Panchito in *The Three Caballeros* (1944), Band in *Casey At The Bat*, Peter, Sasha, Sonia, Ivan, the Wolf and the Hunters In *Peter And The Wolf*, Willie the Whale in *Make Mine Music* (1946), Jiminy Cricket and Lumpjaw in *Fun and Fancy Free* (1947), Singing Masks, Hoedown Caller, Hoedown Dancers, Indians, and Hoedown Band in *Johnny Appleseed*, Donald Duck, José Carioca, Aracuan Bird, and the Butterflies in *Blame It On The Samba*, Pecos Bill and his Horse, Coyote pups, Various

animals, Rabbit, Rattlesnake, Vultures, Townspeople, Cattle, Rustlers, and Painted Indians in *Pecos Bill* in *Melody Time* (1948), train chase sequence and Ichabod Crane and his horse in *The Adventures of Ichabod and Mr. Toad* (1949), Indian Chief, Squaw and her baby, Girl, Brave, Mother-In-Law, John Darling, Captain Hook in *Peter Pan* (1953), Ludwig Von Drake in Walt Disney's *Wonderful World of Color* (1961), and the Pearly Band in *Mary Poppins* (1964). His work was often "wilder" than the other Disney animators and was unique. Ward actually modeled Lucifer after his own cat. You can see an animated depiction of Ward in the animated short *The Nifty Nineties* (1941) alongside fellow animator Fred Moore. He became a Disney Legend in 1989. *Disneyland* dedicated its newly acquired *Disneyland Railroad* engine number 5 to him in 2005.

6. **Eric Larson** (September 3, 1905 – October 25, 1988) joined in 1933. One of the top animators at Disney, he animated notable characters such as Peg in *Lady and The Tramp* (1955), the Vultures in *The Jungle Book* (1967), Peter Pan's flight over London to Neverland in *Peter Pan* (1953), and Brer Rabbit, Brer Fox, and Brer Bear in *Song of the South* (1946). Because of Larson's demeanor and ability to train new talent, Larson was given the task to spot and train new animators at Disney in the 1970's. Many of the top talents at Disney today were trained by Eric in the '70s and '80s.

7. **John Lounsbery** (March 9, 1911 – February 13, 1976) started in 1935 and, working under Norm 'Fergy' Ferguson, quickly became a star animator. Lounsbery, affectionately known as 'Louns' by his fellow animators, was an incredibly strong draftsman who inspired many animators over the years. His animation was noted for its squashy, stretchy feel. Lounsbery animated Ben Ali Gator in *Fantasia* (1940), George Darling in *Peter Pan* (1953), Tony, Joe, and some of the dogs in *Lady and The Tramp* (1955), The Kings in *Sleeping Beauty* (1959), the elephants in *The Jungle Book* (1967), and many, many others. In the 1970's, Louns was promoted to director and co-directed *Winnie the Pooh and Tigger Too* (1974) and his last film, *The Rescuers* (1977).

8. **Wolfgang Reitherman** (June 26, 1909 – May 22, 1985) joined Disney in 1933 as an animator and director. He directed all the animated Disney films after Walt's death until his retirement. Some of his work includes Monstro in *Pinocchio* (1940), Tic-Tock the crocodile in *Peter Pan* (1953), Maleficent as the dragon in *Sleeping Beauty* (1959), and the Rat in *Lady and the Tramp* (1955).

9. **Frank Thomas** (September 5, 1912 – September 8, 2004) joined Disney in 1934. He went on to author the animator's bible, *The Illusion of Life with Ollie Johnston*. His work included the wicked Stepmother in *Cinderella* (1950), the Queen of Hearts in *Alice in Wonderland* (1951), Captain Hook in *Peter Pan* (1953), the dwarfs crying over Snow White's "dead" body, Pinocchio singing at the marionette theatre, Bambi and Thumper on the ice, Lady and the Tramp eating spaghetti, the three fairies in *Sleeping Beauty*, Merlin and Arthur as squirrels and the "wizard's duel" between Merlin and Madam Mim in *The Sword in the Stone*, the animation sequence of King Louie and Baloo in *The*

Jungle Book singing "I Wanna Be Like You," the dancing penguins in *Mary Poppins*, and Winnie The Pooh and Piglet in *Winnie the Pooh and the Blustery Day* and *Winnie the Pooh and Tigger Too*.

Frank and Ollie Johnston were represented by computer animated characters with their likeness in *The Incredibles* (2004), which they provided the voices for. Frank said "Ya see that? That's the way to do it. That's old school." To which Ollie replied "Yeah. No school like the old school." These comments were to reflect on their own pasts when they used to hand draw cartoons the "old school" way, before computer animation existed. Ollie and Frank were also represented in *The Iron Giant* (1999) with their likenesses and voices as the train engineers. Both *The Incredibles* and *The Iron Giant* were directed by Brad Bird who they were an inspiration to. Brad did the voice of Edna 'E' Mode in *The Incredibles*.

E-TICKET

I'm sure if you haven't already heard someone say, "That's an E-ticket ride," then you will at some point. They are making reference to the long-gone ticket books sold in the park prior to 1982. When Disneyland first opened, they would charge an entrance fee of $1.00 to get into the park, and then charge money again, to go on individual attractions. By October 1955, Disney started a "Value Book" system that was sold to patrons after they paid their way into the park. Originally, there were only "A-B-C" tickets. The smaller attractions like *King Arthur Carrousel* and the *Main Street Fire Wagon* used an "A-Ticket." In 1956, they added "D" to the books and upgraded certain "C" attractions to "D" attractions like the *Jungle Cruise*. In June 1959, they introduced the "E-Ticket." This ticket covered attractions like *Matterhorn Bobsleds, Submarine Voyage, Monorail, Disneyland Railroad, Rocket to the Moon, Rainbow Ridge Pack Mules, Rainbow Mountain Stage Coaches, Mark Twain Riverboat, Sailing Ship Columbia, Rafts to Tom Sawyer Island*, and *Jungle Cruise*. The *Matterhorn* was the first ever "E-Ticket" attraction built in the park.

Technically they aren't even called tickets; they are officially called coupons. The guests started calling them tickets because they were being sold at the ticket booths. The "Value Book" system was gradually weened out in the late-1970s with all-day use tickets. This was partially because of the competion started when *Magic Mountain* opened in Valencia, California, in 1971. By 1982, the ticket system was outdated and discontinued. From then on, when someone paid to enter the park, they had full access to all the attractions and shows.

To this day, people still refer to the big popular attractions as "E-Tickets." In fact, during an interview, astronaut Sally Ride (first American woman in space), had commented on her trip to a space station. She said "Ever been to *Disneyland*?

...That was definitely an E ticket!"

Disney offers a printable *Disneyland* pass online. They parody the term "E-Ticket" and use it to refer to "electronic ticket."

In 1966, Disney only charged $2.00 for admission to the park. You could see all the shows and walk through attractions, but no rides without purchasing the ticket books. The ticket costs were A-10¢, B-25¢, C-35¢, D-45¢, and E-60¢. By 1972, the ticket prices were A-10¢, B-25¢, C-40¢, D-70¢, and E-85¢. When Disney discontinued the ticket books, the cost to enter the park and go on all the attractions was only $12.00. Adjusted for inflation, the ticket would by $13.14 in 2017.

MICKEY MOUSE CLUB

The Mickey Mouse Club is an American variety television show that aired intermittently from 1955 to 1996. Created by Walt Disney and produced by Walt Disney Productions, the program was first televised from 1955 to 1960 by ABC, featuring a regular but ever-changing cast of child performers. Reruns were broadcast by ABC on weekday afternoons during the 1960s, right after American Bandstand. The show was reformatted and reimagined after its initial 1955–1959 run on ABC, first from 1977 to 1979 for CBS, and again, from 1989 to 1996 on The Disney Channel.

Mickey Mouse Club was hosted by Jimmie Dodd, a songwriter and the Head Mouseketeer, who provided leadership both on and off screen. In addition to his other contributions, he often provided short segments encouraging young viewers to make the right moral choices. These little homilies became known as "Doddisms." Roy Williams, a staff artist at Disney, also appeared in the show as the Big Mouseketeer. Roy suggested the Mickey and Minnie Mouse ears worn by the cast members, which he helped create along with Chuck Keehne, Hal Adelquist, and Bill Walsh. He got the idea for the ear hats from the Mickey short *The Karnival Kid* (1992), in which he removed and tipped the top part of his head like a Mickey ear hat.

The cast members were called Mouseketeers, and they performed a variety of musical and dance numbers, as well as some informational segments. The most popular of the Mouseketeers comprised the so-called Red Team, which consisted of the following:

- Nancy Abbate
- Sharon Baird
- Bobby Burgess
- Lonnie Burr
- Tommy Cole
- Johnny Crawford
- Dennis Day Margaret Frawley
- Annette Funicello
- Darlene Gillespie
- Cheryl Holdridge
- Cubby O'Brien

- Karen Pendleton
- Mike Smith
- Jay-Jay Solari
- Doreen Tracey
- Don Underhill

Major serials included the following:

- Spin and Marty (1955, 1956, 1957)
- The Hardy Boys (1956, 1957)
- Corky and White Shadow (1956)
- Walt Disney Presents: Annette (1958)
- Adventure in Dairyland (1956)
- Jiminy Cricket "I'm No Fool" serials teach children what to do when faced with certain situations. The "You and Your" serials teach children about the human body.

·I'm No Fool With A Bicycle (10/06/55)	·You - the Human Animal (10/20/55)
·I'm No Fool With Fire (12/01/55)	·You - and Your Five Senses (12/15/55)
·I'm No Fool As A Pedestrian (10/08/56)	·You - and Your Eyes (11/07/56)
·I'm No Fool with Water (11/15/56)	·You - and Your Food (4/18/57)
·I'm No Fool Having Fun (12/15/56)	·You - the Living Machine (5/01/57)
·I'm No Fool with Electricity (10/1973)	·You - and Your Ears (10/03/57)
·I'm No Fool in Unsafe Places (1/1991)	·You - and Your Sense of Touch (1964)
·I'm No Fool on Wheels (1/1991)	·You - and Your Sense of Smell and Taste (4/01/77)
·I'm No Fool with Safety at School (1/1991)	
·I'm No Fool in a Car (3/1992)	
·I'm No Fool in an Emergency (3/1992)	
·I'm No Fool in Unsafe Places II (3/1992)	

- The Adventures of Clint and Mac (1957)
- Boys of the Western Sea (1956-1957)

Each day of the week had a special show theme. The themes were:

- Monday – Fun with Music
- Tuesday – Guest Star
- Wednesday – Anything Can Happen
- Thursday – Circus
- Friday – Talent Round-up

There was a *Mickey Mouse Club* revival and the shoe was brought back and re-named The *All-New Mickey Mouse Club* (1989-1994). It starred a young and talented cast of kids like Keri Russell, Britney Spears, Justin Timberlake, Christina Aguilera, and Ryan Gosling. There were visiting guests like Bill Nye, Bob Saget, John Stamos, Jodie Sweetin, Donald Trump, Annette Funicello, Jonathan Brandis, and Wil Wheaton.

The theme song, "Mickey Mouse March," was written by Jimmie Dodd. Want to sing along with the clubs that's been made for you and me? Unfortunately, due to copyright reasons, I had to remove the lyrics from this edition of my book. If you would like to see the lyrics to sing along, please visit… discoveringthemagickingdom.com/apps/blog/show/44592323-song-lyrics.

WONDERFUL WORLD OF DISNEY

Although Walt was an established film producer and director, well let's face it, he was Walt Disney. He always wanted to do the next big thing and one-up everyone. Television was created and it gave people the ability to watch shows in their own homes. No more going to the theaters for video news reports. The only time people saw the Mickey Mouse shorts was in the theaters before big title films. Walt wanted to harness this new genre of production and make it his own. On March 29, 1954, Walt entered a contract with ABC Television. He wanted a way to finance his upcoming project, *Disneyland*. He used the television studio to show television series produced specifically for the program, animated shorts, and re-runs of his older films that were cut down into 1-hour segments. He would use the show to promote upcoming films like *20,000 Leagues Under the Sea* (1954) and *Darby O'Gill and the Little People* (1959).

The name of the show underwent many changes:

- *Disneyland* (aka *Walt Disney's Disneyland*) (1954–1958) on ABC
- *Walt Disney Presents* (1958–1961) on ABC
- *Walt Disney's Wonderful World of Color* (1961–1969) on NBC
- *The Wonderful World of Disney* (1969–1979) on NBC
- *Disney's Wonderful World* (1979–1981) on NBC
- *Walt Disney* (1981–1983) on CBS
- *The Disney Sunday Movie* (1986–1988) on ABC
- *The Magical World of Disney* (1988–1990) on NBC
- *The Wonderful World of Disney* (1997–2008) on ABC

FUN FACTS

Walt and Roy contacted ABC at the end of 1953 to make a deal with them to make them a financier of the *Disneyland* project. **Walt wanted ABC to invest $500,000** and offer a guarantee for future loans in the amount of $4.5 million that would be used for the park and to fund programming.

One of the **first shows aired was *The Mickey Mouse Club*** (1955-1958).

This is the **show that gave us Fess Parker as *Davy Crockett*** (1954-1956 & 1959) and Guy Williams as *Zorro* (1957-1962). Davy Crockett was a huge success at the time, which is why he made guest appearances in *Disneyland* on opening day and thereafter.

Disney **primarily used the show to promote his upcoming park**, and then new things that would be going on in the future. He would take the viewers behind the scenes, either in his office to show them plans, or take them down to the workshop to interact with Imagineers and see what was coming up.

In the Tencennial edition from 1965, season 11 episode 14, **they visited the Imagineers working on their new projects**. Both projects Walt would never see completed. They talked with Rolly Crump who was working on concepts for the *Museum of the Weird* (a segment of *Haunted Mansion*), Mary Blair working on the *it's a small world* facade for its return from the World's Fair, Harriet Burns working on the *Plaza Inn* exterior model, John Hench working on a detailed interior model of the *Plaza Inn*, Marc Davis working on the *House of Illusions* (later renamed *Haunted Mansion*)

281

changing portraits and stretching portraits, Blaine Gibson sculpting the faces for the pirates in *Pirates of the Caribbean*, and Claud Coats working on the models for *Pirates of the Caribbean*.

🎬 This was **Walt's last time on camera opening for the show**. The episode was for Alaska's 100th anniversary and was titled *A Salute to Alaska* (1967). It aired April 2, 1967, four months after Walt died.

🎬 **Walt was in 317 episodes** of this show as the host.

🎬 **Tinker Bell was the mascot** of the show.

🎬 The last time Walt was on the show, it was called *Walt Disney's Wonderful World of Color* (1961–1969), and was **the inspiration for the nightly water show** in *California Adventure, World of Color*.

MAIN STREET WINDOWS

The *Main Street, U.S.A.* windows are located above all the shops and are dedicated to the Imagineers, animators, artists, or other people that had a hand in making Disneyland the wonderful place it is today. There are currently eighty-seven windows commemorating the achievemnts of the aforementioned people. According to Marty Sklar, "*To add a name on a window today, there are three requirements: 1. Only on or after ones retirement. 2. Only the highest level of service/respect/achievement. 3. Agreement between top individual park management and Walt Disney Imagineering, which creates the design and copy concepts.*" I have photos of almost all of the windows in the park.

Milt Albright	Milt Albright - Entrepreneur - No Job Too Big - No Job Too Small	Opera House
Charles Alexander	Carpenters & Joiners - George Mills - Ray Conway - Chas Alexander	Market House
C.F. Allen	C. F. Allen, MD - C. V. Patterson, MD	New Century Timepieces
Hideo Amemiya	Happiest Dreams on Earth - International School of Hospitality - Hideo Amemiya, Headmaster - "We put people first"	Disney Showcase
Ken Anderson	Ken Anderson - Bait Co.	Market House
X Atencio	The Musical Quill - Lyrics and Librettos by X. Atencio	Opera House
Renie Bardeau	Kingdom Photo Services - Renie Bardeau Photographer, Archivist	Main Street Photo Supply
H. Draegart Barnard	Real Estate—Houses Bought and Sold, H. Draegart Barnard	Disney Clothiers
Tony Baxter	Main Street Marvels - Tony Baxter Inventor "Imagination is at the heart of our Creations"	Magic Shoppe
Wally Boag	Golden Vaudeville Routines - Wally Boag - Prop.	Carnation Company
Chuck Boyajian	Royal Care Co. - We Keep Your Castle Shining - Chuck Boyajian - Prop.	Market House

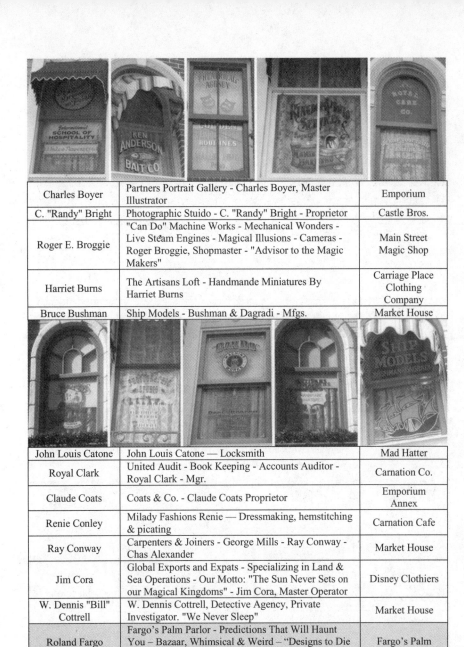

Charles Boyer	Partners Portrait Gallery - Charles Boyer, Master Illustrator	Emporium
C. "Randy" Bright	Photographic Stuido - C. "Randy" Bright - Proprietor	Castle Bros.
Roger E. Broggie	"Can Do" Machine Works - Mechanical Wonders - Live Steam Engines - Magical Illusions - Cameras - Roger Broggie, Shopmaster - "Advisor to the Magic Makers"	Main Street Magic Shop
Harriet Burns	The Artisans Loft - Handmande Miniatures By Harriet Burns	Carriage Place Clothing Company
Bruce Bushman	Ship Models - Bushman & Dagradi - Mfgs.	Market House

John Louis Catone	John Louis Catone — Locksmith	Mad Hatter
Royal Clark	United Audit - Book Keeping - Accounts Auditor - Royal Clark - Mgr.	Carnation Co.
Claude Coats	Coats & Co. - Claude Coats Proprietor	Emporium Annex
Renie Conley	Milady Fashions Renie — Dressmaking, hemstitching & picating	Carnation Cafe
Ray Conway	Carpenters & Joiners - George Mills - Ray Conway - Chas Alexander	Market House
Jim Cora	Global Exports and Expats - Specializing in Land & Sea Operations - Our Motto: "The Sun Never Sets on our Magical Kingdoms" - Jim Cora, Master Operator	Disney Clothiers
W. Dennis "Bill" Cottrell	W. Dennis Cottrell, Detective Agency, Private Investigator. "We Never Sleep"	Market House
Roland Fargo "Rolly" Crump	Fargo's Palm Parlor - Predictions That Will Haunt You – Bazaar, Whimsical & Weird – "Designs to Die For" – Roland F. Crump – Assistant to the Palm Reader	Fargo's Palm Parlor

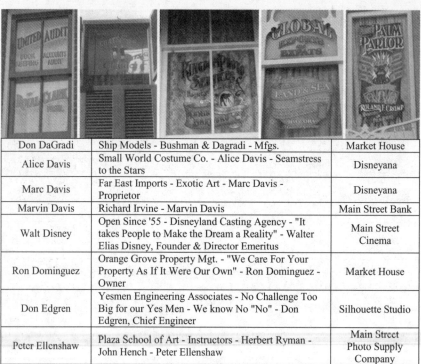

Don DaGradi	Ship Models - Bushman & Dagradi - Mfgs.	Market House
Alice Davis	Small World Costume Co. - Alice Davis - Seamstress to the Stars	Disneyana
Marc Davis	Far East Imports - Exotic Art - Marc Davis - Proprietor	Disneyana
Marvin Davis	Richard Irvine - Marvin Davis	Main Street Bank
Walt Disney	Open Since '55 - Disneyland Casting Agency - "It takes People to Make the Dream a Reality" - Walter Elias Disney, Founder & Director Emeritus	Main Street Cinema
Ron Dominguez	Orange Grove Property Mgt. - "We Care For Your Property As If It Were Our Own" - Ron Dominguez - Owner	Market House
Don Edgren	Yesmen Engineering Associates - No Challenge Too Big for our Yes Men - We know No "No" - Don Edgren, Chief Engineer	Silhouette Studio
Peter Ellenshaw	Plaza School of Art - Instructors - Herbert Ryman - John Hench - Peter Ellenshaw	Main Street Photo Supply Company
Greg A. Emmer	The Cast Doctor Celebrating Our 50th - Operating in Many Lands Around the World - "Every Cast a Perfect Fit" - Greg A. Emmer - Specializing in Casting Since '68	Main Street Cinema
Morgan "Bill" Evans	Evans Gardens - Exotic & Rare Species - Freeway Collections - Est. 1910 - Morgan (Bill) Evans - Senior Partner	Opera House
Orlando Ferrante	Pico Organization - Installation & Coordination of World Class Projects - "We Never Sleep - In Any Time Zone" - Orlando Ferrante, Founder	Market House
Van Arsdale France	Van Arsdale France - Founder and Professor Emeritus - Disney Universities	Main Street Magic Shop
Blaine Gibson	The Busy Hands School - Sculpting, Whittling & Soap Carving & Blaine Gibson - The Eternal Pursuit of the Artists Craft	Opera House
D. S. Gilmore	D. S. Gilmore, MD - E. G. Upjohn, MD	New Century Timepieces

Bob Gurr	Leading the rare to the future – Meteor Cycle Co. – Our vehicles pass the test of time – Fast, Faultless, and Fadless – Bob Gurr – Design Impresario	Disney Clothiers
J. S. Hamel	J.S. Hamel - Consulting Engineer	Main Street Bank
John Hench	Plaza School of Art - Instructors - Herbert Ryman - John Hench - Peter Ellenshaw	Main Street Photo Supply Company
Alexander R. Irvine	Alexander Irvine, M.D.	Baby Care Center

Richard Irvine	Richard Irvine - Marvin Davis	Main Street Bank
Robert F. Jani	Main Street Electrical Parade World Headquarters – Robert F Jani, Master Showman	Opera House
Fred Joerger	Decorative Fountains and Watercolor - By Fred Joerger	Carnation Co.
Bill Justice	New Century Character Company - Custom Character Design and Parade Illuminations - Bill Justice, Master Delineator	Main Street Cone Shop
Emile Kuri	Emile Kuri - Interior Decorator	Market House
Fred Leopold	Attorney at Law - Youngman & Leopold	Disneyana
Gunther R. Lessing	Gunther R. Lessing, Esq.	Disneyana Shop
Jack Lindquist	J. B. Lindquist - Honorary Mayor of Disneyland - "Jack of All Trades. Master of Fun"	City Hall
Mary Anne Mang	Good Neighbor Foundation - "Caring and Giving Come From the Heart" - Mrs. M. A. Mang - Director	New Century Timepieces

Ivan Martin	Buena Vista Construction Co. - Jack Rorex - Ivan Martin - Cash Shockey	Market House
Wilson "Bill" Martin	Wilson Martin - Gabriel Scognamillo	Main Street Bank
Sam McKim	Cartography Masterworks – Sam McKim – Map Maker to the Kingdom – "There's Magic in the Details"	Main Street Photo Supply Company
Edward T. Meck	The Disneyland News - Edward T. Meck - Editor In Chief	China Closet
Christopher D. Miller	Christopher D. Miller - Turkish Baths	Carnation Co.

George Mills	Carpenters & Joiners - George Mills - Ray Conway - Chas Alexander	Market House

Seb Morey	Seb Morey - Taxidermist	Market House
Dick Nunis	Coast to Coast Peoplemoving, World Leader in Leisure Management, Dick Nunis Proprietor	Disney Showcase
George Patrick	Wade B. Rubotton - George Patrick	Main Street Bank
C. V. Patterson	C. F. Allen, MD - C. V. Patterson, MD	New Century Timepieces
Bob Penfield	Club 55 School of Golf - Bob Penfield, Instructor	Coca-Cola Refreshment Corner
Harrison "Buzz" Price	Founded 1953 - Price Is Right Land Company - Call On Our Numbers Man For The Best Price! - Harrison "Buzz" Price - Founder & Finder - We Never Say "No" "Yes" Makes More Cents!	Front of the former Guided Tours building
Cicely Rigdon	Ambassador Finishing School - Cicely Rigdon - Instructor	Disney Showcase

Wathel Rogers	"You'll Cut A Fine Figure" - Wathel Rogers - Menswear	New Century Jewelry
Jack Rorex	Buena Vista Construction Co. - Jack Rorex - Ivan Martin - Cash Shockey	Market House
L. H. Roth	Surveying & Engineering - L. H. Roth	Market House
Wade B. Rubottom	Wade B. Rubotton - George Patrick	Main Street Bank
Herbert Ryman	Plaza School of Art - Instructors - Herbert Ryman - John Hench - Peter Ellenshaw	Main Street Photo Supply Company
Gabriel Scognamillo	Wilson Martin - Gabriel Scognamillo	Main Street Bank
Richard M. Sherman	Two Brothers Tunemakers - Richard M. Sherman and Robert B. Sherman - "We'll Write Your Tune For A Song!"	20th Century Music Company
Robert B. Sherman	Two Brothers Tunemakers - Richard M. Sherman and Robert B. Sherman - "We'll Write Your Tune For A Song!"	20th Century Music Company

286

Cash Shockey	Buena Vista Construction Co. - Jack Rorex - Ivan Martin - Cash Shockey	Market House
Marty Sklar	Main Street College of Arts & Sciences - Martin A. Sklar, Dean	City Hall
E. G. Upjohn	D. S. Gilmore, MD - E. G. Upjohn, MD	Fortuosity Shop
Ray Van De Warker	Ragin Ray's – River Rafting Expeditions – Experienced Guides Since '55 – Ray Van De Warker – Owner-Guide	Mad Hatter
Robert Washo	Robert Washo – Stone Mason	Market House
Frank Wells	Seven Summits Expeditions - Frank G. Wells, President - For Those Who Want To Do It All	Main Street Bank
William T. Wheeler	William T. Wheeler - John Wise - Structural Engineers	Main Street Bank
George Whitney	Geo. Whitney - Guns	Market House

Ed Winger	Old Settlers - Gold Dredging - Ed Winger - Proprietor	Carnation Co.
John Wise	William T. Wheeler - John Wise - Structural Engineers	Main Street Bank
Gordon Youngman	Attorney at Law - Youngman & Leopold	Disneyana
Glenn Hicks	Texas Glenn's Honey Bee Farm—"Our Bees are Real Hummers"—Glenn Hicks Proprietor	Frontierland-Bonanza Outfitters
Fess Parker	Davy Crockett - Coonskin Cap Supply Co - Fess Parker Proprietor	Frontierland-Pioneer Mercantile
Harper Goff	Oriental Tattooing by Prof. Harper Goff - Banjo Lessons	Adventureland-The Bazaar
Walter Elias Disney	Laugh-O-gram Films, Inc. - A Reel of Fun - W.E. Disney, Directing Animator	Toontown-City Hall & the Five & Dime
Elias Disney	Elias Disney – Contractor Est. 1895	Emporium

IMAGINEERS MINI BIOGRAPHIES

The following are a few biographies of some of the Imagineers, musicians, and animators that have contributed a lot to the *Disneyland* parks or Disney films. The term Imagineer is a portmanteau, or combination of words, imagination and engineering. The word was first used in 1940 by Alcoa Inc. (a company that produces aluminum). Walt used it to describe the Walt Disney Imagineering (WDI) branch of his company in 1952 when he started the project of *Disneyland*. There are hundreds of people who should be in this section, but I can only list a few. There are currently about 2,200 Imagineers working for Disney. These were/are some of the most creative and talented individuals in their field, which is why Walt wanted them working on his projects. Most of these people you won't recognize, but should know who they are and what they had to do with your favorite place to visit and favorite films to watch.

Anderson, Ken – (Born March 17, 1909, in Seattle, Washington – Died January 13, 1993). After finishing architecture school in Europe, Ken returned to the states and became a sketch artist for MGM (Metro-Goldwin-Mayer) on films such as *The Painted Veil* (1934). In 1934, Ken was driving past the Disney Studios and decided to just drop in and apply for a job. He was hired instantly and worked on the Silly Symphony shorts like *The Goddess of Spring* (1934) and *Three Orphaned Kittens* (1935). Walt nicknamed Ken "Jack of All Trades" because of his skillset as an animator, architect, artist, storyteller, and designer. His first big animation role was as the art director for *Snow White and the Seven Dwarfs* (1937). He built models for the animators to work from while animating, like the dwarfs' cottage. They even animated Dopey's wiggling ears off of Ken's ability to do so. He followed that with *Pinocchio* (1940), *Fantasia* (1940), and *The Reluctant Dragon* (1941).

While working on *Song of The South*, he helped to innovate the technology needed to produce the live-action/animated crossover process. This process he improved upon while working on *Pete's Dragon* (1977). Ken worked as a layout artist on films such as *Lady and the Tramp* (1955), *Peter Pan* (1953), *Alice in Wonderland* (1951), *Fun & Fancy Free* (1947), *Pedro* (1943), *Saludos Amigos* (1942), and *Ferdinand the Bull* (1938). Ken was also credited for writing the stories for some of our favorite films including *The Rescuers* (1977), *The Many Adventures of Winnie the Pooh* (1977), *Robin Hood* (1973), *The Aristocats* (1970), *The Jungle Book* (1967), *Winnie the Pooh and the Honey Tree* (1966), *So Dear to My Heart* (1948), *Cinderella* (1950), and *Melody Time* (1948). Being an art director is an important job. Ken was the art director for eight Disney films, the ones listed above and also *The Sword in the Stone* (1963), *101 Dalmatians* (1961), *Ben and Me* (1953), and *Ferdinand the Bull* (1938). He was also the production designer on *Sleeping Beauty* (1959), *The Aristocats* (1970), and *101 Dalmatians* (1961).

Because of his architecture expertise, Walt asked Ken to help design some of the concepts for *Disneyland*. Some of his concepts went to design *Peter Pan's Flight*, *Mr. Toad's Wild Ride*, and *Storybook Land Canal Boats*. The final look of the *Haunted Mansion* was modeled after a mansion Ken had seen in a catalogue. The design was originally rejected by Walt, as he wanted all the building in *New Orleans Square* to be designed in the same style. Ken was calling the pre-Mansion designs "Bloodmere Manor." In the end, Walt went with his design. He worked for the Disney Company for 44 years and became a Disney Legend in 1991

Atencio, Xavier "X" – (Born September 4, 1919, in Walsenburg, Colorado). He started out with Disney as an artist in 1938 for the movie *Fantasia* (1940). He became an Imagineer for Disney when *Disneyland* was being built and designed the *Primeval World Diorama* that you pass while riding the *Disneyland Railroad* past *Tomorrowland*. X is also responsible for writing all of the dialogue spoken in the *Haunted Mansion* and in *Pirates of the Caribbean*. He also wrote all the lyrics for two of our favorite *Disneyland* songs, "Yo Ho, A Pirates Life For Me" and "Grim Grinning Ghosts." The voice of the talking Jolly Roger skull on the archway above the first drop for *Pirates* is voiced by Xavier, along with the skeleton in the *Haunted Mansion* that is trying to escape his coffin saying, "Hey, let me outta here." While touring through the *Mansion*, if your doom buggy comes to a halt, you can hear his voice ringing out "Playful spooks have interrupted our tour. Please remain seated in your Doom Buggies." He also wrote the script for the past attraction *Adventure Thru Inner Space*. He did voice work on the original *Submarine Voyage* including "Bridge: Aye, aye, all ahead one third. Stand by the mooring lines." He also wrote the lyrics to Buddy Baker's catchy music for the retired *Walt Disney World* attraction *If You Had Wings*. He retired in 1984 and was named a Disney Legend in 1996.

Baker, Norman "Buddy" – (Born January 4, 1918 in Springfield, Missouri – Died July 26, 2002). Buddy was a music composer for Disney movies and theme park attractions. At the time of his death, he was the last contracted music staff composer still on contract at any studio. He started his career with Disney by composing the musical score for *Davy Crockett and the River Pirates* (1956). After that he went on to create the music for many other films including the *I'm No Fool* shorts starring Jiminy Cricket in 1956 and 1957, *Zorro* (1958-1959), *Swiss Family Robinson* (1960), *Summer Magic* (1963), *The Monkey's Uncle* (1965), *The Gnome-Mobile* (1967), *The Million Dollar Duck* (1971), *The Apple Dumpling Gang* (1975), *The Best of Walt Disney's True-Life Adventures* (1975), *No Deposit, No Return* (1976), *The Mickey Mouse Club* (1955-1996), *The Shaggy D.A.* (1976), *The Many Adventures of Winnie the Pooh* (1977), *Hot Lead and Cold Feet* (1978), *The Apple Dumpling Gang Rides Again* (1979), *The Fox and the Hound* (1981), and *Walt Disney's Wonderful World of Color* (1957-1983).

You can hear his musical scores in the parks on attractions like the *Haunted Mansion*, *Tarzan's Treehouse*, *The Many Adventures of Winnie the Pooh*, and others.

Blair, Mary – (Born October 21, 1911 in McAlester, Oklahoma – Died July 26, 1978). Mary was a concept designer and artist. She started out in the animation industry working in Ub Iwerks animation studio (read further ahead for info on Ub) with her husband Lee Everett Blair before he got hired by Harman and Ising (read further ahead for info on Harman and Ising), the founding fathers of Warner Brothers Animation. Lee got hired on at Disney in 1934 and was joined by Mary in 1940. Mary was an Imagineer for *Disneyland* and designed *it's a small world* for the World's Fair in 1964. Mary was known for her extravagant designs with colors and shapes. There is a doll dedicated to Mary in *it's a small world* known as The Mary Blair Doll. The doll that is dedicated to her is located on top of the Eifel Tower holding a balloon and wearing a yellow rain poncho to mimic

Mary's real life outlandish and wild attire. (*see photo*) Mary also worked on several Disney films including *Saludos Amigos* (1942), *The Three Caballeros* (1944), *Song of the South* (1946), *Fun and Fancy Free* (1947), *Melody Time* (1948), *Make Mine Music* (1946), *So Dear to My Heart* (1948), *The Adventures of Ichabod and Mr. Toad* (1949), *Cinderella* (1950), *Alice In Wonderland* (1951), and *Peter Pan* (1953). Her design usage of bright vibrant colors is what led to *Alice In Wonderland's* nationwide use as a focal for people who were using drugs like LSD in the 1960's during the "hippie era." After her retirement from Disney after *Peter Pan*, she became a freelance graphic designer and illustrator. She worked on creating advertising campaigns for companies such as Nabisco, Maxwell House, Pepsodent, Beatrice Foods, and other companies. She also illustrated in several Little Golden Books for the publisher Simon & Schuster, which can still be found in print today.

Walt requested that Mary come back to the Disney Company to design *it's a small world* for the World's Fair. Her tile mosaics could be found around *Tomorrowland* until the one above *Adventures Through Inner Space* was covered for *Star Tours* in 1987, and the other one was changed from *Circle-Vision 360°* to *Rocket Rods*. Her final tile mural, which was completed in 1971, can still be found today in *Disney's Contemporary Resort* hotel in *Walt Disney World*. She also has some work on display at the Walt Disney Family Museum in San Francisco (*see photo*). Mary Blair became a Disney Legend in 1991.

Broggie, Roger – (October 22, 1908 in Pittsfield, Massachusetts - Died November 4, 1991). Roger was the first official Imagineer. Roger joined the Disney Company in 1939. He worked on the multiplane camera, which was used by Ub Iwerks to make animated films. He also worked on the special effects for *20,000 Leagues Under the Sea* (1954). Walt had Roger design the ½ mile railroad track and design The Lilly Belle, a one-eighth-scale-size of a working steam locomotive, for the Disney's backyard. Roger and his machinist team created the first human audio-animatronic, the sitting Abraham Lincoln for the World's Fair in 1963. He also oversaw the development of the *Santa Fe & Disneyland Railroad*, the *Disneyland Monorail*, and the *Matterhorn Bobsleds*. He was honored with a window on Main Street that says, "*Can Do Machine Works / Mechanical Wonders / Live Steam Engines / Magical Illusions / Cameras / Roger Broggie, Shopmaster / Advisor to the Magic Makers*". Roger was made a Disney Legend in 1990, one year before passing away.

Burns, Harriet – (Born August 20, 1928, in San Antonio, Texas – Died July 25, 2008). Harriet Burns was the first female Imagineer that Walt hired. She started out her career designing sets for television shows, one of those being *The Colgate Comedy Hour* in the early 1950's. In 1955, she was then hired by Walt and was responsible for painting the set and props for the *Mickey Mouse Club* television show. Harriet began designing scale models for a future *Disneyland* project. At the time, the Imagineering department consisted of only three people, Harriet Burns, Fred Joerger, and Wathel Rogers. Her first assignment as an Imagineer was to design a scale model of *Sleeping Beauty Castle*. She continued making models for attractions that would later expand *Disneyland*, including one for the *Matterhorn Bobsleds*, *Pirates of the Caribbean*, and *Haunted Mansion*. One of her other jobs as an Imagineer was "figure-finishing." This is where she comes in at the end of a project and does the finishing touches to the figures or animatronic characters, like the pirates on *Pirates of the Caribbean*, the characters in the *Haunted Mansion*, and all the underwater creatures on the original *Submarine Voyage*. She was involved with some of the design for *Great Moments with Mr. Lincoln* as well. On of the ideas she was proud of was the creation of the chest plates for the *Enchanted Tiki Room* birds. She was having problems with the look of realistic breathing. She was given the remedy idea after seeing Walt wearing a cashmere sweater that bent just right at the elbow. Because Walt was so impressed with her, he featured her on several episodes of *The Wonderful World of Color* behind the scenes of *Disneyland*. She was honored with a window on *Main Street U.S.A.* that says, "*The Artisans Loft - Handmade Miniatures by Harriet Burns.*" She

291

was the first woman in Disney history to receive this honor. She became a Disney Legend in 2000.

🌀 **Coats, Claude** – (Born January 17, 1913, in San Francisco, California - Died January 9, 1992). Claude attended the University of Southern California as an architecture student, but later received his bachelor degree in drawing in 1934. He studied watercolor, which put him on Disney's radar and got him hired as a background artist in 1935. His earliest film work included the animated shorts *Mickey's Fire Brigade* (1935) and *Pluto's Judgment Day* (1935). He also painted sets for the *Silly Symphony* musical shorts, which earned him a membership to the Academy of Motion Picture Arts and Sciences. You can see some of his distinctive work in the academy award winning films *The Old Mill* (1937) and *Ferdinand the Bull* (1936). Walt personally selected him to paint the sets for the first full-length animated feature film, *Snow White and the Seven Dwarfs* (1937). In 1955, Walt asked Claude to join his Imagineers with designing attractions for *Disneyland*. He joined in and designed *Mr. Toad's Wild Ride, Snow White's Scary Adventures, Pirates of the Caribbean,* the *Grand Canyon* and *Primeval World* dioramas on the *Disneyland Railroad, Space Station X-1, Rainbow Caverns, Alice in Wonderland, Submarine Voyage, Adventure Thru Inner Space,* and the more eerie side to the *Haunted Mansion,* opposite of Marc Davis' comedic side. Claude retired in 1989, but stayed on to help design attractions in all the Disney parks (at that time) around the world to include *Magic Kingdom, EPCOT, Tokyo Disneyland,* and *Disneyland Paris.*

Here are some of the films he was involved with.

Snow White and the Seven Dwarfs (1937)	*Fun & Fancy Free* (1947)
Pinocchio (1940)	*Melody Time* (1948)
Fantasia (1940)	*The Adventures of Ichabod and Mr. Toad* (1949)
Dumbo (1941)	*Cinderella* (1950)
Saludos Amigos (1942)	*Alice in Wonderland* (1951)
The Three Caballeros (1944)	*Peter Pan* (1953)
Make Mine Music (1946)	*Lady and the Tramp* (1955)
Song of the South (1946)	

Claude was honored with a window on *Main Street, U.S.A.* that says "*Coats & Co. – Claude Coats Proprietor.*" He became a Disney Legend in 1991.

🌀 **Crump, Rolly** - (Born February 27, 1930, in Alhambra, California) – Rolly started out his career as a "dipper" in a ceramic factory before getting hired on at Disney in 1952. He only had six Saturdays of art instruction at Chouinard Art Institute under his belt. Disney had an open-door policy, so he wandered away from animation to check out the other departments and learned from other artists, sculptors, and Imagineers. With practice and tutelage, he was able to hone his skills. He worked as an in-betweener and later, assistant animator, on the films *Peter Pan* (1953), *Lady and the Tramp*

(1955), *101 Dalmations* (1961), *Sleeping Beauty* (1959) and others until becoming an Imagineer in 1959.

Rolly loved making propellers and mobiles. He had them on display in the studio's library. Ward Kimball told Walt to go check out Rolly's display because it was magnificent. After Walt saw what Rolly could do, he moved him over to Walt Disney Imagineering, but at the time it was WED. Walt was just starting to build up his WED department when he added Rolly who, at the time, was the youngest Imagineer there.

Walt met with five of his Imagineers and told them he wanted a restaurant/dinner show themed with Tahitian décor. That is how Rolly was added to *The Enchanted Tiki Room* project around 1962. Rolly helped come up with the design of the attraction with Imagineer John Hench. Rolly sculpted about 70% of the tikis used in the attraction, the "bird mobile," and the fountain. He was also credited with designing the *Tiki Room Preshow* out in the waiting area. After all that work, Walt thought the restaurant was too good to be just a dinner show, so he made it an attraction.

Due to his design work with windmills and mobiles, Rolly was put in charge of designing the 120-foot-tall *Tower of the Four Winds* for the World's Fair outside of the *it's a small world* attraction in 1964. He was with the *small world* project from day one. He designed and constructed over 200 of the "toys" on the attraction out of Styrofoam and paper-mâché, some of which are still on the attraction today. After the World's Fair ended and *small world* moved into *Disneyland*, Rolly assisted with the setup and layout of the attraction for the park and created the giant clock out front.

Rolly was also one of the key designers on the *Haunted Mansion* project in 1961. He and Yale Gracey spent a year coming up with ideas for the M*ansion's* interior. Rolly came up with a multitude of concepts for the *Museum of the Weird*, which was to be an area for crowds to walk through, but was scrapped when the idea of a walk-thru was changed to a ride-thru. Rolly and Yale were pulled off the project to work on The World's Fair projects. After the Fair is when things changed for the *Mansion's* layout and and design, because of the addition of the Doombuggies. This would take away the need for *The Museum of the Weird*. In Rolly's estimation, only about 25% of his ideas were used in the final attraction, including the séance room, phantom organ player, the changing portraits, moving busts, and a few others. One of the big losses was the nixing of the *Sea Captain's Room*, which was set to have a handful of special effects. The only remaining idea of the Sea Captain can be found as a portrait hanging in the *Haunted Mansion* in *Disney World's Magic Kingdom*. Rolly came up with the first sketches of the "stretching portraits," but then that aspect of the attraction was taken over by Marc Davis who drew the portraits, or a variation thereof, that you see today. Rolly also had concept sketches of faces for the hallway wallpaper, but that too was done by Marc Davis, who designed his wallpaper similarly to Rolly's. (see *The Haunted Mansion* Fun Facts on page 481 for more information)

Rolly worked on the design for the *Magic Kingdom's Mr. Toad's Wild Ride*. The attraction's tracks would split into two and the two cars would race each other. But that attraction was removed to make way for the *Winnie The Pooh* attraction.

Chris Crump is also an Imagineer and the son of Rolly. The only project the two of them worked on together was the *Wonders of Life* attraction in *Epcot*, which existed from 1989 to 2007. Chris recently worked on *The Little Mermaid: Ariel's Undersea Adventure* in *California Adventure*.

Rolly worked on and off for Disney over the decades before his retirement in 1996. He is still an artist today and even has a book out titled *It's Kind Of A Cute Story*, in which he tells stories of his experiences working with Walt and for the Disney company. Rolly had so many stories to tell about his time with Disney that he released a CD series called *More Cute Stories*.

Rolly became a Disney Legend in 2004 and has a dedication window on Main Street that says *"Fargo's Palm Parlor - Predictions That Will Haunt You – Bazaar, Whimsical & Weird – "Designs to Die For" – Roland F. Crump – Assistant to the Palm Reader."*

To hear Rolly speak, check out my podcast, *The Magic Behind The Ears Podcast*, and look up episode #3. It can be found on iTunes, SoundCloud, the podcast app, FaceBook, or you can listen right from online at www.ThemeParkology.com/podcast.

Davis, Alice – (Born in 1929 in Escalon, CA) Alice attempted to get into the Couinard Art Institute to learn how to be an animator since her passion was drawing; but, the Art Institute didn't accept girls. They did, however, accept her to teach her to be a costume designer. Her first class was Fine Art, where they taught her about human anatomy and how muscles worked. The class instructor was Marc Davis. Alice began her career designing women's lingerie and undergarments for the Beverly Vogue & Lingerie House in Los Angeles. It wasn't until after she graduated and began working that she started up a friendship with Marc, whom she ended up marrying in 1956 at the age of 27. She quickly became the head designer. In the mid-1950's, Alice got a call from Marc requesting her to design a dress for Helene Stanley to wear as the live-action model for Briar Rose in *Sleeping Beauty* (1959). Walt was impressed with her work and brought Alice on full time to work on the costumes for *Toby Tyler* (1960) and other Disney television shows. Later in 1963, Walt had her working on the costumes for *it's a small world* for the World's Fair. She worked alongside Imagineer Mary Blair and studied all the different cultures to come up with 150 outfits. She also made all the period clothing for the characters in the *Carousel of Progress*, which can still be seen in *Magic Kingdom*. During the *small world* project, Alice established an audio-animatronic costume manufacturing area, refurbishing techniques, and quality control system which are still in use by Imagineers today. Alice had said that she "*went from sweet little children, to dirty old men overnight*" with the wardrobe creations for *Pirates of the Caribbean,* for which she designed 47 different period costumes that date back to the late-1700's. She had to convert her husband's animated pirate sketches to real life. Walt visited her in the studio and was able to see The Auctioneer pirate in full attire. Then the following day or two he went into the hospital before passing away. He never got to see any of the other pirates. Along with the *Pirates* project, she worked on the costumes for the refurbishment of *Flight to the Moon* in *Tomorrowland*. Alice retired with Marc in 1978, but was still contacted for consulting purposes, like for the film *Up* (2009). She has a window dedicated to her right next to Marc's on *Main Street, USA*, and she became a Disney Legend in 2004.

Davis, Marc - (see *Disney Things Explained: Nine Old Men on page 275*)

Evans, Morgan "Bill" – (Born June 10, 1910 in Santa Monica, California – Died August 16, 2002). Bill was a horticulturalist who guided the landscape design of Disney theme parks for over 50 years. Bill joined the marines and traveled all over the world and collected exotic plant seeds. After leaving the Marines, he went to school and majored in geology. During the depression, he left school to help his father start a nursery. Bill was working at his father's nursery in Santa Monica selling exotic plants to the rich and famous and landscaping their properties. One of his clients was Walt Disney, who had Bill landscape his home in Holmby Hills near Hollywood. Walt was so impressed with Bill's work that he asked him and his brother, Jim, to plan the landscaping of what was to be *Disneyland*.

Bill debunked the rumor of the colorblind tractor operator who bulldozed the trees with the colored ribbons during the building of *Disneyland*. He said he hadn't heard of the rumor until a few years after the opening of the park. He said the rumor was started by Marty Sklar who was a copy writer for Disney and was hurting for stories that were interesting at the time. Aside from landscaping the park, his major project was making the *Jungle Cruise* densely populated with exotic plant life. To help in this endeavor, he planted orange trees upside down, exposing their roots to appear as mangled tree branches. After the park opened, he stayed on as an Imagineer as a landscape planner, consultant, and maintenance supervisor. Disney made him the director of landscape architecture. He went on to oversee the horticulture of *Wald Disney World* and *EPCOT*. Evans retired from Disney in 1975, but continued his work for Disney with the landscape design of *Tokyo Disneyland*, *Hong Kong Disneyland*, *Disneyland Paris,* and additions in *Walt Disney World* such as *Disney's Polynesian Resort*, *Discovery Island*, *Typhoon Lagoon*, *Disney-MGM Studios,* and *Disney's Animal Kingdom*.

After passing away at the age of 92, Bill was awarded the American Society of Landscape Architects Medal in 2002 in recognition of his lifetime achievement in the profession of landscape architecture. He became a Disney Legend in 1992.

Fowler, Joe – (Born July 9, 1894, in Lewiston, Maine – Died December 6, 1993). Joe Fowler was a retired Navy Admiral. He was a good friend of Walt's and a key person behind the construction of *Disneyland*. Walt found him supervising the construction of housing tracts in San Francisco in the 1950's and hired him to construct the *Mark Twain Riverboat*. Fowler went on to supervise the construction of *Disneyland* and *Disney World* and stayed on as an advisor after retirement. He was the general manager of *Disneyland* for the first 10 years of operation. The *Magic Kingdom's* first riverboat was dedicated to him, *The Admiral Joe Fowler*.

Joe oversaw the building of the *Mark Twain Riverboat* and the subs for the *Submarine Voyage* at the Todd Shipyards in San Pedro, California. Walt wanted more traffic on the *Rivers of America,* so he asked Joe to find another ship to accompany The Mark Twain around the island. Joe went all around the US trying to find a memorable ship from our history to become the next attraction on the river. That's when he settled on the "Columbia Rediviva." There was only one known picture of the Columbia, but Disney used it along with historical documents from The Library of Congress to design the final ship. Fowler's Harbor and Fowler's Inn are areas in Critter Country that are dedicated to him. After the final drop on Splash Mountain, you will pass a doorway that says "Fowler's Cellar." He became a Disney Legend in 1990.

Gracey, Yale – (Born September 3, 1910 - September 5, 1983) – Yale was an animator that worked on over six dozen of the Disney shorts and other films including *The Reluctant Dragon* (1941), *Fantasia* (1940), *Saludos Amigos* (1942), and *The Three Caballeros* (1944). He was also an Imagineer and was responsible for designing a lot of the special effects on *Haunted Mansion*. Yale also designed the "burning fire" on *Pirates of the Caribbean*. The character Master Gracey in the Haunted Mansion was named as such to pay homage to him. He was made a Disney Legend in 1999.

Gibson, Blaine – (Born February 11, 1918, in Rocky Ford, Colorado – Died July 5, 2015). Blaine began drawing, sculpting, and whittling at a young age. He would get clay from a nearby river to sculpt and his mother would fire the clay in the kitchen stove. At the age of 12, he sculpted an elephant out of a bar of soap and won $10 in a contest held by Procter & Gamble (P&G). At 21 years old, Blaine became an animator for Disney, and then later a sculptor. Blane did visual effects and character animations for films such as *Pinocchio* (1940), *Fantasia* (1940), *Bambi* (1942), *Song of the South* (1946), *Fun & Fancy Free* (1947), *Cinderella* (1950), *Alice in Wonderland* (1951), *Peter Pan* (1953), *Casey Bats Again* (1954), *Lady and the Tramp* (1955), *Sleeping Beauty* (1959), *Goliath II* (1960), and *101 Dalmatians* (1961). He ended up becoming an Imagineer when *Disneyland* broke ground after Walt had seen some of his animal sculptures in 1954. Blaine worked as an animator and Imagineer until he became a full-time Imagineer in 1961. He created hundreds of sculptures that were turned into audio-animatronics or bronze statues used at the World's Fair and in the Disney theme parks. He sculpted the face of Abraham Lincoln for *Great Moments with Mr. Lincoln*, the pirates on *Pirates of the Caribbean*, the ghosts in the *Haunted Mansion*, and the tiki birds in *The Enchanted Tiki Room*. He was the lead director for the *Hall of Presidents* project for *Disney*

World and had a hand in creating all the presidents up to George W. Bush in 2001.

After nearly 45 years working for the Disney Company, Blaine retired. He did, however, stay on as a consultant after that for attractions like *The Great Movie Ride* in *Disney's Hollywood Studios*. In 1993, he temporarily came out of retirement to create the bronze "Partners" statue that sits in front of the castles at *Disneyland* and *Magic Kingdom*. He also made one of Roy O. Disney sitting with Minnie Mouse on a bench. In his career, he mentored and inspired many Imagineers and sculptors in the Disney Company. He became a Disney Legend in 1993.

Goff, Harper – (Born March 16, 1911 – Died March 3, 1993) In 1951, Harper was in a model train shop in London and wanted to buy a model train. It just so happened that a certain Walt Disney was also there, which led him to moving to Los Angeles to join The Walt Disney Company. Just above the *Adventureland Bazaar* shop there is a window dedicated to Harper Goff. Harper was responsible for some of the original designs for *Disneyland* and some attractions. He was also a concept artist on many films including *20,000 Leagues Under the Sea* (1954), which he designed the Nautilus exterior and all the interior sets, *Willy Wonka & the Chocolate Factory* (1971), and *The Vikings* (1957). He also worked for Warner Brothers, producing the sets for such memorable films as *Sergeant York* (1941), *Charge of the Light Brigade* (1936), and *Captain Blood* (1935). During WWII, Harper was implemented as an advisor to the army in designing the color palette for camouflage, which he compared to a "paint-by-number" kit. He played the banjo in the *Walt Disney Studios* animation department Dixieland jaz group *The Firehouse Five Plus Two*, along with Ward Kimball (trombone and sound effects), and Frank Thomas (piano). He became a Disney Legend in 1993.

Gurr, Bob - (Born October 25, 1931, in Los Angeles, California) – Bob was hired on to the Walt Disney Imagineering department (WDI) by Walt Disney after he was used as a consultant with the construction of the Autopia cars. He designed most of the ride vehicles for the attractions in the park, about 100 different ride vehicles, including the *Haunted Mansion* doom buggies, *Submarine Voyage*, the *Monorail*, the *Matterhorn Bobsleds*, and so many more. He also worked on the *King Kong Encounter* animatronic for *Universal Studios Hollywood*. He even said, "If it moves on wheels at *Disneyland*, I probably designed it." Bob was given

the honor of giving Vice President Richard Nixon the first ride on the new *Disneyland Monorail* in 1959. In 1964, Bob was designing the animatronic character which was to become Abraham Lincoln for the attraction *Great Moments with Mr. Lincoln,* but it was first given to The World's Fair before returning to the park. Bob was made a Disney Legend in 2004 and given a window on Main Street, U.S.A. that says, "Leading the Race to the Future – Meteor Cycle Co. – Our vehicles pass the test of time – Fast, Faultless and Fadless."

Harman and Ising – (Hugh Harman, born August 31, 1903 – Died November 25, 1982) and Rudolf "Rudy" Carl Ising, born August 7, 1903 – Died July 18, 1992) – Both men were an animation duo that worked in the early years of the Disney studios. They animated for Walt on the *Alice Comedies* and also the *Oswald The Lucky Rabbit* shorts. When *Universal Studios* let Walt go from animating the Oswald cartoons, Harman and Ising stayed to continue animating the series. They later went on to be founding members of the *Warner Brothers* and *Metro-Goldwyn-Mayer* animation studios.

Hench, John – (Born June 29, 1908 – Died February 5, 2004) - John worked for Disney for more than 65 years. Starting in 1939, as a story artist, he worked his way through the animation department in all areas including backgrounds, layout and art direction, effects animation, and special effects. John became the first Imagineer for WED Enterprises. In 1960, he designed the Olympic torch, altering it so it was shorter and adding a gripper under the rim so the runners could carry it easier. John was one of the main designers of the *Haunted Mansion* with Imagineer Rolly Crump. He was the one who commissioned the work for the marble Snow White statues currently found in *Snow White Grotto*, which currently have replicas in their place. In 1961, Jon teamed up with animator Bill Justice to redesign and create the standards for the parks Meet & Greet Mickey Mouse so he was evenly proportionsed and was always the same height. John was one of the writers for the animated short *Destino* (2003), which took 58 years to complete. He has a window on *Main Street, U.S.A.* and became a Disney Legend in 1990.

Irvine, Kim – Kim became an Imagineer in 1970, following in the footsteps of her Imagineer mother, Leota Toombs (the face of Madam Leota). Some of her notable projects are the redesign of the *Plaza Inn* restaurant, the *Disneyland Dream Suite* completion, the 2009 version of *Great Moments with Mr. Lincoln*, the 2008 version of the *Sleeping Beauty Castle* walk-through, the 2008/2009 refurbishment of it*'s a small world*, the 2013/2014 expansion of *Club 33*, and *The Haunted Mansion's* pet cemetery. Both *it's a small world* and *Great Moments with Mr. Lincoln* were originaly created by her mother. When *Disneyland* did the *Haunted Mansion Holiday* makeover, they needed a new face for Madam Leota. Since Leota Tombs had passed away in 1991, Kim stepped up and filled in the spot for her mother. She is still active as the art director for *Disneyland*. Kim married the son of Imagineer Richard Irvine.

Irvine, Richard F. – (Born April 10, 1910 – Died March 30, 1976) Richard was an art director for 20th Century Fox and worked on films such as *Miracle on 34th Street* (1947), *Don't Bother to Knock* (1952), *Apartment for Peggy* (1948), and *The Gunfighter* (1950). Richard was hired by Walt in 1952 to be a liason between an architect firm and Disney with the design of *Disneyland*. Untimately Richard convinced Walt that his animators, sculptors, artists, and designers would be the best choice for designing *Disneyland*. So, the Disney Imagineering arm of the Disney Productions company was created. Richard was a good pick to help lead the design of the park because of his history and experience designing movie sets, creating structures, and establishing timeline settings. He was good at getting that "forced perspective" look to the buildings. Richard was the one who chose the architechs, artists, animators, and sculptors to become Imagineers. In 1967, he was appointed executive vice president and chief operations officer of WED Enterprises (now Walt Disney Imagineering). He headed the planning for all of the attractions in *Disneyland*, Disney's attractions for the World's Fair, *Magic Kingdom*, and *Epcot* until his retirement in 1973. He became a Disney Legend in 1990, and also has a dedication window on *Main Street, U.S.A.* His son married Imagineer Kim Irvine, the daughter of Imagineer Leota Toombs, the face of Madam Leota. One of the ferries that takes people across the *Seven Seas Lagoon* to the *Magic Kingdom* was dedicated to him.

Iwerks, Ub – (Born March 24, 1901, in Kansas City, Missouri – Died July 7, 1971) - Born Ubbe Eert "Ub" Iwerks, Ub was an animator, inventor, character designer, special effects technician, and cartoonist. Ub, pronounced the same as "Up" but with a 'b,' was the co-creator of Oswald the Lucky Rabbit and Mickey Mouse alongside Walt Disney. It is said that Ub would lock himself in his office and put out 300 Mickey Mouse sketches a night. Ub is also said to be Walt's oldest friend. They met in 1919 while working for the Pesmen-Rubin Art Studio in Kansas City.

Walt eventually wanted to start his own animation company and Ub joined him. In 1921, Walt started Laugh-O-Gram in Kansas City, Missouri, and Ub was the chief animator. There they worked on Walt's first animated fairytale, *Little Red Riding Hood* (1922). The company went bankrupt in 1923 following the release of *Alice's Wonderland* (1923), which was the pilot to the series referred to as the *Alice Comedies*. Ub went with Walt to Los Angeles following the bankruptcy. There they worked on the *Alice Comedies*. Ub was the sole animator of the first Oswald cartoon in 1927. After the loss of Oswald, Walt swore he would never animate a character that he didn't own the rights to. That was when Walt came up with Mickey Mouse. He had Ub come up with other characters they might be able to use in the cartoons, and that is how Clarabelle Cow and Horace Horsecollar were born. The first few Mickey Mouse and Silly Symphonies cartoons were animated almost entirely by Iwerks, including *Steamboat Willie* and *Skeleton Dance*.

Ub and Walt had a falling out after Ub demanded more credit since he was the sole animator on Walt's cartoons and felt he wasn't getting what he deserved. Their partnership and friendship were severed and Ub went to work for Pat Powers, an animator who used to work for Walt but broke off and started his own company. Pat Powers became the financial backer for Ub to open his own animation studio, Iwerks Studio, in 1930. Powers suspected that Iwerks was responsible for much of Disney's early success and thought that Ub would do great. His cartoons starring *Flip the Frog* and later *Willie Whopper* were a flop, and couldn't compete with Disney or Fleischer Studios. From 1933 to 1936, he produced a series of shorts in Cinecolor, called ComiColor Cartoons. He also tried his hand at stop-motion pictures and produced the short *The Toy Parade* before the closing of his company. In 1937, Leon Schlesinger Productions contracted Iwerks to produce four Looney Tunes shorts starring Porky Pig and Gabby Goat. Ub returned to Disney in 1940.

Ub primarily worked on special visual effects on films after his return. One of the processes Ub is attributed with is the creation of a process that overlays animation with live action. This process was first used in the film *Song of the South* (1946). He also created the xerographic process adapted for cel animation which was used to save time on repeat animations, like the spots on the dogs in *101 Dalmatians* (1961). Ub worked in the WED Enterprises department, later named Walt Disney Imagineering, to design the park attractions for *Disneyland*.

DC Comics created a character named Doctor Ub'x for the Green Lantern comics in 1986 to honor him. He became a Disney Legend in 1989.

Justice, Bill - (Born February 9, 1914 – Died February 10, 2011) – Bill joined Disney as an animator in 1937. He worked on 19 feature films and 57 animated shorts in his animation career. Some of the titles include *Fantasia* (1940), *Fun & Fancy Free* (1947), *The Three Caballeros* (1944), *The Adventures of Ichabod and Mr. Toad* (1949), *Alice in Wonderland* (1951), and *Peter Pan* (1953). He is best known as the animator of the cute rabbit, Thumper, from *Bambi* (1942), and the chipmunks Chip 'n Dale. He moved up to being an Imagineer in 1965 and was an animatronic programmer for *Great Moments with Mr. Lincoln*, *Pirates of the Caribbean*, *Haunted Mansion*, and *Country Bear Jamboree*. He also did some sketch concepts for what later became the *Main Street Electrical Parade*. Bill started the northern California chapter to the Disneyana clubs, *The Golden Gate Disneyana Club*. He retired in 1979 and became a Disney Legend in 1996. He has an autobiography out called *Justice for Disney*.

Kimball, Ward - (see *Disney Things Explained: Nine Old Men* on page 275)

McKim, Sam – (Born December 20, 1924 – Died July 9, 2004) - Sam started his career at the age of 10 acting as an extra in films. He worked alongside Spencer Tracy, John Wayne, Rita Hayworth, and Gene Autry. He had a total of 62 credits to his name, including *Sergeant York* (1941), *Mr. Smith Goes to Washington* (1939), and *The Adventures of Mark Twain*

(1944). While in high school, he decided that he wanted to work behind the camera instead of in front of it, so he sent in sketches to Disney and they responded with offering him a job in the traffic department. Not wanting to do that, he joined the US Army and served during World War II. After he got out, he attended Art Center College of Design in Los Angeles. Upon graduation, he was drafted to fight in the Korean War for 14 months. He was awarded the Distinguished Service Cross and the Bronze Star. When he returned to the United States, he attended Chouinard Art Institute in Los Angeles. In 1953, he got a job working for *20th Century Fox* making story sketches for films. In 1954, just six months before the opening of *Disneyland*, he joined Disney as an Imagineer and began working on the park. He was the "master map maker" and designed the cartoony fun maps that are collected as souvenirs from the park. He designed all the *Disneyland* maps from 1958 to 1964. Following his retirement in 1987, he returned to design the first map for *Disneyland Paris* in 1992. If you look closely at his maps, you can find the initials "S.M." hidden somewhere. He worked on many other projects including *The Golden Horseshoe, Great Moments with Mr. Lincoln, Carousel of Progress, Pirates of the Caribbean*, and *Haunted Mansion*. For *Disney World*, he contributed to the designs of *The Hall of Presidents, Universe of Energy*, and concept art for *MGM Studios* (now *Hollywood Studios*). Along with park designs, Walt had him do storyboard sketches for films such as *Nikki, Wild Dog of the North* (1961), *Big Red* (1962), *Bon Voyage* (1962), *The Gnome-Mobile* (1967), and some episodes of *Zorro* (1957-1959). He has a window on *Main Street. U.S.A.* and became a Disney Legend in 1996.

Moore, Fred "Freddie" – (Born September 7, 1911 – Died November 2, 1952) – Fred had no formal art education. He was a natural artist. He started out animating Mickey Mouse for the shorts. He was later tasked with redesigning Mickey in 1938 for the film *Fantasia* (1940). He worked on the *Brave Little Taylor* (1938) which was the last film Mickey was in with his solid-eyed appearance. After that, he had pupils which was Fred's idea. He was credited with animating the pigs in *The Three Little Pigs* (1933), was the animation director for *Snow White and The Seven Dwarfs* (1937), Lampwick in *Pinocchio* (1940), Timothy Mouse in *Dumbo* (1941), some of the mice scenes in *Cinderella* (1950), some of the oysters and the White Rabbit in *Alice In Wonderland* (1951), and the lost boys and mermaids in the lagoon scene in *Peter Pan* (1953), which were modeled by Margaret Kerry and June Foray.

Fred was known for drawing innocently sexy girls referred to as "Freddy Moore Girls." You could see this when he animated the centaurettes in *Fantasia* (1940), the teenage girls in the "All Cats Join In" segment of *Make Mine Music* (1946), and Casey's daughters in *Casey Bats Again* (1954). His style influenced the look of Ariel in *The Little Mermaid* (1989).

After leaving the Disney studios in 1946, he worked for Walter Lants, the director who took over the Oswald cartoons after Walt Disney was fired, and redesigned Woody Woodpecker. He then returned to Disney in 1948. In

301

November 1952, Fred was in an automobile accident with his wife and passed away at the young age of 41. Fred is often thought to have had the biggest influence on Disney animation. He was involved with animating nearly 35 shorts. You can see an animated depiction of Fred in the animated short *The Nifty Nineties* (1941) alongside fellow animator Ward Kimball. He became a Disney Legend in 1995.

O'Connor, Kendall "Ken" – (Born June 7, 1908, in Perth, Western Australia, Australia – Died May 27, 1998) – Ken Joined the Walt Disney Studios in 1935, where he worked as either art director or layout man on 13 feature-length films and nearly 100 animated shorts. Among the most memorable images he created for films were the magical coach in *Cinderella* (1950), the marching cards in *Alice in Wonderland* (1951), and the dancing hippos in *Fantasia* (1940). His other credits include, *Snow White and the Seven Dwarfs* (1937), *Pinocchio* (1940), *Dumbo* (1941), *Make Mine Music* (1946), *Melody Time* (1948), *Peter Pan* (1953), *Lady and the Tramp* (1955), and many more. Ken's imagination and designs were used in the creation of *Universe of Energy* in *EPCOT,* which was sponsored by Exxon from its opening in 1982-1996. It now houses the *Ellen's Energy Adventure* starring Ellen DeGeneres and Bill Nye, "The Science Guy." Ken worked for Disney for over 30 years and became a Disney Legend in 1992.

Ryman, Herbert "Herb" – (Born June 28, 1910, in Vernon, Illinois - Died February 10, 1989) – After moving to California in 1932, Herb got a job working for MGM as a storyboard illustrator. One memorable project he worked on was the Emerald City in *The Wizard of Oz* (1939), which was also his final project. Herb met Walt at an exhibit of his own artwork at the Chouinard Art Institute in 1938. Walt was so impressed with his art, that he hired him to work for the studio and made him the art director for *Dumbo* (1941) and *Fantasia* (1940). Herb was one of Walt's companions on the three-month goodwill tour of South America, which resulted in the creation of *The Three Caballeros* (1944) and *Saludos Amigos* (1942). In the mid-1940's, he left Disney to go to 20th Century Fox and work on films for them. He took some time off in 1949 and 1951 to travel with the Ringling Brothers Circus and document what he saw in paintings. He became friends with Emmett "Willie the Clown" Kelly. In 1953, Herb received a request from Walt to come back and help him plan a theme park. Walt and Herb worked non-stop through the weekend to come up with a pencil sketch concept of *Disneyland*. It was these drawings that Roy Disney took to New York to show to investors to back the funding of the park. After the park was underway, he developed concept art for many attractions and lands including *Main Street, U.S.A., Sleeping Beauty Castle, New Orleans Square, The Jungle Cruise, Pirates of the Caribbean*, and for attractions featured at the 1964-65 New York World's Fair, including *Great Moments with Mr. Lincoln*. He was the chief designer of the *Cinderella Castle* in *Walt Disney World.*

After 33 years of working for Disney, he retired in 1971. He came out of retirement in 1976 to consult on the design of *EPCOT's The American*

Adventure, the *China Pavillion*, and the *Meet the World* attraction in *Tokyo Disneyland*. His last project for Disney was the concept art for *Main Street* in *Euro Disney*, later named *Disneyland Paris*. He became a Disney Legend in 1990.

FUN FACT: He was the great-great-grandson of the 12ᵗʰ United States President, Zachary Taylor.

Sherman Brothers – The Sherman Brothers is the collective name given to Robert Sherman (Born December 19, 1925, in New York, New York – Died March 6, 2012) and his brother, Richard Sherman (Born June 12, 1928, in New York, New York). They were some of the most talented music composers of all time.

Robert was portrayed by B.J. Novak in the Disney film *Saving Mr. Banks* (2013). In the film, it was mentioned that Robert was limping because he was shot in the leg, but it was never explained as to why. In 1943, Robert obtained permission from his parents to join the army a year early, at age 17. In early April 1945, he led half a squad of men into Dachau concentration camp, the first Allied troops to enter the camp after it had been evacuated by the fleeing German military only hours earlier. On April 12, 1945, the day President Franklin D. Roosevelt died, Robert was shot in the knee, forcing him to walk with a cane for the rest of his life. For his service to his country, he received two Battle Stars, a Combat Infantryman Badge, an American Campaign Medal, a World War II Victory Medal, a European-African-Middle Eastern Campaign Medal, and a Good Conduct Medal. In addition, Robert was also awarded several Army Weapons Qualifications badges including a "Sharpshooter badge" with bars for both rifle and submachine gun, a "Marksman Badge" for carbine, and an "Expert Badge" for rifle and grenade. During his recuperation in Taunton and Bournemouth in the UK, Robert was awarded the Purple Heart medal. On his return to the United States, Robert attended Bard College in upstate New York where he majored in English Literature and Painting. Robert also served as the editor-in-chief of The Bardian, which is the campus newspaper. At Bard, Robert completed his first two novels, *The Best Estate and Music* and *Candy and Painted Eggs*. He graduated in the class of 1949. On May 12, 1990, Sherman received an Honorary Doctorate from Lincoln College.

Richard was drafted into the United States Army in 1953. He received an honorable discharge in 1955. He also went to Bard College and majored in music. Two years after graduating, he began writing songs with his brother, Robert, because of a challenge from their father, Al Sherman. He was a successful popular songwriter in the "Tin Pan Alley" (1885-1930's) days.

In 1958, the brothers had their first Top Ten hit with the song "Tall Paul." It was sung my Mouseketeer Annette Funicello. This was the first time a woman reached the Top Ten list for rock and roll music. This caught the attention of Walt. The first song they composed for Disney was the "Medfield Fight Song" in the film *The Absent-Minded Professor* (1961).

303

They composed music for Walt Disney, and also non-Disney, in many movies. Some of these would include:

Mary Poppins (1964)	*Charlotte's Web* (1973)
The Jungle Book (1967)	*Chitty Chitty Bang Bang* (1968)
The Aristocats (1970)	*Snoopy, Come Home* (1972)
The Parent Trap (1961)	*The Sword in the Stone* (1963)
The Parent Trap (1998)	*The Happiest Millionaire* (1967)
Bedknobs And Broomsticks (1971)	*Tom Sawyer* (1973)
The Many Adventures of Winnie the Pooh (1977)	
Little Nemo: Adventures in Slumberland (1992)	
The One and Only, Genuine, Original Family Band (1968)	

You can hear their musical scores around the parks as well:

Adventure Thru Inner Space
   "Miracles from Molecules"
America on Parade
   "The Glorious Fourth"
Carousel of Progress
   "The Best Time of Your Life"
   "There's a Great Big Beautiful Tomorrow"
CommuniCore
   "The Astuter Computer Revue"
Epcot Center Opening & Dedication

   "The World Showcase March"
Journey into Imagination

   "One Little Spark"
Magic Journeys
   "Magic Journeys"
   "Makin' Memories"

Meet the World in Tokyo Disneyland
   "Meet the World"
   "We Meet the World with Love"
Rocket Rods
   "Magic Highways"
The Great Movie Ride

   "Chim Chim Cher-ee"
The Many Adventures of Winnie the Poo
   "Winnie the Pooh"
   "A Rather Blustery Day"
   "The Wonderful Thing About Tiggers"
   "Heffalumps and Woozles"
   "The Rain Rain Rain Came Down Down Down"
   "Hip Hip Pooh-Ray!"
Walt Disney's Enchanted Tiki Room
   "The Tiki, Tiki, Tiki Room"

One of their most popular songs ever composed is "it's a small world after all" which plays in all of the *it's a small world* attractions in all the Disney parks. Walt wanted the brothers to come up with a song for *it's a small world* when it was an attraction in the World's Fair in 1964. He also wanted it to be able to play in a never-ending loop and translatable into many other languages. The song resides in public domain, so anyone can legally use it.

The documentary *The Boys: The Sherman Brother's Story* (2009) is an excellent film if you want to learn more about them. Walt's favorite song was "Feed the Birds" from *Mary Poppins*. The Sherman Brothers would play it for him whenever he went to their recording studio. On March 11, 2010, they received their own dedication window on *Main Street, U.S.A.* Both brothers became Disney Legends in 1990.

FUN FACT: At the age of 86, Richard Sherman was asked to write the song for the *Disneyland Forever* fireworks show which began May 22, 2015. He titled the song "Goodnight Kiss," to pay homage to Walt's reference of the fireworks show being everyone's goodnight kiss before they leave the park.

Toombs Thomas, Leota "Lee" – (Born Early 1930's - Died December 1991) Leota was a costumer, model builder, finisher, and Imagineer. Leota started working in The Walt Disney Studios in 1940 in the Ink and Paint Department. She transferred to the Animation Department and met Harvey Toombs, whom she wed in 1947. Harvey was an animator from 1940-1962, and worked on such films as *Pinocchio, Dumbo, Bambi, Cinderella, Alice in Wonderland, Peter Pan,* and *Sleeping Beauty.* Leota worked on the human and animal animatronic characters around the park. She had been known to wade into the *Jungle Cruise* water chest deep to adjust an animal. Leota took a break from the Disney Company to raise her two children, Launie and Kim (read about Kim Irvine a few pages back). After returning to Disney in 1962, she joined the Imagineers and helped to work on the *Enchanted Tiki Room,* and then projects for the 1964-1965 World's Fair. She played a pivotal role in the creation of *it's a small world, Great Moments with Mr. Lincoln,* and *Ford's Magic Skyway.* After the World's Fair, she began working on *The Haunted Mansion* and *Pirates of the Caribbean.*

Yale Gracey was experimenting with different techniques for some gypsy head in a ball for *The Haunted Mansion.* He had Leota pose for him and he liked how it turned out. Leota said it was because her eyes were the proper distance apart for the face. Blaine Gibson made a life mask of her face, then Yale and Wathel Rogers filmed her in full makeup to create Madam Leota. Leota didn't provide the voice for Madam Leota; that voice over was provided by Eleanor Audley. Yale did, however, have Leota provide the face and the voice for Little Leota, the little bride that you pass as you exit the attraction. Kim said that it was because they wanted a higher voice for the smaller figure, and her mom's voice made her sound like a little girl.

Her husband, Harvey, passed away in 1968. Leota transferred to the Imagineering Department in *Walt Disney World* in 1971. She started up the team that would maintain the attractions and shows there. She also worked on attractions like *The Hall of Presidents,* among others. While inspecting the progress of the *Jungle Cruise,* she met Hugh Thomas, a gardener, who was working on setting up the plants on the river banks. They fell in love, later got married, and lived in Orlando. She returned to Imagineering in California in 1979 and continued to train the future figure finishers and artisans. She started a ceramics company with her husband called *Thomas Ceramics Company.* Along with being an Imagineer, Leota would design the molds, and Hugh ran the company. Their products were offered for sale in the *Lillian Vernon Catalog.* She became a Disney Legend in 2009. In 2001, Disney dedicated a tombstone to Leota by the entrance to *Magic Kingdom's Haunted Mansion.* It is inscribed with *"Dear sweet Leota, beloved by all, in regions beyond now, but having a ball."* If you stare at

the face on her tombstone long enough, the eyes open and close and the head moves. (*see photo*)

Wagner, Jack "The Voice of *Disneyland*" – (Born December 17, 1925, in Los Angeles, CA – Died June 16, 1995) Jack started doing recordings for *Disneyland* in 1955. He became the full-time park announcer in 1970. Disney installed a recording studio in his own home, which was only two miles from the park, making it one of the first remote audio links from a remote location. He also did some voice work in *Walt Disney World* and *Tokyo Disneyland*. His voice could be heard if an attraction broke down, or if he was giving instructions for that evening's fireworks. He did voice work on Disneyland TV specials, commercials, and Cast Member training videos. Besides working for Disney, Jack worked for KNX radio in Los Angeles as an announcer. He dabbled in television acting as well, being visiting characters on shows such as *The Adventures of Ozzie and Harriet* on which he made 1,244 appearances, *The Ann Sothern Show*, *Sea Hunt*, and *Dragnet*. His most famous line can be heard on the *Matterhorn Bobsleds*, "*Remain seated, please; permanecer sentados por favor.*" You can also hear this recording in the nighttime fireworks, "*Remember... Dreams Come True,*" and on the *Disneyland Monorail Mark VI* saying "*Please stand clear of the doors.*" Because he could be heard just about everywhere, it earned him the nickname "The Voice of *Disneyland*." He retired from his regular voice work in 1991 following a vocal cord surgery, but still did small announcements up until 1993. He became a Disney Legend in 2005.

Rogers, Wathel – (Born June 29, 1919, in Stratton, CO – Died August 25, 2000) After leaving the Couinard Art Institute, Wathel joined The Walt Disney Studios in 1939. He began working as an assistant animator, and later as an animator on such films as *Bambi* and *Pinocchio*. He left the studio for a brief time when he joined the United States Marine Corps in 1943. After World War II, he returned to the studio and worked on films like *Alice in Wonderland, Cinderella, Peter Pan, Lady and the Tramp*, and *Sleeping Beauty*. Wathel liked to sculpt and build toys in his spare time, including model trains, which caught Walt's eye. He was asked to help work on sculpting projects for the studio and made props and miniatures for films like *The Absent-Minded Professor* and *Darby O'Gill and the Little People* as well as television shows including *Mickey Mouse Club* and *Zorro*. One of Wathel's greatest challenges came in 1951, when Walt asked him to make a 9" tall audio-animatronic figure. The project was called "Project Little Man." (*see photo*) This was the precursor to all audio-animatronic which you see in the parks today. To program it, they had actor/dancer Buddy Ebson (*Davy Crockett* (1955), *The Beverly Hillbillies* (1962-1971), and the original Tin Man from *The Wizard of Oz* (1939)) dance around while they etched the movements onto giant discs like records. As the discs turned they would trigger the individual movements. Wathel was then referred to as "Mr.

306

Audio-Animatronics." In 1954, Walt asked him to help set up a model shop for the planning of *Disneyland*. He became one of the top Imagineers and assisted in the architectural models for the park in the development phase. When the 1960's rolled around Wathel created the Abraham Lincoln that was used in the *Great Moments with Mr. Lincoln* exhibit for the World's Fair, and then in *Disneyland*. This all led the way to work on *Pirates of the Caribbean*, *The Enchanted Tiki Room*, and *Jungle Cruise*. He later made the first walking audio-animatronics character for *American Adventure* at *EPCOT*, Benjamin Franklin. He became a Disney Legend in 1995.

DISNEY FILM COMPANY ASSETS

PIXAR

History

Pixar was founded as the Graphics Group, one third of the Computer Division of Lucasfilm that was launched in 1979 with the hiring of Dr. Ed Catmull from the New York Institute of Technology (NYIT). At NYIT, the researchers worked on an experimental film called *The Works*. When the group moved to Lucasfilm, the team worked on creating the precursor to RenderMan, called Motion Doctor, which allowed traditional cel animators to use computer animation with minimal training.

Eventually, the team began working on film sequences, produced by Lucasfilm, or worked collectively with Industrial Light and Magic on special effects. After years of research, and key milestones in films such as *Star Trek II: The Wrath of Khan* and *Young Sherlock Holmes*, the group was purchased in 1986 by Steve Jobs shortly after he left Apple Computer (the company he founded with Steve Wozniak). He paid $5 million to George Lucas and put $5 million as capital into the company, and the Computer Division was renamed Pixar, a fake Spanish word that means "to make pictures," "to make pixels." A contributing factor to the sale was an increase in cash flow difficulties following Lucas' 1983 divorce, which coincided with the sudden drop off in revenues from *Star Wars* licenses following the release of *Return of the Jedi* and the disastrous box office performance of *Howard the Duck*. The newly independent company was headed by Dr. Edwin Catmull, President and CEO, and Dr. Alvy Ray Smith, Executive Vice President and Director. Jobs served as Chairman and Chief Executive Officer of Pixar.

Initially, Pixar was a high-end computer hardware company whose core product was the Pixar Image Computer, a system primarily sold to government agencies and the medical community. One of the leading buyers of Pixar Image Computers was Disney studios, which was using the device as part of their secretive CAPS project, using the machine and custom software to migrate the laborious Ink and Paint part of the 2D animation process to a more automated and thus efficient method. The Image Computer never sold well. In a bid to drive sales of the system, Pixar employee John Lasseter—who had long been creating short demonstration animations, such as *Luxo Jr.*, to show off the

307

device's capabilities—premiered his creations at SIGGRAPH, the computer graphics industry's largest convention, to great fanfare.

As poor sales of Pixar's computers threatened to put the company out of business, Lasseter's animation department began producing computer-animated commercials for outside companies. Early successes included campaigns for;

California Lottery	Life Savers	Toppan Printing
Chips Ahoy	Listerine	Toys "R" Us
Fleischmann's	McDonalds	Trident
Hershey	Paramount Pictures	Tropicana
IBM	Pillsbury	Twizzlers
Kellogg's All-Bran	Sesame Street	Unicef
Levi's Jeans	Tetra Pak Drink Boxes	Volkswagen

During this period, Pixar continued its relationship with *Walt Disney Feature Animation*, a studio whose corporate parent would ultimately become its most important partner. In 1991, after substantial layoffs in the company's computer department, Pixar made a $26 million deal with Disney to produce three computer-animated feature films, the first of which was *Toy Story*. Despite this, the company was costing Jobs so much money that he considered selling it. Only after confirming that Disney would distribute *Toy Story* for the 1995 holiday season, did he decide to give it another chance. Pixar was re-incorporated on December 9, 1995.

Disney

Pixar and Disney had disagreements after the production of *Toy Story 2*. Originally intended as a straight-to-video release (and thus not part of Pixar's three picture deal), the film was eventually upgraded to a theatrical release during production. Pixar demanded that the film then be counted toward the three- picture agreement, but Disney refused. Pixar's first five feature films have collectively grossed more than $2.5 billion, equivalent to the highest per-film average gross in the industry. Though profitable for both, Pixar later complained that the arrangement was not equitable. Pixar was responsible for creation and production, while Disney handled marketing and distribution. Profits and production costs were split 50-50, but Disney exclusively owned all story and sequel rights and also collected a distribution fee. The lack of story and sequel rights was perhaps the most onerous to Pixar and set the stage for a contentious relationship.

The two companies attempted to reach a new agreement in early 2004. The new deal would be only for distribution, as Pixar intended to control production and own the resulting film properties themselves. The company also wanted to finance their films on their own and collect 100 percent of the profits, paying Disney only the 10 to 15 percent distribution fee. More importantly, as part of any distribution agreement with Disney, Pixar demanded control over films already in production under their old agreement, including *The Incredibles* and *Cars*. These conditions were unacceptable to Disney, but Pixar would not concede.

Disagreements between Steve Jobs and Disney Chairman and CEO Michael Eisner made the negotiations more difficult than they otherwise might have been. They broke down completely in mid-2004, with Jobs declaring that Pixar was actively seeking partners other than Disney. However, Pixar did not enter negotiations with other distributors, since other partners saw Pixar's terms as too demanding. After a lengthy hiatus, negotiations between the two companies resumed following the departure of Eisner from Disney in September of 2005. In preparation for potential fallout between Pixar and Disney, Jobs announced in late 2004 that Pixar would no longer release movies at the Disney-dictated November time frame, but during the more lucrative early summer months. This would also allow Pixar to release DVDs for their major releases during the Christmas shopping season. An added benefit of delaying *Cars* was to extend the time frame remaining on the Pixar-Disney contract to see how things would play out between the two companies.

Pending the Disney acquisition of Pixar, the two companies created a distribution deal for the intended 2007 release of *Ratatouille*, in case the acquisition fell through, to ensure that this one film would still be released through Disney's distribution channels. In contrast to the earlier Disney/Pixar deal *Ratatouille* was to remain a Pixar property and Disney would have received only a distribution fee. The completion of Disney's Pixar acquisition, nullified this distribution arrangement.

Acquired by Disney

Disney announced on January 24, 2006, that it had agreed to buy Pixar for approximately $7.4 billion in an all-stock deal. Following Pixar shareholder approval, the acquisition was completed May 5, 2006. The transaction catapulted Steve Jobs, who was the majority shareholder of Pixar with 50.1%, to Disney's largest individual shareholder with 7% and a new seat on its board of directors. Jobs' new Disney holdings outpace holdings belonging to ex-CEO Michael Eisner, the previous top shareholder who still held 1.7%, and Disney Director Emeritus Roy E. Disney who held almost 1% of the corporation's shares. Roy Disney's criticisms of Eisner included the soured Pixar relationship and accelerated Eisner's ouster.

As part of the deal, Lasseter, Pixar Executive Vice President and co-founder, became Chief Creative Officer (reporting to President and CEO Robert Iger and consulting with Disney Director Roy Disney) of both Disney and Pixar Animation Studios, as well as the Principal Creative Adviser at Walt Disney Imagineering, which designs and builds the company's theme parks. Catmull retained his position as President of Pixar, while also becoming President of Disney Studios, reporting to Bob Iger and Dick Cook, chairman of Walt Disney Studio Entertainment. Steve Jobs' position as Pixar's Chairman and Chief Executive Officer was also removed; instead, he took a place on the Disney board of directors.

Lasseter and Catmull's oversight of both the Disney and Pixar studios did not mean that the two studios were merging, however. In fact, additional conditions were laid out as part of the deal to ensure that Pixar remained a separate entity, a concern that analysts had about the Disney deal. Some of those conditions were that Pixar HR policies would remain intact, including the lack of employment contracts. Also, the Pixar name was guaranteed to continue, and the studio would remain in its current Emeryville, California, location with the "Pixar" sign. Finally, branding of films made post-merger would be "Disney•Pixar" (beginning with *Cars*).

Today, Edwin Catmull serves as president of the combined Disney-Pixar animation studios, and John Lasseter serves as the studios' Chief Creative Officer. Catmull reports to Robert Iger as well as Walt Disney Studios' chairman, Dick Cook. Lasseter, who has greenlight authority on all new films, also reports to Iger as well as consulting with Roy E. Disney.

Traditions

While some of Pixar's first animators were former cel animators, including John Lasseter, they also came from stop motion animation, computer animation, or had recently graduated from college. A large number of animators that make up the animation department at Pixar were hired around the time Pixar released *A Bug's Life* and *Toy Story 2*. At the time, while *Toy Story* was a successful film, Pixar had only made one feature film. The majority of the animation industry is located in Los Angeles, California, while Pixar is 300 miles (480 km) north in the San Francisco Bay Area. Also, traditional 2-D animation was still the dominant medium for feature animated films. Not many Los Angeles-based animators were willing to move their families 300 miles (480 km) north, give up traditional animation, and try computer animation. Partly because of this, animators hired at Pixar around this time either came directly from college, or had worked outside of feature animation. For those who had traditional animation skills, the Pixar animation software (Marionette) is designed so that traditional animators would require a minimum of training before becoming productive. According to an interview with John Lasseter with PBS talk show host Tavis Smiley, Pixar films follow the same theme of self improvement. With the help of friends or family, a character ventures out into the real world and learns to appreciate his friends and family. At the core, according to John Lasseter, "it's gotta be about the growth of the main character, and how he changes."

Pixar has created extra content for each of their films since *A Bug's Life* that is not part of the main story. For their early theatrical releases, this content was in the form of "movie outtakes" and appeared as part of the movie's credits. For each of their films since *Monsters, Inc.* (*Finding Nemo* excluded), this content was a short made exclusively for the DVD release of the film. Every Pixar film has included cameo appearances of characters or objects from Pixar's other movies or short films, as well as characters voiced by John Ratzenberger. Ratzenberger has been called "Pixar's good luck charm" since he has played a role in each Pixar feature.

Locations

Pizza Planet is a fictional pizza restaurant that appears in *Toy Story*. It is a large, sci-fi themed restaurant with arcade games. There is a reference to Pizza Planet in every Pixar film to date, either the restaurant itself or the Pizza Planet delivery truck which is stolen by the toys in *Toy Story 2* and has a ride hitched on it by Buzz and Woody in *Toy Story*. It can also be seen in *A Bug's Life*, in the scene where one insect tells another not to touch the motor home light, and *Monsters, Inc.*, when Randall is getting beat up with the shovel; it can be seen on the far left. The company runs a fleet of beat up Toyota Hilux pickup trucks, as seen in *Toy Story 1 and 2* (though in *Toy Story 2*, the truck model is called a "Gyoza"). In *Finding Nemo*, while Gill is explaining his plan to escape from the office, a yellow Pizza Planet truck drives by. In the movie *Cars*, there is a Pizza Planet truck in the end at the stadium. Pizza Planet restaurants at *Walt Disney World's Disney's Hollywood Studios* and *Disneyland Paris* are named after the restaurant in the film and are designed to resemble it as much as possible.

Dinoco is a fictional oil company that first appeared in *Toy Story* as a small gas station and later had more prominent visibility in *Cars*. The company's logo is a dinosaur (a reference to Sinclair Oil, which uses a very similar dinosaur logo). In *Cars*, the company's signature color is a pale blue shade referred to as "Dinoco blue" that was originally created for Richard Petty's racecar, Gulf Oil. Dinoco is a sponsor of the Piston cup, and is the main sponsor of The King, a veteran racer on the verge of retirement. The company's lavish sponsorship is highly sought after by the main character, Lightning McQueen, and rival Chick Hicks. The Dinoco brand has also been featured in much *Cars*-related merchandise.

THEATRICALLY RELEASED (Worldwide Gross estimated June 2017)

NO.	MOVIE	YEAR	BUDGET IN MILLIONS	WORLDWIDE GROSS IN MILLIONS
1	Toy Story	1995	$30	$373.6
2	A Bug's Life	1998	$45	$363.3
3	Toy Story 2	1999	$90	$497.4
4	Monsters, Inc.	2001	$115	$525.4
5	Finding Nemo	2003	$94	$867.9
6	The Incredibles	2004	$92	$633.0
7	Cars	2006	$120	$462.2
8	Ratatouille	2007	$150	$620.7
9	Wall-E	2008	$180	$533.3
10	Up	2009	$175	$735.1
11	Toy Story 3	2010	$200	$1,067.0
12	Cars 2	2011	$200	$562.1
13	Brave	2012	$185	$540.4
14	Monsters University	2013	$200	$744.2
15	Inside Out	2015	$175	$857.6
16	The Good Dinosaur	2015	$200	$332.2
17	Finding Dory	2016	$200	$1,028.6
18	Cars 3	2017	$0	$0
19	Coco	2017	$0	$0
Total Grosses			**$2,451.0**	**$10,744.0**

IN PRODUCTION

MOVIE	PROJECTED RELEASE
The Incredibles 2	June 15, 2018
Toy Story 4	June 21, 2019
Untitled Pixar Film	March 13, 2020
Untitled Pixar Film	June 19, 2020
Untitled Pixar Film	June 18, 2021

SHORT FILMS

SHORT	YEAR	MOVIE RELEASED WITH	DVD RELEASED WITH
The Adventures of André and Wally B	1984	N/A	Pixar Collection 1
Luxo Jr.	1986	*Toy Story 2*	
Red's Dream	1987	N/A	Pixar Collection 1
Tin Toy	1988	*Toy Story*	
Knick Knack	1989	*Finding Nemo*	
Geri's Game	1997	*A Bug's Life*	
For the Birds	2000	*Monsters, Inc.*	
Mike's New Car	2002	*Monsters, Inc.*	
Boundin'	2003	*The Incredibles*	
Jack-Jack Attack	2005	N/A	*The Incredibles*
One Man Band	2005	*Cars*	
Mater and the Ghostlight	2006	N/A	*Cars*
Lifted	2006	*Ratatouille*	
Your Friend the Rat	2007	N/A	*Ratatouille*
Presto	2008	*WALL-E*	
BURN-E	2008	N/A	*WALL-E*
Rescue Squad Mater	2008	N/A	*Toon Disney*
Mater the Greater	2008	N/A	*Toon Disney*
El Materdor	2008	N/A	*Toon Disney*
Tokyo Mater	2008	*Bolt*	
Unidentified Flying Mater	2009	N/A	*Disney Channel*
Partly Cloudy	2009	*Up*	
Dug's Special Mission	2009	N/A	*Up*
George & A.J.	2009	N/A	Pixar Collection 2
Monster Truck Mater	2010	N/A	*Disney Channel*
Heavy Metal Mater	2010	N/A	*Disney Channel*
Moon Mater	2010	N/A	*Mater's Tall Tales*
Mater Private Eye	2010	N/A	*Mater's Tall Tales*
Day & Night	2010	*Toy Story 3*	
Ken Dress Up	2010	N/A	*Toy Story 3*
Air Mater	2011	N/A	*Cars 2*
La Luna	2011	*Brave*	
The Wind	2011	N/A	
Hawaiian Vacation	2011	*Cars 2*	
Small Fry	2011	*The Muppets*	Pixar Collection 2
Time Travel Mater	2012	N/A	*Disney Channel*
The Legend of Mor'du	2012	N/A	*Brave*
Partysaures Rex	2012	*Finding Nemo 3D*	*Monsters*, Inc.
The Blue Umbrella	2013	*Monsters University*	
Party Central	2013	*Muppets Most Wanted*	
Hiccups	2013	N/A	*Disney Channel*

Spinning	2013	N/A	*Disney Channel*
Bugged	2013	N/A	*Disney Channel*
Toy Story of Terror!	2013	N/A	*ABC*
The Radiator Springs 500 ½	2014	N/A	Disney Movies Anywhere
Toy Story That Time Forgot	2014	N/A	*ABC*
Lava	2015	*Inside Out*	
Sanjay's Super Team	2015	*The Good Dinosaur*	
Piper	2016	*Finding Dory*	
Lou	2017	*Cars3*	
Olaf's Frozen Adventure	2017	*Coco*	

Pixar released *Pixar Short Films Collection - Volume 1*, a collection of their short films, on DVD and Blu-ray on November 6, 2007. The disc is an updated version of the earlier-released VHS tape *Tiny Toy Stories*, and includes all of Pixar's shorts through 2006's *Lifted*. As of 2006, many of the short films, except the DVD exclusives, are available to purchase on Apple's iTunes Store. They then released *Pixar Short Films Collection - Volume 2* on November 13ᵗʰ, 2012.

Pixar Short Films Collection Volume 1	Pixar Short Films Collection Volume 2
Adventures of André and Wally B. (1984)	*Your Friend the Rat* (2007)
Luxo Jr. (1986)	*Presto* (2008)
Red's Dream (1987)	*BURN-E* (2008)
Tin Toy (1988)	*Partly Cloudy* (2009)
Knick Knack (1989)	*Dug's Special Mission* (2009)
Geri's Game (1997)	*George & A.J.* (2009)
For the Birds (2000)	*Day & Night* (2010)
Mike's New Car (2002)	*La Luna* (2011)
Boundin' (2003)	*Hawaiian Vacation* (2011)
Jack-Jack Attack (2005)	*Air Mater* (2011)
One Man Band (2005)	*Small Fry* (2011)
Mater and the Ghostlight (2006)	*Time Travel Mater* (2012)
Lifted (2006)	-

FILM ACCOMPLISHMENTS

FILM	YEAR	WORLDWIDE GROSS	AWARDS
Toy Story	1995	$370,638,993	Academy Special Achievement Award winner, Best Song Oscar nominee, Best Original or Musical Comedy Score Oscar nominee, Best Original Screenplay Oscar nominee.
A Bug's Life	1998	$363,398,565	Best Original Score Oscar nominee.
Toy Story 2	1999	$490,728,379	Best Song Oscar nominee, Best Motion Picture Comedy/Musical, Golden Globe winner.
Monsters, Inc.	2001	$562,816,256	Best Animated Feature Oscar nominee, Best Song Oscar Winner.
Finding Nemo	2003	$936,743,261	Best Animated Feature Oscar winner
The Incredibles	2004	$631,442,092	Best Animated Feature Oscar winner, Best Sound Editing Oscar winner, Best Original Screenplay nominee.
Cars	2006	$461,983,149	Best Animated Feature Oscar nominee, Best Song Oscar nominee, Inaugural Best Animated Feature Golden Globe winner.

Ratatouille	2007	$623,722,818	Best Animated Feature Oscar winner, Best Original Screenplay nominee, Best Original Score nominee, Best Sound Mixing nominee, Best Sound Editing nominee, Best Animated Feature Golden Globe winner.
Wall-E	2008	$521,311,860	N/A
Up	2009	$731,342,744	Nominatoed for Best Picture, Won Best Animated Feature, Won Original Score, Nominated Best Sound Editing
Toy Story 3	2010	$1,063,171,911	Nominatoed for Best Picture, Won Best Animated Feature, Won Original Song, Nominated Best Sound Editing, Nominated Best Adapted Screenplay
Cars 2	2011	$559,852,396	No Nominations
Brave	2012	$538,983,207	Won Best Animated Feature
Monster University	2013	$743,559,607	No Nominations
Inside Out	2015	$374,585,774	Won Best Animated Feature

PIXAR FUN FACTS

★Pixar **animated a series of clips featuring Luxo and Luxo Jr.** for *Sesame Street*, including *Light and Heavy*, *Up & Down*, *Front & Back*, and *Surprise*. Pixar also produced numerous animation tests, commonly confused as shorts, including *Beach Chair* and *Flag and Waves*.

★To date, *Toy Story, Cars, Finding Nemo,* and *Monsters, Inc.* are **the only Pixar films to have a sequel**. In 2018, *The Incredibles 2* will be released as a sequel.

★Clocking in at 23-minutes, *Olaf's Frozen Adventure* (2017) is **the longest short Pixar has ever released**. There hasn't been a short with a run time like this since *The Prince and the Pauper* (1990).

★ *Toy Story 2* (1999) was **commissioned by Disney as a direct-to-video**, 60-minute film. When Disney executives saw how impressive the work-in-progress imagery for the sequel was, they decided it should be reworked as a theatrical release. The resulting change in status of *Toy Story 2* was one of the major causes of the disagreement between the two companies that nearly led to their split. *Toy Story 3* was the second theatrical sequel when it was released in June 2010, *Cars 2*, was released in June 2011, and *Monsters University* was released in June 2013.

★Pixar is not against sequels, but believe that **they should only be made if they can come up with a story** as good as the original. Following the release of *Toy Story 2*, Pixar and Disney had a gentlemen's agreement that Disney would not make any sequels without Pixar's involvement, despite their right to do so. In 2004, after Pixar announced their failure to make a new deal, Disney announced that they would go ahead with sequels to Pixar's films with or without Pixar, although they stated they would prefer Pixar to agree to work on them. *Toy Story 3* was put into pre-production at the new CGI division of Walt Disney Feature Animation, Circle 7 Animation.

★When Lasseter was placed in charge of all Disney and Pixar animation following the merger, he stated that **all sequels were immediately to be put**

on hold, with Disney going so far as to actually state that *Toy Story 3* had been cancelled. However, in May of 2006, it was announced that *Toy Story 3* was back in pre-production, then under Pixar's control.

⭐*Toy Story* is also the **only Pixar film to be extended onto television,** with the *Buzz Lightyear of Star Command* film and TV series. *Pixar* created the opening sequence, but the hand-drawn animation was done by *Walt Disney Television Animation.*

⭐*Monsters University* is the **first prequel that Pixar has ever worked on.**

⭐**A film entitled *Newt* was planned** for a 2012 release, but was later canceled. John Lasseter noted that the film's proposed plot, the story of two blue-footed newts trying to find each other to save their species, was similar to that of another film, *Rio* (2011), which was produced by *Blue Sky Studios*. The idea was reworked, pitched again, and was turned into what ended up being *Inside Out* (2015).

⭐*Inside Out* (2015) is **the second top grossing film on an opening weekend** from the Pixar films taking in over $91 million. The first is *Toy Story 3* (2010) taking in over $110.3 million.

⭐The award for **biggest opening weekend of all time for a non-sequel/prequel** (an original story) goes to *Inside Out* (2015).

⭐At the ending of *Cars* (2005) right before the credits roll, the camera pans past the telephone wires showing a line of birds hanging out. **They are the birds from the Pixar short *For the Birds*** (2000), which was released in theaters with *Monster's, Inc.* (2000).

⭐*Toy Story* (1996) and *Toy Story 2* (1999) **both have a 100% rating** on RottenTomatoes.com

⭐Pixar has been utilizing the vocal talents in every single film it has created. **John Ratzenberger can be heard in every Pixar film.** He has also done voice work for Walt Disney Animation films, and also television series. He reprises his characters for video games as well. Back before he was famous, John had a minor role as an air traffic controller in *Superman* (1978) and *Superman II* (1980), and as Rebel Force Major Derlin in *Star Wars: Episode V – The Empire Strikes Back* (1980). He appeared on Walt Disney's Wonderful World of Color in 1990 as Cliff Clavin, a character he would become popular for on the long running television series Cheers (1982-1993). Can you recognize his voice in these Pixar films?

Toy Story (1995) - Hamm	*Up* (2009) - Construction Foreman Tom
A Bug's Life (1998) - P.T. Flea	*Toy Story 3* (2010) - Hamm
Toy Story 2 (1999) - Hamm	*Cars 2* (2011) - Mack Truck
Monsters, Inc. (2001) - Yeti	*Brave* (2012) - Gordon
Finding Nemo (2003) - Fish School	*Monsters University* (2013) - Yeti
The Incredibles (2004) - Underminer	*Inside Out* (2015) - Fritz Repair Man
Cars (2006) – Mack Truck	*The Good Dinosaur* (2015) - Earl
Ratatouille (2007) - Mustafa	*Finding Dory* (2016) - Husband Crab
Wall-E (2008) - John	*Cars 3* (2017) - Mack Truck

✪John Ratzenberger **can be heard portraying four characters** in *Cars* (2006); Mack Truck, Piggy Truck, Abominable Snow Plow, and P.T. Flea Bug.

✪*Cars 2* (2011) **has the lowest rating** on RottenTomatoes.com at 39%.

✪For a **list of the Fun Facts** for all the Pixar films, see *Movie Fun Facts By Individual Film* on page 165.

MARVEL

On August 31, 2009, Disney bought Marvel Entertainment for $4 billion. Stan Lee, the creator of so many Marvel characters, was once the chairman of Marvel Entertainment and was the key behind the sale of the company's characters to Disney. The films have made Disney $11.74 billion.

With this new franchise in their arsenal, Disney went to work making one of the most complex universes in cinematic history. So far, Disney has release fifteen films that are all tied together in one giant story, with another nine planned for the near future. It is unknown how many more Disney will do after that. They have also taken over Netflix with their Marvel television series, and on Disney XD they have created several animated series.

What about the X-Men? Back in 1994, Marvel sold their film rights of the X-Men to 20th Century Fox. The stipulation was that Fox had to utilize their rights to the characters, otherwise the property use rights would revert back to Marvel. After Fox made *Daredevil* (2003) and *Elektra* (2005), they failed to use the characters in anything else. So, Marvel got the characters back, and Disney made the television series *Daredevil* (2015-present) on Netflix.

Due to this stipulation, Disney isn't allowed to use any characters from the X-Men universe, or coin the term "mutant," as that is reserved for the X-Men films. 20th Century Fox owns New World Pictures, which was the company that produced the first X-Men film *Generation X* (1996), and only starred secondary X-Men characters like Jubilee, Banshee, Emma Frost, and Skin. Years started passing and Fox was going to lose the X-Men if they didn't utilize their rights to the characters. After years of trying to make an X-Man film, they released *X-Men* (2000) and gave us all the main characters that we expected in an X-Men film, like Wolverine, Cyclopse, Jean Grey, Professor X, and Storm. Since then they have/will release:

X2: X-Men United (2003)	*Deadpool* (2016)
X-Men: The Last Stand (2006)	*X-Men: Apocalypse* (2016)
X-Men Origins: Wolverine (2009)	*Logan* (2017)
X-Men: First Class (2011)	*X-Men: The New Mutants* (2018)
The Wolverine (2013)	*Deadpool 2* (2018)
X-Men: Days of Future Past (2014)	*X-Men: Dark Phoenix* (2018)

Since part of the stipulation with Marvel/Disney has the rights to the characters that were with The Avengers team, it created a "grey area" when it came to the characters of Quicksilver and Scarlet Witch. Scarlet Witch (Wanda Maximoff) joined The Avengers in 1965 with her twin brother Quicksilver (Pietro

Maximoff) in The Avengers comic issue #16. X-Men used Quicksilver (Evan Peters) in the movie *X-Men: Days of Future Past* (2014) because he is a villain from the X-Men universe. Since Disney exercised their right to also use him as a character, they had to recast the character and used actor Aaron Taylor-Johnson to portray Quicksilver in *The Avengers: Age of Ultron* (2014).

What about our favorite web-head Spider-man? He actually belongs to *Sony Pictures Entertainment*, which is the parent company of *Columbia Pictures*. In 1985, *Marvel* was looking to sell off some of their characters for their film rights, as superhero movies were on a downfall after the box-office flop of *Superman III* (1983). Superhero movies weren't a thing yet. A small company named *The Cannon Group* purchased the rights to Spider-man for $250,000, which they would pay over a five-year span, along with a percentage of the profits from their Spider-man movie that they planned on making in the late 1986. The company was started in 1967 by Dennis Friedland and Chris Dewey. They ran into financial troubles in 1979 and sold the company to Manhem Golan for $500,000, who was the one responsible for the deal with *Marvel* in 1985. *The Cannon Group* was going to film *Masters of the Universe 2* at the same time as *Spider-Man*. Manhem Golan ended up using the sets and costumes to film *Cyborg* (1989) instead of *Masters of the Universe 2*. He had planned to have Dolph Lundgren portray the Green Goblin, since Manhem had worked with Dolph on the *Masters of the Universe* (1987) film. Stan Lee was even set to have a cameo as J. Jonah Jameson. *The Cannon Group* ran into financial troubles and was bought out by *Pathé,* who renamed the company *Pathé Communications*. Manhem left the company, and as part of his severance package, they gave him Spider-Man, Captain America, and the film company *21st Century Distribution Corporation*. Manhem still planned on making a Spider-Man film, but instead released *Captain America* (1990) first. He couldn't get funding for Spider-Man, so he sold the character's television rights to *Viacom*, the home-video rights to *Columbia*, and the theatrical rights to *Carolco*. In 1995, due to lawsuits, a judge deemed the character be returned to his home at *Marvel*. *21st Century* filed bankruptcy in 1996 and all of its film assets were acquired by *Metro-Goldwyn-Meyer* (MGM). More lawsuits ensued and Marvel reclaimed the rights to Spider-Man. They then sold him to *Sony Pictures* for $7 million in 1999. Sony finally released the first Spider-Man films:

Spider-Man (2002)	*The Amazing Spider-Man* (2012)
Spider-Man 2 (2004)	*The Amazing Spider-Man 2* (2014)
Spider-Man 3 (2007)	

There was a plan to release a *Spider-Man 4* in 2011, but plans got scrapped because of the much-needed reboot. The first teenage Spider-Man was portrayed by 27-year-old Tobey Maguire. By the time the third film was released, he was 32. Spider-Man is a teenager in high school. Sony felt it best to just reboot the franchise with 29-year-old actor Andrew Garfield. This, too, was a mistake. The film did very well in the worldwide box office, taking in a staggering $3.96 billion. Domestically, they gradually took in less and less with each film released.

In 2013, there was a planned third installment to the rebooted Spider-Man franchise. Disney wanted to make a deal with Sony to use Spider-Man in *Captain America: Civil War* (2016). Sony agreed to the deal as it would revitalize the character again and they would be compensated in the process. There was huge fan approval with this newly-cast, 19-year-old, Tom Holland, to play the awkward teenage Peter Parker. Tom will reprise his role in *Spider-Man: Homecoming* (2017), alongside Iron Man, and in *Avengers: Infinity War Part 1* (2018). Will Sony just sell Spider-Man back to Disney? Probably not. He is a huge cash cow for them at the moment.

Another character owned by Sony Pictures is Silver Surfer. He only appeared on the big screen alongside another superhero team in *Fantastic Four: Rise of the Silver Surfer* (2007). Speaking of Fantastic Four, that is another team owned by Sony. They only utilized the team in the films *Fantastic Four* (2005), and in the reboot *Fantastic Four* (2015). The latter was a box office flop.

What about the bad-mouthed Deadpool? His film raked in $783 million, awarding it the honor of biggest opening weekend for an R-rated film, taking in $132 million in three days. He, too, belongs to Fox. He is from the X-Men universe. Because of his character's nature to be violent and vulgar, he more than likely won't join the MCU. It won't do his character justice to tone him down. Fox will be releasing *Deadpool 2* (2018).

This might come as a surprise to you, but the Hulk doesn't completely belong to *Marvel/Disney*. He belongs to Universal. At least his "distribution rights" do. That means if *Disney* makes a solo Hulk film, *Universal* has the rights to distribute it. Which is why there hasn't been a solo Hulk film since *The Incredible Hulk* (2008). Disney has a sorted history with Universal since they "took" Oswald the Lucky Rabbit from his creator, Walt Disney, in 1929 and didn't return him until 2006. *Disney* bought *Marvel* in 2009, after the film was made. Universal had the "production rights" to Hulk and made *Hulk* (2003). Since they didn't utilize their rights to him as a character, the rights reverted back to Marvel and they produced *The Incredible Hulk* but contracted Universal with the distribution rights. Then Disney bought Marvel in 2009 and had to recast the actor of Hulk from Edward Norton to Mark Ruffalo. Disney didn't make the first two films in the MCU, *Iron Man* (2008) and *The Incredible Hulk* (2008). *The Incredible Hulk* did have that teaser in the credits of Captain America's shield; a tease at a film that wouldn't get made until *Captain America: The First Avenger* (2011).

Disney finally came along in 2009 and set Marvel on the path to greatness with the Marvel Cinematic Universe (MCU). The MCU is divided into three phases:

❖ Phase One: Avengers Assembled (2008-2012)
- *Iron Man* (2008)
- *The Incredible Hulk* (2008)
- *Iron Man 2* (2010)
- *Thor* (2011)
- *Captain America: The First Avenger* (2011)
- *The Avengers* (2012)

❖ Phase Two (2013-2015)
- *Iron Man 3* (2013)
- *Thor: The Dark* World (2013)
- *Captain America: The Winter Soldier* (2014)
- *Guardians of the Galaxy* (2014)
- *Avengers: Age of Ultron* (2015)
- *Ant-Man* (2015)

❖ Phase Three (2016-2019)
- *Captain America: Civil War* (2016)
- *Doctor Strange* (2016)
- *Guardians of the Galaxy Vol. 2* (2017)
- *Spider-Man: Homecoming* (2017)
- *Thor: Ragnarok* (2017)
- *Black Panther* (2018)
- *Avengers: Infinity War Part 1* (2018) (working title)
- *Ant-Man and the Wasp* (2018)
- *Captain Marvel* (2019)
- *Avengers: Infinity War Part 2* (2019) (working title)

❖ Phase 4 (Future) (2019-unknown)
- *Spider-Man: Homecoming 2* (2019)
- *Guardians of the Galaxy Vol. 3* (TBA)

The **One Shots** are a series of short films that connect the theatrical films together:

- **The Consultant** (2011) – Takes place after *The Incredible Hulk* (2008) and connects it to *Iron Man 2* (2010). Agent Phil Coulson and Agent Sitwell plan to derail General Ross from interfering with S.H.I.E.L.D. by bringing in Tony Stark to talk to him.

- **A Funny Thing Happened on the Way to Thor's Hammer** (2011) – Takes place at the end of *Iron Man 2* (2010) and before *Thor* (2011). Agent Coulson stops at a gas station on his way to Thor's hammer, which is the end credit scene in *Iron Man 2*, when he runs into two robbers trying to hold up the station.

- **Item 47** (2012) – Takes place right after the events of *The Avengers* (2012). Among the shattered city wreckage, a down-on-their-luck couple finds one of the Chitauri weapons and goes on a bank heist spree. Agent Sitwell and Agent Blake are sent to retrieve the couple and their weapon. This 12-minute short was the inspiration for the television series *Agents of S.H.I.E.L.D.* (2013-present).

- **Agent Carter** (2013) – Takes place one year after the disappearance of Captain Steve Rogers, aka Captain America, in *Captain America: The First Avenger* (2011) which is set in 1945 after World War II. Agent Peggy Carter is now a member of the Strategic Scientific Reserve, and is stuck compiling data instead of working in the field. She solves a case by herself and gets reprimanded for not seeking assistance on the case. Instead of getting disciplined, Howard Stark calls in and says that Agent Carter is now the head of the newly-formed Agents of S.H.I.E.L.D. This 15-minute short led into the two-season series *Agent Carter* (2015-2016).

- **All Hail the King** (2014) – Takes place after the end of *Iron Man 3* (2013) when Trevor Slattery (Ben Kingsley) gets put in prison and is living

319

luxuriously. Justin Hammer is in there as well, looking on and wondering what the big deal is with Trevor. Trevor is interviewing for a documentary with Jackson Norris (worked with The Defenders), who is a member of the Ten Rings terrorist group that is not pleased with Trevor's portrayal of the Mandarin. Jackson was there interviewing him to bust him out of prison and take him to the real Mandarin.

Since the Disney purchase of Marvel, there have been multiple live-action television series released starring lesser-known characters or characters from the MCU films:

- *Agents of S.H.I.E.L.D* (2013-present)
- *Agent Carter* (2015-2016)
- *Daredevil* (2015-present)
- *Jessica Jones* (2015-present)
- *Marvel's Agents of S.H.I.E.L.D.: Double Agent* (2015)
- *Luke Cage* (2016-present)
- *Agents of S.H.I.E.L.D.: Slingshot* (2016)
- *Iron Fist* (2017-present)
- *The Defenders* (2017-present)
- *The Punisher* (2017-present)
- *Inhumans* (2017-present)
- *Cloak & Dagger* (2018)
- *New Warriors* (2018)
- *Runaways* (2018)
- *Empire of the Dead* (TBA)
- *Damage Control* (TBA)
- *Marvel's Most Wanted* (2016) (pilot only)

There have been a handful of animated series as well:

- *The Spectacular Spider-*Man (2008–2009) (ended with Disney buyout)
- *Wolverine and the X-Men* (2008–2009) (ended with Disney buyout)
- *Iron Man: Armored Adventures* (2009–2012)
- *The Super Hero Squad Show* (2009–2011)
- *The Avengers: Earth's Mightiest Heroes* (2010–2013)
- *Marvel Anime* (2011–2012)
- *Ultimate Spider-Man* (2012–2017)
- *Hulk and the Agents of S.M.A.S.H.* (2013–2015)
- *Marvel Disk Wars: The Avengers* (2014–2015)
- *Avengers Assemble* (2013–present)
- *Guardians of the Galaxy* (2015–present)
- *Big Hero 6* (2017)
- *Spider-Man* (2017)
- *Marvel Future Avengers* (2017)

What about the attractions in the Disney parks? That is a little tricky. *Universal* holds the rights to the *Marvel* characters in theme parks to the west and east of the Mississippi River as of March 22, 1994. If you have ever been to *Universal Orlando Resort*, you would see *The Incredible Hulk Coaster, The Amazing Adventures of Spider-Man*, and other *Marvel* things ~~around~~. *Universal* can continue to use the rights as long as they keep paying for property usage. *Marvel* can terminate the contract if they feel *Universal* is making their brand suffer. Until then, *Disney* can build attractions in *Disneyland* but not in *Disney World* under the contract guidelines. *Universal* failed to utilize the characters on the west coast. *Disney* can build in the *Disneyland Resort*, but is not allowed to use the name *Marvel* in the title of the attractions. That is why the first *Marvel* attraction isn't called *Marvel's Guardians of the Galaxy – Mission Breakout!*

FUN FACTS

1. The **first Marvel movie ever released was *Howard the Duck*** (1986), which was co-produced with Lucasfilm Ltd. And was distributed by Universal. We see Howard as an Easter Egg in both *Guardians of the Galaxy* films.

2. There are **about 450 pieces that make up the suit for Iron Man**.

3. Tony **named his computer system after Edward Jarvis**, his butler while growing up. Edward Jarvis can be seen in the series *Agent Carter* (2015-2016).

4. Sebastian Stan originally auditioned and was considered for the role of Captain America. The director and producer attempted to convince Chris Evans to take the role of Captain America on multiple occasions. When he finally did accept, **Sebastian was offered the role of Bucky Barnes**, the Winter Soldier.

5. **Lou Ferrigno was the bodybuilder who played the original Hulk** in *The Incredible Hulk* (1977-1982), *The Incredible Hulk Returns* (1988), *The Trial of the Incredible Hulk* (1989), *The Death Of The Incredible Hulk* (1990), and even the voice of Hulk in the animated series *The Incredible Hulk* (1996-1997). He had a cameo appearance as a security guard in *Hulk* (2003) alongside Stan Lee. He returned as the voice of Hulk for *The Incredible Hulk* (2008), along with a cameo appearance as another security guard. Lou would perform the voice of Hulk in *The Avengers* (2012), *The Avengers: Age of Ultron* (2015), and *Thor: Ragnarok* (2017).

6. Stan Lee (*see photo*), Disney Legend in 2017, was the creator of the majority of the Marvel characters. **He has a cameo appearance in almost all of the Marvel movies:**

   - *The Trial Of The Incredible Hulk* (1989) - He plays a jury member in his first cameo appearance.
   - *X-Men* (2000) - A hot dog vendor seen when Robert Kelly emerges from the sea after escaping Magneto.
   - *Spider-Man* (2002) - Saves a young girl from falling debris during Spider-Man's fight with the Green Goblin.
   - *Daredevil* (2003) - Matt stops him from walking in front of a truck.
   - *Hulk* (2003) - Security guard along with Lou Ferrigno.*
   - *Spider-Man 2* (2004) - A man that saves a woman from a falling piece of concrete during the battle of Spider-Man and Doc Ock.
   - *Fantastic Four* (2005) - Willie Lumpkin, Reed Richards' mailman. Willie Lumpkin was his only time he played one of his actual comic book characters.

321

- *X-Men: The Last Stand* (2006) - Jean Grey's neighbor with the water hose.
- *Fantastic Four: Rise of the Silver Surfer* (2007) - Himself, a wedding guest who is turned away.
- *Spider-Man 3* (2007) - A man in Times Square, who shortly comments to Peter Parker about Spider-Man.
- *Iron Man* (2008) - Hugh Hefner
- *The Incredible Hulk* (2008) - The man poisoned by a drink laced with the Hulk's blood.
- *Iron Man 2* (2010) - Larry King
- *Thor* (2011) - "Stan the Man," who tries to pull Thor's hammer using his truck.
- *Captain America: The First Avenger* (2012) - an elderly general.
- *The Avengers* (2012) - a man being interviewed on television who dismisses the idea of superheroes existing in New York.
- *The Avengers* deleted scene (2012) - a man sitting in a bar, calling Steve Rogers a moron for not understanding that Beth the waitress was coming on to him.
- *The Amazing Spider-Man* (2012) - the Midtown Science High School Librarian.
- *Iron Man 3* (2013) - a beauty pageant judge.
- *Thor: The Dark World* (2013) - man in mental hospital.
- *Agents of S.H.I.E.L.D.* (2014) - Episode #13 T.R.A.C.K.S. - man on the train.
- *Captain America: Winter Soldier* (2014) - a Smithsonian guard
- *The Amazing Spider-Man 2* (2014) - a graduation guest who says, "I think I know that guy."
- *Guardians of the Galaxy* (2014) - Xandarian ladies' man
- *Big Hero 6* (2014) - provides the voice for Fred's dad
- *Agent Carter* (2015) - man on bench getting his shoes polished
- *The Avengers: Age of Ultron* (2015) - veteran in the bar
- *Ant-Man* (2015) - bartender
- *Jessica Jones* (2015-present) - Captain Irving Forbush on a Poster at 15th Precinct
- *Deadpool* (2016) - a DJ at the strip club
- *Captain America: Civil War* (2016) - FedEx driver that says, "Are you Tony Stank?"
- *X-Men: Apocalypse* (2016) – old man holding his wife on his front porch; the woman is Joan Lee, his real wife
- *Luke Cage* (2016-present) - Captain Irving Forbush on a Police Advertisement Campaign Poster
- *Doctor Strange* (2016) - bus passenger
- *Agents of S.H.I.E.L.D.: Slingshot* (2016) - Man in photograph in Coulson's Box
- *Guardians of the Galaxy Vol. 2* (2017) - Watcher Informant

- *Spider-Man: Homecoming* (2017) - unknown
- *Thor: Ragnarok* (2017) - unknown
- *Black Panther* (2018) - unknown
- Stan didn't make an appearance in *The Wolverine* (2013) because they were filming in Australia and Stan couldn't make it there.

7. *Captain America: The First Avenger* (2011) was **not the first time Captain America made a live appearance**. *Captain America* (1944) was a grouping of serials totaling over four hours long. This was also the first filming based on a Marvel comic character. Cap wouldn't show up again in a live-action film until *Captain America* (1979) and its sequel, *Captain America II: Death Too Soon* (1979).

8. **Adrianne Palicki can't catch a break**. *Marvel's Most Wanted* (2016), a spin-off from *Agents of S.H.I.E.L.D.*, was the third superhero pilot episode that she starred in that was not put into production. The first was *Aquaman* (2006), and the second was *Wonder Woman* (2011). All of them were shot down.

LUCASFILM

George Lucas, owner and creator of Lucasfilm Ltd. LLC, sold his company to Disney for $4.05 billion on October 30, 2012. They spent a year and a half working on the deal. George decided he wanted to retire and settled on an agreement. George also received $40 million in Disney shares, making him the second-largest, non-institutional shareholder, second to that of the trust of Steve Jobs. Steve Jobs had received $4.14 billion for his share of Pixar and holds a 7% stake in the Disney Company. This buyout is Disney's fourth largest deal. It spent $19.7 billion on Capital Cities/ABC, $7.6 billion on Pixar, and $5.2 billion on Fox Family.

Along with Lucasfilm, Disney bought the rights to Industrial Light & Magic (ILM), Skywalker Sound, and its videogame branch LucasArts. After the purchase, Disney opted to leave the company's headquarters where they are; ILM is in the San Francisco Presidio, and Skywalker Sound and Lucasfilm are in Marin County.

Before Disney purchased the company, Lucasfilm was one of the largest film franchises in existence. The first being the *Marvel Universe* which took in almost $11.7 billion, the second is the *Harry Potter* Universe films which made $8.6 billion, and the third is the *James Bond* films which made $7.07 billion. The *Star Wars* films have made $7.03 billion so far, and will soon be in third, or even second place, after the release of *Star Wars* Episode IX at the end of 2017.

Here is a listing of all the Star Wars films before the Disney buyout:
- *Star Wars: Episode IV - A New Hope* (5/25/77)
- *Star Wars: Episode V - The Empire Strikes Back* (5/21/80)
- *Star Wars: Episode VI - Return of the Jedi* (5/25/83)
- *Star Wars: Episode I - The Phantom Menace* (5/19/99)
- *Star Wars: Episode II - Attack of the Clones* (5/16/02)
- *Star Wars: Episode III - Revenge of the Sith* (5/19/05)

Here is the listing of the Star Wars films released by Disney, and future films:

- *Star Wars: Episode VII - The Force Awakens* (12/18/15)
- *Rogue One: A Star Wars Story* (12/16/16)
- *Star Wars: Episode VIII - The Last Jedi* (12/15/17)
- *Han Solo Star Wars Anthology Film* (05/25/18)
- *Star Wars: Episode IX* (05/24/19)
- *Star Wars Anthology Film* (2020)

Here is a listing of the films and documentaries that aren't from the saga or directly related to the film's story lines. Some were made by Lego and are either full-length movies, or a 22-minute television special:
- *The Star Wars Holiday Special* (11/17/78)
- *Return of the Ewok* (1982)
- *Caravan of Courage: An Ewok Adventure* (1984)
- *Ewoks: The Battle for Endor* (1985)
- *The Great Heep* (1986)
- *Star Wars: Droids - The Pirates and the Prince* (1997)
- *Star Wars: Ewoks – The Haunted Village* (1997)
- *R2-D2: Beneath the Dome* (2001)
- *Star Wars: Ewoks - Tales from the Endor Woods* (2004)
- *Star Wars: Clone Wars* (2008)
- *Lego Star Wars: The Empire Strikes Out* (2012)

Lucasfilm didn't just release films; they released television shows as well:
- *Star Wars: Droids* (1985-1986)
- *Star Wars: Ewoks* (1985-1987)
- *Star Wars: Clone Wars* (2003-2005)
- *Star Wars: The Clone Wars* (2008-2015)
- *Lego Star Wars: The Yoda Chronicles* (2013-2014)
- *Star Wars Rebels* (2014-present)
- *Lego Star Wars: Droid Tales* (2015) (shorts)
- *Lego Star Wars: The Freemaker Adventures* (2016-present)
- *Star Wars Forces of Destiny* (2017-present) (shorts)
- *Star Wars Detours* (2017-present)

There was also a handful of animated shorts created by Lego:
- *Lego Star Wars: Revenge of the Brick* (2005)
- *Lego Star Wars: The Quest for R2-D2* (2009)
- *Lego Star Wars: Bombad Bounty* (2010)
- *Lego Star Wars: The Padawan Menace* (2011)
- *Lego Star Wars: The Yoda Chronicles - The Dark Side Rises* (2013)

It is said that George Lucas loves his fans and welcomes fan art or fan films. There have been quite a few fan films made over the past 40 years. Lucas created the Official Star Wars Fan Film Awards in 2002. They would award the best fan film. It was discontinued after the 2011 festival, due to the fact that they were bought by Disney in 2012. Lucas started the festival again for 2015-2016. They are either shorts, short films, spoofs, or a trailer for a film that would never get made. The majority of them can be seen on YouTube.com. Here are just some of them:
- *Broken Allegiance* (2002) 23-minutes
- *Brooklyn Force* (2008) 13-minutes
- *Chad Vader: Day Shift Manager* (2006-2012) series 4-11-minutes
- *Crazy Watto* (2000) 2-minutes
- *The Dark Redemption* (1999) 35-minutes
- *Dark Resurrection* (2007) 61-minutes
- *Darth Vader's Psychic Hotline* (2002) 4-minutes

324

- *Duality* (2001) 6-minutes
- *The Formula* (2002) 53-minutes
- *George Lucas in Love* (1999) 8-minutes
- *Hardware Wars* (1978) 13-minutes (spoof made $1 million in Box Office)
- *Harmy's Despecialized Edition* (2011) a re-editing of the original trilogy
- *How the Sith Stole Christmas* (2002) 17-minutes
- *The Jedi Hunter* (2002) 8-minutes
- *Knightquest* (2001) 40-minutes
- *Padmé* (2008) 4 -minutes
- *The Phantom Edit* (2000) a fan re-edit of *Star Wars: Episode 1 – The Phantom Menace* (1999)
- *Pink Five* (2002) 4-minutes
- *Pink Five Strikes Back* (2004) 9-minutes
- *Return of Pink Five Vol. 1* (2006) 13-minutes
- *Return of Pink Five Vol. 2* (2006) 14-minutes
- *Star Wars: Revelations* (2005) 47-minutes
- *Ryan vs. Dorkman* (2003) 5-minutes
- *Ryan vs. Dorkman 2* (2007) 10-minutes
- *Saving Star Wars* (2004) 117-minutes
- *Sith Apprentice* (2005) 12-minutes
- *Star Dudes* (2000) 5-minutes, a four-episode series
- *Star Wars Gangsta Rap* (2000) 4-minutes
- *Star Wars Uncut* (2010) 124-minutes
- *Star Wars: Storm in the Glass* (2004) 133-minutes
- *Star Wars: The Emperor's New Clones* (2006) 65-minutes
- *Star Wars: Threads of Destiny* (2014)
- *Thumb Wars* (1999)
- *Trooper Clerks* (2003)
- *Troops* (1997)

THE JIM HENSON COMPANY

On November 20, 1958, Jim Henson founded *Muppets, Inc.* They had produced one film called *Time Piece* (1965) and created puppets for commercials, variety shows, and a few films. They were discovered by this upcoming show, *Sesame Street* (1969-present), in 1968 and were tasked with making and manipulating puppets for the soon-to-be hugely popular children's show that would run for more than 48 years.

FUN FACTS

🐸 **Rowlf the Dog was the first regular character** on television. He made his first appearance in Purina Dog Chow in 1962. He starred opposite Baskerville, a dog named after the Sherlock Holmes novel *The Hound of the Baskervilles*. Both the dogs were voiced by Jim Henson and Baskerville had the distinct voice of Kermit the Frog.

🐸 Jim Henson's **puppets picked up in popularity in 1977,** with the airing of *The Muppet Show* which ran until 1981. It was a show intended to be more for adults than their work on *Sesame Street*.

🐸 Jim Henson made movies and television shows until his death in 1990:

The Frog Prince (1971)	*The Tale of the Bunny Picnic* (1986)
Emmet Otter's Jug-Band Christmas (1977)	*The Muppets: A Celebration of 30 Years* (1986)
The Muppet Movie (1979)	*The Christmas Toy* (1986)

- *Muppet Babies* (1984-1991) had *Marvel Productions* as a co-producer and *Disney Television Animation* to air the episodes on television. Disney's company *Buena Vista Television* was in charge of distribution.

- In August 1989, Jim Henson and the Disney CEO Michael Eisner announced that they were planning on **buying out *The Jim Henson Company* for $150 million** and would allow for a 15-year contract with Jim Henson to use his creative services. The sale would not include the Sesame Street characters.

- Before a deal could be made, on **May 16, 1990, Jim Henson died suddenly** of organ failure caused by streptococcal toxic shock syndrome which was induced by Streptococcus pyogenes. It was basically a type of strep throat.

- The deal fell through and the Henson family maintained the company. **Brian Henson signed a deal with Disney** to allow them to have television rights to *The Jim Henson Company* characters.

- The **last project that Jim Henson worked on** was *Muppet*Vision 3D* for *Disney's Hollywood Studios* in *Disney World*. This would be the last film in which he provided the voice of Kermit the Frog. He also was in an episode of *Walt Disney's Wonderful World of Color* (1954–1991) called  *The Muppets at Walt Disney World,* which aired May 6, 1990. He was the voices of Kermit the Frog, Rowlf, Dr. Teeth, Waldorf, Swedish Chef, and Link Hogthrob.

- Disney co-**produced the television series *Dinosaurs*** (1991-1994) with *The Jim Henson Company*.

- Disney **Imagineer Terri Hardin worked on this show**. She was the arms of Baby Sinclair for the first three seasons, and was the puppeteer for the face of Needlenose. She went on to puppeteer in the films *The Flintstones* (1994), *The Indian in the Cupboard* (1995), and *The Country Bears* (2002). She was also a puppeteer for the small world dolls in the ending scene of *Muppet*Vision 3D*.

- *Muppet*Vision 3D* **would be housed in *California Adventure*** from 2001-2013. The attraction still remains in *Disney World*.

- In the 1990's, The Jim Henson Company co-**produced two films with Walt Disney Pictures**, *The Muppet Christmas Carol* (1992) and *Muppet Treasure Island* (1996).

- In 2000, the **Henson family sold the company to *EM.TV & Merchandising AG***, for $680 million. The new owner was facing financial difficulty by the end of 2000 and put the company up for sale in 2001. *The Walt Disney Company, Viacom, HIT Entertainment, AOL Time Warner, Haim Saban, Classic Media,* as well as the Henson management, were all said to be interested in purchasing it.

- The company entered a deal in December 2002, but it fell through March 2003. The **Henson family was able to just buy the company back** in mid-2003 for $74 million.

- In 2004, **the family sold *The Muppets*** and *Bear in the Big Blue House* (1997-1999, 2002, 2003, and 2006) to *The Walt Disney Company* for an undisclosed amount of money. They stated it is what their father would have wanted.

- Away from Disney, the Henson's are **finally able to produce their long-planned prequel series** to *The Dark Crystal* (1982). *The Dark Crystal: Age of Resistance* (2018) will take place several hundred years before the time of the movie. *Fraggle Rock: The Movie* is planned in the near future.

- When **Kermit the Frog was originally created, he was more of a lizard**. It wasn't until he made more appearances that he became more of a frog.

- Jim Henson's **last performance as Rowlf was on *The Arsenio Hall Show*** in 1990, twelve days before he passed away.

- **Rowlf was Jim Henson's favorite character**. Rowlf was retired after Jim's death until 1996, when Bill Baretta (voice of Earl Sinclair on Dinosaurs) was allowed to voice him. He still does it to this day.

- The Jim Henson Company **had released other films** besides the ones mentioned above:

Buddy (1997)	*MirrorMask* (2005)
Muppets from Space (1999)	*Alexander and the Terrible, Horrible, No*
The Adventures of Elmo in Grouchland (1999)	*Good, Very Bad Day* (2014)
Rat (2000)	*The Star* (2017)
Good Boy! (2003)	*Fraggle Rock: The Movie (TBA)*
Five Children and It (2004)	*The Happytime Murders* (TBA)

DISNEY ON BROADWAY

Walt Disney Theatrical Productions, informally known as *Disney Theatrical*, is the stage play and musical production arm of *The Walt Disney Company*. It advertises as *Disney on Broadway* in New York City.

1. Beauty and the Beast	1994-2007
2. The Lion King	1997-PRESENT
3. King David	1997 ONLY
4. Aida	1998-PRESENT
5. The Hunchback of Notre Dame	1999-2002
6. Elton John and Tim Rice's Aida	1998-2009
7. On The Record	2004-2005
8. Mary Poppins	2004-2014
9. Tarzan	2006-2009
10. High School Musical On Stage!	2007-2009
11. The Little Mermaid	2007-2009
12. High School Musical 2: On Stage!	2008-2011
13. Peter and the Starcatcher	2009 ONLY
14. Peter and the Starcatcher	2012-2013
15. Camp Rock	2010-PRESENT
16. Newsies	2011-2014
17. Shakespear In Love	2013-2015
18. Aladdin The Musical	2014-PRESENT
19. Frozen	COMING SOON
20. The Jungle Book	COMING SOON
21. Pinocchio	COMING SOON
22. The Muppets	COMING SOON
23. The Princess Bride	COMING SOON
24. Alice In Wonderland	COMING SOON
25. Father Of The Bride	COMING SOON
26. Freaky Friday	COMING SOON

What's Inside

PREPARING FOR ENTRY

Over preparation

It has been seen time and time again, moms and dads walking into the theme parks with their maps, time guides, and notepads handy. They want to hit up the *Finding Nemo Submarine Voyage* at 8:15, break for lunch at 12:30, and ride *Pirates of the Caribbean* at 3:30. This is not going to happen. You can never predict lines, the size of the crowd, or other things that will come up during the day (i.e. an attraction closure for a technical malfunction, bad weather, parades, special events, stopping to watch sideshows, etc). To avoid making the common mistake of over preparation, I suggest that it is best to be prepared and to do your research on things that you would ideally like to see and possibly even a method on how you would like to accomplish everything. But, setting a rigid schedule only sets your family up for failure and many arguments throughout the day. If someone wants to get back in line after having a great time on an attraction, it is ok. The parks are full of things to do and see that will not be a part of your itinerary, such as street performers and character meet-and-greets. My best advice is to go into the parks with a goal in mind, but be ready to be flexible.

Under preparation

As often as you see the over-prepared family, you also see the under-prepared aimlessly walking around. As mentioned above, there are countless attractions, shops, and restaurants in *Disneyland* and *California Adventure*. It is a good idea to do your research beforehand, whether through online sites like *disneyland.com* or by purchasing a Disney vacation book like this one. But, if you have no agenda whatsoever or no idea where any attraction is, you could waste valuable time and miss out on the things that your family would truly like to do and see.

Forgetting to set a budget

Expect a hamburger and fries in the park to cost much more than you'd pay in your hometown (see *Cost to Eat In The Park* on page 38). Families often go over budget while on vacation, and it is easy to see why. Theme park food and merchandise can be very expensive, with a fast food meal easily costing your family the same as a sit-down back home. You can avoid this common mistake by setting up a realistic budget for your family ahead of time – allow each person in the family a certain amount of money per day to spend on snacks and souvenirs, and plan to be shelling out extra cash if you are eating in the parks. Better yet, you can plan ahead to take an afternoon break from the parks to have lunch in your hotel room, or even take food into the park from the store down the street. You can find countless restaurants outside of Disney that have more affordable dining options than inside the parks.

SPECIAL NEEDS OR DISABILITIES

➤ If you have **an assistance dog**, please see *Kennel Club & Service Dogs* on page 60.

➤ **Disney Resorts offer what is called a <u>Guest Assistance Card</u>** (GAC), or sometimes referred to as the <u>Special Assistance Pass</u> (SAP). Disney changed the name from SAP to GAC when people thought the word "Pass" meant "pass to the front of the line," so the name was changed. This card is used for people who have a non-visible handicap or disability that makes it difficult to stand in line for long periods of time.

➤ In the past, **people with these disabilities or disorders qualified** for a GAC: ADD/ADHD, Auditory or visual impairments, Autism Spectrum Disorders (ASD), Cerebral Palsy, Epilepsy, Heart Conditions, Lupus, or Multiple Sclerosis.

➤ To get a GAC, or to get more information about it, you can **visit *City Hall*** in *Disneyland* or *Guest Relations* to the left after entering *California Adventure*. The Cast Member will ask you how they can assist you, your child, or adult, and how many people are in your party. You can just say your child/adult has Autism, a heart condition, or whatever the case may be, and how many people are in your party. This is not a "skip to the front of th line pass." It just shows that you need special assistance when you get to an attraction, but you still have to wait. Some attractions have a quiet waiting area for you to sit and wait your turn. This is what Disney said is the purpose of the GAC:

"The Guest Assistance Card is a tool provided at all of the Disney Resort Theme Parks to enhance the service we provide to our Guests with disabilities. It was designed to alert our Cast about those Guests who may need additional assistance. ***The intent of these cards is to keep Guests from having to explain their service needs each time they visit an attraction.***

The Guest Assistance Card is available to our Guests with non-apparent, special assistance needs (i.e., autism, heart condition, etc.). Depending on a Guest's need, this card may provide a variety of assistance, such as allowing Guests to wait in a shaded area, or providing admission to our attractions through auxiliary entrances, where applicable. However, the intention of this card has never been to bypass attraction wait times, or to be used by Guests with a noticeable service need.

Guests with an apparent mobility concern, such as Guests using wheelchairs, canes, crutches, etc., or Guests with service animals, do NOT need a Guest Assistance Card. These Guests should be directed to follow the attraction entrance procedures for guests using wheelchairs, as outlined in the Guidebook for Guests with Disabilities.

A Guest with a specific need for assistance can request a Guest Assistance Card at any Theme Park Guest Relations location upon arrival. To

330

accommodate the individual needs of our Guests, we ask that all Guests discuss their assistance requests with a Guest Relations Cast Member prior to the card being issued. The Guest Relations Cast Member will discuss the available service options with the Guest and provide written instructions for our cast on the Guest Assistance Card. The Guest will be directed to present the Guest Assistance Card to the Greeter or first available Cast Member at the attraction and await further directions for their experience."

➤ If you have more than one special-needs person in your party, **get a card for each of them**. You can keep the card for your whole visit, and if you decide to split up your group, you will want each special-needs person to have their own.

➤ **Hang onto your used card for your next trip**, then hand it over the the Cast Member so they can make a duplicate one for the same use.

➤ As you approach each attraction, look for the Cast Member; usually at the entrance or at the Fast Pass entrance. **Tell them what assistance you need**, like an alternate route for a wheelchair, a separate waiting area with less noise, or a way to avoid the stairs.

➤ If you have problems walking up and down stairs, **you can acquire a handicap pass** in *City Hall* at the front of *Disneyland* or *Guest Services*, to the left in the front of *California Adventure*. This pass has a "stair" logo stamped on it. This will allow you to cut past the parts of the lines that have stairs like *Indiana Jones* (just bypass the stairs part), *Jungle Cruise*, *Splash Mountain*, *Big Thunder Railroad*, and some others. The pass is good for your whole party of up to six people. Just tell them you can't use stairs; no other questions asked.

➤ If you use a wheelchair, **the handicap pass has a "handicap" logo on it**. This too, is not a skip to the front of the line pass; you will just have your own waiting area or separate line. You can rent a wheelchair for $12 with a $20 refundable deposit, or an ECV for $50 with a $20 deposit. As a warning though, there have been a few times that the wheelchair line had a longer wait than the actual line. If you do not get a handicap pass, the wheelchair, walker, cane, crutches or whatever else you may be using work as a "visual handicap pass." Just walk in the handicap entrance and a Cast Member will direct you where to go and what to do. Keep in mind that you can only have six people in the group, including the handicapped person. This is a strict rule. If you hear differently, I promise you it is only 6. If there are more than six people in a group, the handicapped person may enter the handicap line and wait there comfortably while the rest of the group wait in the regular line. Or, the handicapped person can make two trips on the attraction by taking half the group at a time.

➤ If you are **dependent of any sort of insulin** or have any kind of medication that needs to be refrigerated, take it to the First Aid station. There are RNs on duty to assist and have a refrigerator available to hold such things. There are also sharps containers available in the bathrooms, if you need to dispose of any sort of needles. (see page 334 for First Aid station locations)

➤ In 2010, Disneyland **started having sign language interpreters** for shows and attractions that have a lot of dialogue to interpret for deaf people. They are only available a few days out of the week. Check with *City Hall* to find out where and when they can be found.

➤ **Assistive Listening systems**, Reflective Captioning, Sign Language interpretation, Text Typewriter telephones, Handheld Captioning, Video Captioning, and written aids are available to help Guests with hearing disabilities to enjoy the *Disneyland* Resort.

➤ **Audio Description devices**, Braille guidebooks, and digital audio tours are available to help Guests with visual disabilities.

➤ **Parking for Guests with disabilities** is available throughout the *Disneyland* Resort, including the *Mickey and Friends Parking Structure* and the *Toy Story Parking Area* off of Harbor Boulevard. A valid disability parking permit is required.

TIPS AND TRICKS

If you see a line wait time that says (for example) 60 minutes, this usually means 45 minutes. **Most of the wait times are rounded up**. The lines at *Fantasyland* attractions average 10 to 20 minutes, with the exception of *Peter Pan's Flight* which is usually 30 to 40 minutes. *Dumbo* is usually 30 to 50 minutes. During the week, there is usually a minimal wait for attractions.

There are lots of **special little things** for kids to do:

- Ride in the front car of the monorail
- Ride in the front of the train in the tinder box
- Ride in the wheelhouse of the *Mark Twain* and actually ring the bell, blow the whistle, steer, and get a special certificate
- Go UP in the *Haunted Mansion* elevator. That's how wheelchair bound people get back up.
- Anyone can wake up Jose in the *Tiki Room* and catch a glimpse of how it works by just asking.
- Want a view? Get a waterside table in the *Blue Bayou Restaurant* by just asking.

Tie a large ribbon, piece of fabric, scarf, or other identifier onto your stroller or wheelchair, making it easier to pick out of a crowd.

If you have to get a stroller for the young ones, **it can be taken back and forth between *Disneyland* and *California Adventure***. It must be turned in prior to entering *Downtown Disney*. A stroller is $15 for the day or $25 for two for the day.

You can also get strollers from an outside company that can deliver and pickup from your hotel. Over a span of a few days, this way is cheaper. **Visit *www.citystrollerrentals.com* and check out the pricing**. At the time this was written, a 3-day rental is $35 for a single-wide, and $45 for a double-wide. They also have triples and special needs available as well. Their strollers are nicer than in the park as well.

- **Write your cell phone number** on the back of your child's wrist, and paint over it with liquid bandage to keep it from washing off. You can also put a "Hello my name is…" name tag on your child's back with your phone number.

- Don't lose track of your child. There are **blue tooth microchips available**, called *Stick-N-Find Bluetooth Location Tracker*, to clip on your child's shoe or clothing and you can use your smart phone's blue tooth capability to track their location in a crowd like during a show, parade, fireworks, *Fantasmic*, or *World Of Color*.

- **Tweet @DisneylandToday and @DCAToday** to get quick responses to your park-related questions.

- To help avoid problems when you get to the front of the lines, **know your child's height**, and the height requirement of each attraction so your child doesn't get their hopes up. You can find the listing of *Height Requirements* on page 69.

- Use this time to **train your children on how to read a map**. Have them follow the fun *Disneyland* map to lead you from attraction to attraction.

- **Don't get stuck paying ATM fees** while in the park. If you need to get cash to spend at *Disneyland* for popcorn, balloons, etc., simply stop by *City Hall* (located on the west side of *Main Street, U.S.A*) and purchase Disney Dollars. They are bills that come in ones, fives, and tens and can be used as cash (the same dollar for dollar exchange) at the *Disneyland* Resort. At the end of your visit, you can cash in any unused dollars for regular cash or save a few for souvenirs.

- **I suggest just purchasing a Disney gift card**. You can use it to pay for everything in the park and won't have to worry about going outside your budget or having to balance your bank account with all the transactions of the day.

  NOTE: Companies that are under contract to be there, like Starbucks or Ghirardelli, don't accept the Disney gift cards.

- If you have a large group and plan to split up, **plan on taking walkie-talkies** for better communication, or just text, like everybody does nowdays.

- Also, a good idea is to **pick a group leader**. Someone in charge of carrying the map and show schedules and who can figure out planning for show times and to give suggestions to the others in the group of what to do next.

- If you are a small family with just one child, or two children who are far apart in age, **consider taking a friend of each child's age** so they can experience everything together. Make sure it is a child who respects you so there are no problems in dealing with them in the park.

- For **people who develop motion sickness** and have to turn down a ride on *Space Mountain* or *Big Thunder Railroad*, take in a bottle of peppermint oil to put a droplet on your tongue. The peppermint relaxes the muscles in the stomach and esophagus to relieve the feeling of motion sickness. This can be found at most pharmacies (read specified directions before use for possible side effects).

If you start to feel under the weather, have a headache, are dehydrated, scraped your knee, twisted your ankle, or even get a blister on your foot, **stop by the *First Aid* station** for some help. The registered nurse on duty will be happy to help with anything. They can provide a bed for you to recover from heat exhaustion and even have over-the-counter drugs to take, if need be. There is no charge for any of their assistance or medical supplies. If you have a severe-enough condition and need a transport to a local hospital, they can provide that as well (not sure if they charge or not). There are three locations for *First Aid*:

- *Disneyland*: Located at the end of *Main Street, U.S.A.,* across from the *Central Plaza,* and next to the *Baby Center*.
- *California Adventure*: Located next to the Chamber of Commerce on Buena Vista Street.
- *Downtown Disney*: Se the nearest Cast Member for assistance.

You are not a mule. **Don't try to carry everything you own** around the park all day. All you will be left with is a sore back. Utilize the lockers. In *Disneyland, they are located on Main Street, U.S.A. or just outside the entrance;* in *California Adventure,* they are to the right after you enter the park. Keep the majority of your stuff (jackets, scarves, lunch, extra water bottles) in the locker and only carry around what you need. Locker rentals are $7, $10, $11, $12 and $15 per day, depending on the locker size and you have unlimited access for the day, so use them.

Disneyland just converted 18 of their small lockers into **phone charging lockers**. These lockers were designed with two spaced-apart power outlets inside them for charging small devices like cell phones, iPads, iPhones, laptops, camera batteries, and other rechargeable devices. If you do not have your charging adaptor for your iPhone/iTouch/iPad, they have them installed into a few of the lockers for you. The instructions at the beginning with ask you. There is also a micro USB adaptor that fits most other brands of cell phones, Androids, and BlackBerry phones. Right now, the cost is $2.00 per hour to charge your devices. You prepay for the first hour and then pay again to retrieve your item. These lockers are very popular later in the evening as people's phones start to die from use during the day. It will be worse on days when the park is open longer.

When you get to the park, **tell your kids how to find you** if you get separated. Tell your child to find a Cast Member by looking for their name tags. Memorize what clothing your child is wearing for the day and keep a photo with you just incase. If you are with older kids, set up a spot to meet if there is a separation. Many people use the "Partners" statue at the head of *Main Street, U.S.A.* in front of the castle because it is a good central area.

If your Mickey balloon pops while in the park, *Disneyland* will replace it anywhere they sell balloons, even if you find a "dead" balloon in the park or bring an old one back inside. I have heard the same thing for souvenirs. If you hop on *Big Thunder Mountain Railroad* and your flashy light wand breaks, take it back to the store for a replacement.

If you do not speak English (then you probably won't be reading this book), but need to talk to someone else who speaks your language, just look for Cast Members who have a pin with that country's flag. Those Cast Members speak that language. They also have park maps available in many languages as well as in Braille.

Stop by the information center in *City Hall* on *Main Street, U.S.A.* in *Disneyland* or in the main entrance in *California Adventure* to **pick up a free button for celebration**. They have a button for Birthday, 1st Time Visitor, Honorary Citizen, Engagement, Big Dreams, Family Reunion, Just Married, Celebration and others. Go there first thing because they can run out.

When you are in City Hall, a **Cast Member can phone a character for your child** to talk to for their birthday or special event.

If you want to **best utilize your time in the park,** you could download the RideMax program to your computer or the app for your iPhone. This program can be set with whatever attractions you want to visit and organizes them so that they can be done in an efficient order to avoid lines and crowds.

There is **an app called Disney Wait Times Free** that you can download that is considered to be the most accurate for telling attraction wait times. Disneyland also now has their own app called *Disneyland*.

🌐 **Save all your receipts** for souvenirs while on your trip. If you need to return or exchange anything while you are there, any store can take a return from another store.

🌐 If you want souveniers but can't carry them with you on your trip, you can order items and have them sent to your house. **Just use the *Shop Disney Parks* app**. You can even use it to scan barcodes and save items for later.

🌐 Buy a **cup of coffee** on *Main Street, U.S.A.* in the *Market House*. When finished, be sure to save your cup and receipt. Return to get a free refill.

🌐 Try and **get in the park early** with *Magic Morning* (see page 65).

🌐 Get a *Disney Chase* credit card. For anything you charge with it, you earn points called "**Disney Dream Reward Dollars.**" These can be exchanged for a variety of things including:
- Free DVDs and toys
- Half-price stroller rentals
- Discounts on hotels, restaurants, merchandise, and tours
- Early access to special event tickets plus discounts on those tickets. Other rewards can vary and change:
  - Or get free invitations to preview a new Disney movie.
  - Get a private Meet 'n Greet with the Disney characters.
  - First dibs at buying Disney on Ice tickets.

🌐 On a cold day, head for the *Grand Californian Hotel* and **curl up by their huge outdoor fireplace**. It's totally free and you don't need to be a guest staying there.

🌐 Also, a **lot of the vendors sell hot chocolate** to warm you up. Nothing like walking down *Main Street, U.S.A.* sipping on a hot cocoa with whipped cream.

🌐 If you are visiting on one of Anaheim's 105° days, **take plenty of shade breaks** to avoid exhaustion. Frequent the cool bathrooms and splash water on your face to cool off.

THE SMOKING ZONES

There are **a total of three designated smoking areas** inside *Disneyland* and two smoking areas inside *California Adventure*. The park does not allow smoking anywhere else except these predesignated areas. If you are caught smoking anywhere else or smoking and walking, security will tell you to put it out. It is difficult for non-smokers to avoid smokers if they are standing in a line and can't avoid it. The smoking areas are indicated by a smoking logo in this book for easy reference.

Disneyland Designated Areas:

- **Frontierland** - To the left of the loading dock for the *Rafts to Tom Sawyer Island*.

- **Frontierland** - Near the backside of *Big Thunder Mountain Railroad* near the bridge.

- **Fantasyland** - To the east of the Matterhorn Bobsleds near the water.

California Adventure Designated Areas:

- **Hollywood Land** – Near the exit of *Muppet Vision 3D*.

- **Paradise Pier** – On the walkway where *California Screamin'* takes off from.

EXPECTANT MOTHERS

Are you pregnant and sill want to enjoy a full experience of The Happiest Place on Earth? I know that sometimes when planning a trip in advance, you can't always know the future and may be expecting a child at the time of your getaway. Here are some tips to help you plan your trip better.

➤ There is a misconception about all the attractions being safe for pregnant women because they are "little kid rides." This isn't true. The reasoning behind the restrictions for pregnant women to avoid riding certain attractions isn't just a cautionary on Disney's side to avoid lawsuits. Some of the attractions are **known for being very rough and jerky**. Some attractions have **minor to extreme G-forces** and some make sudden stops. In the case of *Autopia* you could get rear-ended without expecting it. There haven't been any known miscarriages directly linked to specific attractions as of yet. Doctors say that if a miscarriage happens, it was going to happen anyway with or without the help of the drop on *Pirates of the Caribbean*. Chances are the car ride to the park is rougher than some of the attractions in the park, but these are the attractions recommended by Disney not to ride:

Disneyland	California Adventure
Autopia	Grizzly River Run
Gadget's Go Coaster	California Screamin'
Matterhorn Bobsleds	Golden Zephyr
Big Thunder Mountain	Jumpin' Jellyfish
Star Tours	Goofy's Sky School
Splash Mountain	Silly Symphony Swings
Indiana Jones Adventure	Mickey's Fun Wheel (non stationary)
Space Mountain	

➤ There are other attractions to keep in mind besides just the recommended ones. For instance, some of the slow-paced ones such as *Pirates of the Caribbean* or *it's a small world* can bump and **get bumped by other boats** causing you to jerk.

➤ Make sure you take plenty of rest breaks. Standing too long in lines on the cement can cause back pains. If it starts to be a problem, you can always **rent a wheelchair** (see *Special Needs* on page 330).

➤ You don't want to overdue it. Being around so many people, seeing shows, and having fun will distract you from how tired you are getting. Take a break in the middle of the day for a **nap at the hotel**.

➤ Some attractions have **lap bars that can get in the way** if you are further along and showing, even though they may be safer for 1st or 2nd trimesters. The attractions with lap bars are:

Disneyland	Pinocchio's Daring Journey
Haunted Mansion	Snow White's Scary Adventure
Winnie The Pooh	
Roger Rabbit's Cartoon Spin	**California Adventure**
Alice In Wonderland	Tuck and Roll's Drive'Em Buggies
Mr. Toad's Wild Ride	Ariel's Undersea Adventure
Peter Pan's Flight	Toy Story Midway Mania!

➤ Drink plenty of water. Being pregnant, you will need more water than normal. **Being hydrated will help to reduce** swelling, dry, itchy skin, and will reduce the possibility of sore muscles.

➤ If you find the 105° Anaheim weather to be unbearable, then **take shade breaks**. Sit on a bench under the trees. You may even meet another expectant mother to swap stories with. This time will also give the other people in your party, like a significant other, the chance to go on an attraction that you can't go on. They can utilize the Single Rider option to skip the lines if they are going solo. There are many things to do to keep out of the heat.

- Watch the *Enchanted Tiki Room* show.

- Listen to Abraham Lincoln give his speech in *Great Moments with Mr. Lincoln*.

- Go into the *Disney Animation Studio* in *Hollywood Pictures Backlot* and watch the film clips projected onto the wall or watch the little kids talk to Crush in *Turtle Talk with Crush*.

- Stop in the *Main Street Cinema* to see Mickey Mouse in his old black & white cartoons from the 1920's.

VISITING WITH INFANTS

I wouldn't take a newborn under one-year-old in the park because of all the germs and the hot weather in the summer. With a newborn, it greatly restricts what you can do and see. Some of the shows are too loud for infants. Also, you can't take them on most of the attractions. Sometimes a trip to Disneyland with an infant can't be avoided.

If you do decide to go to the parks with a newborn, here are some things to know.

🚼 **Visit the *Carnation Baby Care Center*.** This is a place that might be overlooked (even though this station appears on the maps, people may not go to check it out). Those visiting the *Disneyland* Resort with babies and small children should definitely take advantage of "*The Gerber Station*." It is located in *Disneyland* at the end of *Main Street, U.S.A.* on the right, and in *California Adventure* next to the *Ghirardelli Soda Fountain and*

338

Chocolate Shop. They have just about anything someone might need for an infant or toddler.

- Toddler-sized toilets
- Nice changing tables complete with wipes
- A quiet little room for moms to sit in and nurse (wicker chairs in *Disneyland*, and rocking chairs in *DCA*)
- Highchairs for feeding
- Sitting areas with power outlets for using pumps
- A little kitchen with microwave for heating bottles
- Gerber baby food, formula (regular or soy), over-the-counter medicines, pacifiers, bottles, diapers, diaper rash ointment, baby powder, and sunscreen available at a little shop inside
- A Cast Member is on hand for assistance
- A waiting area with tables, chairs, and a television for other family members

They will only allow one adult per child to enter the station. Dads are not allowed into the nursing area. There is a Cast Member that makes sure only a few people come in at a time to ensure this peaceful, non-chaotic place remains that way. A wonderful retreat when the baby just needs to calm down from a day of over-stimulation. Note that the shop inside only accepts cash.

Take hand sanitizer. The railings and everything else that is touchable in the park are covered with germs. Not everyone washes up after using the restroom. Then you touch the railings, then your baby. So, use the sanitizer, a lot.

Utilize the Switch Pass. If you have a young member of your party that is afraid of a particular attraction, or doesn't meet the requirements of an attraction, you can use a "switch pass". You can acquire a "switch pass" from a Cast Member by the **FP** entrance or by and exit. Explain to them that you have a child in your party who can't ride and they will hand you a pass. You will wait in line with the rest of your party while the child who doesn't want to or can't ride waits with an adult by the exit or around the area. When you exit the attraction, have the adult who waited with the child use the pass to then go down the exit and wait for a Cast Member to motion them on the attraction. Check with the Cast Member at the time you get the pass to find out where to re-enter; some attractions are different. This pass is good for three people in your party. You must have the child present with you at the time of acquiring the pass. It must also be used the same day to receive it.

Utilize the Single Rider. If mommy and daddy are there with just the infant and no other child to take on an attraction, they can utilize the "single rider" option that is available on certain attractions (see *FastPass, MaxPass, Switch Pass, and Single Rider* on page 340). This way the little family won't have to separate for long.

Have the baby covered. Anaheim has a bright, hot sun in the summer time. You don't want the baby's face to get sunburned.

FASTPASS, MAXPASS, SWITCH PASS, AND SINGLE RIDER

FASTPASS

Disney's **FastPass** is a FREE service that allows you to make a reservation and enjoy specific Disneyland Resort attractions with little or no wait. Just look for the **FastPass** machines at the attractions listed below and check on the **FastPass** return time. This will be the time you will be able to return and use your **FastPass**. If this time will work for you, insert your park admission ticket (Park Hopper, One-Day Pass, or Annual Pass) into the machine and you will receive your **FastPass** ticket with the time for your return. Be sure to keep this ticket; you will need it to enter the **FastPass** line. Now, you are ready to go and enjoy other attractions until your return time. On the list of "Attractions" in each land, the use of a **FastPass** will be marked with an  FP.

- **FastPass** can sell out, so try to get yours as early in the day as possible. Each distribution area is set to give

- Your time will be within a one-hour span (example 4:45-5:45). You may return any time within that hour with an additional fifteen minutes beyond that as a grace period. Sometimes people are delayed in returning due to parades and other obsticals. (*see photo*)

- Don't worry if you are delayed and can't make it back during your specified hour; you can still use your **FastPass** anytime during that day, and it will expire at the park's closing time.

  NOTE: This information has been changing back and forth with Disney. One time they say the hour window is your only time to return, and other times they say you can return any time after the start time on the ticket throughout the day. Check with *City Hall* when you arrive to see what Disney is doing at that point.

- When you return, there will be two lines (Stand-by and **FastPass**). Enter through the **FastPass** line and show the Cast Member your **FastPass** ticket.

- There are several **FastPass** machines at each **FastPass** attraction.

340

- You should always have at least one **FastPass** on you at all times. This is the best strategy of trying to ride everything efficiently.

- If you are in a large group, send one person with everyone's tickets to get all the **FastPasses**. This decreases the crowding that occurs at the kiosks.

- When one person is sent from the group to retrieve the **FastPasses**, the rest of the group should go ahead to the next attraction line to wait and have the retriever join them in line after getting the tickets.

See the chart further ahead for the attractions that offer the **FastPasses**.

NOTE: A **FastPass** for *World of Color* in *California Adventure* doesn't interfere with getting a **FastPass** for something else; it is generated on a separate computer system. Also, if you get an earlier showing and there are going to be multiple showings that night, you can talk to a Cast Member about switching for a later showing, which will be less crowded.

For a short period of time during the "Year of a Million Dreams" certain Disney employees would hand out a "**Dream FastPass**" to random people in the park. This consisted of a lanyard with a card attached containing removable tabs, one for each attraction offering **FastPass**. I'm not sure if they are still doing this. I have not seen it recently, but keep your eyes open.

Another kind of **FastPass** is a "**Surprise FastPass**." These are spit out of the machines at random. For example: You stick your pass in the kiosk for a **FastPass** to *Indiana Jones Adventures* and the machine produces a ticket for *Indiana Jones* and then also spits out a ticket for *Space Mountain*. This happens at random and if there is low attendance at that other attraction.

For a short period, there was a pass offered called an "**Enhanced FastPass**" or "**Unlimited FastPass**." This was offered through AAA and was purchased separately from an admission ticket. You were basically able to buy your way to the front of the line to ride as many times as you wanted. This is not offered anymore, but who knows what the future holds.

The **FastPass** systems were removed from *Pirates of The Caribbean, Buzz Lightyear Astroblasters, The Many Adventures of Winnie the Pooh,* and *It's Tough to be a Bug.* The kiosks for *The Haunted Mansion* are only in operation during Halloween time when the *Mansion* is converted into the *Haunted Mansion Holiday,* October through December.

MAXPASS

The **MaxPass** is a $10 a day per person service that allows you to make **FastPass** reservations through the Disneyland app. This makes it so you don't have to bolt across the park to get **FastPass** tickets for your next attraction. A new pass can be acquired while waiting in line somewhere else. You can have one person's app manage all the tickets in the group for ease of reservations. One of the perks is the ability to view photos taken within the park from the **PhotoPass** that is built into each ticket. This is all a new system that will be implemented in summer 2017. One of the ways Disney is preparing for this new system is by eliminating the return tickets with the scan able barcodes on it. Each **FastPass** acquired will be attached to each individual park ticket or season pass. The ticket from the kiosk will just serve as a reminder as to your return time. The park pass or season pass will then be scanned so you may enter the FASTPASS line. This will also eliminate the kindness of others free FASTPASS tickets if they are leaving the park and wanting to give their unused tickets to someone else. Since they will be attached to the passes instead of a ticket. Things could change over time since this is a new system.

SWITCH PASS

If you have a young member of your party that is afraid of a particular attraction, or doesn't meet the requirements of an attraction, you can use a "**Switch Pass.**" You can acquire a "switch pass" from a Cast Member by the **FP** entrance or by the exit. Explain to them that you have a child in your party who can't ride and they will hand you a pass. You will wait in line with the rest of your party while the child who doesn't want to or can't ride waits with an adult by the exit or around the area. When you exit the attraction, have the adult who waited with the child use the pass to then go down the exit and wait for a Cast Member to motion them on the attraction. Check with the Cast Member at the time you get the pass to find out where to re-enter; some attractions are different. This pass is good for 3 people in your party. You must have the child present with you at the time of acquiring the pass. It must also be used the same day you receive it. See the chart further ahead for the attractions that offer the **Switch Pass.**

SINGLE RIDER

Although **FastPass** is a great way to beat the long lines, Disneyland also offers "**single rider**" lines. If you're willing to split up your party, you will be seated in any open seats on the attraction. Availability of Single Rider for each attraction will be marked as **SR**.

The below attractions currently offer the **SR** option. If you can't locate the single rider line, see the Cast Member at the entrance, and they will direct you. This is great if you have teenagers who tend to ride the same attraction over and over again. Sometimes the Cast Member will give you a Single Rider ticket. **SP**=Switch Pass, **FP**=FastPass, **SR**=Single Rider

SP	FP	SR	*Disneyland* Attraction
X	X		Autopia (Tomorrowland)
X	X		Big Thunder Mountain Railroad (Frontierland)
X			Gadget's Go Coaster (Toontown)
X	X		Haunted Mansion (New Orleans Square)
X	X	X	Indiana Jones Adventure (Adventureland)
X			Matterhorn Bobsleds (Fantasyland)
X	X		Roger Rabbit's Cartoon Spin (Toontown)
X	X		Space Mountain (Tomorrowland)
X	X	X	Splash Mountain (Critter Country)
X	X		Star Tours: The Adventures Continue (Tomorrowland)
SP	**FP**	**SR**	*California Adventure* Attraction
X	X	X	California Screamin' (Paradise Pier)

X	X	X	*Goofy Sky School (Paradise Pier)*
X	X	X	*Grizzly River Run (Grizzly Creek)*
X			*Monsters, Inc. Mike & Sulley to the Rescue! (Hollywood Land)*
X		X	*Radiator Springs Racers (Cars Land)*
X			*Silly Symphony Swings (Paradise Pier)*
X	X	X	*Soarin' Over California (Condor Flats)*
X			*The Little Mermaid: Ariel's Undersea Adventure (Paradise Pier)*
X			*Toy Story Mania! (Paradise Pier)*
X			*Tuck and Roll's Drive 'Em Buggies (a bug's land)*
X	X		*Twilight Zone Tower of Terror (Hollywood Land)*
	X		*World of Color (Paradise Pier)*

PHOTO PASS

There are quite a few Cast Members walking around the park offering to take pictures of patrons in front of some of the attractions. When you get your first photo, they will give you a card, like a credit card, unless you have a season pass, which has one built in. This card has a specific QR code on it for accessing your digital photos. At the end of your day, you can decide to go to the front to pay for a CD or printouts of your photos. Or, you can go to the website listed on the back of the card to purchase the photos, or just save your photos directly from the site, *www.DisneyPhotoPass.com*. This card can be used over and over again, every time you go, and in both parks. You can also attach multiple cards to your account if you end up with more than one.

Sometimes you can discreetly mention to a photographer to capture special moments, like a proposal by the *Snow White Wishing Well*, or in front of the castle.

There are several attractions in the parks where your photo is taken automatically. You can purchase these pictures at the exit of that attraction. Or, you can do what I do. Take a picture of the screen with your photo on it, unless you want to pay $14.99 for a quality printout. The PhotoPass also works for the "in-ride" photos as well. The attractions that take your photo will be marked with **PHOTO**. Here is the list of attractions that take your photo;

Disneyland
- *Splash Mountain*
- *Space Mountain*
- *Buzz Lightyear*

California Adventure
- *California Screamin'*
- *Radiator Springs Racers*
- *Guardians of the Galaxy*

LITTLE THINGS TO DO JUST FOR THE MEMORIES

Disneyland

➤ Savor a Dole Whip while enjoying the *Tiki Room* show and Pre-Show.

➤ Have a Churro.

➤ Eat some freshly made fudge or brittle.

➤ Get a bread bowl with clam chowder, chili, or gumbo (the bread is made fresh at California Adventure).

➤ Have something for breakfast that you would normally never have—like an ice cream cone!

➤ Press a penny (There are over 50 machines which costs 51¢ to press – makes a nice little souvenir collection).

➤ Smell your hand after you get a hand stamp; ask what character it is.

➤ Then smear it on your face so it will glow on the dark-rides with black lights.

➤ Look at whomever you are with during the "black light" portions of the dark-rides and see how they glow in the dark.

➤ Visit the *Disney Gallery* to the right when you enter the park. You can see all sorts of paintings and other artwork by licensed Disney artists. Art can be purchased and sent to your house so you don't have to worry about it on your trip.

➤ Spend time watching the villain characters interacting with the guests.

➤ Enjoy some *Disneyland* Resort popcorn.

➤ Talk to the Cast Members when you are standing in line or waiting for a parade.

➤ Try the frozen lemonade.

➤ Take time out in *New Orleans Square* to listen to the Jazz Bands or the singing Pirates.

➤ Get to Disneyland early one day so you're right by the rope at the end of *Main Street* for rope drop. When they finally drop the rope and let everyone in, dash ahead to the Partners statue. Turn around and watch the mass of people coming toward you.

➤ Stop at *Main Street City Hall* for a collector's button. They have one for everything: Birthday, First Time Visitor, Honeymoon, Anniversary, Family Reunion, and many more.

➤ Look at the petrified tree in *Frontierland* by the Rivers of America. Walt Disney saw it for sale in Colorado and bought it for Lillian Disney as an anniversary present in 1956. Lillian had it installed by the *Rivers of America* because she thought it would

344

look better there, than in her rose garden. Or is there another story? (see *Disney Myths* on page 264) (*see photo*)

➤ While in line for *Peter Pan*, watch the window above *Snow White*. You will see the evil queen come out. Wave to her.

➤ Sit and watch the ducks in *Rivers of America* and imagine what it is like to live at *Disneyland*.

➤ Check out the little characters that are in the outdoor popcorn carts turning the popcorn. Each land and popcorn cart has a different one.

➤ At the *Market Store* on *Main Street, U.S.A.* there are old phones. Pick one up and listen to the party line.

➤ Watch the flag retreat ceremony at dusk in *Town Square*.

➤ Touch the brass apple at the entrance to *Snow White*.

➤ Listen to the activity coming from the windows near the lockers of *Main Street, U.S.A.* and by the train station *New Orleans Square*.

➤ Check out the interesting things in the bazaar store in *Adventureland*. Find the brass lamp in the store and listen to its secrets (50¢).

➤ Ask politely to ride in the caboose on the *Disneyland Railroad*.

➤ At the rope drop, dash ahead and be the first through the castle. You will feel just like Walt must have, strolling all alone through the archway of the castle in the morning.

➤ Enter *Disneyland* through the left tunnel the first time through.

➤ Enter *Disneyland* through the right tunnel the second time through.

➤ Enjoy a teriyaki stick at *Bengal's Barbecue* at *Adventureland*.

➤ Get a coke at *Coke Corner*; sit back and listen to the piano tunes.

➤ Go on *Pirates of the Caribbean* on a weekday night. It is a different experience when there is no other boat in the same room.

➤ Go to the *Mad Hatter's Hat Shop* in *Fantasyland*. Check out the mirror on the back wall. Watch carefully.

➤ Talk to "Push" the trash can at *Tomorrowland* (sometimes in *California Adventure*).

➤ Turn the 1000-pound marble ball floating on water by *Space Mountain*.

➤ Keep a close eye out for Disney kitties.

➤ Knock on the door of the wheelhouse of the *Mark Twain* and ask politely if you can ride up there.

➤ Drink a mint julep at *New Orleans Square*.

➤ Check out the windows on *Main Street, U.S.A.* – Look for Ron Dominguez Orange Grove – Walt Disney bought the land for *Disneyland* from his father, and he worked for *Disneyland*.

➤ Look for the horseshoe prints in the ground in *Frontierland*.

➤ Shoot at targets in the *Shooting Gallery*.

➤ Play with the interactive elements on *Tarzan's Treehouse*.

➤ Start your day at the *Blue Ribbon Bakery* on *Main Street*. Grab a latte and then go to the porch across *Main Street, U.S.A.* and sit in the rocking chairs. Relax and people watch.

➤ Look at the reflection of the castle in the moat at night.

➤ Look for the abominable snowman's footprint around the *Matterhorn*.

➤ Look for the brass spike in the ground. (Hint: Somewhere in *Fantasyland* near the castle).

➤ Make a wish at Snow White's wishing well; listen for her singing.

➤ Read the dedication plaque at *Town Square*.

➤ Ride the following at night for a different experience: *Casey Jr., Splash Mountain, Matterhorn Bobsleds, Autopia, Storybook Land Canal Boats, Jungle Cruise,* and *Big Thunder Mountain RR*.

➤ Check out the light in Walt's apartment above the *Fire Department* on *Main Street*. (*see photo*)

➤ Spend time in *Toon Town*: open the mailboxes, drink some Goofy water, pull on knobs, and take in the silly architecture.

➤ Stop to admire the swans in the moat around *Sleeping Beauty's Castle*.

➤ Stroll through the park at night when the twinkle lights come on.

➤ Take a ride down *Main Street, U.S.A.* on any of the vehicles.

➤ Try to pull the sword out of the stone by the *King Arthur Carrousel*.

➤ Use the prince/princess bathrooms in *Fantasyland* and feel royal on the throne.

➤ Visit Walt and Mickey's statue (called "Partners") at the hub. Look for Walt's Mickey ring.

➤ Walk around the back way from *Fantasyland* going left which circles around back by the barbeque area to *Big Thunder Mountain*.

➤ Watch the black and white Mickey short cartoons at *Main Street Cinema*.

➤ Find Jingles, the lead horse, on the *King Arthur Carrousel*.

➤ Find the address 33 Royal St. in *New Orleans Square* – that is the entrance to the exclusive *Club 33*.

➤ Ride the *Columbia Ship* and go below to the crews' quarters to check out the museum.

➤ Find the hidden treasure in the caves on *Pirate's Lair on Tom Sawyer's Island*.

➤ Look for the giant microscope on *Star Tours* just before you leave the hangar – it is from the original attraction in the same spot called *"Adventures Through Inner Space."*

➤ Read the time capsule plaque, which is on the ground before passing under the castle.

➤ If you notice that you are about to be in the background of someone's photo, make a funny face for the people to discover after they develop the film.

California Adventure

➤ Visit the *River Creek Challenge Trail* area next to *Grizzly River Run*, especially if you have small children.

➤ In *Flik's Fun Fair*, look for the only four-leaf clover.

➤ Chill out with a glass of wine as you walk through the *Blue Sky Cellar* to cool off and see all the future projects that Disney is working on.

➤ Take time for the tours through the *Ghirardelli Chocolate Factory* and the *Boudin Bread Factory*. You get a free chocolate and sour dough bread sample.

➤ If it is hot, stand under the Space Shuttle engine and wait for a misty surprise.

➤ When you ride *Soarin' Over California*, ask the Cast Member if you could ride in the front row.

➤ Sit on a bench enjoying a frozen lemonade and watch *California Screamin'* launch across the bay.

➤ Take in some of the little shows at *Redwood Exploration Trail*.

➤ Look for the Hidden Mickey on *Soarin' Over California*, when Michael Eisner hits the golf ball.

➤ Take time to enjoy the *Muppet's 3D* queue and preshow.

➤ Go to the *Off the Page* store and look for the characters who have escaped off the pages. They're all around the store.

➤ Watch one of the improvisational groups in *Hollywood Land*.

➤ Check out the symbols in the *Sorcerer's Workshop* at the Animation Building – find Walt Disney's picture. Look at the details in the Beast's library and watch the picture change.

Downtown Disney

➤ Check out the street performers in *Downtown Disney* at night.

➤ Learn about the macaws and cockatoos in front of the *Rainforest Café*.

➤ Take a ride on the *Monorail* into *Disneyland's Tomorrowland*.

➤ Watch a movie at the **AMC** THEATRES (call 888-262-4386 for show times).

Disneyland Resort Hotels

➤ Take the free Arts & Crafts Tour at the *Grand Californian Hotel*.

➤ Enjoy the Native American story time at the *Grand Californian* fireplace.

➤ Check out the memorabilia in the main building of the *Disneyland Hotel*.

➤ Look for Hidden Mickeys at the *Grand Californian Grand Lobby*.

➤ Relax to the piano player in the *Grand Californian's Great Hall*.

➤ There is a waiting room inside the lobby of the *Disneyland Hotel* that is used for *Goofy's Kitchen* restaurant. Disney movies are shown in the air-conditioned room. Sit, relax, and cool off.

CLOSURES

Disneyland stays open 365 days a year now. There have been a few instances when *Disneyland* had unplanned closures. In the beginning, *Disneyland* wasn't even open every day of the week.

The unscheduled closures include:

1. In 1963, due to President Kennedy's assassination.

2. In 1970, due to an "invasion" and demonstration by hippies in August. The stated reason for the attack was because Bank of America, a sponsor of Disneyland, was financing the Vietnam War, which they opposed.

3. In 1994, for inspection after the January 17, 1994, Northridge earthquake, which had a 6.7 magnitude and was the costliest natural disaster in U.S. history, causing more than $20 billion in property damage.

4. In 2001, following the terrorist attacks of September 11, 2001, both of the resort's parks did not open for the day.

Scheduled closures include:

1. In the early years, the park was often scheduled to be closed on Mondays and Tuesdays during the off-season. This was in cooperation with nearby Knott's Berry Farm, which closed on Wednesdays and Thursdays to keep costs down for both parks, while offering Orange County visitors a place to go 7 days a week.

2. On May 4, 2005, for the 50th Anniversary Celebration media event.

3. Due to various special events, the park has closed unusually early to accommodate them, such as special press events, tour groups, VIP groups, private parties, etc. It was common for a corporation to rent the entire park for the evening. The corporation's guests would be issued special passes, which were good for admission to all rides and attractions. In the late afternoon, park employees would announce that the park was closing, then clear the park of everyone without the special corporate passes.

THE HIDDEN MICKEYS

A Hidden Mickey is a partial or complete impression of Mickey Mouse placed by the Imagineers and artists to blend into the designs of Disney attractions, hotels, restaurants, and other areas.

The most common Hidden Mickey form is the tri-circle Mickey frontal silhouette: three circles that form Mickey's round head and adjoining round ears.

There are also hidden Disney characters. They aren't as common as Mickeys, but you will see them just the same. They are basically characters in a place or on an attraction that they don't belong, like Mrs. Potts and Chip from *Beauty and the Beast* can be found on *Tarzan's Tree House*. (*see photo*)

In the *Carnation Baby Care Center* window on *Main Street, U.S.A.*, there is a hidden Walt Disney in the form of a baby photo.

This is a culmination of the Mickey's that I have heard about, seen, or researched on my own from places like *findingmickey.com, hiddenmickeyguy.com, The Hidden Mickeys of Disneyland* book by Bill Scollon, or Mickeys found by guests. Keep in mind that some of the Mickeys can move locations or even be removed altogether, depending on what the Cast Members and the Imagineers want. With the expanding and changing of the park, the Mickeys may end up getting removed or relocated. For instance, *Star Wars Land*. Places were removed to make way for the new sci-fi land. There are said to be over 300 hundred Mickeys out there in the entire resort, and they are waiting for you to find them. I am only listing Mickeys that are part of the structures, attractions, or the décor. Some Hidden Mickey guides will count the Mickey-shaped waffles, pancakes, ice cream bars, personal birthday cakes, balloons, rice crispy treats, beignets, and other Mickey- shaped foods.

For this section, the initials HM stands for Hidden Mickey, not *Haunted Mansion*.

1. Inside *Minnie's House* in *Toontown*.

2. In the ride queue for *Roger Rabbit's Cartoon Spin*.

3. Lamp post in *Toontown*.

4. On the attraction *Big Thunder Railroad* in *Frontierland*.

5. In the stone wall of the attraction queue to *Gadgets Go Coaster*.

6. In the parking structure Daisy between 3A & 3B.

AROUND THE RESORT

Hidden Mickey's can be found before you even enter the park or hotel areas.

1. While traveling north up Disneyland Drive, check out the sidewalk near Disneyland Way. The sidewalk reroutes around the bushes. You can't tell from the ground level, but from Google earth you can see that the sidewalk is actually forming the ears of this resort's largest Hidden Mickey, which is 250 feet across. If you were to walk the whole thing, and jay walk, it would be about 800 feet. Some people are under the misconception that this is the world's largest HM. It is not. There was one larger in *Disney World*. Attached to the *Magic Kingdom's* parking lot was the *Walt Disney World Speedway*. In the middle of the raceway there was a gigantic Mickey-shaped pond (450 feet across) dubbed "Lake Mickey." It was all removed in August 2015 to expand the parking lot, but images can still be seen from space. Larger still, is the 22-acre solar farm west of EPCOT, where solar panels all form a giant Mickey. The world's largest HM is the *Mickey Mouse Forest* south of Clermont, Florida (five miles as Dumbo flies, or 12 miles driving from *Magic Kingdom*), off of Schofield Rd, which is 50-acres, or 2,000 feet across. The 60,000 pine trees that form the Mickey were planted by Disney employees in 1992.

2. If you are in the parking structure, go to the Daisy level and look at the ground between the pillars marked 3A and 3B. The swirl pattern made with the trowel makes circles to form a Mickey. It is about two feet in diameter.

DISNEY RESORT PLAZA

This is the area between *Disneyland* and *California Adventure* after you go through the security checkpoint.

3. If you go to the center of the plaza, there is a giant compass mosaic on the ground containing four Mickeys.

4. There are several signposts with directions to *Downtown Disney, Parking Lot Trams*, etc. On the tops of the poles there are Mickeys.

5. Keep an eye out for the street lamps. Those, too, have Mickeys on top.

6. Disney used to offer commemorative bricks. On the bricks, there are three different versions of Mickey to see, a complete outline, a Mickey head hidden as a wedding bell clacker, and an outline of Mickey's head with the castle in the middle of it.

7. If you need to take a break, have a seat on one of the benches and take note of the supports on the sides.

8. While purchasing your park ticket, take a look at the brackets supporting the counters.

9. The green tree enclosures that look like big bird cages have Mickey-looking bolts holding them together.

10. On the backs of turnstiles as you enter the park, there is a Mickey head speaker.

NOTE: Remember, HM stands for Hidden Mickey, not *Haunted Mansion*.

NOTE: An * after a HM description indicates that there is a photo to coincide with it.

DISNEYLAND

Main Street, U.S.A.

11. The Hidden Mickey is in the window of the *Main Street Photo Supply Co*. It is on one of the cameras on display. In the middle window, on the left-hand side there is one camera; the lens makes the head and two black gear things make the ears.

12. In the window dioramas, there is at least one Mickey in each scene. These windows can change around, so keep a sharp eye.

13. If you hop on the train Engine No. 3, "Fred Gurley," there is a Mickey drilled into one of the brackets up by the tender.

14. Train Engine No. 5, "Ward Kimball," also has a Mickey in the tender, and you can see it from the front row looking through the window.

15. In *City Hall* there is a painting of Mickey walking with a child and an adult into *Fantasyland*. On the adult's shirt, there is a Mickey.

16. Also inside *City Hall,* there is a book case with faux books bearing Disney movie titles. The one titled *Mickey Mouse* has a Mickey head on it. *

17. Above the *Guided Tours* building, there is a flying flag with a Mickey on it.

18. The faux door at the top of the steps that says *Disneyland Casting Agency* "Open since '55" has two Mickeys in the flourishing pattern.

19. The *Main Street Train Station* is also flying a Mickey flag.

351

20. In the *Emporium* behind the cash register, there is a painting with different articles and a gold table with a blue snow globe on it with Sorcerer Mickey painted on it.

21. The fruit cart just off of *Main Street, U.S.A.* has a Mickey in the metal work down near the wheels.

22. In the *Magic Shop* window, there is a deck of magic cards; one of the ace cards has a Mickey instead of a club.

23. Near the Houdini window display, there are three magic balls arranged to form a Mickey.

24. In the display case inside the *Magic Shop*, there is a magic rope coiled to look like a Mickey.

25. If you enter the *20th Century Music Company* store and look above the counter at the display of musical instruments, you will see three tambourines set up to look like a Mickey.

26. In the back of the *Market House,* there is a wrought iron wall hanging with Mickeys on it.

27. The woodwork in the *Fortuosity Shop* has an oblong Mickey decoratively carved into it.

28. Inside the *Penny Arcade,* there is a Pinocchio marionette that you can make dance by pressing buttons. In between those buttons is a Mickey head in the flourishes.

29. As you enter the *Main Street, U.S.A. Cinema,* look down at the lights illuminating the steps. *

30. There is a painting of roses in the *Plaza Inn Restaurant.* On the right side, there is a Mickey painted on one of the petals.

31. In the *Carnation Baby Care Center* window on *Main Street, U.S.A.*, there is a hidden Walt Disney in the form of a baby photo.

Adventureland

32. In the *Bazaar* shop, in the left side entrance, there is a Mickey head on the wall painted in a dirt sifter. *

33. There is a long rope that has been intertwined to form a HM on the wall above the clothing rack. *

❖ **Jungle Cruise**

34. Aboard the "Suwannee Lady," there is a Mickey on a cast-iron frying pan.

❖ Indiana Jones and the Temple of The Forbidden Eye

35. On the well cover, there are hieroglyphs with a Mickey. This one has a tendency to disappear because so many people touch it, but it returns every now and again. *

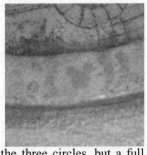

36. There is a hidden Eeyore parking lot sign above the queue in the projection room.

37. If you are looking at the wall above the snake's body just before you're told to "watch out for anything that slithers," you will see a large Hidden Mickey. This Mickey is not just the three circles, but a full profile, nose and all. Mickey is facing the direction the car is going. It is made of cracks in the wall and shadows. *

38. There is a big Mickey on the wall in the projection room. It is outlined with the shapes of the cracks and "mildew" on the wall.

39. Right when you take off on your adventure, there is a giant idol of Mara. Don't look into her eyes, but she has an indentation in her upper lip and her nostrils that form a HM.

40. The *Life Magazine* cover in Indy's office has a picture of Mickey on the front of it. *

41. There is a skeleton wearing personalized Mickey ears, when you drive past the skeleton tomb (sometimes it isn't there).

42. If you translate the glyphs on the walls in the queue, there is a set that translates into MM, for Mickey Mouse.

43. After you go up the steps, there is a wall full of hieroglyphics to translate. Under the message is a carving of a snake. The coils of the snake form a Mickey.

44. After exiting you will pass a truck with equipment in the back. One of the items is an oil lamp with a Mickey on the glass chimney.

❖ Tarzan's Tree House

45. The curtain hooks are Mickey heads.

46. There are three steel drums in a cluster that form a HM.

47. Look for a steamer trunk. The rivets around the keyhole form a Mickey.

48. Check out the teapot and teacup. It is Mrs. Potts and Chip from *Beauty and the Beast* (1991). This is actually a nod to the film *Tarzan* (1999), in which Mrs. Potts and Chip appear in the *Trashin' The Camp* musical number.

❖ Enchanted Tiki Room

49. During the pre-show, Tangaroa lowers the new gods from his branches. One of the new gods to the left of him has a Mickey painted on its belly.

50. High (about nine feet up) on the Southwest wall inside the *Tiki Room* is an orange circle approximately six inches in diameter. It clearly shows Mickey's head and ears.

51. On one of the perches, a feather is suspended from a bamboo Hidden Mickey.

52. Check out the Cast Members' costumes. Their Hawaiian shirt print pattern has a Mickey head on the image of the shield.

New Orleans Square

53. In the *Blue Bayou Restaurant* there is a stained glass in the lobby with a Mickey head pattern.

54. In *Club 33*, the server's vests have a Mickey head in the print pattern.

55. In the *Disney Dream Suite,* there is a pattern in the rugs consisting of red roses. Some of those red roses make a Mickey head.

56. In that same rug, you can also see a pattern with three blue circles to make the Mickey head.

57. On the right side of the entrance to *La Mascarade d'Orleans*, there is a giant bronze plaque with a peacock on it. Look near the base of his tail to see a HM in the feather pattern. *

58. When you are in the master bathroom of the *Dream Suite*, there is a starry pattern above the tub. The stars will appear and make a Mickey head.

❖ Haunted Mansion

59. When you are in the entryway, stand under the candelabra on the wall and look up. The base for the three candles makes a Mickey.

60. There are Mickey heads all over the wallpaper in the art gallery before you board the doom buggy. *

61. In the ballroom birthday party scene, on the dining table, the first place setting to the left of the birthday girl has a large dinner plate and two saucers just above and to either side of the plate arranged in the form of Mickey's head. This is the only setting on the table like this.

❖ Haunted Mansion Holiday

62. In the ballroom where the carriage crashed through the wall, there is a Mickey shaped out of the piles of snow on the floor.

354

63. In the stained glass art of the Christmas tree with the red ornaments in the Stretching Room.

64. In the ballroom, look for a Halloween-themed place setting shaped like a Mickey.*

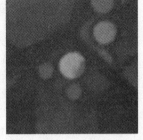

❖ **Pirates of the Caribbean**

65. When you first leave the dock and drop into the water, look to the right to find a cluster of lily pads that form a Mickey.

66. At the beginning of the attraction as you pass the *Blue Bayou* restaurant, if you look to your left at the second house, just before the old man in the rocking chair, there is a silhouette of Mickey on the moon painted on the wall.

67. As you float through the "transition tunnel," you will see a projected image of Davey Jones on a fog screen. On the front point of his hat, to his right side, you will see a little gold Mickey head. *

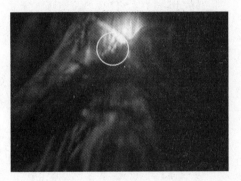

68. After the storm scene, in the room with the oil painting of the wench, there is a table with a pitcher and two mugs, laid out in a Hidden Mickey setting.

69. On the little beach after you drop down, there are shells that make up the Mickey head.

70. In the treasure room, one of the treasure chests has a Mickey-shaped lock.

71. In the battle scene, there are cannon ball holes in the side of the fort in the rock. *

72. There is a mini Mickey head on the armor chest plate in the last scene with the drunken pirates. You have to look to the left and back to see it. It is the size of a half dollar.

73. On the treasure chest in Jack's treasure room.

Frontierland

Note: The two Mickey's found in *Big Thunder Ranch* were removed with the construction of *Star Wars Land*.

74. At the base of the flagpole, there are three rocks placed and proportioned like Mickey.

75. In *Rancho del Zocalo,* there is a pole near the condiment bar that has the Mickey pattern embedded in it.

76. While dining in the *River Belle Terrace*, look at the mural on the wall with the flowers and berries. On the right side of the floral arrangement resides a cluster of three berries that form a Mickey.

77. If you check out the high chairs in the *River Belle Terrace*, check out the back; it's a cut out HM.

❖ Frontierland Shootin' Exposition

78. Near the tombstone targets, look for the cacti that form a Mickey.

❖ Golden Horseshoe Stage

79. The center stage vent has a Mickey pattern hidden among the normal pattern.

80. Out front there is a poster with the dancers on it. There is a flourish on the bottom of the vignette that resembles a squashed Mickey head.

❖ S.S. Mark Twain

81. Mickey head in the ironwork between the smokestacks.

82. *S.S. Mark Twain River Excursions* sign has a Hidden Mickey silhouette on board.

❖ Pirate's Lair on Tom Sawyer Island

83. Above the cave entrance to the left, after you exit the raft.

84. There is a Mickey in the cement on top of the chimney.

85. Near the pile of pirate treasure, there are three doubloons (coins) permanently stuck in the Mickey head pattern.

❖ Rivers of America

86. There is a set of the river rocks that form the Mickey. (NOTE: These may not be there after the construction of Star Wars land.)

❖ Big Thunder Mountain Railroad

87. After you pass the first turn, walk about 10-15 steps and turn to the right stone wall. (If you looked over the wall, you should be looking at the entrance). Look at the center top about knee level. There are three stones that stand out as a Mickey. If this helps, the right ear is a black stone.

88. When you are in *Rainbow Cavers* on the first lift, look to the left at the cut-off stalagmites; three short ones form a Mickey.

89. When you are going up the second lift, before the rattlesnakes, look to the ground on the left at the giant cogs. It is upside down, but the Mickey is there.

Critter Country

90. In *The Briar Patch Gift* Shop, near the Critter Country entrance, you can find three cabbages in the rafters positioned to form a HM. *

91. In that same shop, look to the right near the ceiling. The logs used to make the wall form a Mickey when looking at them from the end.

92. In *Pooh's Corner* look for the lollipop rack. The holes in the rack for the posts to hold the lollypops are little Mickey heads.

❖ Splash Mountain

93. The knot on the height requirement sign.

94. Also on the height requirement sign, there is a swirl pattern on the lower part of it with a cluster of berries that makes the Mickey. *

95. After you enter the barn, look for some gears on old equipment that form a Mickey.

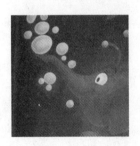

96. On the last turn just before you disembark, look on the wall to the left of the screen showing you a preview of your own photo. There is a photo on the wall of Mickey going down the drop.

❖ Many Adventures of Winnie the Pooh

97. Mickey is hidden in the wood grain to the right side of the entrance.

98. There is a Mickey ears hat on the bookcase behind sleeping Pooh. It is movable, so it may not always be there.

99. Right before the party scene, under the purple heffalump's trunk, there are three yellow honey bubbles that form a Mickey. *

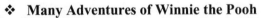

Fantasyland

❖ Alice in Wonderland

100. When you get to the part where the cards are painting the roses red, look down by his feet and you will see a Mickey head made out of the paint splatters. *

101. To the right of Tweedledee and Tweedledum is the

White Rabbit's house. Look through the second floor window to spot the HM on the picture frame.

❖ Casey Jr Circus Train

102. On the first hill of CASEY Jr., look at the house. The windmill of the house is in the shape of Mickey Mouse.

103. The gauges on the locomotive control panel form a Mickey.

❖ It's a Small World

104. Mickey hidden on Santa hat on clock face (holiday season only).

105. Holly berries on the "Peace on Earth" sign form a HM (holiday season only).

106. While waiting in the queue, you will notice the three platforms with the umbrellas for the Cast Members. If you can see them from an aerial view, they form a HM.

❖ King Arthur Carrousel

107. There is a three-jeweled HM on Jingles, the horse. That is the one dedicated to Julie Andrews.

❖ Mad Hatter Shop

108. If you look up at the shop sign, there is a set of Mickey ears to the right.

❖ Matterhorn Bobsleds

109. Look beside the second abominable snowman; Harold. Mickey is carved into the wall. (You have to ride on the attraction to the right, not the left one.)

110. On the post as you wait in the right-side queue, the red and black coat of arms, for the canton of Obwalden, has a small HM in the center of it.

111. When you pass the Wells Expedition area, look on the ground at the rope that coils around to form a Mickey. Sometimes it isn't there.

❖ Mr. Toad's Wild Ride

112. In the queue there are wood carving designs on the arches above. There are clusters of berries that form a Mickey.

113. The Toad statue in the queue has a small HM pointed on his left eye. *

114. Near the beginning, you go through some double doors with stained glass. On the bottom, left in the stained glass, there is a side-profile Mickey in the pink diamond.

115. After you go through the fireplace and then U-turn, there are pictures along both walls. The second picture on the left side has a Hidden Mickey at the top of the picture frame, but it's upside down.

116. The mural painting on the back wall from the loading area has a train in the back ground. Walt is driving the train.

117. When you go through the tavern, look at the left spinning mug in Winky's hand. There is a HM in the foam.

❖ Peter Pan's Flight

118. If you look closely, you'll notice there's a picture of Mickey Mouse on the wall of the nursery.

119. Hidden Mickey teddy bear paws, 2nd floor window, outer façade.

120. You can see Mickey standing in one of the windows on the *Big Ben* clock tower as you fly over the city. *

121. On the exterior to the right of the attraction there is a black Mail Box. On the designs painted on the front, you can see a Mickey.

❖ Pinocchio's Daring Adventure

122. Right as you are boarding, look up at the coke bottle style window above the ride operator. The circles form HMs.

123. At the beginning, there is a dancing Pinocchio puppet. As he is dancing, look at the shadows his feet are casting on the floor; they form a Hidden Mickey.

124. There is a popcorn Mickey in the popcorn machine painted on the wall in the Pleasure Island scene, as well as a popcorn Mickey on the floor near the ride vehicle path. *

125. Just as you pass Geppetto and Pinocchio at the end, you pass by a ship in a bottle; the frame holding the bottle has a Mickey in the top center of it.

126. Look closely at the Pleasure Island painting. On the archway above the gate there is a Mickey head.

❖ Pixie Hollow

127. At the base of the sign that says "Fairies Welcome," you can find a HM in the bark.

128. If you walk around the outside on the pathways along the water, you can spot a tri-circle of fountains that create a swirl pattern to make a Mickey. *

❖ Sleeping Beauty Castle

129. At the top of the castle, there are several gold crowns located near the top of the mast. The design on the crown is that of a HM.

130. Outside the *Castle Heraldry Shoppe,* there is a mailbox with a HM.

131. Inside the *Castle Heraldry Shoppe,* you can find a vase with a cluster of grapes on it; the three on the bottom form a HM.

❖ Snow White's Scary Adventure

132. On the windows when you are boarding. *

133. On the outside, it's the metal decoration on a lamp in the handicapped entrance. Go to the main entrance from *Fantasyland* to the *Toy Shoppe* and look to your right. The Mickey is on the bottom of the lamp that is mounted on the ceiling.

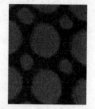

134. There are Hidden Mickey trees on the wall when you are boarding to the left side.

135. There are three red jewels in one of the barrels in the dwarfs' mine that form a HM. *

❖ Storybook Land Canals Boat Ride

136. In the Cinderella section on the *Storybook Land Canal Boats*, there is a Hidden Mickey. If you look at all of the houses in that scene, you'll notice that they have three circles in the shape of an upside-down Mickey. On one of the houses, the circles are right-side-up, with a big circle and two on top for the ears. You can't see it at night because they don't have it lit up, but during the day it's easy to see.

137. There are three jewels in the *Cave of Wonders*.

138. On the stern (backside) of the "Wendy" boat, there is a HM. *

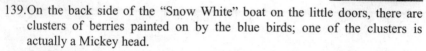

139. On the back side of the "Snow White" boat on the little doors, there are clusters of berries painted on by the blue birds; one of the clusters is actually a Mickey head.

140. On the back of the "Flora" boat, there is a pink Mickey head painted in the flowers.

❖ Village Haus Restaurant

141. There are stained glass windows inside the restaurant. One of them has a Pinocchio in it. On his shorts there are several HM.

142. There is a shelf on the wall with several wooden toys on it; one being a three-masted ship. On the stern side, there is a golden Mickey head. It is hard to see because it is facing the wall.

Mickey's Toontown

143. Above the entrance, there is a seal with a Mickey that says "Order Of The Mouse."

144. Next to the *Fireworks Building*, there is a Gym sign in the shape of a punching bag. On this bag is a large orange circle and inside the circle is Horace Horsecollar holding up a barbell. The two black circles and the large orange circle complete the Mickey.

145. At the *Firework Shop*, there is a carving of Mickey on the side of the building.

146. You can spot a little blue Mickey on the pink firework busting out of the building.

147. *Clarabelle's Frozen Yogurt* has a Mickey on the door that can only be seen when the shop is closed. It is meant to pay homage to Mickey Moo, *Disneyland's* cow mascot from the late 1980's. *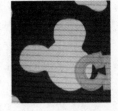

148. The Cast Member exit has a stone Mickey on the wall.

149. *Toontown Post Office* has a letter-shaped sign with a Mickey on the stamp.

150. *Mickey's P.O. Box* and the others feature each character's own silhouette.

151. On the *Toontown* telephones, there are Mickeys in the center of the rotary dial.

152. *Toontown's Third Little Piggy Bank* has Mickey-faced coins on the sign when decorated for Christmas.

153. The manhole covers.

154. On the lamp posts around the land.

155. The safety sign that says "Supervise Children At All Times" has Mickey ears on the child figure.

156. Hidden Mickeys on the hubcaps of the car parked at the gas station.

157. In the *Five & Dime* shop there is a hat rack on a stand shaped like a Mickey.

❖ Gadget's Go Coaster

158. As you pass the first bend in the queue, you can spot three stones in the wall that form a Mickey.

159. There is a second rock Mickey as you turn the last bend.

160. Look on Gadget's workshop wall for the blueprints. Partially covered is a full upper-torso shot of Mickey above the words "Dog & Pony For Mickey At 4pm."

❖ Roger Rabbit's Cartoon Spin

161. While waiting in the queue, you pass a faux alley way with a can of paint; the swirls form the three circles of Mickey.

162. There is a Mickey hidden on the hubcap in the loading area.

163. In the room with buildings, there is a Mickey at the back of the double doors.

164. To the left of the attraction entrance, there is a door knob with eyes. It is the door knob from the *Alice in Wonderland* (1951) film. Which, incidentally, was added to the film by the animators as it didn't exist in the book.

❖ Mickey's House

165. Mickey welcome mat.

166. The window on his front door is a Mickey.

167. In the living room on the bookshelf, the publisher's mark on the bindery of the book titled "My Fair Mouse" is a Mickey.

168. One of the books on the shelf has a hidden Goofy.

169. On the globe in his house, the continent of Australia is shaped like the basic, three-circle Mickey.

170. In the bookshelf with a glass front on the left as you enter the living room, the publisher's mark on the binding of the book titled "2001: A Mouse Odyssey" is two Mickeys.

171. A Mickey-shaped mailbox.

172. "Meet Mickey" sign.

173. Mickey-shaped window on front door.

174. Various books feature Mickey on their spines. *

175. Surrealist Mickey artwork.

176. The notepad on Mickey's desk.

177. A photo of Walt Disney and Mickey.

178. The metronome on Mickey's piano.

179. Mickey-shaped holes in the player piano.

180. There is one hidden Donald in the player piano rotating on the sheet inside.

181. There is also one hidden Goofy in the player piano on the sheet inside. *

182. In Donald's painting area, there are two paint splotches in the shape of a HM. One is in the green paint, the other is in the red.

183. On the movie screen, there is a Mickey head for the countdown.

184. There is a Mickey on the giant paintbrush in Mickey's photo area.

185. In the photo area there are music sheets. Some of the notes are shaped like Mickey.

186. While meeting Sorcerer Mickey, look at the starry backdrop; among the little white stars is a black Mickey head.

❖ Minnie's House

187. The orange book on Minnie's bookcase has a Mickey.

188. Minnie's balls of yarn form a Mickey.

189. Mickey on the front of Minnie's fridge.

190. On the relish jar inside Minnie's fridge.

191. Above her stove is a gathering of pots and pans that form a Mickey.

192. Next to Minnie's house is a Cast Member exit. On the wall, there is a Mickey formed by stones.

Tomorrowland

193. Inside *Pizza Port*, there are Mickey molecules on the *Adventure Thru Inner Space* poster.

194. Inside the *Star Trader,* there is a red Mickey in the center of an atom on top of some display shelves.

❖ Autopia

195. As you enter the "Car Park," you pass through a wrought iron gate. If you look at the pinnacle of the gate, there are three pieces of metal bent into three swirls. This may be a Mickey profile silhouette. The reason this part of the gate sticks out from the rest is because the rest of the gate is symmetrical, except for this one part.

196. The license plates have Mickey expiration tag stickers on them.

197. There is a "Mickey Mouse Crossing" street sign.

❖ Buzz Lightyear Astro Blasters

198. On the wall in the queue, there is a picture on the map of a planet called Ska-densii. *

199. There is a giant mural on the exterior of the building. Look closely at the orange planet on the far left. The markings on it form a Mickey head.

200. There is a Mickey on an orange block in the first shooting room. *

201. While shooting, keep an eye out for a green planet with green/blue swirl Mickey head patterns. *

❖ Finding Nemo Submarine Voyage

202. While you are boarding the submarine, look down at the dock. Sometimes Cast Members will lay rope down in the shape of a Mickey, but this isn't always the case.

❖ Innoventions

203. At the entrance, there are Mickeys above the doors.

204. Tom Morrow has Mickey shoelaces and Mickey pens in his pocket. (NOTE: Not sure if he is permanently gone. Building houses for the Marvel and Star Wars *Meet and Greet*)

205. The ironwork railing inside have a HM in the design. *

206. In the glass floor upstairs, there is a bead Hidden Mickey.

207. When walking down the ramp after exiting, look toward the *Tomorrow Landing Shop;* above that is the satellite dishes from the old *Rocket Rods* loading area. While at rest, they form a Mickey.

❖ Monorail

208. While walking down the exit ramp in *Tomorrowland*, look near the base of the cement corral. There is a three-circle pattern.

❖ Space Mountain

209. The speakers in the coaster cars form a Mickey. *

❖ Star Tours

210. When you are standing in the queue, there is a projection wall that shows silhouettes of people and androids passing by. Watch carefully as there is an R2 unit that puts out two satellite dishes on its head and turns to face you, making them appear to be Mickey ears. *

211. In the queue, you can see a Mickey on the readout in front of C3-PO. *

212. Across from the scanning droid there is a shadow on the wall that makes it look like the droid is wearing Mickey ears. *

213. Pay close attention to the scanning droid's baggage scans. A Mickey plush is in one of them. (NOTE: There are many other hidden characters or nods; to see that list, go to the *Star Tours* fun fact section)

214. One of the bags he scans also has a Sorcerer Mickey hat in it. *

  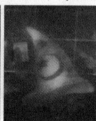 

ᛒuena ᛘista Street

❖ Oswald's Filling Station

215. Inside *Oswald's Filling Station*. On the back wall, there is an alarm bell shaped like a Mickey.

216. To the right side of *Oswald's,* there is the *Guest Relations* counter. Above that on the side of the building on the brick wall, there is a painted-on billboard for Elias & Company. On the right-hand side of the billboard, there is a flourish that has a Mickey hidden in it. It is just to the right of the "N" from "OPEN." *

❖ Julius Katz & Sons

217. In the window, there is a little TV with a test card on the screen with a Mickey in the middle of it.

218. Also in the window is an empty glass watch face with two little watch faces near it to form a Mickey.

219. Inside on top of a shelf is an old-fashioned film splicer. The rollers form a Mickey head.

220. In the exterior window there is a set of two old fashioned cameras with a HM formed by the lenses. *

❖ Elias & Company

221. Inside there are some iron railing patterns with a Mickey shape.

222. Inside there is some beautiful art deco work near the ceiling with the Mickey pattern.

❖ Clarabelle's Ice Cream Shop

223. On the shelves above the waffle ice cream bowls, there are old-fashioned milk bottles with the *Clarabelle's Ice Cream Shop* logo on them and a Holstein cow donning a Mickey-head print on her side. This pattern was done intentionally to pay homage to the once-popular *Disneyland* petting zoo cow, Mickey Moo, who also donned the Mickey-head pattern. She lived in *Disneyland* from 1988-1993.

❖ Carthay Circle Restaurant

224. There is a little white HM just outside the entrance on the ground in the terrazzo-style flooring near the circle logo. *

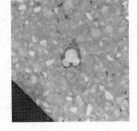

❖ **The Five & Dime Band**

225. The tire treads have the Mickey head in the design.

❖ **Trolley Treats**

226. In the window there is a big mountain of rock candy. If you are inside the store, you can see a section of the mountain boarded up. Look between the boards to see a snowman wearing Mickey ears.

Hollywood Land

227. If you stop in at *Schmoozies*, take a look at the mural on the wall. There are a few Mickey hidden within.

❖ **Off The Page**

228. Outside in the display window, one of the Dalmatian pups has a Mickey-head spot pattern.

229. Inside there are animations hanging from the ceiling. One of them features Tick-Tock The Crock. Near his shadow is a cluster of three pebbles that form a Mickey.

❖ **Monsters Inc. Mike & Sully To The Rescue**

230. When you are watching the video, a monster taxi appears with multiple lights on the front. Three of them form a HM. It is the taxi logo, and it is located all around the queue area.

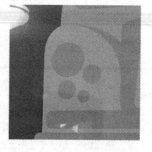

231. In the queue area there is a giant poster of the taxi with the three headlights that form a HM. *

232. Right as you start the ride, look at the city scape for a silhouette of the Earful Tower, the water tower with Mickey ears from *Hollywood Studios* in *Disney World*.

233. When crashing through Harry Hausen's, look for a full-side shot of Mickey's silhouette in the window.

234. Sully has a purple spot on his fur in the shape of a Mickey, when he is hanging from the door holding Boo.

235. Color-changing Randall has a purple Mickey head spot on his green skin, when Boo is beating him with the baseball bat.

236. The control panel on the Monstropolis news van has a Mickey made out of the dials.

❖ **Animation Building**

237. At the tip top of the pole atop the front of the building, there dwells a HM.

238. In the front window, there is a Dalmatian puppy with a HM spot.

239. On the shelf in the *Animation Academy,* you can spot a plush Mickey Mouse.

240. Draw your own animation while following the instructions on how to draw a Mickey Balloon in the *Sorcerers Workshop*.

241. On the wall in the *Sorcerer's Workshop,* there is a relief of Sorcerer Mickey surrounded by multiple HMs.

242. While in the *Sorcerer's Workshop*, warm yourself at the hearth below Prince Adam's portrait; it's a Mickey.

243. Before leaving the *Sorcerer's Workshop,* you can see another relief on the wall. This one is of a treble clef shaped like a side profile Mickey. *

244. The huge mural outside the doors of *Turtle Talk with Crush* has a HM amongst the coral patterns.

245. When leaving the animation building, look at the patterns on the wall to see a Mickey in the speckles.

❖ **Hyperion Theater**

246. While exiting, look at the top of the archway to see a HM.

❖ **Sunset Showcase Theater**

- None have been found yet.

❖ **Red Car Trolley**

247. At the end of the line near *The Guardians of The Galaxy – Mission: Breakout!*, look for a picture of a giant post card. The reflection of the *Mickey's Fun Wheel* is a Mickey head.

❖**The Guardians of The Galaxy – Mission: Breakout!**

248. On the exterior of the building, there are half silver orbs all over the décor. They are upside down HM's. *

249. While in The Collector's office, look in the caged shelves for a plate and a vase ordained with flowers. There is a Mickey figure behind the vase.

A Bug's Land

250. On the cold beverage cart, there is a picture of fruit. There are three cherries that form a HM.

❖ **Heimlich's Chew Chew Train**

251. Just near the end of the attraction before exiting, look at the wall; there are three stones clustered to form a HM.

❖ **A Bug's Life Theater**

252. As you enter the theater, look up and to the left side of the theater while facing front about five rows back from the screen. There are three flower pods that form a HM.

❖ **Flik's Flyers**

253. There are circles, one is a light, embedded in the ground that form a HM.

Cars Land

254. Check out the Cars Land sign at the entrance. Planted beneath are three hook barrel cacti that form a Mickey.

255. In front of the fire station are some power lines with a HM in a tangled stretch of wire.

❖ **Mater's Junkyard Jamboree**

256. While in the queue, look toward the ceiling to find three hubcaps that form a HM. *

❖ **Radiator Springs Curios**

257. In front of the shop to the left, there is a big round yellow sign that says "Pump." Look closely at the chipped paint that reveals a HM.

258. Inside the shop to the right is a yellow sign that reads "Service" and has two break lights above it. *

259. While still inside the shop, look toward the ceiling tiles. One of them has a pattern to form a HM.

260. On one of the shelves is a collection of snow globes. One of those is the snow globe with Knick Knack from the Pixar short.

❖ **Luigi's Rollickin' Roadsters**

261. In the glass cabinet there is a Lightning McQueen antenna ball with a little Mickey ears hat on (which is for sale in the shops). *

262. While inside in the queue, look in the glass cabinet at all the photos. There is what looks like a white business card near the top that says *Topolino*. In Italian, it means "little mouse," but has been used as the name of Mickey Mouse in the Italian Mickey Mouse comics since 1932.

263. On Luigi's desk, there is a little toy Lightning McQueen toy car with Mickey ears and a nose.

❖ **Ramone's House Of Body Art**

264. Inside the shop there is a giant purple hood that says *Ramone's*. On the right side in the purple flames there is a Mickey head about the size of a quarter.

265. In the exterior windows there are seven differently-painted hoods. Each one has a HM somewhere on it.

266. Inside there is a giant box used for a display that has paint splatter all over it. There are three paint

rings that make up a HM.

267. There are more box displays around the edge of the store above display racks that have more HM's in the paint splatters. *

268. On some of the design work along the wall, there is pinstriping with a HM worked into it. *

❖ **Radiator Springs Racers**

269. Once you enter the queue, look down to the right for an arrangement of three hook barrel cactuses. *

270. Before you head up the ramp to load, there is another arrangement of three hook barrel cactuses. Sometimes they are replanted elsewhere as cactuses have a tendency to grow.

271. There is a photo hanging inside one of the garages in the queue of Stanley and Lizzie's wedding day. Lizzie's tiara has multiple gears on top of it and three of them form a HM.

272. On the sod of *The Amazing Oil Bottle House* there is a cluster of bottles that form a Mickey. The ears are made by two blue bottles. *

273. There is a piece of equipment on a shelf, next to a red barrel, that has a pressure gauge on it with a small HM.

274. When entering in the FastPass queue, look on the tops of the fence posts for a stamped HM.

275. While on the attraction tractor tipping, you will pass bushes with projected lights on the wall which contain several HM.

276. At one point, you will come to a fork in the track. If you enter the left side to *Guido's Casa Della Tires,* you will receive new tires. After exiting the showroom, there will be a red tool chest on the right side with HM pinstriping.

277. If you split to the right, you will enter *Ramone's*

House of Body Art. To the left side of the track there, is a white fuse box with pinstriping to form a HM. *

278. There are painted car hoods along the walls of Ramon's that have little HMs on them.

Grizzly Peak

279. There is a stage set up next to *Fly-N-Buy* for Minnie's Fly Girls. There is a Mickey head formed with clouds in the logo.

280. In *Taste Pilot's Grill,* there is a photo on the wall showing some equipment that form a Mickey.

281. When you enter the *Rushin' River Outfitters* shop, look for the display with all the plush bears. The paw pad design is of a Mickey.

282. If you go on the *Boudin Bakery Tour*, you can spot some Mickey sourdough bread loaves right when you enter.

❖ Grizzly River Run

283. If you walk around the trail, you will spot some rusty old machinery with giant gears. When approaching it, the gears appear to form a Mickey.

❖ Soarin' Around The World

284. During the safety video, you can see a pair of Mickey ears on the head of a disappointed man.

❖ Redwood Creek Challenge Trail

285. There is a map posted out front. There are three HM's on it. The Ahwanee Camp Circle Mickey is made with the stumps in front of the stage.

286. The Hoot-N-Holler Logs Slide dust forms a Mickey near one of the wolves tumbling out.

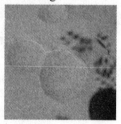

287. The Hibernation Hollow River has three stones to form a Mickey, which is an accurate portrayal of what you will find in that actual spot.

288. While hopping across the *Hibernation Hollow River*, look where you step, and maybe you will be hopping across the river by stepping on a Mickey. *

Paradise Pier

289. While in *Sideshow Shirts*, look for a painting of a man lying on a bed of nails. On the bottom of the painting there is a HM painted to look like a knot. *

290. Enter *Sideshow Shirts* and look for the hanging portrait of Betty Ducks. Just below the barrel of her gun is a HM painted into the frame's woodwork. *

291. Inside *Point Mugu Tattoo*. There is another sign with a flaming surfboard that says DCA and has a Mickey on it as well. *

292. Inside *Point Mugu Tattoo,* on the back wall, is a sign that says *Paradise Pier*. In between the words is a tattoo design with a Mickey head worked into it. *

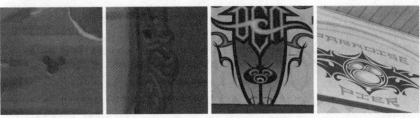

293. On this shops exterior, there is a painting of a woman with a snake around her neck. It isn't just any snake. It is Kaa from *The Jungle Book* (1967). *

294. Look at the facade for *Paradise Pier Amusements Co*. Just under the upper eaves, the are HMs in the Victorian gingerbread accents. *

295. Inside the *Treasures in Paradise* shop, there is a painting of Azalea, the fabulous female illusionist. Her belt has a HM right in the middle. *

296. Also, look for a painting of a carousel lion with a saddle. The saddle has a HM on it. *

297. In the *Man Hat'n Beach* shop there is a giant purple octopus. On the back of his head, you can see a HM in his spots.

298. In *Dumbo's Bucket Brigade* on the left wall behind the buckets of prizes, there is a HM painted into the red paint.

299. Also, on the front of the burning building near Dumbo, there are plumes of smoke billowing out from the fire. There are three clouds of smoke that form a HM.

300. There is a drink stand across from *Toy Story Mania*. On the stand, there is a stack of imitation newspapers that have Mickey from *Steamboat Willie* on the front page.

301. If you catch a bite to eat in *Ariel's Grotto*, go to the stairs and look for a photo area. There is a cluster of bubbles that form a Mickey painted on it.

302. Across from *Ariel's Grotto* is the *Duffy the Bear Meet and Greet* area. The red banners on the support columns have Duffy's paw print on them, which is a Mickey head.

303. While inside meeting Duffy, look at the back wall for a Mickey formed by a ships helm and two porthole- shaped lights.

304. Grab a drink at *Cove Bar* and take a look at the backs of the chairs to find Mickey in the metalwork.

305. Near the bar is a gazebo used for character *Meet and Greets*. On the backdrop, there is a Mickey formed from three life rings.

306. There is also a giant treasure chest with Duffy Bear inside it. Take a close look at his face. Squint if you have to. The outline of his face is a HM.

307. There are footprints leading up to the chest as well. They have a HM in the pad prints.

308. On your way to *California Screamin'* you will pass a billboard with a collection of beach umbrellas in the bottom right corner. One cluster forms a Mickey.

309. Walk up to the *Seaside Souvenir Shop* and look at the mural painted on the wall behind the register. There are two HMs on it in the form of a red balloon and a green balloon.

❖ California Screamin'

310. Directly under the loop, there is a support column that has a white Mickey head at the base. You can only see them if you look toward the ground when you are upside down.

❖ World Of Color

311. There is an orange Mickey balloon that floats before the house in the *Up* scene.

❖ Ariel's Undersea Adventure

312. When you get in the queue, look up at the ironwork in the canopy covering the line. There is a HM. *

313. Right after you load, but before you enter the first room to see Scuttle, there is a HM on the wall to the right. *

314. In the *Under the Sea* scene, there is an octopus with a pink HM spot on its head.

315. In the *Kiss the Girl* scene, the kissing frogs have blue patches on their backs that form an oblong HM.

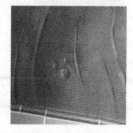

316. Just before you disembark, look at the little cabinet on the wall to the left. There is a little picture of the Little Mermaid statue from the Copenhagen Harbor in Denmark. That is where the story *The Little Mermaid* was written in 1837 by Hans Christian

Andersen.

317. The other picture on the cabinets is a silhouette of Hans Christian Andersen himself.

❖ Jumpin' Jellyfish

318. On the main pole holding up the attraction, you can see a HM formed by the painted-on bubbles.

❖ Goofy's Sky School

319. On the bulletin boards there is a letter that says "Dear Teach." Peeking out from behind the letter is a HM.

320. On the second board next to the upside down notice, there is another HM peeking out.

321. Once you board, you will see a service room with a bunch of tools. The wrench to the far right, hanging on the rack, has a HM.

322. In that same area, there are gauges on the wall that form a HM.

323. While riding on the track, you take a sharp curve and avoid smashing through a billboard that says "How to Turn." The holes in the billboard form a HM.

❖ Mickey's Fun Wheel

324. This is one of the easiest to find. It is also one of the largest in the resort. Look on the front of the wheel. You can't miss the gigantic Mickey head.

❖ Toy Story Midway Mania

325. Prior to boarding, look on the back wall for a grouping of three rings with Jessie, Bullseye, and Rex hanging out of them. *

326. While waiting in the queue, look for the *Dino Darts* poster. Trixie has a HM on the left side of her face.

327. While playing the *Dino Darts* segment, look for the three-circle HM behind the orange 1000-point balloon.

328. While in the *Green Army Men Shoot Camp* segment, look for the three plates front and center that form a HM.

329. After you exit and walk up the stairs through Andy's room, look at the box on the floor. It is there to imply that you were playing the game as if you were the size of the toys. Even the front of the box has the same HM as the one in the loading area with Jessie, Bullseye, and Rex. *

Pacific Wharf

❖ **The Bakery Tour**

330. While walking through the facility, look for a pile of different sourdough loafs. One of them is a Mickey face.

❖ **Blue Sky Cellar**

331. The *Blue Sky Cellar* sign is surrounded by magical pixie dust. Some of the dust particles are Mickey heads.

332. If you walk inside, look at the sign just inside the doors. There is a Sorcerer Mickey formed in the clouds.

333. On one of the displays, there is a painter's palette. The purple paint on the palette makes a Mickey.

❖ **Golden Vine Winery**

334. There is a little information plaque out front that says Pinot Grigio. There is a cluster of grapes that form a Mickey.

Downtown Disney District

335. **D Street** – The walls inside have Mickey-shaped graffiti images. One of the Mickeys has a HM on his belt buckle.

336. **D Street** – There are exposed bricks on the back wall with portraits covering it. The bricks form a Mickey.

337. **Disney Vault 28** – When entering the store, you will see a giant faux vault door. On the upper corner there is a Mickey formed from the rivets, the same down below, but upside down.

338. **Disney Vault 28** – Behind the shop's marquee there is graffiti. In the graffiti patterns you will spot several Mickey heads.

339. **Disney Vault 28** – On the exterior brickwork there is a Mickey carved into it. Look closely; it's the size of a half dollar.

340. **Disney Vault 28** – On the interior walls there is graffiti with a Mickey in the Jolly Roger (skull and cross bones) style.

341. **Disney Vault 28** - There is an old newspaper rack used as a display case with several Mickeys spray painted on it.

342. **Downtown Disney Kiosks** – Multiple venues inhabit the kiosks throughout Downtown Disney. There is a Mickey in the ironwork on top of the signs and supporting the eaves.

343. **Marceline's Confectionary Marquee** - The Mickey is artfully hidden in the decorative swirls between the M & C.

344. **Naples Ristorante E Pizzeria** – Check out the flames in the brick oven on the restaurant's sign. There is a Mickey head in the center that is hard to find.

345. **Ridemakerz** – All over the walls and the windows there is a circle design sticker with RM in the middle. Three stickers are clustered to form the Mickey.

346. **World of Disney** – The exterior awnings above the windows have giant Mickey heads on them.

347. **World of Disney** – On the marquee out front of the western entrance, there are blue Mickey heads on either side under Tweedledee and Tweedledum.

348. **World of Disney** - On this same sign, look up under the umbrella at the gold knob for a HM.

349. **World of Disney** – On the marquee out front of the northern entrance, there are blue Mickey heads on either side under Mickey, Minnie, and Pluto in their flying contraption.

350. **World of Disney** – On the marquee out front of the eastern entrance, there are blue Mickey heads on either side under Huey, Dewey, and Louie with their giant spy glass.

351. **World of Disney** – There is a dishwashing mural painted on the wall with some Mickey-shaped bubbles.

352. **World of Disney** – Behind one of the register sections, there is a giant stained-glass window map. There are little Mickey heads that mark the locations of the Disney parks.

353. **World of Disney** – On that same map, look at the bottom, right for the compass. The post holding the compass has a Mickey head.

354. **World of Disney** – At the top of the map there is a scroll with Mickey heads on the ends.

355. **World of Disney** – The stanchion belts (the queue belts) at the registers have Mickey heads on them.

356. **World of Disney** – The cylindrical display bins around the store have Mickey-shaped patterns in them.

357. **World of Disney** – Look at the base of those storage bins to find a Mickey-shaped support base.

358. **World of Disney** – Around the Sleeping Beauty display, there is pink metal edging with Mickey ear hats cut out.

359. **World of Disney** – There are murals painted around the walls inside. Look for the one with Goofy steering a gondola holding Mickey and Minnie. There is a HM on the archway of the bridge.

360. **World of Disney** – There is a painting with Mickey, Minnie, Goofy, and the Dalmatians in front of the Chinese Theater. Above the theater entrance is a HM.

DISNEY HOTELS

❖ **Disney's Grand Californian Hotel & Spa**

361. Look closely at the *Grand Californian's* sign. Look at the redwood tree with the light green highlights for the HM.

362. That same tree can be seen on the light posts out front along the driveway.

363. The tree is also on the planters out front.

364. Out front there is also the hotel's logo made out of tile, with the same HM. You can find it on multiple folk art relief tile sculptures. *

365. Take a close look at the artwork hanging in the hallways. Actually, look at the corners of the frames for a HM. *

366. The fire place in the main lobby has three roundish stones among the rectangular ones on the left side that form a Mickey. *

367. There is a map of the complex on the lobby wall. Take a close look at the children's pool. The pool has ears. *

   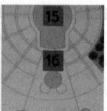

368. The sculpture that has the three trees has a full Mickey face etched into an open spot between the branches about 2/3 of the way up the main tree.

369. When entering, look to the rug on the floor. HM in the tree there as well.

370. At the front counter's center, one of the tiles has a full frontal HM with a side profile of his face. You can even see the buttons on his shorts.

371. One of the green tiles has a hidden Tinker Bell.

372. There is a fabric wall hanging behind the front desk with Mickey sewn into it.

373. At the end of the main lobby there is a desk. Look under the lip of the desk for a tri-circle Mickey-shaped hole.

374. Look for an ornate grandfather clock. Look at the copper clock face to see the HM behind the hands.

375. The light fixtures in the *Hearthstone Lounge* have Mickey on them.

376. In the *Storyteller's Café,* there are cutout Mickey circles on the backs of the highchairs.

377. In the guest rooms, you can see Mickey hidden all over in the carpet pattern. *

378. Look at the lamps in the exterior corridors for Mickey.

❖ **Disney's Paradise Pier Hotel**

379. Look down at the carpet for a swirly Mickey-head pattern.

380. The map on the wall in the lobby says "You are here" and has a Mickey head to indicate your location.

381. Go into the arcade and look for palm tree accents on the walls. The tops are Mickey heads.

382. The rooms have artwork hanging on the walls. A certain picture of *California Adventure's Paradise Pier* displays the old Mickey head in the *California Screamin'* loop.

383. Halfway down the hallway to the back there is a painting on the wall that says "Hot Dog" in it. Look at the designs to either side of the sign for the Mickey.

384. The toiletries, like the shampoo bottles, have Mickey head caps.

385. The beds have a bed scarf with Mickey-head circle patterns.

386. The elevator walls have surf boards painted on them. Look closely at the designs on some of the boards to spot a Mickey.

387. The hallway carpet has little Mickey speckled about.

388. When you take a dip in the pool, check out the railing surrounding it.

389. On the doors to the gym, there is a Mickey-shaped window cutout. There are also Mickey heads around the door frame.

390. Along the sidewalk behind the hotel there are Mickey heads on top of the barrier posts.

391. The entry doors to *Disney's PCH Grill* have art designs on them and hidden within the patterns is a Mickey.

392. Inside *Disney's PCH Grill,* a Mickey head can be found on the heat lamps above the buffet line.

393. Some of the molding around the walls in *Disney's PCH Grill* have Mickey designs on them.

394. The condiment holders on the tables in *Disney's PCH Grill* have a Mickey head for a handle.

395. While enjoying your food in *Disney's PCH Grill*, check out the kites toward the ceiling. One of them has a HM.

❖ **Disneyland Hotel - Adventure Tower** (previously *Dreams* Tower, previously *Sierra* Tower)

- *NOTE*: No Mickeys noted since the tower changed from *Dreams* to *Adventure* after the renovation.

❖ **Disneyland Hotel - Frontier Tower** (previously *Wonder* Tower, previously *Bonita* Tower)

396. The Driveway gate has a Mickey on the face of it.

397. In the lobby, you can find clusters of foot stools surrounding lounge chairs that form Mickey.

398. There is a model of *Big Thunder Mountain Railroad* in the lobby. Look at the first big lift. There is a Mickey made out of cogs. This actually represents a Mickey found on the real attraction in the same spot.

399. Down the hall from the lobby there is a western street scene painting on the wall. Look for the woman walking with two small children. Now, look at the polka dots on her dress.

400. Go up the stairwell to check out the painting on the wall of the past attractions. Look at the passengers of the *Mine Train Ride* for a pair of Mickey ears.

401. On the same painting, check out the *Stage Coach Ride* for another pair of Mickey ears.

402. Near this painting there is a Cast Member-only door with a half Mickey head push plate on it.

❖ **Disneyland Hotel - Fantasy Tower** (previously *Magic* Tower, previously *Marina* Tower)

403. Just off of the main tower is the *Grand Ballroom*. The blue carpet in the lobby has a giant golden HM.

404. All throughout the tower, you can find gold swirl patterns in the blue carpet that are HMs.

405. The blue, red, and gold chairs in the *Convention Center* have little golden Mickey on the tassel pattern.

406. Near the lobby there is a Disneyana Display with lots of Disney merchandise from the past almost 90 years. Look closely to find HMs hidden within the antiques.

407. The hot tub in front of the tower is shaped like a Minnie head with the blue cement and brickwork. You can even spot Minnie's polka dot bow.

408. Pop into *Goofy's Theater* to watch a film, or check out the Mickey in the carpet pattern.

409. On the ceiling at the top of the stairwell that connects *Fantasy Tower* to the *Sleeping Beauty Pavilion,* there is a giant Mickey head surrounded by smaller Mickey heads.

410. At the top of this banister, there is a brass Mickey head next to the railing.

411. Just outside the tower, you can spot a topiary (shaped and trimmed bush/plant) of Mickey, Minnie, and Pluto.

412. The bellman luggage carts have Mickey heads near the handles.

413. The hotel's parking lot has old-fashioned light poles with Mickey heads on top.

414. In the guest rooms, the headboards have etchings in the wood. If you find the one with the Sleeping Beauty Castle, check out the fireworks. One pattern forms a Mickey.

415. In the guest bathrooms, the faucet handles have Mickey heads.

416. On both sides of the bathroom mirror are lamps with Mickey heads in the lamp shades. You can also see Mickey's hand holding the lamps.

417. The bedroom's desk lamp has a Mickey head in the metal work of the lamp's base.

418. The lamp hoods above the pay phones have little holes punched in them to release the light. They are in the shape of a Mickey.

419. If you can actually make it into the penthouse, the inset ceiling is a Mickey, with color-changing mood lighting.

PARADES

Disneyland and *California Adventure* have had many parades come and go over the years. This list is almost impossible to keep current. Check the show schedules when you arrive at the park or online to find out what will be running at that time.

One time, Disney held a parade outside the park. It was in New Orleans. Disney held a parade through the French Quarter before having the premier of *The Hunchback of Notre Dame* on six giant screens in the Superdome on June 19, 1996.

I am please to share with you a full listing of all the parades, with most of their descriptions provided by Chris Lyndon. He is the Disney historian, site moderator, and producer for *DisneyChris.com*. His website has full audio tracks from just about every location in the park, with new audio adventures getting added all the time. The current inventory is at 1,300 audio tracks.

1. Main Street March - The Disneyland Band

Heard here is the original Disneyland Band conducted by Vessy Walker. This march was composed especially for *Main Street, U.S.A.* back in the 1950's. It was first heard on the 1954 broadcast of the Disneyland TV series as Walt showed a scale model of Main Street. The Band would often play it live in the park, as well, during the earlier years.

2. Disneyland Grand Opening Parade - National Emblem March

Disneyland's very first parade was held on opening day, July 17th 1955. At the head of the procession was the United States Marine Corp Band, who played the familiar "National Emblem March" as they made their way down Main Street, U.S.A. They were then followed by many costumed representatives from each of the four lands in the park.

3. The Firehouse 5 Plus 2 - Main Street Parade

One of the first musical groups to perform in a Disneyland parade, which, in the beginning only had live music, was a group of Dixielanders known as the *Firehouse 5 Plus 2*. This talented troupe was comprised of members from Walt Disney's animation staff, and were favorite parade guest stars from opening day, well into the 1970's.

4. The Disneyland Circus Calliope

A genuine 1907, steam-powered, 20-whistle circus calliope was personally purchased by Walt Disney for use in *Disneyland*, and was fully restored for its first appearance in the 1955 Mickey Mouse Club Circus Parade. It would also appear in the 1960 feature film "Toby Tyler" and is often used for parades and special events to this day.

5. Automobile Club Parade

Throughout the 1950's, Walt Disney invited local antique automobile restoration club members to *Disneyland* to participate in processions down Main Street, U.S.A. sporting their vintage cars while dressed in period appropriate costumes.

Due to their popularity, these events also became part of the annual Easter Parade tradition.

6. Christmas in Many Lands Parade

Beginning in 1957, an annual parade was held during the Christmas season, featuring the dances, costumes, music, and customs of many foriegn nations. Dozens of civic organizations were invited to participate, many traveling to *Disneyland* from their home countries. International sections were also featured in many other early parades.

7. Zorro Days Parade

Zorro was a highly-rated weekly TV show produced by the Disney Studio for prime-time television in the 1950's. During the run of this popular program, the actual stars of the show, including the masked avenger himself, portrayed by Guy Williams, made special guest appearances in *Disneyland* which always included a parade down Main Street, U.S.A.

8. Disneyland '59 - Gala Day Parade

To herald in a major expansion of *Disneyland* in 1959, a lavish parade was presented for live TV. In addition to a land-by-land tribute, and a parade of many land segments, three special floats represented the new attractions that were officially dedicated that day, including the *Monorail* System, *Matterhorn Bobsleds* and *Submarine Voyage*.

9. Mickey at the Movies Parade - Disneyland Parade Anthem 1960-1964

Disneyland's first regularly-scheduled daily parade was known as the "Mickey at the Movie's Parade," which included a colorful cavalcade of Disney characters from Walt Disney's film classics. For the first time, the parade was led off by The Big Bass Drum, which would become a *Disneyland* parade tradition in the years to follow.

10. Parade of the Toys

During the 1960 Christmas season, *Disneyland* would present its very first, regularly-scheduled holiday parade, featuring many of the giant toy props that had been created for the upcoming theatrical release of "Babes in Toyland," which was still in production. This was also the first appearance by *Disneyland's* iconic marching wooden soldiers.

11. Anaheim High School Marching Band

Yet another parade tradition began by Walt Disney was the inclusion of many local high school marching bands. Naturally, one of the most frequent participants in these events was the local Anaheim High School. Over time, these invitations would extend well beyond Southern California to include bands from all over the United States.

12. Fantasy on Parade - Introduction

The first Fantasy on Parade was held during the 1965 Christmas season and became a long-standing holiday time tradition for decades to come. The parade always featured dozens upon dozens of classic Disney characters, and concluded with the march of the toy soldiers from Babes in Toyland, followed by Santa Claus and his jolly reindeer.

13. Fantasy on Parade 1965-1976

Fantasy on Parade was showcased on TV, in its entirety, on a 1966 episode of the *Wonderful World of Color* entitled, "Disneyland Around the Seasons." At this time, the music heard during the actual parade was all performed live, but for the special TV broadcast, a fully-orchestrated musical score provided the accompaniment.

14. Small World Opening Day Parade

To usher in the premiere of *it's a small world* in *Disneyland*, a gala parade was held in 1966. It included echoes of parades past by yet again inviting local civic organizations to share the customs of their native lands through costume dance and procession. The event culminated in a special opening day ceremony at the Small World waterways.

15. The Love Bug Parade

In 1969, a special parade was held to promote the new Disney live-action comedy *The Love Bug*. Anyone who wanted to participate was invited to decorate their own Volkswagen Beetle for entry in a contest for most original design. The parade proved so popular, that it returned in 1974 to promote the film's sequel... *Herbie Rides Again*.

16. The Kids of the Kingdom - I Love a Parade

The young singing troupe, known as the Kids of the Kingdom, were featured in many parades over the years, often providing vocals for various prerecorded soundtracks. For their album produced for *Buena Vista Records*, they recorded many songs they often performed live in the park, including the definitive parade anthem, "I Love a Parade."

17. The Disneyland Band - Main Street Marching Medley

The Disneyland Band has been marching all over *Disneyland* since the very day it first opened in 1955, and the electric thrill of seeing them promenade down Main Street, U.S.A. has most certainly not diminished over time. Often, Mickey Mouse himself will lead the procession as excited on-lookers have to fight not to crack a wide-eyed grin.

18. Fantasy on Parade - Walt Disney Production's 50th Anniversary

The annual Fantasy on Parade remained a holiday tradition throughout the 1970's as new scenes were added every year. In 1973, the parade was led off by a special float honoring the 50th anniversary of *Walt Disney Productions* and included characters from the latest animated feature, *Robin Hood*, with Prince John's royal procession.

19. The Mike Curb Congregation - The Best of Disney

In the mid-1970's, the popular singing group Mike Curb Congregation released a hit record covering the "Mickey Mouse Club March" with a contemporary beat, followed by an entire album of Disney songs. To stay current, *Disneyland*

382

adapted their music for use in many of its character parades throughout the 1970's.

20. Mickey's Character Parade

The much-publicized splendor of a *Disneyland* parade gave guests an expectation that one would be presented on the day of their visit, be it any day throughout the year. This gave rise to the afternoon Character Parade, which involved prerecorded music, simple, albeit colorfully-decorated floats, and dozens of costumed Disney characters.

21. The Kids of the Kingdom - America on Parade Medley

The ever-popular Kids of the Kingdom were the lead act to *Disneyland's* bicentennial extravaganza, America on Parade. On a pre-show float decorated with stars and stripes, they performed two songs as they traveled down Main Street, U.S.A., a new song by the Sherman Brothers called "The Glorious Fourth," and a Broadway showtune called "Freedom."

22. America on Parade 1975

America on Parade is one of *Disneyland's* most fondly-remembered parades of all time. This bicentennial extravaganza was also one of the most elaborate parades that Disney has ever staged. Each float represented an important event in American history, and was surrounded by hundreds of stylized costumed figures with giant-sized heads.

23. The Sadie Mae

America on Parade also featured the musical sounds of the Sadie Mae, a fully restored, antique carousel band organ. It was shipped from its Missouri home to a sound studio in Nashville, where the entire soundtrack was recorded. The music was then enhanced with electronic synthesized elements, but heard here is the original unaltered version.

24. Pooh for President Parade

America's favorite bear first tossed his hat into the presidential ring in 1968, and ran again for the following two elections. For his 1972 campaign, a special parade was held in *Disneyland*, featuring Pooh and all his friends from the Hundred Acre Wood. The parade returned again in 1976, with a catchy new campaign song by Larry Groce.

25. Festival Japan Parade

Special weekend events were often presented during *Disneyland's* off-season to attract guests with limited time to the park for unique, entertainment offerings. Festival Japan was one of many annual events started in the 1970's, celebrating the culture of other world nations, each with historical and demographical ties to Southern California.

26. Festival Mexico Parade

Festival Mexico was another annual event held during *Disneyland's* off-season, which celebrated both the culture of another nation and the diversity of Southern California. Each of these festivals included traditional folk music, arts and crafts displays with native artisans, and naturally, everything culminated in a special parade.

27. Mickey Mouse 50th Birthday Parade

One of *Disneyland's* most memorable parades was held in honor of Mickey's 50th birthday in 1978. It was the highlight of several special events held throughout the park celebrating the Main Mouse's big 5-0. It also began the tradition of staging parades to mark significant Disney milestones that continues to this day.

28. The Disneyland Parade Song

The memorable theme song originally featured in the Mickey Mouse 50th birthday parade truly did epitomize the spirit of a *Disneyland* parade, and so, with slightly altered lyrics it would outlive the run of the birthday parade. Over time, it has become a sort-of theme song, often used to represent *Disneyland* parades for special promotions.

29. Dumbo Circus Parade

In 1979, Disneyland presented a colorful parade filled with the many memorable circus characters from Walt Disney's 1941 animated classic *Dumbo*. The parade also featured live animals, silly clowns, acrobatic stunts, and a special appearance by Dumbo, located atop a burning firehouse tower, poised to take flight with his magic feather.

30. *Disneyland's* 25th Anniversary Family Reunion Parade 1980

Disneyland's 25th Anniversary Parade mirrored the original 1955 opening day parade in that it also contained sections representing each of the park's themed lands. In addition to live music, several pre-recorded medleys accompanied the floats for each themed section, and tieing it together was the original theme song... "Disneyland is Your Land."

31. The All-American College Marching Band

Every summer, *Disneyland* hosts a performing arts internship program, and undergrad students are given real-world experience as they perform in various venues throughout the park. A crowd favorite is the All-American College Marching Band. In addition to traditional marches, they perform popular songs in a range of musical styles.

32. It's a Small World Parade

Harkening back to the earlier Christmas in Many Lands parades, in 1981 *Disneyland* presented yet another internationally-themed daily procession down Main Street, U.S.A. Dancers as well as Disney characters were dressed in costumes from countries around the world, and "It's a Small World" served as appropriate theme music.

33. Flights of Fantasy Parade 1983

When *Disneyland's* all-new *Fantasyland* premeired in 1983, a special parade was held to commemorate the grand opening event. The procession was filled with colorful, giant balloons, dozens of beloved Disney characters, and

384

whimsical floats representing scenes straight out of the classic animated films represented in the new *Fantasyland*.

34. American Gazette Parade

The American Gazette Parade was a celebration of the ever-evolving musical genres and popular dance styles that spanned the decades of the 20th century. Setting this parade apart from all others produced during this time, the music was performed entirely live, calling on the talents of *Disneyland's* many in-house musical groups.

35. Donald Duck's 50th Birthday Parade 1984

In 1984, Donald Duck celebrated his 50th birthday. To commemorate this milestone event, a colorful new parade was held at *Disneyland* honoring everyone's favorite web-footed friend. The parade's infectious theme song, "Happy, Happy Birthday to You," was originally featured on the popular 1983 *Disneyland* record album... *Splashdance*.

36. Disneyland's 30th Anniversary Parade

1985 marked the 30th anniversary year of *Disneyland*. In commemoration, a year-long celebration was held throughout the entire park. Every 30th guest was awarded a special prize from the Gift-Giver Extraordinaire located at the main entrance turnstile, and highlighting the entire event was a colorful parade down Main Street, U.S.A.

37. Disneyland's 30th Anniversary - Disney Family Cavalcade

As part of the 30th anniversary festivities, *Disneyland* held a special event in order to recognize the many thousands of workers who had brought magic to millions of visitors over the past three decades. Along with their families, all past and present Cast Members were invited to participate in a parade down Main Street, U.S.A.

38. Circus Fantasy - Come to the Circus Parade

In 1986, the tradition, splendor and color of an old-fashioned circus parade returned to *Disneyland* as part of a park-wide special promotional event called Circus Fantasy. The parade included live animals, including marching elephants with Minnie riding atop the lead pachyderm. Goofy played the strong man and Mickey the Ringmaster.

39. Totally Minnie Parade 1986

Minnie was always more than happy to be Mickey's romantic sidekick, but in 1986 it was finally her turn to be in the spotlight. It was declared the "Year of Minnie," and a contemporary pop music album entitled *Totally Minnie* was released on Disneyland Records. A special Minnie parade was also featured at *Disneyland* all year long.

40. The Disneyland State Fair - Come to the Fair Parade 1987-1988

In 1987, a special park-wide promotional event took place called the *Disneyland* State Fair. Throughout the park, venues were overlayed with traditional state fair exhibits and themed entertainment. A highlight was the State Fair Parade, which included dancing farm crops, Minnie's blue ribbon pies, and barnyard animals.

385

41. Snow White's Golden Anniversary Celebration Parade 1987

In 1987, the first ever full-length animated feature, Walt Disney's *Snow White and the Seven Dwarfs*, celebrated its 50th anniversary. During the year, a special cavalcade was presented featuring all of the beloved characters and memorable music from the classic film. Goofy would introduce the processsion with a royal proclamation.

42. The Very Merry Christmas Parade 1965-1976

After a three-year hiatus, the popular Fantasy on Parade would return to *Disneyland* for the 1980 holiday season, and like its predecessor, the parade included several scenes from classic Disney films. The parade remained much the same when it became the Very Merry Christmas Parade in 1987, but additional scenes were added over time.

43. Blast to the Past Parade 1988

In 1988, Disneyland joined the "Back to the Future" craze with a special event held park-wide known as the Blast to the Past. A central element of this celebration of 1950's music and pop culture was a lively parade featuring a giant jukebox, drag racers and a far-out finale with Martian monsters and Mickey blasting off in a Rocket Ship.

44. Blast to the Past Parade - TV Land Medley

Perhaps the most nostalgic moment from season one of the Blast to the Past parade, was a segment dedicated to classic 1950's TV, featuring a procession of performers dressed as classic characters from television shows of the past, including *The Lone Ranger*, *The Three Stooges*, *Superman*, the *Mickey Mouse Club* and *I Love Lucy*.

45. Blast to the Past Parade - Encore Season

After a successful first year, Blast to the Past would return for a second season in 1989. A brand-new parade was presented with an upbeat new soundtrack that incorporated familiar songs from the musicals *Grease* and *Hairspray* along with several classic rock'n roll tunes. The parade ended with Goofy dressed as Elvis Presley.

46. Blast to the Past - The Main Street Hop

In addition to a traditional parade, the Blast to the Past event also hosted a '50's style sock hop street party. Twice daily, a series of jukebox-shaped floats stopped along the center of Main Street, U.S.A. as bobby sox girls in poodle skirts and guys in letterman sweaters danced along to many memorable tunes from the early days of Rock 'n' Roll.

47. The Main Street Parade

This short-lived mini parade, or cavalcade which paid tribute to Main Street, U.S.A. featured the song, "I'm Walking Right Down the Middle of Main Street, U.S.A." and other 20th century musical standards. Disney characters were dressed in period costumes and Mickey tickled the ivories on a special piano fashioned with bicycle wheels.

386

48. Mickey's 60th Birthday Parade 1988-1989

In 1988, Mickey celebrated his 60th Birthday, and again, an elaborate procession was presented daily up and down Main Street, U.S.A., honoring the lovable mouse who started it all. The parade featured zany costumes and silly mice from around the world, traveling by train, boat, auto, and airplane, to join the Big Cheese in his *Disneyland* celebration.

49. Mickey's 60th Birthday Bash

During Mickey's 60th Birthday event, between showings of the afternoon parade, a special birthday party was staged along Main Street, U.S.A. twice every day. A large birthday cake topped by Mickey Mouse and filled with Mouseketeer-costumed dancers would stop at several points along the parade route for a live, 15-minute musical show.

- Movie Premiere Pre-Parades -

Disney frequently leads off its full-scale parades with what are often referred to as pre-parades. These are used to entertain guests while they wait for the main event, and often promote the studio's latest releases coming to theaters soon. For many, this would be their first introduction to the songs and characters from these future classics. For a time in the 1980's, re-releases of classic animated features also had special pre-parades.

50. The Little Mermaid - Pre-Parade

51. The Jungle Book - Pre-Parade

52. Peter Pan - Pre-Parade

53. Ratatouille - Pre-Parade

54. Chronicles of Narnia: Prince Caspian - Pre-Parade

55. Hooray for Disney Stars Parade

In 1989, Disneyland presented a special parade featuring the stars from its new lineup of popular animated TV series, including *Ducktales*, *Chip 'n Dale's Rescue Rangers*, and the *Adventures of the Gummi Bears*. Also included was movie producer Roger Rabbit and other Disney characters dressed in Hollywood grand premiere attire.

- Tournament of Roses Parade -

Disneyland has had a long relationship with the famous Tournament of Roses Parade held in nearby Pasadena, California, every January, with its first float entry in 1955 announcing the impending premiere of *Disneyland* that following summer. Walt Disney himself was the parade Grand Marshall in 1966, and Mickey Mouse received the same honor in 2005 as part of *Disneyland's* 50th anniversary celebration.

56. Tournament of Roses - The Royal Court

57. Tournament of Roses - 35 Years of Magic

58. Tournament of Roses - Welcome to Toontown

59. Tournament of Roses - 40 Years of Adventure

60. Tournament of Roses - Welcome to Our Family

61. Tournament of Roses - 60 Years of Magic

62. Party Gras Parade 1990

Disneyland's 35th anniversary was celebrated with a lavish parade recreating the fun and excitement of a South American carnival, where guests were encouraged to come out into the streets and dance along to the Latin beat. Another memorable feature were the towering floats that carried inflated Disney characters measuring over 40 feet high.

63. Desert Storm Parade

Disneyland has always been considered one of the most patriotic places in the United States, and over the years it has often celebrated the brave men and woman who have served in the U.S. armed services. A special parade was held in 1991 when battlefront troops returned home from the Gulf War following the end of Operation Desert Storm.

64. Celebration USA Parade 1991

By the early '90's, as the demand for daily parades grew, there arose a slight dilemma. Most of the parades at this time had been tied into special anniversary milestones, so when these anniversaries ended, temporary parades had to be quickly put together as inbetweeners. Celebration USA is a good example of one of these short-lived parades.

65. Disney Afternoon Cavalcade

Coinciding with a 1991 promotional overlay located in northern *Fantasyland*, a small procession was presented several times daily, traveling down "Afternoon Avenue" and Main Street, U.S.A. The mini-parade featured everyone's favorite characters from Disney's *Gummi Bears*, *Ducktales*, *Tale Spin* and *Chip 'n Dale's Rescue Rangers*.

66. The World According to Goofy Parade 1992

1992 marked the 60th birthday of Goofy, and it was finally his turn to have a special parade dedicated in his honor. Quite appropriately, the parade took on a comical tone, following the evolution of Goofy's ancestors from the Stone Age to the present, where a modern-day Goofy ran as a candidate for president of *Disneyland*.

67. Aladdin's Royal Caravan 1993-1994

This popular parade was based on a scene straight out of the 1992 animated feature film *Aladdin*, in which the magic Genie organizes an over-the-top royal procession for Aladdin to impress the Princess Jasmine. Upon the success of this parade, a tradition began of producing parades to usher in their latest animated release.

68. Lion King Celebration Parade 1994-1997

This musical celebration brought to life all of the memorable scenes and characters from the 1994 Disney blockbuster film *The Lion King*. The process of transforming what was originally an animated feature into a three-dimensional live performance would later inspire the production of a 1997 Tony Award winning Broadway musical.

69. Cruisin' the Kingdom Parade 1997

Another short-lived, and yet quite popular inbetween parade, was the aptly named Cruisin' the Kingdom cavalcade. The procession featured an array of familiar Disney charcters, each seated in their own souped-up and fully restored classic model hot rod, as they cruised their way up and down *Matterhorn Way* and *Main Street, U.S.A.*

70. Hunchback of Notre Dame Topsy Turvy Cavalcade

Disney's 34th full-length animated feature, The Hunchback of Notre Dame, became the subject matter for a very popular live outdoor arena show presented in the northern end of *Frontierland*. To promote the show, several performers would be featured in a small cavalcade down Main Street, U.S.A, recreating the colorful Festival of Fools scene.

71. Hercules Victory Parade 1997-1998

This colorful and comical parade was based on the 1997 animated feature *Hercules*, and although it was set in ancient Greece, like the film, the parade featured all manor of modern-day references and tongue-in-cheek humor. The musical score came directly from the film as well, featuring several uplifting Gospe- inspired numbers.

72. Mulan Parade 1998-1999

Inspired by the 1998 Disney animated feature *Mulan*, this parade took its thematic inspiration from the ancient traditions of China. In addition to the characters from the film, the procession also presented traditional Chinese dancers in authentic costumes, skilled tumblers and acrobats, colorful dragons, and marching Chinese warriors.

73. Rainy Day Cavalcade

To brighten the day of those visiting *Disneyland* during inclement weather, a convoy of Main Street vehicles is packed with colorful Disney friends for a special mini-parade. Since this practice began around the year 2000, various pieces of music, originally produced for other live events, have been borrowed for this small procession.

74. Parade of the Stars (45 Years Of Magic Parade) 2000-2005

This long-running parade, celebrating many of Walt Disney's animated film classics, debuted in the year 2000 as the "45 Years of Magic Parade." When *Disneyland's* 45th anniversary year ended, by popular demand it was given an extended engagement, and continued for another four years under the name... Parade of the Stars.

75. Mickey's Shining Star Cavalcade

Because guests expect a parade every day they visit Disneyland, in 2004 a series of cavalcades, or mini parades, were presented on weekdays and in the off-season as *Disneyland* slowly phased out its long-running Parade of the Stars and preparations were underway for an all-new parade in honor of the upcoming 50th anniversary.

76. Mickey's Magic Kingdom Celebration

There were three interim cavalcades held during various periods throughout 2004. One of these was known as Mickey's Magic Kingdom Celebration, which was a musical tribute to the themed lands of *Disneyland*. A choreographed dance number, with the Disney characters, was performed at various points along the parade route.

77. Disneyland's 50th Anniversary - Parade of Dreams 2005-2009

2005 would mark the 50th magical year of *Disneyland*. In celebration of this milestone, an all-new parade was staged featuring everyone's favorite Disney friends in a magical musical march down Main Street, U.S.A. The parade's lively and welcoming theme song was originally featured in the 2003 Disney animated feature film... *Brother Bear*.

78. Year of a Million Dreams - Grand Marshal Cavalcade

Running from October 2007 through December 2008, *Disneyland* celebrated what was called "A Year of a Million Dreams," a promotional campaign granting park Guests an array of prizes, from free vacations to overnight stays inside the park. Each day one lucky family was chosen to be honorary grand marshals in the Main Street parade.

79. Celebrate! A Street Party

In 2009, a new street show, honoring the personal celebrations of that day's *Disneyland* Guests, was presented along the traditional parade route. The procession would pause at three prime viewing locations where an energeric dance show would ensue, encouraging spectators to dance and sing along to popular hits and Disney favorites.

80. Frozen Pre-Parade

The overwhelming and unexpected box office success of Disney's 2013 animated feature *Frozen,* sparked a high public demand to meet the new Princesses Anna and Elsa. In order to give all park Guests a chance to see these popular new Disney stars, a special pre-parade became the prelude to the Soundsational Parade beginning in 2014.

81. Mickey's Soundsational Parade

Disneyland's newest daytime parade ranks as one of its all-time most popular. This energetic and colorful extravaganza showcases some of the greatest musical moments from Walt Disney's classic films, and features countless Disney characters, both old and new, in an eye-popping celebration of musical styles from around the world.

82. **Candlelight Procession 1958**

83. **Main Street Electrical Parade 1972-1975**

84. **Main Street Electrical Parade 1977-1983**

85. **Main Street Electrical Parade 1985-1996**

86. **Disney's Electrical Parade 2001-2010**

87. **Main Street Electrical Parade 2017**

88. **Paint The Night 2015-2016**

89. **Fantasy On Parade 1980-1985**

90. **Very Merry Christmas Parade 1983**

91. **Hooray For Disneywood! 1989-1990**

92. **A Christmas Fantasy Parade 1994**

93. **A Christmas Fantasy Parade 2004**

94. **Light Magic 1997**

95. **Circus On Parade 1986-1988**

PARADES OF CALIFORNIA ADVENTURE

96. **Disney's Eureka! A California Parade 2001–2002**

A parade celebrating diversity and cultures of California.

97. **Disney's Electrical Parade 2001–2010**

A nighttime parade featuring floats covered in lights. Originally known as the Main Street Electrical Parade, this parade ran at Disneyland from 1972–1996 and at Walt Disney World's Magic Kingdom from 1999–2001. After its run at Disney California Adventure ended, the parade relocated back to the Magic Kingdom, where it ran, under its original name, from 2010-2016. It currently runs at Disneyland Park until August 2017

98. **Block Party Bash 2005–2008**

A parade featuring characters and floats based on Pixar films. The parade relocated to Disney's Hollywood Studios after its run at Disney California Adventure ended, and ran there until 2011.

99. **High School Musical Pep Rally 2006–2007**

A traveling street show based on the High School Musical film.

100. **High School Musical 2: School's Out! 2007–2008**

A traveling street show based on the High School Musical 2 film.

101. **High School Musical 3 Senior Year! 2008–2010**

Themed for "*High School Musical 3: Senior Year,*" the show features a traveling rock concert stage with stacked speakers and rows of lights. The cast of 14 singers and dancers will perform songs from the latest High School Musical movie.

102. Pixar Play Parade – 2008-Present

The Pixar Play Parade was introduced in March 2008 as part of the *Disneyland* Resort's Year of a Million Dreams celebration. The parade features characters from all of the Disney-Pixar movies, many of them aboard playful floats outfitted with a number of surprises to delight and entertain guests. The talents of dancers, stilt walkers, acrobats, puppeteers, and bungee-jumpers are also featured.

103. Phineas and Ferb's Rockin' Rollin' Dance Party 2011–2014

A traveling street show based on the series Phineas and Ferb.

PENNY SMASHING & OTHER SOUVIENERS

If you like to collect Disney things, this is an awesome place to get them. I collect shot glasses, magnets, smashed pennies, antenna balls, and little figurines. Each time you visit the parks, you will always find new items to buy or collect. The cheapest souvenirs to collect are the smashed pennies. They cost 51¢ to make. There are (I was told by a Cast Member) about 50 different penny-smashing machines around the parks. Each one smashes a different looking penny. There are also quarter smashing machines; they cost $1.00 in quarters. The *Penny Arcade* on *Main Street, U.S.A.* has lots of these machines. The rest are scattered throughout the different lands in both parks. From a gift shop, you can also purchase a smashed penny passport (booklet)

with little pockets in it to store the pennies.

A more expensive but permanent souvenir was the paver stone. The stones are located in the space between *Disneyland* and *California Adventure*. But, in 2010

392

they discontinued this offer. Keep an eye open for the future in case they offer them again.

For a free souvenir, you can go to the *Main Street City Hall* or the *Customer Service Center* in *California Adventure* and tell them you are there for a special engagement. You will receive a free button. They have many to choose from and many added all the time.

Birthday	1st Time Visitor	Honorary Citizen
Engagement	Big Dreams	Family Reunion
Just Married	Celebration	Fairy Tale Fantasy

If you have a Birthday, Engagement or Just Married button on, all the Cast Members say congratulations or happy birthday to you all day.

If you enjoyed the music from all the shows and attractions inside *Disneyland*, there is a 6-disc CD set that you can purchase called *A Musical History of Disneyland*. They have the recordings of the entire attraction, including the animatronics dialogue, like in *Pirates of the Caribbean*, *The Tiki Room* and *The Haunted Mansion*. You may be able to find them inside the stores in the park or you may have to look online.

The Mickey Ears hats are considered to be the most popular *Disneyland* souvenier.

(magnets, shot glasses, antennae balls)

If there is a specific item or souvenir that you wanted or forgot to pick up, call DelivEARS at 1-800-362-4533 to have it shipped via UPS. They will find the item and mail it to you.

PIN TRADING

Disney Pin Trading is the buying and trading of collectible pins and related items featuring Disney characters, attractions, icons, and other elements. Many thousands of unique pins have been created over the years.

Pins are available for a limited time; the base price for a pin is **$8.99**. Limited edition pins, and special pins (e.g. pins that have a dangle, pin-on-pin, flocking, lenticular, light-up, moving element, 3-D element, etc.) cost up to **$14.99**. Featured Artist and Jumbo Pins cost between **$20** and **$35** and Super Jumbo pins cost upwards of, and sometimes beyond, **$75**. Each guest may purchase up to two pins of each style per day. Pins are frequently released at special events, movie premiers, pin trading events, or to commemorate the opening day of a new attraction. Some pins have appreciated well on the secondary market and have reached prices of over **$500** at venues such as eBay. Most Disney pins are enamel or enamel cloisonné with a metal base. If you need cheap pins to trade with Cast Members or other collectors in the park, search on Ebay or Amazon. It could be the difference between spending $1 and $8 for a pin that you will be trading. Also, make sure that the pins you are purchasing are authentic Disney pins and not knock-offs.

You can also find Disney pin trading or selling Facebook groups. Most of them are private groups that you can ask to join and wait to be approved. The pins for sale generally go up for bid and the one offering the most at the end of the auction wins the pin. I have seen some rare pins sell for over $150 on there.

WARNING: Do not try to collect ALL of the Disney pins as there are over 100,000 and it is pretty much impossible. But please feel free to make an attempt at it.

HISTORY

The first Disney pins showed up in the 1930's with Mickey on them. They were just die-cast with a clasp or brooch-style back. Pins have always been present at Disney parks. But, it wasn't until October 1999, as part of the Millennium Celebration, that Paul Pressler introduced Disney Pin Trading at the *Disneyland* Resort. The next year, the craze spread to the *Walt Disney World Resort*, which has become the home of most Pin Trading events. Since then, Pin Trading has spread to *Disneyland Resort Paris*, *Tokyo Disney Resort*, *Hong Kong Disneyland Resort*, *Disney Cruise Lines*, and *Shanghai Disney*, with each location creating their own pins and traditions. Although the trading of pins has been suspended in *Tokyo Disney Resort*, pins are still offered as prizes at carnival games, and a relatively small number of pins are available. The Cast Member trading lanyards were introduced in 2002 to encourage Guests to trade with them.

PRESENT

In all Disney resorts, a large variety of pins are available for purchase and trade. Most merchandise Cast Members wear pins on lanyards around their necks, or on a pin display card (a 4" by 5" piece of colored nylon fabric) clipped to their belt. Additional Cast Members may wear lanyards if pin trading does not distract from their responsibilities; some managers choose to wear lanyards, but attraction operators are not permitted to do so. Some Cast Members wear a teal-colored lanyard at *Disneyland* and a green lanyard at *Walt Disney World* with pins only tradable to children (12 years or younger). Each lanyard contains around a dozen unique pins, and Cast Members must trade with guests if they are presented with an acceptable pin. Each guest may only trade with the same Cast Member twice in one day.

Pin Collectors can customize displaying their pins because of the wide variety of pin products Disney produces. Lanyards are available in a wide variety of colors and designs as are lanyard medals. There are many ways to store and display collectable pins: pin bags, notebooks, frames, and cork boards. Collectors can be very creative in displaying their pins and are often easy to spot in the parks with their pin-covered vests, hats, lanyards, and fanny packs.

LOCATIONS

Pins can now be found in almost all of the resort's 50+ boutiques around the world, but several locations have been given the special privilege to host "Pin Trading Super Stations," where a much larger collection is available, along with facilities for trading and displaying the latest releases. These can currently be found at:

- Little Green Men Store Command: *Tomorrowland*
- The Star Trader: *Tomorrowland*
- The Emporium: *Main Street USA*
- Guest Relations: *Main Street USA* (they keep a pin book for trading)
- Pin Cart: *Main Street USA* (near *Gibson Girl Ice Cream Parlor*)
- Pooh Corner: *Critter Country*
- Westward Ho: *Frontierland*
- Pioneer Merchantile: *Frontierland*
- Gag Factory/Toontown Five and Dime: *Toontown*
- Adventureland Bazarr: *Adventureland*
- Julius Katz and Sons: *Buena Vista Street*
- Big Top Toys: *Buena Vista Street*
- Fly and Buy: *Grizzly Peak and Grizzly Peak Airfield*
- Rushin' River Outfitters: *Grizzly Peak* and *Grizzly Peak Airfield*
- Off the Page: *Hollywood area*
- Embarcadero Store: *Pacific Wharf Area*
- Sideshow Shirts: *Paradise Pier*

TRADING ETIQUETTE

When you're out and about Pin Trading in the parks, don't forget the following etiquette when you ask to trade with a fellow Guest or Cast Member:

- Only Disney pins will be accepted for trading: they must be made of metal and represent a Disney event, place, character, movie, or icon.
- Pins should be in good, undamaged condition.
- Trade one pin at a time, hand to hand, with the backs attached.
- Guests may trade a maximum of two pins with each Cast Member per day, and only one pin of the same style.
- When trading with Cast Members, guests can only offer a pin that is not already displayed on the Cast Member's lanyard.
- Refrain from touching another person's pins or lanyard. If you need a closer look, ask the person wearing the lanyard if they can show it to you.

PIN TYPES

There are many different types of pins. Each pin is valued differently. Try to do your research online before making a trade to find the value of a pin. These are the most common types of pins.

◊ **Cast Exclusive Pin / Cast Lanyard:** Cast Exclusive pins are only available for Cast Members to purchase backstage, whilst Cast Lanyard pins are given to Cast Members to place on their lanyards to trade with guests.

◊ **Chaser Pin:** These pins are rare and induce a "chase" to find them. They look like a pin from a set of pins, but they aren't colored in. It is just metal. (*see photo*)

◊ **Dangle Pin:** A pin with extra metal elements dangling from the pin by one or more loops or chains. (*see photo*)

◊ **Embedded Pin:** These pins generaly have jewels or hard plastic pieces, like a rose that Belle holds.

◊ **F.R.E.E.-D Pin:** Free-D stands for "Fastened Rubber Element for Extra Dimension." A pin that feature Free-D elements sometimes have discoloring issues and extra precautions should be taken to make sure that the Free-D element is not dirtied.

◊ **Glow Pin:** These pins will glow in the dark after being exposed to light or blacklight.

◊ **Hidden Mickey Pin:** These pins have a little Mickey Head somewhere on them. They are usually part of a set and will say 1 of 6, 2 of 5, etc. Generally, they are sold through "Mystery Packs," but can then be found through trading with other park guests, Cast Members, or on online auctions. (*see photo*)

◊ **Jumbo Pin:** These pins are very large in comparison to the other pins. They can be three to six inches big. They are also more intricately designed. Most jumbo pins can sell for $20-$40. They are also from a more limited release, sometimes 500-750 of a single design. (*see photo*–4 ¾" x 4 ¼" jumbo

pin-on-pin)

◊ **Hinge Pin:** This pin has an element on it that has a little hinge to open the whole face, or just part of the pin. (*see photo*)

◊ **Fantasy Pin:** A pin commissioned or produced by Disney pin collectors that contains similarities to Disney pins, but has not been created or endorsed by Disney. This could include mixing characters in the same pin, like Mushu and Elsa together, or Stitch with pretty much any other charater. These pins are not allowed to be traded with Cast Members, although collectors may trade for these pins amongst themselves. From time to time, Disney will produce a pin that is very similar to a fantasy pin. Fantasy Pins are not to be mistaken for Scrapper pins because Scrappers are knock-offs of existing Disney-created pins and Fantasy Pins are original and aren't sold as authentic Disney pins. Some Fantasy pin backs even have the artist's website, or some other signature. Fantasy pins can be custom ordered but usually require a minimum of 100 pieces. There are websites you can visit to place a custom order of your own design like *condorcreations.com,* *signaturepins.com,* *montereycompany.com,* or *madebycooper.com.* You can pretty much only find Fantasy Pins on Etsy.com, eBay.com, or in Facebook Fantasy Pin Groups. Just go to those sites and search "Disney Fantasy Pin" and add in a specific character you are looking for. (*see photos*)

◊ **Lenticular Pin:** This pin has two or more images that can change when it is tilted back and forth. (*see photo*)

◊ **Light-Up Pin:** A pin featuring one or more flashing LED elements activated via a small button.

◊ **Limited Edition Pin:** A special pin produced only in limited amounts. The amount and pin number will usually be printed on the back. Generally they will limit you to a certain amount while perchasing.

◊ **Musical Pin:** A pin with a button or switch-activated musical element.

◊ **Mystery Pack Pin:** A new series of pins whereby the only way to purchase the limited releases is through special 'Mystery Pack' boxes or bags. Guests do not know which pin they will receive. Duplicate pins can then be worn on lanyards to trade. Some mystery pins are only available to purchase with another purchase of $30, or similar value.

◊ **Open Edition Pin:** A standard pin with no limited edition value.

◊ **Piece of Disney Movie:** This pin frames a cut of film strip from a peticular movie.

◊ **Piece of History Pin:** A series of pins were produced featuring an attraction along with a piece of the attraction that was removed either during refurbishment or when the attraction was dismantled. The piece of the attraction (which could be a splinter, cut of fabric, crushed plastic, piece of glass, or something else) is secured in a little bubble on the front of the pin. (*see photo*)

◊ **Pin-on-Pin:** A pin with an additional layer, or layers, of metal design on top of the main backing piece, used for 3D effect. (*see photo*)

◊ **Rack Pin:** This is another name for the "Open Edition" pins.

◊ **Scrapper Pin, Bootleg Pin, and Junk Pin:** All names for the same type of pin. These pins are unauthorized pins. Many of the molds Disney uses to make pins are not destroyed after the creation of their pin order. These are the molds used by Disney but then are later used to create bootlegs or knock-offs.

These pins have wormed their way into the parks and secondary markets like eBay with cheap imitations. Some are sold on eBay or found in the parks before the real pins are even released. How you can tell if it's a fake:
• The easiest way to tell is to look at the waffle pattern on the back side. The most common pattern is the Mickey Head,

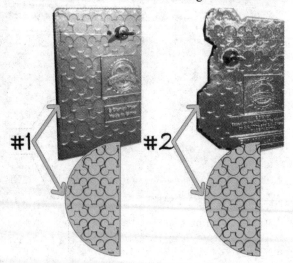

but there can also be Sorcerer Mickey Hats and even ice cream cones. On the real pins, the stamp goes all the way to the edges. On the scrappers, they are cut short of the edge. (*see photo*)

- The colors may not be as bright and vibrant as the real thing.
- The stamp on the back should be legible. Even if the print is small, it can still be read on a real pin.
- On the back of a real pin, there is a prong at the base of the post that is used to keep the pin from spinning.
- The edges of the pin will be sharp. Disney smoothes down their edges.
- Check *pinpics.com* and *disneypins.com* to verify if a pin is real or fake. You can compare the pin in your possession to the one on the site.

◊ **Slider Pin:** A pin with a moveable element that can slide back and forth or pivot across the pin. (*see photo*)

◊ **Spinner Pin:** A pin with an additional element that can be rotated 360°. (*see photo*)

◊ **Spring Pin:** This pin has an element on it that is like a "pin-on-pin" except it is attached with a tiny spring that causes the attached part to bounce around with movement. (*see photo*)

◊ **Surprise/Mystery Pin:** A pin released without first being announced on the official release schedules. Some are part of a special 'Mystery Pins' series, released periodically throughout the year.

CHASER   SPRING   DANGLE   SPINNER   PIN-ON-PIN

SLIDER   HIDDEN MICKEY   PIECE OF HISTORY   VINYLMATION   3D VINYLMATION

F.R.E.E-D   LENTICULAR   GLOW & EMBEDDED   HINGE

◊ **Vinylmation Pins:** The Vinylmation pins are designed after the Vinylmation figures that you can purchase in the parks. Most of them are like the regular metal pins, and some of them are raised with the vinylmation figures mounted on the front to give them the 3D appearance. They are generally released in a collection series. There are over 600 different designs so far. (*see photo*)

PIN TERMINOLOGY

◊ **Artist Proof:** Artist Proof pins (or AP pins) are created during a manufacturing run to verify quality. AP pins have an AP stamped on their back. Generally, 20-24 AP pins are made of each pin per run. Some collectors may value AP pins more than others. You can generally find these on the lanyards of Cast Members.

◊ **Back Stamp:** The stamp on the back of a pin featuring the manufacturer, edition size, and other information.

◊ **Build-A-Pin:** The Build-A-Pin program was introduced in 2002. Guests could personalize pin bases with character add-ons. After selecting their favorite base and add on, the pin was assembled with a special machine. The Build-A-Pin program was retired in summer 2004.

◊ **Cloisonné:** A French word meaning "partitioned." It refers to a style of pin in which the surface decoration is set in designated sections, one color at a time. Cloisonné also refers to a pin type in which crushed minerals and pigments are used to create coloring on a pin. You generally do not find these in *Disneyland*.

◊ **Continuing the Pin Trading Tradition Pin:** Also known as a CTT pin, these annual pins were created for Guest recognition by Cast Members. Guests may be awarded a Continuing the Pin Trading Tradition pin for demonstrating positive Disney Pin Trading etiquette and promoting Disney Pin Trading.

◊ **Die Cast:** Die Cast pins are cast from brass zinc alloy using high-quality hand engraved dies which create an eye-catching, three-dimensional image.

◊ **Epoxy Coating:** Epoxy coating is a glassy, opaque substance used as a decorative or protective coating. When the coating drys, it forms a smooth, glossy surface.

◊ **Flocking:** A flocked pin has an area that is fuzzy.

◊ **Grail Pin:** This is a term used by traders who are looking for a specific pin, a once-in-a-lifetime pin for them. The "Holy grail" of pins to them. It is usually a hard pin to find and the one searching for it is willing to trade lots of pins to get it.

◊ **GWP:** A GWP, or Gift with Purchase, pin is a bonus pin given to Guests who buy at least $25 of pin merchandise in one transaction. The *Disneyland* Resort designates the first Sunday of every month GWP Sunday, and has two collections each year of six pins each. The pins are often traded as lanyard fillers, and as a result they are not valuable initially. *Walt Disney World* has promotions where GWPs are available for $1 each with a $30 purchase.

◊ **Hard Enamel:** Hard Enamel is sometimes called the new cloisonné. It not only retains the characteristics of classic cloisonné, but also provides a much wider selection of colors. Just as with cloisonné, each pin is hand-crafted in a process that begins with a flat piece of brass or nickel which is die-struck and then filled with enamel colors. This pin is then heated, causing the paint to expand. The surface is then hand-polished to give it a smooth, flat finish.

◊ **Lanyard:** A fabric neck band used by Guests and Cast Members to display their pins for trading.

◊ **Limited-Edition Pins:** Limited-Edition pins are just as the name implies, limited. This means there will be an exact number of pins manufactured and sold. The "back stamp" (the text on the back) on the pin will list the edition size. Sometimes, a Limited-Edition pin will be individually-numbered, meaning it will be #XXX of XXX depending on edition size.

◊ **Locking Pin Backs:** These are little metal stubs that replace the rubber backing and have a hex pin that locks down on the stud to keep the pin from easily coming off.

◊ **Mickey's Mystery Pin Machine:** Debuting at *Mouse Gear* in *Epcot* at *WDW* in late 2007, the machines were a modified Gravity Hill arcade machine that dispensed a pin regardless of the outcome. The pins were part of small collections consisting of five pins each. Although the pins originally cost $5 and were distributed randomly, remaining pins were sold as GWP pins and the machines have now been designated as inactive and removed.

◊ **Name Pins:** Name Pins are pins that have a name engraved on them, and may not be traded with Cast Members.

◊ **Pre-Production** or **Prototype Pin:** PP pins are received by product developers prior to a pin being manufactured. These pins sometimes contain different coloring, fills, or features that the final production pin doesn't have. The number depends on what the final product will be, as these pins may be different in size, texture, color, etc. The developers use these "test" pins to determine what the final product will be. Pins from late 2007 now contain a PP stamp on the back. Pins prior to late 2007 may contain a Pre-Production label signifying it is a pre-production pin. Some pins may contain no identification that it is a pre-production pin at all.

◊ **Rack Pins:** Rack pins, also called Open Edition (OE) or core pins, are pins introduced and sold until they are discontinued or retired. These pins are re-ordered for up to several consecutive years. The starting retail price for these pins is typically $8.99 (for a flat pin). Depending upon the number of features on the pin (such as pin-on-pin), the retail price will increase to either $9.99 - $14.99. Some OE pins have a high secondary value, such as the Soda Pop Series pins which can sell in the $20 range.

◊ **Retired Pins:** Retired, or discontinued pins, are pins that are no longer in production. Disney periodically "retires" pins so they can introduce new pins.

◊ **PTN:** Pin Trading Nights are monthly meetings of Disney Pin Traders at *Disneyland*, *Walt Disney World*, or *Disneyland Paris* resorts. The Pin Trading

Team provides pin games and gives traders the opportunity to trade and socialize. Often, a Limited-Edition pin is created to commemorate the occasion.

◊ **Soft Enamel:** A soft enamel pin has the design stamped into the base metal. These pins are filled with enamel colors and baked for durability. A final clear epoxy dome is applied to protect the finish. Typically, a thinner pin than hard enamel pins.

◊ **Surprise or Mystery Pins:** These pins usually feature a low, Limited-Edition size. Typically, the back stamp will include the words "Surprise Pin." The release of this pin happens randomly at various merchandise locations within the Disney Theme Parks and Resorts. Although Surprise Pins have continued at the *Disneyland* Resort, *WDW* rarely releases Surprise Pins.

JEDI TRAINING ACADEMY

For this 15-minute show, 16 or more children are chosen from the audience as Jedi trainees to participate in a training session by the Jedi Master. They are provided training lightsabers and Jedi robes. As the master completes the instruction of a simple combination of lightsaber attacks with the children, Darth Vader, Darth Maul, and a pair of stormtroopers appear. Each Jedi trainee faces off in turn with either Maul or Vader until the villains retreat back to the stage, outnumbered. The children then return the training lightsabers and robes, and are given a diploma for their participation. This interactive show takes place several times a day located on the stage at *Buzz Café*. If you would like your own Jedi or Sith attire, you can go to the *Star Trader* gift shop. There is a section where you can design and build your own lightsaber.

As a Jedi Knight Padawan, you will:

➤ take the Jedi oath

➤ master lightsaber skills

➤ learn moves such as the joust, parry, and block

➤ battle the forces of the dark side, including Stormtroopers, Darth Maul, and Darth Vader

➤ receive a diploma for participation

BIBBIDI BOBBIDI BOUTIQUE

In the *Sleeping Beauty Castle,* there is a very special beauty salon where little girls are transformed from head to toe into little princesses! Your child will feel like royalty with the help of her Fairy Godmother and Fairy Godmothers-in-training. They will put magical touches on everything from hair and make-up to princess gowns and accessories. Make the royal treatment complete with professional photographs of this enchanting Disney princess experience.

Girls 3 years old and above can choose from four hair styles: Fairytale Princess, Disney Diva, Pop Princess, and Color Star; each style is available in four packages (prices are current as of 6/2017 and information from disneyland.com):

➤ The **Coach Package** includes hairstyle, shimmering make-up, princess sash, princess cinch sac, and body jewels for $54.95 plus tax.

NOTE: This package wasn't on the website anymore. I am not sure if it was discontinued or if Disney just didn't have it listed.

➤ The **Crown Package** includes hairstyle, shimmering make-up, princess sash, princess cinch sac, face gem, and nail polish for $59 plus tax.

➤ The **Courtyard Package** includes shimmering make-up, nail polish, face gem, Bibbidi Bobbidi Boutique t-shirt, trendy tutu, princess sash, and princess cinch bag starting at $99 plus tax.

➤ The **Castle Package** includes hairstyle, shimmering make-up, princess sash, princess cinch sac, face gem, nail polish, princess gown of choice, wand, crown, and portrait package courtesy of Disney's PhotoPass Service: photo taken near Cinderella's carriage and assorted prints presented in a themed folder. Determined by the choice of princess gown, prices start at $199 plus tax.

- Continue your Disney Princess experience! Newly-transformed Castle Package princesses are personally escorted on a mini processional—where the young lady is the star!—from the Bibbidi Bobbidi Boutique to the enchanting Fantasy Faire.

- Upon arrival, enjoy the priority entrance (skip the line) to the Royal Hall where beloved and beautiful Disney Princesses from such timeless tales as *The Little Mermaid, Cinderella* and *Sleeping Beauty* eagerly await your visit. Have your autograph books and cameras ready!

➤ The **Knight Package** (for boys) includes hairstyling and a sword plus shield, starting at $19.95 plus tax.

➤ The **Disney Frozen Package** features an Anna or Elsa hairstyle and matching costume starting at $164.95 plus tax.

➤ The **Disney Frozen Crown Package** features an Anna or Elsa hairstyle and for children who already have their own costume, starting at $114.95 plus tax.

Please remember that Guests must be 3 to 12 years of age. Merchandise is available in children sizes only. Selection may vary. Children must be accompanied by an adult age 18 years or older during the **entire** experience. All prices, packages, and information are subject to change without notice. Merchandise available while supplies last. Separate theme park admission is required.

For reservations, please call (714) 781-STYLE or (714) 781-7895. Please notify Disney of any cancellations at least 48 hours prior to your appointment.

FUN FACT: If you look closely on the outside on the shop's front, you will see carvings of Captain Hook, Tick-Tock (the croc) and Mr. Smee. They were left behind as a reminder that the shop used to house *Tinker Bell's Toy Shop*. It later became *Once Upon A Time Disney Princess Shoppe* until April 17, 2007, when they had the grand opening of the *Bibbidi Bobbidi Boutique*.

MEET AND GREET CHARACTERS

Some years back when attendance was high, Cast Members were sent to the parks to survey the guests. Among the questions asked was what the guests wanted most out of their visits to the parks. Beyond collecting that information, Cast Members also queried guests on what improvements could be made regarding guest experience in the parks.

You might have seen the results of this survey. One was the arrival of the FastPass system. The other was the change in the number of character meet-and-greet opportunities. Today, guests can pretty much expect to run into a character just about wherever they venture into the parks.

Character Search

As a result of the survey, Disney decided to add in more characters for park guests to interact with. You can get a schedule of the character's locations from the *Guest Relations* up front. Sometimes the *Guest Relations* Cast Member can make a phone call to the proper department to request the exact time and location to meet your favorite character. This way you can better plan your day.

Character Protocol

After you find out where to find your character, you need to know how to act around them. Help teach your children how to interact with the characters.

➤ **Be patient** – Characters are pretty popular so you can bet that there will be long lines of guests waiting to see their favorite character. Many guests plan a year in advance to get to see their favorite characters, so waiting a few minutes more should not be difficult.

➤ **Respect other guests** – Imagine how you would want to be treated by other guests. That's how you should treat them. This means not cutting in line, and giving those in front of you ample time to enjoy their moment with the characters.

➤ **Addressing the characters** – You know how you enjoy people calling you by name. The same is true for the characters. When you see Mickey, give him a big, "Hiya Mickey!" Or when you see Goofy, be sure and shout out his name. When you speak to the characters, it helps to be in front of them so they can see who is talking to them.

➤ **Obey the greeters** – Each character normally has a greeter to assist in crowd control and answer any questions the guests might have. The greeter also informs the guests when it's time for the character to take a break. Guests should abide by the greeter's instructions so that everyone has an enjoyable experience.

➤ **Cameras at the ready** – Once you are next in line, it's a good idea to have your camera ready for that special photograph. That means turning your camera on, taking the lens cap off, and being prepared to just point and shoot. If you want to, there's no harm in taking two photos. Utilize your photo pass.

➤ **Carry a big pen** – Have you ever tried writing while wearing a pair of mittens? It's somewhat difficult unless you have a thick pen. With that in mind, those characters who are wearing gloves or who have large paws will appreciate using thick pens to sign autographs in your autograph book.

TIP: I purchase postcards with the character on it and then have them autograph it with a permanent pen.

➤ **Show your appreciation** – Think of the patience exhibited by the characters and how hard they try to make your family's moment with them as special as possible. Be sure to thank them if you get a chance and tell them they are doing a good job.

FUN FACTS

🌐 There **are two different types of characters**:
- The first are those who have on a mask, like Mickey, Pluto, Chip and Dale, Minnie, and lots more. These characters are not allowed to talk to you. They can only make gestures and mime.
- The second type of character is called a "face character," which are actors playing the part. They ARE allowed to talk to people while they are out and about and don't wear a mask. They resemble the characters they are portraying. Some of these would include Aladdin, Mary Poppins, Alice, Snow White, Ariel, Aurora, Belle, Jasmine, Cinderella, Tiana, Tarzan, Tinker Bell, and many more.

🌐 The **phrase "duck duty"** is a term given to Cast Members who are in character costumes for *Meet and Greets*.

🌐 In the summer, some of the bigger costumes, like Tigger and Pooh, **can reach up to 150 degrees**.

- Generally, **once a day, Alice and the Mad Hatter meet** at *Coke Corner* to play a game of musical chairs with the kids. This isn't listed in any of the planning guides, but you can ask a Cast Member at *Coke Corner* for the time, which is usually around 2:30 pm.

- Jack Skellington in the **only character who is a half-mask and half-face character**. Above his mouth and the rest of his head is a mask, while his mouth and chin are exposed and allowed to move so he can interact with the Guests.

- Face characters **used to have the ability to converse with park Guests** up until the early 1970's when Disney decided it was too hard for people to understand the muffled talking. They reserved the right-to-talk-to-Guests to the regular characters, like the princesses and other face characters.

- In 2013, the *Toy Story* characters, Woody, Jessie, and Buzz Lightyear, started a tradition of **falling to the ground when someone shouted "Andy is coming."** Disney had to put a stop to it because it could be dangerous for a character to fall to the ground without being able to see well, or the characters could lose their heads. Also, can you just imagine how many times people would be shouting, "Andy is coming," just to see them fall? It would get tiring. But they will sometimes freeze or go limp, if it is shouted now.

- A **brief history of The Mouse**. The first known appearance of Mickey Mouse as portrayed by an actor was in the Fanchon and Marco traveling stage show "*Mickey Mouse Idea*," that premiered March 12, 1931, in Los Angeles. Popular vaudeville performer "Toots" Novelle was the man inside The Mouse. Mickey's second appearance was at the premier of the first full-length color animated film, *Snow White and the Seven Dwarfs* (1937) on December 21, 1937. The permanent appearance of Mickey Mouse, among other Disney characters, was at the grand opening of *Disneyland* on July 17, 1955. Disney didn't have official character costumes yet, so he borrowed them from the Ice Capades. Since they were originally intended for ice skaters, there had obnoxious-looking holes in the face to provide the skater with visibility. The body part of the costume was also meant for a skater, so it was more humanoid than cartoon. Upon the parks opening, Walt had never intended to have characters permanently walk around and greet people, says Disney Legend and *Disneyland* attraction designer John Hench, who designed the torch for the 1960 Winter Olympics. After seeing how enthusiastic people were to see the characters, Walt decided to make them permanent. The costume didn't have set measurements and would sometimes be six feet tall, depending on the performer. It wasn't until the 1961 design done by Bill Justice and John Hench did the costume increase in quality and appearance. With these new standards, Disney cast Paul Castle as a permanent Mickey Mouse performer. Paul had performed as Mickey Mouse in the Ice Capades. In the 1960's there were a set of 10-12 full-time performers that worked five days a week (*Disneyland* used to be closed on Mondays and Tuesdays) in the characters, and another 40 part-time performers to work nights, weekends, and holidays. The newest

Mickey Mouse was added in 2010 and could move his mouth and blink his eyes in synchronization with shows and performances, which later carried over to *Meet and Greets* in 2013, but only in *Disney World*. Hopefully soon he will make his way to *Disneyland*.

- A Cast Member is under **no circumstances allowed to take off the character's head**. Even if they are feeling nauseous. They alert the Cast Member that is chaperoning them of a problem, they raise an arm in the air and cover one eye, then the Cast Member escorts them away.

- Under no circumstances are **two of the same character allowed to be seen together,** lest they be fired. For example: if Snow White is seen changing out places with Snow White.

- The Cast Members are not allowed to say which character they portray in the parks. They can say that they are "friends with," or that they "hang out with." Never that they are said character.

- They are also not allowed to take pictures of themselves in costume, lest they end up on social media. This is a firable offense.

- Disney has some strict requirements to be accepted as a Disney princess.
  - One must be between 5'4" and 5'7."
  - Be under a size 10.
  - Be at least 18 years old.
  - Most princesses are between 18 and 23 years old.
  - It's not uncommon to see a princess that is over 25 years old, but only if she has been there awhile.
  - Princesses are supplied with their own make-up and shown how to apply it to themselves so that they resemble the other girls who have taken on that character.
  - Training consists of five days where the princess discusses in depth her character's movie, supporting characters, mannerisms, and learns the signature.
  - Princesses can't acknowledge the existence of other characters outside of the Disney universe. Ariel can say she is friends with Snow White, but she can't say that she knows who SpongeBob is.
  - The princesses must be able to handle being in the heat and the cold, depending on the season. Not all princesses can stay stationed inside.
  - Princesses have to be great at improvisation, as kids ask the darndest questions.
  - The princess must smile at all times; there is no room for sadness in the Happiest Place on Earth.

Since people come in all heights, there is a character available somewhere for them to portray.

FACE CHARACTERS

PRINCESSES		FAIRIES	
5'3"- 5'7"	Rapunzel, Cinderella, Aurora, Belle	4'10"- 5'2"	Tinker Bell
5'3"- 5'7"	Ariel, Snow White, Jasmine	5'2"- 5'5"	Fawn, Vidia, Periwinkle
5'2"- 5'6"	Mulan	5'2"- 5'5"	Iridessa, Rosetta, Silvermist
5'5"- 5'8"	Tiana	5'4"- 5'6"	Fairy Godmother
FEMALE VILLAINS		OTHER WOMEN	
5'6"-5'10"	Wicked Step-Mother	5'5"- 5'8"	Mary Poppins
5'6"-5'10"	Step-Sisters, Malefacent	5'2"- 5'4"	Alice and Wendy

PRINCES		FAIRIES	
5'10"- 6'	The Prince, Prince Eric, Aladdin	5'4"- 5'7"	Terrence
5'10"- 6'	Prince Naveen, Prince Charming	OTHER MEN	
5'10"- 6'	Flynn Rider, Prince Adam	4'10"- 5'2"	Peter Pan
MALE VILLAINS		5'4"- 5'6"	Mad Hatter
6'0"- 6'6"	Dr. Facilier	5'8"- 6'1"	Jack Sparrow
5'11"-6'3"	Gaston	5'8"- 6'1"	Bert

FUR/MASKED CHARACTERS

4'8"- 5'2"	Mickey Mouse and Minnie Mouse	5'0"- 5'2"	White Rabbit, Pooh
4'6"- 4'10"	Daisy and Donald	5'2"- 5'4"	Suzy, Perla, Jessie, Bullseye
5'2"- 5'4"	Chip and Dale	5'6"- 5'8"	Rafiki, Flick
5'6"- 5'8"	Pluto	5'6"-5'8"	Buzz Lightyear
6'0"- 6'3"	Goofy	5'7"- 5'9"	Eeyore
4'0"- 4'6"	Huey, Dewey, Louie	5'10"- 6'	Tigger
4'9"-4'11"	Lilo and Stitch	5'10"-6'	Green Army Men
4'8"-4'10"	Dopey	6'0"- 6'2"	Captain Hook, Genie
4'10"-5'0"	Piglet	6'2"- 6'4"	Beast, Woody, Jafar

HOLIDAY MAKEOVER

Each year *Disneyland* goes all out to celebrate some of our favorite holidays with decorations and themes. Check *Disneyland's* website for the exact start and end times for the holidays as they may change from year to year. Special celebrations can change from year to year. What was there in 2014, may not be there in 2016.

Leap Year

Starting in 2012, they created *Disney Leap Day* to celebrate Leap Year. The park opened at 6:00 a.m. on February 29th and remained open until 6:00 a.m. on March 1st. There was only one other time Disneyland stayed open for a whole 24 hours and it was for the grand opening of *Star Tours* in 1987. Mark your calendars for February 29, 2016, so you, too, can be in the crowds of people enjoying a full 24-hour visit inside the park. In 2012, there was no extra charge to be in the park for the entire day, but who knows for 2016.

Independence Day

- In *Disney California Adventure*, immediately prior to each *World of Color* performance, *Paradise Pier* will come to life with a patriotic spectacular in honor of our nation's independence.

- In *Disneyland, Disney's Celebrate America! A Fourth of July Concert in the Sky* will celebrate the land of the free and the home of the brave with patriotic music and colorful fireworks.

- Also at *Disneyland,* the 3rd Marine Aircraft Wing Band will perform in honor of Independence Day at the Flag Retreat Ceremony, marching performance prior to Mickey's Soundsational Parade, and in Big Thunder Ranch Jamboree.

- The "Voices of Liberty" singing group appear in the *Main Street Opera House* (*Great Moments with Mr. Lincoln*) for a limited engagement.

- A special fireworks show.

Easter

- *Disneyland* and *California Adventure* have an Easter Egg-stravaganza. It is an egg hunt where you take a special map around the park looking for hidden character eggs. When you find the hidden egg, you place a special sticker on the map indicating where you found it. At the end, you turn in your map for a special prize.

- There is a special *Meet and Greet* with your favorite Disney rabbits, Thumper, Rabbit, Br'er Rabbit, Roger Rabbit, and The White Rabbit.

- They have cookie decorating kits for $6.00.

- At the Big Thunder Ranch Jamboree in *Frontierland* they have the Springtime Roundup event. There are lots of flowers and seasonal décor. You can meet characters, enjoy sweet treats, bunny hop and get as crafty as a hare.

Halloween

- At the beginning of *Main Street, U.S.A.,* there is a giant 12-foot-high Mickey Mouse-shaped Jack-O'-Lantern for taking photos by.

- Jack Skellington and his friends take over the *Haunted Mansion* attraction turning it into the **Haunted Mansion Holiday**. It has a complete makeover on the outside and the inside. The temporary look of the whole attraction is based off of Tim Burton's groundbreaking stop-motion film *Nightmare Before Christmas* (1993). The attraction is closed for two weeks in September for the Cast Members to change everything over. It will last October through the first two weeks of January, followed by 2 weeks of being closed to change the attraction back. For more details about the *Haunted Mansion Holiday*, see page 498.

- There is a *Nightmare Before Christmas* gift shop in *New Orleans Square*, but it is there all year long.

- You can find Oogie Boogie, the villain from *Nightmare Before Christmas* (1993), working in one of the popcorn carts.

410

- Some of the *Meet and Greet* characters will be dressed up in the Halloween costumes as their regular outfits.
- Big Thunder Ranch employs professional pumpkin carvers to design and carve some of the most exotic and fanciful looking jack-o'-lanterns around.
- *Space Mountain* is changed into *Space Mountain Ghost Galaxy* for an even more exciting and adventurous trip around space. For more details about *Space Mountain Ghost Galaxy*, see page 602.
- *Mickey's Halloween Party* starts the second week in September and runs through the end of October. You must purchase a special admittance ticket for this. It is sponsored by Nestle and whole candy bars are given out at trick-or-treat stations, along with healthy alternatives. This is the only time adults are allowed to dress up and enter the park.

Christmas

Each year Disney does a complete makeover of the park to celebrate Christmas and the holiday time. They start putting up the decorations after the Halloween ones are removed, about November 12th (varies from year-to-year). The festivities begin by the third week in November.

- *Sleeping Beauty's Castle* gets new snow-covered spires and everything gets covered with icicles and lights.
- The *it's a small world* gets a whole facelift. It takes a crew of 20 technical-service Cast Members spending 17 days straight, 10 to 12 hours a day, to change over the interior. The outside is covered in 50,000 C-7 lights, the same kind you would string up on your own house, in 6 different colors, plus an additional 2,000 clear flashing bulbs. All this added together equals about 350,000 watts of light. On the trees, hedges and topiaries, bushes shaped like animals or other things, they use about 150,000 mini lights. In all, 60,000 cable ties, 3,000 connectors, 25,000 feet of extension cables, and 18,000 feet of electrical tape are used. The music is changed from the normal song to "Jingle Bells," but it is sung in different languages as you float around the "world."
- *Visit Big Thunder Ranch* in *Frontierland* to see **Santa's Reindeer Round-Up**. Sit on Santa's lap and tell him what you want for Christmas, chat it up with Mrs. Claus, or just sit and do some crafts. Whatever you do, don't miss visiting the reindeer in the corral.
- Save yourself a spot on *Main Street, U.S.A.* to watch *A Christmas Fantasy Parade* go by with lots of Disney characters and even Santa Claus. This exciting parade first began in November of 1994.
- After dark, line up in front of *Sleeping Beauty's Castle* and gaze into the sky to be amazed by the **Believe... In Holiday Magic** fireworks extravaganza. While you watch the bursts of color in the sky, snow is sprinkled down upon everyone. This firework show lasts for the Christmas season through the first week in January.

- Because the **Haunted Mansion Holiday** is a crossover of Halloween and Christmas, it is all still in effect until the beginning of January.
- The **first time they used an artificial tree was in 2008**. Before that they used one large tree and de-branched multiple other trees to fill it out.

New Year's Eve

- New Year's Eve is **one of the busiest days of the year**. For the most part, they reach maximum capacity, about 60,000 guests, around lunch time and won't allow re-entry if you need to go out to your vehicle for anything. Wear all the clothes you are going to wear for the day. You can rent a locker to leave them in, if need be. Take all your food with you, unless you plan on eating in the park.
- Other than *Disney Leap Day*, this is **the longest open day of the year lasting 18 hours**. *Disneyland* and *California Adventure* open at 8:00 a.m., *California Adventure* closes at 1:00 a.m. and *Disneyland* closes at 2:00 a.m.. TIP: Make sure you are in a line for a popular attraction by 1:59 a.m. so that the park can clear out by the time you exit.
- They have **special bands** that come into the park to play.
- You can purchase **special souvenirs** that can only be found at this time. There are special hats and party favors that the park hands out.
- There is a special **fireworks show that lights up the sky** at midnight.

PRO TIP: Show up to the park early. It is not uncommon for Disneyland to turn gueasts away as early at 10:00 am.

Grad Nights

- Grad nights take place May-June and is available to highschool seniors.
- Tickets for the 2017 season were $92 each for a park hopper.
- The special event takes place from 10:00pm-2:00am, but kids can enter the parks earlier in the day.
- The party takes place in *California Adventure* once it is 10:00pm and only certain parts of the park are open

SPECIAL DAYS IN THE PARK

There are special days here you can visit the park and participate in events that are not put on by Disney. Always check online first to find out an exact date and time. These events are put on by small groups of people who have a shared interest with others. Some of the special days listed are official Disney sponsored days.

Gay Days	October	Unofficial	gaydaysanaheim.com
This event was established in 1998 and attracted 2,500 visitors the first time around. Now every year there are around 30,000 visitors that show up just for Gay Days. In Disney World they are getting about 80,000 visitors.			
Bats Day (Goth Day)	May	Unofficial	batsday.net
This event was established in 1999 and originally attracted 80 visitors its first year. Since then it has increased into the hundreds. On this day everyone dressed up in their goth-wear show up to celebrate together.			
Dapper Day	Multiple	Unofficial	dapperday.com
This event was established in 2011 and invites visitors to go to the park all dressed up in their very best attire, mostly themed from the 1920's.			
Star Wars Day	June	Unofficial	starwarsdisneyland.com
This event was established in 2002 as a protest against Disney for not having Star Wars Days in Disneyland like they do in Disney World.			
Tron Fan Day	April	Unofficial	None
This event was established in 2011 and ran for two years. It's following seemed to have died out with the removal of ElecTRONica from California Adventure.			
Raver Day	June	Unofficial	None
This event was established in 2002 for people to meet up in the park all dressed up in their neon clothes, wild hair, and tons of necklaces and bracelets.			
Harry Potter Day	November	Unofficial	potterday.org
This event was established in 2006 for the fans of the widely popular book series and movie franchise of Harry Potter. People dress up as their favorite HP character. Disneyland doesn't allow face masks or wands in the park.			
Yippy Day	August	Unofficial	None
On August 6, 1970, 300 Yippies (members of the Youth International Party, a radical branch of the anti-Vietnam War movement) converged on Disneyland to "liberate Minnie Mouse," as well as protest the park's longstanding, unwritten policy against letting long-haired people inside.			
Annual Autism Awareness Day	April	Unofficial	None
This special day was started in 2008, and is used for people who have, or just want to promote autism awareness.			
Epilepsy Awareness Day	November	Unofficial	epilepsyfoundation.org
This special day was started in 2013, and is used for people who have, or just want to promote epilepsy awareness.			
Tinker Bell Half Marathon Weekend	January	Official	None
This half marathon focused on women will take you through the Disneyland Resort and the streets of Anaheim, California. Each finisher receives an exclusive Tinker Bell-inspired medal, long-sleeve tech shirt, goody bag, and more! Other events during the weekend include the Never Land Family Fun Run 5K, the Tinker Bell 10K (new for 2014), kid's races and an Expo.			

Valentines' Day	February	Official	None
Restaurants around the Disneyland Resort will offer special menus for Valentine's Day.			
Disney's California Food and Wine Festival	Mar-April	Official	disneyparks.disney.go.com
A food and drink festival that takes place each spring in Disney California Adventure			
Cinco de Mayo	May	Official	disneyparks.disney.go.com
Special Cinco de Mayo menus will celebrate Mexican-American heritage at Tortilla Jo's and House of Blues			
Mother's Day at the Disneyland Resort	May	Official	disneyparks.disney.go.com
Celebrate Mother's Day With Special Dining at Disneyland Resort			
AIDS Walk Orange County	May	Official	None
Walk around California Adventure and Downtown Disney to support the battle with AIDS			
Tiki Day	October	Unofficial	facebook.com/pg/TikiDayAtThePark
An unofficial Disneyland gathering that celebrates the love of Tiki! Join our Ohana for a day at the park and don your best Tiki duds!			
Villain's Day	February	Unofficial	None
Show up and Disneybound as your favorite Disney villain.			
Haunted Mansion Fashion	October	Unofficial	None
Dress formally like you belong in the Haunted Mansion.			
Steam Day	November	Unofficial	facebook.com/SteamDay
Grab your cogs, gears and aviator goggles — Steam Day celebrates "steampunk," that science fiction genre that embraces steam-powered machinery over Tomorrowland tech.			
Galliday	September	Unofficial	galliday.com
Hundreds and hundreds of Whovians have been descending on Disneyland for periodic events to celebrate their love of sci-fi institution Doctor Who.			
Pinup Parade in the Park	May	Unofficial	facebook.com/pinupgirlclothing
This event is similar to Dapper Days, where participants dress up in vintage-inspired outfits, but this one is more focused on the glamorous bombshell pinup look of the 1940s to 1960s.			
Disney Leap Day	Leap Year	Official	None
Disney has, in the past, held a special Disney Leap Day. It is a day when guests can enter the park for 24 hours over the leap year of February 29th.			
Rock Around the Park (Rock-a-Billy Day)	November	Unofficial	None
People meet up dressed in 60's rock and roll attire. Generally the day starts off with breakfast and a car show.			

THE ORIGINAL ATTRACTIONS

There were only 25 attractions in *Disneyland* on opening day. Some of the attractions started out with names that were later changed into what we know them as today.

Main Street, U.S.A.
Horse-drawn Fire Wagon
Horse-drawn Street Cars
Horse-drawn Surreys
Main Street Cinema
Main Street Arcade (now primarily a shop)
Santa Fe and Disneyland Railroad (renamed Disneyland Railroad, 1974)
Main Street Shooting Gallery (removed 1962)

Tomorrowland
Autopia
Circarama
Space Station X-1

Adventureland
Jungle Cruise

Fantasyland
Canal Boats of the World (became Storybook Land Canal Boats, 1956)
King Arthur Carrousel (in the old location)
Mad Tea Party (in the old location)
Mr. Toad's Wild Ride
Snow White's Adventures (became Snow White's Scary Adventures, 1983)
Peter Pan's Flight

Frontierland
Davy Crockett Arcade
Golden Horseshoe Revue
Mark Twain Steamboat
Mule Pack
Stage Coach

The only 15 attractions that can still be found in the park today are:

Autopia
Disneyland Railroad
Frontierland Shootin' Exposition
Golden Horseshoe Stage
Horse-drawn Street Cars
Jungle Cruise
King Arthur Carrousel
Mad Tea Party

Main Street Cinema
Mark Twain Riverboat
Mr. Toad's Wild Ride
Peter Pan Flight
Sleeping Beauty Castle
Snow White's Scary Adventures
Storybook Land Canal Boats

THE SHARED ATTRACTIONS

As you may know, there are six Disney resorts around the world containing 13 Disney-themed parks. There are now only three attractions that can be found in all 5 of the resorts. They are:

- *Astro Orbitor*
- *Buzz Lightyear Astro Blasters*
- *Dumbo the Flying Elephant*

Throughout the different parks that share attractions, they may have a different name or a slight variation of the names used in *Disneyland*, but they are still the same basic attraction. Like in *Disneyland*, *Tarzan's Treehouse* used to be *Swiss Family Treehouse;* it was re-themed, but the attraction concept is still the same. In *Disneyland* we have the *Astro Orbitor*, in *Magic Kingdom* it's called *Astro Orbiter*, in *Disneyland Paris* it's *Orbitron Machines Volantes*, in *Tokyo Disneyland* it's *Star Jets,* and in *Disneyland Hong Kong* it's *Orbitron*. All have different names, but all are the same attraction.

The following list indicates the shared attractions between the different parks. It is current as of 2017. After *Shanghai Disneyland* had its grand opening in June

2016, the list changed and there are only three attractions that are shared. Prior to the opening, there were seven. The highlighted attractions aren't shared anywhere; they can only be experienced in the original "Magic Kingdom."

	Disneyland Resort	Magic Kingdom	Epcot	Tokyo Disneyland	Hollywood Studios	Disneyland Paris	Animal Kingdom	California Adventure	Disneyland Hong Kong	Shanghai Disney Resort
Alice in Wonderland	X									
Animation Academy								X		
Astro Orbitor	X	X		X		X			X	X
Autopia	X	X				X			X	
Bakery Tour, The								X		
Big Thunder Mountain Railroad	X	X		X		X				
Buzz Lightyear Astro Blasters	X	X		X		X			X	X
California Screamin'								X		
Casey Jr. Circus Train	X					X				
Character Close-up								X	X	
Chip 'n Dale's Treehouse	X			X						
Davy Crockett's Explorer Canoes	X									
Disney Junior: Live on Stage					X			X		
Disney Princess Fantasy Faire	X									
Disneyland Monorail	X	X	X	X						
Disneyland Railroad	X					X				
Donald's Boat	X			X						
Dumbo the Flying Elephant	X	X		X		X			X	X
Enchanted Tiki Room	X	X		X						
Fantasmic!	X				X					
Finding Nemo Submarine Voyage	X									
Flik's Flyers								X		
Francis' Ladybug Boogie								X		
Frontierland Shooting Exposition	X	X		X		X				
Frozen-Live at the Hyperion								X		
Gadget's Go Coaster	X			X						
Ghirardelli Chocolate Factory Tour								X		
Golden Horseshoe Stage, The	X	X								
Golden Zephyr								X		
Goofy's Playhouse	X			X						
Goofy's Sky School								X		
Grizzly River Run								X		

	1	2	3	4	5	6	7	8	9	10
Guardians of the Galaxy - Mission:Breakout!					X					
Haunted Mansion	X	X		X		X				
Haunted Mansion Holiday	X									
Heimlich's Chew Chew Train								X		
Indiana Jones Adventure	X									
Innoventions	X		X							
It's a Small World	X	X		X		X			X	
It's Tough to be a Bug!							X	X		
Jedi Training Academy	X				X					
Jumpin' Jellyfish								X		
Jungle Cruise	X	X		X					X	
King Arthur Carrousel	X			X					X	
King Triton's Carousel of the Sea								X		
Little Mermaid: Ariel's Undersea Adventure								X		
Luigi's Rollickin' Roadsters								X		
Mad Tea Party	X	X		X		X			X	
Many Adventures of Winnie the Pooh, The	X	X		X					X	X
Mark Twain Riverboat	X	X		X						
Mater's Junkyard Jamboree								X		
Matterhorn Bobsleds	X									
Mickey's Fun Wheel								X		
Mickey's House and Meet Mickey	X			X						
Minnie's House	X			X						
Monsters, Inc. Mike & Sulley to the Rescue!				X				X		
Mr. Toad's Wild Ride	X									
Peter Pan's Flight	X	X		X		X				X
Pinocchio's Daring Journey	X			X		X				
Pirates of the Caribbean	X	X		X		X				
Pirate's Lair on Tom Sawyer Island	X	X		X						
Pixie Hollow	X								X	
Princess Dot Puddle Park								X		
Radiator Springs Racers								X		
Rafts to Tom Sawyer's Island	X			X					X	
Red Car Trolley								X		
Redwood Creek Challenge Trail								X		
Roger Rabbit's Car Toon Spin	X			X						
Sailing Ship Columbia	X									
Silly Symphony Swings								X		
Sleeping Beauty Castle	X					X			X	
Snow White Grotto	X			X					X	
Snow White's Scary Adventures	X			X		X				
Soarin' Around The World			X					X		X
Sorcerer's Workshop								X		
Space Mountain	X	X		X		X			X	
Splash Mountain	X	X							X	

Star Tours: The Adventures Continue	X			X	X	X			
Storybook Land Canal Boats	X					X			
Tarzan's Treehouse	X	X		X		X		X	
Toy Story Midway Mania!					X		X		
Tuck and Roll's Drive'Em Buggies							X		
Turtle Talk with Crush			X				X		
Walt Disney Imagineering Blue Sky Cellar							X		
World of Color							X		

SCAVENGER HUNT

Here is something fun to do for a day while exploring Disneyland. Try to locate the objects or locations listed below. Ask a Cast Member, ask a stranger, or look in this book (I talk about all of them in here) for clues or information leading to the items listed below. Your job is to locate and photograph them as proof that you found them all. You can use the photos later to show friends. Time yourself. Copy the list and break your group into two teams and make it a competition. READY, SET, GO! *(for the answers,* see page 699)

01.__ A great surveyor's point
02.__ A spare Dumbo
03.__ 33 is only by the front door
04.__ A robot that once was a goose
05.__ Gadgets queue Hidden Mickey
06.__ A log cabin that burns no more
07.__ Man-eating piranhas
08.__ A lair with tons of loot
09.__ Meet Mickey
10.__ A giant ball made of marble that can float
11.__ A yeti footprint
12.__ Wrong-handed Hook
13.__ Get a photo taken with a character
14.__ "I am Tangaroa, father of all gods and goddesses."
15.__ An air-blowing cheetah
16.__ Find a disappearing-reappearing head
17.__ Aladdin's palace is so small
18.__ Roger Rabbit as a fountain
19.__ Time capsule
20.__ Trunks are all packed
21.__ Three mounted heads of the long-gone *Country Bear Jamboree*
22.__ A stone tree
23.__ *"Who so pulleth out this sword of this stone and anvil is rightwise ruler born of England."*
24.__ Dinosaurs in *Disneyland*
25.__ Bushes cut to resemble animals
26.__ A car fountain
27.__ A talking mobile *Buzz Lightyear of Star Command*
28.__ "The wildest ride in the wilderness."
29.__ A peeping evil queen
30.__ Pluto's doggy door
31.__ An invisible horse
32.__ "Turn me loose. I said turn me loose."
33.__ Snow White has a wishing well
34.__ Best "partnership" ever

419

DISNEY WORLD RESORT TRIVIA

1. The *Walt Disney World Resort* is the **world's largest and most visited** recreational resort, covering a 25,000-acre (47 sq. mi.) area southwest of Orlando, Florida.

2. It **opened on October 1, 1971,** with only the *Magic Kingdom* theme park, and has since added *Epcot, Disney's Hollywood Studios,* and *Disney's Animal Kingdom.*

3. The resort encompasses **4 theme parks** and 2 water parks (*Typhoon Lagoon* 1989 and *Blizzard Beach* 1995).

4. When the *Magic Kingdom* opened in 1971, the site employed about 5,500 Cast Members. Today the resort **employs more than 66,000** people.

5. Disney spends more than **$1.2 billion on payroll** and $474 million on benefits each year.

6. They are the **largest single-site employer** in the United States.

7. *Walt Disney World* **has more than 3,700 job classifications**. The resort also sponsors and operates the *Walt Disney World* College Program, an internship program that offers American college students the opportunity to live about 15 miles off-site in the four Disney-owned apartment complexes and work at the resort, providing much of the theme park and resort "front line" Cast Members. There is also the *Walt Disney World* International College Program, an internship program that offers international college students from all over the world the same opportunity.

8. More than **5,000 Cast Members are dedicated to maintenance and engineering**, including 750 horticulturists and 600 painters.

9. The **streets in all the parks are steam cleaned** every night to maintain cleanliness.

10. There are **Cast Members permanently assigned to painting** the antique carousel horses; they use genuine gold leaf.

11. There is a **tree farm on site** so that when a mature tree needs to be replaced, a 30-year-old tree will be available to replace it.

12. In 1997, Cast Members found a minute-old abandoned baby girl in the bathroom in *Magic Kingdom's Toontown*. The nurses at the hospital named her Princess Jasmine.

13. There are **28 on-site themed resort hotels** excluding 8 that are on-site, but not owned by the Walt Disney Company, two health spas and fitness centers, and other recreational venues and entertainment.

14. Despite marketing claims and popular misconceptions, the **Disney World Resort is not located within Orlando** city limits. It is actually located about 21 miles southwest of Orlando within southwestern Orange County with the remainder in adjacent Osceola County.

15. The **total number of Guests that visited** in 2016, keeping in mind that Disneyland saw 17.9 million and Californina Adventure saw 9.3 million guests:
    - *Magic Kingdom* – 20.395 million
    - *Epcot* – 11.712 million
    - *Disney's Hollywood Studios* – 10.776 million
    - *Disney's Animal Kingdom* – 10.844 million

Magic Kingdom

16. It **opened** on October 1, 1971.

17. The **first park built** at the resort.

18. Because of the similarity to *Disneyland*, **there was some confusion on the name of the park**. *The Magic Kingdom* was (and occasionally, still is) used as an unofficial nickname for *Disneyland* before the Walt Disney World Resort was built; however, the official nickname of *Disneyland* is "The Happiest Place on Earth." The *Magic Kingdom's* nickname is similar "The Most Magical Place on Earth." Despite the confusion, the park's tickets have always borne the official name of *The Magic Kingdom*. In 1994, in order to differentiate it from *Disneyland*, the park was officially renamed "Magic Kingdom Park."

19. The Walt Disney Company began construction on the *Magic Kingdom* and the entire resort in **1967 after the death of Walt Disney**; however, Walt was very involved in planning The Florida Project in the years prior to his death. The park itself was initially built similar to the existing *Disneyland* in California; however, the *Magic Kingdom* was built in a larger area.

20. Disney **spends more than $100 million every year** on maintenance at the *Magic Kingdom*.

21. Listed as **the most-visited themed park** in the world.

Epcot

22. It **opened** on October 1, 1982.

23. The park is **dedicated to international culture** and technological innovation.

24. The **second park built** at the resort.

25. Total cost to build *Epcot* was $1.4 billion and **took three years to construct**, which, at the time, was the largest construction project on Earth.

26. It is 300 acres, making it **more than twice the size** of *The Magic Kingdom*.

27. Listed as **the sixth most-visited themed park** in the world.

28. *EPCOT stands for Experimental Prototype Community of Tomorrow.*

Disney's Hollywood Studios

29. It **opened on May 1, 1989,** as *Disney-MGM Studios*.

30. This park's **theme is show business.** It draws inspiration from the heyday of Hollywood in the 1930's – 40's.

31. It **covers 135 acres** in size.

32. It was the **third park built** at the resort.

33. The park is **represented by The Sorcerer's Hat**, a stylized version of the magical hat from *Fantasia*. It replaced the *Earful Tower* as the park's icon in 2001.

34. The park **consists of six themed areas**. Unlike the other *Walt Disney World* parks, this one does not have a defined layout; it is more a mass of streets and buildings that blend into each other much like a real motion picture studio would.

35. Listed as **the eighth most-visited themed park** in the world.

Disney's Animal Kingdom

36. It **opened** on April 22, 1998.

37. This park is an **animal theme park**.

38. It was the **fourth park built** at the resort.

39. It is the **largest single Disney theme park in the world**, covering more than 500 acres.

40. It is also the **first Disney theme park to be themed entirely around animal** conservation, a philosophy once pioneered by Walt Disney himself.

41. It is **accredited by the Association of Zoos and Aquariums**, meaning they have met and exceeded the standards in education, conservation, and research.

42. Shortly after the park opened, Disney advertised **the park using the fictional word "nahtazu."** Pronounced "not a zoo," the word emphasized that the park was more than animal displays found in a typical city zoo. Disney stopped using the phrase in January 2006.

43. The **Tree of Life, a sculpted 14-story** (145-foot-tall, 50-foot-wide) tree, is the centerpiece and icon in the park. Tourists can walk around the whole tree to see all 325 animals carved in the "bark" (cement) of this massive tree attraction.

44. **Jiminy Cricket is the mascot** for the park. He represents recycling, environment, and conservation.

45. Listed as **the seventh most-visited themed park** in the world.

DISNEYLAND RESORT FUN FACTS

1. **There are only two "rides" in the park**, *Mr. Toad's Wild Ride*, and *Big Thunder Railroad*, because of the quote "This here's the wildest ride in the wilderness." All the other so called "rides" in the park are considered "attractions."

2. The term **"Imagineer" is a combination of imagination and engineering**, a blend of creative fantasy and technical understanding necessary to build a Disney attraction. This division of the Walt Disney Company is a prestigious organization of only about 1,000 people.

3. When Disney was creating concepts for his upcoming project of *Disneyland*, he **created a company called WED Enterprises**. WED stands for Walter Elias Disney. Under this company name, Walt placed his Imagineers. These are the original Imagineers: Harper Goff, Marvin Davis, John Hench, Ken Anderson, Marc Davis, Roger Broggie, CV Wood, Bill Evans, Joe Fowler, Dick Irvine, Herb Ryman, Bob Gurr, Bill Cottrell, Emile Kuri, Fred Joerger, Sam McKim, Wathel Rogers, Yale Gracey, Claude Coats, and X Atencio. Some of them have biographies in the *Imagineers Mini Biography* section on page 287. Later, the company was renamed WDI, or Walt Disney Imagineering.

4. When the park opened, more than $500,000 was spent on **landscape and irrigation** systems. More than 1,200 full size trees and 9,000 shrubs were brought into the park. Today, a large staff of gardeners care for the park's 800 species of flats from more than 40 nations. The landscape includes nearly 1 million plants (including the plants that are rotated out), which includes shrubs and perennials and 4,500 trees. Ninety percent of the landscape is not indigenous to California. The park has year-round color. Every three months, the flower beds are replanted with new blooms.

5. The 16 trams used to transport the guests from the parking structure to the park's entrance area **run on clean-burning Compressed Natural Gas (CNG)**. Now that the trams use CNG, Disney has eliminated the use of diesel fuel, thereby cutting out about 200,000 gallons of diesel every year. There are a few other transportation units that run on CNG as well, including *Sailing Ship Columbia*, the *Jungle Cruise* boats, and all the vehicles on *Main Street, U.S.A.*

6. One of the **most photographed spots in the world** is the Mickey flower bed at the entrance of the park. (*see photo*)

7. There are more than 600 employees on staff just to **keep the park clean**. Every night all the streets get pressure washed. On a busy day, custodians collect 30 tons of garbage. The resort can recycle 510 tons of paper and 15 tons of aluminum cans in a single year. The money they collect is donated to the non-profit group Canine Companions for Independence. From 2005 to 2011, they have raised over a quarter of a million dollars for them.

423

8. There are more than 19 million **gallons of water** in the 10 water areas. Scuba divers go down to retrieve lost items and to inspect mechanical parts and underwater tracking systems.

9. To be cast as a **Meet and Greet Disney Princess**, you must meet the height requirement of 5 feet 1 inch tall or taller to be considered for the part.

10. *Disneyland* maintains a large staff of electricians. One crew's sole job is to change the lights that edge the rooflines. There are more than **100,000 light bulbs** in *Disneyland* including the 11,000 bulbs trimming the buildings on *Main Street, USA*. The light bulbs are changed when they reach 80% of their life expectancy.

11. *Disneyland* employs **54 full-time electricians**.

12. *Disneyland* uses more than **20,000 gallons of paint** every year.

13. There are 300 professional **costume designers** on staff to keep up the maintenance on the costumes. The wardrobe collection includes more than 500,000 pieces including attraction hosts' and parade costumes, maintenance crew uniforms' and audio-animatronic figures.

14. The **parking structure** was built in 1999. It includes 10,240 parking spaces on six levels and was the second largest parking structure in the world. It is now the sixth largest in the world and it is named the *Mickey and Friends Parking Strucure*.

15. Walt Disney once said, "I love the nostalgic myself. I hope we never lose some of the things of the past." He created *Main Street, U.S.A.* to make sure we could always embrace those wonderful feelings of days gone by. From the decor in the old-time specialty shops to the music in *Central Plaza* to the taste of the ice cream sundaes, ***Main Street, U.S.A.* is pure Americana**.

16. Among the first guests at *Disneyland* in 1955 was 11-year-old **George Lucas** and his family.

17. *Disneyland* can welcome about **65,000 guests** in a single day and welcomes between 14-16 million guests over the course of a year.

18. Walt Disney had to sell his beloved **Smoke Tree Ranch** in order to complete *Disneyland*, but later bought it back. The initials of STR are what appear on his tie on the "Partners" statue in the plaza at the end of *Main Street, U.S.A.*

19. *Main Street's* setting is 1910; *Tomorrowland* is 1986. These years were picked because they were the years of **Hailey's Comet**.

20. Walt originally designed the park so when you **pass from land to land**, you wouldn't see the others, or at least have minimal view of them.

21. **Walt Disney wanted female tour guides** for guests when they entered the park. Possibly because men used to be the main controller of the household income and, therefore, would make the decision to hire a guide. It is

rumored that Walt would only hire women who were naturally beautiful like fairy tale princesses because they weren't allowed to wear makeup.

22. **The tour guides had to weigh in** to make sure they were under the maximum weight requirement specified by Walt. Since then, times have changed and so has the Disney standard. This was told to me by an actual tour guide.

23. Construction at the park offered constant challenges to the city of Anaheim. The Municipal Building Codes did not anticipate what operating standards should **apply to submarines** within city limits.

24. At the time it was built, the **Matterhorn was the tallest** structure in the city of Anaheim.

25. All recorded **music and sounds that you hear in the attractions and throughout the park constantly run**. It costs more for *Disneyland* to shut the sound off and restart the system every day. The only time sound actually gets shut off is when there is an emergency stop or large system failure, ie. a massive power loss, emergency shut down, or other sorts of emergencies. Most notable is *it's a small world* - the dolls may stop moving, but the music still plays and the *Haunted Mansion* -the buggies stop and the animatronics still move and the voiceover says, "there is a ghoul in the system," with no music, but when the music does resume after the voiceover, it has continued playing. There was no pause in it at all. Luckily for cleaning and maintenance crews, they can turn it down so they won't get sick of hearing it.

26. Walt intended for visitors to enter a new world once they go through the tunnel at the entrance. He achieved what he wanted. **Nowhere in the park could you see outside the park**. That was then. Since *Toontown* was built, trees have been ripped out and some other changes make it possible to see outside, if you really tried. In the beginning, Walt had an arrangement with the city of Anaheim that they wouldn't build any buildings close enough or tall enough to be visible from inside the park.

27. There is **at least one Hidden Mickey** in each attraction.

28. On the evening before opening day, some **workers left the park early** after disconnecting the electricity completely throughout the park. Workers were still there, though and had to install a huge African elephant for the *Jungle Cruise* in total darkness.

29. Prior to opening day, Walt visited a few of the local churches and invited a handful of the **best-behaved children** from the Sunday school classes to attend the opening day festivities.

30. The day that *Disneyland* opened, the **asphalt had not quite hardened**, and ladies' heels sunk into it. The women got a free pair of moccasins because those were the only shoes *Disneyland* had for adults.

31. The **first ticket** for *Disneyland* was sold to Walt's brother, Roy, for $1.

32. Walt called the **employees of *Disneyland*** "Cast Members."

33. When the park first opened, Disney employed 1,300 Cast Members. By 1970, that number had increased to 6,200. Now the ***Disneyland* Resort employs over 23,000 people**, making it the largest single employer in Orange County.

34. The *Disneyland* shops inside the park take every kind of **foreign currency** as long as it can be traded into dollars. If a guest shows up with Yen, the Cast Member has to call to get the trading rate, take the amount needed for the equivalent amount of dollars, and make note of when the transaction happened.

35. The water, known to *Disneyland* as the **"Dark Waters,"** actually:
   - starts where the *Motor Boat Cruise* used to be (just north of the *Matterhorn*)
   - travels south near the *Matterhorn* to *Snow White's Grotto*
   - is used in the moat around *Sleeping Beauty's Castle*
   - travels under the bridges around the *Carnation Plaza*
   - goes down past the *Tiki Room*
   - flows into the *Jungle Cruise* lagoon
   - travels under the walk way in front of the *Pirates of the Caribbean* (that whole area is kind of like a bridge)
   - flows into the *Rivers of America*
   - is pumped from an area behind where the *Sailing Ship Columbia* and the *Mark Twain* pick up passengers
   - returns the water to the *Motor Boat Cruise* area, at which point it starts its journey all over again

36. You can tell when you enter a new land because **the ground changes** (*Fantasyland* has a smooth green asphalt. *New Orleans Square* has a kind of cobblestone. *Frontierland* has bricks or something to that effect, etc.)

37. You can also identify which land you are in by looking at the **garbage cans**.

38. Cast Member **Radio Codes**:
   - 100 - Delayed opening
   - 101 - Attraction is down - Routine
   - 101G - Attraction is down due to guest activities
   - 102 - Attraction is up - Routine
   - 103 – Attraction is down - Emergency
   - 104 - Attraction is operating at reduced capacity (running fewer units, trains, cars)
   - 105 - Attraction is operating at full capacity
   - 514 - 'Look out for' or 'Check it out'
   - 902 - Traffic Accident
   - 904 - Fire
   - 90 - Temperature has reached 90 degrees; loosen clothing
   - PXX - VIP importance where P stands for Priority and the X's indicate importance
   - "V" is called when a certain attraction does not agree with one's stomach
   - "P" is called when there is urine left by a passenger
   - "U" is an alternate for "P"
   - Code "H" means one of the *Main Street* horses left some "recycled hay" behind

39. *Disneyland* spends about **$41,000 per night on the fireworks show** above *Sleeping Beauty's Castle*.

40. It takes at least 20 minutes to **restart a smaller attraction** and around an hour to start a bigger attraction due to computer and safety protocols.

41. In order to do **"plainclothes" security**, you have to serve in uniformed security for two years.

42. *Disneyland* has its own plain clothes security detail which monitors potential trouble guests. *Disneyland* has **more security people than the City of Anaheim** has police. At last report, Anaheim has 285 police and *Disneyland* has in excess of 300.

43. Security makes a point to follow and watch guests who have already **stolen items** from the park. They count the value, waiting until it reaches the point where it becomes grand theft rather than petty theft, and then they will apprehend them.

44. The biggest **shoplifting offenders** are parents with baby carriages, as they throw toys in with the kids.

45. You cannot walk down the parade route without **being on at least one camera**. These are hidden well, but can be found. One obvious camera is in what looks like a light fixture on the top of a speaker pole next to *Pixi Hollow* (in front of the temporary Christmas parade spot tower). The camera shoots down the dog leg towards *it's a small world*. These cameras are primarily used for spotting the parades, but security has a feed too.

46. The security **cameras in many of the attractions are infrared** based and can be seen next to the infrared lights (the things that glow red) by turning around in such attractions as *Pirates of The Caribbean*, *Splash Mountain*, and other attractions that are in the dark.

47. Landscapers replant the **giant Mickey** in the front of *Main Street, U.S.A.* about nine times a year.

48. The **first "performer" Mickey Mouse** character at the park was Paul Castle, a former ice capades performer who skated with Sonja Henie and was hired personally by Walt Disney.

49. There's a **tunnel that leads from below** the *Innoventions* building to the area opposite the *Matterhorn* (south). Trash is removed from *Club Buzz* (formally *Tomorrowland Terrace*) via this tunnel. The tunnel is big enough to drive a car through. The entrance to this tunnel is backstage near the backside of the *Innoventions* building. Small trucks full of trash use an elevator to get to the tunnel, and there is also a set of stairs that lead down to the tunnel. The tunnel houses a break room and some dressing rooms, offices and storage space, along with trash compactors. The end of the tunnel is across from the *Matterhorn*, right behind the phones. The building is actually the backside of *Buzz Lightyear* and another door leads into that attraction. The tunnel is also used to get the band from off stage to the rising *Club Buzz* stage.

50. The **costumes that the Cast Members wear** come from a huge building in the back, and are washed daily. Some of the Cast Members might be heard complaining about the costuming department for never having the right sizes.

51. After months of rodent infestation, *Disneyland* finally sought to check the rodent population by natural selection. **They brought in cats to hunt them down.** "Wild" cats still roam the park to this day, appearing late at night and early in the mornings, wisely hiding from the public during business hours. *Disneyland* has always had a problem with cats. It is said that the castle's 1957 makeover, when they added the walkthrough attraction, revealed  almost 100 feral cats living in it. Since then they have been fed and cared for by the Cast Members. In 2001, the TNR (Trap, Neuter, and Return) groups *Best Friends, Catnippers,* and *FixNation* got involved with Disney to have the cats altered to prevent breeding. If kittens did manage to show up, they were adopted out to good homes. There is said to be around 200 cats living on the property now. There are five feeding stations around the parks that look like dog houses, for the cats to eat in. Cats have been seen on *Main Street, U.S.A.* in the bushes behind the food counter area of *Carnation Plaza Gardens*. One of the best places to see them was in *Thunder Ranch BBQ* area, but  that area is gone now because of *Star Wars Land*. They have even stopped the *Big Thunder Railroad* by tripping sensors and confusing the computers. It is definitely weird to watch the cats playing in what they call their home while tourists are eating, shopping, and riding the attractions in *Disneyland* and *California Adventure*. The photo of the long-haired tortoiseshell is of a cat referred to as Francisco (*see photo*). There is an Instagram page for photos of all of the cats called "DisneylandCats." You can also check out DisneylandCats.com. There are feed stations around the park. They look like dog houses, but they have food and water in them. (*see photo*)

52. Although there are plenty of birds and other animals at *Disneyland*, Disney **augments their sounds** throughout the park.

53. When the park closes at night, **big lights, similar to those in a stadium**, rise up from behind the buildings on *Main Street, U.S.A.* so that workers

428

can see better when they clean. At 6:30 a.m., right before the park opens for early entry; the lights turn off and lower back behind the buildings.

54. The **address to *Disneyland*** is 1313 S. Harbor Blvd. The 13th letter of the alphabet is "M"...leading one to believe that the address stands for the park's most famous resident's initials...M.M.

55. All of the Disney **3D Adventure Shows**, such as *Muppet Vision 3D*, and *Captain EO*, *It's Tough to Be A Bug*, as well as the since-past show *Magic Journeys,* use the same principle of presentation. Unlike normal 3D show (red/blue lenses), these films use a process of reverse polarization every other frame. The clear glasses are reversed polarized, which allow your eyes to detect the difference of angle between the two frames. This method is cheap for filming, and it can be added after filming is done. It also adds a higher degree of control on the 3D effects.

56. There is a large fixture in the *Carnation Baby Care Center's* changing room. It isn't a sink or a toilet, it's actually a combination of both. **It's called a Hopper**. The fixture was used to wash and rinse soiled cloth diapers. It was installed in the 1950's, before disposable diapers were invented.

57. It took only **364 days** to build Disneyland.

58. All the garbage cans are **20 paces** apart from each other. Walt Disney started walking while eating a hot dog. After he ate the whole thing, he counted how many paces he went.

59. Due to the fact that two people died on the (since removed) ***People Mover*,** **Cast Members nicknamed** the attraction the "People Re-Mover." Also for how secluded the individual cars were, people have been caught "fooling around" in them, gaining it the nickname "People Maker."

60. The **parrot sitting on the giant map** in the queue for *Pirates of the Caribbean* makes the same whistle sound as the re-entry turnstiles to the park and the bluebird from the "Zip-A-Dee-Doo-Dah" song in *Song Of The South*.

61. **Tinker Bell flies from the top of the *Matterhorn*** during fireworks shows. Tinker Bell is not wearing just a wig, she is wearing a helmet that looks like a wig from far away. Both male and female aerialists have been known to play her during the show. At the end of the zip line, on a platform behind *Village Haus* restaurant, there are Cast Members holding a mattress for her to fly into. It's the best way to slow her down. There was a short period of time in 1966 when they had Mary Poppins fly across, and more recently Dumbo, Zero, and Nemo have flown as well. In *Disney* 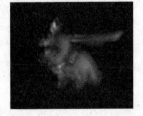 *World,* Tink wears a full-face mask to look more like the animated pixie.

62. The **first Tinker Bell to take flight off the top of the Matterhorn was 70- year-old Tiny Kline**. Kline was a 4 foot 10-inch-tall former circus aerialist for Ringling Bros. and Barnum & Bailey Circus in Hungary. The first time Tinker Bell flew was in 1961. It is rumored that Tinker Bell makes $650 a night for her flight now. Kline retired in 1964 due to health reasons and passed on the job to Mimi Zerbini, a 19-year-old French circus acrobat who flew across the skies for only one summer. The next year it went to Judy Kaye who did it for over a decade, then to Gina Rock in 1983.

63. **Gina Rock**. She flew for 21 ½ years from 1983 to 2005. I got to know Gina very well in recent years. In November 2015, she emailed me asking if I could write an article about what she has been doing since she retired her wings. My article about her was published in the *Disneyana Newsletter*. The following summer she asked me to be her Public Relations Manager, to which I obliged. I connected her with podcasts and interviews. She had me sell her autographed photos on Etsy and eBay. Gina led a fantastic life. She has many stories to tell. Look her up on my website and read about her accomplishments in my blog. There are also links to her interviews. (*see photo*)

64. The Arribas Brothers met Walt Disney at New York's World's Fair in 1964. They had their own glass blowing/sculpting and crystal collectables business. They opened their first crystal shop in *New Orleans Square* in 1967. **It is the oldest company contracted by Disney** to be in the parks. They have two shops; one is in *New Orleans Square* called *Cristal D'Orleans*, and the other is on *Main Street, U.S.A.* and is called *Crystal Arts*. (*see photo*)

65. There is a "Cast Member only" **dining facility that is located in-between** *Main Street, U.S.A.* and *Tomorrowland* **called "The Inn Between."** It was also a sly reference to the animation term "in betweener," referring to an artist who fills in the drawings between the animator's key drawings. "The Inn Between" was the first employee cafeteria in *Disneyland* and the only one open for graveyard shift. It is located at the rear of the *Red Wagon Inn*.

66. In 1955, it cost **$17 million to build** *Disneyland.* Taking into account inflation, it would equal about $116 million with today's rates. It puts things into perspective, knowing that Disney spent $1.1 billion just to give *California Adventure* a makeover.

67. Part of *Disneyland's* **dress code set in the 1950's** prevented men from having beards, moustaches, and even long hair. Disney wanted everyone

clean cut. In the 1960's, people associated long hair on men with hippies and Disney didn't want that. Cast Members at the park gates were also required to turn away park visitors who had long hair, stating that it was an "unwritten" requirement to enter the park as part of the dress code. In the early 2000's, after a 43-year ban, Disney relaxed their policy and allowed men to sport a neatly-trimmed moustache, as pointed out by a Cast Member, "That is what Mr. Disney had." As of February 3, 2012, employees can grow beards or goatees as long as the hair is shorter than a quarter of an inch, and not a "soul patch." In 2010, Disney said women didn't have to wear pantyhose with skirts. They were also allowed to wear sleeveless tops with shoulder straps that were at least 3 inches wide. Men were also allowed to wear untucked, casual shirts. *Disneyland* reviews dress codes among other things to keep up with the times, but despite the wave of changes, there are still plenty of personal appearance choices that Disney doesn't allow. Those would be visible tattoos, body piercings (other than the ears for women), "extreme" hair styles or colors, and muttonchops (big sideburns like Wolverine). A shaved head is acceptable for a man but not for a woman.

68. ***Children's Fairyland* in Oakland, California,** was one of Walt's inspirations for *Disneyland*. He even went so far as to hire *Fairyland's* first director, Dorothy Manes, to work for him in *Disneyland*. On one of Walt's visits, he painted a picture of Mickey Mouse on one of the walls in the park.

69. ABC television studios were **one of the original financial backers** for *Disneyland* and owned shares of the park. Disney bought full ownership of ABC in 1995 for $19 billion.

70. **Walt Disney never owned *Disneyland*.** He was the creative genius behind the concept and had stock in the company, but he never owned a controlling share.

71. At the entrance to the park there is **a plaque that reads,** "Here you leave today and enter the world of yesterday, tomorrow and fantasy."

72. *Disneyland* **doesn't sell chewing gum.** It is a problem for people to litter and spit the gum on the ground, making it difficult to clean up.

73. *Disneyland* has a contract to **sell only Coca-Cola** in the parks.

74. Mickey Mouse **never appears in two places at the same time** in the park. The *Movie Barn* in his *Toontown* house is closed for photos when Mickey has a parade or show.

75. There have been **16,000,000 autograph books** and about 7,000,000 autograph pens sold in *Disneyland* since it opened in 1955.

76. They originally **planned to have a "Land of Oz."** At the time of planning, Disney owned the rights to the L. Frank Baum's books, but still ended up scrapping the idea.

77. When in the planning stages, *Tom Sawyer Island* **was originally going to be called *Mickey Mouse Island*.** Walt decided against it because if

Disneyland was going to be a failure, he didn't want his prized star connected with the project. This is also the reason why he had Tinker Bell as the mascot for the television show *Disneyland*, also known as *Walt Disney's Wonderful World of Color* and has been on the air for 52 seasons.

78. The fireworks show *"Remember... Dreams Come True"* was such a big secret that **Disney did the show tests in the Gobi Desert** in China to prevent people from finding out.

79. The **fireworks show above the castle costs roughly $41,000** every night.

80. New **Cast Members are sent through a three- to five-day training course** called "Traditions," where they are taught that *Disneyland* isn't just an everyday job, but rather, it is a show and to act like they are on stage for everyone to see.

81. **Cast Members are required to use the "Disney Point."** When someone normally points toward something, they use their pointer finger. Some cultures consider this to be a rude gesture, so Disney requires all Cast Members to point with their pointer finger and middle finger at the same time, so they are two-finger pointing. They can also use their whole hand for pointing.

82. Disneyland **goes through 500 brooms** every year to keep the park clean.

83. Disneyland **collects 30 tons of garbage** in an average day.

84. Disney is proud of its recycling program. There are Cast Members hired just to sort through the garbage and recyclables to separate the bottles and cans to **collect a total of 22 tons a DAY**. The recycling program at the park was suggested by a Cast Member in 1988, and the proceeds from the recycling are donated to *Canine Companions For Independence*. That totals over $250K. Because of this program, there have been more than 35 assistance dogs assigned to human companions with disabilities.
   • There are over 650 recycling containers around the resort.
   • They recycle enough aluminum each year to make a soda can about 1,000 times taller than the Matterhorn.
   • More glass is recycled each year than the weight of eight steam trains.
   • And enough paper each year to create a trail from *Disneyland* Resort to *Walt Disney World* Resort and back, twice!
   • The paper napkins and plastic merchandise bags used by Guests are made from 100% recycled content.
   • More than 600,000 plastic cards, from hotel room keys to Main Entrance passes, get collected for recycling each year.
   • *Disneyland* Resort partners with *Clean the World* to donate more than 1,000 pounds of partially-used soaps and bottled amenities per month from its hotels, which are sanitized and recycled into hygiene products for people around the globe.

85. Name tags are worn by all Cast Members signifying their first name and the city from which they originated. Even higher-up management have name tags. This is

432

because **Walt disliked being called "Mr. Disney,"** so he wore his name tag stating his name was 'Walt.' Even the animals around the park have name tags. (*see photo*)

86. **Doritos were invented in *Disneyland*.** There was a restaurant in *Frontierland* called *Casa De Frito*, which is now *Rancho del Zocalo Restaurante*, and was sponsored by Frito-Lay and opened shortly after the park did in 1955. This was a sit-down restaurant and was well known for its Frito Pie. At the end of the day, the restaurant would throw out old corn tortillas supplied by Alex Foods. A distributor for Alex Foods noticed this happening and suggested to the chef to turn the unwanted corn tortillas into corn chips. The chef did this and added seasonings to the final product to resemble the Mexican chilaquiles. Over time, they became so popular that the restaurant began selling them in bags for 5¢ in 1964. The Frito Kid was the mascot and had a statue standing near the restaurant while people inserted their money into the "vending machine." The Frito Kid had two locations from which you could purchase the chips. One was by the entrance to *Casa De Frito* and the second was at *Aunt Jemima's Pancake House* near *Pirates of the Caribbean*.

Frito-Lay figured out that they could mass produce these phenomenal chips and wanted to make them available outside the park. Up until now, Frito-Lay didn't have any corn-based chips in their arsenal of products available elsewhere; their main seller was potato chips. In 1966, Frito-Lay made "Doritos" available nationwide, making it the first nationally-distributed corn chip. Not sure if this part is true, but when the original logo was made, it resembled the original *Disneyland* entrance sign.

In 2012, Taco Bell celebrated their 50th anniversary and entered a partnership with Frito-Lay to sell Doritos Locos Tacos on their menu.

87. The orange grove property that Walt bought **covered 160 acres**.

88. The **record for most Guests in one day** was set on July 4, 1987, with over 87,000 people in the park. That record was broken in 1996 when The Electrical Parade had its final performances.

89. In the 1950's, **Disney printed a *Disneyland Souvenir Guide*** to sell to Guests. They cost 24¢ each to print and the park only sold them for 25¢. Walt said he didn't want to raise the price because this way people would have them on their coffee table and it would advertise the park.

90. When you hear, **"What are you doing next?" "I'm going to *Disneyland*,"** you should know that the saying was started by aviator pilots Dick Rutan and Jeana Yeager. These two had just set the record for first non-stop flight around the world on December 23, 1986. The following January, Michael Eisner had them over for dinner with his wife, Jane. Jane had said, "What are you doing next?" To which they responded with, "Well, we're going to *Disneyland*." Jane suggested to Michael that they use it for advertising. Which they did that year following Super Bowl

XXI when they paid $75,000 to the quarterback for the Giants, Phil Simms, to respond with "I'm going to *Disneyland*," after being asked what he was going to do now that he had won the Super Bowl. They did alternating takes with him saying "*Disney World*" and "*Disneyland*."

91. All the Disney parks have a high volume of attendance. Disney parks alone take up the **top eight spots in world popularity**. All the parks have a 2011 combined attendance of <u>121,405,000</u> people. There are/have been 1,498 themed parks on this planet. The following is a listing of worldwide popularity based on attendance.

World Ranking in Themed Park Attendance		
RANK	PARK	2011 ATTENDANCE
1	Magic Kingdom (Florida)	17,142,000
2	Disneyland (California)	16,140,000
3	Tokyo Disneyland (Japan)	13,996,000
4	Tokyo DisneySea (Japan)	11,930,000
5	Disneyland Paris (Paris)	10,990,000
6	Epcot (Florida)	10,825,000
7	Animal Kingdom (Florida)	9,783,000
8	Hollywood Studios (Florida)	9,699,000
13	California Adventure (California)	6,341,000
15	Hong Kong Disneyland (China)	5,900,000
20	Walt Disney Studios Park (Paris)	4,710,000
-	Shanghai Disney (China)	0
World Ranking in Water Park Attendance		
RANK	PARK	2011 ATTENDANCE
1	Typhoon Lagoon (Florida)	2,058,000
3	Blizzard Beach (Florida)	1,891,000

92. The **shortest-lived attraction in *Disneyland*** was the ***Mickey Mouse Club Circus***. Disney brought the entire Gil Gray Circus show from the Midwest, including their elephants, camels, llamas, and ponies. The show also starred the kids, including Annette Funicello, from the *Mickey Mouse Club*. Debuting November 24, 1955, and ending January 8, 1956, makes it the shortest-lived attraction, only lasting 46 days before closing due to lack of interest. Guests skipped seeing the circus because they could see that anytime; the other Disney attractions they could not. After the Circus closed, *Keller's Jungle Killers* took its place for another seven months before its closing and removal. The two $48,000 candy-striped circus tents were located near where the *Matterhorn* is today. After the attraction was removed, the tents were sent over to *Holidayland*, the future site of *New Orleans Square*, to provide shade. The circus wagons that Disney rounded up and refurbished for this attraction were then sent to the Disney studio to be used in the film *Toby Tyler* (1960), and then later donated to the Circus World Museum in Baraboo, Wisconsin. One of the Imagineers on this project was Richard Irvine, who's son married Kim Thomas (Leota Tombs' daughter), who's name was then changed to Kim Irvine, the current face of Madame Leota in the *Haunted Mansion Holiday*.

93. **Disneyland once had an airport**. It was connected to the Los Angeles International Airport. Los Angeles Airways would bring in visitors or VIPs

via helicopter. The original location of the heliport was just outside *Tomorrowland* over the east wall near Highway 5 and Harbor Blvd. The heliport was operational before *Disneyland* opened in 1955 until it was moved two years later to make way for the realined *Disneyland Railroad* tracks. It was then moved 140 yards south by where the tram pick up/drop off area is now. After three years at that location, it was moved 1,000 yards west to the other side of the resort which is now the *Disneyland Hotel* parking lot. The heliport funchioned in its three locations for a total of 15 years before closing down after the Los Angeles Airways lost funding for it, due to the cost not being feasible. There were also two major accidents that occurred in that time. The first accident was on May 22, 1968, when 23 people died after the helicopter crashed due to the rotar blades coming off. The second accident was on August 14, 1968, when the chopper went down from a fatigue fracture on the blade spindle killing 21 passengers, including the 13-year old grandson of Clarence Belinn, the founder & president of Los Angeles Airways.

94. The *Disneyland* park announcer is Bill Rodgers, and has been since 1991. The announcer for *California Adventure* is Camille Dixon. **Both park announcers are actually married to each other** and live near the park. They have a recording studio in their home so they can make announcements straight from there and send them on over to Disney.

95. Walt **Disney liked spending time with his park Guests** and could sometimes be found waiting in line with them.

96. There have been **three babies born on Disneyland** property since its opening.
   • Born on July 4, 1979, to Teresa Salcedo. The baby received a *Disneyland* birth certificate and was presented it by Mickey Mouse.
   • Born on December 2, 1984, to Margarita Granados. Margarita waited in Tomorrowland for her husband to ride on *Space Mountain*. When Juan returned to her, he had a new daughter.
   • Born on March 11, 2012, to an unnamed mother in the *Toy Story Parking Lot*.

97. When new Cast Members are hired, they have thr**ee days to memorize all of their diologue** down to the letter and inflection.

98. Before fame hit them, so**me celebrities started out working in a Disney park**.
   • Steve Martin – Magic Shop
   • Robin Williams – *Jungle Cruise* Skipper (Rumored)
   • Michelle Pfeiffer – Portrayed Alice in the Main Street Electrical Parade
   • Kevin Costner - *Jungle Cruise* Skipper (his wife Cindy Silva was portraying Snow White when they met and were married 1978-1994)
   • Wayne Brady - Tigger at *Walt Disney World*
   • Teri Garr – Dancer in the Disneyland Parades
   • Joanna Kerns – Portrayed the Blue Fairy in the Main Street Electrical Parade

- Taye Diggs - Dancer in *Sebastian's Caribbean Carnival* at *Tokyo Disneyland*
- John Lasseter - *Jungle Cruise* Skipper (1977-1978)
- Kevin Richardson (The Backstreet Boys) – Was Aladdin in one of the shows
- Richard Carpenter (The Carpenters) – Played the piano on *Main Street, U.S.A.*
- Alyson Reed – Portrayed Alice in the park
- Leanza Cornett (Miss America 1993) – Portrayed Ariel in *Disney World* in 1991
- Ron Ziegler (Richard Nixon's White House Press Secretary) - *Jungle Cruise* Skipper
- Sarah Butler – Portrayed Belle in the park
- Kara Monaco - Portrayed Alice, Ariel, Cinderella, and Snow White at *Walt Disney World*.
- John McEuen (Nitty Gritty Dirt Band) – Was a musician in the park, and taught Steve Martin how to play the banjo.
- Kathryn Joosten – A street performer in Disney's Hollywood Studios

99. During the New Year's Event in 1999, **Disney handed out glow sticks to the Guests and referred to them as "wishing wands."** They did this because of the theory that all the computers would crash at midnight. They thought they would possibly lose power. There were about 80,000 Guests in the park that day. Picture 80,000 glow sticks all out at the same time. Cast Members who weren't working attractions were ordered to leave their posts and go backstage in case the power did go out and there was a Guest stampeed.

100. If someone is being rude to a Cast Member and you hear them say **"Have a Disney Day,"** what they are really saying is "Go s**ew yourself."

101. **Cast Members aren't allowed to say "I don't know."** If they truly don't know the answer to a Guest's question, they must find someone who does know the answer.

102. Originally, **Walt refered to the "Lands" of the park as "Realms."**

103. If you go to *Coke Corner* at the end of *Main Street, U.S.A.*, look up at the lights above the doorway. Every other light is red/white. **The corner light is actually painted** because the lights didn't match up. Half is white and the other half is painted red.

104. Don't think that because Disney World is bigger, that **there are more attractions**. Here are the number of attractions for comparison.

Walt Disney World Resort

Magic Kingdom	37	
EPCOT	31	
Hollywood Studios	19	TOTAL
Animal Kingdom	22	109

Disneyland Resort

Disneyland Attractions	53	TOTAL
California Adventure	36	89

Disneyland Fun Facts

MAIN STREET, U.S.A.

Main Street, U.S.A. is the first land you pass through after entering the park. A lot of shopping and dining can be done in this land, along with watching some entertaining street shows. All of the parades travel down the center of this street during show time. The *City Hall*, which serves as the *Customer Service Center*, can be found on the left side of the street next to the *Disneyland Fire Department*, just after you enter the park.

FUN FACTS

- **General Electric installed their first industrial air conditioner prototype** unit in the Walt Disney Animation Studio in 1939.

- *Main Street, U.S.A.* was designed to **resemble a turn-of-the-century town** in the 1920's.

- The original plans **mirrored the town of Marceline, Missouri**. A depiction of this town can also be seen in the animated film *Lady and the Tramp* (1955). Walt incorporated some of the look of the Colorado town, Fort Collins. Harper Goff (see *Imagineer Mini Biographies on page 288*) showed Walt some of his childhood photos of the town and Walt used them to create the look. Harper even designed *City Hall* to look like the one from his home town.

- The **"hub and spoke" design at the end of** *Main Street, U.S.A.,* in front of the castle, was created by Walt to help patrons go to the land of their choosing faster and more efficiently. By standing in the middle of the hub, you can go in any direction entering into a different land. Other theme parks just have a pathway design where there is a starting point and you have to go through certain sections to get to other sections.

- **Walt Disney stated**, "*For those of us who remember the carefree time it recreates, Main Street will bring back happy memories. For younger visitors, it is an adventure in turning back the calendar to the days of their grandfather's youth.*"

- The lamp that you see burning in the window above the **fire department** is kept burning all the time in tribute to Walt. That room was once his apartment. It is fully furnished, but is not open to the public.

- *Main Street, U.S.A.* is a **real street** listed in the Orange County Thomas Guide.

- The *Main Street, U.S.A.* entrance was **designed to look like a red carpet** with red bricks, instead of asphalt or cement like the rest of the park. It is said that Walt Disney originally wanted to put in actual red carpet for people to walk on, but his Cast Members talked him out of it, stating that it would get dirty really fast with the large volume of foot traffic.

- Have you ever tried to walk down the sidewalks of *Main Street, U.S.A.* while looking at the castle? You can't because the **trees were strategically placed** so that, when you are walking down the sidewalks, you are forced to look into the shops and windows. But when you are walking down the middle of the street, you are forced to look at the castle and the trees partially obstruct the view of the windows.

- There is reasoning behind *Main Street, U.S.A.* being **the only street that is paved with asphalt**. In the summer time when crowds are at their peak, the ground gets hot and radiates heat, thereby forcing people to continue to proceed toward the lands where the ground is cool cement. This is so that people don't "clog" up the entrance, referred to as "the bottleneck."

- **Sound tracks can be heard in the windows** on the side street heading to the lockers. The sound effects coming out of the D*entist's Office* are said to be from the dentist's office in the mining town of Rainbow Ridge. It was from the old *Nature's Wonderland* train ride, which has parts now located at the end of *Big Thunder Mountain Railroad*.

- On the way to the lockers there is **a building called *Hotel Marceline***. A tribute to Walt Disney's home town of Marceline, Missouri, the town he moved to in 1906.

- When *Disneyland* was first built, Disney tried to keep as many of the original trees as they possibly could. Over the course of over a half century, all of the original orange trees have died off. The **only remaining original trees are the eucalyptus trees** (and one palm tree in *Adventureland*) behind the *City Hall*. These were first planted by the farmers to protect the orange grove trees from strong winds.

438

🏰 There are **singing quartette groups** that can be found along *Main Street, U.S.A.* Check with *City Hall* if you want to find out the next time and location of their performance.

🏰 The *Partners* **statue is located in the center of the hub** at the end of *Main Street, U.S.A.* There is usually a photographer there to take photos of guests. The bronze statue was first put there November 18, 1993, to commemorate Mickey's 65th birthday. The statue is surrounded by smaller bronze statues representing different Disney characters. They are: Goofy, Dumbo, Donald, Chip & Dale, Pinocchio, Minnie, and the White Rabbit. It was sculpted by Imagineer Blaine Gibson. (*see photo*)

🏰 In the coffee shop, *Market House*, there are **old-fashioned telephones** that have a recording of random chatter and conversations. Pick one up and listen.

🏰 The **second story windows have the names** of some of the important people who contributed to make *Disneyland* what it is today. One window is a tribute to Elias Disney, Walt's father.

🏰 The ring that Walt Disney wears on his right ring finger **on the "*Partners*" statue is called a Claddagh ring.** It is an Irish ring first made popular in the village of Claddagh (near Galway) in the 17th century. It represents love, loyalty, and friendship (the hands represent friendship, the heart represents love, and the crown represents loyalty). Walt was known for wearing one, which is why 45-year veteran Imagineer Blaine Gibson (sculptor, painter, artist) designed the statue with him wearing it. Blaine was

attributed with sculpting many of the characters that were made into animatronics or bronze statues. He sculpted the 3D models for characters on *Pirates of the Caribbean, Great Moments with Mr. Lincoln, Haunted Mansion*, and *Enchanted Tiki Room*. Blaine retired in 1983 and was named a Disney legend in 1993; that same year he designed the "*Partners*" statue. I am unsure as to why Blaine designed the ring with the heart facing outward as that symbolizes "single and may be looking for love." The other meanings are:

- On the right hand with the point of the heart toward the wrist, the wearer is in a relationship.
- On the left hand with the point of the heart toward the fingertips, the wearer is engaged.
- On the left hand with the point of the heart toward the wrist, the wearer is married.

🏰 If you notice along *Main Street, U.S.A.,* there are

hitching posts in the shape of horse heads. There is no real use for them today, but at the turn of the 20th century, people still rode horses and had to tie them up while they went inside shops. One of the hitching posts is shaped to look like a tree and is in front of the *China Closet Shop*. (*see photo*)

The picture used on the "Lost Parents Inquire Here for Children" sign in front of *City Hall* is a **portrait of Mr. & Mrs. Darling from *Peter Pan*** (1953). Their children were lost in Neverland.

The *Little Red Wagon* vendor is there to pay **homage to the late *Red Wagon Inn*** that used to reside in the space now occupied by the *Plaza Inn Restaurant*.

Back when *Disneyland* opened, there weren't any ATMs for people to withdraw money from their bank accounts. ***Bank of America*** **had a branch in the park** available to Guests every day the park was open from 1955-1998. *Bank of America* was one of the investors in the park, and were responsible for giving Walt his loan to make *Snow White and the Seven Dwarfs* (1937).

The new *Jolly Holiday Bakery Café* opened in January 2012, replacing *Blue Ribbon Bakery* as the source of baked goods. The building housed the A*nnual Pass Holder Center*. On the top of the building is a Mary Poppins weathervane showing Mary with her popular carpet bag in her hand. **Inside the bag are actually two pennies** placed there by the Imagineers. One was minted in 1955 to represent the opening of the park, and the other is from 2012 to represent the opening of the new bakery.

There is a **use of forced perception** with the *Main Street, U.S.A.* buildings. The second floors are shorter than the first floors, while the third floors are shorter than the second floors, making the buildings appear bigger than they actually are.

It is said that Emile Kuri, set director for films like *20,000 Leagues Under the Sea* (1954), *The Absent-Minded Professor* (1961), *Mary Poppins* (1964), *Bedknobs and Broomsticks* (1971), and *It's A Wonderful Life* (1946), witnessed an automobile accident that dislodged a light post. He offered the city $5 for the broken lamp post. **That lamp post was used for the base of the flagpole** at the train station at the front of the park. (*see photo*)

All of the **stone sidewalks used to have Mickey heads** on them, but over the years they have worn away. If you look closely at the less traveled areas, you may be able to make out a Mickey.

440

When facing the entrance to the locker rental area, look to the right. Do you see the brick wall? Notice the variety of bricks. This wall **is called "*The Test Brick Wall*."** It is said that this is where they tested different bricks and layouts for the park in 1954-55. After it was all said and done, the brick wall was left behind due to lack of time and money to remove it. Since then, the wall has been left up to pay tribute to the creation of the park.

The fortune teller, Esmerelda, in the *Penny Arcade,* is **using a *Haunted Mansion*-themed deck of playing cards** to tell fortunes. The cards have pictures of the stretching portraits and the head of Madam Leota. (*see photo*)

There are no longer signs on *Main Street, U.S.A.* that mark **the intersection for Center Street and Plaza Street.** Plaza Street is on the left and was taken over by Carnation Café, and Plaza Street is occupied by the fruit cart. The lockers are found at the end of this street.

Above the *Penny Arcade* sign, there is a **giant Indian head penny**. The year it was "minted" was 1901. That is for the year Walt was born. The *Penny Arcade* opened on July 22, 1955, along with the *Candy Palace*, only five days after the park opened. (*see photo*)

Outside the *Candy Palace,* there are vents to pump out scents. **This technologically-advanced machine is called the Smellitzer**. It was invented by Imagineer Bob McCarthy in the 1980's for the *Spaceship Earth* attraction in *Epcot* to simulate the smell of smoke. It is used elsewhere around the park, like on *Soarin' Around the World*, or *Heimlich's Chew Chew Train,* to make you smell fresh grass or animal crackers. It is also said that they are used to make *Haunted Mansion* and *Pirates of the Caribbean* smell musty and old. When *Disneyland* first opened, they just had fans to blow out the smell of fresh-baked cookies to lure in tourists. Now they use the Smellitzer to pump out the smell of vanilla, and at Christmas time they use peppermint.

The gas lamps that are located on the sidewalks down *Main Street, U.S.A.* were found in 1955 by *Disneyland* designer Emile Kuri. **The gas lamps were 150 years old** at the time and were in a scrap yard in Baltimore, Maryland. Some of the other lamps were purchased in St. Louis, Missouri, and Philadelphia, Pennsylvania. Back when *Disneyland* opened, they used to have a Cast Member dressed up like a 19th century lamplighter who would go around and light them all at dusk.

Disneyland had a monthly **newspaper that they printed called *The Disneyland News,*** which lasted from July 1955 until March 1957. The

Disneyland News spoke of *Disneyland* events, news, and ads from the park's contracted shops. From 1959 to 1968 the paper was printed sporadically, and was never published more than once in a quarter. After 1968, the paper was inactive. But special issues were printed in 1985 for the park's 30th anniversary and in 1988 for the *Splash Mountain* unveiling.

The **bench that Walt sat on in Griffith Park,** when he came up with the spectacular idea for *Disneyland,* can be seen in the *Opera House*. It currently houses *Great Moments with Mr. Lincoln*. (*see photo*)

Main Street, U.S.A. **once had a pharmacy.** It was called the *Upjohn Pharmacy*, and was located where the *New Century Jewelry* shop is now. Visitors used to get free samples of vitamins handed out in little glass bottles. It, too, was designed to look like a turn-of-the-century pharmacy with lots of detail, down to the container of wiggling leeches on the counter. Throughout the decades, this shop has gone through many names: *Upjohn Pharmacy* (1955-1970), *Hurricane Lamp Shop* (1972-1976), *Disneyana* (1976-1986), *Century Watches and Clocks*, aka *New Century Timepieces,* aka *New Century Jewelry* (1972-present).

Disneyland used to house the *Disneyland Tobacco Shop*. There is a **wooden looking Native American statue on** *Main Street, U.S.A.* in front of the now *20th Century Music Company* to pay homage to the long extinct shop. The shop sold cigarettes, tobacco products, and even offered complimentary *Disneyland* matchbooks, until it closed in 1991. The "Tobacco Indian" was first created in a time where most people were illiterate. The statue showed that tobacco was located in that store, just like giant keys represented locksmiths, red-and-white-striped poles represented barbers, giant scissors for tailors, and anvils for blacksmiths. The Indian is not even wood. The original wooden one was the model for the fiberglass one that is there today. I guess closing the store in 1991 was a good thing, since the California smoking ban went into effect January 1995. (*see photo*)

The **two cannons** (*see photo*) **on** *Main Street, U.S.A.* **were actual working cannons** from the 19th century and were used by the French Army.

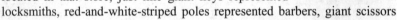

- One of the stores that used to reside on *Main Street, U.S.A.* was **a shop for women called the,** also known as "The Wizard of Bras." It was only open for six months.

- To **help encourage customers to purchase warm clothing articles** and sweaters, the *Main Street, U.S.A. Disney Store* is kept several degrees cooler than the other stores.

- It is said that **Walt wanted curves to his sidewalks** instead of harsh corners, to make them feel more inviting.

- In the development stage, Walt wanted two streets added onto *Main Street, U.S.A.* that were never built. A street called ***Edison Square* was going to jet off of *Main Street, U.S.A.*** up by the *Plaza Inn*. **The second street was going to be called *Liberty Street***, and was going to be located to the left of *Great Moments with Mr. Lincoln*, where the parade exits the street. Both the streets would have been between the buildings on *Main Street, U.S.A.* and *Tomorrowland*, which then had *20,000 Leagues Exhibit*, but now has *Space Mountain*. There was a variation of the street built in *Walt Disney World's Magic Kingdom* called *Liberty Square*.

- People do not really notice the windows on *Main Street, U.S.A.* Each window on the second floor along the street is dedicated to individuals who had a huge influence with the construction or concepts of the park.

- For a **list of this attractions Hidden Mickeys,** see page 349.

- For a **list of Disneyland's Attractions of the Past**, see page 660.

Attractions

Disneyland Railroad

Opened July 17, 1955 - Duration: 18:00

A train ride that circles *Disneyland*.

FUN FACTS

- It was **originally called the *Santa Fe & Disneyland Railroad*** until 1974.

- There are a total of five engines in *Disneyland:*
  - #1 C.K. Holliday
  - #2 E.P. Ripley
  - #3 Fred G. Gurley
  - #4 Ernest S. Marsh
  - #5 Ward Kimball

- There were **two locomotives originally built** at the Disney Studio, the *E.P. Ripley* and the *C.K. Holliday*. Both were named after founders of the Santa Fe Railroad.

🚂 It wasn't until 1958 that **Disneyland had to add a third locomotive**, the *Fred G. Gurley*, named after the (at the time) chairman of the railroad. Instead of creating a whole new locomotive from scratch, the Disney designers found a Baldwin model in use that was built in 1894. It was originally used to haul sugar cane in Louisiana. Disney purchased it for a little over $37,000.

🚂 In 1959, a **fourth locomotive was found hauling lumber in New England** and was repurposed for travel around the park. This one was named the *Ernest S. Marsh* after the president of the railroad. It had been built in 1925.

🚂 Engine #5 was added in June 2005, and was named the *Ward Kimball*, after the animator Ward Kimball. He also had a model train set that was rideable in his backyard just like Walt. **Ward's train was actually the inspiration for Walt to make his own**. Because of his train knowledge, Ward was a consultant on the creation and building of the *Disneyland Railroad*.

🚂 The **train station announcer is usually the first thing you hear** after you enter the park. You can hear it from the Mickey head flowerbed area. The announcement is as follows; *"Your attention please. The Disneyland Limited, now arriving from a trip around Walt Disney's Magic Kingdom. Passengers will stand by to board. Your attention please. The Disneyland limited, now leaving for a grand circle tour of the Magic Kingdom, with stops at New Orleans Square, Mickey's Toontown, and Tomorrowland. All passengers BOARD!"* The announcer's voice belongs to Peter Renaday, the same voice you hear for the narration in *The Many Adventures of Winnie The Pooh* (read further ahead in *Haunted Mansion* for more information about Peter).

🚂 When it first opened in 1955, **there were only two stops for the train**, *Main Street, U.S.A.* and *Frontierland*. In 1956, the *Fantasyland* station was added (renamed *Toontown Station* in 1994) and *Tomorrowland* in 1958.

🚂 The **Santa Fe Railroad Company** was the only company that responded to a solicited request for sponsorship of the railroad. Walt did this to help offset building costs.

🚂 From the years 1955 until 1974, when sponsorship ended, the **Santa Fe "rail pass"** was honored in lieu of a required "D" ticket.

🚂 The **narration provided inside** the cars at multiple points throughout the ride around the park once featured the voice of actor Vic Perrin (original narrator for *Spaceship Earth* in *Epcot* at *Disney World* and opening narrations for *The Outer Limits* television series), then later, Thurl Ravenscroft (see *Who Does That Voice on page 147*), and also Jack "The Voice Of *Disneyland*" Wagner.

🚂 *Disneyland* estimates that the train makes about **13,000 trips** around the park annually.

🚂 This is considered the **longest attraction** in the park, taking 18 minutes to circle the park and make all four stops.

- **There are 11 numbered markers along the tracks**. These number the eleven sections of the track. There cannot be more than one train in a section at a time. This is why you see the red or green lights along the track as well. Green means the section is clear. Red means the train stops until the light is green and can proceed into the next section.
- Since the train first started its operation in 1955, it has covered enough track to **circle the globe** 150 times.
- The first time any of the trains have been **viewed off-site** was May 6-7, 2006, at the annual Fullerton Railroad Days in Fullerton, California. People were able to view the *E.P. Ripley*.
- The conductors have their own **codes with the whistle blows**:
  - One Short – Attention
  - Two Short – Forward movement
  - Three Short – Reverse movement
  - One Long, One Short – Approaching station
  - One Long, Two Short – Crew spotted along track (also used as a general greeting)
  - Two Long, One Short, One Long – Public crossing ahead (with bell)
  - Two Long, One Short – Meeting point (Junction)
  - One Long – Stop immediately or emergency stop
  - Four Long – Train in distress
- When the original two trains were built, they **cost about $240,000 to construct,** with each locomotive engine costing about $40,000.
- The *Lilly Belle* **is a special caboose Walt named after his wife**. She was responsible for the Victorian era décor inside. It used to be open for the general public by reservation when it was opened for a trip around the park four times a day. But in March 2014, Disney made it only available for VIP tours, like a *"Walk in Walt's Disneyland Footsteps" Tour* (see *Take A Tour* on page 62), Club 33 members, or celebrities visiting the park. (*see photo*)

- The **first passengers to ride in the *Lilly Belle*** during its first official trip around the park on October 8, 1975, were Japanese Emperor Hirohito and his wife, Empress Nagako.
- The *Lilly Belle* is **pulled by the *C.K. Holliday*** engine.
- When you ride by the *Grand Canyon Diorama* (while traveling from *Tomorrowland* to *Main Street, U.S.A.*) you can spot **many native wildlife** in the form of taxidermied trophies: deer, mountain lion, turkeys, porcupines, skunks, a golden eagle, and mountain sheep.
- There are also **many species of dinosaurs** located in the *Primeval World Diorama* that follows the Grand Canyon. They are the brontosaurus, stegosaurus, tyrannosaurus rex, triceratops, pteranodons (the flying ones), edaphosaurus (fan back), and ornithomimus (the skinny ones drinking the

water). This diorama was designed by Xavier Atencio (see *Imagineer Mini Biographies* on page 288).

According to fossils recovered by paleontologists, the T-Rex has two fingers, but **the one in the diorama has three**. It is said that Walt liked the dinosaur better with three fingers, rather than two. This specific scene was modeled after an equivalent scene in the film *Fantasia* (1940) called "Rite of Spring." which depicts these same two dinosaurs and a three fingered T-Rex fighting. Since Xavier Atencio was also an animator for *Fantasia*, it might have been his idea to have three fingers to begin with.

FIRE ENGINE
Opened August 16, 1958

Disneyland's very own fire engine. Ride it from one end of *Main Street, U.S.A.* to the other. It's a one-way trip.

FUN FACTS

It is **modeled after** fire engines that were used in the early 1900's.

The **predecessor to this was the** *Fire Wagon* that made its appearance on opening day in 1955 and lasted until 1960, when it was placed in the Fire Station for viewing. It was pulled by horses.

This is another attraction that was designed by Bob Gurr (see *Imagineer Mini Biographies* on page 288). It is **slated as being Bob's attraction**. As Bob stated at the Walt Disney Imagineering Fan Club in April 2000, "*One day in the spring of 1958, Walt comes into my office as he usually does and he just sort of sits there and I looked at him and I said, 'Walt, you know there's one thing we haven't got in Disneyland! We don't have a fire engine on Main Street!' And he said, 'Yeah, we don't have a fire engine.'*

Privately, I wanted a fire engine and I knew that everybody else told me that the only thing that ever goes into Disneyland...those ideas come from Walt; they don't come from anybody else. But I wanted a fire engine. Anyway, he goes away and a little while later Accounting phones up and says, 'The charge number for the Fire Engine is....' So, I knew that Walt had gone to Accounting and had decided we're going to have a fire engine. That's the only attraction in Disneyland that's my attraction."

GREAT MOMENTS WITH MR. LINCOLN

Opened July 18, 1965

See America's 16th president, Abraham Lincoln, recite some of his famous speeches as an Audio-Animatronic character. The first of its kind, this human Audio-Animatronic broke ground for the attractions *Pirates of the Caribbean* and *Haunted Mansion*.

FUN FACTS

- Mr. Lincoln **first appeared in New York City's World's Fair** from April 22, 1964, to October 17, 1965. Robert Moses, who designed the World's Fair, approached Walt and asked if he had anything he wanted to contribute. At the time, Imagineer Bob Gurr (see *Imagineer Mini Biographies* on page 288) was designing Abe for the attraction and that is what Walt donated. They added it to the Illinois section at the fair.

- It was the **first human Audio-Animatronic** figure ever attempted by Walt Disney. One of the original designers was Imagineer and 2004 Disney Legend Bob Gurr. (*see photo*)

- The actor to provide the **voice of Abe is Royal Dano**. Dano was best known for his acting in western films and for his portrayal of President Lincoln in the television mini-series *Mr. Lincoln* (1952-1953).

- Dano had to **deliver his speech multiple times** until he was worn out because it did not meet Walt's expectations.

- The face of the animatronic Abe was copied from **an actual life mask made from Abe himself** in 1860 by the famous American sculptor, Leonard Volk (1828-1895). Mr. Lincoln sat and let Volk lay plaster strips on his face to harden.

- When the Imagineers were making the rubber face for Abraham Lincoln, they turned the face around so it was inside out **and realized that the eyes would follow them from side to side** because the face was concave. This is how they came up with the idea for the busts in *Haunted Mansion,* whose eyes follow the patrons to the loading platform.

447

- While the Imagineers were attempting to install Abe at the pavilion, they kept running into problems with the wiring and fuses malfunctioning. Marc Davis had said, *"Do you suppose God is mad at Walt for creating man in his own image?"*

- During a pre-performance, Abe again ran into difficulties which prompted Walt to say, *"If you're not ready, don't open the curtain."* This would be one of the Imagineers mottos for decades to come.

- Before Abe was created, Walt wanted to add an **extension onto** *Main Street, U.S.A.* **and call it** *Liberty Street.* It was to be a look back at Colonial era America. As the main showcase to this new land section, Walt wanted to have a Presidential Hall to showcase animatronic figures of all the U.S. presidents. Due to limited technology and resources, they scrapped the idea and focused only on Mr. Lincoln. Later, on October 1, 1971, *The Hall Of Presidents* opened in *Disney's Magic Kingdom*.

- The attraction was **originally sponsored by** *Lincoln Savings and Loan Association* until January 1, 1973.

- In the spring of 1973, the attraction was changed. Abe was removed and was replaced with a movie screen that showed the **23-minute film, *The Walt Disney Story***, narrated by Peter Renaday (read about him in the *Haunted Mansion* section). Peter provided the voice for Abraham Lincoln in *The Hall of Presidents* in *Magic Kingdom* from 1993-2008, until it was updated and archive recordings of Royal Dano were used again.

- At one point, they were **thinking of adding in Mark Twain** to have conversations with Mr. Lincoln, but it never came to fruition.

- In 1991, there were **talks about adding the** *Muppet*Vision 3D* **show** to this theater because it was new in *Disney's Hollywood Studios*. After Jim Henson passed away, some of the deals he was making with Disney ceased. Later on, they were able to add the show into the new *California Adventure*, thereby leaving the Lincoln theater alone.

- **Over the years, people complained about missing Lincoln**, so on June 12, 1975, it was reopened as *The Walt Disney Story Featuring Great Moments with Mr. Lincoln*.

- It was updated in 1984 with a **completely new Abraham Lincoln** Audio-Animatronic character. The same audio recordings were used, but some of the lines were removed.

- **Cast Members would attend pre-screening**s of Disney films in this theater. The tradition lasted until the *AMC* opened in *Downtown Disney*, which is where they go now.

- In 2001, the **story line changed by adding a segment before Lincoln's speech** at Gettysburg. Abe's dialogue was then provided by voice actor Warren Burton (known for his voice work in 17 video games over the past 16 years and his appearance as the First Guardian in the recent *Green Lantern* film). (2011) The audience wore headphones while watching a movie screen and assumed the role of a fictitious Union soldier named John Cunningham. The headphones created the surround-sound effects. John went to see Mathew Brady (a real-life photographer known for taking photos of the first 19 U.S. Presidents with the exception of the 9th president, William Henry Harrison) to get his photo taken before heading off to war. In the battle, John is wounded and is then able to meet President Lincoln and attend the Gettysburg Address. Then the curtains rose to show the Audio-Animatronic Lincoln present his speech. This version also had the opening narration voiced by Corey Burton (see *Imagineer Mini Biographies* page 287).

- It closed in February 2005 to make way for *Disneyland: The First 50 Magical Years*, an informational film starring **Donald Duck and the *Main Street Magic Shop's* ex-employee, Steve Martin**. This lasted until March 15, 2009.

- On December 18, 2009, Abe returned to the attraction renamed *The Disneyland Story presenting Great Moments with Mr. Lincoln*. The Lincoln Audio-Animatronic figure was replaced with an electronic Autonomatronic figure, meaning it can move and seem more lifelike. Disney found original recordings from the attraction's beginnings and was able to have **Royal Dano reprise his role**.

- This is also the **first use of a human electronic Autonomatronic** character for Disney. This technology was also created by Disney Imagineers and succeeded the Audio-Animatronic technology.

Horse-Drawn Streetcar
Opened July 17, 1955

Old time horse-drawn streetcar. Ride it from one end of *Main Street, U.S.A.* to the other. It's a one-way trip.

FUN FACTS

- It carries **30 passengers**.
- The **speed at which you travel** on the horses is 4.4 miles per hour.
- The only attraction in *Disneyland* **that utilizes the Belgian horses.**
- This attraction **also opened in *The Magic Kingdom*** in 1971 and in *Disneyland Paris* in 1992.
- The **horses have a polyurethane coating on their horse shoes** to increase the "clip clop" sound they make when they walk. It also

increases their traction.

- The **length of a one-way trip** is about 1,080 feet or 0.2 miles.
- **Every *Disneyland* Cast Member wears a name tag**, even the large draft horses that pull the streetcars up and down the tracks on *Main Street, U.S.A.*

- Disneyland originally used Percherons or Belgians; those two breeds of draft horses usually have relaxed temperaments. Right now, **they currently operate five different horse breeds:** Percherons, Belgians, Clydesdales, Shires, and the Spotted Draft. (*see photo*)

Horseless Carriage

Opened May 12, 1956

A vintage open-air car. Ride it from one end of *Main Street, U.S.A.* to the other. It's a one-way trip.

FUN FACTS

- They are **outfitted with tractor engines** to give them their authentic antique sounds.

- It is modeled after **the authentic 1903 vehicles**. The horn goes "Ah-oo-ga!"

Main Street Cinema

Opened July 17, 1955

The theater is modeled after a 20th Century Theater. The attraction shows Walt Disney's first six Mickey Mouse animated cartoons.

FUN FACTS

- The following is the list of **films that were shown on Opening Day**. They were to set the mood of the 1920's *Main Street. U.S.A.* setting. Take note that none of them were Disney films as Walt himself was only 17 when the most recent one was released.
  - *Fatima's Dance* (1903)
  - *A Dash Through the Clouds* (1912)
  - *Gertie the Dinosaur* (1914)
  - *The Noise of Bombs* (1914)
  - *Dealing for Daisy* (1915)
  - *Shifting Sands* (1918)

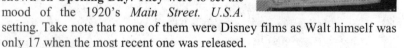

450

🌐 The short **films that are shown today** are all Disney films.
- *Plane Crazy* (May 15, 1928)
- *Steamboat Willie* (November 18, 1928)
- *Traffic Troubles* (March 17, 1931)
- *The Moose Hunt* (May 8, 1931)
- *The Dognapper* (November 17, 1934)
- *Mickey's Polo Team* (January 4, 1936)

🌐 Fun Facts for *Plane Crazy*.
- Technically. this is the **first Mickey Mouse cartoon released**, May 1928. When it was first released. it didn't have a sound track. *Steamboat Willie* was released with sound in November 1928. then *Plane Crazy* had its audio track added December 29, 1928.
- A **budget was set at $3,528** to produce the film.
- This is the **first cartoon to show Mickey**, Minnie, and Clarabelle Cow.
- **Ub Iwerks was the main animator** for this film and all of the Mickey cartoons up to *The Cactus Kid* (1930). He was also the animator for all the *Alice Comedies* from the early 1920's. It is said that Ub put out up to 700 animations a day for this film.

🌐 Fun Facts for *Steamboat Willie*.
- This is **everybody's favorite** out of all six films.
- The version of *Steamboat Willie* they show here **has some scenes edited out** to appease the easily offended. For the 55th anniversary in 2010, the entire film was shown without editing.
- The title is **a parody of the Buster Keaton film**, *Steamboat Bill Jr (1928)*.
- This was the first film when you could see **Mickey and Minnie together** with sound.
- This was the **first synchronized-sound** Disney cartoon.
- Contrary to popular belief, **this was not the first cartoon with sound**. Animators, and Disney's rivals, Dave & Max Fleischer (*Superman, Popeye The Saylor, and Betty Boop*) had been creating cartoons with sound for years before Mickey Mouse came along. Their first film with sound was *My Old Kentucky Home* (1926). It was part of a series called *Ko-Ko Song Car-Tunes*, which featured a bouncing ball on screen so people watching could sing along. This created the saying, "Follow the bouncing ball." The music for the cartoon was from the song "My Old Kentucky Home" composed in 1853.
- This wasn't the first cartoon to have sound, but this was **the first film to have integrated the click track technology**. This technique produced better synchronism, whereas before the sound would sometimes be off.
- When this film was first released, it was **shown in theaters with the movie *Gang War*** (1928). People left the theater uninterested in *Gang War*, but they were all talking about *Steamboat Willie*.

- *The Jazz Singer* (1927), the first feature-length movie with audible dialogue, also referred to as a "talkie," is said to have been **the inspiration for Walt to add sound** to his cartoons.
- The **copyright for this film will expire in 2023** and will be available for public use.

🐭 Fun Facts for *Traffic Troubles*.
- It is said that **Walt got the idea for this film** from a bumpy taxi ride.

🐭 Fun Facts for *The Moose Hunt*.
- This is the first film where **Pluto is referred to as Pluto**. Before this he was called Rover, and he belonged to Minnie Mouse.
- Pinto Colvig provides the voice of Pluto. This is the **only time Pluto actually has dialogue**. He says "Kiss me." Because he was a newly developing character, they hadn't decided on whether or not to have him speak.

🐭 Fun Facts for *The Dognapper*.
- This is the **second film that Mickey and Donald** starred in together.

🐭 Fun Facts for *Mickey's Polo Team*.
- In this film, **many classic actors are portrayed by cartoon counterparts:** Jack Holt, Shirley Temple, Charles Laughton, Eddie Cantor, Harold Lloyd, W.C. Fields, Greta Garbo, Oliver Hardy, Stan Laurel, Harpo Marx, Charlie Chaplin, Edna May Oliver, and Clark Gable.

🐭 Walt Disney provides the **voice for Mickey and Minnie in the 3 movies** released in 1928; the Minnie voice was then passed on to Marcellite Garner. Marcellite was an ink and paint girl for the Disney Company. She auditioned for the role of Minnie Mouse and was partially chosen for the role because she was only one of two women there who could speak Spanish for the film *The Cactus Kid* (1930). The other woman didn't want to sing, so Marcellite acquired the role. She voiced Minnie Mouse in 50 films over an 11-year span, and that was the extent of her acting career. She is attributed for giving Minnie the personality that she has today.

🐭 There is a **"Cast Member" inside the ticket booth named Tilly**. Her name tag says that she is from Marceline, Missouri. It is fitting considering that *Main Street, U.S.A.* was inspired by said town (Walt's hometown). (*see photo*)

🐭 This is a great **place for a break** when it is hot out on *Main Street, U.S.A.* Duck into the dark air-conditioned space to cool off.

🐭 Show up whenever you want. The shows **run continuously**.

🐭 For a **list of this attractions Hidden Mickeys**, see page 349.

⒪MNIBUS

Opened August 24, 1956

A double-decker bus. Ride it from one end of *Main Street, U.S.A.* to the other. It's a one-way trip.

FUN FACTS

🌐 The Omnibus is capable of **reaching speeds** of 60 miles per hour.

🌐 A 45-passenger bus recreated to resemble a 1920's **New York City double-decker**.

ADVENTURELAND

It is designed and themed to **resemble the wild jungles** in Africa, Asia, the Middle East, South America, and the South Pacific. "To create a land that would make this dream reality," said Walt Disney, "we pictured ourselves far from civilization, in the remote jungles of Asia and Africa."

FUN FACTS

- *Adventureland* provides a 1950's view of an exotic adventure, capitalizing on the **post-war Tiki craze**.

- *Adventureland* has **been through the least amount of changes** out of all the lands.

- This **land was inspired by Walt Disney's short films** called *True-Life Adventures* (1948-1960).

- In fact, on Herb Ryman's original 1953 concept art map, **the name for the land was *True-Life Adventureland.*** It was also located where *Tomorrowland* is now. It was going to fit snug, sort of between *Main Street, U.S.A.* and *Tomorrowland*. Imagineer Bill Evans convinced Walt to move it to where it is now, so that the grove of eucalyptus trees behind *City Hall* could be the backdrop of their *Jungle Cruise*.

- Lush vegetation **resembles jungles,** while elements of the "other" surround the visitor. Tribal masks, Congo drums, non-American totem poles, exotic animal statues, and architecture of Pacific influence make for a closed area where industry and technology take a back seat to uncharted nature.

- The phrase "*See no evil, hear no evil, speak no evil,*" originated around the 8th century in Japan. It is from the parable "Three Wise Monkeys." They took the Chinese phrase "*Look not at what is contrary to propriety; listen* not to what is contrary to propriety; speak not what is contrary to propriety; make no movement which is contrary to propriety," from the 4th century BC and turned it into what we know today. The monkeys are named Mizaru, Kikazaru, and Iwazaru, in the order mentioned in the phrase. These **three monkeys can be found in *Bengal Barbeque*.**

Though obviously rooted in Polynesia and the American idea of jungle "other," *Adventureland* goes beyond that by **not explicitly or obviously labeling anything**. Middle-eastern architectural motifs, African "primitive" elements, and North African building styles mix *Adventureland* into a culture native to nowhere. An intentional lack of cultural explanation plays into the space as a tourist's relief from reality. Walt Disney's original intent was to bring the "unusual" foreign experiences to Americans attending his park.

As you enter under the *Adventureland* entrance sign, look up to see the **torches that burn all day** and into the night. Most people don't notice them during the day.

One of the few remaining original trees that existed before *Disneyland* is located between the *Indian Jones Adventure* exit and the entrance to the *Indiana Jones Adventure* FastPass distribution stations. It is a giant Canary Date Palm. **It is called *The Dominguez Palm*** by Cast Members, in reference to the farm owners before the park was built. The tree was planted in 1896. Part of the agreement when purchasing the land was for Disney to leave the tree, as it was originally a wedding gift to the Dominguez family. It was located in another part of the property and relocated to its current spot. (*see photo*)

Ron Dominguez's grandparents owned the pre-Disney property, and are the namesakes of the tree. Ron was actually born in 1935 in the house that Disney used as an administrative office. It stood about where *Pirates of the Caribbean* is now. **Ron was hired by Disney four days before the park opened to be a ticket taker** on opening day. He worked his way up in the company to become Vice President of Walt Disney Attractions until his retirement in 1994. He started the groundwork for what would become the second Disney park of Southern California, *California Adventure*.

Have you ever heard the tale of *The Little Man of Disneyland*? When *Disneyland* opened in 1955, there was a book published by Little Golden Books titled *The Little Man of Disneyland*. Donald Duck is on the front cover. In the story, Patrick Begorra, a leprechaun, walked out of his house, which was in the trunk of an

455

orange tree, to discover people walking around his orange grove. It was Donald, Mickey, Goofy, and Pluto. They said they were digging up the trees to build *Disneyland*. Patrick would have nothing to do with it. He tried to stop them. Mickey told him about a rocket trip, a Wild West stagecoach, and flying pirate ships. Patrick did not believe him, so Mickey flew him in their helicopter to the studio to show him the concept art for the park. Patrick agreed to let them build *Disneyland* there as long as he was able to keep a house in one of the trees near the roots. Mickey shook on it and flew him back to the park. Every day Patrick watched the construction of *Disneyland*, until the very end when Mickey approached him and said it was time to remove his orange tree and move him to a new house. Patrick did not want to have anything to do with it so he packed up his stuff and left. During the daytime, he would rest in the shade; and in the safety of the darkness of the night, he would roam around the park looking for the perfect place to live. Nobody knew where he lived. Until now. In the summer of 2015, for the 60th anniversary celebration, Disney installed a little house for Patrick at the base of a tree next to the Indiana Jones entrance sign. If you look closely at the front mat, you can see the initials P.B. for Patrick Begorra.

- In 1955, a company called *Oceanic Arts*, from Whittier, California, **custom made all the Tiki masks** you see along the entrance as you pass by the Tiki Room.

- Just above the *Adventureland Bazaar* shop there is a **window dedicated to Harper Goff** (see *Imagineer Mini Biographies* on page 288).

- For a **list of Disneyland's Attractions of the Past**, see page 660.

- For a **list of this lands Hidden Mickeys**, see page 349.

Attractions

Enchanted Tiki Room Pre-show

June 23, 1963 - Duration: 3:58

This pre-show was designed to entertain Guests while they pass the time in the waiting area. This is the area where most people get their highly-anticipated *Dole Whip* or *Dole Whip Floats* from the Dole Bar.

FUN FACTS

- A brief documentary of **the history of the pineapple** is presented in the waiting area out front. The story, filmed in the early 1960's and updated at the end with a Macromedia Flash presentation of a parade of Dole products, is shown on a screen on the rear of the roof of the Dole snack bar at the entrance to the lanai. The name of the film is "The Flavor of Hawaii."

While waiting outside in a lanai area for the show to start, visitors are serenaded by Hawaiian music, which at one time included that of Martin Denny and Bud Tutmarc. **Hawaiian gods are represented,** as well, around the perimeter of the lanai and each has a rhyming legend to tell via Audio-Animatronics. Some include Hina, goddess of rain; Rongo, god of agriculture; Maui, who roped the playful sun; and Tangaroa, father of all gods and goddesses (voiced by Thurl Ravenscroft). The dialogue for the gods and goddesses is as follows:

MAUI: "My name is Maui. Natives call me "The Mighty One." I tamed the playful sun and gave my people time. Now they set their clocks by mine, for I am tropic standard time."

KORO: "Aloooooooooha! Wahine makune mana (basic translation: Hello! Ladies and gentlemen). I am Koro, midnight dancer! Today my magic feet no move. My head sore! But last night, all tiki gods have big time. Some luau! When drums begin to pound, my head full, biiiiiiig sound!"

RONGO: " Ua mau ke ea o ka aina i ka pono (This is the state motto of Hawaii, it means, "The life of the land is preserved in righteousness"). Me Rongo, god of agriculture. My land so good to me, I got time for sport. I fly kite. Me number one kite flier! Too bad I no have key, then me, I find electricity!"

PELE: "I am Pele, goddess of fire and volcanoes. Some say I torment poor Ngendi, the earth balancer, for when my violent temper rises, the earth trembles on its foundation!"

NGENDI: "Legends say I'm balancing the earth, but sad to say, I'm just hanging on."

PELE: "I'm the one who's really sad. When I smile, it comes out maaaad!"

TANGAROA-RU: "They call me Tangaroa-Ru, the east wiiiiiiiind!"

HINA: "And I am Hina, goddess of rain."

TANGAROA-RU: "We often travel together, wind and rain, through tropic lands, across the seven seeeeeeeeeeas."

HINA: "Come closer so that you may see, what magic there is, in fantasy."

TANGAROA: "I am Tangaroa, father of all gods and goddesses. Here in this land of enchantment, I appear before you as a mighty tree. Stand back! Oh, mystic powers, hear my call. From my limbs, let new life fall!"

This attraction was **so advanced with its technology by 1963** standards, that an Audio-Animatronic talking "barker" bird (Juan, cousin of José), once located near the walkway to beckon visitors inside, and had to be removed. It caused enormous traffic jams of visitors trying to catch a glimpse of it. He was voiced by Wally Boag (see *Who Does That Voice* page 149).

The **tiki gods were designed and created by Rolly Crump** (see *Imagineers Mini Biographies* page 287).

Rolly was given the task, by Walt, of creating a pre-show for the Guests to entertain them while they wait for dinner service, which was later changed to just a show. Rolly found **a book called "*Whispers on the Wind*"** that was written by missionaries about the Polynesian mythology and about tikis. He used this book to come up with ideas for his tiki god sketches.

When Rolly took his concept art to Blaine Gibson (see *Imagineers Mini Biographies* page 287) to sculpt, Blaine said he was too busy and for him to do it himself. Rolly told him he had **never sculpted before, so Blaine gave him a crash course in sculpting**. Rolly's first sculpts ever were these tiki gods. The warehouse where he was sculpting was so cold it was difficult to sculpt, so he would roll the clay outside where it was warm and sculpt out there.

458

- The **plaques displayed near each god, and their dialogue**, were done by Marty Sklar (see *Imagineers Mini Biographies* page 287).
- For a **list of this attractions Hidden Mickeys**, see page 349.

Walt Disney's Enchanted Tiki Room

June 23, 1963 - Duration: 15:36

A showcase of animatronic technology, featuring singing birds, flowers, and tiki poles. *The Enchanted Tiki Room* was the first *Disneyland* attraction to run entirely by Audio-Animatronics.

FUN FACTS

- While visiting New Orleans, **Walt found a little mechanical bird in a little cage in a curio shop**. He brought it back with him and asked Imagineer Wathel Rogers to take a look inside it to see how it worked. Walt asked if a magnetic recording tape could be used to program the bird's movement and talking. And so, the production of the Tiki Room began.

- When it was first created, the Tiki Room was to be a sit down and dine show. That is why it is the **only attraction with restrooms**.

- This attraction **was originally the *Bird Cafe***. The idea developed after an idea for a Chinese restaurant for *Main Street, U.S.A.*, with a talking Confucius (or just an old Chinese man), was dropped. The Tahitian Terrace was remodeled in 1962 with outdoor terraces and a private dining room (the *Bird Cafe*). I have heard that the idea was to hide microphones on the tables so that the birds could interact with the Guests. You will see a handgrip controller used with prototype birds in old videos. The Tiki Room opened in 1963 in its present form, except with both the audio and animation recorded on audio tape. The "interactive" version moved to the Trophy Room at Club 33.

- Because it was going to be a dining attraction, **Walt had already purchased tables and bamboo chairs**. They ended up just using the chairs for Guests to sit in until the 2005 refurbishment for *Disneyland's* 50th anniversary, when they added the padded benches.

- This was going to have a shared kitchen with the *Tahitian Terrace*, which is now gone. In fact, the **base of the fountain is actually a coffee bar**, with usable cabinets inside it. Rolly Crump sculpted it.

- This was *Disneyland's* **first fully-functional animatronic attraction**.

- Walt attributed the **technological advances of this attraction to the Polaris Missile** control computer developed by the U.S. Navy. He had said that if the Navy had not spent the money on its development, it would never have been done.

- Due to sponsoring, **there was a 75¢ charge to enter** when it first opened.

- While this attraction was being constructed, Disney was working on the film *Mary Poppins* (1964). They were able to use the **same technology to animate the animatronic bird on Mary Poppin's hand** and her talking umbrella.

- The first generation of birds on this attraction **were actually air pneumatic**. The movements of the birds were recorded on a magnetic tape roll, like a VHS tape. When the computer got to each mark on the tape, it would trigger a charge that would shoot a puff of air pneumatically to each part of the bird that needed to move. It is a pun when Fritz says, "We better start the show rolling."

- This was *Disneyland's* **first fully air-conditioned attraction** due to the need of keeping the animatronics cool.

- Only **232 guests can be seated** per showing.

- This attraction was sponsored by United Air Lines from 1964-1973. Hawaii joined the United States in 1959, so Hawaiian style was very popular throughout the 1960's. United Air Lines benefited from its Tiki Room sponsorship because its airlines offered flights to Hawaii during this period of peak popularity. In 1976, sponsorship was taken over **by Dole Pineapple and has been the sponsor** ever since.

- Imagineer **Rolly Crump** (see *Imagineer Mini Biographies* on page 288) was responsible for designing and carving **about 70% of the tikis** in this attraction and in the pre-show.

- Other than the removal of a minor musical number set to the "Barcarolle" from Jacques Offenbach's *Opera Tales of Hoffmann*, and the final verse of "The Tiki Tiki Tiki Room," the **show has remained otherwise unchanged** since its 1963 inception. This is due to a stipulation in the sponsorship contract with Dole that the attraction remain unchanged.

- According to the book "*Disneyland Detective*" by Kendra Trahan, **the "cast list"** breaks down as follows:
  - 54 singing orchids
  - 4 totem poles
  - 12 tiki drummers
  - 24 singing masks
  - 7 birds of paradise (the plant variety)
  - 8 macaws
  - 12 toucans
  - 9 forktail birds
  - 6 cockatoos
  - 20 assorted tropical birds

🐦 There are over **150 animatronic** characters.

🐦 "*Let's All Sing Like the Birdies Sing*" is **mentioned in the computer-animated movie** *Happy Feet* (2006).

🐦 The **voices of the tiki birds** were done by:
- Wally Boag as "Jose" (Hispanic accent)
- Thurl Ravenscroft as "Fritz" (German accent)(see *Who Does That Voice on page 147*)
- Fulton Burley as "Michael" (Irish accent)
- Ernie Newton as "Pierre" (French accent)

🐦 The colored feathers used on each of the birds were **designed to resemble the colors** of their individual country-of-origin's flag.
- "Michael" is from Ireland – green, white, and orange
- "Pierre" is from France – blue, white, and red
- "Jose" is from Mexico – green, white, red, and yellow
- "Fritz" is from Germany – yellow, red, and black

🐦 Both Wally Boag (Pecos Bill) and Fulton Burley (The Irish Tenor) were in the ***Golden Horseshoe Review* together** in the *Golden Horseshoe Saloon* for decades. (*see photo*)

🐦 An article published in 2013 by D23 for the attraction's 50th anniversary listed **the voice actors responsible for some of the other voice work**. Some of the background birds are voiced by Clarence Nash (Donald Duck), Maurice Marcelino, Marion Darlington (*Bambi, Snow White, Pinocchio, Cinderella*), and Purv Pullen (*Snow White, Sleeping Beauty, Who Killed Cock Robin*). Ernest Taveres voiced the Tikis in the Hawiian War Chant, Maui, Ngendi, Rongo, and Koro from the pre-show. Pele and Tangaroa-Ru are voiced by Ginny Tyler (*Mary Poppins, Sword in the Stone, Son of Flubber*) and Anne Essex voiced Hina.

🐦 Wally Boag, Thurl Ravenscroft, and Fulton Burley **all reprised their roles** for *Disney World's Tiki Room: Under New Management* in 1998, which

461

later reverted back to the original show in August, 2011, with a shortened performance to accommodate the bustling crowd of *Magic Kingdom*.

- Apparently, there were supposed to be **seven female sulphur-crested cockatoos** who sing "*Let's All Sing like the Birdies Sing*" on the bird mobile. Jose comments on how Rosita is missing. The other six are Collette, Susette, Mimi, Gigi, Fifi, and Josephine.

- Rolly Crump was lifted 15 feet into the air on a Raymond lift for days on end so he could **work on the bird mobile**. He said he was allowed to come down to go to the bathroom or have lunch.

- The most popular song "The Tiki Tiki Tiki Room" was **written by the Sherman Brothers** (see *Imagineer Mini Biographies* page 287). It had a predecessor song written by the Sherman Brothers titled "Swiss Family Robinson Calypso." If you speed up the song and change the lyrics, it sounds like the Tiki Room song. They wrote the song for *Walt Disney Presents* (1958-1961) in the episode *Escape to Paradise* which aired December 18, 1960, only two days before the release of *Swiss Family Robinson* (1960), for which it was promoting and showing behind-the- scenes footage.

- **Who can resist singing along with all the birdies**? Unfortunately, due to copyright reasons, I had to remove the lyrics from this edition of my book. If you would like to see the lyrics to sing along, please visit… discoveringthemagickingdom.com/apps/blog/show/44592323-song-lyrics.

- The **Hawaiian lyrics** to "Hawaiian War Chant" (sung by the totem poles):

Tahuwai la a tahuwai wai la, Ehu hene la a pili koo lua la, Pututui lua ite toe la, Hanu lipo ita paalai. Au we ta hua la. Au we ta hua la.

The lyrics in **English, translated** by Caesar M. of San Jose, CA:

You and I in the sea spray such joy, the two of us together embracing tightly in the coolness breathing deep of the palai fern. Oh such spray. Oh such spray.

- The birds' chests are **covered in custom-woven cashmere** which allows the figures to "breathe" in a lifelike manner. The choice came quite by accident in a planning meeting. Harriet Burns (see *Imagineer Mini Biographies* page 287), the very first female Imagineer, noticed a cashmere sweater that Walt Disney was wearing which moved at the elbows exactly the way the engineers envisioned.

- The exit song **lyrics for the Tiki Room Heigh Ho exit song were written by Wally Boag** and set to the tune of "*Heigh Ho*" from *Snow White and the Seven Dwarfs* (1937) which was written by Frank Churchill. Sing along as you march out into the sunlight. Unfortunately, due to copyright reasons, I had to remove the lyrics from this edition of my book. If you would like to see the lyrics to sing along, please visit… discoveringthemagickingdom.com/apps/blog/show/44592323-song-lyrics.

462

For a **list of this attractions Hidden Mickeys**, see page 349.

PRO TIP: When you first enter the show room, find the Cast Member and ask if your child can awaken Jose to start the show.

INDIANA JONES ADVENTURE:
TEMPLE OF THE FORBIDDEN EYE
Opened March 4, 1995 - Duration: 3:25

An attraction based on the popular Indiana Jones franchise. It is an extremely elaborate combination of the dark-rides and a motion simulator (the jeep you ride in has a motion-control device that moves and shakes the upper section of the vehicle). The basic concept is that looking into "the Eye of Mara" will cause untold calamity and, of course, it is virtually impossible not to look. Among many other dangers, the attraction climaxes with a re-creation of the gigantic boulder from *Raiders of the Lost Ark* (1981).

FUN FACTS

- The **timeline for the attraction was set in 1935,** in the *Temple of the Forbidden Eye* on the lost Delta of India.

- Apparently, **the attraction takes place before** *Raiders of the Lost Ark* (1981), which takes place in 1936. On Indy's desk in his office, there are letters from "Abner Ravenwood." In the beginning of the *Raiders* film, Marion tells Indy that Abner is dead. This leads us to believe that the attraction happens before the film. *Indiana Jones and the Temple of Doom* (1984) takes place in 1935, though.

- One of the concepts for tha attraction was to **close** *The Jungle Cruise* and use the boats to transport guests to the *Indiana Jones Adventure*.

- In the queue, **there is a fake gas generator**. It fades in and out, causing the lights above the queue to flicker. It is easy to tell if you are standing outside and can hear the generator slow down and watch the lights go out with it simultaneously. In case of an emergency shutdown, the lights go up to their full brightness and stay up until the attraction is ready to resume. The lights are not actually powered by the wires they are hanging from. There is a separate power source going into each bulb socket.

- The **budget for constructing** *Indiana Jones* was around $200 million and took about seven years to complete from planning through its construction.

- In 1989, the live-action **stunt show** *Indiana Jones Epic Stunt Spectacular!* was built in *Disney World's Hollywood Studios*. *Disneyland* wanted something similar there as well, so they worked with George Lucas to come up with the concept of the attraction as it is today.

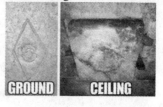

- **Take note at the diamonds on the ground in the queue**. You are warned not to step on them because they are booby trapped. If you look at the ceiling above each diamond, there is a stone being held by pieces of wood.

- This attraction **has the same track layout** and EMV's (Enhanced Motion Vehicle) as the attraction *Dinosaur* in *Disney World's Animal Kingdom*.

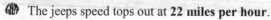

- In the queue, **Mara has her eyes closed** in all the pictures or statues. But during the ride, she has her eyes open in all of the pictures and statues.

- Apparently, when *Indiana Jones Adventure* first opened, **the queue got so long it went out into** *Adventureland*, through *Frontierland,* and ended in *Fantasyland* near the castle.

- The jeeps speed tops out at **22 miles per hour**.

- The animatronic faces of Indiana Jones were not **molded from Harrison Ford's** face as he denied the request by Disney. Imagineers molded a generic face that looks similar to his face and gave him vocals similar to Harrison's, but not his.

- When you first take off from the loading area, you randomly go through **one of three doors**. The door to the left enters "The Observatory of The Future," the middle door is "The Chamber of Earthly Riches," and the door to the right is "The Fountain of Eternal Youth."

- After you watch the "Eye on the Globe" video in the projection room, you will enter a room with a caged off area with artifacts in it. In that room, there is a wooden crate marked **"Deliver To: Club Obi Wan."** This is a reference to "Club Obi Wan," where Indiana Jones gets in a fight at the beginning of *Indiana Jones and the Temple of Doom* (1984). George Lucas put this in his movie as a reference to the *Star Wars* (1977) character Obi-Wan Kenobi.

- There is another **crate marked with the numbers "990 6753."** This is the number marked on the crate that stored the Ark of the Covenant in *Raiders of the Lost Ark* (1981).
- Part of the building was **built over the "Eeyore" parking lot**. You can still see an "Eeyore" parking lot sign on the wall up behind the projector in the queue.
- There are well over **4,000 different possibilities** for this attraction, as in different combinations of things that you may experience each time you ride.

- The queue begins outside where Guests walk past a 2.5 ton Mercedes-Benz troop transport truck. This truck is **the actual truck used** in the famous desert chase scene in *Raiders of the Lost Ark* (1981). Take note at how the hood ornament is still missing. The license plate still says WH-11204, but the spare tire has been changed out. There was also a handle added to the right side for the stunt men to use while filming.
- Near the exit is one of the **ore mining cart props** from Indiana *Jones and the Temple of Doom* (1984).
- Many of the items in Indy's office are **props from the films**.

- **John Rhys-Davies** is the narrator of the short safety film that you watch in the queue. He is the actor who portrayed "*Sallah*" in *Raiders of the Lost Ark* (1981) and *Indiana Jones and the Last Crusade* (1989).* He has been in over 180 films and television series episodes. You might also remember him as the battle axe wielding dwarf "*Gimli*" from the "*Lord of the Rings*" trilogy or as *Professor Maximilian Arturo* from the television series "*Sliders.*"
- Even though John Rhys-Davies is the Sallah you see in the safety video, he isn't the one who voices Sallah. The **voice of Sallah was done by voice actor Bob Joles**. He also does the voices of Gimli in several *Lord of the Rings* video games.
- The whole **queue length** for the attraction is almost a ½ mile long. When the park gets really crowded, they have the queue work its way across the top of the *Jungle Cruise* line then back down and through the regular queue.
- The attraction was **sponsored by AT&T** up until 2002. It has no sponsor at present.
- The attractions interior has **168,000 square feet of hand carved surfaces**.
- **There are 1,995 skulls** on the attraction. The 1,995 stands for the year the attraction opened, 1995.

465

The original 50-foot **American-made king cobra snake** was green. Due to frequent break downs, they replaced it with one from Japan that was yellow. After so many issues with the yellow one, they installed the tan and brown one that was made in America.

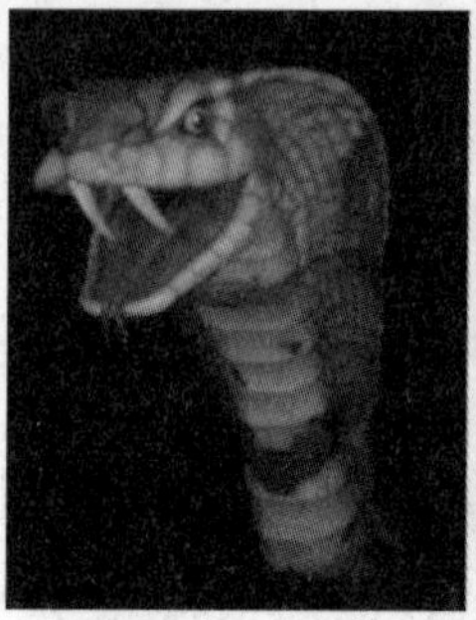

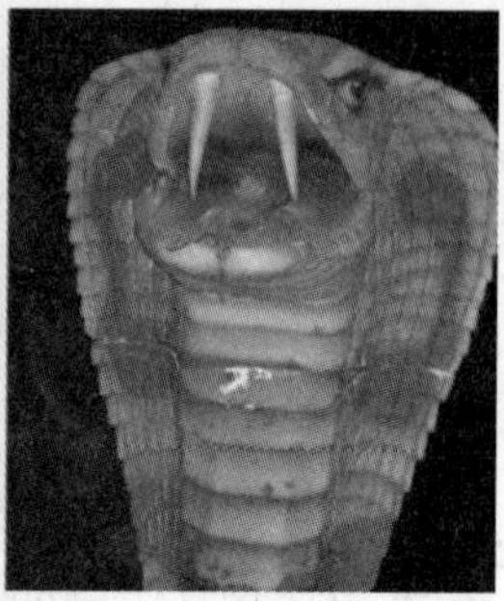

During the part when the boulder is crashing toward you, the car seems to be moving backwards, but actually, the **room is moving forward**.

There are **hieroglyphics in the caves** as you wait in line called "Maraglyphics." Since FP was added, most of them are passed. When the attraction first opened, they handed out little cards from AT&T with the translation codes on it. Below is the hieroglyphics translation chart for you to try out for yourself. The photo below is of the wall at the top of the stairs just before you descend the other side to board the jeeps.

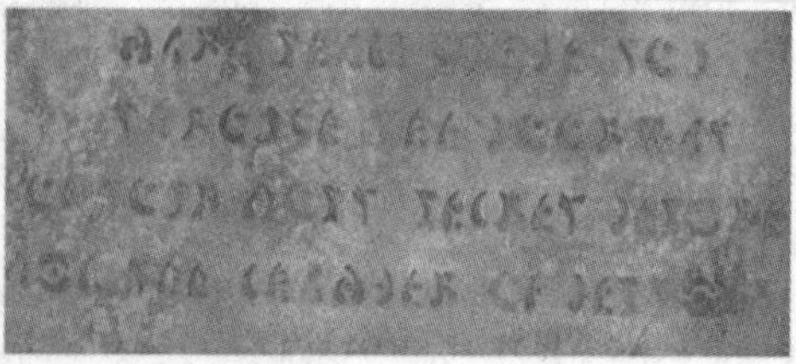

"Mara shall guide you through the doorway of your most secret desire in the chamber of destiny."

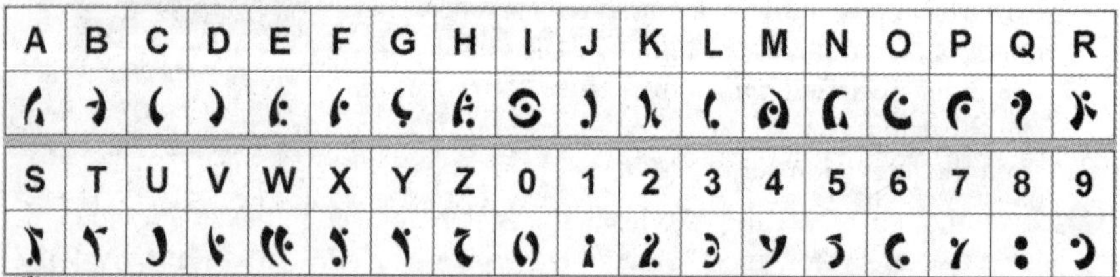
A B C D E F G H I J K L M N O P Q R
S T U V W X Y Z 0 1 2 3 4 5 6 7 8 9

For a **list of this attractions Hidden Mickeys**, see page 349.

All of the **music on the attraction was a compilation** of the music from the Indiana Jones movie series. All the original music scores were composed by John Williams (see *Disney Movie Trivia* page 156), but were re-scored by composer Richard Bellis.

In 2012, Indy was closed from September to December for some major special effects updates. Some of them included **adding a projection face to the Mara** statue head at the beginning,

There are several **different quotes** from Indiana Jones; they might be different every time you go. At the end with the crashed boulder he says:

- "Not bad, for tourists!"

- "Next time, you wear blindfolds, okay?"
- "There! That wasn't so bad, was it?"
- "Next time, you're on your own."
- "Don't tell me that wasn't big fun!"
- "Tourists, why'd it have to be tourists?"

For a **list of this attractions Hidden Mickeys, see page 349**.

Jungle Cruise

Opened July 17, 1955 - Duration: 9:05

A skipper pilots a boat (actually on an underwater rail) through a jungle inhabited by wild animals and hostile natives. The river is set in a jungle, combining African, South American, and Indian elements. It simulates a sightseeing tour in the early 20th century, around the 1930's.

FUN FACTS

This was **one of the original attractions** that opened with the park.

They **went through several names in concept** and production; *Explorer Boat Ride, Riverboat Ride, Jungle Riverboat Safari, Jungle Cruise Boat Ride*, and *Jungle Riverboat*.

The final name of *Jungle Cruise* **has been used since 1959**.

The **Nile River, Congo River, and the Mekong River** were the inspirations for the look of this attraction's waterways.

This was one of **Walt Disney's favorite** attractions.

The night before the grand opening, the engineers **had to install a recently-delivered 900-pound elephant in the dark** because the power was shut off.

The attraction **was based off of a television series called *True Life Adventures*** (1948-1960). The dialogue spoken by the skippers was not comedic, but rather informative, like a documentary.

The skippers originally followed a **straight-forward script** that was serious and more like a nature documentary when it first opened. But after Walt Disney heard some guests commenting that they didn't need to go on the attraction again because there was nothing more to see, he advised the skippers to improvise jokes and puns to make it more appealing. Thurl Ravenscroft (see *Who Does*

467

That Voice on page 147) did a voice-over of the attractions dialogue for *Walt Disney's Wonderful World of Color*.

- The river you float down **is referred to as** the *The Rivers of the World*.

- In the beginning, there was a pen near the attraction's queue that **was used to house several live alligators** for spectators. There were several occasions when the gators escaped into the waters of the attraction, so the pens were removed. I haven't been able to find photos of the real alligators, but the information was published in *Disneyland Secrets* by Gavin Doyle in 2015.

- A total of **six lions** have been removed since the attraction opened in 1955. One from the original opening that simply growled, two lionesses in the veldt that were fighting over a bloody strand of zebra meat, a lion and a lioness that each had a zebra leg in their mouth and looked up from the bushes at the boats, and one lion that was originally dead and hanging upside down over a fire in the native village.

- Originally, African **wild dogs** resided in the African veldt and were barking at the lions, but they were removed as well.

- Walt brought Marc Davis over from animation to WED to work on the attractions. The first project he worked on was *The Jungle Cruise*. Walt wanted comedic scenes added. **The first scene and project Marc designed was the elephant pool**.

- Other changes that were made since it's opening:
  - 1957 - Addition of the rainforest, a pair of menacing gorillas, native war party and dancing natives, and Trader Sam shows up.
  - 1961 – The original two-story boathouse was removed because the trees grew too tall to see over, and the open waterway between the *Jungle Cruise* and the *Rivers of America* was filled in to create space for the *Swiss Family Treehouse* walk-through attraction, which is now *Tarzan's Treehouse*.
  - 1962 - Addition of the Indian Elephant pool (concepts by Marc Davis) and the Ganesha, lost city, and Cambodian ruins scene along the bank.
  - 1964 - Addition of African Veldt and Lost Safari scenes (concepts by Marc Davis) were added in.
  - 1976 – Addition of crocodiles snapping at a hornbill, safari camp being overrun by gorillas, Bengal tiger and cobras added to Cambodian ruins, a gorilla battling a crocodile, a python threatening a water buffalo calf (it replaced gorillas hiding in the underbrush near the river banks), baboons on termite mounds, and the lions feasting on the zebra was moved into the new rock den.
  - 1993 – The boats were repainted and made to look weathered to match the look of the upcoming Indian Jones attraction.
  - 1994 - Addition of the boathouse second floor queue, the queue was re-themed to resemble a setting in the mid-1930's to coincide with the *Indiana Jones Adventure*

- 1995 – Rerouting of the river to accommodate the *Indiana Jones Adventure*
- 1997 - Replacement of the original attraction boats with longer boats
- 1997 – The canvas boat covers that used to be striped became solid
- 2005 - Various replacements and reconstructions, addition of piranhas, updates to the Gorilla Camp scene, and a replacement of Schweitzer Falls.
- 2010 - After 55 years of growth and care, *Disneyland's* man-made jungle is declared "real" and complete with its own ecosystem.
- 2013 – This year began the annual overlay of the *Jingle Cruise*, a Christmas-themed variation to the original.
- 2016 – The attraction was closed for four months so a new dock could be added which would stabilize the boats for ease of boarding.

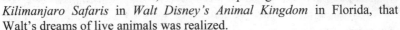 These animals are the precursor to the Audio-Animatronic animals that we know today. **They were simply just mechanical animals**. They had very limited movement. It wasn't until after the creation of the 1963 Tiki birds that we began to see a better animatronic animal on the *Jungle Cruise*.

The 1962 Elephant Pool expansion **displaced the Magnolia Park gazebo**.

Walt Disney really **wanted an authentic safari attraction with live animals**. But his Imagineers talked him out of it because of the small amount of space and the fact that most animals sleep during the day and wouldn't be very interesting for people to see. So, this was the mechanical version of what Walt was looking for. It wasn't until 1998, with the opening of *Kilimanjaro Safaris* in *Walt Disney's Animal Kingdom* in Florida, that Walt's dreams of live animals was realized.

There are **12 boats total in the fleet**:
- Amazon Belle
- Congo Queen (gold-painted for 50th anniversary)
- Ganges Gal
- Rio Hondo Hattie
- Irrawaddy Woman
- Kissimmee Kate
- Nile Princess
- Orinoco Adventuress
- Suwannee Lady
- Ucayali Una (Wheelchair accessible)
- Yangtze Lotus
- Zambezi Miss

- *Magdalena Maiden* (decommissioned in 1997)
- *Mekong Maiden* (decommissioned in 1997)

On opening day of the park, **there were only two boats in use**, the Ganges Gal and the Congo Queen.

There can only be **9 boats on the river** at one time.

The African Queen **(1952) starring Humphrey Bogart** and Katherine Hepburn was the inspiration behind the look and feel of the boats.

Some of the orange trees that died when *Disneyland* took over the orange grove were **recycled by planting them upside down** to look like vines along the shore.

The **native village** wasn't a village on opening day but a dense jungle with tikis, masks, and several natives that popped up from the bushes and trees.

During the scene with the hippos, the skipper **fires off two shots** with his gun to scare away a hippo. This also works as notification system for the employees.

1 shot – the second shot was a misfire
2 shots – everything is normal
3 shots – need assistance
4 shots – emergency
5 shots – nothing
6 shots – boat came off track and has run aground

For a short period of time the guns were taken off the attraction. But when Michael Eisner was riding on the attraction and the skippers didn't shoot at the hippos he decided that the attraction needed that element back, so **he had the guns returned to the attraction**.

The hand guns used by the skipper to fend off the charging hippos **is an actual Smith & Wesson .38 Special**. But they have been altered so that no live rounds can be placed in them.

The **guns are registered with the FBI**. No skipper can go home at the end of the night until all the guns are accounted for.

Trader Sam once wore a mask, and a gorilla across the water would try to grab his merchandise.

Next to Trader Sam there was, for a brief time, **a tablet with an alien skull on it**. It was a tie in to the recent film *Indiana Jones and the Kingdom of the Crystal Skull* (2008). After the hype of the movie died down, the tile was removed.

An indoor jeep attraction with the same scenes of the *Jungle Cruise* called **Jungle Expedition** was planned for *Disneyland Paris*, but the plans were scrapped.

There is a **shield in front of one of the native's tee pees** with the "*Lion King Musical*" logo on it.

- *Jungle Cruise* was parodied on **Timon and Pumbaa's** Virtual Safari on *The Lion King Special Edition*.

- They **have to add dye to the water** to make it not only look more realistic, but to also hide the fact that the water is only a few feet deep in some areas.

- You can **ask the skipper for a map of the *Jungle Cruise*** when exiting, but it may cost you an animal impersonation.

- The water **used to be connected to the *Rivers of America***.

- The islands in the middle are called **Manhattan Island and Catalina Island** by the Cast Members.

- The **hornbill in the rafters above the queue stairs** used to be on the attraction near the snapping crocodiles. (*see photo*)

- **There is an Elvis hidden on this attraction**. Apparently hiding Elvis was a thing for the Imagineers to do. Just like the Hidden Mickeys. The only difference is the Elvis' were only visible to the employees and not to Guests on the attractions. On this attraction, Elvis can be seen painted as one of the giraffe's spots, but it is on the opposite side of the Guests. You would have to be standing on the land looking toward the boats to see it. There is also a picture of him somewhere in the attic of *Haunted Mansion*, and there used to be one in the Christmas tree during *it's a small world's* Christmas overlay.

- The hippo pool measures 14 feet deep; it is the **deepest part**.

- These are **all the animals** that you encounter on the attraction:

African elephant	crocodile	hyena	tiger
African lion	giraffe	Indian elephant	vulture
antelope	gorilla	king cobra	water buffalo
baboon	hippo	piranha	wildebeest
butterfly	hornbill	python	zebra
cow (skull)	human	rhino	

- At the last turn, there is **Arabic writing up on the side of the building**, which is actually the boat storage. It says, *"Fine Food, Fine Dining, Fine Entertainment."* Although, sometimes the skipper will tell you it is the contact information for the complaint department. (*see photo*)

- A **film adaptation of the attraction was in the works** with a 2007 release starring Tom Hanks and Tim Allen, but ran into some issues and was scrapped. The filming plans reformed with a 2019 release and will star Dwayne "The Rock" Johnson. It is said to be modeled after the film *The African Queen* (1951), which was the original inspiration for this attraction.

🐭 Rumors are circulating that some of **the attraction will be altered to match up with the new movie**, much as they did with *Pirates of the Caribbean*. It all depends on how well the movie does in theaters. Dwayne Johnson mentioned in a tweet that he was talking with Imagineering about his input.

🐭 For a **list of this attractions Hidden Mickeys, see page 349**.

PRO TIP: Right before you board the line splits into two lines, keep your group together in the same line. The line to the **left boards slightly faster**, but then you get seated on the left side of the boat. This side has a lot **less animatronic animals** to view while the ride is in motion.

Tarzan's Treehouse

Opened June 23, 1999 - Duration: N A

A re-creation of the treehouse built by Tarzan's parents in the big hit animated film *Tarzan* (1999). It is a complete walk-through attraction. It was the product of a redesign of the former *Swiss Family Treehouse*.

FUN FACTS

🐭 In February 1999, *Disneyland* closed the **Swiss Family Treehouse** and Imagineers re-themed the attraction to coincide with the soon-to-be released Disney film *Tarzan* (1999).

🐭 There are **450 branches** and limbs with 6,000 hand-applied vinyl green leaves.

🐭 The **Latin name for this species of tree** is *Disneyodendron Semperflorens Grandis*. Translated to English it means *Large, Ever-Blooming Disney Tree*.

🐭 It weighs in at **150 tons**. It is made up of steel, concrete, and stucco.

🐭 Imagineer Bill Martin was placed in charge of the project. **Wolfgang Reitherman helped to design the treehouse**, just as he did for the set of the *Swiss Family Robinson* (1960) film.

🐭 There is **a sign located near a low-hanging branch** that reads, "Mind Thy Head." This pays homage to the *Swiss Family Treehouse* that had the sign hanging there from 1962 up to 1999 when the tree was re-themed.

🐭 In the base of the tree, at the entrance stairs, it appears as if **Jabba the Hutt is molded into the bark**.

🐭 The **phonograph plays the *"Swisskapolka"***

that played in the house when it was the *Swiss Family Treehouse* as well. The *"Swisskapolka"* was written for the movie *Swiss Family Robinson* (1960) by music composer Buddy Baker (see *Imagineer Mini Biographies* page 287).

When walking up the stairs, **you will come across Sabor** (the spotted leopard). Get as close to him as possible to see what happens.

One of the few attractions shared among all five Disney resorts around the world. It still goes by its original name and theme of *Swiss Family*

Treehouse in *Disneyland Paris*, *Tokyo Disneyland,* and *Magic Kingdom.*

The tree is actually **designed after the Moreton Bay Fig tree**. Walt saw one near *Disneyland* and had his Imagineers check the tree out as a reference back in 1962. The tree was planted around 1876 and can still be found today in Founders Park, only 2 1/5 miles north of *Disneyland* at 410 N. West Street, Anaheim.

The tree is **70 feet tall**.

For a **list of this attractions Hidden Mickeys, see page 349**.

NEW ORLEANS SQUARE

It was the **first new "land" added** and is based on 19th century New Orleans. The land was opened to the public on July 24, 1966, and despite its age, it is still very popular with *Disneyland* guests. When it was designed, *New Orleans Square* was meant to be just that - a perfect square - although nowadays it is not exactly clear where *New Orleans Square* borders with *Frontierland*. Walt Disney was very involved in the design and implementation.

FUN FACTS

🎷 If you look at the **balconies, you can see props** that belong to the "inhabitants" of the apartments and indicate what their occupation is: musical instruments, a typewriter, and voodoo supplies.

🎷 Some of the **iron work further up is actually painted plastic**. It is said this was done because iron has a tendency to breakdown with the elements.

🎷 If you look above the *Royal Street Veranda* restaurant, you can see the **gold lettering initials of Walt** and

Roy Disney in the wrought-iron railings. They used to be the same color as the rest of the wrought-iron, until the remodel of the upper levels into the *Dream Suite* when they were painted gold. (*see photo*)

🎷 If you look past the rooftops you can see the **flagpole that sports the Louisiana state flag** with a pelican on it.

🎷 If you stand down by the *Rivers of America* in front of *Pirates Of The Caribbean*, you can see **the top of a ship's mast with sails** over the rooftops down Royal Street. This was done to make it look as if the buildings were up against the ocean with ships anchored. You can also see

this by standing near the entrance to the *Disneyland Railroad* on Front Street.

When *New Orleans Square* was in the process of being constructed, Walt Disney took the television viewers of *Walt Disney's Wonderful World of Color* (1961-1969) on an **exclusive behind-the-scenes tour** with his newly-appointed *Disneyland* Ambassador, and *Disneyland's* Miss Tencennial, Julie Reihm. Julie was originally a tour guide for *Disneyland*.

The **four streets that make up** *New Orleans Square* are Royal Street, Front Street, Orleans Square, and Esplanade Road. (*see photo*)

Many people believe **there are hidden tunnels underground** throughout the park. This isn't true. It is for *Disney World*, but not here. There are, however, basements below the restaurants and shops in *New Orleans Square*. These basements are connected by doorways and little hallways to get from one room to the next. *The Blue Bayou* kitchen is down there as well as an employee cafeteria. If you think about it, the basements aren't really below ground level. When you enter *New Orleans Square* you have to walk uphill to get to it.

The *Blue Bayou Restaurant* **can be found in only three Disney parks:** *Disneyland*, *Tokyo Disneyland*, and *Disneyland Paris*. The one in *Disneyland Paris* is called *The Blue Lagoon*.

The rock wall area by *Rivers of America* is made out of cement to resemble stones. It is common practice for **stone masons to date the keystone** (the one in the top middle) when an archway is completed. During the river front makeover in the early 1990's, the construction workers didn't know what to put, so they used the birth year of Imagineer Matt McKim, the son of Imagineer Sam McKim, the concept artist of *New Orleans Square*, and subtracted 200 years, leaving it with the year 1764.

There is **an anchor from the ship** of infamous pirate Jean Lafitte. The plaque at the base reads, "*Lafitte's Anchor: Said to be from a pirate ship commanded by Jean Lafitte in the battle of New Orleans January 8, 1815. It is also said that Lafitte's privateering ships left a wake of blood from the mainland to Barataria Bay. But don't believe everything you read.*" This anchor has been in *Disneyland* since it first opened. It was last located in front of *The Golden Horseshoe*. (*see photo*)

At one point, there was a concept that would **connect *Pirates of the Caribbean*, *Haunted Mansion*, and *Tom Sawyer's Island*** all together under one main theme. That theme was Jean Lafitte.

475

- In the *Pieces of Eight* shop there is an odd-looking **chandelier shaped like a monkey**. It is believed that this was the inspiration behind Captain Barbossa's Capuchin monkey side kick in the *Pirates of the Caribbean* films.

- Walt **started the planning stages for *New Orleans Square* in 1957** with concept art by Imagineer Sam McKim. When Disney printed the souvenir maps in 1958, they included the "district" of New Orleans to be part of *Frontierland*.

- There was, at one point, a **Captain Jack Sparrow voodoo doll** in the *Pieces of Eight* shop window.

- *New Orleans Square* is the only land in *Disneyland* that is **named after a real place**.

- The land of *New Orleans Square* **exists only in *Disneyland*** in California; it can't be found in any other Disney park around the world.

- The area now occupied by the *Dream Suite* was originally **intended to be a private apartment** for the Disney family, much larger than the one above the *Main Street Fire Station*.

- *Cristal D'Orleans* is a tiny shop located at 32 Royal St. There is a long history for this shop that goes back to The World's Fair in 1964-65 when Walt Disney met Alfonso and Tomas, the Arribas Brothers. They were attending the World's Fair to represent their home city, La Coruña of Spain, with their glass blowing and glass cutting art. Walt was very impressed with them and asked if they wanted a shop in *Disneyland*. On June 15, 1967, they opened a little shop in the *Sleeping Beauty Castle* in *Fantasyland*. After the shop became successful, their younger brother Manuel Arribas joined them and they moved to Cristal d'Orleans in New Orleans Square. They have grown to 14 shops in all the Disney parks worldwide, and even have a shop on *Main Street, U.S.A*. The Arribas Bros are the longest-running leasees in the park. The Arribas Brothers were **the only thing Walt Disney brought back from The World's Fair** that he didn't originally take there himself.

- **Right at the exit of *Pirates of the Caribbean* sat the *Pirate's Arcade Museum*.** It was part of the *Pieces of Eight* shop. It opened around the same time as *Pieces of Eight* in 1967, a few weeks before *Pirates of the Caribbean* opened. It was not a museum at all. It contained vintage arcade games, created well before video games came into being. For only a dime, you could play a shooting game. There were several of them, like "Freebooter Shooter," "Cap n Black," "Captain Hook," and "Pirate Shoot." One machine would press your

476

choice of wording onto a Spanish doubloon, and another contraption that would spit out post cards with Marc Davis' pirate concept art on it. "Fortune Red" is a machine that can still be found there to this day (*see photo*). A red-bearded pirate would tell you your fortune and spit out a card. Through the glass, you can see him holding a treasure map. Sam McKim, the original artist of the *Disneyland* maps, drew that map. The arcade closed in 1980.

In *Le Bat en Rouge,* **there was once an Old Hag in a cage**. She was originaly created by WED to display in the *Emporium* window in *Magic Kingdom* back in 1975 to promote *Snow White and the Seven Dwarfs*. When the *Disneyana* shop opened on *Disneyland's Main Street, U.S.A.* in 1976, she was sent to the shop as a centerpiece. As an Audio-Animatronic figure, she would move around begging passers by to let her out, or else they would regret it. She was later moved to the *Villain's Lair Shop* in *Fantasyland* and then to her spot in *New Orleans Square*. Where is she now?

For a **list of this lands Hidden Mickeys, see page 349**.

For a **list of Disneyland's Attractions of the Past**, see page 660.

Attractions
DISNEYLAND RAILROAD
Opened 1966 - Duration: 18:00

The *Disneyland Railroad* has a station in *New Orleans Square*. See other details in the description from *Main Street, U.S.A.*

FUN FACTS

- The *Frontierland* railroad station was **re-themed and renamed** when *New Orleans Square* opened in 1966.

- This Station Master's Office is **modeled after the station in the Walt Disney film** *So Dear to My Heart* (1949).

- The sound of **the telegraph heard at the train station** is the first two sentences of Walt Disney's speech on *Disneyland's* opening day, July 17, 1955. It is done in landline telegraphy, the predecessor of Morse code, which was used for train station operators to communicate. The first two sentences: *"To all who come to this happy place; welcome. Disneyland is your land."*

- It is rumored that when the telegraphy was first installed at the train station, it was an old Irish bar joke. Apparently, in the 1920's, **Lillian Disney used to be a telegrapher in her early adult life** at the train station in her hometown in Idaho, so she noticed what was being tapped out. She advised Walt of this code as being inappropriate for a family place, so Walt had it changed to his opening day speech.

- *Disneyland's* steam trains sometimes have a **longer stop** at the *New Orleans Square Station*, since that's where they refill them with water.

Fantasmic!

Opened May 13, 1992 - Duration: 22:00

Fantasmic! is a long-running Disney nighttime show at both *Disneyland* and *Disney's Hollywood Studios*, Florida. The show features fireworks, live actors, water effects, fire, music, several boats, decorated rafts, and projections onto large mist screens featuring reworked Disney animation. It originated at *Disneyland* in 1992 after *Disneyland's* entertainment department was asked to create a nighttime spectacular involving water and  fireworks to invigorate the space in front of the *Rivers of America*. Disneyland Entertainment employed the resources of Walt Disney Feature Animation and Walt Disney Imagineering as collaborators. Much of the area around the *Rivers of America* needed to be reworked, including terracing the walkways to accommodate viewing and modifying part of *Tom Sawyer Island* so that it could act as a stage for much of the show's live action.

The show is located on the waters of the *Rivers of America* and on a stage across the waterway on the front of *Tom Sawyer Island*. A tavern and tall trees act as a backdrop for the show. To begin, lights around the *Rivers of America* fade and the female voice of Linda Gary narrates the shows introduction;

"Welcome to Fantasmic! Tonight, our friend and host Mickey Mouse uses his vivid imagination to create magical imagery for all to enjoy. Nothing is more wonderful than the imagination for, in a moment, you can experience a beautiful fantasy or an exciting adventure. But beware, nothing is more powerful than the imagination, for it can also expand your greatest fears into an overwhelming nightmare. Are the powers of Mickey's incredible imagination strong enough and bright enough to withstand the evil forces that invade Mickey's dream? You are about to find out. For we now invite you to join Mickey, and experience Fantasmic!... a journey beyond your wildest imagination."

Linda also provided the voice of Maleficent in *Fantasmic!*. She can also be heard in many animated series throughout the 1980's and 1990's, including; *Spider-Man, The Land Before Time II, III, & IV, The Tick, The Little Mermaid, Batman: The Animated Series, Bonkers, The Pirates of Dark Water, Rugrats, Darkwing Duck, Adventures of the Gummi Bears, TaleSpin, DuckTales, Superman, BraveStarr, The Transformers, Ghostbusters, Pound Puppies, He-Man and the Masters of the Universe, Smurfs, Tarzan, Lord of the Jungle, Scooby-Doo and Scrappy-Doo,* and *The Legend of Prince Valiant.*

479

FUN FACTS

- **Official debut**: May 13, 1992
- **Show cost**: approx. $33,000 per evening.
- **Heroes**: Mickey Mouse, Peter Pan, Belle, Ariel, Snow White, Prince Phillip
- **Villains**: The Evil Queen, Ursula, Flotsam, Jetsam, Chernabog, Maleficent, Captain Hook, Mr. Smee, Kaa, Monstro, and Pink Elephants on Parade
- The 20-foot-tall **Ursula is no longer a part of the show**. It was too costly to maintain. A budget was given to replace Ursula when *Fantasmic!* received its new barges in 2007, but the replacement never happened when the barges went over budget.
- The **Ursula sequence now features Flotsam and Jetsam**, in the form of jet-ski-based floats which snake through the water. These provide a replacement for the Ursula float.
- The Peter Pan sequence was given **a new mechanical crocodile** (Tick-Tock), which, though smaller, is more animated than its predecessor and can now interact with the action during the scene.
- A **new Audio-Animatronic dragon** (code-named Murphy) was built to replace the previous dragon (code-named Bucky), which was a mechanical dragon's head on a JLG cherry picker. The new dragon was designed to be a full-bodied replica of Maleficent's final form in *Sleeping Beauty* (1959), standing at 45 feet tall. The dragon had initial problems before a scheduled debut date and was unable to operate on said date. The new dragon premiered on September 1, 2009.
- In early February 2010, **the entire *Rivers of America* were drained**. Both the *Mark Twain* and the *Sailing Ship Columbia* underwent refurbishment, and the track along which the ships travel was replaced. The show's underwater effects underwent maintenance as well, and the laser effects for the finale were upgraded. In early May, the refurbishment was completed, and the rivers were restored. *Fantasmic!* was scheduled to return for the summer season on May 28, 2010.
- On August 28, 2010, the second generation **dragon (Murphy) broke again**. It partly collapsed during a performance. It was restored to the show on November 12, 2010.
- The **fire-on-water effect is created by natural gas lines** running beneath the river. The gas simply bubbles up to the surface and 6 flame throwers along the banks of the river ignite the gas. With the original dragon, it initially would be the source of ignition for the water. This would cause the face of the dragon to burn and so three flame throwers were added. The new dragon's style of flame thrower sprays the stream of fuel, and then ignites it after it is all airborne, opposed to igniting the fuel as it sprays out. This allows the flame to throw further, aerosolize, and overall be more impressive.
- The video and audio playback was **originally mastered to laserdisc**.

480

- The **voice cast is as follows**;
  - Wayne Allwine - Mickey Mouse
  - Louise Chamis - Evil Queen/Old Hag
  - Tony Jay - Magic Mirror, Judge Claude Frollo
  - Eddie Carroll - Jiminy Cricket
  - Corey Burton - Chernabog, Captain Hook, Pirates
  - Linda Gary - Maleficent
  - Pat Carroll - Ursula

- *Disneyland's* **version has** Mickey, Minnie, Chip, Dale, Goofy, Pluto, Donald, Cinderella, Perla and Suzy, Snow White and her Prince, Dopey, Princess Aurora, Prince Phillip, Aladdin, Jasmine, Princess Tiana, Ariel, Prince Eric, Belle, the Beast, Mary Poppins, Alice, The White Rabbit, The Mad Hatter, Tweedle Dee and Tweedle Dum, Woody, Buzz Lightyear, Jessie, and two soldiers from *Toy Story*.

- After a long period of being closed for the construction of *Star Wars Land*, *Fantasmic* will re-open some changes. Most will be seen after the re-opening happens. One change that is known for now is that the **Peter Pan sequence is being removed** and replaced with a Pirates of the Caribbean sequence.

Haunted Mansion

Opened August 9, 1969 - Duration: 10:00 **FP**

Go on a "scary" ride through a haunted mansion in 19th century New Orleans. The riders are taken throughout the house, the attic and out the attic window into the graveyard.

FUN FACTS

- This is **one of the most popular attractions** in the whole park.

- Before this attraction was constructed, they had to remove the **previously- existing building which housed the *Chicken Plantation Restaurant***. They served fried chicken from *Disneyland's* opening day until 1962. That was back when this area was part of Frontierland and could fit the antebellum themed restaurant exterior.

- On opening day back in 1969, **they set a record for park attendance reaching 82,516 Guests**. The queue was so long it stretched through *New Orleans Square* and ended in the hub near where the *Partners* statue is now. The average wait was about three hours to get on.

The hearse was added to the outside queue during the refurbishment in 1995 (read the "Disney Myth" about it at the end of this section). Disney purchased the hearse from Dale Rickards, a collector of sorts from Malibu, California. Dale didn't have the  documents of authenticity which were lost with the passing of the previous owner, Robert Cottle, so its history can't be traced. The manufacturer's plate was also missing, making it impossible to trace that way. It is thought that the hearse was constructed around the 1890's. (*see photo*)

When still planned as a walkthrough attraction, **Walt and his Imagineers went up to the Winchester Mystery House** in San Jose, California, to observe how the guided tours worked to see if his Haunted Mansion would work like *The Jungle Cruise* with a live Cast Member talking to the Guests.

Originally, the queue didn't have a switchback area. The area that now has the switchbacks used to be a graveyard with headstones. Guests would just walk on the other side of that wall and head straight to the mansion. After nine months of being open, Disney realized they needed more wait room, so the graveyard was removed and replaced with railings in May 1970.

In 1969, **Disney released a record album to coincide with the opening of the attraction titled *The Story and Song of the Haunted Mansion*.** It was a promotional and collectable record that immersed the listeners in the story of the attraction. Thurl Ravenscroft (the  fallen bust in the graveyard-*see photo*) narrated the record and had the voice of the Ghost Host provided by Peter Renaday (read his mini biography further ahead). The story followed two teenagers as they walked through *Haunted Mansion* after seeking refuge inside during a storm. The voice of the teenage boy, Mike, was provided by 15-year-old Ron Howard, only a year after the ending of *The Andy Griffith Show* (1960-1968). The voice of the teenage girl, Karen, was provided by Robie Lester, who was 44 years old (read her mini biography further ahead).

Robie Lester (singing voice for Duchess in *The AristoCats* and for Bianca in *The Rescuers*) was the voice of the girl. She was the *Disneyland* Story Reader and recorded lots of read-along-records for Disney and is most

482

notable for the phrase *"...when Tinker Bell rings her little bells like this (chime sounds), turn the page."*

🎤 **Peter Renaday was planned to be the voice of the Ghost Host** for the completed attraction, just as he did for the record, but Disney decided to use Paul Frees instead. Paul's voice can be heard elsewhere around the park in the past and present, and also in other Disney parks. In fact, he is the first voice you hear entering the park as the announcer on the *Disneyland Railroad*, *"Your attention please...."* He also voiced Max and Henry the Bear in *Country Bear Jamboree*, he is the narrator for *The Many Adventures of Winnie the Pooh*, the safety announcer for *Astro Orbiter*, the narrator of the past *Walt Disney Story* shown in the *Great Moments with Mr. Lincoln* theater, Abraham Lincoln in the *Magic Kingdom's Hall Of Presidents* from 1993-2008, Captain Nemo for *Magic Kingdom's 20,000 Leagues Under The Sea: Submarine Voyage*, and the voice of Mark Twain on the *Mark Twain Riverboat*. Other attractions from the past would include *Adventure Thru Inner Space*, *Tomorrowland Transit Authority* (*The People Mover*), *Snow White's Scary Adventures* as The Huntsman in *Magic Kingdom*, *Rocket To The Moon*, and *Mission To Mars*. Aside from his work in the parks, he has been an actor and voice actor for Disney in such films as;

Lt. Robin Crusoe USN (1966)	Pilot
The One and Only, Genuine, Original Family Band (1968)	Dakota Townsman
The Love Bug (1968)	Policeman on Bridge
The Computer Wore Tennis Shoes (1969)	Lt. Hannah
The Aristocats (1970)	The Milkman and the Le Petit Cafe Chef
The Barefoot Executive (1971)	Policeman
The Million Dollar Duck (1971)	Mr. Beckert
The Strongest Man in the World (1975)	Reporter
The Shaggy D.A. (1976)	Roller Derby Ticket-Taker
The Rescuers (1977)	American Delegate
The Cat from Outer Space (1978)	Bailiff
The Apple Dumpling Gang Rides Again (1979)	Jailer at Fort
The Last Flight of Noah's Ark (1980)	Irate Pilot
The Devil and Max Devlin (1981)	Studio Engineer
The Black Cauldron (1985)	Henchman
Mulan (1998)	Additional Voices
The Lion King II: Simba's Pride (1998)	Additional Voices
Howl's Moving Castle (2004)	Additional Voices
Nausicaa of the Valley of the Wind (2005)	Additional Voices
The Princess and the Frog (2009)	Additional Voices
Walt Disney's Wonderful World of Color (1972-1974)	Reporter and Stan
DuckTales (1987)	Additional Voices
TaleSpin (1990)	Captain William Stansbury
Darkwing Duck (1992)	Derek Blunt
Aladdin (1994-1995)	Man
Gargoyles (1994-1995)	Commander, Father and Fortress I Captain

In addition to his Disney roles, he was the first to voice Master Splinter in the series *Teenage Mutant Ninja Turtles* (1987-1996) for nearly a decade.

🎤 The *Haunted Mansion* construction first broke ground in 1962 with the laying of the foundation, and had the exterior completed by 1963. But the

entire attraction wasn't completed and opened for seven years. There was a big hiatus starting in 1964 when Walt put his Imagineers on projects for the World's Fair instead of this.

- **Originally Walt put Yale Gracey in charge of the *Haunted Mansion* project** along with Rolly Crump. The production of the Mansion got put on hold as Walt deferred his Imagineering team to the production of the World's Fair projects. After the Fair, they picked it back up. Other Imagineers joined the team along the way including Marc Davis, Claude Coats, X Atencio, Bill Justice, Harper Goff, Ken Anderson, Bob Gurr, Blaine Gibson, Marvin Davis, and Harriet Burns, who all played important roles with the design and construction of *Haunted Mansion*. To read their see *Imagineer Mini Biographies* page 287.

- Hints of a "ghost house" attraction for **Walt's *Disneyland* began back in 1951** when Walt asked Harper Goff to draw up some conceptual designs.

- Imagineer Marvin Davis **originally designed the Mansion to be a rickety old house** up on a hill leading off of *Main Street, U.S.A.* down a long crooked path.

- The **final look of the *Mansion* was modeled after a mansion seen in a catalogue** by Imagineer Ken Anderson, which was also originally rejected by Walt, as he wanted all the buildings in *New Orleans Square* to be designed in the same style. Ken was calling the pre-Mansion designs "Bloodmere Manor."

- During the planning of the *Mansion*, **Walt referred to his Imagineers as Illusioneers**, seeing as the attraction was going to be called the "Museum Of Illusions."

- While the Imagineers were creating the characters for *Haunted Mansion*, they would sometimes **rig them so that they would turn on and "come to life"** at nighttime when the cleaning crews went through the studio.

- The vehicles you sit in while traveling through the mansion **are called "doom buggies."** This design of moving large quantities through an attraction at one time was used for the newly-constructed *The Little Mermaid: Ariel's Undersea Adventure* in *California Adventure*.

- The **"doom buggies" were designed by Imagineers Roger E. Broggie,** Bert Brundage, and Bob Gurr who called the ride system the "omnimover" which is a portmanteau of omnirange and PeopleMover. They were named doom buggies by Yale Gracey. They were inspired by their omnimover design of ride vehicles for the World's Fair on the Ford's Magic Skyway, except those vehicles could not individually rotate. The design was upgraded and retooled for *Adventure through Inner Space,* which was the predecessor to the doom buggies.

- **Walt was the one who came up with the idea for The Omnimover** System when he visited the Ford Motor Company plant and saw their production line conveyor system and asked if they could put a chair on it.

- There are **131 "doom buggies" spaced six feet apart that can pass about 2,400** Guests through per hour. That is a little over 38,000 people on a summer day.

- It takes about **10 minutes to completely travel the 786-foot track** throughout the *Mansion*.

- Blaine Gibson only sculpted a certain amount of faces for this attraction. **Disney face-shared between multiple attractions to cut costs.** You can see recognizable faces divided between *Haunted Mansion*, *Pirates of the Caribbean*, *Jungle Cruise*, and the late *Carousel of Progress* (now only in *Magic Kingdom*).

- In its original concept, ***Haunted Mansion* was going to be a walk-through** attraction with several scenes for people to stand in front of in order to view. To help speed up the viewing process, the "doom buggies" were added. This also prevented the public from vandalizing. Walt said he wanted it to be similar to taking a tour of Hearst Castle in San Simeon.

- **Harriet Burns designed three concept models** of the Mansion's exterior. Two of them had a haunted theme and one had a normal exterior.

- The exterior of the Mansion was **modeled after a mansion built in 1803** in Baltimore, Maryland, called the Shipley-Lydecker House. For a long time, people believed it was the Evergreen House built in 1857, which is also located in Baltimore, Maryland.

- While the Mansion was being constructed, Walt said, *"We'll take care of the outside, and the ghosts will take care of the inside."*

- A film that was a huge **inspiration for elements in the *Mansion* was *The Haunting* (1963)** directed by Robert Wise and starred Julie Harris, the actress that Walt originally wanted to play Mary Poppins until he met Julie Andrews. One noticeable aspect is the *Corridor of Doors* where you can see the doors bulging out toward the Guests to make it appear as if something is trying to escape. The tops of the door jams have facial features, not unlike the door jams in the film. In fact, there was an inter-office communication memo, sent out by Richard Irvine, for all the Imagineers working on the project to go to a private screening at the Disney Studios in January 1965. Richard specifically sent it to Marc Davis, Wathel Rogers, Yale Gracey, Chuck Mayall, Jack Ferges, Rolly Crump, Marty Sklar, and Blane Gibson.

- In the *Corridor of Doors*, you can see portraits of some of the ghosts that you see while on the attraction. **These portraits are actually the concept sketches** done by the artists. You can even spot the Hatbox Ghost in them. (*see photo*)

When Imagineer Rolly Crump was designing *Haunted Mansion*, **he used aspects from the film *Beauty and the Beast*** (1946), also called "*La belle et la bête*," as an inspiration for the feel and look that he wanted for this new attraction. Some of the architecture included human-looking body parts, like the arm holding the torch in the crypt (*see photo*). The continuation of the projects design was later handed off to Imagineer and artist Marc Davis.

One of Rolly's characters that didn't make it into the *Mansion* was "**the candle man**," who was made entirely out of wax and had his fingers burning like wicks.

Rolly came up with the first sketches of the "stretching portraits," but then that aspect of the attraction was taken over by Marc Davis who drew the portraits, or a variation thereof, that you see today. Rolly had said he did not mind Marc taking over the art aspect, as he was a great animator.

Rolly was also working on **a project called *The Museum of the Weird*** with Yale Gracey, which was to be in the spill area, but was scrapped when the attraction turned into a ride-thru. They still wanted some of Rolly's ideas in the attraction anyway, so the changing portraits, the phantom organ player, the séance chamber, the moving busts, faces in the décor (*see photo*), and some others were used. Rolly once said in an interview that about 25% of his ideas actually made it into the final *Mansion*. He also came up with the idea of an enchanted gypsy wagon, which was later turned into Madame Leota's Cart in *Walt Disney World*.

Seekers of The Weird **is a comic book series published by Marvel Comics** for Disney. The first issue was published January 15, 2014. *Seekers of the Weird* was named after the *Haunted Mansion* concept, *Museum of the Weird,* which was first planned as a spillover area for the Guests exiting the walk-through attraction *Haunted Mansion*. Since the *Mansion* became a ride-through attraction, due to the invention of the Doom Buggies, the museum was no longer needed. All of the odd concepts that were going to be in the museum were created by aforementioned Rolly Crump. You can still see some of his creations in the *Mansion* today, like the face wallpaper, the armchair with the face, and the stretching portraits to name a few, although that last one was redrawn by animator Marc Davis. Marvel contacted Rolly to see if it would be alright to create a comic series based on his concepts. Rolly was thrilled that his concept projects were going to be put to use after nearly five decades. The comics follow Maxwell and Melody after their parents get kidnapped. They are thrust into a thrilling race through the world's strangest and dangerous museum as they unite with their mysterious and swashbuckling uncle to save their family and the world from an evil secret society. The uncle was named Rolly to pay homage to the inventive Imagineer. There are currently five issues available with the most recent released in 2016.

🎪 Rolly also **had concept sketches of faces for the hallway wallpaper**, but that too was done by Marc Davis, who designed his wallpaper similarly to Rolly's. However, if you look closely at the faces on the wallpaper, you can clearly recognize Rolly's artistic style.

🎪 While Rolly and Yale were working in the warehouse on the Mansion characters, they received a call from custodial advising them to leave the lights on as there would be a janitor going in to clean that night. Before they left, **they set up some of the characters to come to life**. The next day, Rolly and Yale arrived to a lonely broom lying in the middle of the floor and a phone call from custodial advising them that they would have to clean their own workspace from now on.

🎪 **Claude Coats** (see *Imagineer Mini Biographies* page 287) **was responsible for the creepy and moody first-half of the attraction**. Claude was mainly a background artist and designer, not a character designer. He did design a few ghosts for this attraction, and the only one that made it into the finished product was the ghost in the crypt toward the end of the graveyard scene.

🎪 Imagineer Yale Gracey came up with an idea by **projecting a loop video of a face onto the face of a Beethoven statue** that made it appear as if it were talking. Later the idea became what we know as Madam Leotta.

🎪 One of the **most famous lines from this attraction** that you can hear people repeating around the park is spoken by the disembodied Ghost Host, "*Welcome, foolish mortals, to the Haunted Mansion! I am your host, your ghost host.*"

🎪 This attraction features the voice of the late **Paul Frees** as the disembodied "ghost host" (see *Imagineer Mini Biographies* page 287).

🎪 You can **see the Ghost Host in the beginning as the hanging corpse** above the stretching room. He offers up to the Guest the suggestion of taking his way out as he said, "*Which offers you this chilling challenge. To find a way out. Ha ha ha ha. Of course, there's always my way.*" Lightning strikes and you can see him swinging from the rafters as Guests scream.

🎪 All of the dialogue for the entire attraction, including the lyrics to "The Grim Grinning Ghosts" song **was written by Xavier Atencio**. He was also responsible for doing the same thing for *Pirates of the Caribbean*. You can hear his voice emanating from the coffin in the hallway of doors saying, "*Hey, let me outta here!*"

🎪 Walt had a hand in creating this attraction, but **never got to see it completed** because of his death. He wanted the exterior to be clean and neat like the rest of the park, but he would let the ghosts take care of the cleanliness inside.

- In the graveyard scene, you can hear a gruff sounding **laugh that resembles the rhinos** from *Robin Hood* (1973). That's because they were all voiced by Candy Candido (see *Who Does That Voice* on page 147). You can also hear the laughing as you exit the building when you go up the PeopleMover at the end.

- Check out the **tombstones while you are in the queue** outside, they have funny names on them.

- When you enter the stretching room and begin to lower down, **you only go down four feet**. The rest of it is the ceiling rising. This is to get the Guests low enough to go under the train tracks and enter the show building outside the perimeter of the park. The raised ceiling actually goes up into what would be considered the attic of the house.

- I described earlier what a stock sound was. It is a generic sound used in multiple movies or in multiple places. **You can hear the stock sound "Castle Thunder #2" after the Ghost Host** says, *"Of course there's always my way."* You can hear that same thunder in *101 Dalmatians, The Jungle Book, Pete's Dragon, The Fox and the Hound, Mickey's Christmas Carol, Frankenweenie, The Gummi Bears* intro, *The Great Mouse Detective, The Brave Little Toaster,* and *The Little Mermaid.*

- Yale Gracey was the one who came up with the brilliant concept of an elevator.

- The **elevator in the stretching room can carry six tons going down**, and only one ton coming back up.

- You **see a raven four times** throughout the attraction. Each time it appears it is a signal to the riders that they will be hearing the voice of the Ghost Host. This is because Disney intended to have the raven be the voice speaking to you as you passed by, but then later went with the Ghost Host.

- When the Imagineers were making the rubber face for Abraham Lincoln, in *Great Moments with Mr. Lincoln*, they turned the face inside out **and realized that the eyes would follow them from side to side** because the face was concave. This is how Rolly came up with the idea for the busts in the entrance whose eyes follow the patrons to the loading platform.

- The 2003 movie, ***The Haunted Mansion*** (starring Eddie Murphy), was based on this attraction.

- The whole attraction **was originally based on a story** of a man and a woman who were to be married. The woman wanted to go back east to visit her family before her marriage. While she was gone, her fiancé built a huge mansion for her. As soon as he was done building the mansion, it became haunted by a phantom. The phantom had fallen in love with the man's fiancée as well. The soon-to-be groom planned to have a huge party and wedding for his bride as soon as she returned from visiting her family. She promised him that she would arrive in her wedding dress ready to get

488

married. Right before she arrived, the phantom hung the groom in the tower (you see him in the stretching room as the lightning strikes). The phantom (the one playing the organ in the Ballroom) condemned the bride to spend an eternity with him. All the party guest ghosts are the ghosts you see in the ballroom scene and in the graveyard. After the Imagineers changed the attraction around, they made the bride out to be the killer who had many grooms. So, the story doesn't really fit anymore.

The **first conceptual story was about a sea captain** who drowned at sea, but whose ghost returned home in a murderous rage to kill his wife. Rolly Crump and Yale Gracey set up models of what a scene would look like with the sea captain dripping with water and burying his wife behind a brick wall in the house, only to disappear and leave behind a water puddle as the skeletal ghost of his wife flew out of the wall toward the audience. Marc Davis' conceptual art for the sea captain can still be seen in *Disney World's Haunted Mansion*. This scene was only possible if the audience was stationary, and since the attraction became a ride-thru, it was cut.

Every holiday season, *Haunted Mansion* is **transformed into Haunted Mansion Holiday**. This crossover, based on Tim Burton's *The Nightmare Before Christmas* (1993), began in 2001. *Haunted Mansion* is closed every September for a few weeks as they revamp the attraction, replacing many of the props and Audio-Animatronics with characters and themes from the movie. The attraction is closed again in January when it is returned to the regular *Haunted Mansion*.

Thurl Ravenscroft sings as part of a group of singing busts in the graveyard scene; he is the broken bust lying on its side. Many people believe this bust to be of Walt himself, but it is not (see *Who Does That Voice on page 147*).

After you go down the stretching room and hop on the attraction, you will actually be going **outside the perimeter** of the park. You are under ground, so you don't even notice.

An important part of Disney history is located in the grand hall scene. For those of you who may remember, in the original attraction **the pipe organ** on the far left of the scene is the original prop from the studio's 1954 release, *20,000 Leagues Under the Sea*. (*see photo*)

Unless you rode on *Haunted Mansion* within its first few days after opening in 1969, **you will never have seen the Hatbox Ghost**. Yale Gracey's plan was to have his head disappear and reappear inside the hatbox that he was holding. He was located in the attic scene across from the bride. There was a

489

black light used to illuminate his head. When the light would go out, another would come on in the box revealing his head's new location. The problem was there was too much light in the attic already, so his head would never totally disappear. Thus, the character was a flop and it was removed. There is only one known photo and a few seconds of a recorded home movie of him in existence. Nobody knows where the unused character's body is now, but it is rumored that the animatronic parts were used to create Sam the Eagle in the *America Sings* attraction from 1973. You can still find his head in use today as Ezra, one of the hitchhikers as you are about to disembark the attraction. (*see photo*)

🦇 The **Hatbox Ghost was themed to be the groom of the bride**. The narrative of *Haunted Mansion* LP record, published in 1969, as read by Thurl Ravenscroft states as follows, "*As they turned to run out of the door, another ghostly manifestation appeared and blocked their way. He was a cloaked figure with an evil, grinning face. A hatbox hung from his hand. With each beat of his bride's heart, his head disappeared from his body, and appeared in the hatbox.*"

🦇 With the removal of the Hatbox Ghost, the ghost count for the Mansion technically **dropped to 998 happy haunts**.

🦇 In May 2015, **Disney reintroduced the Hatbox Ghost** for the 60th anniversary of the park. The Imagineers created all new special effects to get the character to do what was originally intended back in 1969. (*see photo, and also back cover*)

🦇 Imagineer **Patrick Romandy Simmons was responsible for the rematerialization** of the Hatbox Ghost back to the attic by sculpting him. He had these fun facts to say about the popular ghost:
- Patrick designed the ghost to be of Irish descent.
- The walking stick he holds is a shillelagh, which is a thick walking stick with a knob at the end, typically used in Ireland as a weapon.
- The shillelagh measures 30" long.
- He stands 5' 3" tall hunched over.
- The late 1800's shoes they found for him are a size 12.
- The size of his top hat is a 7.

🦇 In the summer of 1982, a **live person began walking around in the Corridor of Doors**, the area between the coffin and Madam Leota's Séance Room dressed in a suit of armor. This live character was referred to as the "Knight in Armor." It was an awesome and easy special effect to add into the Mansion. Cast Member David Mink was the first to portray the Knight and test out its impact on the Guests. In the beginning, the Knight was given a six-foot battle axe to swing toward the Guests, bang on the floor, tap on the back of the Doom Buggy, or hook around the edge of the buggy to scare

Guests. People were hitting and doing other things to the Cast Members. There were also guest complaints that it was too scary. One Knight even got his nose broken by an overly scared teenage girl cheerleader after accidently touching her. After that incident, Disney implemented a new rule of staying at least six feet away from the Guests, and then later added no scaring senior citizens or small children. The Knights, like the other CMs, were given an emergency shut-off button, much like a garage door opener. One CM had to use it to get a woman back on her Doom Buggy after she jumped out to throw her purse at him. This effect was so popular that there were two shifts added for the Knights. The a.m. shift would consist of two Knights that would rotate out every 30 minutes, and a p.m. shift also containing two knights that would swap out every 30 minutes. Even though the compliments outweighed the complaints, the added feature of the Knight was removed because it was reportedly getting too costly for the Character Department (the Cast Members who portray face characters like Mickey Mouse, Genie, Chip & Dale, etc.). It was discontinued in late 1985.

⚜ There was **talk about adding a live groom in the attic scene,** for which they had already made a costume, but it would never come to fruition. In the works were also a planned phantom in the endless hallway and a specter in *the graveyard; both also never came into existence.*

⚜ In the séance room, the floating **effect used to make Madame Leota's crystal ball float** around was added in 2005.

⚜ On June 26, 1999, *Disneyland* **celebrated the 30ᵗʰ anniversary of *Haunted Mansion*.** They held a special gathering in the *Mansion* at midnight following a night of panel discussions with Imagineers Rolly Crump, Marc Davis, X Atencio, Buddy Baker, and Sam McKim, for which a limited quantity of 1,000 tickets were sold. As an intro to the panel, which was held in the *Fantasyland Theater*, Guest were treated to a little stage show performed by costumed characters from the *Mansion*, including the bride, the caretaker, the three hitchhiking ghosts, and a full-bodied Madam Leotta. The visitors could purchase special *Haunted Mansion* items and limited-edition items created by Imagineers Eric Robinson and Terri Hardin. For  those who rode the *Mansion* at midnight, they had a special greeting by Cast Member Maynard (*see photo*) before entering the *Mansion*. Once in the stretching room, Guests were met by X Atencio, Buddy Baker, and Sam McKim. Later on, Guests could catch a glimpse of Marc and Alice Davis waiving to passersby from the *Ball Room's* dining table. There were also multiple new costumed characters added, including ghostly bridesmaids, vampires, phantoms, the return of the Knight in Armor, and a few other spooks.

⚜ On October 21, 2004, a bidder on a Disney-sponsored auction on eBay won the right to be the first non-*Disneyland* employee to have his name added to

491

an attraction. Cary Sharp, a doctor and health-care attorney from Baton Rouge, Louisiana, placed a winning bid of $37,400 to become **Disneyland's one thousandth ghost** with the addition of his nickname, a joke eulogy, and the signatures of Disney Imagineers on a tombstone to be displayed in the attraction. Its placement is guaranteed for ten years and will remain as a permanent exhibit. According to the Los Angeles Times, the opening bid of $750 was placed by horror novelist Clive Barker. Sharp, who had only visited *Disneyland* once before, placed the bid in good faith as a way to entertain his friends and never expected to win. The tombstone is located near the beginning of the graveyard scene and can be seen just as the vehicle enters the graveyard gates to the left. The name on the tombstone is "Jay." The money has been donated to the *Boys and Girls Club*. Half went to the local Anaheim

chapter of the main charity while the other half went to the Baton Rouge chapter.

- In the ballroom scene, there are two portraits hanging on the back wall. They depict two men who are about to have a duel. Their ghosts appear, shoot at each other, and then disappear. In 1974, **someone actually shot at the portraits** with a .22 caliber gun. Some people believe it was a child with a sling shot. This left a hole in the glass (the second to the last on your way through the scene next to the pillar). The Disney Imagineers used a fake spider and webs to cover the hole. To replace the whole pane of glass, they would have had to remove the roof to lower it in.

- Because of the cost cutting by Disney with the "face sharing," the face of **the dueling ghost on the left is the same face as the auctioneer pirate** on *Pirates of the Caribbean*, as well as the captain ghost coming through the wall in the ballroom.

- The effect used to show riders the ghosts dancing in the ballroom is **called the Pepper's Ghost Effect**. It was invented by English engineer Henry Dircks (1806–1873), but was later popularized by John Henry Pepper (1821-1900), a British scientist and inventor who entertained the public and royalty with the trick. The effect has an object out of view from the rider, but has it on the same side of a sheet of glass. When the object is lit up, it makes it look like it has just appeared out of thin air. This same trick is used for the Blue Fairy on *Pinnochio's Daring Journey*.

- In the fourth photo of Constance with her husband, you will notice her husband sitting in a fancy chair. This is **the chair you see Jack Sparrow sitting in** in his treasure room when you are going up the lift to leave *Pirates of the Caribbean*. It was also the prop chair in the Disney movie *The Haunted Mansion* (2003). Master Gracey (played by Nathaniel Parker) is sitting in it during dinner.

🚋 While riding through the attic, you may notice something peculiar about the portraits of Constance with her different husbands. Her first husband is dressed simply, while the following husbands increase in their wealth. Along with her increase of wealth, Constance Hatchaway, the "Black Widow Bride," **gains a new string of pearls with each husband**.

🚋 While looking at the portraits, take note that she **wears the same wedding dress** at each of her weddings.

🚋 The **actress who portrays the "Black Widow Bride" Constance Hatchaway in the attic** scene is Kathryn "Kat" Cressida, the current voice of Wendy and Alice in the Disney parks. Disney motion captured her face and computer altered the video for the projection onto the bride's face. You can also hear Kat in the *Tower of Terror* queue as the little girl crying on the out-of-tune radio on the workbench.

🚋 The **actress who modeled for the portraits of Constance**, with her multiple husbands scattered around the attic, is Julia Lee (from *Buffy the Vampire Slayer*). (*see photo*)

🚋 It is said that Ken Anderson's **inspiration for the bride was the photo of the "Brown Lady of Raynham Hall."** The Brown Lady, or Ghost of Raynham Hall, was the title of a photo taken in 1936 by Country Life magazine. It is a photo of the staircase in Raynham Hall that has a ghostly woman in the middle of it appearing to be dressed as a bride. It is speculated that it was the spirit of the late Lady Dorothy Walpole (1686-1726) who died in the estate from smallpox. Prior to her death, she was confined to her home by her husband, Charles Townshend, because he caught her having an affair. After that, she remained in the dwelling until her death, and even after that.

🚋 In Ken's original concept art, **the bride would have been down a corridor** leading up some stairs, much like the Endless Hall with the floating candelabra.

🚋 **The bride has gone through multiple changes since her first appearance** in 1969. The first bride guests met was named "The Corpse Bride." She had a heartbeat with a visible red beating heart and a skeletal face with glowing eyes. She held a candle and a bouquet of flowers for over two decades until a blue-faced bride replaced her in the early 1990's. The Imagineers decided that the bride needed a face. This bride's face more resembles the concept art of Marc Davis. She haunted the attic until the *Mansion* update in 2006 when Constance Hatchaway appeared. She is known as "The Black Widow Bride," as she leaves behind the corpses of her late husbands. They are as follows;

- Ambrose Harper (married in 1869)
- Frank Banks (married in 1872)

- The Marquis de Doom (married in 1874)
- Reginald Caine (married in 1875)
- George Hightower (married in 1877)

🦇 **Constance can be seen earlier in the attraction**. When you enter the stretching room, she can be seen as an old woman holding a rose. As the portrait stretches, she is revealed to be sitting on the headstone of her last husband, George Hightower.

🦇 The following is the **narration for the entire attraction**:

- **Foyer:**
  - When hinges creak in door less chambers, and strange and frightening sounds echo through the halls. Whenever candlelights flicker where the air is deathly still. That is the time when ghosts are present, practicing their terror with ghoulish delight!
- **Portrait Gallery:**
  - Welcome, foolish mortals, to the Haunted Mansion! I am your host, your ghost host. Kindly step all the way in please and make room for everyone. There's no turning back now.
  - Our tour begins here in this gallery where you see paintings of some of our guests as they appeared in their corruptible, mortal state.
  - Your cadaverous pallor betrays an aura of foreboding, almost as though you sense a disquieting metamorphosis. Is this haunted room actually stretching? Or is it your imagination, hmm? And consider this dismaying observation: This chamber has no windows and no doors, which offers you this chilling challenge: to find a way out!
  - Of course, there's always my way.
- **Portrait Hall:**
  - Oh, I didn't mean to frighten you prematurely; the real chills come later. Now, as they say, look alive, and we'll continue our little tour. And let's all stay together, please. There are several prominent ghosts who have retired here from creepy old crypts from all over the world. Actually, we have 999 happy haunts here, but there's room for a thousand. Any volunteers? If you insist on lagging behind, you may not need to volunteer. The carriage that will carry you into the moldering sanctum of the spirit world will accommodate you and one or two loved ones. Kindly watch your step as you board, please. We spirits haunt our best in gloomy darkness, so remember, no flash pictures, please.
  - And now, a carriage approaches to carry you into the boundless realm of the supernatural. Take your loved ones by the hand, please, and kindly watch your step. Oh yes, and no flash pictures, please! We spirits are frightfully sensitive to bright lights.
  - Do not pull down on the safety bar, please; I will lower it for you. And heed this warning: the spirits will materialize only if you remain quietly seated at all times.

494

- **Doom Buggies:**
  - o We find it delightfully unlivable here in this ghostly retreat. Every room has wall-to-wall creeps, and hot and cold running chills. Shhh, listen!
  - o All our ghosts have been dying to meet you! This one can hardly contain himself!
  - o Unfortunately, they all seem to have trouble getting through. Perhaps Madame Leota can establish contact. She has a remarkable head for materializing the disembodied.
- **Madame Leota: (see her quotes below)**
- **Grand Ballroom:**
  - o The happy haunts have received your sympathetic vibrations and are beginning to materialize. They're assembling for a swinging wake, and they'll be expecting me. I'll see you all a little later.
- **The Attic: (see the bride's quotes below)**
- **Grim Grinning Ghosts: (see the lyrics below)**
- **Ghost Host:**
  - o Ah, there you are, and just in time! There's a little matter I forgot to mention. Beware of hitchhiking ghosts! They have selected you to fill our quota, and they'll haunt you until you return! Now I will raise the safety bar, and a ghost will follow you home!
  - o If you would like to join our jamboree, there's a simple rule that's compulsory. Mortals pay a token fee. Rest in peace, the haunting's free; so hurry back, we would like your company!
- **Little Leota:**
  - o Hurry back! Hurry back! Be sure to bring your death certificate, if you decide to join us. Make final arrangements now! We've been dying to have you!

The face and voice of the small ghost hostess at the end is that of **Imagineer Leota Toombs**. Some fans refer to her as "Little Leota." She is also Madame Leota, the face in the crystal ball. **Eleanor Audley is the voice** of Madam Leota (she also voiced Maleficent in *Sleeping Beauty* and Lady Tremain in *Cinderella*). Her voice in the crystal ball chants:

- "Serpents and spiders, tail of a rat, call in the spirits wherever they're at."
- "Rap on a table, it's time to respond, send us a message from somewhere beyond."
- "Goblins and ghoulies from last Halloween awaken the spirits with your tambourine."
- "Creepies and crawlies, toads in a pond, let there be music from regions beyond."
- "Wizards and witches, wherever you dwell, give us a hint by ringing a bell."

🏰 There were two lines **cut from Madame Leota's dialogue**, but were still recorded.

- "Horn toads and lizards, fiddle and strum. Please answer the roll by beating a drum."
- "Ghost friends and furies, old friends and new. Blow on a horn, so we'll know that it's you."

🏰 The bride, **Constance**, in the attic repeats these quotes:

- "I do, I do...I did"
- "You may now kiss the bride"
- "And we lived happily ever after"
- "As long as we both shall live"
- "For better or for worse"
- "Here comes the bride"
- "Till death do us part"
- "Through sickness and in...wealth"

🏰 **"Grim Grinning Ghosts" is sung by a barbershop-type quartet** consisting of Thurl Ravenscroft, Jay Meyer, Chuck Schroeder, Verne Rowe, and Bob Ebright who were called *The Phantom Five*, a mixture of five excellent singers. It was composed by Buddy Baker, with the lyrics written by X Atencio, and was recorded February 14, 1969.

🏰 **Want to sing along with the creepy singing busts?** Unfortunately, due to copyright reasons, I had to remove the lyrics from this edition of my book. If you would like to see the lyrics to sing along, please visit... discoveringthemagickingdom.com/apps/blog/show/44592323-song-lyrics.

🏰 Cast Members used to **hand out Death Certificates to Guests who asked**, but stopped doing that in 2012. If you still want one, you can download and print it from DoomBuggys.com.

🏰 **There are unofficial names for each bust**. They are, from left to right, Rollo Rumkin (Verne Rowe), Uncle Theodore (Thurl Ravenscroft), Cousin Algernon (Chuck Schroeder), Ned Nub (Jay Meyer), and Phineas P. Pock (Bob Ebright).

🏰 In January 2014, there **was a comic book series created by Disney and Marvel** called *Seekers Of The Weird*. It followed two kids who have to wander through the *Museum of The Weird*. One of the main characters in the comic series is Uncle Rolly, named after the Imagineer Rolly Crump, who first imagined all the weirdness that the comics would contain.

- **The hitchhiking ghosts at the end also have unofficial names**. Phineas is the one in the top hat holding the bag, Ezra is the skeletal one with the same face as the Hatbox Ghost, and Gus is the short-bearded one with the ball and chain.

- For a **list of this attractions Hidden Mickeys, see page 349**.

DISNEY MYTHS

- Although it is widely rumored that *Disneyland* acquired the coach that carried **Mormon Pioneer Brigham Young's body** to its grave in 1877, it happens that this is just another one of the many myths that surround *Haunted Mansion*. According to Glen M. Leonard, director of The Church of Jesus Christ of Latter-day Saints' Museum of Church History and Art, historical records are conclusive that the hearse couldn't possibly have been used for Young. "Historical evidence shows no hearse was used," he said, although he allowed for the possibility that the vehicle may be an authentic carriage from Young's era that originated in Utah. The truth of the hearse's origins may never be known, but it can be said with reasonable certainty that neither Brigham Young nor Joseph Smith, the Latter-Day Saints church founder, for that matter, were ever transported in this particular coach. It is also reasonably certain that no carriages throughout history have ever been pulled by invisible horses, though we give *Disneyland* extra credit for including the horseshoes in this clever display. (*see photo*)

- One Disney myth that has been floating around is that the **Ghost Host was voiced by the late and great horror film actor Vincent Price**. Although he did not voice the Ghost Host in *Disneyland*, he did voice the Ghost Host in the *Haunted Manor* in *Disneyland Paris*. Although, that voice track has since been updated with a different actor.

PRO TIP: *If the queue splits into two lines, take the line to the right; it's faster.*

497

Haunted Mansion Holiday

Opened October 3, 2001 - Duration: 10:00

Haunted Mansion Holiday is a seasonal overlay of the *Haunted Mansion* attraction. It blends the settings and characters of the original *Haunted Mansion* with those of Tim Burton's *The Nightmare Before Christmas* (1993). *Haunted Mansion* typically closes for two and half weeks in September so it can be converted into *Haunted Mansion Holiday*. The overlaid attraction is then open to Guests from late-September through early-January, before being closed again during January so the overlay can be removed.

HISTORY

Two similar overlays, the past *Country Bear Christmas Special* and current *it's a small world Holiday,* had already been successful for some time when *Haunted Mansion Holiday* was developed. Initially, Disney considered doing a retelling of *A Christmas Carol*, but decided against it due to the attraction's setting in *New Orleans Square* and the incongruity of bringing Santa Claus into the eerie environment of *Haunted Mansion*. Instead, they decided to base it on *The Nightmare Before Christmas,* after considering which Disney character would celebrate Christmas in *Haunted Mansion*, should Santa Claus ever land there on his journey. Steve Davison took the idea and worked with Walt Disney Creative Entertainment to develop the overlay.

STORYLINE

Jack Skellington, usually in charge of the spectacular Halloween celebrations in Halloween Town, grows tired of these annual routines. One day, he accidentally discovers Christmas Town and is inspired by the new ideas and sensations. He then sets out to take over for "Sandy Claws" and run the Mansion's Christmas celebrations in his own twisted style, with the help of the citizens of Halloween Town.

SOUNDTRACK

The attraction's musical score was originally composed by Gordon Goodwin. It was replaced in 2002 with an adapted score by John Debney, based on themes from the film's soundtrack composed by Danny Elfman. Since 2003, Goodwin's original music has been used in the stretching rooms and the exit crypt (where Goodwin's attic music is used), while the rest of Debney's score remains. Several characters in the ride are voiced by the original actors from the film, and the various sound effects are an admixture of tracks from the original attraction and new ones.

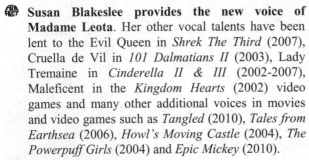

FUN FACTS

🏚 Leota Toombs, whose face was used for Madame Leota, passed away in 1991. **Her daughter Kim Irvine** (see *Imagineer Mini Biographies* page 287), who was also an Imagineer (who created the pet cemetery by the handicap entrance to *Haunted Mansion*), had such a close resemblance to Leota that the Imagineers used her face for the new face of Madame Leota. (*see photo*)

🏚 **Susan Blakeslee provides the new voice of Madame Leota**. Her other vocal talents have been lent to the Evil Queen in *Shrek The Third* (2007), Cruella de Vil in *101 Dalmatians II* (2003), Lady Tremaine in *Cinderella II & III* (2002-2007), Maleficent in the *Kingdom Hearts* (2002) video games and many other additional voices in movies and video games such as *Tangled* (2010), *Tales from Earthsea* (2006), *Howl's Moving Castle* (2004), *The Powerpuff Girls* (2004) and *Epic Mickey* (2010).

🏚 In the attic scene, only **three names are marked naughty** on the list: Tim (reference to Tim Burton), Leota (for Madam Leota), and Vincent (from the short film of the same name, and Vincent Price, famous horror actor and friend of Tim Burton. He also provided the original *Phantom Manor* narration in *Disneyland Paris*).

🏚 After *Haunted Mansion Holiday* opened, it quickly became so popular with Guests that **Disney had to re-open the FastPass** machines.

🏚 A Smellitzer (a machine used to pump out fabricated smells) is used to **pour artificial gingerbread scent** into the hallway as you pass by the Gingerbread House in the ball room.

- The **gingerbread house in the ballroom** scene is made with 100% real gingerbread. A new unique sculpture is created annually at Disney's local bakery.

- In 2016, there was a **Hidden Mickey on the gingerbread house's roof** design. (see photo)

- The gingerbread house that was created in 2012 holds the record as being the **tallest gingerbread house they have created** so far, measuring 9 feet tall.

- The **voice talent**:
  - Jack Skellington - Chris Sarandon
  - Oogie Boogie - Ken Page
  - Ghost Host - Corey Burton
  - Sally - Catherine O'Hara
  - Madame Leota's voice - Susanne Blakeslee
  - Madame Leota's face - Kim Irvine

- To get the part of the Ghost Host, Corey Burton went down to the studio to audition. He was excited to be a part of the project because Paul Frees, the original Ghost Host, was an idol and inspiration to him. Disney liked the voice Corey provided, so **they ended up recording for 2 ½ hours** and had all of the dialogue recorded for the attraction. Disney ended up just using the demo recording as the final product for the attraction, which they recorded only six months before the overlay's opening.

- In 2010, the **floating Leota effect** from the 2005 refurbishment was kept for the holidays, along with several glowing bottles surrounding Leota.

- In the pet cemetery out front, **a grave was added for "Sparky"** from Tim Burton's *Frankenweenie* (2012). But the grave is all dug up to follow the story line of the film. (*see photo*)

- The **new stretching portraits are just placed over top of the original ones**, as they proved too difficult to remove without damaging them.

- This attraction **was originally proposed as its own dark ride** in 1996. Since the movie lacked popularity, Disney did not want to spend a lot of money creating an entire attraction. If this one flopped, they could just discontinue the overlay. The movie and attraction developed a cult following and became very popular. So popular that the overlay has been going on for over one and a half decades.

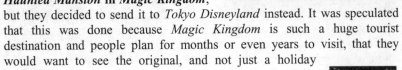

- The original Oogie Boogie was **a repurposed animatronic skeleton of Big Al** from *The Country Bear Jamboree*. *The Country Bears* closed on September 9, 2001, just one month before the opening of this overlay. (*see photo*)

- There was going to be an **overlay for *Haunted Mansion* in *Magic Kingdom***, but they decided to send it to *Tokyo Disneyland* instead. It was speculated that this was done because *Magic Kingdom* is such a huge tourist destination and people plan for months or even years to visit, that they would want to see the original, and not just a holiday overlay.

- **Garner Holt Productions made the animatronic characters** for the overlay. They also made the animatronics for *Ariel's Undersea Adventure* and *Cars Land*.

- When the attraction in 2016 with the overlay, there was a new character added to the graveyard scene. **Sally can be found daydreaming** on a headstone. (*see photo*)

- For a **list of this attractions Hidden Mickeys, see page 349**.

PRO TIP: *If the queue splits into two lines, take the line to the right; it's faster.*

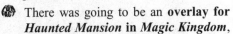

PIRATES OF THE CARIBBEAN
Opened March 18, 1967 - Duration: 16:30

An over sixteen-minute dark-ride, in a boat, through a gallery of animatronic pirates. This was the largest Audio-Animatronic attraction ever created and still ranks among the largest today. It was set in the 1700's in the West Indies. The

attraction seems to be expressing the message that piracy, though initially attractive, will ultimately bring about one's downfall (although as initially conceived and executed, the attraction was more purely a trip through scenes of violence and adventure, without any particular moral message). The 2003 movie, *Pirates of the Caribbean: The Curse of the Black Pearl* and subsequent films, were very loosely based on this attraction.

FUN FACTS - THE BASICS

- Above the entrance, there is an **American flag with only 30 stars** on it, which would indicate the setting to be 1848-1851. (*see photo*)

- The exterior of the **building was modeled after The Cabildo**, the Louisiana State Museum, located at 701 Chartres St. New Orleans, LA. It is the building in which the Louisiana Purchase was signed in 1803.

- This attraction is **actually three stories tall**. The loading area is on the equivalent of the third floor. Below that is the actual attraction itself and offices.

- The attraction can handle **3,400 guests per hour**.

- The entire **boat flume measures 1,838 feet long**.

- The boats float in a flume **containing 750,000 gallons of water**.

- The **combination of both drops** is 52 feet long at a 21-degree angle; the *Splash Mountain* drop is 52.5 feet at a 47-degree angle.

- When the boat slides down the drop, it is only going down **14 feet into the ground**.

- The second floor at *The Blue Bayou* looks like a facade to complete the appearance of an outdoor patio. Actually, **it is part of *Club 33***.

- When it first opened, this attraction had a total of **64 animatronic humans** including pirates, enemies, and townspeople. There are also **55**

animatronic animals. These numbers have varied over time as animals and people have been taken out or added in.

- The whole attraction **footprint covers 112,826 square feet** within the two show buildings.
- **The *Pirates* attraction cost $8 million.** That totaled more than 50% of the whole $15 million budget of the whole *New Orleans Square* project.
- This attraction **inspired the highest-grossing, live-action film franchise** in Disney's history taking in $4.26 billion worldwide. The film series includes five movies currently released. Totals were calculated three weeks after the release of *Pirates 5* on 06/11/17.
  - *Pirates of the Caribbean: Curse of the Black Pearl* (2003) - $654.3 million
  - *Pirates of the Caribbean: Dead Man's Chest* (2006) - $1.07 billion
  - *Pirates of the Caribbean: At World's End* (2007) - $963.4 million
  - *Pirates of the Caribbean: On Stranger Tides* (2011) - $1.05 billion
  - *Pirates of the Caribbean: Dead Men Tell No Tales* (2017) - $528.8 million
- The *Pirates of the Caribbean* film series is the top-grossing franchise with only five films, so far, and it is the ninth top-grossing franchise in film history. The numbers are as of 06/11/17;
  - 1-*Marvel Cinematic Universe* (15 films) - $11.75 billion (soon to be 23 films)
  - 2-*Harry Potter Universe* (9 films) - $8.54 billion (soon to be 13 films)
  - 3-*Star Wars* (8 films) - $7.76 billion (soon to be 10 films)
  - 4-*James Bond* (26 films) - $7.07 billion (soon to be 27 films)
  - 5-Middle Earth (*The Hobbit/Lord of The Rings*) (6 films) - $5.85 billion
  - 6-*Fast and Furious* (8 films) - $5.13 billion (soon to be 10 films)
  - 7-*X-Men* (10 films) - $4.99 billion (soon to be 11 films)
  - 8-*Batman* (11 films) $4.9 billion (soon to be 12 films)
  - 9-*Pirates of the Caribbean* (5 films) - $4.26 billion
  - 10-*Spider-Man* (5 films) - $3.96 billion (6th film is in the MCU)
  - 11-*Transformers* (5 films) - $3.78 billion (6 films on 6/21/17)

FUN FACTS - THE HISTORY

- Imagineer Herb Ryman was working on concept sketches for the park in 1954 and came up with a land called *True-Life Land*, which was named for Disney's *True-Life Adventures* (1948-1960) series. It was going to be modeled after *New Orleans,* but with a pirate theme. There was to be a shipwreck with overflowing treasure chests, a store/restaurant called *Pieces of Eight*, and a store/restaurant called *Blue Beards Den*. This was to all be added onto *Frontierland*. This concept all predates *Disneyland*, but **shows that Walt had an interest in adding pirates to his park**. Walt's dream of a completely themed pirates land wouldn't be realized until the construction of *Treasure Cove* in *Shanghai Disney*, which opened June 16, 2016.
- **Walt inadvertently named the attraction** in 1961 when he said he wanted it to show pirates of the Caribbean. The name stayed.
- **Construction for *New Orleans Square* and *Pirates* began in 1961**, after seven years of on-again, off-again design and development.

503

⚜ They had **originally intended for this to be a wax museum**, and then later changed it to Audio-Animatronics.

⚜ Originally, the **attraction was going to be called *The Rogues' Gallery***, but was later changed to the *Pirate Wax Museum*.

⚜ The basement of the *Blue Bayou*, then **called the *Blue Bayou Mart***, was going to house the wax museum.

⚜ The production of the wax museum halted, along with *Haunted Mansion*, to work on attractions for the World's Fair in 1964. The creation of the Abraham Lincoln Audio-Animatronic figure **led to the upgrade from wax to fully-functional pirates**.

⚜ The **creation of the attraction was a culmination of creativity and ingenuity from a multitude of multifaceted Imagineers.** They had diverse talents with multiple backgrounds to bring to the project to life, including Marc Davis, Herb Ryman, Dorthea Redmond, Claude Coats, Bill Justice, Yale Gracey, Dick Irvine, Blaine Gibson, Alice Davis, Wathel Rogers, and X Atencio.

⚜ Wathel Rogers became **the lead Audio-Animatronic programmer** at WED, which earned him the unofficial title of "Mister Audio-Animatronic."

⚜ Marc Davis **took his pirate design inspirations from author and artist Howard Pyle**. More specifically, his final work *Howard Pyle's Book of Pirates*, published in 1921. We see and design pirates today because of Howard's artistic outlook of them. Howard published a total of 24 books in his short lifetime, some of which were tales of King Arthur and Robin Hood.

⚜ **Marc Davis came up with a copious amount of ideas for scenes** with the pirates. Only a small portion was actually used in the final attraction. Once the decision was made to make the pirates move, it freed up Marc to create gags that required movement. But the new ideas were fewer due to the cost of making the new design of pirates.

⚜ This was a new concept for the Imagineers to create **an attraction without a story line**. The attraction would just consist of scenes showing what it was like to be a pirate. The characters do not even repeat. There is no beginning and no end to a story. What happened to the city after the fire? We would never find out.

⚜ Imagineer **Claude Coats was in charge of the set design and layout** in which Marc would place his comedic scenes.

⚜ Walt brought in sketch animator Xavier Atencio to make him an Imagineer for the writing of the script. **Xavier had never done a script before**. To get a feel for the pirate jargon, he watched *Treasure Island* (1950), *Captain Blood* (1935), *The Sea Hawk* (1940), *Captain Kidd* (1945), *Blackbeard the Pirate* (1952), and *The Buccaneer* (1958).

⚜ The **first scene X Atencio wrote was the Auction Scene**. He used the dialogue to soften the scene of auctioning off women. They also created a big banner that said, *"Auction - Take a Wench for a Bride"* to imply the pirates were purchasing for marriage. He showed the dialogue to Walt and he loved it, so X went on to write the rest of the attraction.

Atencio was **inspired to write the song from the phrase "Yo-ho-ho and a bottle of rum."** He told Walt that there needed to be a song that would show cohesiveness within the attraction.

Like its equally great counterpart, *Haunted Mansion*, this attraction's creation also went on a hiatus while the Imagineers directed their attention to the World's Fair projects. It is a good thing too, because like *Haunted Mansion*, this too was to be a walk-through attraction. Thanks to the expediency of *it's a small world's* ability to traverse 3,000 guests per hour, **Imagineers visited the idea of making *Pirates* a boat ride**.

This attraction was **originally planned to be a walk-through attraction**. Then again, so was *it's a small world*. And, like *it's a small world,* Walt decided to go with the whole boat idea, convinced that no one would want to walk through an attraction. They actually used the same flat bottom boats on *Pirates* as they did in *small world*.

At the time, **the basement for the attraction had been partially constructed** with steel and girders. The area was going to be too small for Walt's idea. He decided to tunnel under the train tracks. It was a huge waste of money to rip it all out and start over, but Walt knew what he was doing.

The show building, which houses a large section of the attraction outside the berm, **displaced what they called *Holiday Land***. It was more of a picnic area for corporate events. Right where the building sits used to be a baseball diamond.

After you go down the drop past the little beach, and see the skeleton scene with the lightning, the chess-playing skeletons, the captain's quarters, and the treasure room, you actually leave the park. **The transition tunnel takes you under the train tracks**. All those scenes I just listed were crammed into the area that was to house all of the original *Pirates Wax Museum*. After you pass the last of the burning buildings, you go back under the train tracks.

In 1965, just after returning from the World's Fair, **MAPO was founded**. MAPO was founded with the profits made from *Mary Poppins* (1964) and was called Manufacturing and Production Organization. They were responsible for the production and creation of all the prototype and finished products of the Audio-Animatronics. After the attraction's opening, there was a souvenir magazine sold in the park that credited MAPO with the prototype research, testing, development, and fabrication of the Audio-Animatronics characters and systems.

Imagineering had the ability to program the Audio-Animatronics to do **so much more than they ended up doing**. They kept it simple on purpose, mostly because of the forced simplicity and elegance of programming Mr. Lincoln.

Each animatronic character is programmed with movements. One figure can be programmed with up to 37 different movements, including the moving of fingers, bending of elbows, blinking of eyes, moving of mouths, etc. The average pirate/villager was programmed with 7-8 movements. Some only had 3-4 movements. When the attraction first opened, there were only 12 characters that had more than 10 movements. One was the captain at the well dunking Carlos with 14 movements, and **the auctioneer pirate with 25 motions**. Of course, this has all changed with the progression of technology since 1967.

The glistening of Carlos is **caused by mineral oil** on his face and clothes.

Because of the cost cutting by Disney with "face sharing," the **face of the auctioneer pirate has the same face as the dueling ghost** on the left in Haunted Mansion and the same face as the sea captain ghost coming through the wall in Haunted Mansion's ballroom scene.

Yale Gracey made the moving cloud effects for the World's Fair in the *General Electric*-sponsored attraction *Skydome Spectacular*. It was so believable, that Yale was able to implement its use in the *Pirates* attraction to further convince riders that they are actually outside at night time.

Harriet Burns had said that **Yale originally made the fire effect with an old hubcap** that he had found and crinkly Mylar.

The fire sequence was **so convincing that Anaheim Fire Chief Edward Stringer was going to shut the ride down**. After he was shown how the effects worked, he ordered that the effects shut off in the case of a real fire so as not to mislead the firefighters.

In Marc's original concepts for the wax museum, he had a burning city. Walt still wanted to keep the burning seaport. Claude Coats saw Yale's fire effect and was impressed with it so much that **he was able to design an entire scene surrounding that one effect**.

Walt asked **Alice Davis to come in and design the wardrobe for the pirates**. She last worked on the "it's a small world" attraction for the World's Fair. She had said, "*I went from sweet little children to dirty old men overnight.*" The pirates were a challenge for her because they did not move like people in order to put clothing on. She used a lot of Velcro so that the clothing could be taken off and replaced quickly. She also learned from her *small world* experience that the fabric wears down in certain areas from constant rubbing, and leaking hydraulic fluid and oil is also a problem.

It took Alice and a **team of four seamstresses less than one year to create the sewing patterns and wardrobe** for all of the pirates.

Alice said that they needed a backup wardrobe for each of the pirates. The Accounting Department would not approve the extra spending. To get what she wanted, Alice had given projection costs of double what it actually cost so that she could make two of each costume. This foresight was a miracle as **there was a fire in the Burning Town scene just about two months after opening**. The fire destroyed three costumes, and several more were damaged by the emergency sprinkler system. Dick Irvine called up Alice in a panic and asked how quickly she could make another set of the costumes. She said she could change them out overnight.

The **Imagineers created a mock-up of the Auction scene** in the Glendale studio. They could not create a mock-up of the whole attraction as they did with the "dark rides" because of the massive scale. For this moment, the *Pirates of the Caribbean* was actually a walk-through.

Before everything was built in the location it is in today, **a mock-up had to be built to get the feel of the attraction concept**. Dick Irvine was in charge of the project as the design director. He delegated out tasks to the individual Imagineers to do a full-scale re-creation of the Auction Scene as created by concept artist Marc Davis. Claude Coats was in charge of scenic design, Blane Gibson sculpted the characters, Yale Gracey was the special effects artist, Alice Davis was the costume designer, Wathel Rogers and Bill Justice were in charge of the animation of the Audio-Animatronic figures created by Roger Broggie, X Atencio wrote the dialogue and musical lyrics for the whole attraction, and John Hench created a wooden boat on wheels with wooden benches. This whole assignment was for one purpose, to get Walt's approval. They pushed Walt seated in the boat through the Auction Scene at a predestinated pace of two feet per second. The results were that he loved it so much; he considered it his favorite attraction. Sadly, Walt never got to ride the completed attraction due to his death, four months before the grand opening. (*see photo*)

X Atencio apologized for all of the sounds and dialogue coming from all directions. It seemed a bit much. Walt replied with, "*Don't worry about it. It's like a cocktail party. People come to cocktail parties and they tune in a conversation over here, then a conversation over there. Each time the Guests come through here, they'll hear something completely different. That'll bring them back time and again.*"

On November 2, Walt had x-rays that revealed a tumor in his left lung. Doctors gave Walt six months to two years to live. After a two-week stay in the hospital, he returned to WED to check up on the projects. Walt asked Roger Broggie how the *Pirates* attraction was doing. At this point, all of the animatronics had been sent to the show building in the park. He said the

507

company was pressuring them for a Christmas opening. Walt asked if they were ready for it, and Roger said they still had a few more bugs to work out. Walt then decreed that it would not open until it was done right. **This would be Walt's final executive decision.** A decision that would put off the opening of *Pirates* so that he would never see it open to the public. Walt had said before, *"If you're not ready, don't open the curtain."* This will go on to always be the Imagineers adage.

🧠 Walt visited the show building in *Disneyland* and went on a tour with Marc Davis and a few other Imagineers. The boats' water channel was not filled yet and all the sets were frame worked, so they were able to walk through. The Auction Scene was set up with the Auctioneer moving about. **This would be the last Walt ever saw of the attraction's sets,** because of his failing health and then eventually his death.

🧠 In addition, on what would be Walt's last visit to the studio, he visited Marc Davis to look over the concept art for other attractions. **Marc showed him sketches for the upcoming attraction *The Country Bear Jamboree*.** Marc said that as long as he kept showing stuff to Walt, he would keep commenting and laughing with him.

🧠 Dick Irvine and John Hench then joined Walt and Marc to go over the mock-up for the *Flight to the Moon* attraction. He gave his input and suggestions as usual. They could tell there was something wrong with Walt. He looked tired and worn out on his first day back to the studio. At this point, only Walt's immediate family knew how sick he was. He kept playing off his gaunt haggardly look by attributing it to an old polo injury. When he was leaving the office, the **last thing Walt said to Marc was "Good-bye, Marc,"** which was odd because he always said, "see you later" or "keep up the good work."

🧠 Walt put a lot of work into this attraction. It had the most elaborate use of Audio-Animatronic figures than any other attraction. Sadly, **Walt passed away four months before** the attraction began operation.

🧠 *Pirates* would not **open to the public until four months after the passing of Walt**.

🧠 The *Blue Bayou* **restaurant was completed,** but was delayed because *Pirates* was not yet ready to open.

🧠 Not wanting to complete the attraction without Walt's approval, Marc and **Claude kept moving the parrot sitting next to the drunk pirate** with dangling leg. It did not seem right to continue on without Walt making the final decisions. In the end, they decided that they had to get it open and as Walt always said, "Go back and plus it later."

🧠 On opening day, there was a huge press event. Reporters from television programs and newspapers, photographers, and other VIPs were aboard the *Sailing Ship Columbia*. On their journey around the island with the crew, pirates who approached in a rowboat overtook them. **They were led by the pirate captain, played by the *Golden Horseshoe Saloon's* Wally Boag** (also the voice of Jose in the *Enchanted Tiki Room*). They all had sword fights and tossed the old crew overboard into the river. They all celebrated with the reporters by drinking mead, dancing on the deck, and having a merry ol' time. They then disembarked and led the way to the entrance of the long-awaited attraction, where the pirates had to battle with the soldiers guarding the doors. After the soldiers were taken down, the pirates rammed the door open and let everyone in.

The anchor of Jean Lafitte was once located closer to the entrance of the *Sailing Ship Columbia* in *Frontierland*. It was **christened with a bottle of Mississippi River** water by beautiful actress Dorothy Lamour just before the *Pirates* attraction was overtaken.

FUN FACTS WHILE ON BOARD

When you first enter the *Pirates* building, while waiting in the queue, you will see cartoon-looking paintings of pirates on the walls. All those pirates existed in history. Marc Davis (see *Imagineer Mini Biographies* page 287) studied real pirates for inspiration behind this attraction, which was originally supposed to be a walk-through attraction before they settled on using boats to move large crowds through it.

- **Anne Bonny** (March 8, 1700 - possibly April 25, 1782) – Anne is famous mostly in part to being only one of two known women to be convicted of piracy in the Caribbean. She married famous pirate *James Bonny*, and also had a relationship with the pirate *John "Calico Jack" Rackham*. She later hooked up with *Mary Read* and they became a trio of pirates with Calico Jack until they were captured in October 1720.

- **Mary Read** (1670-1698, no one knows for sure - 1721) - Mary grew up being dressed as a boy by her mother, to disguise the fact that she was a girl. She became a deck hand, married a Flemish soldier, dressed as a woman until he passed away, and then started dressing like a man again. Her ship was taken over by Calico Jack and Anne Bonny. Mary joined their crew and became friends with Anne. Mary, Anne, and Jack terrorized the Caribbean until their capture in October 1720. She later passed away in prison during child birth.

- **Sir Francis Verney** (1584 - 1615) - Sir Francis Verney came from a wealthy background. After being forced to marry his step-sister in an arranged marriage to save the family wealth at the age of 14, he went away to Trinity College in Oxford England. He was knighted in London at the age of 19. He left his inheritance, wife, and estate behind to get into piracy. One of the ride boats is named after him. He died at the age of 31.

- **Sir Henry Mainwaring** (1587 - 1653) - Sir Mainwaring was also born to a wealthy and military-based family. He graduated from Oxford University when he was only 15 with a law degree. His career on the sea began at the age of 24, when he was hired by England's *Charles Howard, 1st Earl of Nottingham*, to hunt down the famed pirate *Peter Easton* (1570-1620). He began plundering Spanish, Portuguese, and French ships for supplies, becoming a pirate himself. In exchange for a full pardon, he ended up working for the Spanish government. Britain also granted him a full pardon. He later wrote the book *Discourse of Pirates* in 1618, was knighted, and became a Vice-Admiral in 1618.

- **Charles Gibbs** (November 5, 1798 - April 22, 1831) - Charles Gibbs' real name was James D. Jeffers and he was born in Newport, Rhode Island. He was one of the last active pirates in the Caribbean and one of the last executed. He claims to have had as many as 400 victims and his legend grew after his death. He started his career in the United States Navy before turning pirate.

- **Edward "Ned" Low** (1690 - 1724) – As an adolescent, Ned was a pickpocket and a burglar. After losing his wife during childbirth, he set out to sea to become a pirate. He was a very successful pirate who captured at least a hundred ships in his short-lived, three-year pirating career.

The **parrot sitting next to the giant map** in the queue makes the same whistle sound as the re-entry turnstiles to the park and the bluebird from the "Zip-A-Dee-Doo-Dah" song in *Song of the South*.

The **parrot used to be mostly green** with yellow prior to the 2006 update. Instead of the map that is there now, there was a map with fiber optic lights that would light up saying *"Pirates of the Caribbean."* The parrot was replaced with a blue-and-yellow macaw that matches Cotton's parrot from the movies, and he was given considerably more dialogue.

Did you ever notice the names on the boats? **There are 50 boats** to transport Guests to the past and into the world of the pirates. Here is the list of boat names:

01 Amelie	14 Simone	27 Juliet	40 Carlotta
02 Yvette	15 Musetta	28 Gabriella	41 (unknown)
03 Fantine	16 Claudine	29 Francis Verney	42 Muriel
04 Josette	17 Carolina	30 Giselle	43 Blackbeard
05 (unknown)	18 Dominique	31 Lisette	44 Destine
06 Monique	19 Capt. Mainwaring	32 Cap. Kidd	45 Jolie
07 Annabelle	20 Camille	33 Justine	46 Maria
08 Valentina	21 Kimmi	34 Henrietta	47 Mystique
09 Calico Jack	22 (unknown)	35 Fleurette	48 Aimee
10 Marietta	23 Eloise	36 Angelique	49 Sabine
11 Mathilde	24 (unknown)	37 Eugenie	50 Marianne
12 Odette	25 Josephine	38 (unknown)	
13 Stephanie	26 Christine	39 Louisa	

510

🏴 The **loading and unloading announcement** is done by Corey Burton (see *Who Does That Voice* page 149).

🏴 It is rumored that the pirate sitting in the rocking chair at the beginning is **modeled after the infamous pirate Jean Laffite** (1776-1823). Jean terrorized the Gulf of Mexico in the early 1800's. It is said that he had a secret hideout in the swamplands of Louisiana. Since the beginning of *Pirates* is in the Louisiana swamp lands, it all fits together. The fact that when you board the boats the dock is called Laffite's Landing also lends a clue. Jean's place and time of death are rumored and unverifiable as well; perhaps he did live out his life secluded on a houseboat in the swamps. Jean had a crucial role in the creation of New Orleans. In exchange for a pardon for his crimes, Jean assisted General Andrew Jackson (7th president of the United States and is found on the $20 bill) in defending New Orleans against the British in the War Of 1812.

🏴 **The Banjo you hear** right before the big drop is said to be from the recordings of Walt Disney. He is playing "Oh! Susanna" and "Camptown Races."

🏴 There is a **Jolly Roger with a talking skull on the archway** above the first drop voiced by Xavier Atencio (he was an artist and writer for Disney from 1938 to 1984). He was responsible for writing all the dialogue for the whole attraction including the lyrics for the "Yo Ho A Pirates Life For Me" song. He did the same for *Haunted Mansion*. You can also hear him as the pirate with the dangling hairy leg on the bridge after you pass through the Auction Scene.

- *Psst! Avast there! It be too late to alter course, mateys, and there be plundering pirates lurking in every cove, waitin' to board. Sit closer together and keep yer ruddy hands inboard! That be the best way to repel boarders. And mark well me words, mateys, dead men tell no tales! Heh heh heh...*

- *Ye come seeking adventure and salty old pirates, aye? Sure you've come to the proper place. But keep a weather eye open, mates - and hold on tight, with both hands, if you please! There be squalls ahead, and Davy Jones waiting for them what don't obey! heh heh heh.....*

🏴 After the two drops, you hear a **disembodied pirate voice exclaiming "Dead men tell no tales!"** It repeats over and over, echoing through the cave. This is the voice of Paul Frees, the disembodied voice of the Ghost Host in *Haunted Mansion*. Paul also voices the parrot sitting out front (pre-2006 update), the auctioneer, Carlos dunking in the well, the "pooped pirate"

511

(pre-1997 update), one of the prisoner pirates, and the captain on the Wicked Wench (pre-2006 when it became Captain Barbossa).

It is believed that Walt's inspiration behind the rock caves after the drop came from his visit to **Carlsbad Caverns in New Mexico**.

It is said that **the likeness and mention of some of the most notorious pirates** in history can be found here. This is rumored:

- *Edward "Blackbeard" Teach* (1680-1718) - the original captain on the *Wicked Wench* pirate ship in the Battle Scene, and now added to the fog screen projection; one of the ride boats is named for him as well. (*see photo*)
- *Captain William Kidd* (165-1701) - pirate in the red coat dunking Carlos in the well (before getting a hook for a hand); one of the ride boats is named for him as well. The posters around the park of the pirate in the red coat has a treasure chest at his feet. The initials on the chest read W.K. for William Kidd.
- *Admiral Sir Henry Morgan "Captain Morgan"* (1635-1638).
- *Jean Laffite* (1766-1823) - sitting in the rocking chair in the bayou; named on the loading platform sign.

One of the **most famous songs of the park** is "*Yo Ho A Pirates Life For Me*." The music was written and composed by George Bruns, but the lyrics were written by Xavier Atencio. The origins are partly derived from the sea-chanty "Dead Man's Chest" in the novel *Treasure Island*, published in 1881 by Robert Louis Stevenson.

Grab a tankard of rum or mead and **sing along with the tipsy scallywags**. Unfortunately, due to copyright reasons, I had to remove the lyrics from this edition of my book. If you would like to see the lyrics, please visit... discoveringthemagickingdom.com/apps/blog/show/44592323-song-lyrics.

J. Pat O'Malley voiced the captain pirate (before the addition of his hook hand) at the well dunking Carlos, and one of the jailed pirates. You will also recognize his voice as Otto the hound dog in *Robin Hood* (1973), Colonel Hathi and Buzzie in *The Jungle Book* (1967), he was the pearly drummer that said the memorable line "*For example, one night I said it to me girl, and now me girls my wife*," the master of the hounds, and a huntsman in *Mary Poppins* (1964), Colonel and Jasper in *101 Dalmatians* (1961), Goliath Sr. in the animated short *Goliath II* (1960), the Walrus, the Carpenter, Tweedle Dee/Tweedle Dum and Mother Oyster in *Alice In Wonderland* (1951), but his first job for Disney was the voice of Winkie, a police man, and Cyril Proudbottom, the horse in *The Adventures Of Ichabod and Mr. Toad* (1949).

🏴 Marc Davis originally designed the chess game being played by the two pirate skeletons to be **set as a stale-mate game** when he was doing concepts for *Pirates* in *Magic Kingdom*. Neither pirate would win without one of them forfeiting, so they would be there forever. They were originally designed for *Magic Kingdom's Pirates* and were later added into the *Pirates* in *Disneyland* around 2006. In *Magic Kingdom*, the pieces kept getting moved around until someone discovered the original sketches by Marc, and the pieces were fixed and returned to a stalemate in 1990. There is still always the possibility that they will be moved again one day. (*see photo*)

🏴 In the room where the skeletons are drinking, there is a **painting of a redhead.** This is supposed to be the same redhead you see later being sold at the bride auction as it is showing the future. The painting was done by Marc Davis  and is titled *"Portrait of Things to Come."*

🏴 Some people have thought that the painting of the red-haired pirate in the skeleton's tavern and the portrait of the girl that turns into Medusa in *Haunted Mansion* are **paintings of the same girl**. They are not of the same girl; they have different color eyes and some facial features, but the same artist; legendary animator Marc Davis did them both.

🏴 In 2006, they **refurbished parts of the attraction** to better coincide with the *Pirates of The Caribbean* movie series; this included three Audio-Animatronic figures of Captain Jack Sparrow, one of Hector Barbossa (who replaced the original captain of the *Wicked Wench* ship Edward "Blackbeard" Teach, and the projected characters of Davey Jones and Blackbeard during the transition tunnel. All FOUR characters are voiced by the actors who portrayed them in the movies, Johnny Depp, Geoffrey Rush, Ian McShane, and Bill Nighy.

🏴 The **only real human skull** on the entire attraction is the one hanging above the bed in the Captain's Quarters Scene. There used to be a lot more human bones on the attraction, acquired from UCLA, of human research bodies because lifelike plastic hadn't been invented yet. (*see photo*)

🏴 The **treasure chest** in the Treasure Room Scene is the actual prop from *Pirates Of The Caribbean: Curse Of The Black Pearl*. (*see photo*)

The woman who shouts out of the window by the well, "Don't tell him, Carlos," was **voiced by June Foray**, better known as the voice of Granny on Looney Tunes (see *Who Does That Voice* page 149)

Pirates would go live in the bayou **after retirement** from piracy. That's why the pirate sitting on the rocking chair in the beginning has the same face as the pirate playing the stringed instrument in the three singing pirates group. *(see photo)*

The pirate auctioneer is said to be a re-located Audio-Animatronic **character of Abraham Lincoln** from *Great Moments with Mr. Lincoln*. The auctioneer is the mark III model that was then replaced with the mark IV model.

The **dog whining in the Jail Cell** Scene is the same whimpering recording as Andrew the dog's whimper in the movie *Mary Poppins* (1964). It was the scene when Mary was taking the children to see Uncle Albert (played by Ed Wynn). Incidentally the whimper was vocalized by Thurl Ravenscroft (see *Who Does That Voice on page 147*).

It is said that **Walt Disney's face was molded** onto the drunken pirate hanging from the lamp post. He is the one behind the pirate wearing all the hats while getting into the boat.

The pirate on the left of the imprisoned pirates, attempting to get the jail cell keys away from the dog, has the **likeness of comedian and actor Sid Caesar,** who was Coach Calhoun in *Grease* (1978) and *Grease 2* (1982).

514

There are **instances of "face sharing"** with the pirates. The Imagineers could save time and money by just making more than one face from a mold. If you look closely at the face of the Spanish soldier in the fort on the left, he has the same face as Carlos (the mayor being dunked in the well) and the pirate trying to keep a basket of food from a dog and donkey.

The **chair Captain Jack Sparrow is tipping back in,** when you go up the final lift, is the prop chair from the Disney movie *The Haunted Mansion* (2003). Master Gracey (played by Nathaniel Parker) is sitting in it during dinner. You can also spot the chair in the *Haunted Mansion* Attic Scene. Constance's fourth husband is sitting in it in their portrait.

Sometimes **Johnny Depp will dress up as Captain Jack Sparrow** and insert himself into the attraction to interact with Guests. The most recent occurrence of this was April 26, 2017. (*see photo*) (photo supplied by Robert Peacock of Mission Viejo, CA)

This attraction can be found in five of the six Disney Resorts around the world. *Hong Kong Disneyland* doesn't have one.

What **instances from this attraction made it into the films**? This list does not count the representations from the film added TO the attraction from the movie;

● *Pirates of the Caribbean: Curse of the Black Pearl* (2003)
  ○ The promotional poster for the film was the skeleton at the ship's helm.
  ○ A whole scene with a bride auction, including the auctioneer, was filmed as an extra opening scene in 2011. It explains the reason why the two wenches slap Jack when they see him in Tortuga, and that the redhead removed spikes from Jack's boat causing it to sink when Jack makes his first appearance. Cotton also shows up and swears not to speak of what happened, lest his tongue be cut out.
  ○ Young Elizabeth Swann in the beginning of the film sings the "Yo Ho" song; again later when she is marooned on the island with Jack Sparrow; and then finally Jack sings it solo at the end of the film.
  ○ When Jack is locked in the jail, the dog is there holding the keys.

- When Jack arrives in Tortuga you can see a drunkard drinking from a barrel that's spilling through its bullet holes, the redhead slaps Jack in the face, and the drunk pirates are randomly firing off guns.
- Jack dumps a bucket of water on Mr. Gibbs, who is sleeping with the swine.
- On the Black Pearl, the skeletal Barbossa drinks red wine and it pours right through him.
- The monkey also shows up. He was inspired by the chandelier in the *Pieces of Eight* shop at the *Pirates of the Caribbean* exit.
- While on the Isle de Muerta, you can see their piles of gold.

- *Pirates of the Caribbean: Dead Man's Chest* (2006)
  - When the pirates make their way through the bayou and arrive at Tia Dalma's house, you can see the design of it is similar to the beginning of the attraction.
  - When Jack and Gibbs arrive on Tortuga, there is a magistrate getting dunked in a well and spitting out water, a man tied up shaking in his nightgown, a pirate trio playing instruments, and a woman chasing a pirate who has taken a pig. This scene was originally filmed for part one.

- *Pirates of the Caribbean: At World's End* (2007)
  - When they all plummet down the edge of the world, Barbossa quotes the echoes in the caves, *"You may not survive to pass this way again and these be the last friendly words you'll hear!"*
  - Going over the edge of the world simulates the drop at the beginning of the attraction. They fall into darkness and you hear music from the attraction and the lines, *"Strike yer colors, ya bloomin' cockaroaches," "Shift yer cargo, dearie, show 'em your larboard side," "Dead men tell no tales...tales....tales."*

- *Pirates of the Caribbean: On Stranger Tides* (2011)
  - In Ponce de Leon's bed, Jack and Barbossa sit next to a skeleton that is looking at a map with a magnifying glass, below a headboard that has a skull and crossbones.
  - When Jack is in the middle of a sword fight with Angelica, the scene resembles the burning city because of the beam balancing, the smoke, and all the fire.
  - The character of Black Beard. Black Beard was once on the Wicked Wench before Barbossa was added.

- *Pirates of the Caribbean: Dead Men Tell No Tales* (2017)
  - The title of the film references the echoing line from the attraction.
  - Here we have the introduction of the Wicked Wench.

The following is a list of the changes made for *Disneyland's* 30th anniversary facelift in 1985:

🏴 The skeleton in the Captain's Quarters now has the **magnifying glass** adjusted so his eye socket is seen through the glass as you float by.

🏴 In its original form, the *Disneyland* attraction contained a scene in which pirates were shown chasing attractive females in circles (achieved by simply placing figures on rotating platforms hidden below Guests' view), along with a comical reversal in which an overweight woman was seen chasing a pirate. Some **Guests were offended** by this depiction, and, in response, Disney initially changed the woman chasing the pirate by having her try to hit him with a rolling pin. In 1997, this sequence was changed so that the pirates pursued women holding pies, and the large woman is chasing a pirate with a stolen ham.

🏴 The shadow **projection of the dueling sword fighters** is now projected on the smaller, left-hand fort in the bombardment scene. The projection was originally seen above the pirate with the pigs in the burning city.

🏴 The **auctioneer has been re-programmed**. He now gestures to his men when he wants them to blast the bidding pirates. He gestures to the redhead and to the gravitationally-challenged wench, as he refers to them. He now has a much more fluid motion. The female goat behind the auctioneer is from *World of Motion* in *Walt Disney World*, replacing the male goat.

🏴 The first chase **turntable was removed**. In its place is a horse (from *World of Motion*) and a pirate (also from *World of Motion*). The pirate is moving the basket of fruit he is holding back and forth, trying to keep it from the horse and goat. This pirate was riding an ostrich in the Animal Power Scene of *World of Motion*.

🏴 Originally, one overweight pirate (sometimes known as the "**Pooped Pirate**," but then changed to the "Gluttonous Pirate" or "Stuffed Pirate") was shown exhausted from his pursuit of an unwilling teenaged female. He brandished a petticoat as Guests floated past and uttered suggestive dialogue, including *"It's sore I be to hoist me colors upon the likes of that shy little wench,"* and *"I be willing to share, I be."* Behind him, the woman he had been pursuing would peer out from  her hiding place inside a barrel. This scene was altered in the American parks, but it remains unchanged in the versions at *Tokyo Disneyland* and *Disneyland Paris*. He is also newly voiced by **Corey Burton** (see *Who Does That Voice* page 149) who is doing a phenomenal job of imitating **Paul Frees** (see *Who Does That Voice* page 149). (*see photo*)

🏴 The **pirate on the barrels** (from the Arsenal Scene just before the up ramp, last on left) is on the stairs behind a stuffed pirate. The barrels have rum now, not dynamite, and they have been pierced, causing a fountain flow of amber rum into the mugs of two pirates on the steps below him. Both of these are from *World of Motion*, and one of them was riding a camel. This

517

scene was originally drawn by **Marc Davis** 30 years ago, but was not put into *Pirates of the Caribbean* then.

🔹 The second **turntable lost its wench**; now the pirate has a net and is chasing several chickens. Recent drawings had him holding an axe, but that was nixed. The chickens came from the chicken turntable, which was around the fountain at the top of the stairs (between 2nd and 3rd turntable). The third turntable has the wench holding food on a tray, but still running from the pirate. The fourth turntable has the old pirate with food and loaves of bread under his arm, being chased by yet another gravitationally-challenged wench.

🔹 In the **Burning City Scene**, the pigs wallowing on the right with the pirate now sing in sync with the "*Yo Ho*" music. They had never been in sync; they just grunted aimlessly before.

🔹 There is **a new skeleton** in the first of the three jail cells. It is lit a little differently from the two cells with pirates. It adds a tension, an overshadowing of imminent doom if those pirates do not get the key from the dog. Now there seems to be much more terror, the fact that a dumb dog literally holds the key to these pirates' lives.

🔹 In the **Arsenal Scene**, the pirate on the winch to the right now has the bar of the winch across his chest, in front of his shirt and lacy collar. It no longer looks like it is going clean through his body.

🔹 In the place of the pirate on the barrels on the left, there were two pirates from *World of Motion* (where they were in Animal Power trying to push/pull a stubborn zebra). They were trying to leverage a huge Jolly Roger flag full of treasure up the ramp, but were not helping each other. They pulled and pushed out of sync with each other, not cooperating, as if they might have broken out in a fight any minute. This whole scene was replaced with a **Jack Sparrow Scene,** having him sitting in a chair surrounded by his treasure.

🔹 Heard overhead is the reprise of the Grotto warning "**Dead Men Tell No Tales**." This is the most important part of the whole upgrade, the end of the story. Instead of laughing it up and getting away with all their destruction and theft, the pirates are doomed to DIE! Just as the skeletons seen in the earlier part of the attraction, the circle is now complete and they are living the curse; crime doesn't pay!

🔹 Another thing to note is that **all seven deadly sins** are represented: Anger, Pride, Greed, Lust, Envy, Sloth, and Gluttony.

🔹 Technically, the attraction **control system** was completely replaced with a newer, more complex system. In addition, much of the down and up ramp flume-canals have been replaced, since they were leaking very badly.

Rehabilitation a year later offered the additional enhancements listed below:

🔹 While in line, look at the new **dedication plaque** they have installed in the queue area directly below the entrance door. It commemorates this as the

518

"original" *Pirates* attraction and lists all the Imagineers who worked so hard to put it all together originally.

🏴 Inside you will see the **shooting star has returned** to the sky above the bayou, and that the first drop now takes place in almost total darkness. New, more colorful lighting illuminates many of the caves with the ghost pirates, and the treasure in the treasure room has been pulled back some, away from nearby boats and prying fingers.

🏴 A literal fog bank envelops the huge pirate ship attacking the town. The **projection of the sword fight is much clearer now** on the fort's walls. Mayor Carlos has been fixed and is now spitting up more of the well water, but the goat is missing; it now is in the redone Chase Scene further on.

FUN FACTS – PIRATES AROUND THE WORLD

🏴 On December 15, 1973, *Magic Kingdom* **opened up their** *Pirates of the Caribbean* attraction, seven years to the day after the death of Walt Disney.

- This version is **located in** *Adventureland*.
- This version's **ride duration is 8 ½ minutes**.
- The **Guests had complained that there were no pirates** in their east coast theme park. To oblige, Disney opened one out there.
- They had Marc Davis work on the concept for the *Magic Kingdom*, but to cut time they just had Marc make **an almost duplicate attraction to the one in Anaheim**. Marc was upset at this fact because he had so many other ideas he wanted to do. One of those was to be a pirate changing into a skeleton using the Pepper's Ghost Effect, the same effect used in *Haunted Mansion* to show the ghosts. That never happened. The movie *Pirates of the Caribbean: Curse of The Black Pearl* (2003) took that idea and ran with it.

🏴 On April 15, 1983, *Tokyo Disneyland* **opened up their** *Pirates of the Caribbean*.

- This version is **located in** *Adventureland*.
- This version's **ride duration is 9 ½ minutes.**
- This version **lacks the Captain's Quarters** Scene.
- It has the **original scene with the pirates chasing the women** (altered in Anaheim).
- It has a **variant ending** with the drunken pirate shootout.
- Also, Guests go down **only one drop** and then disembark the boat before the boats go up the ramp to load new guests.
- Imagineers wanted to alter the attraction so that it better fit with Japanese culture and to reflect their pirate history. Japan wanted it to remain the same as Anaheim because that is how it is nostalgic to them and has American culture in it. The whole **ride is in the same English language that Anaheim has**, except the Jolly Roger before the drop;

519

he is speaking in Japanese. That voice was provided by Teichiro Hori, who was also the voice of *Tokyo Disneyland's Haunted Mansion* Ghost Host.

⊛ On April 12, 1992, **Disneyland Paris**, formerly *Euro Disney*, **opened its version of** *Pirates of the Caribbean*.

- This version is **located in** *Adventureland*.

- This version's **ride duration is 10 ½ minutes.**

- This version **also has two drops**, one is near the middle, and one is near the end.

- On this version, we see the pirates pillaging, plundering, and setting the village on fire before going down the second drop and ending up in the section that shows the pirates after their demise, in their skeletal forms. This is **backwards from the** *Disneyland* **version**.

⊛ On June 16, 2016, **Shanghai Disneyland opened up its version of** *Pirates of the Caribbean*.

- This version is located in **its own pirate-themed land**, *Treasure Cove*.

- This attraction's run time is 8 ½ minutes, making it the **shortest** *Pirates* **attraction**.

- This is the **first version to have a different name**, *Pirates of the Caribbean: Battle for The Sunken Treasure.*

- All the **dialogue spoken on the attraction is in Chinese**.

- It is also the **most hi-tech attraction out of all of them**. There are giant movie screens that scenes are projected onto that show huge battles between ships.

- The Shanghai version **does not have any drops to enter the attraction;** the drop happens toward the end.

- They have the Three-Jailed Pirates Scene with the **jailer dog, but they are all skeletons**.

- They have similar scenes to the original, but once you are past the beginning of the attraction the **story line focuses on the characters and setting from the movies** with Captain Jack Sparrow and Davey Jones.

- The only *Pirates* to have **the mermaids from the film.**

- Unlike the other *Pirates* boats, **this one has the boats on a track;** they are not free floating. This is imperative to make the Guests face where you want them. The boat can go forward, backward, and even sideways.

⊛ For a **list of this attractions Hidden Mickeys**, see page 349.

PRO TIP: *If the queue splits into two lines, take the line to the right; it's faster.*

CRITTER COUNTRY

The area now known as *Critter Country* was **first called the Indian Village** and featured Native American shows and attractions. In 1972, it became *Bear Country*, a land themed to the forests of the Pacific Northwest. It was home to the new *Country Bear Jamboree*. *Bear Country* was renamed to *Critter Country* in 1988 in anticipation of *Splash Mountain's* January 1989 opening. In 2001, the *Country Bear Jamboree* was replaced with *The Many Adventures of Winnie the Pooh*. *Critter Country* is also home to *Davy Crockett's Explorer Canoes*.

Critter Country **is somewhat small** when compared to *Disneyland's* larger lands. This westernmost area features a single pathway that wraps around the footprint of *Splash Mountain*, starting near *Haunted Mansion* and ending in a series of shops nestled against the *Splash Mountain* show building.

FUN FACTS

- Inside *Pooh's Corner* store in the confections area, **there are two portraits of Winnie The Pooh** with two recognizable bears. The one playing the piano is Gomer and the one on the swing is Teddi Barra from the greatly-missed *County Bear Jamboree*. The swing Teddi used to sit on during the show now has Pooh sitting on it in the attraction, over a swirling vortex of honey.

- The shop **sign for *Pooh Corner* was carved by woodcarver Raymond Kinman**. He carved the original sign that once hung above the entrance to Country Bear Playhouse. He then carved the *Many Adventures of Winnie the Pooh* that subsequently replaced it. He also did the *Splash Mountain* sign with Br'er  Rabbit for *Disneyland* and *Magic Kingdom*. Outside the *Hungry Bear Restaurant,* you can find a carving he did of a "butler" bear holding up a serving tray along with a happy beaver leaning against a sign that reads "*Hungry*?" There was once a tubby bear carved by Raymond that was sitting on a log about to eat a burger with a sign on him that said "*Eat at the Hungry Bear!*" Over in *Adventureland*, he carved the *Indiana Jones Adventure Outpost* sign. If you are grabbing a bite to eat at *Rancho del Zocalo Restaurante*, check out the sign, because he did that one as well.

- There is a **little birdhouse outside the store** that says "Mr. Bluebird's House" on it. It is a tie-in to *Splash Mountain*, the attraction themed after the U.S. banned film *Song Of The South* (1946) that sings about "...*Mr. Bluebird on my shoulder*..."

- Fowler's Harbor, Fowler's Inn and Fowler's Cellar are **areas dedicated to retired Navy Officer Admiral Joe Fowler**. He was a good friend of Walt's and a key person behind the construction of *Disneyland*. Walt found him supervising the construction of housing tracts in San Francisco in the 1950's and hired him to construct the *Mark Twain Riverboat*. Fowler went on to supervise the construction of *Disneyland* and *Disney World* and stayed on as an advisor after retirement. He was the general manager of *Disneyland* for the first 10 years of operation. The *Magic Kingdom's* first riverboat was dedicated to him. After adding a second riverboat, the *Admiral Joe Fowler* was accidently damaged beyond repair and left the *Richard F. Irvine* to be the soul boat on the river. The *Irvine* was dedicated to the Imagineer Richard Irvine, whose son was married to Kim Irvine, the daughter of Imagineer Leota Toombs (the face of Madame Leota in *Haunted Mansion*). Kim Irvine is the current face of Madame Leota in *Haunted Mansion Holiday* from September, Halloween time, to the beginning of January, Christmas time.

- For a **list of this lands Hidden Mickeys, see page 349**.

- For a **list of Disneyland's Attractions of the Past**, see page 660.

Attractions
Davy Crockett's Explorer Canoes

Opened May 19, 1971 - Duration: 10:00

Guests paddle canoes in the *Rivers of America* around *Pirate's Lair on Tom Sawyer Island*.

FUN FACTS

- It is **2,400 feet around** the entire island.

- There are nine fiberglass canoes to ride in, all **measuring 35 feet in length**.

- This is the only attraction in the park that is **powered by the visitors**.

- After you experience this attraction, your **arms will hurt** the rest of the day if you're not in shape.

- It is **themed after the Disney television series** *Davy Crockett* (1954-1956)

- This is one of the two attractions that **has been in three different lands** without ever changing its location. In the past, it has been considered part of *Frontierland*, *Bear Country*, and *Critter Country*.
- Originally **called *Indian War Canoes***, the attraction opened on July 4, 1956, as part of *Frontierland's Indian Village* expansion with real American Indian guides aboard every canoe.
- The *Indian War Canoes* closed with *Indian Village* in 1971 but **reopened on May 19th, 1971, as *Davy Crockett's Explorer Canoes***, inspired by the *Davy Crockett Disneyland* television shows, with the guides now wearing coonskin caps.
- *Davy Crockett's Explorer Canoes* **operates on busier days** only, primarily in the summer and on weekends.
- Canoe Cast Members sometimes take trips early in the morning called "Deadheads" before the park opens. One of the great *Disneyland* traditions is the **canoe races** which are held during the summer season. Trophies are awarded to teams that complete a lap in the fastest time. The finals day course is once around *Tom Sawyer Island* in the opposite direction of normal river traffic with the start/finish line at the south end of the canoe dock. Only two men teams have ever broken the 4:00 barrier since the addition of the *River Stage* and *Fantasmic!* show.

The Many Adventures of Winnie the Pooh

Opened April 11, 2003 - Duration: 3:10

An attraction that recreates memorable scenes from several of the Winnie the Pooh cartoons.

FUN FACTS

- This attraction was originally **supposed to go in *Toontown***, where the attraction *Roger Rabbit's Car Toon Spin* is now located. Passengers would have been in spinning honey pots, much like the *Mad Tea Party* cups.

- The **entrance sign was carved by woodcarver Raymond Kinman**. He had also done the *Country Bear Playhouse* that was mounted right where the new sign is now.

- During the mid-1990's, the Imagineers **planned on making it a boat ride**, much like *it's a small world*. But by 1999, the plans were scrapped and they started working on a "dark ride."

- The estimated **budget to build was $30 million**.

- **Plans for this attraction started in the late 1970's**. The Imagineers originally wanted it to be built in *Fantasyland* when it had the makeover in 1983, but this didn't happen.

- The **trophy heads** of Max the Buck, Buff the Buffalo, and Melvin the Moose, Audio-Animatronics from *Country Bear Jamboree*, may be spotted if one looks up and backwards while leaving the Heffalump and Woozle room. The heads were taken from Theatre Two of the *Country Bear Playhouse*. (*see photo*)

- **The voice of the narrator is provided by** Peter Renaday (see the *Haunted Mansion* section for mini bio). Peter once voiced characters that resided in this space before. They were that of Henry the Bear, and Max (*see photo*) from the past *Country Bear Jamboree*.

- The vehicle you ride in is **called a "beehicle."**

- There is **usually a short line for this attraction**, due to the fact that it is located in the back corner of the park next to a "big kid" attraction far away from all the "little kid" attractions in *Fantasyland*.

- Both Jim Cummings, who voices Winnie The Pooh (1988-present), and Peter Cullen, who voices Eeyore (1989-2009), **both reprised their roles for this attraction.**

- Paul Winchell came out of retirement at the age of 81 to **reprise his role of Tigger**. He voiced Tigger in the Pooh films from 1968 to 1999. This was his last recorded voice before he passed away, with the exception of a sing-along video in 2003.

- It is said that the lift, that **Winnie the Pooh hangs** from over the swirling vortex of honey, is the same lift that was used in the *Country Bear Jamboree* as a swing for Teddi Barra. (*see photo*)

- For a **list of this attractions Hidden Mickeys, see page 349.**

524

Splash Mountain

Opened July 17, 1989 - Duration: 9:21

An attraction based on the film *Song of the South* (1946). Riders travel on water in "logs", and the attraction alternates between cheerful singing animals from the movie and steep drops for thrills. It has been one of the most popular attractions in *Disneyland* since its inception. Many of the Audio-Animatronics used in the attraction were recycled from *Tomorrowland's America Sings*.

FUN FACTS

🐰 The day this attraction opened **marked the 34ᵗʰ anniversary** of *Disneyland*.

🐰 *Song of the South* (1946) was Walt Disney's **first live-action film**, though it also contains major segments of animation. The film has never been released on home video in the U.S. because of content which Disney executives believe would be construed by some as racially insensitive towards African Americans and is thus subject to much rumor, although it does exist on home video in the UK.

🐰 Most of **the Audio-Animatronic characters were reassigned from the *America Sings*** attraction in *Tomorrowland* that ran from 1974 through 1988. One of the reasons they were used was because attendance for *America Sings* had dropped and was losing popularity. The construction for *Splash Mountain* was over budget, so, to save some money, the characters were re-themed.

🐰 It took **3 months just to re-wire and test the characters** after they were installed. The engineers spent about 80 hours on each character to synchronize them. Each character has about 45 seconds of preset movements before the settings loop and do it all again.

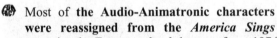

🐰 The song "How Do You Do?" was **recorded specially for this attraction** in 1988 by The Floozies. They are a 29-piece band from Oregon.

🐰 The **singing bullfrog was voiced by Thurl Ravenscroft** (see *Who Does That Voice on page 147*).

In 1987, **Disney used 75 Cast Members to record the song** "Zip-A-Dee-Doo-Dah".

The attraction can handle **2,008 guests** per hour.

At the time it was built, *Splash Mountain* was the **most expensive attraction** ever built, with an estimated cost of $75 million.

Br'er Fox and **Br'er Rabbit are voiced by actor Jess Harnell,** who is best known for his role as Wakko Warner on *Animaniacs* (1993), Captain Hero on *Drawn Together* (2004), the announcer on *America's Funniest Home Videos* (1998), and so many more cartoons and video games. He also provided the voices for Ironhide and Barricade in the *Transformers* film franchise (2007, 2009, 2011) and is the only actor to portray a good guy (Autobot) and bad guy (Decepticon) in the same film (only 2007).

Almost five decades after the film *Song Of The South* (1946) was created, **Nick Stewart returned to reprise his role** as the dumbfounded Br'er Bear for this attraction. Actually, the last project he ever worked on was the voice of Br'er Bear in the *Splash Mountain* video game (1989) for play in the *Sega Dreamcast*. (*see photo*)

It holds **965,000 gallons** of water.

They can run **50 to 54 logs at a time**.

The final drop is **52.5 feet long** at a 47-degree angle.

Originally, the attraction's scene "Sticky Situation," which portrays Br'er Rabbit stuck in honey, was planned to be the infamous **Tar Baby Scene** from *Song of the South*. The scene was changed to avoid the same notorious racial controversies that have plagued the banned film. (*see photo*)

Rumors state that this attraction was originally going to be named *Zip-a-Dee River Run*. In 1984, **Touchstone Pictures released a movie named Splash**. The studio executives wanted the Imagineers to put Madison, the mermaid played by Daryl Hannah, into a scene. The Imagineers refused to do it because the movie's theme didn't fit with the *Song of the South* story. They ended up naming it *Splash Mountain* instead.

There are 36 hidden cameras, so the Cast Members can monitor the attraction. There is an infra-red intrusion system should someone step out of a log (anywhere), an alarm notifies the Cast Member in the tower and an automatic camera shot of that area of the attraction pops up on one of the 18 monitors that a Cast Member in the tower is watching (like in *Haunted Mansion*).

526

- Hoping to make illicit use of the **in-ride photographs** that Disney later sells to ride patrons, some riders briefly expose themselves (e.g., a woman baring her chest) during the final drop. They prevent people from viewing these photos, but they can be seen online on a website called *flashmountain.net* from the mid-to-late 1990's through today.

- The top of *Splash Mountain* is **known as Chickapin Hill**. This is the home of Br'er Fox and Br'er Bear in the film.

- The white riverboat you pass just before the end is **called the Zip-A-Dee Lady**.

- There is a cave you float by before the first drop that is the cave for Br'er Bear. If you listen closely, Br'er **Bear can be heard snoring** from his cave. That snoring used to play near the entrance to *Bear Country* and it was Rufus the bear from *Country Bear Jamboree* snoring. (*see photo*)

- After the plunge, you will pass **a doorway that says "Fowler's Cellar."** It is a dedication to one of Walt's good friends, and a key person in the reason why *Disneyland* was possible, retired

Navy Officer Admiral Joe Fowler. (*see photo*)

- In the Riverboat Scene **you can see Mr. Bluebird** from the song sitting on a thorny vine to the right of the boat.

- For a **list of this attractions Hidden Mickeys, see page 349**.

FRONTIERLAND

Frontierland first appeared in *Disneyland* as **one of five original themed lands**. Conceived by Walt Disney, the land did not initially contain many attractions, but centered around open expanses of wilderness, which could be traversed by guests via stagecoach, pack mules, and walking trails. *The Mine Train Thru Nature's Wonderland* opened in 1961, consisting of a sedate train ride around various western landscape dioramas. The *Mine Train* closed in 1977 to make way for the new attraction, *Big Thunder Mountain Railroad*, which opened in 1979.

FUN FACTS

🐭 The land's long shoreline along the *Rivers of America* is considered a **prime viewing location** for the nighttime *Fantasmic!* show. The docks to both the *Mark Twain Riverboat* and the *Sailing Ship Columbia*, (a replica of American explorer Robert Gray's 18th century ship that circumnavigated the globe) are located here, and *Pirates Lair on Tom Sawyer Island* in the river's center is also considered a property of *Frontierland*.

🐭 *Frontierland* borders *Fantasyland* (via the *Big Thunder Trail*), *New Orleans Square*, and *Adventureland* and connects to the *Central Plaza* through an iconic set of fort-style gates.

🐭 There used to be a *Frontierland Railroad Station*. It was located further to the left of where the *New Orleans Square Railroad Station* is now. It was closer to *The Jungle Cruise*. The **station was moved and renamed in the mid-1960's** when *New Orleans Square* was built.

🐭 There used to be a **Marshal's office** to honor Willard P. Bounds. He was Walt's father-in-law and was actually a U.S. Marshal.

🐭 The front gates of *Frontierland* are **made out of Ponderosa pine** logs.

🐭 There are **deer and elk antlers on the front** of the *Westward Ho Trading Company* store. It was common practice in western times to places antlers on the front of the general stores so that cowboys riding into town would know where to get supplies.

🐭 There is a **window that honors Fess Parker** in front of the *Crockett and Russel Hat Co.*; he played Davy Crockett in the TV series. (*see photo*)

🐭 For a **list of this attractions Hidden Mickeys, see**

528

page 349.

For a **list of Disneyland's Attractions of the Past**, see page 660.

To the left of the loading dock for the *Rafts to Tom Sawyer Island*.
Near the backside of *Big Thunder Mountain Railroad* by the bridge.

Attractions

Big Thunder Mountain Railroad

Opened September 2, 1979 - Duration: 3:14

This roller coaster took the place of the more sedate *Mine Train Thru Natures Wonderland* (1960-1977) attraction, and many of its elements were incorporated into *Big Thunder Mountain*.

FUN FACTS

- The design is **based on the *hoodoos*** of *Bryce Canyon National Park* in Utah.

- The **hoodoos are tall columns of rocks formed in elements** and are cause when the top of the pillar has a harder rock to protect the ground beneath it from eroding away. They can range anywhere from the height of a man to 10 stories tall. The word hoodoo means bad luck.

- Top speed is **36 mph**.

- There are **six trains**: U.B. Bold, U.R. Daring, U.R. Courageous, I.M. Loco, I.B. Hearty, and I.M. Fearless. There can only be five on the track at one time.

- The **sound effects** of the actual train ride going on the tracks were used in *"Indiana Jones and the Temple of Doom"* (1984) for the mine cart sequence.

- **There is 2,780 feet of track**. That means you travel a little over ½ mile on the attraction.

- There are sound effects of the train on the attraction, including **the whistle sound**, even though there is no real whistle on the locomotives.

529

The mechanical animals that you go rocketing past **are recycled from the** *Mine Train Thru Natures Wonderland*.

There were **3,000-4,000 gallons of paint** used to paint the mountain.

The entire mountain is made up of **9.5 acres of painted concrete**.

This attraction replaced the *Mine Train Through Nature's Wonderland*. Many of the **animatronics throughout the attraction were originally from** *Nature's Wonderland*. You can see the old animatronic fish jumping out of the pond along *Big Thunder Trail*.

The rock walls on either side of the queue line are **made of 100 tons of gold ore** from the former mining town of Rosamond, CA.

The **dinosaur skeleton is there to pay homage** to the skeletal remains of a dinosaur from the original attraction that were seen embedded in the ground

The little town at the end, before you disembark, was actually the **town of** *Rainbow Ridge* **and was the loading platform** for *Mine Train Through Natures Wonderland*. The train used to go the opposite direction when taking off instead of the direction it does now when it is coming back in.

Just as you enter the mine with the falling rocks, look above the entrance at the **upside-down horseshoe**. An upside-down horseshoe signifies bad luck.

This **attraction cost $16 million to build;** just $1 million

shy of *Disneyland's* original budget.

- There is a **1,200-pound cogwheel** that was originally used for crushing ore. (*see photo*)
- The **10-foot-tall stamp mill** that you see while waiting in line was acquired by the Imagineers at a swap meet and was built in 1880. (*see photo*)
- In the queue is a **train locomotive** used in *Hot Lead and Cold Feet* (1978), starring Don Knotts and Jim Dale. (*see photo*)

- *Big Thunder Mountain Railroad* **was the last "E-ticket ride" ever added**. The first was *The Matterhorn Bobsleds*.
- The **remains of the *Rainbow Caverns*** are seen during the first lift on the attraction. (*see photo*)

- **The safety spiel was done by voice actor Dallas "Dal" McKennon.** He was the laughing voice of the hyenas in the zoo in *Lady and the Tramp* (1955). You can hear this same laughing track for the hyenas on *it's a small world*. In *Lady and the Tramp,* he voiced Pedro, the Chihuahua in the pound, Toughy, the dog that banged his tail on the pail, and the human with the bowler passing the zoo that Tramp tried to pass off as his owner. He also voiced the Angel in the "Johnny Appleseed" segment of *Melody Time* (1948), Cal McNab, Paul's father, in *Paul Bunyan* (1958), the owl that dances with Aurora and also Diablo in *Sleeping Beauty* (1959), random barking dogs in *101 Dalmatians* (1961), the fox and a hunting horse in *Mary*

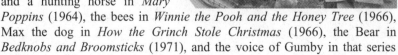

Poppins (1964), the bees in *Winnie the Pooh and the Honey Tree* (1966), Max the dog in *How the Grinch Stole Christmas* (1966), the Bear in *Bedknobs and Broomsticks* (1971), and the voice of Gumby in that series

531

from 1988. In the late attraction, the *Country Bear Jamboree,* he was the voice of Zeke.

For a **list of this attractions Hidden Mickeys, see page 349**.

FRONTIERLAND SHOOTIN' EXPOSITION

Opened July 17, 1957 - Duration: N/A

This is a target shooting range to test out your skills with a laser shooting rifle. It's okay if you don't have any quarters, they have a change machine.

FUN FACTS

- It **first opened as *Frontierland Shooting Gallery*** in 1957. The name was later changed to *Frontierland Shootin' Arcade* in 1985 and has been using its current name since 1996.

- The best time to **go here is at night**.

- In previous years, the **shooting gallery used .54 caliber Hawken rifles to shoot pellets**. Safer infrared laser-emitting guns were added in 1996.

- Before the infrared laser guns were used, the Cast Members had to repaint all the targets every night. This was **using close to 2,000 gallons of paint** every year.

- Sometimes you can see **Western Goofy shooting** at the targets alongside kids, which he did with me. He kept bumping my elbow to make me miss my target.

- This is **one of the original targets** used before the infrared guns were used. (*see photo*)

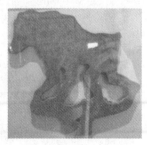

- The guns on the **left side have a lower counter** so they can be used by Guests in wheelchairs or ECVs.

- This **wasn't the only shooting gallery in *Disneyland***. The *Main Street Shooting Gallery* closed in January of 1962. There was also the *Safari Shooting Gallery* that lasted from June 1962 until its closure in 1982. Both galleries closed to make way for shops.

- There are **18 rifles** to shoot at dozens of moving targets. Each target hit triggers movement of a nearby prop.

532

THE GOLDEN HORSESHOE STAGE

Opened July 17, 1955- Duration: Varies

The Golden Horseshoe Stage has been home to a variety of stage shows over its 60-year run. There have been comedy shows and musicals on stage to entertain Guests, and a "saloon" where one  can belly up to the bar and get a soda or an ice cream sundae.

FUN FACTS

- It opened in 1955 as the *Golden Horseshoe Saloon* but **it changed names** to *The Golden Horseshoe Stage* in 1999. I heard they changed the names because a "saloon" promotes drinking.

- The venue for a show features **singing, dancing, joke-telling**, bluegrass music, and general fun and rowdiness, starring *Billy Hill and the Hillbillies*.

- The interior of the **saloon was designed** by Harper Goff (see *Imagineer Mini Biographies* page 287), the same person who designed a saloon set for the movie "*Calamity Jane*" starring Doris Day. Goff was already working on designing exteriors for buildings on *Main Street, U.S.A.,* when asked to work on this project.

- *The Golden Horseshoe* had an **unofficial opening on July 13**, 1955. The special occasion was Walt and Lillian's 30th anniversary. At that time, it was called *The Golden Horseshoe Saloon*, and they had a private viewing of the first showing of *The Golden Horseshoe Revue*.

- On July 16, 1955, **Wally Boag had his first "official" appearance as Pecos Bill** and the Traveling Salesman for a private party for corporate sponsors.

- Finally, on July 17, 1955, the day *Disneyland* opened, the title of the show was ***Slue Foot Sue's Golden Horseshoe Revue***.

- **They are in the Guinness Book of Records**. *"The greatest number of performances of any theatrical presentation is 47,250 [to April 1986] for The Golden Horseshoe Revue, a variety show staged at Disneyland Park, Anaheim, California, U.S.A., from July 16, 1955, to October 12, 1986. It was seen by 16 million people."* Quote from Guinness World Records book, the 2005 publication.

- **There was a movie based off of this show** that was directed by Ron Miller, Walt's son-in-law. It was for *Walt's Disney's Wonderful World Of Color* and was titled *The Golden Horseshoe Revue* (1962). They basically filmed the shows 10,000[th] performance. The movie starred Annette Funicello,

Wally Boag, Betty Taylor, Fulton Burley, Ed Wynn, and even Walt Disney. The music was produced by Buddy Baker.

There were many shows housed here over the past six decades;

- **The Golden Horseshoe Revue:** *The Golden Horseshoe Revue* was the **original and longest-running show** at the saloon playing from July 16, 1955, until October 12, 1986. Over the years, it has starred Wally Boag (see *Imagineer Mini Biographies* page 287), Betty Taylor, Donald Novis, Fulton Burly, Dick Hardwick, Jack Watson, Judy Marsh, Burt Henry, Dana Daniels, Jay Meyer, Kirk Wall, Jimmy Adams, Don Payne, and many others. The stage show features saloon owner Slue Foot Sue and her dance hall girls who welcome the audience with, "*Hello Everybody*," followed by a flirtatious interactive song like "*A Lady Has to Mind Her P's and Q's*" or "*Riverboat Blues*." The show's MC introduces various skits featuring a traveling salesman, played by Wally Boag, and later  Dick Hardwick. Later, the show is interrupted by Pecos Bill himself who sings his self-titled signature song.

- **The Golden Horseshoe Jamboree Show:** This show ran from November 1, 1986, until December 18, 1994. Over the years, it starred Judi Wallace, Eric Gunhus, Don Payne, John Eaden, Heather Paige Kent, Gil Christner, Joe Jacoby, Judy Bell, and many others.

- **Billy Hill and the Hillbillies:** This show ran from December 22, 1994, until January 6, 2014. Over the years, it starred Kirk Wall, Dennis Fetchet, John Marshall, Evan Marshall, John Eaden, Duane Michaels, Rick Storey, Anders Swanson, and many others. It features bluegrass and comedy. After their show was canceled, they moved their performance to Knott's Berry Farm and changed the name of their group to Krazy Kirk and the Hillbillies.

- **The Golden Horseshoe Variety Show:** This show featured the comedy and magic talents of Dana Daniels. It ran from June 13, 1995, until October 8, 2003. It starred Hal Ratliff, Richard Allen, Dana Daniels, and many others.

- **Woody's Round-up:** This child-friendly show ran from November 21, 1999, until July 17, 2000, and featured characters from the Disney/Pixar movie *Toy Story 2* (1999). It sort of returned as *Woody's All-American Roundup* with *Billy Hill and the Hillbillies* on June 14, 2013, but on stage

534

in *Big Thunder Ranch*. That was removed when the area closed to build *Star Wars Land*.

- **Frontierland: The Little Town That Could:** This comedy/melodrama ran occasionally from 2001 until 2003 and featured a supposed history of the founding of *Frontierland*. It starred players from Laughing Stock and Company, including John Eaden, Kevin Gregg, Ken Parks, Danny Roque, and Cory Rouse.

- **Various other evening entertainment** has appeared there over the years, including Alabama, Louis Armstrong, various jazz and gospel groups, and special events. It was also used during the 1950's as a venue for dancing couples during *Disneyland's* Date Nite promotion.

- **A Salute to the Golden Horseshoe Revue:** This short-lived show was created to bring back the family-style musical shows of the past. It only ran Thursday thru Monday from January 10, 2013, to February 4, 2013. It featured songs and dance numbers from the past such as "Hello, Everybody," "A Good Man Is Hard to Find," "Belly Up to the Bar," and "Can-Can."

For a **list of this attractions Hidden Mickeys, see page 349**.

MARK TWAIN RIVERBOAT
Opened July 17, 1955 - Duration: 12:00

A large paddlewheel boat that makes a 12-minute round trip through the *Rivers of America* with a recording that points out various sights.

FUN FACTS

When it first opened in 1955, its **name was the *Mark Twain Steamboat***.

The name Mark Twain is the **pen name for book author Samuel Langhorne Clemens**. He is famous for writing the books *The Adventures of Tom Sawyer* (1876) and its sequel, *Adventures of Huckleberry Finn* (1885). This is how *Tom Sawyer's Island* got its name.

It was **built to a scale** of 5/8 of the real boats.

The **boat is 28 feet high**, 105 feet long, and weighs 150 tons.

It had its **maiden voyage four days before the park opened**. It was used for a private party celebrating Walt and Lillian's 30th wedding anniversary.

The riverboat is **actually powered by the rear-mounted paddle**, but is guided by the same replacement track installed at the install time of *Fantasmic!* It is a real steam-powered sternwheeler, but the steam is

535

regulated by the engineer in the rear of the boat and steam is powered by a biodiesel-fueled boiler. The boiler is regulated at the center of the boat with many gauges and a three-way toggle switch labeled "Slow," "Fast," and "FANTASMIC." The last setting provides the most speed.

The captain's voice you hear giving **the narration of the attraction is done by Rex Allen** (narrator for the 1973 *Charlotte's Web* and the narrator for the 1960's Disney nature series (over 80 films), he is also known as The Arizona Cowboy). The voice of the First Mate is done by Thurl Ravenscroft (see *Who Does That Voice on page 147*).

Off to the starboard side (left side) of the boat you can **catch a glimpse of the extinct *Mine Train* Through Nature's Wonderland** locomotive and cars. It appears as wreckage on shore. (*see photo*)

There are a few former sights that the boat passed along the river. The **Burning Settler's Cabin**, which used propane to simulate burning, was one of them. The cabin burned for more than four decades on the north end of the island. Over the course of the 40 years, the back story changed several times. From its opening in 1956, the cabin owner laid dead on the ground outside of his cabin with an Indian arrow stuck in his back. A line from the old dialogue on the passing *Disneyland Railroad* said, *"Our forefathers, who tamed this great wilderness,s faced constant danger. And there,*

across the river, is proof, a settler's cabin afire! The old pioneer lies nearby, the victim of an Indian arrow." Ed Winger, the Manager of Building, Grounds and Construction in the Maintenance Division (you can see his dedication window on *Main Street*), volunteered to be used to make a plaster mold for the dummy body. In the 1970's, Disney realized this scenario was offensive to some people, so they removed the arrow and stated he was a victim of evil river pirates. There was a period of time with this setting, that the flames were not being used due to an energy crisis. Instead, Disney used fake flame effects similar to the ones in *Pirates of the Caribbean*. These effects were not very convincing and the real flames returned in the mid-1980's. Around this time, the cabin was again redesigned to look like a moonshiner's cabin with his still out front. The body still remained out front on the ground, not dead, but was said to be "too full of his own product." In the early 1990's, an eagle's nest appeared

536

atop a dead tree trunk right next to the cabin. The new story was that the careless settler had accidentally set his own cabin on fire, endangering the nearby nest. The settler was not very smart if he burned down his own cabin. The eagles were even less smart if they built their nest right next to a settler's cabin. In the early 2000's, it is said that the gas pipeline started failing and that was the reason for the flame's departure. The cabin was neglected and forgotten and began to be overgrown with trees until it was fixed up during the islands makeover and was made to look the way it is today. There were plans in 2007 to replace the failed feed and again have the cabin burn. However, the *Pirate's Lair at Tom Sawyer Island* modifications affected these plans. As of now, the burn marks have been removed, the holes patched, and the area cleaned up. The front lawn area now has a table, picnic-like decorations, and clothes on a clothes line. What makes this odd is while the rest of *Tom Sawyer Island* appears as if pirates have invaded it, this part of the island is the only thing not pirate themed.

- Along with the cabin, the Gullywhumper, one of *Disneyland's* **extinct Keel Boats**, is now scenery along the river's bank. (*see photo*)

- During the riverboat's first official voyage, when the crowd moved to one side of the boat to view a passing scene of an Indian encampment or other sight, the boat would list to one side and **water poured over the deck**, as no one had determined the *Mark Twain's* maximum safe passenger capacity. This oversight caused the *Mark Twain* to almost capsize on a voyage a few days later, when attraction operators continued to wave more than 500 guests on board until the deck neared the water line. During the sparsely-vegetated river route, the ship came loose from its track and got stuck in the muddy banks. Immediately, the park established a maximum capacity of 300 passengers, which remains in effect today.

- One of the animatronic characters on shore is a Native American Chief sitting on a horse that is constantly waiving to the boats as they pass by. This earned him the nickname **"Chief Waves-A-Lot."**

- This was **the first paddle wheeler built** in the United States in the past half century.

- The creation of the river boat in Todd Shipyards in San Pedro, California, **was overseen by Joe Fowler,** the retired Navy Admiral who was hired to oversee the construction of *Disneyland* (see *Imagineer Mini Biographies* page 287)

- For a **list of this attractions Hidden**

Mickeys, see page 349.

PRO TIP: If you ask one of the Cast Members nicely, they might **let you go up top to steer the boat** and blow the whistle. They allow four people up at a time for the duration of the trip, and you get a special certificate stating that you got to steer the boat.

PIRATE'S LAIR ON TOM SAWYER ISLAND
Opened May 10, 2007 - Duration: N/A

First came the attraction. Next came the movie. Lastly, the movie found its way into the attraction. Now pirates have taken over another part of *Disneyland* – *Pirate's Lair on Tom Sawyer Island* opened May 10, 2007. All those pirates, including Jack Sparrow, who have been milling around *New Orleans Square* singing sea chanties, posing for pictures, and insulting tourists as

only pirates can, are now permanently stationed on *Tom Sawyer's Island*. Now, you can get as deep into the fantasy of being a pirate as you like. You can spend the whole day on the island, not just 17 minutes like on the ride.

FUN FACTS

- The island **originally opened as Tom Sawyer Island** on June 16, 1956.

- **Walt originally designed** the island's caves and pathways himself.

- It is said that this is the **only attraction that was completely designed by Walt Disney** himself. Apparently, he wasn't thrilled with the plans that Marc Davis drew up, so he took the work home himself, turned it in, and it was built exactly as Walt wanted.

- You can get your photo taken inside **one of the bone cages** modeled after that of the cage from Pirates of the *Caribbean: Dead Man's Chest* (2006).

- *Lafitte's Tavern* **is located on the front of the island**. This tavern directly ties the island to the *Pirates of the Caribbean* attraction in *New Orleans Square* because there they have "Lafitte's Landing" and Jean Lafitte himself. The island itself is said to be where Jean Lafitte hides his treasure.

- The island reopened as *Pirate's Lair on Tom Sawyer Island* to coincide with the theatrical **release of the film** *Pirates of the Caribbean: At World's End* (2007).

- There is a photo op on the back of the island with all of the pirate booty. Sometimes **there are pirates there, or even Jack Sparrow**, to take a photo with.

- There are many new things that **pop out at you** as you explore the caves.

- In one of the treasure caves, **the decaying face of Mister Pintel**, from *Pirates of the Caribbean: Curse of the Black Pearl* (2003) pops up out of the darkness to scare onlookers. Pintel is portrayed by actor Lee Arenberg, who is also well known for his character "Grumpy" on the hit television show *Once Upon a Time* (2011).

- If you locate Dead Man's Grotto, you can find **Davy Jones' heart** in a chest. It has an actual heartbeat.

- Keep touching that gold bar, and the **skeletal hand holding the eye of Ragetti** will drop down to see you.

- This is the only attraction that **you have to ride on one attraction to get to another attraction**.

- For a **list of this attractions Hidden Mickeys**, see page 349.

RAFTS TO
TOM SAWYER ISLAND

Opened June 16, 1956 - Duration: 1:00

Large powered wooden rafts convey visitors to *Pirate's Lair on Tom Sawyer Island*.

FUN FACTS

- At **one time, there was a fishing pier** on the island called *Catfish Cove* where fishing poles and live bait were provided for avid and amateur fisherman alike. Guests were invited to cast their lines and take home all the live fish they could catch.

SAILING SHIP COLUMBIA

Opened June 14, 1958 - Duration: 12:00

A full-scale replica of the first American ship to sail around the world; it follows the same route as the *Mark Twain Riverboat*.

FUN FACTS

- The *Sailing Ship Columbia* operates **only on the park's busiest days**, or when the *Mark Twain* is not operating.

- When it was constructed in 1958, it was the **first three-masted windjammer** to have been built in the United States in more than one century.

- The *Sailing Ship Columbia* is an exact **replica of the ship Columbia Rediviva**. The Columbia Rediviva was the first American ship to circumnavigate the globe in 1790. The Columbia Rediviva's tender ship (a smaller ship used to transport people and supplies to and from land when the larger ship is at sea) was the Lady Washington. In 1989, a replica of the Lady Washington was built and later used in the film *Pirates of the Caribbean: Curse of the Black Pearl* (2003) as the HMS Interceptor and was also Captain Hook's ship in the ABC television series *Once Upon a Time* (2011).

- Walt wanted more traffic on the *Rivers of America,* so he asked *Disneyland's* construction supervisor and former navy admiral, Joe Fowler, to find **another ship to accompany The Mark Twain** around the island. Joe went all around the U.S. trying to find a memorable ship from our history to become the next attraction on the river. That's when he settled on the "Columbia Rediviva." There was only one known picture of the

Columbia, but Disney used it, along with historical documents from The Library of Congress, to design the final ship.

- It is a little-known Disney myth that on its maiden voyage around *Tom Sawyer's Island,* **the Mousketeers acted as the crew** with Admiral Joe Fowler there to christen and captain it. Supposedly, a young 16-year-old Annette Funicello was there with them. In actuality, Gretchen Richmond, wife of Alfred Carroll Richmond then Vice Admiral of the U.S. Coast Guard, did the actual christening. The ship's crew consisted of the Sea Scouts from Redondo Beach, CA. Sea Scouts is a group kind of like the Boy Scouts, but for water activities, and it consisted of boys and girls between the ages of 13-21. Walt Disney and Art Linkletter were also on the ship.

- The **ship was constructed at Todd Shipyards in San Pedro**, California, in the same place where the *Mark Twain's* hull was built.

- Walt put a **silver dollar under each mast** before they were fastened down as it was a custom to do so. Sailors have long believed a coin under the mast brings good luck. The ritual is believed to have started with the Romans to pay Charon, the boatman who ferried the souls of the dead, across the River Styx to Hades.

- Watch for this ship in the nighttime spectacular *Fantasmic!*, when it **stands in as Captain Hook's pirate ship** while he battles Peter Pan.

- The **only major change** that has been made to the ship was when they added the nautical museum below deck in 1964.

- There is a **mini nautical museum below deck**. It depicts what life was like for a crew in 1787. It also has a galley, pantry, dry stores, and sick bay. You can see the quarters for the crew, bosun and bosun's mate, first mate, captain, and surgeon.

- To the top of the main mast, the **ship is 84 feet tall**.
- The length of the **ship is 110 feet**.
- It can hold **up to 300 passengers** at once.
- The **ship is CNG (Compressed Natural Gas) powered**, unlike the bio-diesel which powers the *Mark Twain*.
- The **cannon on deck is a real working cannon** that is used during the Peter Pan segment of *Fantasmic!* Blanks are fired from it.

FANTASYLAND

Fantasyland features a central courtyard dominated by *King Arthur Carrousel* in front of which sits a sword in an anvil. **Several times each day a costumed Merlin** helps a child pull the sword from it. Walt Disney said, "What youngster has not dreamed of flying with Peter Pan over moonlit London, or tumbling into Alice's nonsensical Wonderland? In *Fantasyland*, these classic stories of everyone's youth have become realities for youngsters - of all ages - to participate in."

FUN FACTS

- In 1983, *Fantasyland* **received a major facelift,** dubbed "*New Fantasylan,*" and the attraction facades changed from medieval tents to unique buildings themed to the movies upon which the dark-rides were based.

- If you search for them, **you can find four of the old ticket booths** located in *Fantasyland* that used to sell "A-E Tickets."
  - *Mushroom Ticket Booth* – It is currently located by the entrance to *Alice In Wonderland* as a giant yellow mushroom.
  - *The Kodak Film & Photo Information Station* – It is currently located by *it's a small world*. It used to be the central ticket booth in *Fantasyland* right where *King Arthur Carrousel* is located prior to its re-location.
  - *Casey Junior Circus Train Ticket Booth* – It is located near *Casey Junior Circus Train*. It is a little building with shingles on the roof. It was one of the many things designed by Bruce Bushman, a leading designer of *Disneyland*.
  - *Lighthouse Ticket Booth* – It is located at the entrance to *Storybook Land Canal Boats*.

🐾 This is a **layout of *Fantasyland* as it was before** the 1983 refurbishment. You can compare it to your excursions into the *Fantasyland* of today.

1. *Canal Boats of the World* 1955-1956, renamed *Storybook Land Canal Boats* 1956-present
2. *Chicken of the Sea Pirate Ship and Restaurant* 1955-1969, renamed *Captain Hook's Galley* 1969-1982
3. *Casey Jr. Circus Train* 1955-present
4. *Skyway to Tomorrowland* 1956-1994
5. *Dumbo the Flying Elephant* 1955-present
6. *Mad Tea Party* 1955-present
7. *Alice In Wonderland* 1955-present
8. *King Arthur Carrousel* 1955-present
9. *Mr. Toad's Wild Ride* 1955-present
10. *Mickey Mouse Club Theater* 1955-1964, renamed *Fantasyland Theater* 1964-1981
11. *Peter Pan* 1955-1982, renamed *Peter Pan's Flight* 1983-present
12. *Snow White and Her Adventures* 1955-1982, renamed *Snow White's Scary Adventures* 1983-present.
13. *Sleeping Beauty Castle* 1955-present

🐾 If you have ever heard the phrase **"The Pirate Trio,"** you might think of the singing trio of pirates on *Pirates of the Caribbean*. Actually "The Pirate Trio" was a grouping of three female pirates who sang and played instruments in front of the old *Chicken of the Sea Pirate Ship and Restaurant* in the summers of 1961-1963. It is said they might have been the inspiration behind Marc Davis' design of the three singing pirates on *Pirates of the Caribbean*.

🐾 There are **350 miles of fiber optic lighting** used throughout the land. More than half of them are used on *Peter Pan's Flight* alone.

🐾 For a **list of this attractions Hidden Mickeys, see page 349.**

🐾 For a **list of Disneyland's Attractions of the Past**, see page 660.

The smoking section is located to the east side of the *Matterhorn* near the water.

Attractions

Alice in Wonderland

Opened June 14, 1958 - Duration: 3:40

One of the many so-called "dark-rides" of *Disneyland* (especially *Fantasyland*), this attraction has riders loaded into large brightly-colored caterpillars, which then go through a series of indoor displays that basically tell the story of the movie. An interesting note is that Kathryn Beaumont recorded the voice of Alice for the attraction, as she did in the Disney film. The attraction reopened in 1984 with new and improved special effects, based on the movie of the same name.

FUN FACTS

- Opening on July 26, 1951, **Alice in Wonderland created a huge fan base** because of its bright colors and peculiar story line and characters, which is the film this attraction is based off.

- This attraction is in the **first-person point of view** (meaning you are Alice). There was only one Alice figure on the attraction (in the singing flower garden hidden behind a leaf to the visitor's right). The figure shouldn't even be there, but was added during the 1983 refurbishment. The attraction was closed for four months and reopened on July 4, 2014, with all new special effects and multiple instances that show Alice. (*see photo for original*)

- When the park first opened, it **was intending to have a walk-through Alice attraction** where they ended up placing the *Fantasyland Theater*, which is now *Pinocchio's Daring Journey*. Due to budget restrictions, it never came to be, but then this attraction opened three years after the park.

- This dark ride stood out from all the others because it was the **first one to have an exterior load area that was themed**. The other "dark-rides" had the banner canopies.

- *Disneyland* in California is the **only park to have the *Alice in Wonderland*** attraction.

544

- It is the only "dark-ride" in the park that **has a second story** and the **only one that goes outside**.

- **Originally there was an "oversized room"** and an "upside-down room," but they were both removed in the 1984 refurbishment, and the Unbirthday Scene was moved from before the upper floor exit to the end.

- The sets inside that were based off of the film were **designed by Imagineers Mary Blare and Claude Coats**. Claude was also responsible for the color and styling of *Alice in Wonderland* (1951).

- *Alice* **opened three years after the rest of *Fantasyland*** opened in 1955. Some say it set the tradition established by the White Rabbit of always being late. When the new *Fantasyland* opened in 1983, the new *Alice* didn't open until 1984.

- There are **six color variations of the caterpillar cars** you ride in, yellow/yellow, green/green, pink/pink, yellow/orange, green/blue/green, and pink/purple.

- The ride vehicle of a **caterpillar actually has three wheels** instead of the usual four, because of the sharp turns it has to make.

- The **caterpillar vehicles were designed by Imagineer Bob Gurr**, who designed many other vehicles in the park, like the *Peter Pan Pirate Ships*.

- Kathryn Beaumont (see *Who Does That Voice* page 149) **lent her voice to the animated Alice** in *Alice in Wonderland* (1951) and returned to Disney 33 years later to do the same for Alice on this attraction's refurbishment.

- The large **mushroom near the entrance** is one of the old ticket booths.

- When this "dark-ride" opened in 1958, Disney held a special ceremony on live television. It was hosted by Walt Disney himself and **Mouseketeer Karen Pendleton, who was dressed as Alice**. There was a very cheap White Rabbit costume used in the presentation that must have been thrown together at the last minute.

- This attraction temporarily closed on July 15, 2010, because California's Department of Occupational Safety and Health pointed out that the exterior ramp from the second floor to the first floor needed handrails. **There had been some temporary railings installed** and the attraction re-opened August 3, 2010. After four years, Disney replaced the ugly railings that were on both sides with permanent railings on the door side of the car in the areas where there was a  drop-off. This was done during the 2014 refurbishment.

- They originally planned to **house this attraction in the spot where *Pinocchio*'s *Daring Journey* is now**, which was the spot they made into the Mickey *Mouse Club Theater*.

- It was also **originally planned on being a walk-through attraction** with weird walkways and tilting stairs.
- While winding around on the track, you end up going **over top of *Mr. Toad's Wild Ride.***
- Disney sculptor Blane Gibson, the one who made the *Partners Statue*, **sculpted the Caterpillar.**
- Imagineer **Bob Gurr designed the effects** inside the building.
- The 1984 refurbishment **cost Disney $8 million.**
- The attraction can run **16 caterpillar cars at one time.**
- Of all the "dark-rides," **this one travels at the slowest pace.** It gives you more time to take in the scenery.
- The **current voice credits** are as follows;
  - Kathryn Beaumont - Alice (same as the movie)
  - Corey Burton (*Haunted Mansion Holiday* Ghost Host) - The White Rabbit/Cards
  - Thurl Ravenscroft (*Haunted Mansion* fallen bust) - Ace of Clubs
  - Tony Pope (Goofy 1987-1988) - Cheshire Cat/King of Hearts
  - Tress MacNeille (Chip & Gadget in *Rescue Rangers*) - Queen of Hearts
- For a **list of this attractions Hidden Mickeys, see page 349**.

Casey Jr. Circus Train

Opened July 31, 1955 - Duration: 3:30

Guests ride in various cars of a small "circus train" and see a plethora of miniaturized towns, houses, etc. based on a classic Disney cartoon.

FUN FACTS

- Caser Jr. **is the train from the movie *Dumbo*** (1941).
- Even though this attraction opened in 1955, it was not actually available for riders on opening day; it was still in the testing process. It **opened two weeks later.**
- This attraction was meant to be **the first roller coaster** in the park.
- The locomotive that pulls the train is not actually pulling the train at all. The train is being **pulled by the circus music organ** wagon behind the locomotive. A hidden combustion engine inside the wagon hauls the rest of the train while pushing the locomotive forwards.

🐭 Years ago, the attraction engineers had to make room for more animals on the *King Arthur Carrousel*. In order to do this, they removed **four sleighs from the attraction**. Walt didn't want to just throw them away, so he decided to put them elsewhere in the park. The engineers converted them into train cars for the Casey Jr. Circus Train. There are two trains there, and they each have two sleighs.

🐭 For a **list of this attractions Hidden Mickeys, see page 349**.

Dumbo the Flying Elephant

Opened August 16, 1955 - Duration: 1:35

An attraction similar in design to the *Astro Orbitor*, riders can "fly" in replicas of the title character from the movie *Dumbo*.

FUN FACTS

🐭 A figure of Timothy Mouse rides atop the central hub. The figure originally held a training whip, later replaced with the magic feather. It has since been **changed back to the whip**.

🐭 The voice of Timothy Q. Mouse **was performed by Chris Edgerly**, who also lent his voice to Scuttle on the new *The Little Mermaid: Ariel's Under Sea Adventure* in *California Adventure*.

🐭 Even though this attraction opened in 1955, it was not actually on opening day; it was **opened three months afterward**.

🐭 I was told that during his 1957 visit, former **U.S. President Harry S. Truman** politely declined a ride. Elephants are the symbol of America's Republican Party; Truman was a Democrat.

🐭 The Dumbo attraction was originally planned to have all **pink Dumbo elephants** like in Dumbo's nightmare "Pink Elephants on Parade." It was suggested by one of the *Disneyland* design artists, Bruce Bushman.

🐭 The attraction first had 10 elephants and had the **working title *10 Elephants on Parade*.** Now the attraction has 16 Dumbo carriages to sit in. The six new Dumbo carriages were added back in 1990.

🐭 During the park's 50th anniversary, **one of the Dumbos was donated** to the National Museum of American History.

🐭 **One of the few attractions shared among all five** Disney resorts around the world.

547

- The **band organ that provides background music was built in 1915** and has the capability of being heard up to a mile away. It is rumored to be designed by Gavioli, but that company ceased its production of organs in 1912. It was originally purchased by some American collectors visiting Europe in the 1970's and was intended to be used in the now extinct *Bear Country*, but it sat in storage until the *Fantasyland* makeover in 1983.

- Originally, **Dumbo's ears used to flap up and down** when he flew, but they proved to be too heavy for the mechanical arms to lift, so they were removed.

- At the Disneyana Convention in 1992, one of the original **Dumbo vehicles sold for $16,000.**

- For a **list of this attractions Hidden Mickeys, see page 349.**

Fantasyland Theater

Re-themed in 2009 - Duration: N/A

Located next to Mickey's Toontown, this 5000-square foot amphitheater has had many shows and performances over the years. Its facade has changed many times.

FUN FACTS

- When the amphitheater **first opened in 1985, it was called *Videopolis*.** In 1995, it was dismantled and the *Fantasyland Theater* was built, but it had no top. In 1998, the top was added.

- A lot of the stage that is there now is **left over from the Snow White** show.

- This theater **used to house stage shows** in the past;
  - Sing'in' Dance'in' Heigh Ho (1987)
  - Circus Fantasy (1988)
  - Show Biz Is (1989)
  - One Man's Dream (December 16, 1989 - April 29, 1990)
  - Dick Tracy starring in Diamond Double Cross (June 15, 1990 - December 31, 1990)
  - Plane Crazy (March 15, 1991 - September 1991)
  - Mickey's Nutcracker (Christmas Seasons 1991 & 1992)
  - Beauty and the Beast Live on Stage (April 12, 1992 - April 30, 1995)
  - The Spirit of Pocahontas (June 23, 1995 - September 4, 1997)
  - The Wiggles (1998)
  - Disney's Animazement - The Musical (June 18, 1998 - October 21, 2001)
  - Mickey's Detective School (2002 - 2003)
  - Minnie's Christmas Party (Christmas Seasons 2001 & 2002)

- Snow White: An Enchanting Musical (February 2004 - September 2006)
- Disney Princess Fantasy Faire (October 2006 – August 2012)
- Mickey And the Magical Map (May 25, 2013 - present)

Fantasy Faire

Opened March 12, 2013 - Duration: N/A

This area was newly added as an expansion to *Fantasyland*, but is almost like a "mini land" itself. It is basically a large area for a *Meet and Greet* with a

princess.

FUN FACTS

 There are four main features to the *Fantasy Faire*;

- **The Royal Hall** - A *Meet-and-Greet* area where visitors can visit one-on-one with Cinderella, Aurora, and Ariel. Ariel's previous area was lost to TinkerBell in *Pixie Hollow*.

- **The Royal Theatre** - Three 30-minute plays that are hosted by two thespians on stage named Mr. Smythe and Mr. Jones. They tell jokes and act out the story of *Tangled* with the help of Rapunzel and Flynn Ryder, *Beauty and the Beast* with the help of Belle, and Frozen with the help of Elsa and Anna.

- **Fairy Tale Treasures Shop** – They sell princess costumes and accessories. You can look around and see all the neat decorative props around the store.
- **Maurice's Treats Snack Cart** – This cart sells signature treats that can only be found here. The Boysen Apple Freeze (frozen apple slush, boysenberry syrup, topped with passion fruit-mango foam) comes in second to the park visitor's favorite, Dole Whip. They also have twisted pastry snacks, the strawberry twist and the chocolate twist. If you are not in the mood for sweets, you can get the cheddar garlic bagel twist.

The *Royal Theatre* can seat 300 guests.

The *Meet-and-Greet* **area is actually divided into two halves**. Each half is divided into the three sections for the different princesses. In each half is a duplicate princess of the one in the other half. In other words, there are two Auroras, two Ariels, and two Cinderellas. Disney did this to cut down on the wait time, and only has it available on busy days.

There is a 16-foot rock statue of Rapunzel's tower with her in the upper window. Her **hair is embedded with fiber optic lighting** for a touch of magic at nighttime.

The background music was raised to help **cover the talking of the duplicate princess** on the other side. It was noticed that you could be with Cinderella, but hear Cinderella on the other side of the wall.

- Look very closely inside *Clopin's Music Box*. There are **many hidden Disney characters to be discovered**. Here are some that I have identified so far;
  - Smee – *Peter Pan* (1953)
  - The Coachman – *Pinocchio* (1940)
  - Geppetto – *Pinocchio* (1940)
  - Tony – *Lady and the Tramp* (1955)
  - Maurice – *Beauty and the Beast* (1991)
  - Snow White – *Snow White and the Seven Dwarfs* (1937)
  - Alice – *Alice In Wonderland* (1951)
  - Flynn Rider – *Tangled* (2010)
  - Gaston - *Beauty and the Beast* (1991)
  - TinkerBell – *Peter Pan* (1953)
  - Sleepy - *Snow White and the Seven Dwarfs* (1937)
  - Peter Pan – *Peter Pan* (1953)
  - Doc - *Snow White and the Seven Dwarfs* (1937)
  - Prince Adam (Beast) - *Beauty and the Beast* (1991)
  - Belle - *Beauty and the Beast* (1991)
  - Random person who looks like he is a caricature of someone.

- If you **look closely at the treasure chest on the sign** for the *Fairy Tale Treasures Shop*, you can see an acorn amongst the gold and jewels. It was placed there to pay homage to the woodland creatures who have helped princesses in past fairy tales, since animals do not care about riches.

- Above the exit tunnel is a **gold crest with the initials CPG**. They represent *Carnation Plaza Gardens*, which used to exist in the *Fantasy Faire* spot before construction. (*see photo*)

- On **one of the window ledges, you can see Figaro** and a blue bird. Watch them closely for movement. (*see photo*)

PRO TIP: *When you sit in the Fantasy Theater, and cannot sit up close, sit toward the right or left side. Otherwise, the center beam that holds up the tent will get in the way of viewing.*

551

it's a small world

Opened May 28, 1966 - Duration: 14:23

A boat ride through a tour of displays depicting various world cultures. Animatronic dolls sing the show's famous theme song in many languages.

FUN FACTS

- *it's a small world* is always **spelled with lower case** letters.

- The **original working title** of this attraction was *Children of the World.*

- There are **over 300** animated/unanimated figures.

- The attraction was originally created for the 1964/1965 **New York World's Fair**, and then was transported to *Disneyland* in 1966.

- There is **only one adult character**, which is dressed as nutcracker Mounty from Canada (not counting the new Woody or Jessie). (*see photo*)

- When the attraction was first being created, Rolly Crump (see *Imagineer Mini Biographies* page 287) was one of the Imagineers on the project. He **designed and constructed over 200 of the "toys"** on the attraction out of Styrofoam and paper mache, some of which are still on the attraction today.

- When the attraction was installed in *Disneyland* after leaving the World's Fair, Imagineer **Rolly Crump designed the giant clock** out front.

- The **theme song was written by the *Sherman Brothers*** (see *Imagineer Mini Biographies* page 287). Walt was originally going to play all the individual country's national anthems but it didn't sound right, so he asked the Sherman Brothers to write one song that could easily be translated into other languages, and could play on a loop. They came up with the song "it's a small world after all," later shortened to just "it's a small world" and that's when the name of the attraction changed.

- This is **the single most-performed and widely-translated song in the world**. The tune for the song and the lyrics are not now, nor will they ever be copyrighted. It is the only Disney creation to not be copyrighted. It was requested by UNICEF (*United Nations Children's Fund*, created on December 11, 1946, to provide emergency food and healthcare to children in countries that had been devastated by World War II) to not have them copyrighted. It can be heard worldwide on musical devices ranging from keyboard demos to ice cream trucks, and even public loudspeakers in some parts of Japan that play this song to signal the time; it remains "a gift to the children of the world."

- Marc Davis' wife, **Alice Davis, who was a costume designer for Disney**, and went on to design the pirates' clothing for *Pirates of the Caribbean*, designed the costumes for the dolls.

- There are **100 regions from around the world** represented inside.

- The attraction **has been parodied** often, even in Disney movies such as *The Lion King 1 ½*.

- The **original attraction length** was 30 minutes. Disney noticed people were losing interest quickly, so the water flow speed was increased.

- The gold trim around the facade is actually **22 karat gold**.

- The animatronic dolls that represent **China were not added** to the attraction until 1970, after President Nixon became the first President to visit China.

- There were **only two characters representing America**, a cowboy and a Native American (*see photo*) toward the end of the attraction (not including parts for Hawaii and Alaska). The reason given was that America was the "host" for the attraction and didn't need to have representation for itself, since the attraction resided in America. Since the 2008 makeover, there has been an American Scene added with Woody and Jessie. (*see photo*)

- Other **changes include narrower boats** so that fewer people can fit in a row. The collective weight of the riders was causing the boats to touch bottom in the older version.

- Costumed children from around the world joined Walt to celebrate on opening day, May 28, 1966. The children helped Walt pour **water collected from the "seven seas"** into the waterway, creating a memorable beginning for the "happiest cruise that ever sailed."

- The attraction was closed for a brief time only a month after opening to **add more animation** to some of the characters and to increase the boat's speed.

- It takes anywhere **from three to five years to create a topiary** (bushes shaped like animals). There were 50 gardeners involved in this process. The elephant itself needs four bushes to create his body and head. (*see photo*)

- The **same face mold was used** for all the children dolls to show just how small of a world this is and to show that we are all the same.

553

- One of the few attractions shared among all five Disney resorts around the world.
- The Imagineers have **added several new characters** including:

Timon & Pumbaa	Simba	Dori & Nemo	Three Caballeros
Aladdin & Abu	Jasmine	Peter Pan	Flounder
The White Rabbit	Alice	Lilo & Stitch	Mulan & Mushu
Woody & Jessie	Pinocchio	Cinderella	Jaques & Gus
	Ariel	Jiminy Cricket	TinkerBell

- This attraction was the **first one to use the FastPass system** on November 21, 1999.
- The Christmas overlay is a **tradition dating back to 1997**.
- There is a doll dedicated to Mary Blair (see *Imagineer Mini Biographies* page 287) known as **The Mary Blair Doll."** She was an Imagineer for *Disneyland* and designed *it's a small world* for the World's Fair in 1964. Mary was known for her extravagant designs with color and shapes. The doll that is dedicated to her is located on top of the Eifel Tower holding a balloon and wearing a yellow rain poncho to mimic Mary's real-life outlandish and wild attire. Mary was

554

also the art director for several Disney films including *Dumbo* (1941), *Saludos Amigos* (1942), *The Three Caballeros* (1944), *Song of the South* (1946), *Fun and Fancy Free* (1947), *So Dear to My Heart* (1948), *Cinderella* (1950), *Alice In Wonderland* (1951), *Peter Pan* (1953), and *Lady and The Tramp* (1955). Her designs usage of bright, vibrant colors is what led to *Alice In Wonderland's* nationwide use as a focal for people who were using drugs like LSD in the 1960's during the "hippie era."

Actor Dallas "Dal" McKennon is the voice of the laughing hyenas. This laughing track was actually taken straight from the laughing hyenas in the zoo in *Lady and the Tramp* (1955). In *Lady and the Tramp,* he voiced Pedro, the Chihuahua in the pound, Toughy, the dog that banged his tail on the pail, and the human with the bowler passing the zoo that Tramp tried to pass off as his owner. He also does the safety spiel for *Big Thunder Mountain Railroad*.

At **Christmas time, the entire attraction gets a makeover**. A crew of 20 technical service Cast Members spend 17 days straight, 10 to 12 hours a day, to change over the interior. The outside is covered in 50,000 C-7 lights, the same kind you would string up on your own house, in 6 different colors, plus an additional 2,000 clear flashing bulbs. All this added together equals about 350,000 watts of light. On the trees, hedges and topiaries, bushes shaped like animals, or other things, they use about 150,000 mini lights. In all 60,000 cable ties, 3,000 connectors, 25,000 feet of extension cables, and 18,000 feet of electrical tape are used.

The attraction was given the nick-name "The Asylum" due to the fact that over-exposure to the infamous song, "It's A Small World (After All)," would cause someone to go crazy.

PRO TIP: *If the queue splits into two lines, take the line to the right; it is faster.*

King Arthur Carrousel

Opened July 17, 1955 - Duration: 2:18

A carrousel featuring antique horses and themed to *Sleeping Beauty*.

FUN FACTS

- The carousel **rotates at 2.4 miles per hour**.

- The *King Arthur Carrousel* is located near the center focal of *Disneyland* for a reason. When Walt Disney's daughters were little girls, he used to take them to *Griffith Park* every weekend to ride the carousel. While sitting on a park bench, **he had his first very real thoughts** about having attractions that adults could enjoy, too. A place for every member of the family. It is no mistake that all those dreamed-of attractions surround the *Carrousel* and make up *Disneyland*, as we know it today. As soon as you enter *Main Street, U.S.A.*, the *Carrousel* is the first permanent attraction you can see straight through the entryway of the castle.

- Walt put Imagineer Bruce Bushman in charge of finding the horses for his carousel. **Bruce traveled up to Toronto, Canada, to find horses**. The problem was that there were other animals on the carousel besides the horses. After they were removed, the carousel was short horses. Bruce traveled to Coney Island where he was able to acquire the extra horses. They were found under the boardwalk.

- **The "lead" horse is named Jingles**. The ride operator used this horse as a marker to count how many times the carousel went around. Jingles is the only horse covered in bells. In 2005, he was painted completely gold for the 50th anniversary celebration. In 2008, he was repainted and dedicated to Julie  Andrews for her 50 years of dedication to Disney. In the film *Saving Mr. Banks* (2013), Walt (Tom Hanks) has Mrs. Travers sit on this horse when he tells her he was bet $20 he couldn't get her on a ride.

- **Jingles is considered to be the most popular** and favorite horse of park visitors. He has been recreated in sculptures, art, and even as a Tsum Tsum. (*see photos*)

- When *Disneyland* first opened in 1955 **the carousel was located closer to the castle**. It was shifted further away in 1983 for the *Fantasyland* refurbishment.
- The **carousel has 72 horses**, most carved at the Dentzel factory in Philadelphia, Pennsylvania, in 1875. So technically this is the oldest attraction in the park.
- Recently, four horses were removed to add a bench back onto the attraction, **leaving the carousel with 68 horses.**
- In 1959, there were 4,200 carousels around the U.S.; now there are only 172. Disney`s carousel is in the best condition.
- There are ten shields around the outside that were designed to look like **the shields of the Knights of the Round Table** from the Arthurian Legend, the story of King Arthur. The shields belong to;
  - Sir Kay (older brother of King Arthur, remember him from *Sword in The Stone*?)
  - Sir Garethe (brother of Sir Guaen)
  - Sir Galahad (son of Sir Lancelot, second cousin to Sir Bors and Lyonell)
  - Sir Guaen/Gawaine (brother of Sir Gareth)
  - Sir Lyonell (cousin of Sir Lancelot and brother of Sir Bors)
  - Sir Tristan de Leaunois/Tristram (inspiration for the love story of *Tristan and Isolde*)
  - Sir Lohengrin (known as Knight of the Swan, he is a Knight of the Holy Grail, he is the son of Sir Percival)
  - Sir Bors de Ganis' (cousin of Sir Lancelot and brother of Lyonell)
  - Sir Lancelot (father of Sir Galahad and cousin to Sir Bors and Lyonell)
  - The orange shield with the white chevrons do not seem to have an origin. I have found that these markings are considered generic and could represent anyone.

- There are a **total of 85 horses on hand**. The extras are used to swap out for repairs and touch-up painting.
- The **music that plays** while the horses are in motion is from the animated film *Sleeping Beauty*. The song is *Once Upon a Dream*.
- Supposedly, **Lillian Disney's favorite horse was Doubloon**. He can be found in the outer row of horses and can be identified by his single gold tooth.

557

- The **calliope that was used to play the music** is now located over by *Dumbo*.

- The **horses used to be a variety of colors** until 1975, when they were all painted white.

- The sword in the stone and anvil from *Sword in the Stone* **(1963) out in the front were added in 1975.** This is where they conduct the sword-pulling ceremony with Merlin.

- **There was a band that would play music for** *Fantasyland* and for the sword ceremony called *Make Believe Brass.* They were added to *Fantasyland* in 1983 and stayed as a regular music group into the 1990's.

- For a **list of this attractions Hidden Mickeys, see page 349.**

PRO TIP: *Sit on Jingles, the horse with the bells; it was the one dedicated to Julie Andrews.*

Mad Tea Party

Opened July 17, 1955 - Duration: 1:30

Riders board any one of a number of brightly-colored teacups on a large platform. The platform moves in a circle. The teacups are also on smaller moving circles on the platform, and the riders can turn a wheel in the center of each teacup to make the cup itself spin around. Located adjacent to the *Alice in Wonderland* attraction. Also based on the same animated film from 1951.

FUN FACTS

- The orange diamond cup is **regarded as the fastest spinner,** followed by the purple cup. The two heart cups are the slowest. This could just be a legend as there is no real supporting evidence that this is true.

- This attraction **was the inspiration** for *Roger Rabbit's Cartoon Spin.*

- When *Fantasyland* had its 1983 makeover, this **attraction was moved to its current location**. It used to be in the center of *Fantasyland* where the *King Arthur Carrousel* is now located.

- **One of the few attractions shared among all five** Disney resorts around the world.

- This is the **only teacup attraction between all five** in existence that must close during the rain due to the turntable getting saturated with water, because it isn't covered.

- In 2004, **Disneyland had the teacups altered so that they could not spin as fast** as they once could, claiming it was for safety reasons. The public complained and Disney restored the spinning capabilities, but some say it is not as fast as it once was.

𝔐atterhorn 𝔅obsleds

Opened June 14, 1959 - Duration: 2:07

A roller coaster ride that runs through a 1/100-scale reproduction of the Matterhorn Mountain in the Alps. It is the only structure in *Disneyland* that is easily visible from the freeway. This attraction was the first roller coaster to use tubular steel track. It received several enhancements in 1978.

FUN FACTS

⚜ This attraction can boast about being **the first "thrill ride" in *Disneyland*** because it was one of the first attractions to require an "E-ticket." The other was the *Submarine Voyage*.

⚜ It is based on the Matterhorn, **a mountain in the Swiss Alps** of over 14,000 feet, which has been scaled back to 1/100-scale to fit in with the rest of *Disneyland*.

⚜ When the park first opened, **there was a mountain of dirt located where the Matterhorn is** right now. It was the extra dirt from the excavation for *Sleeping Beauty Castle*. Its nickname was *Holiday Hill* and it had pathways and park benches. Walt intended it to be used as a picnic area. It was alone for a year until the *Skyway* to *Fantasyland* opened and Walt had the idea of building the *Matterhorn*.

⚜ *Matterhorn Bobsleds* is **based on a little-known Disney movie called *Third Man on the Mountain*.** In 1978, the attraction received a major refurbishment, where the abominable snowmen were added and the single-car bobsleds were replaced with two-car bobsleds; it doubled the capacity, and the trackway was better themed as ice tunnels. In 1994, when the *Skyway* closed, the passage through the mountain was filled in.

⚜ One of the changes in 1994 was **the addition of the Wells Expedition scene** in the mountain. It was placed there to pay homage to former Disney President Frank Wells, who had died earlier that year in a helicopter crash after a weekend ski trip with Clint Eastwood.

- It was announced in 2011 that **Disney will be making a movie** based on this attraction called *"The Hill,"* about five teenagers who go on a journey up the mountain and encounter a yeti.

- Until 1970, *Matterhorn Bobsleds* **was listed in park guides as a** *Tomorrowland* attraction; at some point they began to list it as a *Fantasyland* attraction.

- **The inside of the mountain was once bare**. You could see the other tracks and riders. Later on, the snow and ice caves were added.

- The maximum speed is **27 miles per hour**, but has an average speed of 18 miles per hour.

- The Matterhorn Ski Club was the name of the group of ride operators for this attraction. They started collecting spare change and pocket knives that fell out of people's pockets and eventually expanded to collecting cans to **make money for Guide Dogs of the Desert**. Their donations would go toward funding the raising and training of a guide dog for the blind.

- The **yeti's name is "Harold,"** after the computer system that operates the attraction. He was added onto the ride in the early 1970's during one of the rides updates. On May 22, 2015, the attraction re-opened after an extended refurbishment for the park's 60th anniversary and Guests were introduced to the new, updated Harold. There are four of them on the attraction all together. There are two in full form, and two sets of glowing red eyes. (*see photo*)

- In season 1 episode 3 of the *Mickey Mouse* (2013-present) animated series, **the Yeti can be seen with Mickey.** Next to him are smashed up bobsleds that look like the old set that were removed in 2012. The Yeti was voiced by Fred Tatasciore, the voice of Hulk in animated series, animated films, and video game since 2016. He is also the voice of the Yeti in *Animal Kingdom's Expedition Everest*.

- During firework presentations, **Tinker Bell "flies" off the top**.

- The top of the mountain **reaches 147 feet into the air**, making it the third tallest attraction in the resort. The tallest is the Guardians of the Galaxy – Mission: Breakout! tower at 183 feet and the second is *Mickey's Fun Wheel* at 158 feet.

- The **highest the riders will reach** while coasting through the mountain is 100 feet.

In the control booth window, **you can see a plush abominable snowman** named Bumble from the movie *Rudolph the Red-Nosed Reindeer* (1964). (*see photo*)

The mountain is **made out of different layers**: the outer shell is made out of concrete, then there is wire mesh and canvas, that is on a wood superstructure made from enough wood to build 300 new homes, then the center is all made out of steel beams.

The shields, or coat of arms, that you see while in the queue are the **coat of arms for each of Switzerland's cantons** (or states). There are 26 cantons in total. All 26 coats of arms can be found hanging in the queue.

Anywhere from **1,500 to 2,000 visitors** can pass through each hour.

Disneyland California is the **only park to have this attraction**.

When it opened, the *Matterhorn Bobsleds* was the **first coaster to use cylindrical rails** with urethane wheels.

The cylindrical rails **are hollow and are pressurized with air**. There is a sensor that alerts the crew if there is a leak so they know to repair it.

When the attraction first opened, the toboggans **were single cars that only sat four riders**. In 1978, two cars were joined together to make it a two-car toboggan that can seat eight people. They were designed by Bob Gurr.

Since it first opened, the **bobsleds have been changed out** and upgraded several times; in 1978, 1983, 2000, and 2012. On June 15, 2012, guests rode the single seater toboggans. No more lap sitting. Instead of being able to seat eight people to a train, four sets of two lap sitters, they now have to sit singly with six seats per train. (*see photo*)

The altering of the toboggans to becoming single seats **allowed Disney to add a single rider line**.

Other **possible names Walt considered** were *Mount Disneyland, Snow Hill, Snow Mountain, Walterhorn, Disneyland Mountain, Fantasy Mountain, Echo Mountain, Sorcerer's Mountain* (after the mountain in *Fantasia*), and even *Magic Mountain*.

This is only one **of the four mountains in *Disneyland***. The other three are *Splash Mountain, Space Mountain,* and *Big Thunder Mountain*. If you are counting the whole resort, you can add *Grizzly Peak* to the list.

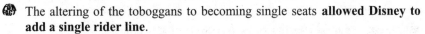

561

- Walt Disney thought more small children would board from *Fantasyland* and teens from *Tomorrowland*; that's why they **decided to have two separate tracks**.

- The track on the *Fantasyland* side is a **smoother track**.

- The left (*Fantasyland*) track of the attraction is **2,037 feet long** with a ride time of 2:07 while the right side (*Tomorrowland*) is 2,134 feet long with a ride time of 2:26.

- There is a **yeti footprint** from "Harold" mounted at the backside of the mountain. (*see photo*)

- Water, also known as the *Alpine Pond*, is used at the end to **slow down the toboggans**.

- The **whistling wind sound effects** are supposed to simulate the real Matterhorn in Switzerland.

- Cast Members **climb the mountain** daily for entertainment purposes (on busy summer days). Sometimes you can even see Mickey or Goofy. (*see photo*)

- There is a **half basketball court in the top** of the mountain. Rumor has it that the reason they built a basketball court in the top of the mountain was because, back in the 1950's, the building codes prohibited any structure from being that tall unless it was a sports structure. It is located about two thirds of the way up. It was actually built as a break room for Cast Members, for the mountain climbers to get ready for their climbs, and for TinkerBell to prepare for her flight during the fireworks. They also added a ping pong table at the request of Gina Rock, the longest flying TinkerBell in *Disneyland* history.

- At the end of the attraction, you hear the now famous "*Remain seated please; Permanecer sentados por favor*" safety announcement; it is one of many recordings by the former **"Voice of Disneyland," Jack Wagner**. He was also the voice that announced the start of *Disneyland's Main Street Electrical Parade*.

- The **Toblerone chocolate bar** uses the Matterhorn as the logo on its packaging.

- A **similar attraction to this can be found** in *Disney's Animal Kingdom* as *Expedition Everest* in Florida. The similarities are a lost expedition coasting through the snow-covered mountains and encountering an abominable snowman.

- They closed down in January 2012 for five months to do a complete makeover of the mountains. The entire mountain was covered with scaffolding and tarps. They used over 800 gallons of paint to redo all of the snow, to make it look more realistic. Since it first opened in 1959, all they have been able to do is touchups. To add a more realistic look, **they added glass beads to the white paint** to make it glisten in the sunlight, just like real snow does.

- The band *No Doubt* **with Gwen Stefani is originally from Anaheim**. They released an album called *Tragic Kingdom* in 1995. On the last track, you can hear a recording of Jack Wagner.

- When it first opened, the Disney family (Walt, Lillian, Sharon, and Diane) **along with Richard Nixon, all rode on it.**

- If you have ever heard **a reference to "Dolly's Dip" on the Matterhorn**, it is because of 48-year-old Dolly Regina Young of Fremont, California. On January 3, 1984, Dolly was thrown from a *Matterhorn Bobsleds* car and was struck by the next oncoming bobsled. An investigation showed that her seat belt was found unbuckled after the accident. It is unclear why she unfastened her belt. It is believed that she removed it to turn around and assist her children.

- For a **list of this attractions Hidden Mickeys, see page 349**.

mr. Toad's Wild Ride

Opened July 17, 1955 - Duration: 2:01

A "dark-ride" attraction based on *The Wind in the Willows* (1949). It reopened with improvements in 1983 as part of the *New Fantasyland*.

FUN FACTS

- This is **one of the original attractions** from *Disneyland's* opening day.

- The book *Wind in the Willows* **was written by Kenneth Grahame** (8 March 1859 – 6 July 1932) in 1908 and turned into a Disney film in 1949. He also wrote the book *The Reluctant Dragon* in 1898, also turned into a Disney film in 1941.

- There is a moose head on the wall in the tavern that **closely resembles Melvin** from the, now gone, *Country Bear Jamboree*.

- When you drive through the town square, there is a **silhouette of Sherlock Holmes** in a second-floor window to the left. as soon as you go through the doors. This pays homage to Basil Rathbone (13 June 1892 – 21 July 1967) who portrayed the detective Sherlock Holmes in 16 Sherlock Holmes films between 1939 and 1953. Basil Rathbone was the narrator for *Wind in the Willows* (1949). He was also the inspiration behind the character Basil of Baker Street in *The Great Mouse Detective* (1986).

- Right next to Sherlock Holmes is a **painting of "Blind Justice."** She is supposed to be blindfolded, but if you look, you can see that she is peeking.

563

In the loading area, there is a mural painted on the wall of a train. If you look closely, **you will see "W.E.D. Railroad"** written on the side. It stands for Walter Elias Disney. Back in the beginning, the Imagineers worked for the company W.E.D. (*see photo*)

The **coat of arms above the entrance reads**, "Toadi Acceleratio Semper Absurda". Translated from Latin it means, "Speeding with Toad is always absurd."

Mr. Toad's full name is *J. Thaddeus Toad, Esquire.*

Mr. Toad **made an appearance in the film** *Who Framed Roger Rabbit* (1988) as a firefighter riding on a fire truck.

Some people say that the painting above the fireplace **resembles the sidewalk chalk art that Bert** draws in *Mary Poppins* (1964), but the film came out 11 years after this attraction did. (*see photo*)

Each character is represented by name on individual cars, Mr. Toad, Toady, Ratty, Moley, MacBadger, Cyril, Winky and Weasel. On Mr.Toad, there is one scene with each of the car names except Ratty. Mr.Toad, in works of art, as a statue in town square. Mole, in the pub, eating fried chicken. Badger, on a ladder in the library. Cyril, holding Toad in the center of town. Weasel, on the chandeliers in the hall after the leaded- glass window. Winkie, in the pub, spinning the beers.

This is the only "dark-ride" attraction that **stuck with the theme of first-person point of view** after the 1983 *Fantasyland* makeover. There are no actual characters of Mr. Toad on this attraction. Whereas on Peter Pan, Snow White, and Alice, they had the title character added in later.

Protesters staged a "Toad-In" day, so everyone showed up and packed in line to ride. Disney was **planning on shutting this attraction down** and replacing it with *The Many Adventures of Winnie the Pooh*. Due to its popularity, Disney ended up putting *Pooh* in the back corner of the park in *Critter Country*. *Magic Kingdom's* version was not so lucky. Theirs was removed and replaced with Pooh. One of the devils from the hell scene was auctioned off and sold to John Stamos, who hung it up in his recording studio.

The statue of Mr. Toad, next to the queue just inside before you board, has his arm behind his back. **He originally had his arm out to hold his monocle**, just like the figure of him on the attraction and on the facade of the building, but people kept putting cigarettes between his fingers, so it was altered. (*see photos*)

🎯 For a **list of this attractions Hidden Mickeys, see page 349**.

𝔓eter 𝔓an's 𝔉light

Opened July 17, 1955 - Duration: 2:10

"*Second star to the right and then straight on till morning.*" This attraction is a unique variation on the dark-ride theme, the rider "flies" in a pirate ship through a creative interpretation of the Disney version of *Peter Pan*, traveling over London and then through Neverland. It reopened in 1983 with improvements as part of the *New Fantasyland*.

FUN FACTS

🎯 When you fly over the blocks, look down on them. **They spell out "PETER PAN."** (*see photo*)

🎯 Look for the stack of blocks in the children's room. From the bottom up, they **spell out "D15NEY."**

🎯 The **voices on this attraction** were performed by:
- Peter Pan - Ronnie McMillan
- Wendy - Kathryn Beaumont (see *Who Does That Voice* page 149).
- Indian Chief - Candy Candido (see *Who Does That Voice* page 149).
- Captain Hook & Mr. Smee - Corey Burton (see *Who Does That Voice* page 149.

🎯 Captain Hook's **left hand is a hook**. The two figures on the attraction have him with his right hand as a hook. In the original book, Captain Hook is missing his right hand, like on this attraction. For the film, the animators decided to make his left hand the hook, as they did for the mural on the wall when you are disembarking. (*see photos*)

🎯 The highly advanced technology used to make the car lights on the freeway was **a bicycle chain with painted headlight dots** and was turning around through gears.

565

- Wendy, in her nightgown, is **the only character wearing real fabric clothing** on the whole attraction. (*see photo*)

- This is one of the **most popular attractions in *Disneyland***, especially for *Fantasyland*. Expect a longer wait, even at the end of the night.

- The original intent of the attraction was for the guests to fly through the attraction, as if they were Peter Pan. Audiences did not quite grasp this concept and were left wondering, *"Why wasn't Peter Pan in the Peter Pan ride?"* In 1983, during *Fantasyland's* remodel, an **Audio-Animatronic Peter Pan was added** to his namesake attraction.

- As you exit your pirate ship, look up at the **hook hanging on the wall** holding a lantern. It was originally in the *Pirate Ship Restaurant* before it was torn down. It was sponsored by Chicken of the Sea until 1969, and then the name was changed to *Captain*

Hook's Galley. It was in *Fantasyland* from 1955 until 1982, when it was bulldozed and replaced with the relocated *Dumbo the Flying Elephant* attraction. (*see photo*)

- When you fly over the mermaid lagoon, **one of the mermaids resembles Ariel** from *The Littler Mermaid* (1989). She was not

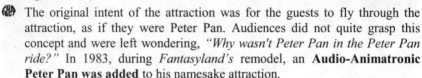

intended to look like Ariel; this is a myth that one hopes to be true. Since this attraction was built in 1955 and refurbished in 1983, the film did not yet exist. On the other hand, the mermaid in the mermaid lagoon in *Magic Kingdom* was made to resemble Ariel.

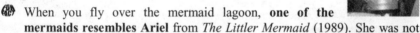

- The attraction **was originally called *Peter Pan***. It was not changed to *Peter Pan's Flight* until after the 1983 refurbishment.

- Prior to the refurbishment, Peter Pan was not on the attraction because the rider WAS Peter Pan. **Only his shadow was seen.**

- With the 1983 refurbishment **they added the Big Ben clock tower** as part of the building's facade. (*see photo*)

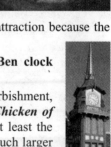

- Captain Hook's ship was added in 1983 after the refurbishment, which led to the rumor of Disney **repurposing the *Chicken of the Sea Pirate Ship*** and using it in this attraction. At least the bridge of the ship. This is false. The restaurant was much larger and the bridge did not look anything like the one in the attraction.

566

For a **list of this attractions Hidden Mickeys, see page 349**.

Pinocchio's Daring Journey

Opened April 15, 1983 - Duration: 2:47

A dark-ride through the story of Pinocchio, which was the studio's second animated feature film.

FUN FACTS

In front of the attraction there is a lamp hanging from an ironwork arm. The name **"Pinocchio" is spelled out** in the filigree.

The poolroom scene, when Lampwick turns into a donkey, was the **first time Imagineers used holograms** at *Disneyland*. (*see photo*)

The **toys sitting on the shelves** at the end before you disembark are reproductions of the ones from the movie.

This attraction **replaced** *The Mickey Mouse Clubhouse Theater* that opened with the park in 1955. In 1964, the name changed to the *Fantasyland Theater*. It closed in 1982 for the New Fantasyland project. In 1983, it opened as what it is today.

The **same mirror illusion** is used here with the appearance of the Blue Fairy as it is in *Haunted Mansion* with the ghosts in the Ballroom Scene. It is called the "Pepper's Ghost" effect.

In the scene of Pleasure Island, **a portrait of Leonardo da Vinci's *Mona Lisa* can be found**. She has a moustache painted on her face. It is believed this was a nod to famous French painter Marcel Duchamp, who in 1919 painted a parody portrait of the Mona Lisa with a moustache. Marcel Duchamp is better known for his surrealist painting *Nude Descending a Staircase, No 2*. (*see photo*)

The voices on this attraction were performed by:
- Pinocchio - Kevin Brando
- Jiminy Cricket - Eddie Carroll
- Stromboli - Ray Templin
- Coachman - Ray Templin
- Monstro – Thurl Ravenscroft (see *Who Does That Voice on page 147*)
- Additional voices - Will Ryan, Candy Candido (see *Who Does That Voice* page 149)

For a **list of this attractions Hidden Mickeys, see page 349**.

567

Pixie Hollow

Opened October 25, 2008 - Duration: N/A

Meet Tinker Bell and her fairy friends, Silvermist, Iridessa, Fawn, and Rosetta in the new *Pixie Hollow*. As you make your journey along a winding pathway that follows the banks of an enchanted pond, you will feel like you have been magically shrunk to fairy size.

FUN FACTS

- This extremely popular *Meet and Greet* area opened in October 2008, but **before it became *Pixie Hollow* it was *Ariel's Grotto***. It was an area for children to meet and greet with Ariel in her mermaid form. (*see photo*)

- There used to be a **fountain located in the pond of King Triton** that would spray water from the end of his trident. That statue was moved and placed on top of the new attraction *The Little Mermaid: Ariel's Undersea Adventure* in *California Adventure*.

- Just beneath the *Pixie Hollow* sign, you can spot a large block of green concrete. Sometimes it is covered with camouflage like in the photo. This cement is the last remaining footprint of the **long-gone Monsanto's House of the Future**. It resided in *Disneyland's Tomorrowland* from 1957-1967. It was too much work to remove the solid cement base, so they left it.

- For a **list of this attractions Hidden Mickeys, see page 349**.

Sleeping Beauty Castle

Opened July 17, 1955 - Duration: N/A

Opened July 17, 1955, the castle is the oldest of all Disney castles. The castle initially featured an empty upper level that was never intended to house an attraction, but Walt Disney was not satisfied with what he viewed as wasted space. He challenged his Imagineers to find some use for the space. Beginning April 29, 1957, visitors were able to walk through the castle and view several dioramas depicting the story of *Sleeping Beauty*. The original dioramas were designed in the style

of Eyvind Earle, production designer for Disney's 1959 film *Sleeping Beauty*, and were then redone in 1977 to resemble the window displays on *Main Street, U.S.A.*

FUN FACTS

- It reaches a **height of 77 feet,** making it the shortest of all the Disney castles, but the same height as the castle in *Hong Kong Disneyland*. *Disneyland Paris* is 167 feet tall, *Magic Kingdom* is 189 feet tall, and *Shanghai Disneyland* is 197 feet tall, making it almost three times taller than the one in *Disneyland*.

- The walk-through was **closed for unspecified reasons** in October 2001. Popular belief claims the September 11th attacks and the potential danger that ensued played a major factor in the closing.

- On July 17, 2008, Disney announced that the *Sleeping Beauty Castle* **walk-through would reopen** in the style of the original Earle dioramas, enhanced with new technology not available in 1957. The walk-through reopened on November 27, 2008, at 5:00 p.m., drawing long lines going as far back as *Main Street, U.S.A.* Unlike previous incarnations, visitors who are unable to climb stairs or navigate the passageways of the castle can still experience the walk-through "virtually" in a special room on the castle's ground floor.

- In celebration of *Disneyland's* 50th anniversary, the **castle was repainted and five turrets were decorated** with stylized crowns, each representing a decade in the park's history. (*see photo*)

- The creation of *Disneyland* is represented by a pair of famous "ears" peeking up over the horizon to see the wonders to come.
- "A World on the Move," otherwise known as the "*New Tomorrowland*" of 1967, is represented by rocket ships and accented by opalescent planets.
- The Blue Fairy represents the debut of the *Main Street Electrical Parade*.
- The *Indiana Jones Adventure* is represented by the evil Eye of Mara, guarded by snakes.
- The 50th Anniversary of *Disneyland* is represented by fireworks and Tinker Bell.

On July 17, 2015, **the park celebrated its 60ᵗʰ anniversary**. To spruce up the castle, Imagineers replaced all the turret rooftops with tops that had been bejeweled. They were eventually taken down because the look of them didn't turn out exactly as planned. (*see photo*)

There is a **gold marker on the ground** that marks the geological center of *Disneyland* (prior to *Toontown*). At least that is what most people believe. Actually, the marker was there as a surveyor's marker and was used to line up the castle with *Main Street, U.S.A.* There are actually several gold markers throughout the park. The center of the park is actually closer to the *"Partners"* statue. (*see photo*)

The drawbridge of the castle is functional, but has been rarely used. It has only been **publicly lowered on two occasions**: when the park opened in 1955, and when *Fantasyland* was rededicated in 1983. The gears that control the drawbridge were removed during a refurbishment in 1996 and have not been replaced. In 2014, the bridge was altered from having chains to having a wooden rail, due to the possibility of a child falling into the water. This addition keeps the bridge from raising up without the removal of the railings.

While walking through the top floor, there is a door with a window that shows a guard peeking in at the end of a long corridor. If you touch the door, **Maleficent's goon pops up with his grunting laugh**. He is voiced by Candy Candido, just like in the movie when he says, "*Yeah, we searched mountains and forests and, uh, houses and... uh, lemme see here... and all the cradles.*" He is also the Indian Chief in *Peter Pan* (1953), and on the attraction, and Fidget in

The Great Mouse Detective (1986). You can also hear Candy's menacing laugh in *Haunted Mansion* in the graveyard and as you exit the building.

While being filmed, **Walt Disney accidentally referred to the castle as Snow White's Castle**. This blooper sparked speculation among fans that the castle was originally going to be called "Snow White's Castle," but was changed to coincide with the release of *Sleeping Beauty* (1959). This rumor is true. Originally, Walt had intended for the castle to be *Snow White's Castle*, but later changed it to help promote the upcoming film. You can tell by looking at the design of it and see how it closely resembles the castle in *Snow White*, rather than the gothic style of the castle in *Sleeping Beauty*.

The production of *Sleeping Beauty* (1959) began in 1951 and ended in 1958. Disney knew of the future release of the film for 1959 and so **named the castle after the film,** even though the film was released four years after the castle opened.

The **family crest over the entry archway** is said to be that of the Disney

family according to Cast Members, tour guides, and seasoned *Disneyland* veterans. I am not sure how accurate that is. From what I can find, the Disney family crest has three fleur-de-lis in the middle of it that represents purity. The crest on the castle has three lions in the middle which represent courage and is the crest for England, since that is the country of origin for Aurora. It was also the crest for King Richard the Lionheart, of England. It was added to the castle in 1960. The photo on the left is the crest on the

571

castle. The center photo is the Disney Family crest from the *Castle Heraldry Shoppe* inside the castle only 30 feet away, which has been in *Disneyland* since 1994, and in its current location since 2008. The photo on the right is the crest logo for *C.R. England: Global Transportation*, a shipping company founded in 1920. (*see photo*)

When the moat surrounding the castle is dredged, **any money retrieved** from it is given to the organization *Boys and Girls Club of America*.

The **castle was originally blue**, like Cinderella's castle, but was then changed to its current pink, gold, and light blue color scheme.

Starting in late October, ***Sleeping Beauty Castle* is slowly transformed** into *Sleeping Beauty's Winter Castle* with over 80,000 LED lights and projections. *Sleeping Beauty's Winter Castle*, first introduced in 2007, is decorated even more elaborately during the holiday season with additional snowdrifts and icicles. After dark, a sensational new holiday lighting and special effects show carries the magic of the holidays from the castle all the way to the Christmas tree in *Town Square*. For the first time in 53 years, the Christmas tree is completely artificial, which enables *Disneyland* to present a holiday light show with more than 62,000 energy-efficient LED lights. The *Sleeping Beauty's Winter Castle* presentation unfolds throughout the evening in three acts, each of them featuring a touch of winter snow on *Main Street, U.S.A.* The finale of the show includes the legendary "Believe... in Holiday Magic" fireworks show, which takes Guests on a journey of sights and sounds of the season and ends with a touching rendition of "White Christmas," along with a climactic snowfall swirling down on *Main Street, U.S.A., small world mall,* and *New Orleans Square.*

It is **modeled after the Neuschwanstein Castle** (pronounced noi-schvan-shtine), a Bavarian castle built from 1882-1886 by King Ludwig II (1869-1886) near the village of Hohenschwangau, Germany. You can catch a glimpse of it over in *California Adventure* on the new *Soarin' Around the World.* (*see photo*)

The front of the castle is actually the back, and the back of the castle is actually the front. Imagineer Herb Ryman designed the castle and Imagineer Fred Jorger created a model. After the model was created of the castle, they were not satisfied with how it looked. The Imagineers were waiting for Walt to come and look at the progress of their projects. Herb decided to take the top of the castle off and flip it around before setting it back down. They liked the look of that better, but did not have a chance to put it back before Walt came in. Walt loved it the way they had it and so it was built that way. Here you can see the real castle and the backside of *Sleeping Beauty Castle*.

The castle uses **"forced perspective" to make the castle appear taller** than it actually is. The stones at the base are larger than they are at the top. You don't notice the gradual shrinkage as you look toward the top. The stones aren't even stones, they are made out of cement, plaster and fiberglass.

There is always **one male and one female swan** in the moat.

The Imagineers **had junipers planted around the moat,** because it is one of the few plants that swans will not eat.

Walt wanted the gold spires to really sparkle. To do so, he wanted **22-karat gold leaf to be used** atop the spires. His brother, Roy, did not want that to happen, so when Roy went on a business trip, Walt had it done.

In the courtyard is a plaque for the **Disneyland Time Capsule**. It was installed in 1995 for the 40th anniversary and is set to be opened in the year 2035 for the 80th anniversary. Inside is said to be Disney pins, buttons, photos, and other Disney memorabilia.

Walt referred to the castle as "the wienie" of the park. It would draw your attention down *Main Street, U.S.A.* toward the central hub. He called it the wienie because of a game he used to play with his poodle, Lady. He would hold out a piece of hot dog, a wienie, and the dog would go wherever he wanted. Then at the end of her obedience, he would reward her with the hot dog. Same with the castle. You will be rewarded with *Fantasyland*.

For a **list of this attractions Hidden Mickeys, see page 349**.

Snow White's
Scary Adventures

Opened July 17, 1955 - Duration: 1:51

A dark-ride based on Disney's first animated film, *Snow White and the Seven Dwarfs* (1937).

FUN FACTS

When the attraction first opened in 1955 **it was called *Snow White and Her Adventures***. Some people found scenes in it to be too frightening for little children, so Disney placed a warning sign at the entrance. During the 1983 *Fantasyland* makeover, they added *"Scary"* to the title just to make sure it was known.

The character of **Snow White did not even appear on the attraction** until the 1983 *Fantasyland* makeover because the attraction was intended to be a first-person experience as someone went from scene to scene as if they themselves were Snow White.

During the makeover, Adriana Caselotti **returned to re-record her singing**. (see *Disney Princess Collection* for biography page 90)

There is an easy way to **recall the names of all seven dwarfs.** There are two D's, two S's and three emotions. They are Dopey, Doc, Sleepy, Sneezy, Happy, Grumpy and Bashful.

If you keep your eyes peeled, you can spot a pie cooling in the window that has been **specially made for Grumpy**.

The attraction **vehicles are all mine cars**, each one named randomly after one of the Seven Dwarfs, just like in the film, where their names are carved on the foot boards of their respective beds.

🐭 In the scene when the witch offers the Guests the poisoned apple, Guests consistently tried (and often succeeded) to steal the apple. When *Fantasyland* was reopened in 1983, they solved the problem of the ever-missing poisoned apple by **replacing it with a 3D image of an apple**. Guests who reach out to steal the apple now find their hands passing through it.

🐭 Next to the entrance door, **there is a golden apple**. Touch the apple and some bloodcurdling cackles are heard.

🐭 The **dwarfs playing their respective instruments** in the Cottage Scene are as follows: Doc on mandolin, Grumpy on organ, Happy on accordion, Bashful on guitar, Sleepy on fiddle, and Dopey is on Sneezy's shoulders.

🐭 Above the entrance there is a window with a pair of curtains in it. Every now and then, **the Queen parts the curtains** and peers out. It is said that there was a moment in the 1990's when the Cast Members removed the Evil Queen's dress to have it cleaned. Somehow the mechanism that open and closes the curtains was left on so that the queen flashed everyone for almost seven hours before management discovered the mistake and turned it off.

🐭 When it opened, **it cost children 25¢** and adults 35¢ to ride.

🐭 For a **list of this attractions Hidden Mickeys, see page 349**.

Snow White Grotto

Opened April 9, 1961 – Duration: N/A

This is a relaxing area to the left of the entrance to *Fantasyland* by *Sleeping Beauty's Castle*. There is a nice little tranquil waterfall and a singing wishing well.

FUN FACTS

🐭 When *Fantasyland* was refurbished in 1983, Adriana Caselotti was asked to come back and re-record her song *"I'm Wishing"* for the wishing well at the age of 67. That is about 46 years after her first recording. This information was confirmed in the book *Snow White and the Seven Dwarfs & the Making of the Classic Film* with the quote from Adriana, *"I was already 67 years old,*

and didn't know if I could sound exactly the same as I did in 1937." (see *Disney Princess Collection* for biography page *90*)

A Disney myth is that Walt Disney was given **marble statues of Snow White and the seven dwarfs** by an anonymous Italian sculptor in 1961. What really happened is they were commissioned by Imagineer and Disney Legend John Hench (animator on *Fantasia, Dumbo, Peter Pan, Cinderella, and Alice In Wonderland*) to be made by sculptor **Leonida Parbla.** Unfortunately, the sculptor

made the dwarfs the same height as Snow White. They were copied from a set of soaps that were licensed to be released at the time, which is why Snow White is the same size. John contacted the sculptor to remedy the size problem, but Leonida wanted $2,000 to redo Snow White, so John worked with what he had and used the technique of "forced perspective." The dwarfs were set up along a waterfall. By setting the Snow White figure at the top of the waterfall, and slightly back, they were able to give the illusion that she was taller than the dwarfs. In order to preserve the original marble pieces, the statues were replaced with fiberglass copies and the marble ones were stored in the Imagineer studio. (*see photo*)

The money that is thrown into the **well is donated to charity**.

This **same spot was recreated for *Hong Kong Disneyland***, but the error of the size difference was corrected to make Snow White taller than the dwarfs. *Hong Kong Disneyland* refused to be different from the original in *Disneyland,* so the mistake was switched back.

Storybook Land Canal Boats

Opened July 17, 1955 - Duration: 6:00

A boat ride with much of the same sights as the *Casey Jr. Circus Train*, but with a different layout and more leisurely pace. At the beginning of the attraction, the boat travels through the mouth of Monstro, the whale from *Pinocchio*.

FUN FACTS

This attraction was **inspired by Walt's fascination** with collecting miniatures.

All the buildings, trees, and other plants were **created in a 1:12 scale**.

The small **village from Switzerland was purposefully placed** in the part of the attraction where the boat approaches it head on with the *Matterhorn* directly in the background, making it appear as if the snowy miniature mountains are a part of the much larger *Matterhorn* (the scene with the wind mills). It is more noticeable to smaller children.

- Almost all of the princesses' respective **castles are shown, except for the castle from *Beauty and the Beast*** (1991). This is odd because the castle in which Jasmine resides while in Agrabah is present, and the film *Aladdin* came out in 1992. Sleeping Beauty's castle is also missing, but this could be because they have the real thing in the center of the park. *Mulan* and *Pocahontas* did not have castles. *Brave* and *Princess and the Frog* came out too recent, and *Frozen* was added because of the popularity of the movie.

- On December 20, 2014, the boats relaunched after a short refurbishment. To Guest's astonishment, **the Old Mill Scene, based on the 9-minute animated short** *The Old Mill* (1937), was absent from this classic attraction. In its stead was the kingdom of Arendelle from the smash hit film *Frozen* (2013).

- The **Madurodam was the inspiration** behind this attraction. Madurodam is a miniature city located in Scheveningen, The Hague, in the Netherlands. It is a Dutch tourist attraction built in 1952. It is a 1:25 scale model of a Dutch city, complete with a miniature airport, city hall, parks and many other buildings and landmarks.

- This is one of only two *Disneyland* Park attractions where **a live host rides with you** and narrates the attraction. The other is the *Jungle Cruise*.

- The canal contains **465,000 gallons of water** which flow via underground pipes to the moat around *Sleeping Beauty Castle*, the *Jungle Cruise*, and to the *Rivers of America* where it is pumped back to *Storybook Land*.

- **The boats are all named after females, except Flower**. He was the boy skunk in *Bambi* (1941).

- **There are 15 boats**: Ariel, Alice, Aurora, Belle, Cinderella, Daisy, Faline, Flora, Fauna, Flower (no longer in use), Katrina (no longer in use), Merryweather, Snow White, Tinker Bell, and Wendy.

- The boats named **Belle and Ariel were not added until 1994**.

- The attraction's 15 boats are **powered by outboard motors**. When not in use, they are stored in a boathouse hidden behind the waterfall containing *Triton's Castle* from the film *The Little Mermaid* (1989).

- The boats are **scaled down versions of the old Dutch**, English, and French style boats.

- The houses in *Storybook Land* are fitted with **six-inch doors and quarter-inch hinges that open and close**, so the Disney electricians can change the light bulbs.

- All the plants on this attraction are **miniatures plants**, including a bonsai tree that *Walt Disney* planted himself.

- When the attraction **first opened, it was called *The Canal Boats of the World***. After 11 months, the attraction was renamed to what it is today.

- One of Walt's unrealized ideas for this attraction was to have **miniature landmarks from around the world**.

- This **project was headed up by Imagineer Ken Anderson.** (see *Imagineers Mini Biographies on page 288*)

- When the attraction first opened, it was not yet completed. The captains would tell people the trees were **so miniature that they could not even be seen**.

- Due to the overabundance of the mud scenery, it earned **the attraction's nickname, *The Mud Bank Ride***.

- The **boats were all built by the Robert Dorris Boat Works**.

- The **first boats were powered by outboard motors**, which often overheated and had to be towed back. Gas engines were so loud that Guests could barely hear the guide's narration.

- With Ken Anderson's design help (and the assistance of Frank Armitage, Walt Peregoy, Harriet Burns, and Fred Joerger), the attraction was re-themed, and re-titled. The **boats opened as we know them on June 16, 1956**, with all the plants and little trees.

- **The American Dairy Princess was brought over to christen the boats** by pouring milk on them. There used to be an exhibit in *Tomorrowland,* next to the *20,000 Leagues Under the Sea* walk-through, which is where *Star Tours* is now. It was called *The Dairy Bar* and was sponsored by the American Dairy Association. It only lasted for a year and a half from January 1956-September 1958. That is where people went to get a tall cool glass of milk, along with a small assortment of other foods. There was also a little walk-through exhibit. The Dairy Princess came from there.

- **The boats' original names** were Nellie Bly, Lady Katrina, Lady of Shalott, Annie Oakley, Gretel, Bold Lockinvar, Lady of the Lake, and Lady Guinevere.

- It is said that Imagineer Fred Joerger would go to the miniature church after his lunch break and **urinate on the new copper roof** to help age the metal.

578

Later the Imagineers came up with a chemical to put on copper to give it an aged look.

🐭 The **lighthouse, which was the old ticket booth, was located near Monstro** the Whale. That is actually where people used to board the boats, right in front of his mouth. (*see photo*)

🐭 The Monstro at the start of the attraction was an idea from Imagineer Bruce Bushman for **the Pinocchio boat ride**, which never came to fruition.

🐭 Ken Anderson heard about **little redwood trees located in Van Damme State Park in Northern California**. He made a trip up there to check them out. The state park would not sell any of the miniature redwoods to him. Apparently, the redwoods growth was stunted because of the limestone in the ground that prevented the trees from getting proper rooting. He ended up finding an area nearby that had the same dwarfism of the redwood trees and was able to bring back about 20 trees. After replanting, two of the trees ended up dying, but Disney kept spraying them green until they could be replaced.

🐭 When it first opened, **male Cast Members steered the boats**. At night, the men had to manually pull the boats into the covered boat dock. Females were gradually taking over until the 1960's when it was just about all females.

🐭 **Electricians eventually installed a two-way switch on the boats**, providing a reverse gear to easily back the boats into the storage tunnel.

🐭 There were **four Mouseketeers present for the re-grand opening**, Darlene, Lonnie, Sharon, and Bobby, who joined a half-dozen other children.

🐭 Another concept that never made it off the drafting table was *Big Rock Candy Mountain*. The boats were to go through the mountain and see **Dorothy having a party in the Land of Oz**.

🐭 Originally, it was **a "C ticket" attraction and was changed to a "D ticket" attraction** by the 1960's and 1970's.

🐭 Before King Triton's Castle was added behind the waterfall, where the boats are docked for the night, **the captain would tell the kids that through the waterfall was Neverland**.

🐭 **Sometimes characters will hop on** this attraction and engage the children while riding. (*see photo*)

🐭 For a **list of this attractions Hidden Mickeys, see page 349**.

MICKEY'S TOONTOWN

Mickey's Toontown opened in *Disneyland* on January 24, 1993. The area is themed after the Toontown Scene in the film, *Who Framed Roger Rabbit* (1988), and resembles a set from the animations of Max Fleischer (1930's *Superman*, *Popeye* and *Betty Boop*). The buildings are stylized and colorful. There are several attractions involving classic cartoon characters, such as the "houses'" of Mickey and Minnie Mouse, and a small kiddie coaster. There are a few interactive gags. Compared to other *Disneyland* areas, there are few large or technically-complex rides or shows, and the houses themselves appeal primarily as playhouses.

FUN FACTS

- Just walk around and touch, press, pull, poke, prod, listen to, talk to, feel, climb, and attempt to do everything you can. Just about **every door, window, knob, handle and everything else can be interacted with**.

- Drink some of the Goofy water from the fountains near the bathrooms; **you can hear voices coming out of the drains**.

- Because Roger Rabbit was such a big hit, **Disney decided to make a land just for him** and other toon characters. It was originally planned to be called *Hollywood Land* and placed behind *Main Street, USA*. There were also plans for a *Mickey's Birthdayland*, to celebrate our favorite mouse's 60th birthday. Therefore, they ended up combining the two ideas into what is there today. The ideas for Baby Herman and Judge Doom to have their own attractions were thrown out.

- *Tokyo Disneyland* is the **only other resort to have a *Toontown*.** There was one in *Magic Kingdom*, but it closed in 2011 to make way for their *Fantasyland* expansion.

- In the library window, there is a **sign to pay homage to the first company** that was started by Walt, "Laugh-O-grams Films Inc." The studio was located in Kansas City, Missouri, and housed Walt's animation studio from 1921-1923. They made a total of 10 short films. After the company went bankrupt, Walt sold his film camera for a one-way ticket to California. He brought along his unfinished final film *Alice's Wonderland*. (*see photo*)

- **Toontown is divided into three sections:** *Downtown Toontown, Mickey's Neighborhood,* and *Toon Square*.

- The name of the **clock above City Hall is called The Clockenspiel**. It starts ringing bells and blowing whistles to announce when a meet-and-greet character is coming out.

- When the Imagineers were designing *Toontown*, they were told no rulers. As you may notice, **there are no straight lines**. Everything is cartoony and looks "poofy."

- Next to *Roger Rabbit's Cartoon Spin,* **you can find the door handle from** *Alice In Wonderland* (1951). Give his knob a turn to make his eyes change.

- There is **a game online called *Disney's Toontown Online***. It is massive multiplayer online role-playing game created by The Walt Disney Company. It is considered the first one designed just for kids and families. It went online in June 2003.

- When you enter this land, **you can almost see it in its entirety** when standing in once place. (*see photo*)

- For a **list of this attractions Hidden Mickeys, see page 349**.
- For a **list of Disneyland's Attractions of the Past**, see page 660.

Attractions

CHIP 'N DALE TREEHOUSE

Opened January 24, 1993 - Duration: N/A

A treehouse based on Chip 'n Dale. Children pass through an opening at the base of the redwood style tree house and climb a staircase that spirals up through the trunk.

DISNEYLAND RAILROAD

Opened July 17, 1955 - Duration: 18:00

The *Disneyland Railroad* has a station in *Mickey's Toontown. See Other Details in The Description From Main Street, U.S.A.*

DONALD'S BOAT

Opened January 24, 1993 - Duration: N/A

A large landed boat that Donald Duck might have. It is named Miss Daisy after Daisy Duck, and it is docked in the lagoon of Mickey's neighborhood. This is a walk-through experience with fun hands-on activities.

FUN FACTS

There were **several parts of the attraction that were changed** because of injuries to children, i.e. the cargo net.

GADGET'S GO COASTER

Opened January 24, 1993 - Duration: 0:51

A roller coaster constructed to appear as if it had been pieced together from human objects by the character Gadget from *Chip 'n Dale Rescue Rangers*. It takes you on an adventure over and around upper *Toon Lake*. This attraction is located in Mickey's neighborhood in an area themed as a rustic, natural setting with a waterfall, rocks, and foliage. The cars resemble trains and are made to look like they were built entirely from *Toontown* discarded parts. The coaster train consists of one lead car with seven trailing cars.

FUN FACTS

This roller coaster made its debut run **3 years after the cancelation** of the famous 65-episode cartoon series *Chip 'n Dale Rescue Rangers* (1989-1990).

This is the only attraction in the Disney Resort that is **based on a cartoon series** from the two-hour television block Disney Afternoon.

On the blueprints stamped with "Rejected", you can see the Three Little Pigs and the name of their construction company, Chinny Chin Chin Construction.

Toontown **characters** (Mickey, Minnie, Goofy) have been known to ride in the cars next to children.

When you reach the peak of the coaster track, **you can see over the back of the *Toontown* wall**, revealing the "outside world." This is one of a few places in the park to do so.

Right when you're about to hop on the train, there is a **poster on the wall** that has a diagram of the giant soup can from the queue. The giant can in the queue says "Acorn Soup," the soup can in the diagram says "Walnut Soup." (*see photo*)

For a **list of this attractions Hidden Mickeys, see page 349**.

GOOFY'S PLAYHOUSE

March 6, 2006 - Duration: N/A

A playhouse for kids based on Goofy's house.

FUN FACTS

- It **used to be called** *Goofy's Bounce House*, and was a giant room that was inflatable. This was changed due to continual air leaks and was only available for little children.

- The pumpkin in the Jack-O-Lantern patch that has a regular face instead of a cut-out face is the **face of Jack Lindquist**, the first president of *Disneyland* from 1990-1993. (*see photo*)

MICKEY'S HOUSE AND MOVIE BARN

Opened January 24, 1993 - Duration: N/A

Mickey's House is in the corner of *Toontown* with a small detached garage to the left. Visitors enter Mickey's living room and walk through his house while viewing personal mementos and show business memorabilia. Check out the screening room, where a continuous film featuring segments from four of Mickey's early cartoons is shown on a bed sheet serving as a screen. Mickey's street address is #1 Mickey's Neighborhood Way. Before exiting the house, visitors have the option to go see Mickey Mouse and get their picture taken with him (this can sometimes be a 5 to a 45-minute wait).

FUN FACTS

- The only house to visit in *Toontown* that **can have a 20-minute** wait just to go inside.

- Mickey's dog, **Pluto, got his name in 1930,** due to the new discovery of the planet, Pluto.

- Mickey's House **contains four movie sets** for the meet and greet: Steamboat Willie, Fantasia, Band Concert and Through the Mirror. You can ask a Cast Member what would be a good time to return if you want a specific set.

- The *Movie Barn* is the section of the house where **you will be meeting Mickey Mouse** for a photo opportunity.

583

- Mickey's **house address is *1 Neighborhood Lane***. You can see this printed on the mail on his table inside.
- Did you notice Mickey's car? His **license plate is MICKEY1**.
- If you look closely around his house, **you can see props from his films**. The plane from *Plane Crazy* (1928), the outfits from *The Band Concert* (1935), the mop carrying buckets from *Fantasia* (1940) and many more.
- For a **list of this attractions Hidden Mickeys, see page 349**.

Minnie's House

Opened January 24, 1993 - Duration: N/A

Minnie's House, where guests could meet Minnie Mouse herself until 2004, now can meet her strolling around *Mickey's* Toontown. Minnie's dream home is right next door to *Mickey's House* in Toontown. Guests walk through *Minnie's House*, which has a delightfully whimsical decor. You'll find pictures of her favorite mouse, Mickey, as you stroll through.

FUN FACTS

- If you drop change in Minnie's wishing well out back, **you will hear her voice** talking back at you. That money is donated to charity.
- Check out **the cheese in Minnie's fridge**. She has Jack, Bob, Mouseerella, True Bleu, Gouda, Not So Gouda, and The Big Cheese.
- On the hills behind her house, you can see **trees in the shape of the letters WDI**, which stands for *Walt Disney Imagineering*.
- For a **list of this attractions Hidden Mickeys, see page 349**.

ROGER RABBIT'S CAR TOON SPIN

Opened January 24, 1994 - Duration: 3:30

Guests enter the *Toontown Cab Company* building which is the queue line for *Roger Rabbit's Car Toon Spin*. You will wander through back alleys, past Baby Herman's apartment, backstage at the *Ink & Paint Club*, and into an underworld hideout where "Dip," a deadly concoction of paint solvent, is secretly being stored in a plot to wipe out *Toontown*. You board a toon taxi and follow Roger and Benny's trail through town pursued by the weasels. Take control of the wheel, spinning your way through the Bullina China Shop, the local Power Plant, and the Gag Warehouse on a fast-paced spinning taxi cab. Guests ride in a car named Lenny,

resembling Benny the Taxi from the movie *Who Framed Roger Rabbit*, and travel through a story line that somewhat resembles that of the film.

FUN FACTS

- "DIP" is **the chemical used by Judge Doom** in the movie to erase toons from existence. It contains one part acetone, one part benzene, and one part turpentine.

- Marvin Acme's "Acme Warehouse" from the film is called the "Gag Warehouse," and the cans of "DIP" in the opening scene of the attraction **are real props from the film**. One has a dent from where Christopher Lloyd kicked it.

- This was the **only new "dark-ride" to open in *Disneyland*** during the whole decade of the 1980's.

- Roger Rabbit was such a popular character after the film's release that there were plans to make **Roger a star of his own land** behind *Main Street, U.S.A.* called *Hollywood Land*.

- Originally, **it was going to be two stories tall** with a similar riding system as *Haunted Mansion*, but they decided to go with a new design, which is what is in use today.

- Roger Rabbit, Judge Doom, and Baby Herman **almost got their own attractions** in *Disney's Hollywood Studios*, but due to budget cutbacks, they were never made.

585

- Unlike all of the other "dark-rides" of its kind, this one **has things to look at behind you, instead of just in front,** like all of the others because this is the only one where you can be facing any direction in a 360° radius.

- There are **several vanity plates hanging on the wall** at the end of the queue and as you exit the attraction.

FAN T C (Fantasy)	CAP 10 HK (Captain Hook)
RS2CAT (Aristocat)	101 DLMN (101 Dalmatians)
MR TOAD (Mr. Toad)	ZPD2DA (Zip-a-dee-doo-dah)
2N TOWN (Toontown)	L MERM8 (The Little Mermaid)
1DRLND (Wonderland)	1D N PTR (Wendy & Peter Pan)
BB WOLF (Big Bad Wolf)	IM L8 (I'm late - The White Rabbit)
3 LIL PIGS (Three Little Pigs)	

- Next to the attraction operator, there is a framed **$1 bill that has Roger Rabbit** on it. (*see photo*)

- In Baby Herman's nursery, you can see the **silhouette wallpaper pattern of Jessica Rabbit**.

- The voice cast reprised their same roles as in the film:
  - Charles Fleischer - Roger Rabbit, Benny the Cab, Greasy, and Psycho
  - Kathleen Turner (*Romancing the Stone*)- Jessica Rabbit
  - Jim Cummings - Baby Herman
  - David Lander (Squiggy from the TV show *Lavern and Shirley*) - Wiseguy
  - Fred Newman (*Doug, Harry And The Hendersons*) - Stupid
  - June Foray (see *Who Does That Voice* page 149) - Wheezy
  - Will Ryan - unnamed weasel

- For a **list of this attractions Hidden Mickeys, see page 349.**

TOMORROWLAND

Tomorrowland is one of the most popular lands in the whole park. This land represents the future, the opposite theme of *Main Street, U.S.A.,* which represents the past. Walt was always striving for the future and future technology as he showed it to the world with his television programs. This land is a representation of what Walt thought the future would hold.

"Tomorrow can be a wonderful age. Our scientists today are opening the doors of the Space Age to achievements that will benefit our children and generations to come. The Tomorrowland attractions have been designed to give you an opportunity to participate in adventures that are a living blueprint of our future." ~Walt Disney

FUN FACTS: 1955-1967

- The first *Tomorrowland* opened at *Disneyland* on July 17, 1955, with **only some of its planned attractions,** due to budget cuts.

- Because the timeline in the first park's construction was rushed, *Tomorrowland* **was the last land to be finished**.

- Walt Disney was reluctant to turn his land into a corporate showcase, but when the time crunch came, he accepted any offer he could. **Monsanto Chemicals, American Motors, Richfield Oil, and Dutch Boy Paint** were some of the many company showcases that were open in *Tomorrowland* in the first few years. For the first four years, most of *Tomorrowland* was generally open space.

- Since the park was on a strict budget, **one cost-cutting idea was to use the sets** from the 1954 movie *20,000 Leagues Under the Sea* as a walk-through attraction, (where *Star Tours* is now) which remained until 1966. A replica set can now be seen in *Disneyland Paris* as *Mysteries of the Nautilus*. The original pipe organ can be seen in the Ballroom Scene in *Haunted Mansion*.

- When it first opened, *Tomorrowland* represented the future. That is if you **count the year of 1986 as being the future**. That year was chosen because that was the year of Halley's Comet, just like for *Main Street, U.S.A.*

- *Tomorrowland* **once showcased the *House of The Future by Monsanto*.** It was made entirely out of plastic. It was a memorable attraction that you can see in old *Disneyland* photos. Its purpose was to show people what living would be like in the future set in 1986. It looked like a giant wheel of cut Brie cheese. The house was there for visitors to peruse from 1957-1967. It is said that during demolition, the wrecking ball bounced off the house. It was located where *Pixie Hollow* stands now. The concrete base was too large to break apart and remove, so Disney painted it green and used it as a planter box. In an effort to revive the "house of the future," Disney added a newer-style futuristic house to *Innoventions* and called it the *Innoventions Dream House*, and it cost $15 million to install.

FUN FACTS: 1967-1998

⚙ Walt Disney died in December of 1966, **almost seven months before** a vast new *Tomorrowland* opened.

⚙ In 1967, **the area was completely rebuilt with new attractions and scenery**. The original layout was demolished, and a new set of buildings was erected. The addition of the *Carousel Theater*, *Flight to the Moon* building, the *Adventure Thru Inner Space* building, a new *Circle-Vision* building, and the *PeopleMover/Rocket Jets* platform gave *Tomorrowland* the "World on the Move" theme. In time, Walt Disney's idea of a Space Port opened as *Space Mountain*. *Star Tours* and *Magic-Eye Theater* opened in places of older attractions.

⚙ During the late-1980's and early-1990's, **the planning phase of Michael Eisner's "Disney Decade"** called for both American *Tomorrowlands* to receive makeovers. "*Tomorrowland* 2055" was slated to be completed by the late-1990's. The back-story of this renovation would be that with mysterious alien relics having been excavated in *Disneyland*, aliens were given the signal that Earth was now ready for intergalactic tourism, and a century after *Disneyland's* opening, *Disneyland* would have become a popular destination for aliens visiting Earth. Within the new land were proposed attractions such as *ExtraTERRORestrial Alien Encounter,* which later made its debut in *Magic Kingdom* in Florida; the *Timekeeper*, the American version of *Disneyland Paris' Le Visionarium; Plectu's Fantastic Intergalactic Revue*, an Audio-Animatronic musical revue, and makeovers for classic attractions. However, due to financial difficulties surrounding the *EuroDisney* project, the plan was cut drastically and plans were shelved until 1997.

FUN FACTS: 1998

⚙ **A new *Tomorrowland* opened in 1998**, loosely based on *Disneyland Paris' Discoveryland* and a "retro-futurist" concept. In place of the slow-moving *PeopleMover* was the ill-fated *Rocket Rods*.

⚙ **Most of the attractions remained the same**, except for the removal of *Circle-Vision 360, Captain EO,* and *Mission to Mars* attraction theaters. The *Rocket Jets* were replaced by a similar attraction called the *Astro Orbitor* placed at the entrance of the land at ground level. The original *Rocket Jets* attraction mechanism remained intact atop the *Rocket Jets* queue, converted into an unmanned show element dubbed the "Observatron." Two Epcot attractions found their place in *Tomorrowland*, "*Honey, I Shrunk the Audience!*" (now gone) and "*Innoventions*." The whole land, including *Space Mountain*, was painted in bronzes, golds, and dark browns with emerald green trim on some attractions.

- The landscaping had apparent vegetable plots planted in some locations that made reference to "neo-agrarian" concepts (**meaning every plant is edible**). Some of these plants are mint, various types of lettuce, kale, artichokes, grapes, corn, beans, thyme, rosemary, chives, bananas, cabbage, strawberries, parsley, cilantro, kumquats, oranges, dwarf apples, and more.

- **The overhaul was unpopular among many fans**, and its flagship new attraction, *Rocket Rods*, closed in September 2000 for financial and mechanical reasons. Many shops and restaurants opened, but few new attractions were built in accordance with policies set by Paul Pressler and Cynthia Harriss, mandating the expansion of retail space. Many Disney fans complained that the space in *Tomorrowland* was poorly used and that lack of maintenance was taking its toll on the land. They also complained that the placement of the *Astro Orbitor* in *Tomorrowland's* entrance led to congestion problems. While some guests were pleased with the new color scheme and shift toward "future-that-never-was" elements, others claimed that *Tomorrowland* had taken a turn for the worse.

FUN FACTS: Present

- *Tomorrowland* has received the most facelifts and changes than any other land.

- In late 2003, Matt Ouimet became president of the *Disneyland* Resort and sought to change **some of the cost-cutting trends** established by the former management. *Space Mountain* was closed for two full years, as the entire attraction was refurbished and a new track was built. The empty *Rocket Rods* queue and the old *Circle-Vision Theater* were converted into *Buzz Lightyear Astro Blasters*.

- In February 2005, Walt Disney Imagineering approved a **repaint of Tomorrowland** for the *Happiest Homecoming on Earth 50th Anniversary Celebration*. The new paint scheme incorporates a mix of blue, white and silver while keeping a little of 1998's gold and bronze colors.

- Most of *Tomorrowland* has been repainted and **new plans are being considered** for the land.

- **There is an X-Wing Starfighter hanging from the ceiling** inside above where the *Starcade* was, adjacent to the upper level queue to *Space Mountain*. It once hung inside the *Star Trader* gift shop until its refurbishment.

- **New monorail trains** opened in late 2007.

- Rumors on some Disney-related internet forums have been abuzz over the **possible return of the *Rocket Rods*** to their original location, as well as plans for the *PeopleMover* track, which may include variable-speed personal gyroscopes, the pod transport system used by Syndrome in *The*

Incredibles, the *PeopleMover* seen in the futuristic city in the movie *Meet the Robinsons*, or a new *PeopleMover* altogether.

Push, the talking trash can, could be found rolling around *Tomorrowland*. Push was an interactive garbage can that could roll around and talk to people. He was remote controlled for an operator who was 10-15 feet away. They would have their hand in a satchel and have a mic near their mouth to control him and talk through the built-in speaker system. He first showed up in 1995 in *Magic Kingdom* and then eventually made his way to *Disneyland*. He could sometimes be found in other lands and even *California Adventure*. Push had his last day in *Magic Kingdom* on February 10, 2014. There was a social media outcry to save Push as people were hashtagging #savePUSH. Some say he retired because the contract with the engineering company that created him was up.

After the buyout of LucasFilm, rumors were also going around about **possibly making a whole *Star Wars* section** of *Tomorrowland* based on the films. Disney ended up deciding on just making a complete new land and placing it behind *Frontierland*. It needed to be in its own section of the park as the whole land will be one quarter the size of *Disneyland*.

Currently, the "Mayor" of *Tomorrowland* in *Disneyland* is an **Audio-Animatronic Robot named Tom Morrow** who is seen at *Innoventions*. He is voiced by actor Nathan Lane, who also voiced Timon in *The Lion King* movies.

Repurposed *PeopleMover* cars can be found in *The Little Green Men Store Command* (pin trader store) as the cashier counters.

Along the pathway going to the train station **there is a billboard that says Agrifuture**, which means "agriculture of the future." The Imagineers believe that in the future, due to shortage of land, people will have plants around their houses that both work as decoration and as food. As you may notice, all the plants in *Tomorrowland* are edible, or produce something edible.

The **Moonliner rocket in front of *Redd Rocket's Pizza Port*** is a replica of the one that stood 80 feet tall in front of *The Rocket to The Moon* (later named *Flight To The Moon*) attraction from 1955-1975.

For a **list of this attractions Hidden Mickeys, see page 349**.

590

Attractions

ASTRO ORBITOR

Opened May 24, 1998 - Duration: 1:30

Similar to the *Rocket Jets* of previous years, this is an attraction in which the Guests board a small, personal "spaceship" which then flies around in a circle in the air, going up and down around a type of high-tech maypole, just like *Dumbo The Flying Elephant*.

FUN FACTS

- 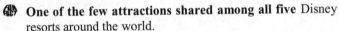 This attraction is **based on the classic attraction**, *Astro Jets*, that was renamed *Tomorrowland Jets* in 1964 after United Airlines (then sponsor of *The Enchanted Tiki Room*) complained by stating that it was free advertising for their opponent's American Airlines' coast-to-coast Astrojet service. It remained *Tomorrowland Jets* until the *Tomorrowland* revamp in 1966 when the attraction closed. It later re-opened in 1967 as *The Rocket Jets*. Then it was located in the center of *Tomorrowland* by the *PeopleMover* platform, which now houses the *Observatron*. One of the old *Rocket Jets* rockets can be found in *The Little Green Men Store Command* (pin trader store). It was converted into a display shelf.

- **One of the few attractions shared among all five** Disney resorts around the world.

- It is **styled after *Disneyland Paris*' version**, the *Orbitron*, which opened in 1992.

- This exact attraction can be found in *Magic Kingdom* as well, **but it is spelled *Orbiter***.

- One of the original designs suggested having people **load from below ground level**. Another suggested having water below, as on *Dumbo;* both were never used.

- It is said that Disney Imagineers used **drawings from Leonardo da Vinci's astrolabe** from nearly 500 years ago to develop a concept design.

- It is also said that this attraction **was built in Italy** and shipped over here.

- Many people agree that it **resembles Aughra's Observatory** (she's the ugly witch) in Jim Henson's *The Dark Crystal* (1982).

591

- The *Rocket Jets* that preceded this attraction **had eight rockets to ride in;** this one has twelve.
- On the 12 rockets, **there are the 12 astrological symbols** for the astrological calendar. Ask a Cast Member if you can sit in the one that represents your month of birth.

⋀UTOPI⋀

Opened July 17, 1955 - Duration: 5:00

Guests drive small cars around a guided track retaining relative freedom, but not the ability to drive off the course (this was a lesson the *Disneyland* officials learned the hard way).

FUN FACTS

- One of the **original attractions** from opening day.
- The **name comes from combing two words**, AUTomobile & utOPIA.
- Each car can top out at speeds pushing **seven miles per hour**.
- Each car **has seven horsepower**.
- There were a **total of three different Autopias**:
  - *Autopia* in *Tomorrowland* 1955-present
  - *Junior Autopia* in *Fantasyland* 1956-1958, then 1959-1999
  - *Midget Autopia* in the *Fantasyland* area which is near *it's a small world* 1957-1966
- When the *Midget Autopia* **was removed, it was donated** to a park in Walt's hometown of Marceline, Missouri. However, because it was too costly to upkeep, they were forced to remove it. One of the green *Midget* cars was donated to the Walt Disney museum in that town. The cars ran there for 11 years before it got too costly to maintain.
- The **current version is a consolidation of the two** former *Autopias*. One was the regular *Autopia* track in *Tomorrowland* and the other was the *Junior Autopia* track in *Fantasyland*. Both attractions were separate until their closure in 1999 and were combined for their re-opening in 2000 with their Chevron sponsor.
- On the left side of the track, shortly after you take off from the loading zone, there is a **bronzed statue of a *Midget Autopia* car** to pay homage to the past attraction. It was one of the working vehicles from Marceline's *Midget Autopia* after it closed. (*see photo*)

- **Imagineer Bob Gurr** (see *Imagineer Mini Biographies* page 287) was brought in as a consultant for the design of these little cars. Walt liked his work so much that he offered him a permanent job. Here is a photo of Bob Gurr sitting in an Autopia car at the Disneyana Convention in July, 2016. (*see photo*)

- This attraction has **been updated several times** since 1955; most recently on June 29, 2000.

- The **"Route 55" signs** on the track pay homage to Autopia's opening year. (*see photo*)

- In 2005, rumors circulated that Disney was planning on developing an overlay that would **tie in with the Pixar film** *Cars*, which would have required the attraction going down sometime in 2006. However, this did not happen. That attraction was moved over to *California Adventure* and the design concepts were changed to make it a high-speed attraction similar to *Test Track* in *Epcot*. It was then named *Radiator Springs Racers*.

- The future prospect for the current *Autopia* cars is to be eventually **replaced with electric cars**, if that system is able to prove itself in the *Hong Kong Disneyland* version of the attraction.

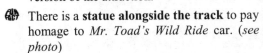

- There is a **statue alongside the track** to pay homage to *Mr. Toad's Wild Ride* car. (*see photo*)

- The **vehicles come in 12 different colors**, including "chromalusion," which is a color that changes, depending on the angle you are looking at it from. To achieve this effect, the paint contains tiny synthetic flakes about one micrometer thick. The flakes are constructed of aluminum coated with glass-like magnesium fluoride embedded in semi-translucent chromium. The aluminum and chrome gives the paint a vibrant metallic sparkle, while the glass-like coating acts like a refracting prism, changing the apparent color of the surface as the observer moves around.

- This is the **last surviving attraction** in *Tomorrowland* that was here on opening day.

- When *Autopia* **first opened, it didn't have a track for the cars to stay on.** There were curbs alongside the race track and bumpers surrounding the cars. It was changed to the current track design with the center rail in 1965 because, if cars hit the curbs hard enough, they would hop out of the track.

- To go along with the original "no track" design, the Imagineers had to **test drive the first cars, with no bumpers**. With all the bumping and crashing, they decided to add the full perimeter bumpers around each car. There was still damage happening to the cars, so the spring-loaded bumpers were added by opening day.

- *Disneyland* **went through several designs and adjustments to the cars' design** in the beginning. The first fleet of cars was dubbed the "Mark I" fleet. From 1955 to 1958 they went through the "Mark I," "Mark II," "Mark III" & "Mark IV" designs. The "Mark V" design came out in 1959 and lasted until the "Mark VI" came out in 1964. In 1967 the "Mark VII" was invented and they lasted until 1999. When the refurbishment occurred for the opening in 2000, they débuted the "Mark VIII," which is the current version.

- Each "Mark VII" **vehicle cost $5,000** to make.

- **Chevron was the sponsor** from 2000-2012.

- The attraction closed on January 11, 2016, for updates and re-opened April 29, 2016, with **Honda as the new sponsor.** It closed and then re-opened again on March 24, 2017, to show that Honda added their android ASIMO, Advanced Step in Innovative Mobility, to scenes around the attraction. ASIMO was once inside *Innoventions*. He has a pet robotic bird with him named "Bird." The project update was headed up by Imagineer Kim Irvine, daughter of Leota Toombs, the face of Madam Leota in *Haunted Mansion*. Kim is the current face of Madam Leota in the *Haunted Mansion Holiday* overlay. (*see photo*)

- For a **list of this attractions Hidden Mickeys, see page 349**.

Buzz Lightyear Astro Blasters

Opened April 15, 2004 - Duration: 5:00

Guests ride in spaceship-like cars armed with infrared laser guns. Guests must shoot at targets and accumulate points to attain high scores.

FUN FACTS

- Emperor Zurg is **voiced by Andrew Stanton**. He also voiced Zurg in *Toy Story 2* (1999) and *Toy Story 3* (2010). He also voiced Crush in the film *Finding Nemo* (2003), and was the director/writer for the film as well. He was involved somehow in all the Pixar films. Andrew's first live-action film to write and direct was *John Carter* (2012). He recently reprised his roles of Crush and Emperor Zurg in the video game *Kinect Disneyland Adventures*.

- This building **used to house *Circle-Vision 360*** and the queue for *Rocket Rods*.

594

There are two Evil Emperor Zurg characters on the attraction. A few inches below the emblem of the "Z" on his chest plate, is a hole about the size of a dime. Shooting in that hole is **worth 50,000 points**.

One of the few attractions shared among all five Disney resorts around the world.

There are **four target shapes**. This list is the order of the point value of each shape.

- Circle - 100 points
- Square – 1,000 points
- Diamond – 5,000 points
- Triangle – 10,000 points
- Zurg's Chest – 50,000 points

When a **target is lit up**, it is worth more points.

If you **shoot a target repeatedly**, it is worth more points.

As you go through the "speed tunnel" before the final room, **there is a target hidden on the wall** to the right when you first enter it and to the left before you exit. There are also two targets on the ceiling. All these targets are difficult to see until they light up. However, when they do, keep shooting to skyrocket your score.

Take note that there are **no targets on any of the good guys**.

The brand name on the batteries on this attraction is "Megavolt." The evil character **Megavolt from the television series Darkwing Duck** (1991-1992) inspired the name. (*see photo*)

The different ranking levels with the qualifying score:

- Level 1 Star Cadet: 0 – 1,000
- Level 2 Space Ace: 1,001 – 10,000
- Level 3 Planetary Pilot: 10,001 – 100,000
- Level 4 Space Scout: 100,001 – 300,000
- Level 5 Ranger 1st Class: 300,001 – 600,000
- Level 6 Cosmic Commando: 600,001 – 999,999
- Level 7 Galactic Hero: 1,000,000 +

Your **score readout can max out at 999,999** points. If you max out, keep shooting; your total score will be visible on the photo they take of you. As you exit the attraction, there are several computer monitors where you can view your picture. Choose your photo, and then email it to yourself. If you scored well, your placing for the day at that point is listed above your photo.

- 🏰 For this attraction, **Pat Fraley does the voice of Buzz** instead of Tim Allen. Pat has done voice work in over 150 films and television shows.

- 🏰 This building **used to house** *the Circle-Vision 360° theater.*

- 🏰 If you look closely at **the giant 9-volt batteries**, they say, "**Made in Glendale, California, USA, Earth, Gamma Quadrant.**" The Walt  Disney Imagineering Department is located in Glendale, California. (*see photo*)

- 🏰 In the final scene where they take your photo and you get one last chance to fire upon Zurg, **there is a cartoon moon and sun** on the wall up toward the ceiling, above the  tunnel that you enter the room through. They are left over from the previous attraction that was housed in here, *Circle-Vision 360* (now located in the China section of *Epcot*) and *Circarama.* (*see photo*)

- 🏰 For a **list of this attractions Hidden Mickeys, see page 349**.

DISNEYLAND MONORAIL

Opened June 14, 1959 - Duration: 13:00

This monorail train currently travels over *Tomorrowland, Fantasyland,* the entrance to *California Adventure,* and the *Downtown Disney District* with stops at *Tomorrowland* and at *Downtown Disney,* near the *Disneyland Hotel.* The *Disneyland* version has had five different series of monorails since 1959 (Marks I, II, III and V). It was recently overhauled again on July 3, 2008, to a Mark VII.

FUN FACTS

- 🏰 It cost **$2,480,000 to build**.

- 🏰 They can reach a **speed of up to 35 miles per hour**.

- 🏰 The **track length is 2.5 miles**.

- 🏰 There are **three trains** - Red, Orange and Blue.

- 🏰 In May 2012, the monorail got a makeover to tie it in with the opening of the new *Cars Land*. **The trains were given faces that resemble characters** from the *Cars* films. Each train has its own name and personality. The train speaks to the passengers with their own voice and accent. The blue train is

596

Mandy Monorail, the orange train is *Mona Monorail,* and the red train is *Manny Monorail*.

- In **the sing-along songs** video *Disneyland Fun*, during "Zip-a-Dee-Doo-Dah," the *Monorail* was briefly seen.

- It was the first daily operating monorail **in the western hemisphere**, as well as the first in the United States.

- There have been five different models of the Monorail since 1959:
  - Mark I - 1959-1961 (built by ALWEG)
    - o 3-car trains
    - o Colors: red and blue

  - Mark II - 1961-1969 (built by ALWEG)
    - o 4-car trains
    - o Bigger dome on top of front car
    - o Colors: red, blue and yellow

  - Mark III - 1969-1987 (built by Walt Disney Imagineering/WED Enterprises)
    - o 5-car trains
    - o 137 feet (41.76 m) long
    - o Colors: red, blue, yellow, and green.

  - Mark V - 1987-2008 (built by Walt Disney Imagineering/WED Enterprises)
    - o 5-car trains
    - o Total number of passengers per train: 132
    - o Colors: red, blue, orange, and purple

  - Mark VII - 2008–Present (built by Dynamic Structures)
    - o Has a new island seating configuration, with one row of inward-facing seating at the front and rear of each car.
    - o The main cabins have a capacity of 22 passengers
    - o Colors: red, blue, and orange

DISNEYLAND RAILROAD

Opened July 17, 1955 - Duration: 18:00

The *Disneyland Railroad* has a station in *Tomorrowland*.

See Other Details in The Description From *Main Street, U.S.A.*

FINDING NEMO

SUBMARINE VOYAGE

Opened June 11, 2007 - Duration: 15:00 – 20:00

A re-theming of the classic *Submarine Voyage* attraction using underwater projections and Audio-Animatronics based on the 2003 Pixar film *Finding Nemo*.

FUN FACTS

- The attraction uses **the same submarines** used in the former *Submarine Voyage* that existed from 1959 to 1998.

- The **submarines do not actually submerge**; they are boats in which the passenger seating area is below the water level.

- When the attraction originally opened as *Submarine Voyage* in **1959, it was one of the first "E-ticket" rides**, along with the *Matterhorn Bobsleds*.

- The creation of the subs in Todd Shipyards in San Pedro, California, **was overseen by Joe Fowler,** the retired Navy Admiral who was hired to oversee the construction of *Disneyland* (see *Imagineer Mini Biographies* page 287).

- Above the loading dock there are some **pipes with "TL59" stenciled on them**. It stands for "Tomorrowland 1959," when the attraction first opened. (*see photo*)

- Originally, it was **never intended to be submarines**, but glass bottomed boats.

- After the closure in 1998, it was said that the attraction would return in 2003 with a **theme based on Disney's 41st animated feature** *Atlantis: The Lost Empire* (2001). Due to its failure in the box office, they scrapped that idea.

- The subs **used to use diesel fuel, but are now electric**. They are charged at the loading dock by "no contact" inductive coils, while the next load of passengers board.

- Submarines **have 40 seats** each, but do allow lap sitting.

- While on the subs, you are taking an ocean tour provided by the **Nautical Exploration and Marine Observation Research Center**, or N.E.M.O. for short.

- A new version of the attraction, the **Marine Observation Outpost**, or "MOO" for short, has been provided for Guests with physical disabilities who cannot navigate the submarine spiral staircases or who are claustrophobic. The observation outpost allows Guests to experience the entire attraction in high definition on a plasma screen.

- There are **6.3 million gallons of water** on the attraction. Originally, it was 9 million; changes were made to conserve water.

- Each submarine **cost about $80,000**.

- Each submarine is **52 feet in length**.

- These submarines **run on electricity**.

- The eight *Disneyland* submarines make up the 8th **largest "submarine" fleet in the world.**

- All the **individual submarine names** are as follows:
  - *Nautilus*
  - *Scout*, formerly Neptune, formerly Seawolf
  - *Voyager*, formerly Sea Star, formerly Skate
  - *Mariner*, formerly Explorer, formerly Skipjack
  - *Seafarer*, formerly Seeker, formerly Triton
  - *Explorer*, formerly Argonaut, formerly George Washington
  - *Neptune*, formerly Triton, formerly Patrick Henry
  - *Argonaut*, formerly Sea Wolf, formerly Ethan Allen

- On the original attraction, the captain would announce that **there was a sea serpent** out the port hole right before you docked. Although the sea serpent is no longer mentioned, it can still be seen. The original goofy-faced serpent was sold at auction, so a stand-in, serpent-shaped stone covered in barnacles remains in its place as a tribute. (*see photo*)

- The coral was **painted with a special technique that uses glass.** *Disneyland* used over 30 tons of recycled glass in 40 different colors to do this. By using this technique, they are permanent and won't have to be repainted, so it saves time and money for the future It also helps the environment. There were several colors created just for the lagoon, including Split Pea, Mango Mud, and Aqua Jazz.

- Walt was first inspired to create *Submarine Voyage* after seeing the footage of the **undersea exploration done by the USS Nautilus** on August 3,

1958. It was completed under the polar ice caps. Some of the attraction simulated that voyage.

🔱 Originally, the subs were painted military grey. When they received a facelift in 1986, **they were painted yellow to represent research subs**, which are also yellow. They are yellow because that is the last color that can be seen at great depths before disappearing.

🔱 From 1965-1967, **there used to be mermaids basking in the sun** on the coral reefs. Not real mermaids, but Cast Members dressed as such. For four hours each day in the summer time, these mermaids would lie around and conduct underwater stunts for passersby. Disney discontinued this when some of the girls started complaining about the diesel fumes from the subs (now they are electric) and the highly chlorinated water. There were also issues with large crowds blocking the walkway between the *Matterhorn* and the lagoon just so they could see them. Men would wrap up quarters with dollar bills and toss them to the sea sirens. There were several instances when young men had to be retrieved from the lagoon once they dove in after the mermaids. I have read that the Cast Members portraying mermaids made $1.65 an hour.

STAR WARS LAUNCH BAY

Opened November 16, 2015 - Duration: N/A

This exhibit is set up in the *Innoventions* building. *Innoventions* vacated the no-longer-rotating facade in 2015. It opened with the kickoff of *Disneyland's Season of the Force*.

FUN FACTS

🔱 Throughout the building and the rest of *Tomorrowland*, you can see weird lettering on plaques and displays. **This alphabet is called Aurebesh**. It is a writing system used to transcribe Galactic Standard, a language most prevalent in the Star Wars universe. You can use this chart to translate for you.

ᛕ	ᗱ	ᛁᛁ	ᚖ	Ⅵ	᚛	ᗡ	ᗃ	1	ᗔ	ᗡ	ᐱ	ᒪ
A	B	C	D	E	F	G	H	I	J	K	L	M
ᗰ	△	ᗪ	ᒋ	ᚖ	ᗔ	↓	ᗇ	Y	◻	△	ᐯ	ᗡ
N	O	P	Q	R	S	T	U	V	W	X	Y	Z

🔱 **Star Wars shared the building with *Super Hero HQ*** and was located in the lower level of the building.

On display, you can **see models of ships and vehicles from the Star Wars universe**, along with character costumes from the films.

When the attraction first opened, g**uests could meet Darth Vader**, Boba Fett, and Chewbacca.

In January 2016, **they introduced Kylo Ren** to greet Guests there by replacing Darth Vader, since they did not exist at the same time in the films.

Boba Fett left when Kylo Ren showed up for these same reasons.

There had been **many complaints from Guests about Kylo Ren's demeanor**. The actor in costume stays in character and is rude and intrusive to Guests, sometimes bringing small children to tears. When you first met him, he got in your face and asked if you are part of the Resistance or the First Order. He would then press you for information on the whereabouts of the droid because it has the plans to the Death Star. Legitimate Star Wars fans loved the character and their interaction with him.

Darth Vader returned and replaced Kylo Ren in October 2016 in preparations for *Rogue One: A Star Wars Story* (2016), as he reappeared in that film. Boba Fett also returned.

SPACE MOUNTAIN

Re-opened July 15, 2005 - Duration: 2:45

An indoor roller coaster in the dark. The original white exterior was painted green/gold in 1997, only to be restored to its original white in late 2003. This is one of the most popular attractions in the whole park.

FUN FACTS

⚙ The attraction **originally opened May 27, 1977**, cost $20 million, and took two years to build. The attraction unexpectedly closed April 10, 2003, for its refurbishment.

⚙ The attraction's **re-opening was part of *Disneyland's* 50th anniversary** celebration.

⚙ It makes **four left hand turns and thirteen right hand turns**.

⚙ It reaches speeds of up to **32 mph**.

⚙ The track **tops out at 128 feet** into the air.

⚙ This is **the tallest "mountain" attraction in *Disneyland***, track wise. You may think it is the *Matterhorn*, but those tracks only go 2/3 of the way up. This one is inside, so you do not even notice how high you are going.

⚙ Its opening weekend was over Memorial Day. The park had an **attendance of 185,500 guests** over that 3-day weekend.

⚙ **There was going to be a *Science Land* behind *Tomorrowland*** back in the late-1950's, but it never happened. It was to be where *Space Mountain* is now. The name was later changed to *Adventures in Science* and was going to have four attractions in it;

- A "Powercade" which was to be an entrance display of motors and gears and sponsored by GM.
- A "time travel" exhibit which more than likely became the *Primeval World* in the diorama on the train.
- An outer space attraction that would surpass the *Rocket to The Moon* attraction.
- A "Micro World" where guests would shrink down and travel into a drop of water. More than likely this was the precursor to the *Adventure Thru Inner Space* in which guests would shrink down and travel through a snow flake.

⚙ The first **soundtrack for the rockets was not added until 1996**. The idea was to fuse together two iconic musical forms of the 1960's, sci-fi horror and surf. For the first half of the track, they used music from Camille Saint-Saëns' (a music composer from the late-1800's and early-1900's) musical work of "The Carnival of the Animals." Guitarist Dick Dale was recorded playing his surfing style music for part of it. The present-day soundtrack was created by composer Michael Giacchino who is credited for composing the music for films like *The Incredibles* (2004) and *Mission Impossible III* (2006).

⚜ The "re-entry" zip noise is actually the sound of a **jet airplane played backwards**.

⚜ Some of the "stars" are actually **made by a disco ball** near the third lift hill. The others are light bulbs on the track and on the supports.

⚜ **Walt Disney actually came up with the concept** for this attraction in the 1960's, but they had to wait 12 years for technology to catch up with Walt's vision to make it happen.

⚜ The track layout is an **exact replica of the original track** built in 1977, but the foundation is 30 feet lower in the ground.

⚜ The **original rockets used to glow in the dark;** these new rockets do not.

⚜ The **first *Space Mountain* built was in *Disney World's* Magic Kingdom** in 1974, but has a two-track system.

⚜ **Fed Ex was one of the sponsors** in the past. They also sponsored the one in Florida.

⚜ **One of the few attractions shared** among all five Disney resorts around the world.

⚜ Among the **first people to ride after its first opening** in 1977 were the first Americans in space, NASA's Mercury Astronauts: Scott Carpenter, Gordon Cooper, John Glenn, Wally Schirra, Alan Shepard, and Deke Slayton.

⚜ At the grand re-opening in 2005 Disney had a **guest speaker, Neil Armstrong**, the first astronaut on the moon.

⚜ Since its first opening, **there have been 170 million *Tomorrowland* "astronauts"** who have ridden it. Total track covered since then has been over 9 million miles. That's enough distance to travel back and forth to the moon 18 times.

⚜ There is a code number above the space ship in the boarding area. It used to read **DL2000, which stands for Disney Land 2000**, meaning the future. Now that the year 2000 has passed, it has been changed to DL3000.

⚜ There are several instances when **you will notice "SMS - 077"** around the queue inside. This stands for "Space Mountain 1977," the year it opened.

⚜ The **ghost story of "Disco Debbie"** is from this attraction. Before they filled in the windows in the queue, where you enter the building, with metal, they were glass and you could see the track inside. It is said that the ghost of Debbie would appear to people peering through the window.

⚜ **This attraction's origins date back to 1964** as an attraction that Walt wanted for his park. He worked with Imagineer John Hench to design an inside thrill ride with four tracks of which they could control the environment.

603

- The **initial name for** *Space Mountain* **was** *Space Port*. It was not until 1966 that the name *Space Mountain* become the permanent title.
- The construction of the mountain **was planned for the 1967** *Tomorrowland* **makeover**, but with Walt passing away, and the lack of space in the area, the project got pushed to the back burner.
- *Space Mountain,* in its various forms, **can be found in all five Disney** parks (pre-*Shanghai Disneyland*). They all opened at different times;
  - *Magic Kingdom* opened January 15, 1975
  - *Disneyland* opened May 27, 1977
  - *Tokyo Disney* opened April 15, 1983
  - *Disneyland Paris* opened June 1, 1995
  - *Hong Kong Disneyland* opened September 12, 2005 (first SM to open with the park)
  - *Shanghai Disneyland* opened June 16, 2016, but did not get a *Space Mountain*. Instead, they got *TRON Lightcycle Power Run*.
- **In 1973, Imagineers re-visited Walt's "Space Port" idea** and broke ground for construction in *Magic Kingdom*. The first *Space Mountain* opened there in 1975.
- Following the success of the first one, *Disneyland* **broke ground just months after** *Magic Kingdom's* **opening**. *Disneyland's* version would open two and a quarter years behind the first one.
- **This version has side-by-side seating**, unlike the *Magic Kingdom* version, which is row seating, like the *Splash Mountain* logs. In addition, the *Magic Kingdom* version has two tracks and can load two cars at a time, like the *Matterhorn Bobsleds*.
- The *Disneyland Paris* version differs from all the others **because it has a launch and an inversion**, like *California Screamin'* and *Hollywood Studio's Rock 'n' Roller Coaster*.
- The original height of the exterior of the mountain was going to be too tall and could have been seen from *Main Street, U.S.A.*, thereby breaking the illusion on the 1920's from that perspective. To remedy this issue, **there was a 17-foot deep hole dug out** for the mountain to be built in. That is equal to about two stories, or about the height of the *Main Street, U.S.A.* buildings.
- The **cost to build such an attraction was a staggering $20 million**. That is $3 million more than the cost of *Disneyland* itself. Accounting for inflation, it would cost over $84 million today.
- The **total track distance is 2/3 of a mile**, making it 60 feet shorter than *Magic Kingdom's*.
- This attraction can pump through **1,800 Guests an hour** in its 12 cars.
- Following the track design of the *Matterhorn Bobsleds*, this too has a **steel cylindrical track containing 100 psi of air** inside it to detect any leaks, or cracks in the track.

604

- Due to the need of projections inside, the **support beams are on the exterior of the mountain**, leaving the ceiling inside smooth. (*see photo*)

- One of the reasons why it feels like you are going so fast is because of the **fans near the track**. They are blowing towards the riders to make it seem like you are going faster than you actually are.

- Aarin Richard and Imagineer Eddie Soto **added the soundtrack in 1996**.

- **Dick Dale, who also did a rendition of Wipe Out**, the opening music to Pulp Fiction, music in *Space Jam, Escape from L.A.,* and *Aloha Scooby-Doo*, composed the music for this attraction.

- After the re-opening on July 15, 2005, a new soundtrack was added. **The new soundtrack was created by composer Michael Giacchino.** Michael is known for composing music for films such as *Mission: Impossible III, The Incredibles, Star Trek, Star Trek Into Darkness, Star Trek Beyond, Ratatouille, Up, Super 8, Cars 2, 50/50, John Carter, Dawn of the Planet of the Apes, Jurassic World, Inside Out, Zootopia, The Muppets' Wizard of Oz, Rogue One: A Star Wars Story, Doctor Strange, Spider-Man: Homecoming, Tomorrowland, Jupiter Ascending, Sky High, War For The Planet Of The Apes, Jurassic World 2, The Incredibles 2, and music for the attraction Star Tours: The Adventures Continue.*

- In 1997, the exterior was painted green, gold, copper, and bronze **to give it a "steampunk" look**. It was changed back to white for the re-opening in 2005.

- The **speed ramps on the front of the attraction facade were removed in 1997** and people had to walk up the ramps after that.

- From 1994 until 2003, **the attraction was sponsored by FedEx**.

- SM TV (Space Mountain Television) was a fake TV station Disney made to play on the televisions while Guests stood in line. It played out much like MTV did. **Mario Lopez was one of the announcers on the show.** Since the attraction was sponsored by FedEx at the time, there were a few commercials that aired to promote them. The whole television set up by FedEx was only there for about 10 years before it was removed.

- **Each spaceship is actually weighed before takeoff**. This is done to properly stagger the takeoff of each ship. The ships that weigh more will travel faster and reach the end sooner than the lighter ones.

- The **order/pickup windows for *Space Place*** were over by where the *Space Mountain* FastPass distribution and entrance is now. Guests had to order their food there and walk up the walkway to where the 670 seats and tables were located. That walkway is now used as the *Space Mountain* queue since the removal of the speed ramp out front. *Space Place* closed in 1996 and was replaced by *Toy Story Funhouse*.

- A transformation takes place during Halloween time when **they change the attraction into *Space Mountain: Ghost Galaxy***. The new attraction was first featured in the 2009 Halloween Time festivities. *Ghost Galaxy* was featured at Hong Kong's version of the attraction in 2008. It is so far unknown if this will continue to be an annual refurbishment like *Haunted Mansion's Christmas/Halloween* transformation. *Space Mountain* will stay decorated from September 25 through November 1, the same time as the Halloween festivities.

- In 2015, Space Mountain received **another overlay in the form of *Hyperspace Mountain***. It opened with the *Seasons of the Force* event on November 14, 2015. In this overlay, Admiral Ackbar sends you into battle on your way to Jakku. This overlay utilizes the projectors installed for *Ghost Galaxy*. An assortment of music composed by John Williams and performed by the London Symphony is played. While soaring through space in the middle of battle you will see X-Wing Starfighters and TIE Fighters, along with a Star Destroyer.

- For a **list of this attractions Hidden Mickeys, see page 349**.

STAR TOURS:

THE ADVENTURES CONTINUE

Opened June 3, 2011 - Show length: 4:30

A motion-simulation attraction based on George Lucas's *Star Wars* universe. Ride it many times, for every experience will be different.

FUN FACTS

- *Adventure Thru Inner Space* **was originally located** inside this building.

- The **original** *Star Tours* **opened January 9, 1987,** and closed on July 27, 2010, to make way for the newly-recorded film and updated technology with 3D viewing and a new cast of characters.

- This version of *Star Tours* **pre-dates the previous version**. Now you will be riding in a StarSpeeder 1000, whereas before you rode in a StarSpeeder 3000.

- The first *Star Tours* **timeline was set after the film** *Star Wars 6: Return of the Jedi* (1983). This one is set in the timeline between *Star Wars 3: Revenge of the Sith* (2005) and *Star Wars 4: A New Hope* (1977). Which would make it set in the same time as *Rogue One: A Star Wars Story* (2016).

- While waiting in line, a voice announcement calls out for an illegally parked speeder, **license number THX-1138**, which is the name of George Lucas' famous USC student film, as well as the name of his first film made for commercial distribution in 1971.

- On the PA system in the waiting area, a voice says, **"Mr. Egroeg Sacul, Mr. Egroeg Sacul."** The name is "George Lucas" spelled backwards.

- On the PA system in the waiting area, **a voice page says "Mr. Tom Morrow,"** who was a character in *Flight to the Moon* (he later became Mr. Johnson for the overhaul called *Mission to Mars*, which closed in 1992). He later became a separate character for the attraction *Innoventions*, which opened in 1998.

- *Disneyland* purchased **four large military flight simulators** for $500,000 each to use as the Starspeeders.

- The finished **cost to build the original attraction in 1987 was $32 million**. That is twice the cost to build all of *Disneyland* in 1954.

- The C-3PO and R2-D2 in the queue are **actual props from the *Star Wars*** movies that have been fitted with Audio-Animatronics. (*see photo*)

The G2 repair droids (a model of droid used for fixing other droids) in the queue line are actually the **skeletons of two goose Audio-Animatronics** from *America Sings*. They were removed from the show for this attraction during the last two years of its run. (*see photo*)

Patrick Warburton provides the voice for the G2-4T droid that is doing the body scans near the end of the queue. Patrick also provides the voice for the AC-38 droid that is supposed to be piloting the ship. You can also see him on the attraction *Soarin' Around the World* in *California Adventure* as the flight attendant. (*see photo*)

While waiting in line, you can see the prototype for the Rex droid that will be piloting the future *Star Tours* StarSpeeder 3000. (*see photo*)

Tom Fitzgerald, the Executive VP and Senior Creative Executive of Walt Disney Imagineering, returned to again **provide the voice for the G2-9T droid** as he did for the first *Star Tours* in 1987. The G2-9T droid is the first droid you pass in the queue, the one doing the baggage security checks.

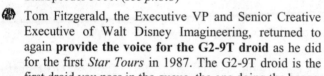

Watch the G2-9T droid as he scans the luggage. There are 71 scans to see and a few little jokes that come along with the scans as stated by the droid. They have changed slightly over the past few years after its opening, but here are a few of them:

- You can see a robotic hand that is said to belong to Luke Skywalker.
- When he sees a Goofy hat he says, "*Souvenir hats in the shape of Jar-Jar Binks, how goofy is that?*"
- Mr. Incredible's super suit.
- Genie's lamp.
- Major Domo and Minor Domo, the drum android, from *Captain EO*.
- Some battle droid heads that say "Rodger," to which the G2 droid says "*You can call me Roger if you want to*," making a reference to Bambi.
- An Ewok playing the drums on the helmet of a Storm Trooper.
- A Buzz Lightyear toy to which G2 says, "*To Tatooine... and beyond!*"
- A prototype droid of the future captain, Rex.
- Lando Calirissian's luggage.
- C3-PO.
- Pod racing gear.

608

- Space helmets. The oxygen tanks are labeled with the old logo for *Space Mountain* and "DASA" (Disneyland Aeronautical and Space Administration) – both from *Disneyland* in the 1970's. G2-9T ignores all that, though. Instead, he sings "*Star Tours, nothing but Star Tours*" which is an adaptation of the "Star Wars" song created by Bill Murray on *Saturday Night Live*.
- Wall-E, and then in a later scan you see Wall-E's stuff: lights, a VHS tape, a shoe with a plant growing in it.
- Some pirate gear, including Hook's hook.
- R2-D2 Mickey Mouse ears.
- A Monster's, Inc. teddy bear.
- Items that look like letters, but make up a riddle, O-bee-wand-key-N-"o"-B (Obi Wan Kenobi).
- Indiana Jones' luggage with contains a fedora and a whip.
- A Madam Leota head from *Haunted Mansion*.
- A microscope and a big snowflake to pay homage to *Star Tours* predecessor *Adventure Thru Inner Space*.
- Another pair of Mickey ears with the name "Luke" stitched on the back.
- A plush

In one of the bags the G2 droid scans **you can see V.I.N.CENT**, the android from the Disney film *The Black Hole* (1979), who was voiced by Roddy McDowall and also known for his voice as Mr. Soil (cranky old ant) from *A Bug's Life* (1998). He also starred in *Bedknobs and Broomsticks* (1971), *Planet of the Apes* (1968), *That Darn Cat!* (1965) and over 250 other films and television series.

After crashing down on Coruscant, the Starspeeder lands on a platform and nearly misses a fuel tanker truck. The truck was placed there to pay homage to the **fuel tanker truck in the original show**.

When entering the asteroid field near the Death Star, C-3PO says, "*I have a bad feeling about this.*" This **was one of the lines that was spoken by Rex** the pilot in the original attraction that was voiced by Paul Reubens.

The voice actress that portrays Aly San San, the android stewardess in **the pre-boarding video, is none other than Alyson Janney**. She is known for her roles in *10 Things I Hate About You* (1999), *Drop Dead Gorgeous* (1999), *American Beauty* (1999), *Nurse Betty* (2000), *Finding Nemo* (2003), *The West Wing* (1999-2006) and dozens more. The most common
place to recognize her is in your car. She is the spokeswoman for *Kaiser Permanente* and can be heard on the radio frequently in their commercials.

The rest of the cast:
  ○ Dee Bradley Baker - Boba Fett (voice)
  ○ Anthony Daniels - C-3PO (voice)
  ○ Carrie Fisher - Princess Leia (new voice with archive footage)
  ○ Tom Fitzgerald - G2-9T (voice)

- ° Sterling Hedgpeth - Rebel pilot
- ° James Earl Jones - Darth Vader (voice)
- ° Tom Kane - Admiral Ackbar (voice)
- ° Marianne McLean - Mon Mothma
- ° Frank Oz - Yoda (voice)
- ° Paul Reubens - RX-24 (voice) (archive sound)
- ° Fred Tatasciore - Gungan captain (voice)
- ° John Boyega - Finn
- ° Marianne McLean - Mon Mothma
- ° Lindsay Schnebly - AC-38 "Ace" (the pilot droid)
- ° Robin Atkin Downes - Security guard
- ° Rob Howe - Rebel pilot
- ° April Royster - Naboo squad leader
- ° Darren Criss - miscellaneous voices

The giant screen you see while waiting in the queue originally had another screen there for the previous attraction, *Adventure Thru Inner Space*. **The screen was used to show Guests a giant, colorful snowflake**.

The queue when you first enter is **still the original attraction queue**. The Omnimover load area was located past where C-3PO is standing.

The giant microscope from *Adventure Thru Inner Space* that **the Omnimover entered was in the spot that houses the Starspeeder**.

In the original film, **you could see a giant microscope prop in the first scene** when you fly out of the hanger. It is just to the right before you exit through the opening into space. Look it up on YouTube.

The FastPass **distribution machines are modeled after the Power Droids** from the *Star Wars* movies. (*see photo*)

There are **54 different possibilities in the story line** on this attraction. The entire attraction's sequence is randomized. This type of experience is known as a "Choose Its Own Adventure" because it has a branching narrative. The system chooses the course of each specific ride, just like in *Indiana Jones Adventure*. This gives *Star Tours* the advantage of different experiences every time a rider boards the attraction, or sometimes the same; it's a gamble. The main priority of delivering the Rebel spy to safety is accomplished no matter what the sequence is. The Rebel spy is chosen from among the riders in each StarSpeeder. In other words, it may be you, or the person sitting next to you. Keep an eye on the screen to the right to see who it is. When referring to the spy, the characters on screen will alter their dialogue, depending on the gender of the person chosen as the spy and refer to the spy as him, her, or them.

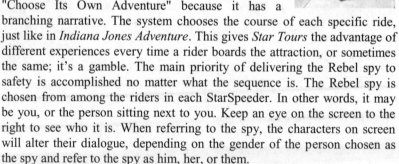

There are 11 random segments of the film. It starts with two opening segments, four primary destination segments, and four hologram message segments followed by four ending destination segments. With the variable possibilities, it makes for 96 different possibilities of combinations.

- The two **main** first scenes:
  - o Darth Vader, Imperial Stormtroopers, and Skytroopers arrive to arrest the Rebel spy aboard the speeder. Vader force grabs the Starspeeder. The Starspeeder fires at Vader causing him to release his grasp.
  - o An Imperial probe droid detects the presence of the Rebel spy onboard the Starspeeder. At the same time, Han Solo starts shooting at a group of Stormtroopers and races up the boarding ramp of the Millennium Falcon.

- The **4 scenes** following the lightspeed jump:
  - o The Starspeeder almost crashes on Hoth, where a battle between Rebels and Imperial AT-ATs is happening. The Starspeeder enters the battle before careening off a cliff.
  - o The Starspeeder reaches Tatooine and enters the pod race alongside the big cheater Sebulba. After the race, the Starspeeder rockets back to space.
  - o The Starspeeder lands on Kashyyyk and is chased by Imperial jet speeders as it speeds past on-looking Wookies. While the jet speeders are chasing Chewbacca and another Wookie, Chewie falls off the back of his vehicle and lands on the Starspeeder's windshield.
  - o The Starspeeder lands on Jakku and follows the Millennium Falcon, piloted by Finn, while being chased by TIE Fighters. The Starspeeder crashes in the wreckage of a Star Destroyer where scavengers rip the *Star Tours* logo off the front of the StarSpeeder.

- Once back in space, an incoming holo transmission gives direction of where to take to Rebel spy by one of **4 characters**:
  - o Admiral Ackbar
  - o Princess Leia
  - o Jedi Master Yoda
  - o BB8

- For the fourth and final scene, there are **3 different outcomes** after R2-D2 sets the coordinates.
  - o The Starspeeder reaches Coruscant, that is under attack by the Republic's Clone troopers. The Starspeeder then plummets through the planet's atmosphere and into the bustling sky traffic of the city planet and lands on a landing platform.
  - o The Starspeeder enters Naboo's space, which is under attack by the last Trade Federation armies. The Starspeeder plummets into the water near Otoh Gunga after speeding past Jar Jar Binks. As it torpedoes through the water, it dodges attacks by giant sea creatures, then surfaces and crashes into a repair hanger.
  - o The Starspeeder exits light speed to enter an asteroid field surrounding the uncompleted Death Star. Boba Fett chases the Starspeeder through

611

the asteroids until they charge through the center of the Death Star and enter light speed again after Boba Fett discharges a sonic bomb. It reaches the Rebel fleet, and lands onboard the Mon Calamari Cruiser.

After *The Force Awakens* was released, **Disney added scenes into the show with Finn, BB8, the Millennium Falcon, and Jakku**. The opening sequence with Darth Vader was removed, as he did not exist in Episode VII. Adding these elements to the show changed the timeline of the experience.

For a **list of this attractions Hidden Mickeys, see page 349**.

CALIFORNIA ADVENTURE FUN FACTS

Found directly across the promenade from *Disneyland*, *Disney's California Adventure Park* opened February 8, 2001.

FUN FACTS

- The Guests had issues with the new entrance of the park. They said it too **closely resembled the entrance to *Disney's Hollywood Studios*** in *Walt Disney World* (*see photo above*). The main street of that park was also themed similarly.

- The style and look of the entrance was **copied from the Pan-Pacific Auditorium** in Los Angeles which stood from 1935 until it burned down in a fire in 1989.

- It was **originally themed after the gorgeous state of California**. The park was popular when it first opened because it was the "new" thing and saw five million Guests. That number dropped the following year to just a little under five million. Over the following six years, the park's attendance never made it out of the five million range. In 2001, *Disneyland* welcomed 12.3 million Guests and increased to 14.72 million by 2008. Meanwhile *DCA* (*Disney's California Adventure*) remained the same, only taking in about one third the attendance as the main park only 400 feet away.

🌐 Disney decided to **completely overhaul *DCA* to make it more appealing** to Guests. They spent $1.1 billion to overhaul the entire park by re-theming the attractions and the lands. It was a gradual process that began in 2007 and ended in 2012, when the park was fully opened as *Disney's California Adventure*, dropping the "Park" off the title, on June 15.

🌐 The original CALIFORNIA **sign was removed and sent to the California State Fair Grounds** in 2013 for their 160th anniversary.

🌐 When the sign was still at the park, **Disney would decorate it for the different holidays**. For Christmas, it would be changed to red-and-white striped peppermint candy canes and had Disney characters around it. For Halloween, the sign changed to orange, yellow, and white and the A's were replaced with giant candy corns.

🌐 When the Anaheim Angels were going to have a rally in *Downtown Disney* in 2002, the **A's were given a red cover-piece and a temporary halo** was bolted into the tops.

BUENA VISTA STREET

This land is the entrance to *California Adventure*. It was originally called *Sunshine Plaze*, but on June 15, 2012, it re-opened as *Buena Vista Street*.

FUN FACTS

- Its name was **established by the address of Walt Disney Studios**, 500 S. Buena Vista Street, Burbank, CA 91521.

- The **land is themed to the 1920's** to resemble what it would have looked like when Walt Disney first arrived.

- The bridge you walk under was **designed after the Glendale-Hyperion Bridge** in Atwater Village, a district of Los Angeles. (*see photo*)

- Atwater borders Forest Lawn Cemetery, which is **where Walt's ashes are kept.**

- In the central plaza area in front of *Carthay Circle Restaurant,* **there is a statue of Walt Disney and Mickey Mouse** referred to as the "*Storytellers*" statue. The plaque on a pillar behind it reads, *"It was July 1923. I packed all of my worldly goods – a pair of trousers, a checkered coat, a lot of drawing materials and the last of the fairy tale reels we had made – in a kind of frayed cardboard suitcase. And with that wonderful audacity of youth, I went to Hollywood, arriving there with just forty dollars. It was a big day the day I got on that Santa Fe California Limited. I was just free and happy!"* – Walt Disney

- It also borders Glendale. Disney expanded its workshops and offices from Burbank and moved some of its divisions to Glendale in the 1960's. **This was the birthplace of Imagineering**, or WED as it was called back then.

- **Buena Vista Pictures Distribution** was a company started by Walt to distribute and promote his films.

- When the street opened, it premiered the Resort's **first Oswald-inspired gift shop**, *Oswald's Filling Station*. Disney had recently re-acquired the rights to Oswald. It fits in the theming here as Oswald was Walt's creation even before Mickey Mouse back in 1927.

- For a **list of DCA's Attractions of the Past**, see page 679.

Attractions

RED CAR TROLLEY

Opened June 15, 2012 - Duration: 3:10

A trolley system that takes passengers from the entrance to *Guardians of the Galaxy – Mission: Breakout!* in *Hollywood Land*.

FUN FACTS

- Was **based on the Pacific Electric Railway** that ran from 1901 to 1961.

- This is the **first transportation attraction** ever installed in *California Adventure*.

- There can be **two trolleys on the track at one time**.

- The trolley **can hold 21 guests** at one time.

- **Brookville Equipment Corporation** in Brookville, Pennsylvania, constructed them.

- **The show *Red Car Trolley News Boys*** is a *Newsies* (1992) themed musical show that uses the trolley. The trolley stops in front of *Carthay Circle Restaurant* and paperboys, along with Mickey Mouse, put on a show. (*see photo*)

- The **charging cable overhead is just for show**. The trolleys are actually battery powered. They are charged with an induction coil system in the ground at the *Sunset Boulevard Stop*.

🐾 The **trolley makes two stops**, not including the start and end point. The first stop is *Carthay Circle Restaurant* in Carthay Circle, the second is the *Animation Academy* on *Hollywood Boulevard*.

GRIZZLY PEAK

This land is themed after the aviation industry of California and its wilderness areas such as Yosemite and its Redwood National Parks. The featured attractions here are *Soarin' Around the World.* This popular attraction simulates a hang glider flight over six different continents and *Grizzly River Run*. Also, in this area is the *Taste Pilot's Grill, a* counter service restaurant.

FUN FACTS

🐾 The **number 47 is used multiple times** through the land. It represents the year 1947 because that is when the sound barrier was first broken.

🐾 This area has a **giant water mister in the shape of a rocket jet**. It makes a great place to relax and cool off.

🐾 In this section of the park, you may see characters from the movies *Up* or *Brother Bear.*

🐾 As you exit the land going toward Pacific Warf, you will pass through a **sub-land that is themed after the San Francisco Bay Area**.

🐾 A special **entrance to Disney's Grand Californian Hotel** is also located in this area.

🐾 Walking down the path is supposed to simulate the drive along **California's beautiful Route 49**.

🐾 If you look down into the creek bed, you might spot **old pans used for panning** for gold.

🐾 Back when the park first opened, **there was a woman known as DeVine**. She would walk on stilts and was covered in grape vines. She would lean against posts and bushes to blend in. People would pass by not even noticing her unless she moved. From what I can find she left the park around 2002, but she can still be found in *Disney's Animal Kingdom* in Florida.

🐾 This part of the park is the best area to look for the **feral cats of Disneyland**. Just about all the cats have been given names. This is a photo of Francisco. She is a domestic long-hair tortoise shell. You can even see her right ear tip to show that she is spayed. If you want to follow the cats of *Disneyland*, just look them up on Instagram under @DisneylandCats.

For a **list of this attractions Hidden Mickeys, see page 349**.

For a **list of DCA's Attractions of the Past**, see page 679.

Attractions

Soarin' Around The World

Opened June 17, 2016 - Duration: 4:45

Soarin' Around the World is a simulator attraction that shows off the breathtaking beauty found all over the world. Riders who are deathly afraid of heights shouldn't ride this. You are not actually that far off the ground, but the film footage and effects make it feel that way.

FUN FACTS

- This attraction replaced *Soarin' Over California*, which was housed here since opening day until its closure on June 16, 2016, **just one day before the new version took over.**

- Just before boarding, Guests will watch a pre-boarding video hosted by their **Chief Flight Attendant, Patrick Warburton** (who also voiced the characters Kronk in *Emperor's New Groove*, Buzz in *Buzz Lightyear Of Star Command*, Joe Swanson on *Family Guy*, Steve Barkin on *Kim Possible,* Ken in *Bee Movie*, and the G2-4T droid that is doing the body scans near the end of the queue on *Star Tours: The Adventures Continue*).

- All of **your senses will be engaged while riding**. Wind will blow in your face. You will have the sensation of flying. You will discover the smell of rose blossoms, fresh cut grass, and the sea breeze. All these effects were added in to make your flight more stimulating by using a Smellitzer.

- If you ask a Cast Member if you may sit in the front, you will have **the best view possible**.

- **This is one of the most visited attractions** at the entire *Disneyland* Resort (facing tough competition from fan favorites over at *Disneyland*) and usually has wait times from 30-150 minutes.

- The attraction can take **87 Guests** at a time on a simulated hang glider tour of the world at the same time.

- The film takes you across six different continents around the world by flying you over:
  - Matterhorn Mountain in Switzerland

- Isfjord, Greenland
- Sydney Harbour, Australia
- Neuschwanstein Castle in Bavaria, Germany
- Kilimanjaro National Park and Mount Kilimanjaro, Tanzania
- The Great Wall, China
- The Great Pyramids, Egypt
- Taj Mahal in Uttar Pradesh, India
- West and East Mitten Buttes in Monument Valley, Utah
- Lau Islands, Fiji
- Iguazu Falls, Argentina
- Eiffel Tower in Paris, France
- *Disneyland*, California

Take a close look at the Neuschwanstein Castle in Bavaria. Does it look familiar to you? It was the model castle for the *Sleeping Beauty Castle* in *Disneyland*.

The Matterhorn Mountain, need I say it, was **the inspiration for the *Matterhorn Bobsleds* in *Disneyland*.**

The **final scene in the Shanghai version ends with *Shanghai Disneyland*,** and the ending for the Epcot version ends in Epcot.

Tinker Bell makes a guest appearance at the end of the film.

Disney **used composer Bruce Broughton** and the London Studio Orchestra for the music. He used the music composed by Jerry Goldsmith, the composer for *Soarin' Over California*, as an inspiration for this attraction update. He is best known for his musical scores in films such as *Harry and the Hendersons, Monster Squad, Betsy's Wedding, The Rescuers Down Under, Honey, I Blew Up the Kid, Stay Tuned, Homeward Bound: The Incredible Journey, So I Married an Axe Murderer, Tombstone, Miracle on 34th Street, Homeward Bound II: Lost in San Francisco, Lost in Space, Mickey, Donald, Goofy: The Three Musketeers,* and *Bambi II.*

This **attraction can be found in Epcot** under the same name, but in *Shanghai Disney,* they call it *Soaring Over the Horizon*. It opened in Shanghai on June 16, 2016, upon the park's opening. *Epcot's* version opened at the same time as *California Adventure's*.

For a **list of this attractions Hidden Mickeys, see page 349**.

GRIZZLY RIVER RUN

Opened February 8, 2001 - Duration: 6:00 **FP** SR

The raft trip around *Grizzly Peak* begins with the rafts being lifted up a wooden conveyor that runs under leaking pipes that spray water on the riders. Upon reaching the top of the conveyor, the rafts are dropped into the water to descend down the peak, passing through a cave, and bumping against a log jam. The climax of the attraction drops the rafts down into a geyser field. The final drop has a unique element in that **the rafts are spun** as they begin their descent.

FUN FACTS

- 🐻 The attraction's **name comes from *Grizzly Peak***, the bear shaped mountain that the rapids flow around. (*see photo*)

- 🐻 *Grizzly Peak* **started out as a 25' X 25' hand-carved** foam model that was scanned into a computer. The computer translated it into the plans of the final version that is steel and cement, carved to look like stone.

- 🐻 The top of *Grizzly Peak* **is 110 feet** from the ground.

- 🐻 When you first hop on, you **ride 300 feet up the lift** toward the top of the mountain to start your journey to the bottom. This is 20 feet higher than any other water rafting ride.

- 🐻 On the final drop, **you descend 21 feet**, while spinning 360°.

- 🐻 The final drop is **called "The Grizzly-Go-Round."**

- 🐻 The **motto for rafters** is, "The wetter, the better."

- 🐻 The wheel alongside the building when you first ride up the ramp is called **The Pelton Wheel**. Lester Pelton invented this style of wheel. (*see photo*)

- 🐻 The theme park attraction design company Intamin, originally from Switzerland but is now located in Maryland, is **responsible for building this attraction,** and also *California Screamin'*.

- 🐻 As with all flume-type attractions, there must be a **location to store or drain the water** in the upper sections of the flumes when the pumps are shut down. The original plan was to create a large, underground basin

620

beneath *Grizzly Peak* to hold water. This would have required costly excavation and construction. Upon looking at the final layout of *California Adventure*, it was noticed that the *Pacific Wharf* area of the park had a water element meant to simulate a tidal basin. The tidal basin is located across a walkway from *Grizzly River Run* and became the catch basin for water from the raft attraction. The rise and fall of water in the tidal basin serves the dual purpose of providing a location to store water and, being a scenic element that simulates a rising and falling tide.

- This attraction **uses 250,000 gallons** of water.

- The attraction is one of **three in American Disney Parks** taking the names of former *Opryland U.S.A.* (1972-1997) attractions. A similar attraction at the now-defunct park in Nashville, Tennessee, was called the *Grizzly River Rampage*.

- You will **get very wet** on this attraction. They sell ponchos.

REDWOOD CREEK
CHALLENGE TRAIL

Opened February 8, 2001 - Duration: N/A

The Redwood Creek Challenge Trail is a large forest-themed play area. The play area appeals to both kids and adults. It has many bird's-eye views of the area with many stairs, cargo net walkways  and buildings leading up several stories. This is the Redwood Creek, so there are many spots on the river and water crossings that give it a lovely appearance. Included is a play area for kids featuring a Mount Shasta wilderness-like setting, and suspension and wire bridges. It also features rock climbing and a *Brother Bear* scene cave. It is designed for adventurous adults.

FUN FACTS

- If you **follow the animal tracks** embedded in the cement, you will discover information about them. These animals are a bighorn sheep, black bear, porcupine, beaver, California quail, king snake, striped skunk, river otter, and a mountain lion. (*see photo*)

- Near the start of the trail, you will find a cross section of a fallen redwood tree from 1937. **The tree dates back to 818 A.D.**

- The **three log ranger stations** were named after the mountains found in California, Mt. Lassen Lookout, Mt. Shasta Lookout, and Mt. Whitney Lookout.
- In 2009, some of the **theming was changed into the Wilderness Explorer Camp** to match up with the Pixar film *Up* (2009). You can meet Russell and Doug.
- For a **list of this attractions Hidden Mickeys, see page 349.**

PARADISE PIER

Paradise Pier is themed **after a California boardwalk**, based on popular coastal boardwalks such as the *Santa Monica Pier* and the *Santa Cruz Beach Boardwalk*. *Paradise Pier's* attractions consist of the classic amusement park attractions found in many boardwalks such as the *Mickey's Fun Wheel* (Ferris Wheel), *California Screamin'* (classic wooden style roller coaster), and the *Silly Symphony Swings* (Wave Swinger). A section of *Paradise Pier* is themed after the Historic Route 66 with a desert road. The *Sunglass Shack* is in the shape of a giant roadside attraction dinosaur.

- For a **list of this attractions Hidden Mickeys, see page 349**.
- For a **list of DCA's Attractions of the Past**, see page 679.

Attractions

California Screamin'

Opened February 8, 2001 - Duration: 2:36 **FP** **PHOTO** **SR**

One of the fastest steel roller coasters in the United States. It is modeled after a traditional boardwalk wooden roller coaster.

FUN FACTS

- Max speed **61 miles per hour**.
- The attraction's name is derived **from the song** *California Dreamin'* released by The Mamas & the Papas in 1965.
- It is the **6th longest roller coaster in the world**, the 2nd longest steel coaster in the United States, and it currently holds the record for the longest coaster in California.
- The **entire track is 6,072 feet long**. That would be 1.15 miles long. Its highest point is 120 feet, followed by a 108-foot drop at a 50° angle.
- This coaster is more **uncommon than most**, as it uses LIMs, or linear induction motors, to launch the train up the first hill, replacing the traditional lift hill chain.
- The seaside launch ramp also sports a **wave-machine** that allows waves to crash alongside the rock base of the ramp, as well as crashing up onto the trains before launch.
- This coaster **was *Disneyland's* fastest attraction**, accelerating Guests from 0 to 55 mph in 4 seconds at the launch. It is the fastest attraction in the resort, closely followed by *Radiator Springs Racers*, installed in 2012, and tops out at 40 mph.
- Like *Space Mountain* and *Rock 'n' Roller Coaster*, in *Disney's Hollywood Studios*, **the roller coaster is set to music.**
- It is the **only inverting (upside-down) outdoor attraction** within the *Disneyland* and *Disney World Resorts*. *Rock 'n' Roller Coaster* in *Disney's Hollywood Studios* goes upside down three times, but it is indoors.
- On December 11, 2006, it was closed and its **loop was temporarily removed** due to construction below for *Toy Story Midway Mania*.
- It contains over **36 miles of electrical wire** and 167 miles of individual conductors.

- It took **5.8 million pounds of steel** to build it. Not all that steel was required for the support, but they were going for the look of a wooden coaster, which has more supports.

- There are **11.5 million pounds of concrete** in the foundations and the "deepest" foundation is 48 feet down.

- Due to the fact that *California Adventure* is located within a residential zone and must adhere to certain noise restriction guidelines, special **"scream" tubes were designed** to muffle the guests' screams during those thrill portions of the attraction.

- **There are a total of 7 trains**. Five trains can hold 24 people. They are colored red, yellow, orange, blue, and purple. Also, two trains, colored green, that can hold 23 riders.

- The Mickey head that was in the giant loop was **the second largest Mickey Head in the whole resort**.

- On November 5, 2010, they changed the safety announcement as you pull away from the station. **You now hear the voice of Neil Patrick Harris** making the attraction that much more "legen… wait for it… dary." He says one of four pre-recorded spiels;
  - "Get ready screamers! Head back, face forward, and hold on like you mean it! Here you go in 5-4-3-2-1!"
  - "Not ready? Too bad! Head back, face forward, and hold on like you mean it! 5-4-3-2-1. GO!"
  - "Second thoughts? Too late! Head back, face forward, and hold on like you mean it! 5-4-3-2-1. SCREAM!"
  - "Second thoughts? Too late! Head back, face forward, and hold on like you mean it! And away you go in 5-4-3-2-1!"

- If you remember the original recordings, those **were provided by Dee Bradley Baker**. He is known for his voice-over work for Momo and Appa in *Avatar: The Last Airbender* (2005), Storm Troopers in *Star Wars: The Clone Wars* (2008), Boba Fette in *Disneyland's* new *Star Tours: The Adventures Continue*, the talking parrot on the attraction *Pirates Of The Caribbean*, and so many others.

- Even though it **looks like a wooden coaster**, it is not. The "fake" wood was left up to look like the old wooden roller coasters of the boardwalks.

- The **music is by Gary Hoey and George Wilkins**. George was also responsible for the music in *Country Bear Vacation Hoedown*, *Roger Rabbit's Car Toon Spin*, *The Enchanted Tiki Room: Under New Management* in *Magic Kingdom*, *It's Tough To Be A Bug*, *Test Track* in *Epcot*, and *Superstar Limo*.

- On January 23, 2007, the **onboard sound track was temporarily changed** to the Red Hot Chili Peppers' "Around The World" song. The attraction was renamed *Rockin' California Screamin'* for the duration of the promotion "Rockin' Both Parks."

- For a **list of this attractions Hidden Mickeys, see page 349**.

624

Games of the Boardwalk

Opened February 8, 2001 - Duration: N/A

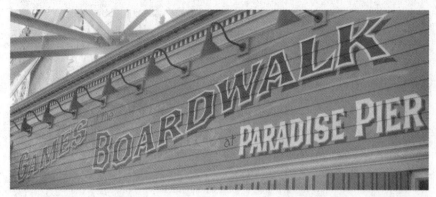

Boardwalk-like pay games.

Golden Zephyr

Opened February 8, 2001 - Duration: 1:30

A spinning attraction similar to *Dumbo the Flying Elephant* and *Astro Orbitor* in neighboring *Disneyland*.

FUN FACTS

- Themed to the Buck Rogers and Flash Gordon style rocket ships, it takes park guests on a relaxing trip. Unlike its cousins *Dumbo The Flying Elephant* and the *Astro Orbitor* next door in *Disneyland*, the rockets are **controlled by centrifugal motion** over *Paradise Bay* and cannot be automatically controlled to go up and down.

- The **design comes from the *Harry Traver Circle Swing*** rides of the early 20th century, specifically the *Aerostat / Strat-O-Stat* ride that operated at *Riverview Park* in Chicago.

- In designing the attraction, Disney **engineers visited *Pleasure Beach*** in Blackpool, England, to examine the *Captive Flying Machines*, a similar (but much larger) ride designed by Sir Hiram Maxim, which has operated there since 1904.

- Unfortunately, the attraction cannot operate at **constant wind speeds over 10 mph**, or gusts over 15 mph.

- The rockets can **reach speeds of 15 miles per hour**.

- The central **tower is 85 feet tall**.

Goofy's Sky School

Opened July 1, 2011 - Duration: 1:45

This is a "wild mouse" mini-roller-coaster type attraction. Riders board a plane and navigate a crash course of flying through sharp turns, steep drops, and sudden stops.

FUN FACTS

- It **replaced the attraction** *Mulholland Madness* during the park's facelift in 2011.

- The attraction is based on Disney's 1940 **animated cartoon** *Goofy's Glider.*

- About **960 passengers can ride in an hour** within the 10 "planes" that fit on the track at one time.

- Riders can reach a **maximum speed of 27 mph**.

- For a **list of this attractions Hidden Mickeys, see page 349**.

Instant Concert...
Just Add Water

Opened June 2012 - Duration: 5:00

This water show will surely bring back childhood memories of watching the Goofy shorts. Check the parks guides for show times and then line up in front of Paradise Bay to watch Maestro Goofy wave his baton to comically conduct the fountains of water.

FUN FACTS

- The show is **narrated in the style of the 1940's** *"How To"* Goofy shorts.

- **Some of the scores Goofy performs**; *"Hungarian Rhapsody No. 2"* and *"Holiday for Strings."*

Jumpin' Jellyfish

Opened February 8, 2001 - Duration: 1:30

A mini-drop attraction.

FUN FACTS

- Each tower **reaches 50 feet** into the air.
- The attraction's name comes from the **jellyfish-themed parachute** attraction vehicles and the bubble and kelp-themed towers.
- Jumpin' Jellyfish has **a sister themed attraction** that opened in September of 2001 in *Tokyo Disney*. This attraction is similar to that of the, now removed, *Maliboomer*, but scaled down to more child-sized proportions and re-themed.
- "Jumpin' Jellyfish" is a phrase **used by Sebastian** in *The Little Mermaid* (1989).
- Disney was **originally going to remove** it during the *California Adventure* makeover, but then decided against it later.
- For a **list of this attractions Hidden Mickeys, see page 349**.

King Triton's Carousel of the Sea

Opened February 8, 2001 - Duration: 2:00

A carousel of sea creatures.

FUN FACTS

- The attraction's name comes from King Triton, **Ariel's father** in *The Little Mermaid*.
- **Unlike the horse arrangement** in *King Arthur Carrousel* in *Disneyland*, this carousel uses sea horses, flying fish, whales, dolphins, sea lions, otters, and Garibaldi (orange fish).
- The carousel sports **56 sea creatures**.
- All the **sea creatures are native to California**. In fact, the Garibaldi is the state fish.
- The **design concept was thought up by John Hench**, a Disney animator and attraction designer who worked for Disney for 65 years, from 1939-2004. He also designed *Cinderella's Castle* in *Magic Kingdom* and *Tokyo Disneyland* and *Space Mountain*. He became a Disney Legend in 1990.

- There are pictures located on the top portion to **represent other California piers**:
  - Abbot Kinney Pier, Venice (1905)
  - Venice of America, Venice (1904)
  - Lick Pier, Ocean Park (1923)
  - Venice Pier, Venice (1925)
  - The Pike, Long Beach (1905)
  - Nu Pike, Long Beach (1950)
  - Looff's Pier, Santa Monica (1908)
  - Fraser's "Million Dollar" Pier, Ocean Park (1912)
  - Pickering Pleasure Pier, Ocean Park (1920)
  - Ocean Park Pier, Ocean Park (1929)
  - Santa Monica Pier, Santa Monica (1909)
  - Pacific Ocean Park, Santa Monica (1958)
  - Virginia Park, Long Beach (1939)
  - Belmont Park, San Diego (1925)
  - Santa Cruz Beach Boardwalk, Santa Cruz (1907)
  - Playland At The Beach, San Francisco (1928)

The Little Mermaid:
Ariel's Undersea Adventure

Opened June 3, 2011 - Duration: 6:15

A "dark-ride" that takes you under the sea on an adventure with Ariel. Experience some of the major scenes and musical numbers from the film in person.

FUN FACTS

- The space now occupied by this attraction **used to house the film** *Golden Dreams* hosted by Whoopi Goldberg. That theater with the restrooms was torn down and built into what it is today.

- The **only "dark-ride"** found in *California Adventure*.

- The **attraction is based on the film** ***The Little Mermaid* (1989)**. It has no references to *The Little Mermaid 2: Return to the Sea* (2000), *The Little Mermaid: Ariels Beginning* (2008), or *The Little Mermaid* (1992) television series.

- The types of **vehicles you ride in are part of a system called omnimovers**, meaning they never stop for loading; they continually move through the attraction. The technology is also used in *Haunted Mansion* as the doom buggies and in *Buzz Lightyear Astro Blasters* as spaceships. However, these are shaped like seashells.

- The **King Triton statue on top of the building was originally** in the pond by *Ariel's Grotto* in *Disneyland*. It was a fountain that would squirt water from the tips of his trident. It was removed in 2008, when the area got converted into *Pixie Hollow*. (*see photo*)

- There **were earlier plans to open a Little Mermaid**-type attraction in the early 1990's, based on the then recently-released 1989 princess film, in *Disneyland Paris* and *Magic Kingdom*. The plans ended up being scrapped.

- Some of **the voice cast is the same** as in the film, Jodi Benson as Ariel and Pat Carroll as Ursula.

- **Corey Burton, the *Haunted Mansion Holiday* Ghost Host**, voiced Flotsam and Jetsam, and Chris Edgerly, Timothy Mouse on *Dumbo the Flying Elephant*, voiced Scuttle.

- **Kevin Michael Richardson provides the voice of Sebastian**. Richardson is best known for providing voices to some other more prevalent character like Jabba The Hutt in *Star Wars: Clone Wars* (2008), Captain Gantu in all the *Lilo & Stitch* films and TV series, Martian Manhunter in *Young Justice* (2010), Cleveland Brown Jr. in *The Cleveland Show* (2009), Kilowog in the *Green Lantern: The Animated Series* (2011) and hundreds more.

- The attraction had not even been open a year before Disney shut it down for a five-day stint to **change out Ariel's hair**. Apparently, people didn't like the way it looked. They said it looked too much like a Dole Whip or ice cream swirl, even though the Imagineers were just copying that

629

sequence from the "Under the Sea" scene in the film. (*see photo*)

You can spot Henry Limpet from the Warner Brother's film *The Incredible Mr. Limpet* (1964) in the "Under the Sea" musical number in *The Little Mermaid* (1989). Because he was in the movie, the Imagineers placed him on this attraction in the scene when Ariel can be seen dancing around for the "Under the Sea" song. In the film, the animators added him to pay homage to the late Disney animation director Vladimir "Bill" Tytla, whose last film was *The Incredible Mr. Limpet*. While directing and animating for Disney, he animated some of the most iconic characters of all time including Stromboli, Yen Sid, Chernabog, Dumbo, and the popular dwarf Grumpy. (*see photo*)

The entrance area is a **replica of The Palace of Fine Arts** and was used as the entrance for Golden Dreams. That part remained, but was redecorated.

At the end of your adventure you will pass two cabinet doors on the left. One of them has **a picture of Hans Christian Andersen**, the author of *The Little Mermaid* (published in 1837). The other picture is that of the Little Mermaid statue found in the harbor of Copenhagen, Denmark. (*see photo*)

For a **list of this attractions Hidden Mickeys, see page 349**.

Mickey's Fun Wheel

Opened May 4, 2009 - Duration: 9:00

A Ferris wheel attraction with both swinging and stationary gondolas.

FUN FACTS

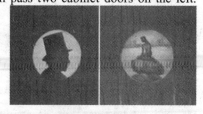

Mickey's Fun Wheel is a Ferris wheel **measuring 160 feet wide** and 158 feet tall, making it the second tallest attraction in the *Disneyland* Resort following *Guardians of the Galaxy – Mission: Breakout! measuring* 183 feet.

The **variation from the standard Ferris wheel** is that the 16 orange and purple gondolas are able to ride on interior rails so that they slide inward and outward with the gravitational force during the wheel's rotational movement. This provides for quite a disorienting and intense experience.

Motion **sickness bags are even provided** in each of the gondolas, due to the disorienting nature of the attraction. If you have an accident, be sure to tell a Cast Member that you had a code "V."

- This is the first "Wonder Wheel" style Ferris wheel **built since 1927,** when the Wonder Wheel was opened at Coney Island in New York.

- The **eight red gondolas**, which are on the outside of the wheel, remain stationary. Guests may choose to ride either the swinging gondolas or the stationary ones upon entering the queue.

- About **960 passengers can ride in an hour** (depending on how many they can fit in one gondola).

- This particular wheel has **the effect of loading the passengers** from below the waterline.

- Only **four of the "Fab Five" characters** can be found on the gondolas, Minnie Mouse, Donald Duck, Pluto, and Goofy. Mickey is found on the whole face of the wheel. (*see photo*)

- An American engineer named **George Washington Gale Ferris Jr. designed the first Ferris wheel** in 1893 for the World's Columbian Exposition in Chicago.

- The attraction was **formerly known as the *Sun Wheel*** (February 8, 2001 - October 14, 2008).

- **The highest you can get in the Disney parks** is at the top of the wheel. You have the best unobstructed view of everything. You can see *Big Thunder Mountain Railroad, Matterhorn Bobsleds, Space Mountain, Soarin' Around the World, Grizzly River Run*, and *Guardians of the Galaxy*. (*see photo*)

Silly Symphony Swings

Opened June 11, 2010 - Duration: 1:30

A "wave swinger" type ride.

FUN FACTS

- The swings were themed after the animated **short film** *The Band Concert* (1935), although The Band Concert was not part of the 75 animated shorts called *"Silly Symphonies"* film series (1929-1939). (*see photo*)

- Riders fly around while listening to **William Tell's Overture "Storm"** By Gioachino Rossini in 1829.

- There can be up to **48 guests riding** at one time.

- This attraction **replaced the** *Orange Stinger* during the *California Adventure* $1.1 billion make-over. (*see photo*)

- The top of the swings rises to **40 feet in the air**.

- For a **list of this attractions Hidden Mickeys, see page 349.**

TOY STORY MIDWAY MANIA!

Opened June 17, 2008 – Duration 6:05

Park guests wear 3-D glasses aboard spinning vehicles that travel through virtual environments, based on classic carnival midway games. Each Guest's score is recorded by an onboard display screen as points are acquired with individual toy cannons firing simulated projectiles at virtual targets. Toy Story characters, including Woody, Hamm, Buzz Lightyear, and Bo Peep, appear during the attraction's different games.

FUN FACTS

- *Toy Story Midway Mania!* was **originally named** *Toy Story Mania!*
- The attraction's vehicles seat up to **four in back-to-back pairs**.
- The attraction **features five mini-games** after a practice round, each of which includes at least one "Easter egg" that can trigger additional targets or gameplay changes.
- **Mini-games**:
  - Hamm & Eggs (egg toss game)
  - Pie Throw Practice Booth (pie toss target practice game; no points awarded)
  - Bo Peep's Baaa-loon Pop (dart throw game)
  - Green Army Men Shoot Camp (baseball throw / plate breaking game)
  - Buzz Lightyear's Flying Tossers (ring toss game)
  - Woody's Rootin' Tootin' Shootin' Gallery (suction cup shooting game)
- The queue features a large Mr. Potato Head Audio-Animatronics figure that interacts with Guests through pre-recorded snippets of **dialogue performed by comedian Don Rickles**, who voiced the character in the *Toy Story* films. The sophisticated figure identifies people in the audience, sings, and tells jokes. (*see photo*)
- Disney Interactive Studios has released **"Toy Story Mania!" the video game**. The game features gameplay and levels similar to those on this attraction, along with original levels and features. The game was released exclusively for the Nintendo Wii console.
- In 2010, Jakks Pacific released their **"Plug It In & Play TV Game"** version of *Toy Story Mania!* with 3D glasses. No console needed. It just plugs into the TV.
- There **used to be a single rider line**, but it closed January 1, 2010.
- This was the **first attraction ever built simultaneously** for two parks, *California Adventure* and *Disney's Hollywood Studios* in Florida.
- The mini game **"Bo Peep's Baaa-loon Pop" was replaced with "Rex and Trixie's Dino Darts"** on May 21, 2010, to better tie in with the film *Toy Story 3* (2010).
- The attraction cost an **estimated $800 million to design** and build.
- Many of the **parts for the attractions control system were supplied** by two of Disney's corporate sponsors, Siemens AG and Hewlett-Packard.

- There are **more than 150 PCs** used to run and control the entire attraction.
- If your vehicle is delayed for whatever reason, **you are allowed to continue playing**. The score isn't kept, but it gives you something to do to pass the time.
- The *Hollywood Studio's* version of this attraction opened on May 18, 2008, to coincide with the launch of the *Discovery* shuttle heading to the *International Space Station*. There was a **Buzz Lightyear toy action figure donated to NASA** to accompany the astronauts into space for experimentation. After spending 15 months in space, Buzz returned and was donated to the Smithsonian Museum by John Lasseter, the original designer of Buzz.
- The queue area has over an hour of different music; this is to reduce repetitive music. The **music was composed by Jennifer Hammond** and recorded at Capitol Studios with a live orchestra. You might recognize some of Jennifer's work in the film *The Smurfs* (2011), *I Am Number Four* (2010), *Tangled* (2010), *Prince of Persia* (2010), *Shrek Forever After* (2010), *Alice in Wonderland* (2009), *Up* (2009), *X-Men Origins: Wolverine* (2009), *High School Musical 3* (2008), *National Treasure: Book of Secrets* (2007), *Shrek the Third* (2007), *Meet the Robins* (2006), *Flushed Away* (2006), *Mission Impossible 3* (2006), *The Chronicles of Narnia* (2005 & 2007), *Lilo & Stitch 2* (2005) and *Pooh's Heffalump Movie* (2005).
- For a **list of this attractions Hidden Mickeys, see page 349**.

PRO TIP: There are secret high value targets that you can make appear during game play. To achieve a score upwards of 300,000 points, you need to shoot frequently over accuracy. It is also best to play solo. The following are some of the secret targets that I know about;

Ham & Eggs (The Barn):

1. On the bottom left, a fox will pop up worth 500 points. Shoot him and two hens will run out, both worth 1,000 points.
2. There are also two pigs that appear above the barn, each worth 100 points. After shooting the pigs, a cat will appear worth 1,000 points. The pigs will show up again, followed by the cat again, but this time the cat is worth more. Keep shooting in that sequence as the cat continues to go up in value.
3. A tiny rat crawls across the barn. Shoot him to reveal a family of rats all worth 1,000 points each.

Rex and Trixie's Dino Darts:

4. Shoot the big balloons in the lava flow at the base of the volcano. This will cause squiggly lava balloons worth 500 points each. After that, there are comets that appear on both sides of the screen. Pop those three times each. They will crash down and cause an explosion that spews high value balloons across the screen.

Green Army Men Shoot Camp (The Plates):

5. Two plates will be tossed into the air worth 2,000. If you break both those plates on the same toss, a tank emerges with six plates worth 5,000 points each.

Buzz Lightyear's Flying Tossers (Ring Toss):

6. You and your teammate have to toss a ring around each little green man in the center of the rocket ship before they each reappear. If you do this, the ship will take off and reveal an opened-mouth robot. Fill his mouth as much as you can. Each time he closes and opens his mouth, the value of the rings you are feeding him goes up.

Woody's Rootin' Tootin' Shootin' Gallery (Suction Cup Darts):

7. With your teammate, shoot the bullseye to make the smaller bullseyes pop up. Make sure you shoot down each one so they all disappear. After you can get them to all disappear, all new bullseyes worth 1,000 and 2,000 points show up.

8. As the mine carts roll towards you, start shooting them from left to right and take out as many as you can. A bat will appear on the ceiling worth 1,000 points. Take him out and continue taking out the mine carts left to right. A second bat will pop up worth 5,000 points; take him out. Take out the rest of the mine carts. If you don't miss any, the last carts will have been worth 5,000 points each.

World Of Color

Opened June 11, 2010 – Duration 29:00

The *World of Color* is a 29-minute nighttime show that is a stunning blend of lights, water, animation and music. With 1,200 fountains that can shoot streams of water as high as 200 feet in the air, awesome fire effects, and appearances from some of your favorite Disney characters, you will be entertained and your heart will be touched. This show must be seen in person to truly be experienced.

FUN FACTS

🔹 The nighttime show *LuminAria* **was a water fireworks show** that was here from November 2001 until January 2002. It never returned after that.

🔹 From the draining of the *Paradise Bay* lagoon until its opening night, **it took 15 months to build**, set up, and complete dry run tests. That is 3 months longer than it took to build all of *Disneyland* 1954-1955.

🔹 It was a **long, drawn-out process** to complete the show:
- Fall 2007 – Announcement of the new water show
- November 3, 2008 – Drained the lagoon
- January 5, 2009 – Construction of the platform began
- November 2009 – The water in *Paradise Bay* was refilled
- January 2010 – The shows testing started after the park closed at night
- June 5, 2010 – The first test show for the Imagineers and their families

🔹 The show has **1,200 fountains that can spurt jets of water** into the air up to 200 feet and each fountain is mounted on an LED light ring, capable of producing multiple colors. This is what the fountains look like raised out of the water. (*see photo*)

🔹 A **wall of mist 380 feet wide** is used as a projection screen for the animated images. A screen that is similar, but smaller, is used for the *Fantasmic!* show.

🔹 It cost Disney **$75 million to create** and build. In 1954-55, it cost $17 million to build all of *Disneyland*.

🔹 Its **opening night** was June 11, 2010, as part of their *Summer Nightastic!*

🔹 On November 1, 2010, **scenes were added into the show** as a promotion for *Tron: Legacy* (2010), but were removed in March 2011.

🔹 **Scenes from the *Pirates of the Caribbean: On Stranger Tides* (2011)** were added in on May 20, 2011.

🔹 With the addition of the "Tron: Legacy" segment to the show, they began doing **projections onto the face of the *California Screamin'*** loop to act as a movie screen. This went for the *Pirates* scenes as well.

636

◀◀ From July 1 through July 4, 2011, they had a special **Independence Day addition with fireworks**, which it normally does not have. It is unknown if this will be a yearly addition.

◀◀ They sell **special Mickey ear hats that light up** in sync with the show. They are available for a mere $40. (*see photo*)

ABOUT THE SHOW

The most complete viewing of the show is available from the *Paradise Park* area, since this area faces the projection screens. Viewing is available from all around *Paradise Bay*, but most of those areas can see the fountains only, or view the projections from the back side.

FASTPASS OPTIONS

Everyone wishing to watch *World of Color* from the *Paradise Park* viewing area must have a *World of Color* FastPass. The viewing area includes all of the space from *Ariel's Grotto* (including the bridge) over to the *Golden Zephyr*. FastPasses are available beginning at park opening at the *Grizzly River Run* FastPass machines until they are all gone. FastPasses for all shows that day (including an additional show that is added due to demand) will be distributed at *Grizzly River Run*. Guests may not select which show they wish to attend. If you get an earlier showing and there are going to be multiple showings that night, you can talk to a Cast Member about switching for a later showing. FastPass tickets are separated into colored sections, corresponding to different sections of the viewing area, and large groups may find themselves split among two or more sections.

Each FastPass ticket will designate the colored section that the bearer is to return to for entrance to the show: blue, red, yellow, green, or orange. Within each section, Guests will have a choice of rows, so they can choose not to go down to the "wet zone" if they do not want to. FastPass tickets will also indicate when Guests can return and be admitted to the viewing area. For those Guests who arrive prior to this time, queuing areas are identified around the area by color. Since the show is still new, the FastPass tickets sell out fast. The queues start filling up more than an hour prior to the start of their scheduled showing.

DINNER PACKAGES WITH FASTPASSES

Get a FastPass by purchasing one of the dining packages.

World of Color **Picnic**: The *World of Color* picnic is a cold boxed meal, which can be ordered on-line at *www.disneyland.com* up to 30 days in advance (subject to availability). Adults have a choice of four meals, with three meals available for kids. Each meal includes a non-alcoholic beverage. Meals are $14.99, ($12.99 for Annual Passholders) which includes a FastPass to the *World of Color* viewing area. Meals can be picked up from 2:00 p.m. until 8:00 p.m. at the *Sonoma Terrace* of the *Golden Vine Winery*. Picnic meals can also be purchased in person (subject to availability) for $13.99 at the *Sonoma Terrace*.

Picnic meals reserved on-line will have tickets to the first show. The meals purchased in person will have tickets to the second show.

World of Color **Prix Fixe Dinners**: Dinner packages, which include a ticket to the preferred reserved viewing area, are available at *Wine Country Trattoria* and *Ariel's Grotto*. These packages can be reserved up to 60 days in advance (subject to availability) by calling *Disneyland Dining*, 714-781-DINE. Each location offers a fixed menu with choice of entree. Prices range from $33.99-$39.99 for adults (depending upon location), and $17.99-$20.99 for kids.

START OF THE SHOW

During peak times, *World of Color* shows twice a night, though on especially busy days, FastPasses will be distributed for a third show. For those who do not have FastPasses, but wish to view the show, they can do so from the *Boardwalk* if there is space. If not, then ask a Cast Member if there is a third show that night.

There was a pre-show called *Carnival of Color* for the first show only. This began about 30 minutes before the show started, and ran about 15 minutes. It included large, lighted "sky puppets" of Genie, Lumiere, Mike Wazowski, Tigger, and Sebastian, corresponding to the colors of the different sections: blue, yellow, green, orange, and red. It is not certain if they will be returning. The entire waterfront area gets very packed and makes it difficult to maneuver around.

There is **no seating** available for the show. Guests should expect to stand for anywhere from 30 minutes to one hour. Cast Members will ask everyone in the viewing area to stand 45-60 minutes before the show begins.

There can be significant mist from the fountains. Those closest to the water (on the lowest level of the viewing area) will get wet, and depending on the wind direction, might get very wet. Everyone in the viewing area should expect to feel at least some mist.

The viewing area is accessible to those in wheelchairs and ECVs. When obtaining FastPasses at the *Grizzly River Run* FastPass machines, see a Cast Member if you or someone in your party is in a wheelchair or ECV. For those with dining packages, please consult a Cast Member when you enter the viewing area to be directed appropriately.

All attractions in the *Paradise Pier* area close about 60 minutes prior to the first show, and remain closed for the evening. If you are in a line waiting to ride an attraction you are fine, they will close the line down behind you. Keep this in mind when planning your route for the day. Everyone that would normally be standing in the lines for *California Screamin, King Triton's Carousel, Toy Story Midway Mania, Mickey's Fun Wheel, Goofy's Sky School, Golden Zephyr, Jumpin' Jellyfish, Silly Symphony Swings* and the *Games of the Boardwalk* will all be in the other areas of the park, thereby making all those lines longer. Basically, try to get everything done in *Paradise Pier* early.

- Children must have their own ticket into the viewing area, and must be accompanied by an adult.
- There are a couple parts of the show that might be disturbing or scary for children.
- This area is very congested. Be sure to keep your children near you at all times.

PACIFIC WHARF

This sub-land is based on Monterey's Cannery Row area, as depicted in John Steinbeck's novels, and also resembles San Francisco's Fisherman's Wharf. This area includes many restaurants, cafes, along with a *Karl Strauss Beer Truck* and a margarita stand. It also features attractions such as *The Boudin Bakery Tour* and the *Ghirardelli Chocolate Factory*, which includes a tour on how chocolate is made. Visitors get a free chocolate square sample.

For a **list of DCA's Attractions of the Past**, see page 679.

The Golden Vine Winery

This sub-land is themed after Northern California's Napa Valley and the wine making industry. Included in this area are two restaurants, *The Vineyard Room*, a fine dining dinner-only table service restaurant which features a great selection of wines, and *Wine Country Trattoria*, a more casual table service dining restaurant which features wines and Italian foods. Attractions in this area include *Blue Sky Cellar*, an area dedicated to showing off the plans Disney has for the park's future. You can see artists' renditions of future attractions and plans, or even scale models. There is a video journal featuring the Imagineers' creative progress and displayed on a spectacular 103-inch plasma television. For interaction, you can answer a variety of trivia questions on one of four interactive video screens to learn more about Walt Disney's adventures in California and how they inspired shows and attractions in *California Adventure*.

FUN FACTS

🐭 Before this land **was used to grow oranges, it grew grapes**. In the 1880's the grapevines were removed due to disease and orange groves were planted. The disease still exists and sometimes affects these vines too, causing Disney to have to replant them.

🐭 There are other wineries out there that produce wine for other known Disney-affiliated people.

- Fess Parker, better known as Davy Crockett, whose label is "Fess Parker." His wine is served in *Club 33* in *Disneyland*.

- Diane Miller, Walt's daughter owned "Silverado Vineyards" in Napa, California, with her husband, Ron Miller.

- Kurt Russell collaborated with "Ampelos Cellars," located in Lompoc (north of Santa Barbara), to create his label "GoGi." Gogi is the nickname Kurt acquired while growing up of how he pronounced his middle name, Vogel.

- John Lasseter owns "Lasseter Family Winery," located in Sonoma County, California.

- Fred MacMurray's ranch has a winery. Fred had always wanted to preserve the agricultural side of the land, so he purchased property in Northern California for farming. Upon his death, the land was purchased by "E & J Gallo" (the largest exporter of California wines) and was turned into a winery. The wine label from this vineyard says "MacMurray Ranch." You can purchase this wine here in the *Wine Country Trattoria*.

- Francis Ford Coppola owns "Rubicon Estate Winery," located in Napa Valley, California. He was the director of the *Tomorrowland* 3D attraction *Captain EO* (1986), starring Michael Jackson.

- Emilio Estevez owned "Casa Dumetz Wines" in Malibu until he sold it in 2016. Emilio was in Disney's *The Mighty Ducks* (1992), *D2: The Mighty Ducks* (1994), and *D3: The Mighty Ducks* (1996).

THE BOUDIN BAKERY TOUR

Opened February 8, 2001 - Duration: 13:00

The Boudin Bakery Tour guides you through the sourdough breadmaking process with Rosie O'Donnell (*The Rosie O'Donnell Show* and 1998's *Tarzan*) and Colin Mochrie (1998's *Whose Line Is It Anyway?*) as video tour guides. A sample of the bread is handed out at the entrance.

FUN FACTS

⚜ **Lactobacillus Sanfrancisco is the only patented live bacteria**. It has been renamed Lactobacillus sanfranciscensis. It is a microorganism in sourdough starter that produces lactic and acetic acids. Leo Kline and T.F. Sugihara received a patent in 1977 for San Francisco Sour Start, freeze-dried natural flour culture that contained live Lactobacillus sanfrancisco, in Richmond, California.

⚜ **The factory makes all the sourdough bread for both parks**. If you get a clam chowder bowl in New Orleans Square, it came from here.

PRO TIP: Get a bread bowl and eat it while you are waiting for *World of Color*, or visit *Ghirardelli* and get an ice cream sundae.

Cars Land

This land features attractions based on the 2006 Pixar film *Cars* that made over $6 billion in itself from ticket sales, DVD/Blu-ray, and toy sales from around the world.

FUN FACTS

⚜ It officially **opened on June 15, 2012**.

⚜ Part of the **$1.1 billion *California Adventure* makeover**, *Cars Land* is bringing the much-needed "Disney" feel to this park.

⚜ *Cars Land* is the **newest land in the whole *Disneyland* Resort** to open since *a bug's land* opened October 2002.

⚜ Walt and Roy started out their animation in 1923 called *Disney Brothers Cartoon Studio*, but was **renamed *Walt Disney Studios* in 1926**. Just like the date on the outside of the *Radiator Springs Curios* shop.

⚜ It is **12 acres** in size.

⚜ In one of the *Radiator Springs Curios* windows is a **neon sign that says "Catmull Oil."** This is to pay homage to Walt Disney Animation Studios President

641

Edwin Catmull. Edwin used to work as the Vice President of the computer graphics division in Lucasfilm and helped to create the digital image compositing technology to make 3D special effects a reality. When Steve Jobs bought this animation division from Lucas, he hired Edward to be the Chief Technical Officer and, under that title, he helped to create RenderMan, the computer rendering software used on films like *Toy Story* and *Finding Nemo*.

PRO TIP: Find out what time sundown is so that you can arrive for the moment the neon lights up the street. This land is beautiful at night with all the neon lights.

🌐 For a **list of this attractions Hidden Mickeys, see page 349**.

🌐 For a **list of DCA's Attractions of the Past**, see page 679.

Attractions

Luigi's Rollickin' Roadsters

Opened March 7, 2016 - Duration: 1:30

Luigi invited his cousins from Carsoli, Italy, to Radiator Springs for a dance festival in the tire yard behind his *Casa Della Tires* shop. The Guests ride in vehicles, as they spin and move around to the Italian music.

FUN FACTS

🌐 In Luigi's office, there is **a set of Foose rims on display**. They are to pay homage to Chip Foose, the famous automotive designer and star of Velocity TV's *Overhaulin'*. He worked as a key consultant in the *Cars Land* creation. Foose and his paint team gave *Cars Land* a gearhead's touch and painted the custom designs on the car hoods hanging in the windows of *Ramone's House of Body Art*. There are Hidden Mickeys painted on them.

642

The following is the **queue track listing of the songs** that were identified by the visitors of the park:

TITLE	ARTIST
"Eh Cumpari"	Julius La Rosa
"Luigi"	Louis Prima
"La Strada Del Bosco"	Claudio Villa
"Che Cosse` L'amor"	Vinicio Capossela
"Funiculi Funicula"	VariousItalia"
"Arrivederci, Roma"	Mario Lanza
"Tie, Ti, Tie Ta"	Claudio Villa
"Volare (Nel Blu Dipinto Di Blu)"	Domenico Modugno
"Carina"	Nicola Arigliano
"Mambo Italiano"	Rosemary Clooney
"La Donna è Mobile (Rigoletto)"	Orchestra Italiana
"That's Amore (That's Love)"	Dean Martin
"Papa Loves Mambo"	Perry Como
"Forget Domani"	Perry Como
"O Sole Mio"	Various
"Soldi, Soldi, Soldi"	Sophia Loren
"Juke Box"	Fred Buscaglione

If you look closely at Luigi's wall, you can see the Periodic Table of Elements, but as the **Periodic Table of Automotive Elements**.

This is the first Disney attraction between the *Disneyland* Resort and *Walt Disney World* to use **a trackless ride system**. This technology is already in use in the Hong Kong, Paris, and Tokyo parks. The first attraction to use a trackless system is *Pooh's Hunny Hunt,* which opened in 2000 across the ocean in *Tokyo Disneyland.*

Each car is different. Just check out the license plates.

While you are waiting in the queue, there are **glass cases with Luigi and Guido's vacation souvenirs**. One of these items is a post card signed from "John Lassetire," to pay homage to John Lasseter, the Chief Creative Officer Disney-Pixar Studios & Walt Disney Animation. (*see photo*)

There is also a **large business card that says "Topolino Gomme."** Topolino is the Italian name for Mickey, and Gomme is the Italian word for gum or rubber. (*see photo*)

There is a mini **movie poster that says, "20,000 Leaks Under the Seal,"** a spoof title to the Disney film *20,000 Leagues Under The Sea* (1954). (*see photo*)

There is **a sign that says "Anti Gelato,"** which means "Against Gelato." Gelato is Italian ice cream. (*see photo*)

For a **list of this attractions Hidden Mickeys, see page 349**.

Mater's Junkyard Jamboree

Opened June 15, 2012 - Duration: 1:30

Hop on as baby tractors pull trailers and whip you around while weaving in and out of each other as Mater sings different redneck songs

FUN FACTS

- 🚗 The design concept **mimics the** *Mad Tea Party* in *Fantasyland*.

- 🚗 Outside the queue area there is a "petting zoo" where you can **pet a baby tractor**. (*see photo*)

- 🚗 There is memorabilia on the walls next to the queue that are **throwbacks to the** *Mater's Tall Tales* (2008) shorts.

🚗 For a **list of this attractions Hidden Mickeys, see page 349**.

Radiator Springs Racers

Opened June 15, 2012 - Duration: 4:22

The attraction will take Guests in a six-person vehicle through a briefing with the characters Doc and Lighting McQueen. Riders will then be launched into the middle of a race, which includes sharp turns and steep banks with Guests eventually racing another guest vehicle with random outcome.

FUN FACTS

- 🚗 This attraction was **modeled after the attraction** *Test Track* in *Disney World's Epcot*.

- 🚗 At the time of its construction, this attraction is the most expensive attraction ever constructed in the *Disneyland* Resort and in the history of Disney. It also held the record for the **most expensive attraction ever built in the whole world.**

- 🚗 After you first take off, there is serene music playing. And as you round the bend, **you**

approach the bridge that Lightning McQueen and Sally Carrera drove over in *Cars* (2006). (*see photo*)

It **cost an estimated $200+ million to build,** which takes about 18% of the *California Adventures* $1.1 billion makeover budget.

Tops out at **40 miles per hour**.

The green steel bridge you walk under was **modeled after the Overholser Steel Truss Bridge** on old Route 66 just west of Bethany, Oklahoma, which was erected in 1925.

The mountain range covers **280,000 square feet and is 125 feet tall** at its peak.

The voice cast is as follows:
- Owen Wilson - Lightning McQueen
- Larry the Cable Guy - Mater
- Bonnie Hunt - Sally Carrera
- John Ratzenberger - Mack
- Tony Shalhoub - Luigi
- Jenifer Lewis - Flo
- Cheech Marin - Ramone
- Edie McClurg - Minny
- Richard Kind - Van
- Corey Burton - Doc Hudson
- Michael Wallis - Sheriff
- Lloyd Sherr - Fillmore
- Paul Dooley - Sarge
- Guido Quaroni - Guido

The cars run on **a track that is similar to a child's electric racecar track**. There are what is called collector shoes on each car that both electrical lines touch to run power to the motor, which is located in the back of the car.

For a **list of this attractions Hidden Mickeys, see page 349.**

"A BUG'S LAND"

Featuring *Flik's Fun Fair* and *It's Tough to be a Bug!,* this whole land is based on the Disney-Pixar film *A Bug's Life* (1998). It opened in 2003 and offers various kid-friendly rides.

- In the beginning, *"a bug's land"* **was going to be called** *"Flick's Fun Fair,"* but now it just refers to the section in the land with the "fair style" attractions.

- There is **only one four leaf clover** in the whole land; it is by the entrance to Francis' Ladybug Boogie. (*see photo*)

- Keep an eye on the bushes for your favorite characters from *A Bug's Life* (1998). If you do not spot Flik or Princess Atta, it's because they come out as Meet and Greet characters. (see photo)

- In 2010, the main street through *Hollywood Pictures Backlot*, now *Hollywood Land*, was closed down to alter it for the nighttime show *Eletronica*. When this happened, there was no way for people to get to the *Hyperion Theater* or *Tower of Terror*, so **a second entrance was added** to the back side of *a bug's land*. This also increased traffic through the land. Lines are a little longer than they used to be. People now get in lines as an impulse because they are already there passing by, when normally people did not go out of their way to go to this land unless they had little children.

646

🐾 At the entrance, you pass through **a giant box of "Cowboy Crunchies."** This is a variation of the "Kanine Krunchies" that were shown in *One Hundred and One Dalmatians* (1961). "Cowboy Crunchies" were first used in *Toy Story 2* (1999).

🐾 For a **list of DCA's Attractions of the Past**, see page 679.

Attractions

It's Tough to Be a Bug!

Opened February 8, 2001 - Duration: 6:00

See the world through a bug's eyes as you peek into the hilarious and dazzling 3-D world of amazing and amusing insects as they astound you with a one-of-a-kind stage show. Laugh at the fun and startling in-theater effects, like overhead giant spiders! The only thing that will "bug" you is if you miss it!

FUN FACTS

🐾 The film was **created for showing in *Disney World's Animal Kingdom*** in 1998, but was then also placed in *California Adventure* when it opened in 2001.

🐾 The first *It's Tough to Be a Bug* was released for public viewing in *Animal Kingdom* seven months **before the actual movie *A Bug's Life* came out.**

🐾 This movie quite possibly acquired its title from the short, **animated film *It's Tough To Be A Bird!*** It was animated in 1969 by Disney to show the difficulties and history of being a bird. It was played in the *Fantasyland Theater* in *Fantasyland* before it was turned into *Pinocchio's Daring Journey* in 1983.

🐾 The film was **not actually created by Pixar**; instead it was created by Rhythm and Hues Studios. Using lighting, 3-D filming techniques, Audio-Animatronics, and various special effects, the show gives the audience an idea of what it would be like to be an insect. Flik, from *A Bug's Life*, hosts the show and educates the viewer on why bugs should not be seen as pests, but more as friends.

647

In the final song, there are a bunch of honey bees singing, "We're pollinators, we're pollinators." **All the voices are male**. In the honey bee world, the male bees stay behind to care for the hive and mate with the queen bee, while the female honey bees go out into the world and pollinate from flower to flower. The voices should be female.

The **cast list** is as follows:
- Dave Foley - Flik
- Kevin Spacey - Hopper
- Cheech Marin - Chili, a Mexican Redknee Tarantula
- French Stewart - The Termite-ator
- Tom Kenny - The Dung Beetle Brothers
- Jason Alexander - Unnamed bug who wreaks havoc
- Corey Burton – The announcer and additional bug voices

It is neat to just wait in line for the show because they play **music in the lobby with insect sounds** instead of instruments. There are also posters around the walls of famous movies but have been altered to be a little "buggy" like "Beauty and the Bees," "Webside Story," and "A Stinkbug Named Desire." This is the track list of songs:

Track	Name	Parody / rendition of
1	"One" (*A Cockroach Line*)	"One" (A Chorus Line)
2	"Beauty and the Bees" (*Beauty and the Bees*)	"Beauty and the Beast" (*Beauty and the Beast*)
3	"Tomorrow" (*Antie*)	"Tomorrow" (*Annie*)
4	"I Feel Pretty" (*Web Side Story*)	"I Feel Pretty" (West Side Story)
5	"Hello Dung Lovers" (*The Sting and I*)	"Hello Young Lovers" (*The King and I*)
6	"Tonight" (*Web Side Story*)	"Tonight" mixed with Flight of the Bumblebee (*West Side Story*)

Disney now **uses this theater to show sneak peaks at upcoming animated Disney films**. Generally, there are figures out from to display and advertise what film they will be showing. They typically show about ten minutes of the film followed by the trailer. (*see photo*)

Flik's Fun Fair

This area opened October 7, 2002. This little area in *"a bug's land"* has smaller attractions for little visitors like the *Fantasyland* portion in *Disneyland*. These attractions are similar to attractions that would be found at a county fair. It is basically like a small land inside of a land.

Flik's Flyers

Opened October 7, 2002 - Duration: 1:30

A swing attraction in which visitors swing in over-sized food boxes.

FUN FACTS

The Chinese food-to-go container is designed after the one used in *A Bug's Life* (1998). It was also used in *Inside Out* (2015).

Francis' Ladybug Boogie

Opened October 7, 2002 - Duration: 1:30

An attraction similar to *Mad Tea Party* in *Disneyland*, except ladybugs are used instead of tea cups.

Heimlich's Chew Chew Train

Opened October 7, 2002 - Duration: 2:11

A train attraction in which visitors see how Heimlich finds food.

FUN FACTS

The **scent of watermelon and animal cracker** are sprayed onto the train as you pass by the corresponding food item by a Smellitzer.

For a **list of this attractions Hidden Mickeys, see page 349**.

649

Princess Dot Puddle Park

Opened October 7, 2002 - Duration: N/A

A water play area for kids that was designed to look like a giant water hose that is full of leaks and spits out random streams of water.

Tuck and Roll's Drive' Em Buggies

Opened October 7, 2002 - Duration: 1:30

A bumper car attraction, but at a slower speed.

FUN FACTS

- Tuck is the **pill bug with one big eyebrow** and Roll is the pill bug with two eyebrows.

HOLLYWOOD LAND

Hollywood Land is an area styled to appear as Hollywood's boulevards and movie backlots with Hollywood, television, and movie-themed attractions.

FUN FACTS

- A **version of the** *Tower of Terror* **attraction** from *Disney World's Hollywood Studios* opened here in 2004, but closed in 2017 to make way for *Guardians of the Galaxy – Mission: Breakout!*.

- This land **used to be called** *Hollywood Pictures Backlot* until the *California Adventure* remodel. It was renamed *Hollywood Land* for its opening June 15, 2012.

- The original name *Hollywood Pictures Backlot* **was derived from the film company created by Disney** in 1990 called Hollywood Pictures. Its first movie released was *Arachnophobia* (1990) starring Jeff Daniels and John Goodman.

- The entrance to the area with the sign *Hollywood Pictures Backlot* was removed after the makeover. It used to feature two **ceramic elephant sculptures atop columns** to pay homage to a huge set constructed for the epic Hollywood film *Intolerance* (1916) directed by D.W. Griffith.

- There were plans to put a *Hollywood Land* in *Disneyland* back in the 1980's following the release of the film *Who Framed Roger Rabbit* (1988) with themed attractions related to the movie. It would have been located between *Main Street, U.S.A.* and *Tomorrowland*.
- For a **list of DCA's Attractions of the Past**, see page 679.

 The smoking area is located near the exit of *Sunset Showcase Theater*.

Attractions

Disney Animation Studio

Inside this building are four interactive attractions.

FUN FACTS

- The size of the building **takes up one acre**.
- There are **11 giant projection screens** and 6 large-scale screens in the "Courtyard Gallery."
- Some images and sketches projected onto the screens can only be seen here and nowhere else as some **were recovered from the archives**.
- For a **list of this attractions Hidden Mickeys, see page 349**.

Turtle Talk with Crush

Opened July 15, 2005 - Duration: 10:00-12:00

A show in which one can interact with Crush from *Finding Nemo* (2003). Guests are seated in a large, movie theater-like room with children encouraged to sit up front on the floor

so Crush can see them better during the show. Crush comes down from the surface of the Ocean to appear in the "Window to the Pacific." A "Hydrophone" is used for the underwater communication with Crush. Guests (especially children) are chosen to ask Crush questions. Crush looks and moves much as he does in the movie, complete with facial expressions and subtle gestures. Crush converses freely with guests using quick wit and humor.

FUN FACTS

- This show **originally started in Florida's *Epcot*** in November 2004.
- The "Window to the Pacific" is in reality a **large rear-projection screen** portraying an animated undersea environment. Sea grasses wave on the ocean floor as fish and other aquatic creatures swim by. The image of Crush

is rendered by voice-activated 3-D animation, projected at 30-frames-per-second, so that the turtle's mouth moves in synchronization with the words of a hidden voice actor portraying the character. The sophisticated system enables the projected turtle to move about the screen, seemingly propelling himself with his flippers, doing somersaults, and hovering, in very convincing maneuvers controlled by the actor.

When engaging a particular child or adult in conversation, Crush will move to the side of the room where the involved guest is seated. The actor **expertly mimics the character voice** from the film, and is extremely adept at improvising clever and amusing reactions to questions and comments of the guests, whom he often addresses as "Dude." Undoubtedly, after playing scores of performances, the actor develops and perhaps writers have scripted, humorous responses and sassy come-backs to the most typical and often repeated audience questions and remarks. The invisible actor sees the audience via a cleverly-hidden camera (or cameras) or by other means, since he refers to the appearance and behavior of particular questioners, as well as their location in the theatre. The show is a cutting-edge blend of sophisticated computer graphic techniques, image projection, and live, interactive, and quick-witted improvisation.

In the film *Finding Nemo* (2003), **Crush was voiced by Andrew Stanton**. Andrew was the director/writer for *Nemo* and many other films. He was also the voice of Emperor Zurg in *Toy Story 2* (1999), *Toy Story 3* (2010) and on the *Buzz Lightyear Astro Blasters* in *Disneyland*. Andrew's first live-action film to write and direct was *John Carter* (2012). He recently reprised his roles of Crush and Emperor Zurg in the video game *Kinect Disneyland Adventures*.

For a **list of this attractions Hidden Mickeys, see page 349**.

Animation Academy

Opened February 8, 2001 - Duration: 10:00

A presentation on how to draw Disney characters such as Jack Skellington, Mickey Mouse, Pluto, Goofy, Tigger, Minnie Mouse, Dopey, Winnie The Pooh, and many  more. Unlike *Disney World's Academy*, the students don't get to choose what character they will be drawing in that particular class. There is a schedule of characters that will be drawn for the day. You can visit a Cast Member at the entrance to the *Academy* and ask to see the list so you know when to return for your favorite character.

When you enter the classroom, you will be given a drafting board, a blank piece of paper, and a pencil with no eraser. A Disney artist will give a presentation about animation, and, until 2005, showed a short video starring *Mushu* from *Mulan*, voiced by Eddie Murphy, and animator Chris Sanders, showing the step-by-step process to making a cartoon. They used *Redfeather* from *Pocahontas*

(1995) as an example of the animators' choosing process. *Redfeather* was supposed to be Pocahontas' side-kick, but was cut before the movie's animations started; he was to be voiced by John Candy. The artist then uses a large projector to show you step by step how to draw a specific character. At the end of the class you get to take home your drawing to keep as a souvenir.

FUN FACTS

- In the old video, Chris Sanders was **the voice of Stitch** from all the *Lilo & Stitch* (2002) movies, and Belt in *The Croods* (2013).

- For a **list of this attractions Hidden Mickeys, see page 349**.

Character Close-Up

Opened February 8, 2001 - Duration: N/A

A gallery where visitors can view all Disney characters close-up. There are many animations hanging around to view, to show the process of elimination, and deciding the final look of a character. This area has been  changed out several times with different themes and things to see.

Sorcerer's Workshop

Opened February 8, 2001 - Duration: N/A

A presentation where visitors can create their own animation. Visitors will be given a chance to do voice-over work for some popular cartoon characters from scenes of their favorite movie, including, *Lion King, Jungle Book, Snow White*, and more.

FUN FACTS

- The magic mirror is **surrounded by the different zodiac signs** along with a Disney character to represent it. The characters are: Sebastian/Cancer, Tweedledee & Tweedledum/Gemini, Phil (from Hercules)/Aries, Djali/Capricorn, Bull (from Lady and the Tramp)/Taurus, Simba/Leo, Robin Hood/Sagittarius, Snow White/Virgo, Fish from Fantasia/Pisces, Lumier/Libra, Leviathan (from Atlantis)/Scorpio.

- In the first section of this attraction, you **learn how animation movement works,** and you can learn how to draw your own animation timeline.

- In the second section, you get to sit at a chair at a computerized book and answer some questions to **find out which Disney character you are most like**. This is hosted my Lumiere and Cogsworth.

In the third section, you get the opportunity to **do voice-over work** for some of your favorite characters. You can either choose to do dialogue or sing a song. It is hosted by non-other than the voice-stealing Ursula.

For a **list of this attractions Hidden Mickeys, see page 349**.

Disney Junior: Live on Stage!

Opened April 11, 2003 - Duration: N/A

A show in which visitors can meet the Playhouse Disney characters live. Playhouse Disney is the brand name for Disney Channel's preschool programs, often airing as its own channel outside of the United States. The target age for this segment of the channel is from age 2 - 6. The brand name was rolled out in 1997 when Disney Channel moved from premium cable to basic cable. It is the main competitor to Nick Jr. in most countries.

FUN FACTS

This theater **show was called** *"Playhouse Disney Live on Stage!"* until 2011, when the name was changed to reflect the name change to the television station name change.

They perform **10 shows a day**.

The show has had **new segments added and changed throughout the years** including Mickey Mouse Clubhouse, Doc McStuffins, Sophia The First, Jake And the Neverland Pirates, Roli Poli Olli, Book of Pooh, Stanley, Bear in the Big Blue House, JoJo's Circus, My Friends Tigger and Pooh, Handy Manny, and Little Einsteins.

HYPERION THEATER

This is a theater in the park to show musicals on stage. The Hyperion has been in the park since it opened in 2001.

FUN FACTS

The *Hyperion Theater* got **its name from Hyperion Boulevard**, which is the name of the street where Walt Disney Studios started out.

- It is **modeled after the Los Angeles Theater** built in 1930 in downtown Los Angeles.
- This is **the first theater of its type** ever built in a Disney park.
- Hyperion Theater **Seating Capacity**: 2,011
- Originally, Disney wanted to use the theater for ceremonies and other events, but due to changes to the original plans, **they removed the lobby and the restrooms**. To use the restrooms, you actually have to leave the building and go back up the main street.
- Across the street, on the building's wall, is a sign for the Walt Disney Studios, based on the **billboard that stood above Walt's 1930's Hollywood Animation studio** on Hyperion Avenue.
- The **world premiere of _The Lone Ranger_** (2013) was held here on June 22, 2013.
- There were rumors going around that during the makeover of _California Adventure_, they were going to end _Aladdin_ and **start _Toy Story the Musical_** like on the cruise ships.
- _Disney's Aladdin: A Musical Spectacular_ had **its last show January 11, 2016,** thirteen years after it first opened. (_see photo_)

- There have been **multiple musicals played here** since its opening;
  - _Step in Time_ 2001-2001
  - _Blast!_ 2001-2002
  - _Disney's Aladdin: A Musical Spectacular_ 2003-2016
  - _Frozen – Live at The Hyperion_ 2016-present

FROZEN

LIVE AT THE HYPERION

Opened May 27, 2016 - Duration: 55:00

This production is a Broadway-type show inspired by the huge hit *Frozen* (2013).

FUN FACTS

- This production replaced *Disney's Aladdin: A Musical Spectacular* which had just **come off a 13- year run**.
- The show has a **cast of about 100 people**.
- When production was doing auditions, there were **over 3,500 people who wanted roles**.
- There are **five performances daily**.
- **New technology was created** for the special effects in the show, like the projection of ice onto Elsa's dress.
- For Elsa's magical dress change, **her ice dress is sewn in under her other dress,** allowing the outer dress to flip away after she pulls on the straps. It is the same trick used for the dress in *Rodgers & Hammerstein's Cinderella* on Broadway.
- A **whole new stage was built** for this production.
- A **2,200-foot screen was added** to the backdrop for the projection of images and backgrounds.
- **Puppet creator Michael Curry**, who designed the puppets for *The Lion King* musical, *Finding Nemo – The Musical*, and *Rivers of Light*, also created the puppets for this production.

MONSTERS, INC.

MIKE & SULLEY TO THE RESCUE!

Opened January 22, 2006 - Duration: 4:05

A "dark-ride" that goes through the scenes of the movie *Monsters, Inc.* (2001).

FUN FACTS

- This **attraction replaced *Superstar Limo***, which was removed due to its unpopularity.
- When you first enter Harryhausen's Restaurant, you **can smell ginger and soy sauce**.
- **Pay attention to Roz at the end** before disembarking. She is interactive and will have witty things to say to you.
- For a **list of this attractions Hidden Mickeys, see page 349**.

Sunset Showcase Theater

Opened May, 2016 - Duration: Varies

The theater is now used to show previews of upcoming Disney films.

FUN FACTS

- The entire theater **can seat 574 people**.
- From 2001 to 2014, **this building housed *Muppet*Vision 3D***.
- ***For the First Time In Forever: A Frozen Sing-Along Celebration*** was here from 2015 until its conversion into what it is now in 2016.

They first **began testing Guest reaction to movie sneak peeks** in here with the release of *Tron: Legacy* (2010). They then showed *Frankenweenie* (2012) and *Oz the Great and Powerful* (2013). It wasn't until the theater conversion in 2016 that they show sneak peels regularly: *Alice Through the Looking Glass* (2016), *Pete's Dragon* (2016), *Doctor Strange* (2016), *Beauty and the Beast* (2017), and *Pirates of the Caribbean: Dead Men Tell No Tales* (2017)

The lobby area is **used to display props** or other articles from the movies to entertain Guests while they wait. This is Belle's dress and the Enchanted Rose.

For a **list of this attractions Hidden Mickeys, see page 349**.

GUARDIANS OF THE GALAXY - BREAKOUT!

Opened May 27, 2017 - Duration: 2:15

A drop attraction based on the characters from the movie *Guardians of the Galaxy* (2014). The exterior of the building is designed to look like the fortress of Taneleea Tivan, "The Collector." He has brought his vast collection to Terra (Earth) for our viewing pleasure. The Collector's main attraction is the Guardians of the Galaxy as he has

imprisoned them in cases. Rocket has escaped and is seeking the help of the riders to free the other Guardians.

FUN FACTS

This 183-foot attraction is **the tallest attraction at the resort**, as well as the tallest building in Anaheim. At least, at the time it was built.

The **attraction opened 22 days after the release of their second film,** *Guardians of the Galaxy Vol. 2* (2017). The belief for the later opening is that the attraction will contain spoilers for the film and the 22 days will give Guests a chance to see the film before visiting the park.

The Collector, **Tanlella Tivan, is holding an orloni**. That is the rodent-type creatures seen in the bar scene in *Guardians of the Galaxy* (2014) when everyone was placing bets. Baby Groot also rides on one in the opening scene of *Guardians of the Galaxy Vol. 2* (2017).

- Chris Pratt (Star-Lord), Zoe Saldana (Gamora), Dave Bautista (Drax), Pom Klementieff (Mantis), and Benicio Del Toro (The Collector) **reprised their roles for the attraction**.

- This is the **first Marvel-themed attraction Disney has made in America**.

- It is the **second Marvel-themed attraction Disney has built in the world**. *Iron Man Experience* opened in *Hong Kong Disneyland* in January 2017.

- Around the exterior queue are plants with their names listed, like Pachypodium Succulentum and Rhipsalis Cruciformis, among others. **These are all real plants**.

- During the pre-boarding video, **Stan Lee makes a cameo appearance**. He says, *"Hey. Do you guys validate?"* Stan Lee has made a cameo in all of the Marvel films made by Disney, and most of the movies prior to Disney. (*photo is of Stan Lee*)

- The pre-boarding room, the room that used to show the video of Rod Serling, now has the most realistic Audio-Animatronic made by Disney. **Rocket Raccoon talks to Guests** while not only moving around fluidly, but also moving left to right. A movement animatronic characters cannot make because they are bolted down. A close rival to this animatronic is that of the shaman Na'vi in *Pandora* in *Animal Kingdom*, who also has realistic and fluid movement.

- When this attraction had its **grand re-opening, there were many big names that showed** up for the presentation, including Zoe Saldana (Gamora), Michael Rooker (Yondu), Pom Klementieff (Mantis), Benicio Del Toro (The Collector), James Gunn (the film's script writer), and Bob Chapek (Disney Company CEO).

- Disney added adult Groot to the cast of characters for a *Meet & Greet* opportunity. The difference between Groot, Mickey, Minnie, Goofy, and all the other characters, is he can talk. However, all he can say is *"I am Groot."* This makes Groot the **first *Meet & Greet* character to be able to talk to the Guests** in the *Disneyland* Resort. *Magic Kingdom* has had a talking Mickey, but *Disneyland* has not. This excludes the "face characters" like Aladdin, Alice, Cinderella, and the other princesses.

- The **adding of adult Groot changes the timeline** of the attraction because Groot was a teenager in post credit scene of *Guardians of the Galaxy Vol. 2* (2017). On the attraction, Groot is still just a little sapling, meaning the timeline of the events of the attraction take place after the movie ends, but before the post credit scene.

In the entry level of the attraction before boarding, **there are lots of "Easter Eggs"** hinting at all of the Marvel films or other Disney things;

- Cosmo the Spacedog - *Guardians of the Galaxy* (2014)
- Hanging in a cage high above is Figment - *Epcot's Journey into Imagination*
- An Ultron sentry that lights up and randomly quotes lines from the movie - *Avengers 2: Age of Ultron* (2015)
- Armor from the Nova Corps - *Guardians of the Galaxy* (2014)
- Armor from the Einherjar, the warriors of Asgard - *Thor* (2011) and *Thor: Dark World* (2013)
- Warlock's Eye from Odin's trophy room, it follows your movement - *Thor* (2011)
- Kree orb - *Agents of S.H.I.E.L.D.* (2013-present) episode *Failed Experiment*
- Dark Elf mask - *Thor: The Dark World* (2013)
- A cocoon, believed to be Adam Warlock's, as seen in *Thor: Dark World* (2013) and *Guardians of the Galaxy* (2014)
- Kree artifacts, as in Ronan's race - *Guardians of the Galaxy* (2014)
- Artifacts from Atlantis, possibly hinting at Prince Namor the Sub-Mariner
- An Asgardian War Hammer that will one day belong to Beta Ray Bill, the one who wins Thor's hammer, Mjolnir. Odin then gives Bill his own hammer, this one, also called Stormbreaker.

- A painting with The Collector and his brother The Grandmaster, played by Jeff Goldblum - *Thor: Ragnarok* (2017)
- The Crimson Bands of Cyttorak are hanging on the wall in the pre-boarding video room. They were the full-body, metal cage used by Doctor Strange to imprison Kaecilius - *Doctor Strange* (2016).
- There is a little figure on The Collector's desk of a ghost dog - *Haunted Mansion*
- A Hydra soldier helmet - *Captain America: The First Avenger* (2011)
- On the shelf behind the open book is a bellhop hat - *Tower of Terror*
- One of the books has a HTH bookmark - *Hollywood Tower Hotel*
- A case of eyes marked "Chitauri" - *The Avengers* (2012)
- A case marked "Orloni" which are little rodent-like creatures - *Guardians of the Galaxy* (2014)

- Just before boarding the lift, you can see <u>Harold,</u> the original Yeti - *Matterhorn Bobsleds*
- <u>The painting</u> that is behind the octopus used to hang in the *Twilight Zone Tower of Terror* on the wall before the pre-boarding video room.
- <u>The octopus</u> is Dolores from the extinct attraction *The Country Bear Vacation Hoedown* (1986-2001) that existed in *Critter Country* until The

Many Adventures of Winnie the Pooh replaced it.

🌐 **Tyler Bates composed the music for the attraction queue**. He also composed the music for both of the *Guardians of the Galaxy* films. Some of his other notable works; *John Wick: Chapter 2* (2017), *John Wick* (2014), *The Darkest Hour* (2011), *Conan the Barbarian* (2011), *Sucker Punch* (2011), *Watchmen* (2009), *Halloween* (2007), *Doomsday* (2008), *Grindhouse* (2007), *300* (2006), and *Get Carter* (2000).

🌐 **There are six randomized possibilities for this attraction**. The drop experience can vary between these six possibilities;
- Drax vs. Beast
- Antigravity
- Escape
- Drones
- Quill vs. Orloni
- Abilisk Attack

🌐 **Along with the randomized drops, there is accompanying music**;
- *"I Want You Back"* by The Jackson 5
- *"Hit Me with Your Best Shot"* by Pat Benatar
- *"Give Up the Funk"* by Parliament
- *"Born to Be Wild"* by Steppenwolf
- *"Burning Love"* by Elvis Presley
- *"Free Ride"* by Edgar Winter Group

🌐 For a **list of this attractions Hidden Mickeys, see page 349**.

DISNEYLAND'S ATTRACTIONS OF THE PAST

main Street, U.S.A.

1955-1962, Main Street Shooting Gallery
1961-1963, Babes in Toyland Exhibit
- Utilizing the sets from the movie of the same name, this walk-through attraction occupied the *Opera House* near the park's entrance.
1970-1973, Legacy of Walt Disney
1973-1989, *Disneyland* Presents a Preview of Coming Attractions
1955-19??, Black Shoe Shine Boys
- They would tap dance and sing as part of their routine, dressed in the *Main Street* era.
2005–2009, *Disneyland*: The First 50 Magical Years
- Narrative film on the history of *Disneyland*, hosted by Steve Martin and Donald Duck

Tomorrowland

1955-1956, Court of Honor
1955-1956, *Tomorrowland Boats* (renamed *Phantom Boats* in 1956)
- It was a man-made lake for children to captain their own motor boats. Disney had too many problems with the boats overheating and smoking, so they remade the engine area covering it better so they wouldn't smoke so much, but then this caused them to overheat faster. Disney also resorted to having a Cast Member be the skipper of each boat and steer the boats around at reasonable speeds. On January 15, 1956, the *Tomorrowland Boats* were re-named *The Phantom Boats*. It was just too costly for Disney to maintain with the needed 17 Cast Members to steer all the boats, and the public lost interest due to not being able to steer themselves. Disney eventually closed it down in August 1956, making it the **first permanent attraction to be removed** from *Disneyland*. The attraction only lasted for 11 months before its partial removal. It was located in the area that now houses the *Finding Nemo Submarine Voyage*. The other part, nearest to *Fantasyland*, was turned into the *Motor Boat Cruise,* which was later re-named *Boat Cruise to Gummi Glen*.
1955-1960, *Space Station X-1* (renamed *Satellite View of America* in 1958)
1955-1960, *The World Beneath Us*
1955-1960, *Aluminum Hall of Fame*
-It was sponsored by Kaiser Aluminum and told the story of the history and creation of aluminum. The center piece in the exhibit was an aluminum pig.
1955-1963, *Dutch Boy Color Gallery*
1955-1966, *Clock of the World*

662

1955-1966, *Monsanto Hall of Chemistry*
 - This facility, which was similar to a fair exhibit, lasted for 11 years. It showed people the importance of chemicals and what impact they can have in our lives in the future. It was eventually replaced by *Adventure Thru Inner Space,* and then *Star Tours* in 1987.
1955-1966, *Rocket to the Moon*
 - Inside a building under a tall futuristic-looking rocket ship, the audience sat in seats around central viewing screens (top and bottom of the center of the room) so that they could see where they were going as they headed away from Earth and towards other worlds. As the real journey to the moon became more likely, the attraction was refurbished as Flight to the Moon from 1967-1975.
1955-1997, *Circarama, U.S.A.* (renamed *Circle-Vision 360°* in 1967)
 - Scenes from around the United States (and, later, China) in 360-degree splendor. Guests stood in a large, circular room and watched a film projected on nine large, contiguous screens that surrounded them. During its run, the attraction was hosted by Bell System, AT&T, Pacific Southwest Airlines, and Delta Air Lines. In 1998, the theater became the attraction-queue for the short-lived *Rocket Rods* attraction. After the closure of *Rocket Rods,* the theater sat empty, except for a short period after September 11, 2001, when the theater opened and "America the Beautiful" was shown. The theater was completely removed in 2004, when construction for *Buzz Lightyear Astro Blasters* began.
  Shows were:
- 1955-1959, "A Tour of the West"
- 1960-1984, "America the Beautiful"
- 1984-1989, "All Because Man Wanted to Fly" (lobby pre-show)
- 1984-1996, "American Journeys"
- 1984-1996, "Wonders of China" (is currently in the *China World Showcase* in *EPCOT*)
- 1996-1997 and after September 11, 2001, "America the Beautiful," again

1955-1966, *20,000 Leagues Under the Sea* **exhibit**
1955-1966, *Flight Circle*
1955-1966, *Art Corner*
1955-1966, *Hobbyland*
1955-1966, *Monsanto Hall of Chemistry*
1955-1999, *Tomorrowland Autopia*
 - In 2000, the expanded *Autopia* opened at the same location, using much of the same infrastructure as the original.
1956-1958, *American Dairy Association Exhibit*
1956-1960, *Crane Company Bathroom of Tomorrow*
1956-1960, *Bathroom of Tomorrow*
1956-1963, *Our Future in Colors*
1956-1966, *Avenue of the Flags*
1956-1994, *Skyway to Fantasyland*
1956-1997, *Jet Ride*; has undergone the following incarnations:
- 1956-1964, *Astro-Jets*
- 1964-1966, *Tomorrowland Jets*

- 1967-1997, *Rocket Jets*
1957-1958, *The Viewliner*
- "The fastest miniature train in the world" ran alongside the *Disneyland Railroad* for just over a year, and therefore has the distinction of being one of the shortest-lived attractions in the park's history. It was located partially where *it's a small world* is now, and stretched over to almost the backside of the *Autopia* tracks.
1957-1967, *Monsanto House of the Future*
- A walk-through tour of a plastic house with plastic furnishings and interior and fascinating modern appliances, such as dishwashers and microwaves. The house was designed in roughly the shape of an X (looking down on it) with high-tech rounded exterior contours, all made from white plastic with large windows. It was outdated almost as soon as it was built. It was anchored to a solid concrete foundation that proved to be so indestructible that, when it was
dismantled, the work crew gave up and left some of the support pilings in place and they can still be seen in *Neptune's Grotto*, now *Pixie Hollow*, between the *Tomorrowland* entrance and *Fantasyland*. Just look behind the entrance sign for the *Pixie Hollow* queue for cammo mesh covering the concrete.
1959; 1965-1967, Mermaids
-The mermaids first appeared at the *Submarine Voyage's* grand opening in 1959 where they were used for promotional purposes. They later returned to the lagoon for the summers of 1965, 1966, and 1967. They would swim around for four hours each day to entertain guests by doing aquatic stunts. Sometimes they would swim up to the people floating by in the submarine and peek through the porthole. They would also perform sychronized swimming. Some of the girls started to complain about the fumes from the, then diesel, subs and the high chlorine content of the water. So, it pressed Disney to remove them. The Cast Member girls who portrayed the lovely mermaids made a reported $1.65 an hour. There were some instances when young men were caught jumping into the water and swimming out to the mermaids, who were basking in the sun on the coral in the middle of the lagoon.
1959-1998, *Submarine Voyage*
- Riders entered the half-submerged miniature submarines by descending through access hatches at either end of the submarine, sat on tiny fold-down seats, and leaned forward to peer out through port holes on either side of the submarine. The submarines moved around a track in the mermaid lagoon and simulated diving by having bubbles rise around it with the purported captain intoning commands over the loudspeaker (they never really submerged). On the trip, riders saw real-looking and imaginary sea life fastened to rocks or floating in the water, a treasure chest of gold, mermaids, a sea serpent, and passed under

664

icebergs at the "North Pole." The submarines were originally military gray, but were repainted high-visibility yellow in the 1980's. The new attraction, *Finding Nemo Submarine Voyage*, replaced the original submarine attraction in 2007.

1960-1966, *The Art of Animation*

1960-1984, *Bell Telephone Systems Phone Exhibits*

1961-1966, *Flying Saucers*

- Sort of a people-sized version of air-hockey. Cars rode on a cushion of air and were steered by shifting body weight. The air cushion was supplied from below through holes that opened when the cars passed over. The attraction was later reimagined as *Luigi's Flying Tires* and opened in *Cars Land*.

1963-1964, *New York World's Fair Exhibit*

1965-1966, *Monsanto's Fashions and Fabrics Through the Ages*

1967-1975, *Flight to The Moon*

1967-1973, *General Electric Carousel of Progress*

- A sit-down show in which the building rotated the audience around a series of stages. The stages had audio-animatronic humans and household appliances showing how appliances and electronics advanced about every 20 years from the turn of the century to the "modern" era of the early 1960's. The audience stopped in front of each stage while the characters joked with each other, described life at the time in history, and demonstrated their kitchen. This attraction originated at the 1964 New York World's Fair and was installed at Disneyland after the fair closed. The transition from stage to stage was accompanied by all the characters singing the upbeat theme song, whose chorus was "There's a great, big beautiful tomorrow shining at the end of every day; there's a great, big, beautiful tomorrow, and tomorrow's just a dream away."

1967-1985, *Adventure Thru Inner Space*

- This attraction, originally sponsored by Monsanto, seemed inspired by *Fantastic Voyage*, a popular film of the year before the attraction was first presented. It was a dark-ride that pretended to shrink the rider gradually down to microscopic size within a snowflake, then further to view a water molecule in the flake, then finally to the point where one could see the throbbing nucleus of a single oxygen atom with electrons zooming all around. The attraction's entryway featured a floor-to-ceiling spiral network of strings down which evenly spaced droplets of oil slowly ran, appearing to be sparkling liquid beads in nearly suspended animation. From the line inside the entry, line-standers could watch other riders in their 3-person cars disappear into a shrinking machine and then see the other shrunken riders appear in perfect synch and then disappear into the attraction. At one point, within the attraction, a gigantic eye perused the riders through a huge microscope lens.

☂ The snowflake props were partially made from styrofoam. People passing by would break pieces off and ruin the experience for other guests. This caused Disney to create the "envelope of protection" on future attractions which is why objects on an attraction are further away from the riders than they used to be.

665

@ Disney created a special ticket for the ticket books specifically for this attraction because teenagers would repeatedly ride the attraction and cause disruptions. Each ticket book only had one ticket to ride it.

@ Some Guests were worried that if Disney shrank them down, they wouldn't be returned to their normal size. They believed that with Disney's advanced technology, they would actually shrink people.

@ One Guest complained to a Cast Member that she never saw her son pass by in the shrunken cars.

1967-1986, *Tomorrowland Stage*
1967-1995, *PeopleMover*
- A scenic, slow-moving attraction high-above *Tomorrowland* that was intended to demonstrate how people could be shuttled around a central urban area without rushing to board individual trains or drive individual cars. It consisted of many dozens of small open-air cars seating up to eight riders, all running continuously on a track above and through the various attractions in *Tomorrowland*. People boarded the *PeopleMover* by stepping onto a moving walkway that brought them up to the speed of the cars, which then took riders all around *Tomorrowland*, providing a preview of all of the *Tomorrowland* attractions. It ran through the entry waiting areas for *CircleVision* and *Adventure Through Inner Space*, down the main promenade, over the *Autopia*, and so on. After the attraction was closed, the track sat vacant for two-and-a-half years until the opening of the ill-fated *Rocket Rods*. A new version is reported to be in the works as part of the "*Tomorrowland* Revitalization Plan," and scheduled to open after the new Finding Nemo attraction.

1967-1995, *Alpine Gardens*
1974-1988, *America Sings*
- A sit-down show in the same building using the same stages as *Carousel of Progress*. Audio-Animatronic animals sang American tunes from different eras. It was described as a "lighthearted journey to Musicland, U.S.A." After the attraction closed in spring of 1988, most of the singing, dancing animals were recycled into the current *Splash Mountain* attraction, except for Sam the eagle and his co-host, Ollie the owl. Earlier in 1987, two geese were removed and their outer skins peeled and used in the *Star Tours* queue as droids. Between the years of 1988 and early 1997, the building was completely empty, except for seats and the old stages. It was then occupied by *Innoventions*, which left in 2015.

1975-1992, *Mission to Mars*
1977-1984, *Space Stage*
1977-2015, *Starcade*
-Originally the arcade took up both the top and bottom floor. The arcade shrunk from over 200 games down to only a few dozen. The games were all crammed into a small corner by the back entrance to make way for the *Star Trader* gift shop expansion. There was an X-Wing Starfighter from the *Star Wars* movie saga hanging in the second floor. It is said to have

been a prop from the movies. The X-Wing can now be seen hanging in the *Star Trader*.

1986-2015, *Captain EO*
was a 3-D film starring Michael Jackson and directed by Francis Ford Coppola, who came up with the name which is Greek for "dawn." After showing in *Tomorrowland* from 1986 to 1997, EO left to make way for *Honey, I shrunk The Audience!* It later returned to the *Magic Eye Theater* on February 23, 2010.

- *Captain EO* first opened September 18, 1986, and closed April 7, 1997.

- The theater can seat 575 people.

- The name EO was derived from the name of the Greek goddess Eos, the goddess of dawn, which is depicted when EO brings light to the queen's land.

- The film's executive producer was George Lucas.

- It is said that Michael Jackson also asked Steven Spielberg to produce it, but he was working on his film *The Color Purple* (1985).

- The film was choreographed by Jeffrey Hornaday and Michael Jackson.

- The film was directed by Francis Ford Coppola as suggested by George Lucas. Some other films he was involved with are *The Godfather* (1972), *American Graffiti* (1973), *The Godfather II* (1974), *Apocalypse Now* (1979), *The Black Stallion* (1979), *The Outsiders* (1983), *The Godfather III* (1990), *Jack* (1996) and *Sleepy Hollow* (1999).

- The score was written by James Horner and featured two songs, "We Are Here to Change the World" and "Another Part of Me;" both written and performed by Michael Jackson. The album was released to CD in 2010 and titled *Captain EO's Voyage;* it contains 12 tracks.

- EO was named as such after the "Goddess of the Dawn" from Greek Mythology, Eos.

- The Supreme Leader was played by Anjelica Huston, better known for her role as Morticia Addams in *The Addams Family* (1991) and *Addams Family Values* (1993). She is also the voice of Queen Clarion in the *Tinker Bell* movie series.

- The rest of the cast list includes:
  - Dick Shawn - Commander Bog
  - Tony Cox – Hooter
    - Ewok in *Star Wars 6: Return of the Jedi* (1983), Limo Driver in *Me, Myself & Irene* (2000), Bink in *Epic Movie* (2007), and Knuck in *Oz the Great and Powerful* (2013).
  - Debbie Lee Carrington - Idee
    - Ewok in *Star Wars 6: Return of the Jedi* (1983), Valerie Vomit in *The Garbage Pail Kids Movie* (1987), Little Bigfoot in *Harry and the Hendersons* (1987), Thumbelina in *Total Recall* (1990), and Kitty Katz in *Tiptoes* (2003).
  - Cindy Sorenson - Odee

- Gary DePew - Major Domo

🐜 *Captain EO* is regarded as the first "4-D" film (4-D being the name given to a 3-D film which incorporates in-theater effects, such as lasers, smoke, frame synced to the film narrative, etc). This innovation was suggested by producer-writer Lemorande, who is sometimes referred to as "The Father of 4-D."

🐜 *Captain EO* made full use of its 3-D effects. The action on the screen extended into the audience, including lasers, laser impacts, smoke effects, and starfields that filled the theater. These effects resulted in the 17-minute film costing an estimated $30 million to produce. At the time, it was the most expensive film ever produced on a per-minute basis, averaging out at $1.76 million per minute.

🐜 The 2010 version does not include the in-theater laser and starfield effects. It does utilize hydraulics previously used for *Honey, I Shrunk the Audience!* to make the seats tilt along with Captain EO's spaceship. They are also used for the bass heavy musical numbers.

🐜 Two new songs appeared in the film. The first is an early mix of "Another Part of Me." The song was re-mixed and later appeared on Jackson's hugely successful *Bad* album. It was released as a single in 1988.

🐜 The song "Another Part of Me" makes a brief appearance in the movie *Rush Hour*, in which Chris Tucker mimics Captain EO after blowing up a car.

🐜 "We Are Here to Change the World" was not officially released until 2004 as part of *Michael Jackson: The Ultimate Collection*. However, this version is a shorter edit of the full-length song.

🐜 Soul/R&B singer Deniece Williams covered the song "We Are Here to Change the World" on her *As Good as It Gets* album in 1988.

🐜 After the death of Michael Jackson on June 25, 2009, *Captain EO* regained popularity on the Internet. For several years, a small group of fans had petitioned Disney to bring back the attraction and Jackson's death had brought this campaign to a peak. Soon afterward, Disney officials were seen in Disneyland at the *Magic Eye Theater* and reportedly held a private screening of *Captain EO* to determine if it could be shown again. It was rumored that Disneyland would announce the return of the attraction at Disneyland in September. However, on September 10, Disney CEO Bob Iger said, "There aren't plans to bring back Captain EO at this time ... We are looking at it. It's the kind of thing that, if we did it, would get a fair amount of attention and we'd want to make sure we do it right."

🐜 On December 18, 2009, it was announced that *Captain EO* would return to *Tomorrowland* at *Disneyland* beginning in February 2010. Social and Print Media Manager, Heather Hust Rivera from Disneyland Resorts, confirmed this on the DisneyParks Blog and stated that *Honey, I Shrunk the Audience!* would be closing. The attraction hosted its final public showing in the *Magic Eye Theater* at midnight on January 4, 2010, to make way for the Michael Jackson film's return.

668

In the scene when the Supreme Leader is lifted into the air, Anjelica Huston had a stand-in stunt double. **This part was played by Terri Hardin, a Disney Imagineer, sculptor, and puppeteer for the *Jim Henson Company*.**  The very talented Terri is noted as one of the top ten puppeteers in California and has done many things for the Disney parks including the model sculpt for the Br'er Fox on *Splash Mountain* in three Disney parks, the Br'er Rabbit log figurehead in *Magic Kingdom's* and *Tokyo Disneyland's Splash Mountain* (*see photo*). In that attraction she also designed the main drop, the puppeteering for Idee and Odee in *Captain Eo*, the puppeteer for the *it's a small world* dolls in *Muppet*Vision 3D*, and designed all of *Dragon's Lair* in *Disneyland Paris*. Some other of her projects included the costumes in *Dune* (1984), puppeteering "The Twins" in *Men In Black* (1997), the puppeteer for Sharkhead and the Worms in *Men In Black 2* (2002), the puppeteer for the face of the Stay Puft Marshmallow Man and the demon dogs in *Ghostbusters* (1984), *The Flintstones* (1994), *The Flintstones In Viva Rock Vegas* (2000), the puppeteer for Baby  Sinclare's arms in *Dinosaurs* (1991), *Indian In The Cupboard* (1995), *Monkeybone* (2001), *The Country Bears* (2002), *Team America* (2004), the facial puppeteer for Molly Rex in *Theodore Rex* (1995), in *Jungle 2 Jungle* (1997). She also created the drugged cat that Tim Allen shot with the blowgun in *Mars Attacks!* (1996); she made the dove of peace and the presidential parakeets for *The Relic* (1997); she made the giant ground sloth skeleton and a second version of it that was  burnable; she designed and built the Foster Imposter chickens for the Foster Farms commercials (*see photo of plushes*), and is the puppeteer for the passenger chicken. Terri was also a figure sculptor for Disney for years designing and creating many of the collector figures that we all like. One of which is Tinker Bell walking along the map to show Captain Hook where to find Peter Pan (*see photo*). Her final project for Disney was a large bronze *Disneyland* puzzle. She also has an instructional DVD titled "*Pumpkin Sculpting with Professional Artist Terri Hardin,*" and a book *Tales from Terri, A Disney Sculptors Life – Volume One*.

669

Still today, she custom sculps figurines for collectors. This Stitch and Remy (*see photo*) were sculpted by her in 2016 and 2017. She still sculpts all the time and sells them on her website ***www.squareup.com/store/terri-hardin-designs-inc***. She is interviewed quite frequently on podcasts, just look her up. Her stories are amazing and she is intriguing to listen to. If you have an opportunity to meet

her in person as a Disney convention, go up and say hello to her. She is very animated when she is talking, it comes from her days as a puppeteer. You will be hanging on her every word.

🔵 The attraction was originally titled *Captain EO*. After its re-opening, the title was changed to *Captain EO Tribute*.

🔵 The area where this theater sits use to house the attraction *Flying Saucers* from 1961-1966. It was the *Tomorrowland Stage* from 1967 until it was removed in 1977 to make way for *Space Mountain*. A smaller stage was built called the *Space Stage* which stood from 1977 until the building of the *Magic Eye Theater* in 1985.

🔵 When the *Magic Eye Theater* opened, it showed off its new 3D technology with the film *Magic Journeys*. *Magic Journeys* played on the *Space Stage* from June 1984 until the opening of *Magic Eye Theater,* when it switched to playing inside.

1986-present, *Magic Eye Theater*, which still exists with current 3-D films, also featured the following:

- 1986, *Magic Journeys*
- 1986-1997, *Captain EO*
- 1997-2010, *Honey, I shrunk The Audience.*
- 2010-2015, *Captain EO Tribute* (brought back in commemoration of Michael Jackson's death)
- 2015-Present, *Star Wars: Path of The Jedi* – A ten-minute recap of the first six Star Wars films designed to remind, or inform, people of the Star Wars films series storyline to prepare them for the release of *Star Wars: The Force Awakens* (2015).
- Since *Captain EO* left, the theater has been used to show previews of upcoming movies like *Tomorrowland*, *Big Hero 6*, and *Guardians of the Galaxy* to build up interest in the films. The theater was renamed *Tomorrowland Theater*.

1987-2010, *Star Tours*

- One of the most popular attractions in *Disneyland* due to the huge following of Star Wars fans. This attraction was replaced with a newer up-to-date version of the same attraction with current technology, special effects, and a new storyline to keeps the fans enthralled and was renamed *Star Tours: The Adventures Continue.*

1996, *Toy Story Funhouse and Hamm's All-Doll Revue*

670

-This short-lived, temporary attraction was located next to the *Magic Eye Theater* entrance. It was where the entrance to *Space Mountain* is now. You could meet with Buzz and Woody for a photo op, interact with the other characters, and play some games. After you exited, there was a stage show called *Hamm's All-Doll Revue*.

1998-2000, *Rocket Rods*

- A short-lived attempt at a thrill attraction using the massive supportive infrastructure and track left from the scenic *PeopleMover* attraction. The line for the *Rocket Rods* was routed through the old *Circle-Vision* theater, where early Disney films about transportation, combined with more recent footage, entertained riders before they continued on to the attraction itself. The retro-styled rockets, each seating up to five riders, traveled along the former *PeopleMover* track, periodically accelerating rapidly until they rose onto their back ends and then decelerating until the front end dropped back to the track. However, ongoing technical problems that resulted in frequent attraction closures were never resolved. After the attraction closed for good, the tracks and supporting structure were left standing unused along the main promenade.

1998-2002, *Cosmic Waves*

1998-2003, *The American Space Experience*

- An exhibit highlighting space exploration in conjunction with NASA's 40th Anniversary. It occupied the former shop location outside of the *Circle-Vision 360* theater. It has been replaced by the FASTPASS Distribution Center and the *Buzz Lightyear Astro Blasters* attraction.

1998-2015, *Innoventions*

-A large round building housing various games and demonstrations of new technologies, much like *Epcot*. It uses the same building that formerly housed the *Carousel of Progress* and *America Sings*. You could spend hours in here playing video games and cooling off out of the sun.

- It made one full revolution every 17 minutes, 40 seconds; it doesn't rotate anymore.
- It rotated at an excessive speed of 1 mile per hour. During testing, it is said the building could reach speeds of 14 to 15 miles per hour.
- The building used to house a previous attraction, *Carousel of Progress* (1967-1973).
- The building also used to house the attraction *America Sings* (1974-1988).
- Tom Morrow was the host for this attraction. Tom was voiced by Nathan Lane (Timon, from *Lion King*). Mr. Tom Morrow used to be the director of the Control Center on *Mission to Mars* until it closed in 1992.
- Tom Morrow sang a quick little line from the "Zip-A-Dee-Do-Dah" song during his speech before you enter. *Innoventions* used to be the building that housed the attraction *America Sings*. Since the changeover, the characters were moved to *Splash Mountain* and are all now singing "Zip-A-Dee-Do-Dah".
- Tom Morrow briefly sang part of the "Great Big Beautiful Tomorrow" song that played in this building when it was the *Carousel of Progress* and was written by The Sherman Brothers (see *Imagineer Mini Biographies* page 287).

671

🏰 Tom Morrow was standing on a grate because he dripped oil.

🏰 After Tom's presentation, he continued to move around without talking until it was time for the next group of people.

🏰 The design of Tom was used to create Timekeeper in the attraction *The Timekeeper* in *Disney World's Magic Kingdom* (1994-2006). He was voiced by Robin Williams.

🏰 The mural painted on the outside showed some attractions from *Tomorrowland's* past, like the *Moonliner*, the *House of the Future,* and the original *Monorails*.

🏰 This building used to house a popular show called *Stitch's Picture Phone,* where a family would go into a small room and talk one-on-one with Stitch. It was removed in the beginning of 2009 due to the cost of upkeep.

🏰 If you planned your time right, you could exit the building when it was time for the fireworks and get a great, unobstructed view from the upper floor.

🏰 The building constantly had new exhibits to see.

- 1998-2000: Honeywell sponsored playground
  - 1998-2000: Silicon Graphics sponsored A Bug's Life Exhibit
  - 1998-2004: General Motors simulator attraction
  - 1998-2007: Hewlett Packard-sponsored free computer game arcade
  - 2000-2007: AT&T–Hyperlink Hopscotch
  - 2000-2007: Pioneer "Virtual Resort", guests experience a virtual reality vacation
  - 2000-2015: St. Joseph Medical Center's Healthy University
  - 2004-2005: Segway Track, where guests 16 and older could ride a Segway (*see photo*)
  - 2005-2007: VMK Central (Vitual Magic Kingdom)
  - 2005-2009: Talk to Stitch, an interactive experience in which guests could talk to Stitch from *Lilo & Stitch* (2002) using technology similar to that of Turtle Talk with Crush in *California Adventure*
  - 2005-2015: Honda ASIMO theater (*see photo*)
  - 2007-2008: Segway Track, it returned for another year (*see photo*)
  - 2007-2015: Siemens AG Project Tomorrow
  - 2008-2011: The Neighborhood at Innoventions, within the five zones guests would watch and sometimes participate in live shows about Taylor Morrison homes, Yamaha musical instruments, ABC multi-format programming, Honda, or Southern California Edison.
  - 2008-2015: Taylor Morrison / Microsoft Innoventions Dream Home (sponsored by HP, Microsoft, and Taylor Morrison), was a house filled with the latest

technology that is either on the market or soon to be available. The house was inhabited by the fictional Elias family, which was hosting an open house to show off their newly acquired technology.

1999-2002, *Radio Disney Broadcast Booth*
2001-2006, *Club Buzz*
2015-2016, *Super Hero HQ*

-This *Meet and Greet* was established in the *Innoventions* building. Some of the exhibits first showed up when it was still *Innoventions* in 2013. It closed in April and moved the *Meet and Greets* to *California Adventure.*

- 2013-2016: Iron Man Tech Presented by Stark Industries, a promotional exhibit to promote the release of *Iron Man 3* (2013), Paul Bettany (Vision in the *Avengers* films) provided the voice of J.A.R.V.I.S. as he did in the films.
- 2013–2016: Thor: Treasures of Asgard, was a promotional exhibit to promote the release of *Thor: The Dark World* (2013).
- 2014–2015: Captain America: The Living Legend and Symbol of Courage, was a promotional exhibit for the release of *Captain America: The Winter Soldier* (2014).
- 2015-2016: V.A.U.L.T. featuring Spider-Man; it was a promotional exhibit to meet with your favorite web slinger. Guests could meet him before his appearance in the upcoming film *Captain America: Civil War* (2016), Spider-Man's first Marvel film with the Disney Company.

Fantasyland

1955, *Canal Boats of the World*
- Renamed *Storybook Land Canal Boats,* which is still an active attraction today.

1955-1964, *Mickey Mouse Club Theater*
- It was renamed *Fantasyland Theatre* in 1964.
- The theater was able to seat 400 guests.
- They generaly showed a 30-minute cartoon.

1955-1956, *Mickey Mouse Club Circus*
- This was an actual circus attraction with acrobats, horses, and other stunts starring professional performers and the kids from the *Mickey Mouse Club*. This was the **shortest-lived attraction, only lasting 46** days before closing due to lack of interest. Guests skipped seeing the circus because they could see that anytime; the other Disney attractions they could not. After the Circus closed, *Keller's Jungle Killers* took its place for another seven months before its closing and removal. The two $48,000 candy-striped circus tents were located near where the *Matterhorn* is today. After the attraction was removed, the tents were sent over to *Holidayland* to provide shade. The circus wagons that Disney rounded up and refurbished for this attraction were then sent to the Disney studio to be used in the film *Toby Tyler* (1960), and then later donated to the Circus World Museum in Baraboo, Wisconsin. One of the Imagineers on this project was Richard Irvine, who's son married Kim Thomas (Leota Toombs' daughter), who's name was then changed to Kim Irvine. She is the current face of Madame Leota in the *Haunted Mansion Holiday*. Richard had the *Richard F. Irvine Riverboat* in *Magic Kingdom* dedicated to him.

1956, *Keller's Jungle Killers*

1955-2001, *Sleeping Beauty Castle* (closed after 9/11 for security reasons).

1956-1994, *Skyway to Tomorrowland*
- This attraction, a typical aerial lift attraction seen in many parks, traveled from a chalet on the west side of *Fantasyland*, through the *Matterhorn*, to a station in *Tomorrowland*. Cabins for up to about six people hung from cables and ran constantly back and forth between the two lands. One difference between this skyway and those in many other parks is that even from above, *Disneyland's* backstage areas were hidden from view. When the *Skyway* closed in 1994, all signs of it, including its huge supporting towers, vanished seemingly overnight. It was closed primarily for financial reasons, as refurbishing it to comply with recently passed safety and accessibility laws would have also necessitated changes to the *Matterhorn* (through which it passed), which was deemed financially prohibitive. The chalet, which still exists on a hillside in *Fantasyland*, was hidden instantly by tall pine trees. One of the two holes on the *Tomorrowland* side of the *Matterhorn* was partly sealed up a few years later. This was all verified by Disney Imagineer Bob Gurr.

1956-1958, *Junior Autopia*

1957-1966, *Midget Autopia*

1957-1991, *Motor Boat Cruise*:
- 1991-1993, Renamed *Motor Boat Cruise to Gummi Glen* (Based on TV show, *Gummi Bears*)

1959-1991, *Fantasyland Autopia*:
- 1991-1993, *Rescue Ranger Raceway*

674

- 1993-2000, *Fantasyland Autopia* (merged with *Tomorrowland Autopia* to become *Autopia* in 2000)

1961-1982, *Skull Rock and Pirate's Cove* (located near the entrance to *Storybook Land* attraction)

1964-1982, *Fantasyland Theatre*
- It was replaced with *Pinocchio's Daring Journey*, which opened in 1983.

1985-1995, *Videopolis* (renamed *Fantasyland Theater*)
- *Sing'in, Dance'in, Heigh Ho* (1987)
- *Circus Fantasy* (1988)
- *One Man's Dream* (December 16, 1989 - April 29, 1990)
- Dick Tracy starring in *Diamond Double Cross* (June 15, 1990 - December 31, 1990)
- *Plane Crazy* (March 15, 1991 - September 1991)
- *Mickey's Nutcracker* (Christmas Seasons 1991 & 1992)
- *Beauty and the Beast Live on Stage* (April 12, 1992 - April 30, 1995)
- *The Spirit of Pocahontas* (June 23, 1995 - September 4, 1997)
- Disney's *Animazment - The Musical* (June 18, 1998 - October 21, 2001)
- *Mickey's Detective School* (2002 - 2003)
- *Minnie's Christmas Party* (Christmas 2002)
- *Snow White: An Enchanting Musical* (February 2004 - September 2006)

1991-1991, *Disney Afternoon Avenue*
-The area between *Storyland Canal Boats* and the *Videopolis*, now the *Toontown* entrance, showcased a set of themed attractions after the Disney Afternoon cartoons. The *Fantasyland Autopia* cars were re-themed as *Rescue Rangers Raceway*, the *Motorboat Cruise* was re-themed as *Motor Boat Cruise to Gummi Glen*, you could visit Baloo from *Tale Spin* in his dressing room, see Scrooge McDucks vault and Duckburg City Hall, learn how Gummi Berry Juice is made, take photos with your favorite characters, and so much more.

Frontierland

1955-1986, *Golden Horseshoe Revue*
- An old-west show featuring singing, dancing, joke-telling, banjo playing, and general fun and rowdiness, starring Slue-foot Sue and a gang of cowpunches. An extremely popular show, it ran in the *Golden Horseshoe Saloon* nearly unchanged for about three decades. It was replaced by:
- 1986-1994, *Golden Horseshoe Variety Show*: A similar show.
- 1999-2000, *All-New Woody's Roundup*: A live-action show featuring characters from *Toy Story*. This shared the *Golden Horseshoe Saloon* with:
- 199?-present, Billy Hill and the Hillbillies (who also performed outdoors in a casual setting at the *Big Thunder Ranch* during show times taken by *Woody's Roundup*).

1955, *Davy Crockett Museum*
- Mostly given over to retail space, with a few exhibits detailing scenes from the television series of the same name.

1955-1956, *Mule Pack*

- Real mules in a line upon which you could ride to view the simulated frontierlands and deserts. After renovations and upgrades, the attraction was renamed:

- 1956-1959, *Rainbow Ridge Mule Pack*
- 1960-1973, *Pack Mules Through Nature's Wonderland*
- 1973, *Big Thunder Mountain Railroad* and *Big Thunder Ranch* replaced *Nature's Wonderland*.

1955-1956, *Stage Coach*
- A real stagecoach drawn by real horses. After new scenic landscaping, it became:

1956-1960, *Rainbow Mountain Stage Coaches*

1955-1960, *Conestoga Wagons*
- A real Conestoga wagon drawn by real animals.

1956-1959, *Rainbow Caverns Mine Train*
- A scale-model train ride through the new Living Desert. The scenery was redone in 1960, it was also upgraded and became *Mine Train Through Nature's Wonderland*.

1960-1977, *Mine Train Through Nature's Wonderland*.
- The *Big Thunder Mountain Railroad* attraction replaced this sedate train ride with a roller-coaster version. The only attraction that remained from the scenic vistas was the mighty waterfall tumbling from Cascade Peak into the *Rivers of America*, visible only from various boat rides around the Rivers. The structure that formed Cascade Peak and its waterfalls was demolished in 1998, after it was found to be suffering structurally from the decades of water that flowed over it.

1956-1963, *Mineral Hall*
- Next to the mine train ride, it displayed rocks which glowed in various colors under black light. You could get souvenir rocks prepackaged and labeled as Walt Disney's Mineral Land. There is a window about its past location to commemorate the rock museum. (*see photo*)

1956-1971, *Indian War Canoes*

1955-1971, *Indian Village*

1986-1996, *Big Thunder Ranch*
- A western-themed casual area for seeing shows, viewing *Disneyland's* horses on their breaks and days off, and dining at Big Thunder Barbecue, which served ribs, chicken, potatoes, beans, and such. The Barbecue remained open for a few more years after the Ranch area became the *Festival of Fools Stage* for *The Hunchback of Notre Dame* show.

1986-2016, *Big Thunder Ranch*
- This quaint, little petting zoo was hiding in the back corner of *Frontierland* behind *Big Thunder Mountain Railroad*.

When it opened in **1986, it was called *Little Patch of Heaven***. It closed in 1996, reopened in 2004, and then became *Big Thunder Ranch* in 2005.

- It was **sponsored by Brawny** paper towels.

- In 1982, there was a Holstein cow born in Maine with a giant Mickey head on its side. Disneyland found out about it and adopted **the friendly bovine and named her "Mickey Moo"** and moved her here in 1988. While she enjoyed her retirement in the "Happiest Place on Earth" she bore a calf who was named "Baby Moo." She passed away at the age of 11 in 1993. She is considered the most famous cow in history.

- It is said that the Hidden Mickey on the sliding door to *Clarabell's Yogurt Shop* in *Mickey's Toontown* was **put there in memory of Mickey Moo**.

- The *Disney World Petting Zoo* **had a similar cow named "Minnie Moo,"** because she had the same Mickey head marking.

- Sometimes you could **catch a glimpse of the draft horses** from the *Horse-Drawn Street Cars* on *Main Street, U.S.A.* taking a break from their hard work.

- There was also a **walk-through cabin containing large tables** inside with crayons and coloring pages to entertain small children.

- At Halloween time, there were **professional pumpkin carvers** that came in to carve the faces of your favorite Disney characters on them.

- For the months of October each year for Halloween, **the ranch got re-themed as *Woody's Halloween Roundup*.** There was even a coinciding stage show starring Jessie and Woody.

- Since November 2005, *Big Thunder Ranch* housed **the yearly Thanksgiving turkey** that was pardoned by the president of the United States.

- In the Christmas season, **the Ranch celebrated with *Santa's Reindeer Round-Up*.** Sit on Santa's lap and tell him what you want for Christmas, chat it up with Mrs. Claus, or just sit and do some crafts. For about seven years, they also brought in reindeer to pet, but discontinued their visits stating *"The reindeer are at the North Pole with Santa."* The real reason is because a federal rule in the Animal Welfare Act stated that the enclosures had to be six feet tall for reindeer, and that is too tall for small visitors.

- It permanently closed on January 11, 2016, to **make way for *Star Wars Land*** opening in 2019.

1955-1994 and 1996-1997, *Mike Fink Keel Boats*

- Shut down due to an accident on May 17, 1997, when the Gullywhumper boat began rocking side-to-side on a trip on the *Rivers of America*. The boat capsized, dumping the 20 passengers into the river. They had gone to the top deck, making it top heavy. The attraction never returned. The Gullywhumper's sister boat, the Bertha Mae, was sold on Disney's auction site. In 2003, the Gullywhumper returned to the *Rivers of America* as a prop and is moored on *Tom Sawyer Island,* where it was visible from the *Mark Twain Riverboat*, the *Sailing Ship Columbia*, and the *Explorer Canoes* until it was removed in 2009.

- The boats were the props from the film *Davey Crockett and the River Pirates* (1956), starring Fess Parker and Buddy Ebsen. In the film, they had to race Mike Fink in a keel boat race down the Mississippi river to New Orleans.

- This attraction had the slowest turnover. Up to forty people could ride at a time and the boats could take five to six loads an hour, making their turnover 400-480 Guests per hour.

- For the first three years, the boats were made out of wood. Then the hulls were replaced with fiberglass, and made to hold a larger capacity.

- It used to be a "C" ticket attraction, back when ticket books were in use.

- They were originally brought into the park because a big boat was needed in case the *Mark Twain Riverboat* ever broke down and needed to be towed. However, it never did happen.

- The boat's engine had 70 horse power.

- The dock that was used for loading and unloading passengers is now the smoking section in front of *Haunted Mansion*.

- There were only two boats, the Gullywhumper and the Bertha Mae.

- After the attraction closed on May 17, 1997, the Bertha Mae was sold on Ebay for $15,000 to Richard Kraft. The Gullywhumper was run ashore as a crashed prop on the island. (*see photo*)

- Most of the river is only about four-feet deep. Out in the middle where the track is for the *Sailing Ship Columbia* and the *Mark Twin Riverboat*, it is eight and a half feet deep.

- On May 17, 1997, one of the boats capsized. There were 20 people on board and all of them went to the second deck, causing the boat to be top heavy and tip over. The boats went 101 (the attraction is down) for the rest of the day, and then never reopened after that.

2004-2005, *Little Patch of Heaven Petting Farm*
1956-2007, *Tom Sawyer Island*
 - An island surrounded by the *Rivers of America*. It contains a western fort and a simulated old-west cemetery, Injun Joe's Cave, the elaborate Tom's Treehouse, barrel and suspension bridges to Smuggler's Cove, and Tom and Huck's Castle Rock; all designed primarily for children to climb and play on, although they are all large and sturdy enough for adventurous adults to follow. The island was changed to *Pirates Lair On Tom Sawyer Island,* based on the *Pirates Of The Caribbean* (2003-2011) movie franchise.

Adventureland

1962-1999, *Swiss Family Treehouse* (renamed and re-themed *Tarzan's Treehouse*).

1962-1992, *Tahitian Terrace* (re-themed *Aladdins Oasis*)
- A dinner show that always had a long line to get in. They served food from places like Hawaii and the Tahitian islands. After dinner, there was a show with Tahitian dancers. It only operated in the busy season and on weekends.

1993-1994, *Aladdin's Oasis* (reworked as *Aladdin and Jasmine's StoryTale Adventures*)
- A dinner show that served exotic delicacies, including papadam wafers with mint chutney sauce, fresh fruit with honey-yogurt sauce, shish-kebobs (beef, chicken, or vegetarian), raisin-nut rice pilaf, tabbouleh, and dessert. The dinner show only lasted two seasons before being shut down. In 1995, it remained just a restaurant without a show. In 1997, it was used just as a storytelling theater, which is how it is today. You can also have a *Meet and Greet* with Aladdin, Jasmine, or Genie out front.

New Orleans Square

1967-1980, *Pirate's Arcade Museum*
1987-2007, *The Disney Gallery*
- A gallery of Disney-related art. The Disney Gallery was the only area listed on Disneyland maps as both an attraction and a retail location. The Gallery sometimes featured preliminary artwork and sketches from certain attractions or movies, sometimes (as in the 100 Mickeys exhibit) the displayed art was associated only with Disney and not with any specific attraction, film, or event. Often, prints from the exhibit were available for purchase via the print on demand system, and the Gallery always featured items such as books about Disney artwork. The Gallery used to sell prints of the attraction posters featured in the tunnels leading to and from *Main Street, U.S.A.* The posters can now be ordered online. The gallery was closed, remodeled, and is now the site of the *Disney Dreams Suite.*

Bear Country (Bear Country opened in 1972; it was renamed

Critter Country in 1988)
1972-1986, *Country Bear Jamboree*
- An Audio-Animatronic show featuring traditional American folk songs sung by a variety of bears and their friends, including Henry the host and Big Al, Shaker (AKA Terrance), Bunny, Bubbles, Beulah, Oscar, Liver-Lips McGrowl, Wendell, Trixie, Teddi Barra, Zeke, Zeb, Ted, Fred, and
Tennessee. The content of the show was replaced by:

- 1986-2001, *Country Bear Vacation Hoedown* at the renamed *Country Bear Playhouse*. They used the same animated figures and redecorated.

1972-1988, *The Mile-Long Bar*
- A snack bar fashioned like an old-west wooden bar with brass footrail and featuring wall-sized mirrors at either end so that it appeared that the bar went on forever.

1972-2003, *Teddi Barra's Swinging Arcade*

1956-1971, *The Indian War Canoes* (reopened as *Davy Crockett's Explorer Canoes*)

mickey's Toontown

1993-2003, *Jolly Trolley*
- A bright trolley with a giant winding key on top. It traversed the length of Mickey's *Toontown*, but the small size of the area prevented operation on all but the most sparsely attended days. One of the trolleys was auctioned on eBay.

1993-2006, *Goofy's Bounce House*
- A bounce house-style attraction themed to the home of Goofy.

1993-1998, *Chip N' Dales' Treehouse and Acorn Crawl*
- After climbing the stairs in the treehouse, children under 48" would go down the slide and end in a pit full of acorn-shaped balls. From January 1993 until its removal in January 1998, Disney had to deal with children using the ball pit as a toilet, and was constantly shutting it down for cleaning.

1993-????, *Toon Park*

Holidayland

1957-1961, *Holidayland*
- *Holidayland*, the "lost" land of *Disneyland*, was a recreation area with a separate entrance before being replaced by *New Orleans Square*.

CALIFORNIA ADVENTURE'S ATTRACTIONS OF THE PAST

A Bug's Land

2001-2010, *Bountiful Valley Farms*
- A water play area for kids that mimics California's irrigation system.

Hollywood Pictures Backlot

2001-2002, *Superstar Limo*
- A dark-ride that took riders through a cartoony version of Hollywood, spotting some celebrities like Regis Philbin, Drew Carey, and Whoopi Goldberg. The attraction closed in 2002, giving it an 11-month lifespan. It sat

dormant until 2005 when it was repurposed and converted into *Monsters, Inc. Mike & Sulley to the Rescue!*

2001-2001, *Step in Time*

- A musical in the Hyperion Theater. It was briefly there before getting replaced with *Blast!*, a shortened version of the instrumental musical *Power of Blast.*

2001-2002, *The Power of Blast*

- A musical in the *Hyperion Theater*. It was briefly there before getting replaced with Disney's Aladdin: A Musical Spectacular. *Blast!* was a shortened version of the instrumental musical *Power of Blast.*

2001-2004, *Who Wants to Be A Millionaire - Play It!*

- Millionaire was an attraction in which park guests played a real game of Millionaire, except with points instead of dollars. Including the ten players in the "Ring of Fire" seats (which included video screens) down on the stage, the entire audience could play the Fastest Finger game, in which players had to put certain items in a certain order, such as "Put these American cities in order from east to west." The game's prizes were:

- 1,000 points - Who Wants to Be A Millionaire - Play It! Baseball Cap
- 32,000 points - Who Wants to Be A Millionaire - Play It! Polo Shirt
- 1,000,000 points - Trip to New York to see filming of actual show (2001-2002)
- 1,000,000 points - Trip for four on the Disney Cruise Line to *Castaway Cay* in the Bahamas (2002-2004).

Every question earned a guest a commemorative pin with the point value of said question on it.

2010-2012, *ElecTRONica*

- A nighttime show that opened on October 8, 2010, as a way to promote the new movie *Tron: Legacy* (2010) due out that following December. They blasted music, performed by Daft Punk, and projected images, from *Tron: Legacy,* and sold glowing-themed items. The show was only supposed to run for a few months, but due to its popularity, it ran until April 15, 2012, to be replaced by *Mad T Party*, a similar show.

2010-2012, *Flynn's Arcade*

- An old 1980's-style video arcade designed to resemble the arcade from *Tron* (1982). It closed down with the *ElecTRONica* show.

2001-2011, *C.A.L.I.F.O.R.N.I.A. Sign*

- The giant letters that used to stand out front of *California Adventure* were removed in July 2011 to make way for the new entrance to *Buena Vista Street*. In 2013, the letters were donated to Cal Expo for the State Fair.

2003-2016, *Disney's Aladdin: A Musical Spectacular*

- The production is a Broadway-type show. Many of the classic scenes and songs from the movie are re-created on stage in the Hyperion Theater, and some of the action even spills out into the aisles, like Prince Ali's jubilant arrival in Agrabah on elephant back. Flying carpets, magic lamps, a wise-cracking genie, a princess, and an evil wizard are all part of this musical production.

681

@ Alan Menken composed a new song for this production called *To Be Free*, which finally gave Jasmine her own princess song.

@ The show was quite popular because, while much of it is scripted, the dialog of the Genie constantly changed to reflect popular culture.

@ Number of scene changes per show: 18

@ Number of costume changes per show: 250

@ Number of Cast Members per show: 28

@ It closed on January 11, 2016, to make way for *Frozen – Live at the Hyperion*.

2001-201, *Muppet*Vision 3D*

- The show was a 3-D film featuring Jim Henson's Muppets. The show was sometimes referred to as Jim Henson's Muppet*Vision 4-D, due to the use of Audio-Animatronics, live full-bodied Muppets, and other similar effects.

@ This **show originated** in *Disney's Hollywood Studios* on May 16, 1991. This date marked the one-year anniversary of Jim Henson's death.

@ This was **the last movie** where Kermit the Frog was voiced by Jim Henson.

@ **Jim Henson was the director** of the film.

@ The **writer of the film was Bill Prady**. He is known for his other works like *The Big Bang Theory* (2007), *Dharma & Greg* (1997), *You Can't Do That on Television* (1979), *Fraggle Rock* (1987), *The Jim Henson Hour* (1989), and over in *Disneyland* he was the writer of the, now replaced with *Captain EO Tribute*, *Honey I Shrunk the Audience* (1994) 3D attraction.

@ At the end of the show when the wall got knocked down, **you could see Pluto** in the crowd of people gathered around outside.

@ There were **10 Audio-Animatronics involved** with the film. They included Bean Bunny, Statler, Waldorf, Swedish Chef, and the penguin orchestra.

@ The entire theater **could seat 574 people**.

@ The **cast list** was as follows:
- Wayne Allwine - Mickey Mouse
- Jim Henson - Kermit the Frog / Swedish Chef / Waldorf
- Frank Oz - Miss Piggy / Fozzie Bear / Sam the Eagle
- Dave Goelz - Dr. Bunsen Honeydew / The Great Gonzo / Zoot the Sax Player
- Jerry Nelson – Camilla, the chicken (Jerry voiced Elmo in the early 1970s when Elmo was just a background monster for *Sesame Street*. Elmo didn't become who he is today until Kevin Clash took over in 1984; before that he had Jerry's deep gravely voice)
- Richard Hunt - Beaker / Scooter / Statler / Sweetums
- Steve Whitmire - Waldo C. Graphic / Bean Bunny / Rizzo the Rat (Steve took over as the voice of Kermit the Frog after Jim Henson's passing in 1990)

- John Henson – Sweetums (puppeteer only)

🎬 The attraction *it's a small world* **was one of Jim Henson's favorite attractions**, so he inserted part of a scene to the final number to pay homage to the attraction.

🎬 *Muppet*Vision 3D,* along with *Captain EO Tribute,* were two Disney 3D attractions which **actually called their glasses "3D Glasses."** For *It's Tough to Be a Bug* they refer to them as "Bug Eyes," on *Star Tours: The Adventures Continue* they are "Flight Glasses," on *Toy Story Midway Mania* they are called "Carnival Games Goggles." Sometime here they were called "3D Safety Goggles."

🎬 Near the end of the main show, during the Muppets' celebration with marching bands and fireworks, some of the band members wear blue Colonial-style hats with red tabs on the side. The tabs have a Hidden Mickey in the center.

🎬 When the wall gets blown up, park patrons gather around outside; some are holding Mickey head balloons.

2004-2017, *The Twilight Zone Tower of Terror*

- A drop-attraction based on the movie *Tower of Terror* (1997) starring Steve Guttenberg and Kirsten Dunst. The attraction was themed to resemble the fictional Hollywood Tower Hotel. The story of the hotel, adapted from elements of the television series, includes the hotel being struck by lightning on October 31, 1939, mysteriously transporting an elevator car full of passengers to the Twilight Zone. The exterior of the attraction resembled an old hotel with a blackened scorch mark across the front of the facade where the lightning destroyed part of the building.

🎬 This 183-foot attraction was the tallest attraction at the resort, as well as the tallest building in Anaheim.

🎬 For Disney's Halloween Time, this attraction received special sound and lighting effects and a fun Halloween makeover of the lobby and exterior.

🎬 All of the Cast Members wore a costume that resembled that of a 1930's bellhop. At over $1,000 per uniform, it was the most expensive costume in the various theme parks.

🎬 The elevators could fall faster than the speed of gravity because they would pull down.

🎬 There were eight elevators that rotated around in three elevator shafts.

🎬 While you were waiting in the line, you could spot props and design elements from the *Twilight Zone* television series (1959-1964). A listing of all the hidden elements can be found at *TowerOfTerror.org*. The items and related episodes are as follows:
- Holding Area

◦ A Gold Thimble - "*The After Hours*"
◦ A Broken Stopwatch - "*A Kind of a Stopwatch*"
◦ Out-of-order elevator #22 - "*22*"
• The Library
  ◦ A Pair of Broken Spectacles -"*Time Enough at Last*"
  ◦ Two White Envelopes containing 1/4" audiotape, labeled "Victoria West" and "Rod Serling" - "*A World of His Own*"
  ◦ A Trumpet - "*Passage for Trumpet*"
  ◦ Miniature Spaceman - "*The Invaders*"
  ◦ The Mystic Seer - "*Nick of Time*"
  ◦ Book titles - episode titles from the Twilight Zone series appear on the bindings of a matched set of volumes.
  ◦ A black book with a note on it - "*To Serve Man*"
  ◦ Footage of Rod Serling on introductory video - "*It's a Good Life*"
  ◦ Shakespeare's Bust - "*The Bard*"
  ◦ Twilight Zone Episode Scripts - In both libraries, you will find on the bookshelves a stack of books that have, on the bindings, names of Episodes of the *Twilight Zone*.
• Boiler Room
  ◦ The Boiler Room contained a notepad with the cryptic rhyme:
  ◦ "It's easy enough to be pleasant, when life hums along like a song. But the man worthwhile, is the man who can smile, when everything goes dead wrong."
  ◦ Chalk Marks on the Wall - "*Little Girl Lost*"
  ◦ Copies of *Popular Mechanics* on workbench in boiler room - "I *Sing the Body Electric*"
• Basement
  ◦ "Modern Wonders" store front along the exit corridor (image capture display area):
  ◦ Red Toy Telephone - "*Long Distance Call*"
  ◦ Box Camera - "*A Most Unusual Camera*"
  ◦ Self typing typwriter with the message "Get out of here, Finchley." - "*A Thing About Machines*"
  ◦ Electric Razor - "*A Thing About Machines*"
  ◦ Antique Radio - "*Static*"
  ◦ Slot Machine - "*The Fever*"
• Other *Twilight Zone* References
  ◦ Anthony Fremont Orchestra poster (Image Capture Area) - "*It's a Good Life*"
  ◦ Willoughby Travel (Shop name, Image Capture Area) - "*A Stop at Willoughby*"
  ◦ "Picture if You Will" (Purchasing counter for Image Capture Photos) - One of Rod Serling's famous catch phrases, from his opening narration.
  ◦ Cadwallader (Signature on Elevator Inspection Certificate, Ride Vehicle) - "*Escape Clause*"

- The chalk markings on the wall in the queue look like the ones in the episode "Little Girl Lost." If you listen to the static on the out of tune radio, you can hear the cries of the lost little girl. This voice is that of voice actress Kathryn "Kat" Cressida. She is the voice of the bride, Constance, in the *Haunted Mansion* attic.
- The first *Tower Of Terror* opened in *Disney World's Hollywood Studios* back in 1994.
- Following the *Twilight Zone* television credit sequence, Rod Serling's opening lines in the introduction video during the queue were as follows: *"Tonight's story on The Twilight Zone is somewhat unique and calls for a different kind of introduction. This as you may recognize is a..."* then this is where it gets tricky. In the original episode titled "It's a Good Life," Rod Serling says *"...is a map of the United States."* They changed that line to *"...is a maintenance service elevator, still in operation, waiting for you..."* Since Rod Serling passed away in 1975, he could not provide the extra narration, so  Disney had Mark Silverman provide the entire voice impersonation of Serling for this particular dialogue sequence. Silverman is known for his voice work in films like *Eragon* (2006), *Tales from Earthsea* (2006-English version), *Howl's Moving Castle* (2004-English version), *Pom Poko* (2003-English version), and *Nausicaä of the Valley of the Wind* (1984-English version).
- Guests were allowed to ride one last time on January 3, 2017, before they shut the doors for good. The attraction was then re-themed into *Guardians of the Galaxy – Mission: BREAKOUT!* The new attraction is housed in the same building as the old attraction, but in the new one you must help Rocket Raccoon rescue the other Guardians from The Collector. It is believed that this was done because the Marvel Land expansion is going into the open space along the backside of the tower and *Cars Land. Mission Breakout* would be by the entrance area. If you want to go on Tower of Terror, you must go to *Hollywood Studios* in Florida.

The Bay Area

2001-2008, *Golden Dreams*

- *Golden Dreams*, a film about the history of California, was featured. It stars film actress Whoopi Goldberg as Califia, the Queen of California. In 2007, it was scheduled for removal to make way for the more frivolous fare of the *"The Little Mermaid: Ariel's Undersea Adventure"* dark-ride attraction. However, the exterior replica of the Bernard Maybeck's Palace of Fine Arts remained.

The Golden Vine Winery

2001–2008, *Seasons of the Vine*

- Film presentation which took viewers through the journey of producing wine in California. Closed due to low attendance and is now the site of *Walt Disney Imagineering Blue Sky Cellar* which features artwork of the future *California Adventure.*

Paradise Pier

2001–2008, *Sun Wheel*

- Ferris wheel inspired by Coney Island's 1927 Wonder Wheel, which featured swinging and stationary gondolas and a large replica of a sun in the center. It was re-themed as *Mickey's Fun Wheel.*

2001–2008, *Orange Stinger*

- Swings that revolve around a giant orange.

2001-2010, *Maliboomer*

- An attraction that launches you 180 feet straight into the air. It was designed to resemble the "high striker" games from boardwalks where a hammer is used to hit a mallet in an attempt to hit the bell at the top. This attraction was removed to make way for the new expansion.

2001-2010, *Mulholland Madness*

- The attraction's name came from the famed Mulholland Drive in Los Angeles, California, named after the famed engineer William Mulholland. This attraction was re-themed as "Goofy's Sky School."

2001-2010, *S.S. Rustworthy*

- A water play area for children. This attraction was removed to make way for the new expansion. It was replaced with a Beer Garden to fit in with the surrounding theme.

Cars Land

2012-2015, *Luigi's Flying Tires*

- This attraction was an updated and safer version of the original *Disneyland* attraction *Flying Saucers.* An adult could ride with a child, but due to the size of adults, if there were multiple adults, they had to ride alone for the bests results.

- The *Flying Saucers* **existed in** *Disneyland* **from 1961** until the *Tomorrowland* update opened without them in 1967. Apparently, they were too costly to maintain.

- The attraction is designed basically like a **giant air hockey table**.

- There are **21 giant tires that float 2 inches** off the ground.

- There are **6,714 air vents built into the ground** that can blow over 1.86 million cubic feet of air per minute to keep the tires floating slightly above the ground.

686

◈ Because of all the air vents, **this attraction is about 10° cooler** while riding than the existing air in the summer time, considering that it is an outside attraction.

Condor Flats

◈ **2001-2017,** *Soarin' Over California*

◈ All of **your senses were engaged while riding.** Wind blew in your face. You would have the sensation of flying. You would discover the smells of orange blossoms, pine, the sea, and sagebrush. All these effects were added in to make your flight more stimulating by using a Smellitzer.

◈ During the **desert scene,** just before the appearance of the USAF Thunderbirds, the path the horseback riders take leads to a cliff edge and a long drop.

◈ As you passed by the cliff face in Yosemite, you could **see six climbers from the Yosemite Mountaineering School** making their way to the top.

◈ *Soarin' Over California* was one of the **most visited** attractions at the entire *Disneyland* Resort (facing tough competition from fan favorites over at *Disneyland*) and usually had wait times from 30-150 minutes.

◈ The attraction took **87 guests** at a time on a simulated hang glider tour of the Golden State, flying over:

San Francisco	Palm Springs	Lake Tahoe
Humboldt County	Camarillo	Malibu
Napa Valley	San Diego	Los Angeles
Monterey	Yosemite National Park	Disneyland
	Anza-Borrego Desert State Park	

◈ The attraction ended with a flight over *Disneyland* **at Christmas,** a Christmas parade traveling down *Main Street, U.S.A.,* decorations on *Sleeping Beauty Castle,* and fireworks.

◈ During the first few seconds of the scene with the aircraft carrier in port in San Diego, the **shadow of the helicopter** with the IMAX camera could be seen on the bottom left of the screen on the side of the ship.

◈ At the time of the Soarin' movie filming, *California Adventure* was **still being built.** *California Adventure* was very dark when the helicopter flew over *Disneyland,* and the old ticket booths were still visible.

◈ Also at the time of filming, the former **Rocket Rods** were still operating. The entrance was visible at the *Disneyland* scene.

◈ In the *Disneyland* Christmas finale, the **parade was not moving.** The toy soldiers marched in place and the floats weree stationary. Producers did this to allow the IMAX helicopter to make several passes.

◈ The Disneyland Christmas finale was **actually filmed during a private family cast holiday party,** closed to the general public.

◈ **Tinker Bell made a guest appearance** at the end of the film.

🐭 Disney **used composer Jerry Goldsmith for the music**. He is best known for his musical scores in movie films such as *The Sand Pebbles, Planet of the Apes, Patton, Chinatown, The Wind and the Lion, The Omen, Hollow Man, Along Came a Spider, The Last Castle, Looney Tunes: Back in Action, The Boys from Brazil, Night Crossing, Alien, Poltergeist, The Secret of NIMH, Gremlins, Hoosiers, Total Recall, Basic Instinct, Rudy, Air Force One, L.A. Confidential, Mulan, The Mummy,* three *Rambo* films, and five *Star Trek* films. It is said that when Goldsmith first rode it, he left in tears and said, "*I'd do anything to be part of this project. I'd even score the film for free.*"

🐭 There was a Hidden Mickey on the golf ball hit by former Disney CEO Michael Eisner.

🐭 During the fireworks finale composed of three strategically placed blooms, you could see a Hidden Mickey.

WALT IS THE MAN

Who He Was

Walter Elias Disney (December 5, 1901 – December 15, 1966) was a multiple Academy Award-winning American film producer, director, screenwriter, voice actor, animator, entrepreneur, and philanthropist. Disney is notable as one of the most influential and innovative figures in the field of entertainment during the 20th century. As the co-founder (with his brother Roy O. Disney) of Walt Disney Productions, Disney became one of the best-known motion picture producers in the world. The corporation he co-founded, now known as The Walt Disney Company, today has annual revenues of approximately $35 billion.

Disney is particularly noted for being a film producer and a popular showman, as well as an innovator in animation and theme park design. He received 59 Academy Award nominations and won 26 Oscars, including a record four in one year. He holds the record for an individual with the most awards and the most nominations. He won 7 Emmy Awards. Disney and his staff created a number of the world's most famous fictional characters, including the one many consider Disney's alter ego, Mickey Mouse. He is the namesake for Disneyland and Walt Disney World Resort theme parks in the United States, Japan, France, and China.

Disney died of lung cancer on December 15, 1966, a few years prior to the opening of his Walt Disney World dream project in Lake Buena Vista, Florida.

The Life Behind the Legend

Walt Elias Disney was born to Elias Disney, an Irish-Canadian, and his mother, Flora Call Disney, who was of German-American descent. His father moved to the United States from Canada after his parents failed at farming there. Walt's first name was given to him to honor his parent's preacher, Walter Parr. His middle name was given to him after his father, Elias. After Walt's birth, Elias, along with his family, moved to Marceline, Missouri. While in Marceline, Disney developed his love for drawing. One of their neighbors, a retired doctor named "Doc" Sherwood, paid him to draw pictures of Sherwood's horse, Rupert. He also developed his love for trains in Marceline, which owed its existence to the Atchison, Topeka, and Santa Fe Railway which ran through town. Walt would put his ear to the tracks in anticipation of the coming train. Then, he would look for his uncle, engineer Michael Martin, running the train.

The Disneys remained in Marceline for four years, then moved to Kansas City in 1910. There, Walt and his sister, Ruth, attended the Benton Grammar School, where he met Walter Pfeiffer. The Pfeiffers were theatre aficionados, and they introduced Walt to the world of vaudeville and motion pictures. Soon, Walt was spending more time at the Pfeiffers' than at home.

Teenage Years

In 1917, Elias acquired shares in the O-Zell jelly factory in Chicago, and moved his family back there. In the fall, Disney began his freshman year at McKinley High School and began taking night courses at the Chicago Art Institute. Disney became the cartoonist for the school newspaper. His cartoons were very patriotic, focusing on World War I. Disney dropped out of high school at the age of 16 to join the Army, but the Army rejected him because he was underage.

After his rejection from the Army, Walt and one of his friends decided to join the Red Cross. Following his joining of The Red Cross, he was sent to France for a year, where he drove an ambulance.

He then moved to Kansas City to begin his artistic career. His brother, Roy, worked at a bank in the area and got a job for him through a friend at the Pesmen-Rubin Art Studio. At Pesmen-Rubin, Disney created ads for newspapers, magazines, and movie theaters. It was here that he met a cartoonist named Ub Iwerks. They became close friends and decided to start their own art business.

In January 1920, Disney and Iwerks formed a company called "Iwerks-Disney Commercial Artists." However, following a rough start, Iwerks left temporarily to earn money at Kansas City Film Ad Company. Disney followed suit after the business venture was taken over by his New York financial backers, Winkler and Mintz.

Hollywood

Together with his brother, Disney pooled their money to set up his first Hollywood cartoon studio in his uncle's garage. Disney sent an unfinished print to New York distributor Margaret Winkler, who promptly wrote back to him. She was keen on a distribution deal with Disney for more live-action/animated shorts based upon Alice's Wonderland.

Alice Comedies

Virginia Davis (the live-action star of Alice's Wonderland) and her family were relocated at Disney's request from Kansas City to Hollywood, as were Iwerks and his family. This was the beginning of the Disney Brothers' Studio. It was located on Hyperion Avenue in the Silver Lake district, where the studio would remain until 1939. In 1925, Disney hired a young woman named Lillian Bounds to ink and paint celluloid. After a brief period of dating her, they were married on July 13, 1925.

The new series, Alice Comedies, was reasonably successful, and featured both Dawn O'Day and Margie Gay as Alice. Lois Hardwick also briefly assumed the role of Alice. By the time the series ended in 1927, the focus was more on the animated characters, in particular a cat named Julius who resembled Felix the Cat, rather than the live-action Alice.

Oswald the Lucky Rabbit

By 1927, Charles B. Mintz had married Margaret Winkler and assumed control of her business, and ordered a new all-animated series to be put into production for distribution through Universal Pictures. The new series, *Oswald the Lucky Rabbit*, was an almost instant success, and the character, Oswald—drawn and created by Iwerks—became a popular figure. The Disney studio expanded, and Walt hired back Harman, Ising, Maxwell, and Freleng from Kansas City.

In February 1928, Disney went to New York to negotiate a higher fee per short from Mintz. Disney was shocked when Mintz announced that he not only wanted to reduce the fee he paid Disney per short, but also that he had most of his main animators, including Harman, Ising, Maxwell, and Freleng (notably excepting Iwerks) under contract and would start his own studio if Disney did not accept the reduced production budgets. Universal, not Disney, owned the Oswald trademark, and could make the films without Disney. Disney declined Mintz's offer and lost most of his animation staff.

It took Disney's company 78 years to get back the rights to the Oswald character. The Walt Disney Company reacquired the rights to *Oswald the Lucky Rabbit* from NBC Universal in 2006.

Mickey Mouse

After losing the rights to Oswald, Disney felt the need to develop a new character to replace him. He based the character on a mouse he had adopted as a pet while working in a Kansas City studio. Ub Iwerks reworked the sketches made by Disney so that it was easier to animate it. However, Mickey's voice and personality were provided by Disney. As many of the old animators have commented, "Ub designed Mickey's physical appearance, but Walt gave him his soul." Besides Oswald and Mickey, a similar mouse-character is seen in Alice Comedies which features a mouse named Ike the Mouse, and the first Flip the Frog cartoon called Fiddlesticks, which showed a Mickey Mouse look-alike playing fiddle. The initial films were animated by Iwerks; his name was prominently featured on the title cards. The mouse was originally named "Mortimer," but later christened "Mickey Mouse" by Lillian Disney, who thought that the name Mortimer did not fit. Mortimer later became the name of Mickey's rival for Minnie, who was taller than his renowned adversary and had a Brooklyn accent.

The first animated short with Mickey in it was titled, *Plane Crazy*, which was, like all of Disney's previous works, a silent film. After failing to find a distributor for *Plane Crazy* or its follow-up, *The Gallopin' Gaucho*, Disney created a Mickey cartoon with sound called *Steamboat Willie*. A businessman named Pat Powers provided Disney with both distribution and Cinephone, a sound-synchronization process. *Steamboat Willie* became a success, and *Plane Crazy*, *The Galloping Gaucho*, and all future Mickey cartoons were released with soundtracks. Disney himself provided the vocal effects for the earliest cartoons and performed as the voice of Mickey Mouse until 1946. After the release of *Steamboat Willie*, Walt Disney would continue to successfully use sound in all of his future cartoons; soon, Mickey eclipsed Felix as the world's most popular cartoon. By 1930, Felix, now in sound, had faded from the screen, as his sound cartoons failed to gain attention. Mickey's popularity would now skyrocket in the early 1930's.

Silly Symphonies

Following the footsteps of the Mickey Mouse series, a series of musical shorts titled *Silly Symphonies* was released in 1929. The first of these was entitled *The Skeleton Dance* and was entirely drawn and animated by Iwerks, who was also responsible for drawing the majority of cartoons released by Disney in 1928 and 1929. Although both series were successful, the Disney studio was not seeing its rightful share of profits from Pat Powers, and in 1930, Disney signed a new distribution deal with Columbia Pictures. The original basis of the cartoons was musical novelty, and Carl Stalling wrote the score for the first Silly Symphony cartoons as well.

Iwerks was soon lured by Powers into opening his own studio with an exclusive contract. Later, Carl Stalling would also leave Disney to join Iwerks' new studio. Iwerks launched his *Flip the Frog* series with the first voice cartoon in color, *Fiddlesticks*, filmed in two-strip Technicolor. Iwerks also created two other series of cartoons, *Willie Whopper* and *Comicolor*. In 1936, Iwerks closed his studio in order to work on various projects dealing with animation technology. He would return to Disney in 1940 and would go on to pioneer a number of film processes and specialized animation technologies in the studio's research and development department.

By 1932, Mickey Mouse had become quite a popular cinema character, but Silly Symphonies was not as successful. The same year also saw competition for Disney grow worse as Max Fleischer's flapper cartoon character, Betty Boop, would gain more popularity among theater audiences. Fleischer was considered to be Disney's main rival in the 1930's, and was also the father of Richard Fleischer, whom Disney would later hire to direct his 1954 film *20,000 Leagues*

Under the Sea. Meanwhile, Columbia Pictures dropped the distribution of Disney cartoons and was replaced by United Artists. In late 1932, Herbert Kalmus, who had just completed work on the first three-strip technicolor camera, approached Walt and convinced him to redo *Flowers and Trees*, which was originally done in black and white, with three-strip Technicolor. *Flowers and Trees* would go on to be a phenomenal success and would also win the first Academy Award for Best Short Subject: Cartoons for 1932. After *Flowers and Trees* was released, all future *Silly Symphony* cartoons were done in color as well. Disney was also able to negotiate a two-year deal with Technicolor, giving him the sole right to use three-strip Technicolor, which would also eventually be extended to five years as well. Through *Silly Symphonies*, Disney would also create his most successful cartoon short of all time, The Three Little Pigs, in 1933. The cartoon ran in theaters for many months, and also featured the hit song that became the anthem of the Great Depression, "Who's Afraid of the Big Bad Wolf."

First Academy Award

In 1932, Disney received a special Academy Award for the creation of "Mickey Mouse," whose series was made into color in 1935 and soon launched spinoff series for supporting characters such as Donald Duck, Goofy, and Pluto; Pluto and Donald would immediately get their individual cartoons in 1937, and Goofy would get solo cartoons in 1939 as well. Of all of Mickey's partners, Donald Duck–who first teamed with Mickey in the 1934 cartoon, *Orphan's Benefit*–was arguably the most popular, and went on to become Disney's second most successful cartoon character of all time.

Children

Disney's first attempt at fatherhood ended up in Lilly having a miscarriage. When Lilly Disney became pregnant again, she gave birth to a daughter, Diane Marie Disney, on December 18, 1933. A few years later, the Disneys adopted Sharon Mae Disney (born December 21, 1934), as their second child.

"Disney's Folly": *Snow White and the Seven Dwarfs*

Disney introduces his popular creations: Mickey, Minnie Mouse, and Pluto to Hansel and Gretel (Dorothy Rodin and Virginia Murray). After the creation of two cartoon series, Disney soon began plans for a full-length feature in 1934. In 1935, opinion polls showed that another cartoon series, Popeye the Sailor, produced by Max Fleischer, was more popular than Mickey Mouse. Disney was, however, able to put Mickey back on top, and also increase Mickey's popularity further by colorizing him and partially redesigning him into what was considered to be his most appealing design up to this point in time. When the film industry came to know about Disney's plans to produce an animated feature-length version of Snow White, they dubbed the project as "Disney's Folly" and were certain that the project would destroy the Disney studio. Both Lillian and Roy tried to talk Disney out of the project, but he continued plans for the feature. He employed Chouinard Art Institute professor Don Graham to start a training operation for the studio staff, and used the Silly Symphonies as a platform for experiments in realistic human animation, distinctive character animation, special effects, and the use of specialized processes and apparatus such as the multiplane camera; Disney would first use this new technique in the 1937 Silly Symphonies short, *The Old Mill*.

All of this development and training was used to elevate the quality of the studio so that it would be able to give the feature film the quality Disney desired. *Snow White and the Seven Dwarfs*, as the feature was named, was in full production from 1934 until mid-1937, when the studio ran out of money. To acquire the funding to complete *Snow White*, Disney had to show a rough cut of the motion picture to loan officers at the Bank of America, who gave the studio the money to finish the picture. The finished film premiered at the *Carthay Circle Theater* on December 21, 1937; at the conclusion of the film, the audience gave *Snow White and the Seven Dwarfs* a standing ovation. Snow White, the first animated full length animated feature in English and Technicolor, was released in February 1938 under a new distribution deal with RKO Radio Pictures; RKO had previously been the distributor for Disney cartoons in 1936, after it closed down the Van Beuren Studios in exchange for distribution. The film became the most successful motion picture of 1938 and earned over $8 million in its original theatrical release. The success of Snow White (for which Disney received one full-size and seven miniature Oscar statuettes), allowed Disney to build a new campus for the Walt Disney Studios in Burbank, which opened for business on December 24, 1939. Snow White was not only the peak of Disney's success, but it also ushered into what was known as the Golden Age of Animation for Disney. The feature animation staff, having just completed *Pinocchio*, continued work on *Fantasia* and *Bambi*, while the shorts staff continued work on the Mickey Mouse, Donald Duck, Goofy, and Pluto cartoon series, ending the Silly Symphonies at this time. Animator Fred Moore had redesigned Mickey Mouse in the late 1930's, when Donald Duck began to gain more popularity among theater audiences than Mickey Mouse.

During World War II

Pinocchio and *Fantasia* followed *Snow White and the Seven Dwarfs* into the movie theaters in 1940, but both were financial disappointments. The inexpensive Dumbo was planned as an income generator, but during production of the new film, most of the animation staff went on strike, permanently straining the relationship between Disney and his artists.

Shortly after the release of *Dumbo* in October 1941, the United States entered World War II. The U.S. Army contracted most of the Disney studio's facilities and had the staff create training and instructional films for the military, home-front morale-boosting shorts, such as *Der Fuehrer's Face* and the feature film *Victory Through Air Power* in 1943. However, the military films did not generate income, and the feature film *Bambi* underperformed when it was released in April 1942. Disney successfully re-issued *Snow White* in 1944, establishing a 7-year re-release tradition for Disney features.

693

The Disney studios also created inexpensive packaged films, containing collections of cartoon shorts, and issued them to theaters during this period. The most notable and successful of these were *Saludos Amigos* (1942), its sequel *The Three Caballeros* (1945), *Fun and Fancy Free* (1947), and *The Adventures of Ichabod and Mr. Toad* (1949). The latter had only two sections: the first based on *The Legend of Sleepy Hollow* by Washington Irving, and the second based on *The Wind in the Willows* by Kenneth Grahame. During this period, Disney also ventured into full-length dramatic films that mixed live action and animated scenes, including *Song of the South* and *So Dear to My Heart*. After the war ended, Mickey's popularity would fade as well.

By the late 1940's, the studio had recovered enough to continue production on the full-length features *Alice in Wonderland* and *Peter Pan*, which had been shelved during the war years, and began work on *Cinderella*, which became Disney's most successful film since *Snow White and the Seven Dwarfs*. The studio also began a series of live-action nature films, entitled *True-Life Adventures*, in 1948 with *On Seal Island*. Despite rebounding success through feature films, Disney's animation shorts were no longer as popular as they used to be, and people began to instead draw attention to Warner Bros and their animation star, Bugs Bunny; by 1942, Warner Bros' Termite Terrace officially became the most popular animation studio. However, while Bugs Bunny's popularity rose in the 1940's, so did Donald Duck's; Donald would also replace Mickey Mouse as Disney's star character in 1949.

Testimony Before Congress

In 1947, during the early years of the Cold War, Disney testified before the House Un-American Activities Committee, where he branded Herbert Sorrell, David Hilberman, and William Pomerance, former animators and labor union organizers, as Communist agitators. All three men denied the allegations. Disney implicated the Screen Actors Guild as a Communist front, and charged that the 1941 strike was part of an organized Communist effort to gain influence in Hollywood. However, no evidence has been discovered to support this.

Carolwood Pacific Railroad

During 1949, Disney and his family moved to a new home on a large piece of property in the Holmby Hills district of Los Angeles, California. With the help of his friends, Ward and Betty Kimball, owners of their own backyard railroad, Disney developed blueprints and immediately set to work on creating a miniature live steam railroad for his backyard. The name of the railroad, Carolwood Pacific Railroad, originated from the address of his home that was located on Carolwood Drive. The railroad's half-mile long layout included a 46-foot (14 m)-long trestle, loops, overpasses, gradients, an elevated dirt berm, and a 90-foot (27 m) tunnel underneath Mrs. Disney's flowerbed. He named the miniature working steam locomotive built by Roger E. Broggie of the Disney Studios, Lilly Belle, in his wife's honor. He had his attorney draw up right-of-way papers giving the railroad a permanent, legal easement through the garden areas, which his wife dutifully signed. However, there is no evidence of the documents ever recorded as a restriction on the property's title.

Planning Disneyland

On a business trip to Chicago in the late-1940's, Disney drew sketches of his ideas for an amusement park where he envisioned his employees spending time with their children. He got his idea for a children's theme park after visiting Children's Fairyland in Oakland, California. This plan was originally meant for a plot located south of the Studio, across the street. The original ideas developed into a concept for a larger enterprise that was to become Disneyland. Disney spent five years of his life developing Disneyland and created a new subsidiary of his company, called WED Enterprises, to carry out the planning and production of the park. A small group of Disney studio employees joined the Disneyland development project as engineers and planners, and were dubbed Imagineers.

When describing one of his earliest plans to Herb Ryman (who created the first aerial drawing of Disneyland, which was presented to the Bank of America while requesting funds), Disney said, "Herbie, I just want it to look like nothing else in the world. And it should be surrounded by a train." Entertaining his daughters and their friends in his backyard and taking them for rides on his Carolwood Pacific Railroad had inspired Disney to include a railroad in the plans for Disneyland.

Expanding into New Areas

As Walt Disney Productions began work on *Disneyland*, it also began expanding its other entertainment operations. In 1950, *Treasure Island became* the studio's first all-live-action feature, and was soon followed by *20,000 Leagues Under the Sea* (in CinemaScope, 1954), *The Shaggy Dog* (1959), and *The Parent Trap* (1961). The Walt Disney Studio produced its first TV special, *One Hour in Wonderland*, in 1950. Disney began hosting a weekly anthology series on ABC named *Disneyland* after the park, where he showed clips of past Disney productions, gave tours of his studio, and familiarized the public with Disneyland as it was being constructed in Anaheim, California. The show also featured a *Davy Crockett* miniseries, which started a craze among the American youth known as the Davy Crockett craze, in which millions of coonskin caps and other Crockett memorabilia were sold across the country. In 1955, the studio's first daily television show, *Mickey Mouse Club* debuted, which would continue in many various incarnations into the 1990's.

Walt Disney meets with Wernher von Braun

As the studio expanded and diversified into other media, Disney devoted less of his attention to the animation department, entrusting most of its operations to his key animators, whom he dubbed the Nine Old Men. During Disney's lifetime, the animation department created the successful *Lady and the Tramp* (in

CinemaScope, 1955), *One Hundred and One Dalmatians* (1961), *Sleeping Beauty* (in Super Technirama 70mm, 1959), and *The Sword in the Stone* (1963).

Production on the short cartoons had kept pace until 1956, when Disney shut down the shorts division. Special shorts projects would continue to be made for the rest of the studio's duration on an irregular basis. These productions were all distributed by Disney's new subsidiary, Buena Vista Distribution, which had assumed all distribution duties for Disney films from RKO by 1955. Disneyland, one of the world's first theme parks, finally opened on July 17, 1955, and was immediately successful. Visitors from around the world came to visit Disneyland, which contained attractions based upon a number of successful Disney properties and films. After 1955, the show, *Disneyland* came to be known as *Walt Disney Presents*. The show transformed from black-and-white to color in 1961 and changed its name to *Walt Disney's Wonderful World of Color*, moving from ABC to NBC, and eventually evolving into its current form as *The Wonderful World of Disney*. It continued to air on NBC until 1981, when CBS picked it up. Since then, it has aired on ABC, NBC, Hallmark Channel, and Cartoon Network via separate broadcast rights deals.

During the mid-1950's, Disney produced a number of educational films on the space program in collaboration with NASA rocket designer, Wernher von Braun: *Man in Space* and *Man and the Moon* in 1955, and *Mars and Beyond* in 1957.

Early 1960's Successes

By the early 1960's, the Disney empire was a major success, and Walt Disney Productions had established itself as the world's leading producer of family entertainment. Walt Disney was the Head of Pageantry for the 1960 Winter Olympics. After decades of pursuing, Disney finally procured the rights to P.L. Travers' books about a magical nanny. *Mary Poppins*, released in 1964, was the most successful Disney film of the 1960's and featured a memorable song score written by Disney favorites, the Sherman Brothers. The same year, Disney debuted a number of exhibits at the 1964 New York World's Fair, including Audio-Animatronic figures, all of which were later integrated into attractions at Disneyland and a new theme park project which was to be established on the East Coast.

Plans for Disney World and EPCOT

Disney World was to include a larger, more elaborate version of *Disneyland*, which was to be called the *Magic Kingdom*. It would also feature a number of golf courses and resort hotels. The heart of *Disney World*, however, was to be the *Experimental Prototype Community of Tomorrow*, or *EPCOT* for short. Cast Members have nicknamed it "Every Paycheck Comes on Thursday." *Epcot* was designed to be an operational city where residents would live, work, and interact using advanced and experimental technology, while scientists would develop and test new technologies to improve human life and health.

Death

Disney's involvement in Disney World ended in late 1966; after many years of chain smoking cigarettes, he was diagnosed with lung cancer. He was admitted to Providence St. Joseph Medical Center across the street from the Disney Studio, where his health began to deteriorate, causing him to suffer cardiac arrest. Just before he was hospitalized, Disney was scheduled to undergo a neck surgery for an old polo injury; Disney was a frequent polo player at The Riveria Club in Hollywood, California, for many years. On November 2, 1966, during pre-surgery x-rays, doctors at St. Joseph's Hospital in Los Angeles discovered that Disney had an enormous tumor on his left lung. Five days later, Disney went back to hospital for surgery, but the tumor had spread to such great extent that doctors had to remove his entire left lung. The doctors then told Disney that he only had six months to a year to live. After several chemotherapy sessions, Disney and his wife spent a short amount of time in Palm Springs, California, before returning home. On November 30, 1966, Disney collapsed in his home, but was revived by paramedics, and was taken back to the hospital, where he died on *December 15, 1966, at 9:30 a.m.*, ten days after his sixty-fifth birthday. He was cremated on December 17, 1966, and his ashes reside at the Forest Lawn Memorial Park in Glendale, California. Roy O. Disney continued to carry out the Florida project, insisting that the name be changed to Walt Disney World in honor of his brother.

Songwriter Robert B. Sherman said about the last time he saw Disney: "He was up in the third floor of the animation building after a run-through of *The Happiest Millionaire*. He usually held court in the hallway afterward for the people involved with the picture. And he started talking to them, telling them what he liked and what they should change, and then, when they were through, he turned to us and with a big smile, he said, 'Keep up the good work, boys.' And he walked to his office. It was the last we ever saw of him."

At the time of Walt's death, he is said to have owned 286,000 shares of Disney Stock. It was estimated to be worth $18 million.

Shortly after the death of Walt Disney in May 1967, satirist Paul Krassner published The Disneyland Memorial Orgy Poster, a cartoon illustration portraying the liberated behavior of the Disney characters.

A long-standing urban legend maintains that Disney was cryogenically frozen, and his frozen corpse was stored underneath the *Pirates of the Caribbean* attraction in *Disneyland*. However, this was discredited due to the fact that Disney was cremated, and the first known instance of cryogenic freezing of a corpse (of Dr. James Bedford) occurred a month later, in January 1967.

The final productions in which Disney had an active role were the animated feature *The Jungle Book* and the live-action musical comedy *The Happiest Millionaire*, both released in 1967.

It is said that Walt's last visit to his "Magic Kingdom" was on October 14, 1966. He hosted a special event that awarded heroic soldiers with The Congressional Medal Of Honor.

Continuing the Vision

After Walt Disney's death, Roy Disney returned from retirement to take full control of Walt Disney Productions and WED Enterprises. In October that year, their families met in front of Cinderella Castle at the Magic Kingdom to officially open the Walt Disney World Resort.

After giving his dedication for *Walt Disney World*, he then asked Lillian Disney to join him. As the orchestra played "When You Wish Upon a Star," she stepped up to the podium accompanied by Mickey Mouse. He then said, "Lilly, you knew all of Walt's ideas and hopes as well as anybody; what would Walt think of it (*Walt Disney World*)?" "I think Walt would have approved," she replied. Roy died from a cerebral hemorrhage on December 20, 1971, the day he was due to open the *Disneyland* Christmas parade.

During the second phase of the *Walt Disney World* theme park, *EPCOT* was translated by Disney's successors into *EPCOT Center*, which opened in 1982. As it currently exists, *EPCOT* is essentially a living world's fair, different from the actual functional city that Disney had envisioned. In 1992, Walt Disney Imagineering took the step closer to Walt's vision and dedicated Celebration, Florida, a town built by the Walt Disney Company adjacent to *Walt Disney World*, that hearkens back to the spirit of *EPCOT*. *EPCOT* was also originally intended to be devoid of Disney characters, which initially limited the appeal of the park to young children, but the company later changed this policy.

The Disney Entertainment Empire

Today, Walt Disney's animation/motion picture studios and theme parks have developed into a multi-billion-dollar television, motion picture, vacation destination and media corporation that carry his name. The Walt Disney Company today owns, among other assets, five vacation resorts, eleven theme parks, two water parks, thirty-nine hotels, eight motion picture studios, six record labels, eleven cable television networks, and one terrestrial television network. As of 2007, the company has an annual revenue of over $35 billion.

Disney Animation today

Traditional hand-drawn animation, with which Walt Disney started his company, no longer continues at the Walt Disney Feature Animation studio. After a stream of financially unsuccessful traditionally-animated features in the late-1990's and early 2000's, the two satellite studios in Paris and Orlando were closed, and the main studio in Burbank was converted to a computer animation production facility. In 2004, Disney released what was announced as their final "traditionally animated" feature film, *Home on the Range*. However, since the 2006 acquisition of Pixar and the resulting rise of John Lasseter to Chief

698

Creative Officer, that position has changed, and the upcoming 2009 film, *The Princess and the Frog*, will mark Disney's return to traditional 2-D animation.

CalArts

In his later years, Disney devoted substantial time towards funding The California Institute of the Arts (CalArts). It was formed in 1961 through a merger of the Los Angeles Conservatory of Music and the Chouinard Art Institute, which had helped in the training of the animation staff during the 1930's. When Disney died, one-fourth of his estate went towards CalArts, which helped in building its campus. In his will, Disney paved the way for creation of several charitable trusts which included one for the California Institute of the Arts and another for the Disney Foundation. He also donated 38 acres of the Golden Oaks ranch in Valencia for the school to be built on. CalArts moved onto the Valencia campus in 1971.

In an early admissions bulletin, Disney explained: "A hundred years ago, Wagner conceived of a perfect and all-embracing art, combining music, drama, painting, and the dance, but in his wildest imagination he had no hint what infinite possibilities were to become commonplace through the invention of recording, radio, cinema, and television. There already have been geniuses combining the arts in the mass-communications media, and they have already given us powerful new art forms. The future holds bright promise for those whoes imaginations are trained to play on the vast orchestra of the art-in-combination. Such supermen will appear most certainly in those environments which provide contact with all the arts, but even those who devote themselves to a single phase of art will benefit from broadened horizons."

SCAVENGER HUNT LOCATIONS

01. A golden spike in the ground under the archway of the castle.

02. At the exit to the Dumbo attraction. It is for taking photos.

03. The entrance to Club 33 located next to The Blue Bayou at the exit of Pirates of the Caribbean.

04. The G2 repair droid in the line for Star Tours. It used to be the skeletons of a goose Audio-Animatronic character from America Sings.

05. When in line for Gadgets Go Coaster, it is in the rock wall on the first turn.

06. While on Mark Twain Riverboat you will pass a log cabin on the backside of Pirates Lair On Tom Sawyer Island.

07. They jump out of the water at you on Jungle Cruise.

08. On Pirates Of The Caribbean you will float past a cave full of gold and treasure.

09. There are several places in the park, but guaranteed to see him in his house in Toon Town.

10. The giant rock ball in the center of Tomorrowland.

11. It is at the backside of the Matterhorn Bobsleds.

12. Captain Hook on Peter Pan's Flight has his hook on the wrong hand.

13. This could be anywhere.

14. The Tree god in the waiting area of The Enchanted Tiki Room.

15. At the top part of Tarzan's Treehouse.

16. In The Haunted Mansion attic.

17. You will see it while riding Storybook Land Canal Boats.

18. Right in front of Roger Rabbit's Cartoon Spin.

19. The plaque is in the ground before you cross the draw bridge to Sleeping Beauty's Castle.

20. Elephants on Jungle Cruise. The Captain makes reference to the elephants having their trunks packed.

21. On The Many Adventures Of Winnie The Pooh, the trophy heads of Max the buck, Buff the buffalo and Melvin the moose, may be spotted if one looks up and backwards while leaving the Heffalump/Woozle room.

22. The petrified tree is located near the loading dock to the riverboat at the Rivers Of America.

23. The sword in the stone and anvil next to King Arthur's Carousel.

24. You will pass them while riding the Disneyland Railroad from the station in Tomorrowland to Main Street.

25. They are located in front of "it's a small world".

26. You will pass it on the right side while riding a car on Autopia.

27. He is in the center of the queue to Buzz Lightyear Astro Blasters.

28. Big Thunder Railroad.

29. The evil queen peers through the upper window above Snow White's Scary Adventure.

30. It is right inside the front door to Mickey's House in Toontown.

31. By the steps going into the Haunted Mansion.

32. Briar Rabbit stuck in the honey in the "sticky situation" scene on Splash Mountain.

33. Located to the right side of Sleeping Beauty's Castle.

34. The Partners statue on Main Street in front of the castle.

"Thank you, Walt Disney, for everything you have done and for bringing us the happiest place on earth." -Joshua Shaffer